Civil Law

**The International Library of Essays in Law and Legal Theory**
*Series Editor: Tom D. Campbell*

*Schools*

**Natural Law, Vols I & II** *John Finnis*
**Justice** *Thomas Morawetz*
**Law and Economics, Vols I & II** *Jules Coleman and Jeffrey Lange*
**Critical Legal Studies** *James Boyle*
**Marxian Legal Theory** *Csaba Varga*
**Legal Reasoning, Vols I & II** *Aulis Aarnio and D. Neil MacCormick*
**Legal Positivism** *Mario Jori*
**American Legal Theory** *Robert Samuel Summers*
**Postmodernism and Law** *Dennis Patterson*
**Law in History, Vols I & II** *David Sugarman*
**Law and Language** *Fred Schauer*
**Sociological Theories of Law** *Kahei Rokumoto*
**Rights** *Carlos Nino*
**Law and Psychology** *Martin Lyon Levine*
**Feminist Legal Theory, Vols I & II** *Frances Olsen*
**Law and Society** *Roger Cotterrell*
**Contemporary Criminological Theory** *Francis T. Cullen and Velmer S. Burton Jr.*

*Areas*

**Criminal Law** *Thomas Morawetz*
**Tort Law** *Ernest J. Weinrib*
**Contract Law, Vols I & II** *Larry Alexander*
**Anti-Discrimination Law** *Christopher McCrudden*
**Consumer Law** *Iain Ramsay*
**International Law** *Martti Koskenniemi*
**Property Law, Vols I & II** *Elizabeth Mensch and Alan Freeman*
**Constitutional Law** *Mark V. Tushnet*
**Procedure** *D.J. Galligan*
**Evidence and Proof** *William Twining and Alex Stein*
**Company Law** *Sally Wheeler*
**Privacy, Vols I & II** *Raymond Wacks*
**Lawyers' Ethics** *David J. Luban*
**Administrative Law** *D.J. Galligan*
**Child Law** *Harry D. Krause*
**Family Law, Vols I & II** *Harry D. Krause*
**Welfare Law** *Peter Robson*
**Medicine and the Law** *Bernard M. Dickens*
**Commercial Law** *Ross Cranston*
**Environmental Law** *Michael C. Blumm*
**Conflict of Laws** *Richard Fentiman*
**Law and Religion** *Wojciech Sadurski*
**Human Rights Law** *Philip Alston*
**European Community Law, Vols I & II** *Francis Snyder*
**Tax Law, Vols I & II** *Patricia D. White*
**Media Law** *Eric Barendt*
**Labour Law** *David L. Gregory*
**Alternative Dispute Resolution** *Michael D.A. Freeman*

*Legal Cultures*

**Comparative Legal Cultures** *Csaba Varga*
**Law and Anthropology** *Peter Sack*
**Hindu Law and Legal Theory** *Ved Nanda*
**Islamic Law and Legal Theory** *Ian Edge*
**Chinese Law and Legal Theory** *Michael Palmer*
**Russian Legal Theory** *W. Butler*
**Common Law** *Michael Arnheim*
**Japanese Law and Legal Theory** *Koichiro Fujikura*
**Law and Development** *Anthony Carty*
**Jewish Law and Legal Theory** *Martin P. Golding*
**Legal Education** *Martin Lyon Levine*
**Civil Law** *Ralf Rogowski*
**African Law and Legal Theory** *Gordon Woodman and Akintunde Obilade*

*Future Volume*
Cumulative index

# Civil Law

*Edited by*

Ralf Rogowski

*University of Warwick*

NEW YORK UNIVERSITY PRESS
REFERENCE COLLECTION

Manufactured in Great Britain

First published in the U.S.A. in 1996 by
NEW YORK UNIVERSITY PRESS
Washington Square
New York NY 10003

**Library of Congress Cataloging-in-Publication Data**
Civil law/edited by Ralf Rogowski.
p. cm. — (International library of essays in law and legal theory. :Legal cultures ; 10)
Includes bibliographical references.
ISBN 0-8147-7465-2
1. Civil law. 2. Procedure (Law) 3. Actions and defenses.
I. Rogowski, Ralf. II. Series.
K623.C58 1995
340.5'6—dc20 95–8007
CIP

# Contents

# Acknowledgements

The editor and publishers wish to thank the following who have kindly given permission for the use of copyright material.

American Association for the Comparative Study of Law for the essays: Wilhelm Karl Geck (1977), 'The Reform of Legal Education in the Federal Republic of Germany', *American Journal of Comparative Law*, **25**, pp. 86–119; Frederick H. Lawson (1977), 'Comparative Judicial Styles', *American Journal of Comparative Law*, **25**, pp. 364–71.

Blackwell Publishers for the essays: Hein Kötz (1987), 'Taking Civil Codes Less Seriously', *Modern Law Review*, **50**, pp. 1–15; Erhard Blankenburg and Ralf Rogowski (1986), 'German Labour Courts and the British Industrial Tribunal System: A Socio-Legal Comparison of Degrees of Judicialisation', *Journal of Law and Society*, **13**, pp. 67–92.

Boston College International and Comparative Law Review for the essay: Franz Wieacker (1981), 'The Importance of Roman Law for Western Civilization and Western Legal Thought', *Boston College International and Comparative Law Review*, **4**, pp. 257–81.

The British Institute of International and Comparative Law for the essay: Peter Herzog and Brigitte Ecolivet Herzog (1973), 'The Reform of the Legal Professions and of Legal Aid in France', *International and Comparative Law Quarterly*, **22**, pp. 462–91.

Cambridge Law Journal for the essay: Basil S. Markesinis (1990), 'Litigation-Mania in England, Germany and the USA: Are We So Very Different?', *Cambridge Law Journal*, **49**, pp. 233–76.

Columbia Journal of Transnational Law Association for the essay: Ernst Benda (1981), 'Constitutional Jurisdiction in Western Germany', *Columbia Journal of Transnational Law*, **19**, pp. 1–13.

Hambledon Press for the essay: Peter Stein (1988), 'The Attraction of the Civil Law in Post-Revolutionary America', in *The Character and Influence of the Roman Civil Law: Historical Essays*, pp. 411–42. Original copyright © 1966 *Virginia Law Review*, **52**, pp. 403–34. Permission also by Virginia Law Review Association and Fred B. Rothman & Company.

Harvard Law Review Association for the essay: Harold J. Berman (1977), 'The Origins of Western Legal Science', *Harvard Law Review*, **90**, pp. 894–943. Copyright © 1977 by The Harvard Law Review Association.

Louisiana Law Review for the essay: George W. Pugh (1962), 'Administration of Criminal Justice in France: An Introductory Analysis', *Louisiana Law Review*, **23**, pp. 1–28.

McGill Law Journal Inc. for the essay: Thomas E. Carbonneau (1980), 'The French Legal Studies Curriculum: Its History and Relevance as a Model for Reform', *McGill Law Journal*, **25**, pp. 445–77.

John Henry Merryman (1975), 'Legal Education There and Here: A Comparison', *Stanford Law Review*, **27**, pp. 859–78. Copyright © 1974 by John Henry Merryman. Permission also granted by Stanford Law Review and Fred B. Rothman & Company.

Michigan Law Review Association for the essay: John P. Dawson (1940), 'The Codification of the French Customs', *Michigan Law Review*, **38**, pp. 765–800.

Tulane Law Review for the essays: Bernard Rudden (1974), 'Courts and Codes in England, France and Soviet Russia', *Tulane Law Review*, **48**, pp. 1010–28. Copyright © 1974, the Tulane Law Review Association. All rights reserved. Konrad Zweigert and Hans-Jürgen Puttfarken (1970), 'Statutory Interpretation – Civilian Style', *Tulane Law Review*, **44**, pp. 704–19. Copyright 1970, the Tulane Law Review Association. All rights reserved. Robert A. Riegert (1970), 'The West German Civil Code, Its Origin and Its Contract Provisions', *Tulane Law Review*, **45**, pp. 48–99. Copyright 1970, the Tulane Law Review Association. All rights reserved. André Tunc (1976), 'Methodology of the Civil Law in France', *Tulane Law Review*, **50**, pp. 459–73. Copyright 1976, the Tulane Law Review Association. All rights reserved.

University of Chicago Law Review for the essay: John H. Langbein (1974), 'Controlling Prosecutorial Discretion in Germany', *University of Chicago Law Review*, **41**, pp. 439–67.

University of Pennsylvania Law Review for the essay: Gerald L. Kock (1960), 'The Machinery of Law Administration in France', *University of Pennsylvania Law Review*, **108**, pp. 366–86.

The Yale Law Journal Company and Fred B. Rothman & Company for the essay: Mirjan Damaška (1975), 'Structures of Authority and Comparative Criminal Procedure', *Yale Law Journal*, **84**, pp. 480–544.

Every effort has been made to trace all the copyright holders but if any have been inadvertently overlooked the publishers will be pleased to make the necessary arrangement at the first opportunity.

# Series Preface

The International Library of Essays in Law and Legal Theory is designed to provide important research materials in an accessible form. Each volume contains essays of central theoretical importance in its subject area. The series as a whole makes available an extensive range of valuable material which will be of considerable interest to those involved in the research, teaching and study of law.

The series has been divided into three sections. The Schools section is intended to represent the main distinctive approaches and topics of special concern to groups of scholars. The Areas section takes in the main branches of law with an emphasis on essays which present analytical and theoretical insights of broad application. The section on Legal Cultures makes available the distinctive legal theories of different legal traditions and takes up topics of general comparative and developmental concern.

I have been delighted and impressed by the way in which the editors of the individual volumes have set about the difficult task of selecting, ordering and presenting essays from the immense quantity of academic legal writing published in journals throughout the world. Editors were asked to pick out those essays from law, philosophy and social science journals which they consider to be fundamental for the understanding of law, as seen from the perspective of a particular approach or sphere of legal interest. This is not an easy task and many difficult decisions have had to be made in order to ensure that a representative sample of the best journal essays available takes account of the scope of each topic or school.

I should like to express my thanks to all the volume editors for their willing participation and scholarly judgement. The interest and enthusiasm which the project has generated is well illustrated by the fact that an original projection of 12 volumes drawn up in 1989 has now become a list of some 60 volumes. I must also acknowledge the vision, persistence and constant cheerfulness of John Irwin and the marvellous work done by Mrs Margaret O'Reilly and Ms Sonia Hubbard.

TOM D. CAMPBELL
Series Editor
*The Faculty of Law*
*The Australian National University*

# Introduction

As a concept, civil law is the opposite of common law. It was invented by common law to characterize the continental European legal system(s). However, civil law is not a distinct field of law, but an umbrella concept for legal cultures on the European continent and in other parts of the world. It is supposed to identify the common thread which creates the 'other' of common law.

The origin of the concept lies in the comparison with private law, hence the name civil law. In its semantic development, the concept has transcended this comparison with private law and now comprises both substantive law and legal institutions. Introductory texts to the field acknowledge that the study of civil law incorporates all aspects of a legal system including doctrinal and procedural law, as well as ordinary and specialized courts of law, the legal profession and legal scholars (see Merryman 1985; see also von Mehren and Gordley 1977).

It is not possible in a collection of essays to cover all these aspects in detail. However, the volume's aim is to provide an introduction to major discussions under the heading of civil law. The essays are taken from a variety of legal periodicals and comprise major contributions to the study of civil law. The collection includes 'classic' texts as well as innovative research which illuminates important aspects of civil law systems.

## Civil Law and Common Law

From a global perspective, civil law constitutes one of the major legal systems of the world (see David and Brierley 1985). Civil law and common law are labels which comparative lawyers use to classify the legal landscape into 'groups' or 'families' of law. However, the distinction between civil law and common law is not arbitrary, the concept of civil law being intricately linked to that of common law. It is civil law in particular which enables the common lawyer to develop an external view of his/her own system. In this sense the field of civil law is in fact the product of common law debates.

Most of the contributions in this book treat the concept of civil law as a tool for common lawyers to analyse legal systems on the European continent and in other parts of the world which have been influenced by civil law systems. The studies take a distinctly academic approach to their subject. Thus the concept of civil law often appears as a theoretical construct which does not necessarily reflect the view of lawyers practising in a civil law system. These practitioners might find other aspects more characteristic of their system than those emphasized by academic studies of civil law.

Within the discourse on civil law, legal practitioners are supported by critical scholars who question the unsophisticated methodology of most civil law studies (see Frankenberg 1985; Gordon 1984). They argue that civil law is often a mere projection of the 'other' of common law and is thus limited by its own world view. From a critical perspective it is precisely the task of the comparative common lawyer to become aware of the limitations which one's own legal system imposes on observations of any other legal system. By becoming self-critical, the common law comparativist can support both the legal practitioner and the legal academic in distancing themselves from the 'dominant legal consciousness' (Frankenberg 1985, pp. 447–8).

The history of civil law studies encompasses a number of self-critical debates. In particular, legal historians have questioned the origin of the split between common law and civil law, with the traditional view blaming England for this divergence. This perspective attributes the dichotomy to the peculiar isolation of English law from the rest of Europe during the Middle Ages. Common law deviated from the scholarly course of using Roman law to establish a unifying concept of law and resisted modernization.[1] However, this traditional interpretation of the divergence thesis has been questioned by eminent scholars (see, for example, the cautious criticism in von Mehren and Gordley 1977, pp. 12–14). In his recent Goodhart lectures, Raoul van Caenegem in turn argued that the common law followed a 'normal' path by modernizing the English judicial system through centralization and by gradually building up new case law without adhering to ancient Roman law principles. In contrast, the continental obsession with the *Corpus Iuris* appears to Caenegem to have been an odd reshaping of all law 'through scholastic glosses, disputations and commentaries on this venerable relic of a defunct world' (Caenegem 1987, p. 126).

There are also attempts to reject the divergence thesis altogether. Fritz Pringsheim, for example, has argued that not only the civil law, but also the common law, were decisively influenced by Roman law. He developed the thesis of an 'inner relationship between Roman law and English law' pertaining to the basic principles of common law. This relationship is particularly clear if one compares Gaius' *Institutes* rather than Justinian's *Corpus Iuris* with English law (Pringsheim 1935).

Reinhart Zimmermann has recently interpreted the development of English common law as being continuously influenced by civil law. Indeed, he contends that these influences justify the claim that English law had a 'European character' throughout its existence (Zimmermann 1993). As evidence for his thesis, Zimmermann variously cites the Norman feudal laws which created the basis of early common law, Bracton's systematic and scientific analysis of common law, Blackstone's 'civilian' approach in compiling the common law rules, English canon law, Scottish contract law, the development of an international Lex Mercatoria in English courts and European influences on the reform of contract law in the 19th century. His continental analysis of English legal development emphasizes in particular the role of English legal scholars who were persistently in intellectual contact with civil law developments and were thus able to shape the understanding of common law.

## Legal Science and Legal Education in Civil Law

Legal historians and comparative lawyers agree that Roman law had an equal impact on common law and civil law in early medieval legal development. Medieval Roman law influenced both the law and scholarly legal writing in England and on the Continent alike. However the situation changed during Tudor times, 'after the Inns of Court had definitely prevailed over academic education in the preparation of barristers, sergeants-at-law and judges' (see Wieacker in Chapter 1, p. 5). The common law resisted domination by Roman law, including the use of scholarly texts and interpretations to mould legal decision-making.

In contrast, the development of civil law was closely linked to a rediscovery of Roman law and the creation of legal science in the 11th century. The renaissance of classical Roman law on the European continent began in Italian law schools, of which Bologna was predominant. Their scholarly approach spread quickly throughout Europe. Legal science had an historical function in developing a comprehensive system of rules in civil law countries. Thus the rediscovery of the Justinian *Corpus Iuris*, the scholastic method of analysing and teaching law in universities, created the basis of the Western tradition of legal science (Berman in Chapter 2).

The scientific character of law has shaped legal education in civil law countries from medieval times to the present. According to Merryman in Chapter 3, legal education on the European continent and in Latin American countries is democratic, public, general and scientific, whereas in common law countries it is meritocratic, private, professional and obsessed with teaching methods. However, according to Merryman, law students in common law countries, in particular the US, have at present an advantage over their colleagues in civil law countries because the system of legal education in the former is more demanding, requiring students to develop an analytical/critical approach.

Indeed, the conditions of learning law differ widely between the US and the UK on the one hand and continental European countries on the other. To a large extent the disadvantage to students in civil law education relates to institutional factors which make the learning experience a rather anonymous affair. The reality of mass legal education on the European continent contradicts the high ideals of civil law legal education. Despite the reform efforts in the 1970s (see Geck in Chapter 4), which were unfortunately abolished in the 1980s, German legal education continues to follow a traditional path of separating university studies from practical training. Legal education in both phases is centred around the abstract idea of studying for a judicial career. University education is almost entirely devoted to a 'scientific' introduction to law and Supreme Court decisions. In the second stage, which is entirely separated from the university, training mainly takes place in the courts (see Brunnée 1992). The academic teaching of law in France seems even more theoretical and impersonal than in German law faculties. Mass lectures prevent students from being taught practical or critical perspectives on the law (see Carbonneau in Chapter 5).

## Codification and Statutory Law

The scientific approach to law also encouraged the compilation of rules into comprehensive codes in civil law countries. We can distinguish three forms of codification. The early approach adopted in medieval times in Germany and elsewhere was to create codes by collecting and listing existing customary law. A famous example is the *Sachsenspiegel* (Mirror of Saxon Law) which was written by a well-educated knight, Eike von Repgow, in the 1220s in order to document the laws of Saxony (Berman 1983, pp. 503–5). A similar attempt to compile and codify customary law was undertaken in the north of France in the 16th century (see Dawson in Chapter 6).

A different concept of codification emerged with the introduction of the great codes around 1800. The *Preußisches Allgemeines Landrecht* (1794) of Saxony and the French *Code Civil*

(1804) were clearly influenced by ideas of the enlightenment period. Although these codes represented political attempts to create a rational society through law, they have been accused of revolutionary democratism and 'rampant rationalism' (Merryman 1985, p. 28). This is because they attempted to grant each citizen knowledge of his or her rights, as well as to provide a complete list of solutions for any legal complaint, thus reducing the role of the judge to the selection of the relevant provision without further powers of judicial interpretation.

A third approach was taken by the German Civil Code, the *Bürgerliches Gesetzbuch* (BGB). Historically oriented, scientific and professional, it combined both Roman law traditions and German law developments. Its provisions appear to be rather abstract and scientific without, however, displaying a rationalist zeal. The BGB acknowledged that there must be some scope for judicial interpretation by incorporating a number of general clauses (von Mehren and Gordley 1977, pp. 75–9; on the origins of the BGB, see also John 1989). Furthermore, later amendments to the BGB and separate regulations of areas not covered by it gave rise to innumerable statutes. Thus the BGB contributed to the rise of statutory law in Germany and to a development which has been described as 'juridification of all major social spheres' (see Teubner 1987).

The French *Code Civil* and the BGB differ fundamentally in the scope they grant for judicial interpretation. Whereas German judges enjoy wide powers to interpret the legislative provisions of the BGB, French judges pay 'literal lip-service to the restrictions' imposed by the *Code Civil*. Somewhat paradoxically, however, by adhering to a restrictive judicial style, the French judges also free themselves from the *Code*. In cases not regulated by the *Code*, they acquire quasi-legislative power (see Rudden in Chapter 7, pp. 220–22 on France).

Although both civil law and common law have 'migrated', their manner of doing so has differed markedly. Whereas the common law migrated through principles of private and public common law and by exporting distinct legal institutions – the jury, the writ of habeas corpus, an independent judiciary and an adversarial procedural system – mainly to other Commonwealth countries (Goodhart 1960, pp. 46–8), the civil law penetrated other systems through its comprehensive, systematic codes. A remarkable example of such migration of civil law was the adoption of the French *Code Civil* in Louisiana and the discussion of civil law as the basis for a particular American jurisprudence (see Stein in Chapter 8). In general, the history of migration of law seems to reveal that civil law has a greater potential for persuasion while common law more often had to rely on coercion.

## The Civil Code and Statutory Interpretation

From a common law perspective, a specific feature of civil law is the role and structure of statutes, codes and codification in general. The common assumption is that civil law systems are ruled by statutes, that these systems make an attempt to unify regulations in single codes for each area of law, and that codification dominates legal policies. In contrast, common law systems seem to be governed by case law and precedents established by courts. Statutes thus play only an auxiliary role to case law developed by the courts.

Both generalizations need to be qualified. On the one hand, case law and judge-made law are a necessary feature of civil law systems. The meaning of provisions of the German BGB is established by case law. This judicial interpretation of statutes is recognized by the BGB in so far as it contains general clauses which can be used for the further development of case law. Furthermore, 'there are large areas of *pure* case law in the civil law system' (Zweigert and Puttfarken, Chapter 9, p. 272).

With respect to common law systems, statutes have become the dominant form of regulation in most areas of law. This fact has led some authors to speculate about a *rapprochement* between English and continental laws (David and Brierley 1985, p. 332; Markesinis 1994). Furthermore, there have been a number of attempts to systematize and 'codify' common law. The American Uniform Commercial Code and the (failed) British attempt to introduce a code in the areas of the law of contract and landlord and tenant are prominent examples to provide comprehensive legal frameworks. The common law of the UK in particular is faced with continuous pressure to introduce new legislation due to its membership of the European Union.

The French *Code Civil* and the German BGB differ with respect to the degree of abstraction of their statutory principles. Whereas the BGB provisions are accused of being too abstract and thus not effective (Riegert, Chapter 10, pp. 287–92), the *Code Civil* is criticized for being too concrete, requiring supplementation by the *droit civil* which is derived from specific statutes, judge-made law and doctrine established by legal academics (see Tunc, Chapter 11).

The lesson which common law can draw from the French and German experience is that codification can adopt different levels of generalization (Kötz, Chapter 12, p. 350). Periods of codification are followed by periods of decodification and fragmentation into special statutes. With increasing complexity, there will again be attempts to recodify in order to make scattered rules more comprehensible. However, the idea of codification has been transformed and no longer rests on a rationalist philosophy which attempts to restructure society by enshrining the rights of citizens. Rather, it has become a bureaucratic device to facilitate administrative and judicial decision-making.

## Constitutional Law and Judicial Review

A distinct feature of civil law systems is their hierarchy of norms, with the written constitution at the apex. In a civil law system, any legislation can be scrutinized for compliance with the constitution. Furthermore, modern constitutions grant citizens human and civil rights which require effective means of enforcement in order to guarantee real protection.

The German judiciary enforces rights in five different court systems. In addition, and most importantly with respect to constitutionally protected rights, there exists a Federal Constitutional Court, the *Bundesverfassungsgericht*. Its far-reaching powers include arbitration of conflicts between organs of the federal state, protection of human rights and judicial review of legislation. The Federal Constitutional Court is not constrained by law from acting of its own volition. However, it would soon encounter opposition and implementation problems if it were to disregard the contemporary political climate. Thus judicial self-restraint is actually a precondition for the court to be effective in its decision-making (Benda, Chapter 13, pp. 371–2).

The French system of judicial enforcement of rights is divided into two sections which have their own appeal structures: the judicial courts and the administrative courts (see Kock, Chapter 14). In addition there exists a Constitutional Council, the *Conseil Constitutionnel.* Its powers are limited and do not include the right to make a constitutional complaint challenging a violation of human or civil rights. The French constitutional court is almost exclusively concerned with questions of the constitutionality of legislative acts before promulgation (see Bell 1992; Finer et al. 1995, pp. 3–12).

## Criminal Courts, Prosecutors and the Inquisitorial Process

The traditional view emphasizes the nonadversarial or inquisitorial character of criminal procedures in civil law countries. At the centre of the trial is the judge who conducts the hearing as an 'active inquisitor' (Merryman 1985, p. 127). It is a contest between the accused and the prosecutor who represents the state. The inquisitorial model is usually contrasted with the common law accusatorial model in which the contest is between the accused and the accuser, with the judge acting as a referee.

The two models have been criticized for concentrating too much on the trial phase. However, if pre-trial prosecution is included, the concepts seem less appropriate to characterize criminal procedure in common law and civil law systems. Mirjan Damaška (Chapter 15) offers an alternative concept: the hierarchical model which characterizes continental criminal procedure, and the coordinate model which characterizes common law criminal procedure. In the hierarchical model the legal expert applies normative standards, whereas in a coordinate model the decision-maker has to find the best solution to a social problem in the light of his/her own political and ethical values.

However, Damaška's concepts operate at a rather abstract level. If one looks at specific legal systems, we detect significant differences in civil law. An outstanding feature of German criminal procedure, for example, is the discretion granted to prosecutors who have sole power in preferring formal charges (Langbein, Chapter 16, pp. 468–9). The prosecutor is in charge of the investigative phase. Although compelled to bring charges in cases where there is a sufficient factual basis (*Legalitätsprinzip*), he/she also has a certain amount of discretion. In some cases the prosecutor can ask for a penal order for the payment of penance monies instead of a formal fine. In addition, prosecutors enjoy explicit discretion granted within the criminal procedure code. They can reject prosecution if the suspect's guilt is minor and if no public interest would thereby be served. These statutory criteria, which at the same time allow and regulate nonprosecution, seem from a comparative point of view a major achievement of the German criminal justice system (Langbein, Chapter 16, pp. 484–7 and 492–3).

In France, for a number of criminal cases, the pre-trial period is split into the investigative phase in which the police make inquiries under the direction of the public prosecutor and into the examining phase conducted by the examining judge (*juge d'instruction*) (Pugh, Chapter 17, pp. 507–8). This distinction was quite common in a number of civil law countries. However, the examining judge has now been abolished in Germany and Italy where most of his former powers were handed to the public prosecutor. Even in France there are discussions to deprive the examining judge of his investigative powers and to reduce his role to supervision of the investigation (Delmas-Marty 1994, pp. 94–5).

## Courts, Lawyers and Litigation in Civil Law Systems

Civil law and common law differ most, perhaps, with respect to judicial practice and administration. In particular, the style of conducting a hearing and finding a decision is linked to general principles and functions of procedure. Whereas common law judgements concentrate on establishing premises, civil law decisions, in particular under French law, concentrate on the law (Lawson, Chapter 18).

The French legal profession was for a long time diversified, with a major distinction existing between legal practitioners who represented clients in court (*avocat*) and those who mainly communicated with clients in writing (*avoué*). This division certainly bore some similarity with that between barristers and solicitors under English law. However, since 1972 this distinction has been abolished and the French legal profession now appears more united than its English counterpart (Herzog and Herzog, Chapter 20).

The German legal profession is probably the most diversified among civil law systems. Four major groups of jurists exist: judges, legal practitioners, administrative lawyers and company lawyers (Blankenburg and Schultz 1988). Three factors characterize German jurists from a comparative point of view: (1) an academic understanding of the law through legal education and legal doctrine, (2) a special emphasis on and communication of experiences through written legal texts and (3) a state-focused understanding of the role of the legal profession, with judges at its centre (see Luhmann, Chapter 21). Surprisingly these features dominate the work and attitudes of legal practitioners, even including the powerful group of German corporate lawyers (see Rogowski 1995).

There is still little lateral mobility between the various subgroups of German jurists. Becoming a judge means entering a separate judicial career immediately after completing legal education. Only to a limited extent do transfers occur between administrative lawyers working for regulatory agencies and practising attorneys. The rule is still that a young jurist begins a judicial, an administrative or a lawyer's career and stays in that chosen track.

A particular feature of the German system is the differentiation of five judicial sub-systems, each enjoying full autonomy with separate levels of final appeal. However, the style of litigation is similar in each of these court systems. Legal practitioners only prepare the claim but do not conduct the hearing. Even in specialized courts like the German labour courts, one fundamental principle applies: the judge is in charge of questioning (Blankenburg and Rogowski, Chapter 19). Other common factors include the professionalization of judges and the preparatory work which is required by judges (see Markesinis, Chapter 22; see also Blankenburg 1985).

## The Function of Theory in Civil Law Studies

The study of civil law is closely linked to developments in comparative law. In particular, methods of comparison have been a topic of continuing debate. In recent times these discussions have evinced a renewed interest in theory.

However, the degree of theoretical emphasis differs according to the comparative approach adopted. We can distinguish four methods: country studies, benchmark, functional, and theoretical or deductive approaches (see Rogowski, 1996, forthcoming). In particular the fourth method – the advanced theoretical approach – offers many possibilities to explore new dimensions in contrasting civil and common law. It enables the establishment of a comprehensive comparative framework; it allows analysis from the position of an external observer of legal systems and it encourages criticism and self-criticism of the comparative frame.

A new commitment to theory transcends the rule-based comparative analysis of law and takes into account the inevitability of the mediating effect of the observer of another legal system. The study of civil law can appear as an attempt of common law **to 'restage'** that legal culture within its own parameters (Legrand 1995). The observer only detects those legal aspects which his/her framework suggests it is relevant to analyse.

One response to these limitations is to broaden the basis of comparison. In particular, legal sociology offers a way forward by transcending the study of law to a comparison of legal cultures (Friedman 1975, pp. 223–67; Friedman 1990, ch. 5; Blankenburg 1985). From this perspective, future studies of civil law need to be interdisciplinary and theoretical in order to grasp diversity and detail, particularities and local deviations.

A similar reaction comes from comparative lawyers who emphasize the importance of case law, judicial practice, the study of specific legal problems and the personalities of comparative lawyers as objects of comparison. By concentrating on these issues, civil law studies promise to attract a wider common law audience (Markesinis 1990). This proposal to highlight fine detail in comparative law would seem to have advantages and disadvantages. It is convincing in so far as it contextualizes the comparative approach and focuses on the essence of an autonomous legal system, i.e. recursive decision-making and the development of binding case law. It opens comparative law to include particularistic aspects of legal history and the cultural context, thus promoting analysis at a concrete level as well as increased interdisciplinarity.

However, there is also a limitation to this approach. Markesinis' above-mentioned list of topics reveals a bias. He falls into the old trap of comparing common law and civil law by using common law and its particularities, especially case law, as the mirror by which to approach the other. The only aspects of civil law that appear in this mirror are those which have a reference point in common law.

The basic problem of a common law approach to civil law is thus the projection of civil law as the 'other' of common law. Recourse to psychoanalysis might reveal insights into the 'subconscious' of common law in order to find a deeper reason for this continued projection.

At another level the philosophical position which the Jewish philosopher Emmanuel Levinas has expounded with respect to the concept of the 'other' could be utilized. In his ethical position, it is necessary to recognize the otherness of the other. Accordingly, common law must treat civil law as totally independent from its own concerns. This approach requires that the other be allowed to speak freely with its own voice.

These ethical claims are translated into theoretical concerns by modern social theory – in particular social systems theory – which argues that differentiation of legal systems is characteristic of their internal as well as external relations. Systems theory uses social theory to distance analysis from a specific legal perspective. It introduces abstract concepts to analyse concrete historical developments (Luhmann, Chapter 21). Legal systems develop by becoming self-critical and self-referential. In realizing their epistemological shortcomings and their limited regulatory capacities, they become reflexive (Teubner 1992; Luhmann 1993; Rogowski and Wilthagen 1994).

## Conclusion

If we return to the question of the convergence or divergence of common and civil law, we can envisage that rules and principles of law might gradually converge. Indeed, there might even be scope for a 'common law of Europe'. However, diversity will always remain. In fact it is the acknowledgement of the virtue of particularistic law which characterizes our modern (or post-modern) legal systems. The legal cultures and the legal mentalities of the people involved may not naturally move towards harmonization. Otto Kahn-Freund has commented on the obstacles to the assimilation of common and civil law: 'The obstacles to mutual understanding are of a different character, different not only in degree but in kind. ... The principal difficulty is created by method and style of law making and legal argument' (Kahn-Freund 1978a, p.138). The study of civil law systems needs to focus on these 'methods and styles' of continental legal institutions, judicial practices and doctrinal approaches. However, in order to be successful, it also needs to develop appropriate theoretical frameworks which can encompass the discrepanies between harmonization of rules and the diversity of legal attitudes and practices. It must become self-critical in order to perceive the limits of external observation and to understand the relativism involved in observing legal systems.

## Note

1. An example of this view is Alan Watson's discussion of the Scottish (Roman law-based) law of contract: 'Because of her connection with the civil law tradition, Scotland accepted a modern system of contract. ... England, which stood outside the civil law tradition, did not achieve a similar modern system or any system approaching that in clarity and efficaciousness until the nineteenth century' (Watson 1981, p.51).

## Bibliography

Bell, J. (1992), *French Constitutional Law*, Oxford: Oxford University Press.
Berman, H.J. (1983), *Law and Revolution: The Formation of the Western Legal Tradition*, Cambridge MA and London: Harvard University Press.
Blankenburg, E. (1985), 'Indikatorenvergleich der Rechtskulturen in der Bundesrepublik und den Niederlanden', *Zeitschrift für Rechtssoziologie,* **6**, 206–54.
Blankenburg, E. and U. Schultz (1988), 'German Advocates: a Highly Regulated Profession', in R. Abel and P. Lewis (eds), *Lawyers in Society* Vol. 2: The Civil Law World, Berkeley: University of California Press, pp.124–59.
Brunnée, J. (1992), 'The Reform of Legal Education in Germany: The Never-Ending Story and European Integration', *Journal of Legal Education*, **42**, 399–426.
Caenegem, R.C. van (1987), *Judges, Legislators and Professors: Chapters in European Legal History*, Cambridge: Cambridge University Press.

Cappelletti, M. (ed.) (1978), *New Perspectives for a Common Law of Europe*, Leiden: Sijthoff.
David, R. and J.E.C. Brierley (1985), *Major Legal Systems in the World Today: An Introduction to the Comparative Study of Law*, 3rd edition, London: Stevens.
Delmas-Marty, M. (1994), 'The *juge d'instruction*: Do the English Really Need Him?' in B. Markesinis (ed.) (1994), pp.46–63.
Finer, S.E., V. Bogdanor and B. Rudden (1995), *Comparing Constitutions*, Oxford: Clarendon.
Frankenberg, G. (1985), 'Critical Comparisons: Re-thinking Comparative Law', *Harvard International Law Journal*, **26**, 411–55.
Friedman, L. (1975), *The Legal System: A Social Science Perspective*, New York: Sage.
Friedman, L. (1990), *The Republic of Choice: Law, Authority, and Culture*, Cambridge MA and London: Harvard University Press.
Glendon, M.A., M.W. Gordon and C. Osakwe (1994), *Comparative Legal Traditions: Text, Materials and Cases on the Civil and Common Law Traditions, with Special Reference to French, German, English and European Law*, 2nd edition, St Pauls: West.
Goodhart, A.L. (1960), 'The Migration of Common Law', *Law Quarterly Review*, **76**, 39–40 and 45–8.
Gordon, R.W. (1984), 'Critical Legal Histories', *Stanford Law Review*, **36**, 57–125.
John, M. (1989), *Politics and the Law in Late Nineteenth-Century Germany: The Origins of the Civil Code*, Oxford: Clarendon Press.
Kahn-Freund, O. (1978a), 'Common Law and Civil Law – Imaginary and Real Obstacles to Assimilation' in M. Cappelletti (ed.) (1978), pp.137–68.
Kahn-Freund, O. (1978b), *Selected Writings*, London: Stevens.
Legrand, P. (1995), 'Comparative Legal Studies and Commitment to Theory', *Modern Law Review*, **58**, 262–73.
Levinas, E. (1989), *The Levinas Reader*, edited by S. Hand, Oxford: Blackwell.
Luhmann, N. (1993), *Das Recht der Gesellschaft*, Frankfurt/Main: Suhrkamp.
Markesinis, B. (1990), 'Comparative Law: A Subject in Search of an Audience', *Modern Law Review*, **53**, 1–21.
Markesinis, B. (ed.) (1994), *The Gradual Convergence: Foreign Ideas, Foreign Influences and English Law on the Eve of the 21st Century*, Oxford: Clarendon.
Mehren, A.T. von and J.R. Gordley (1977), *The Civil Law System: An Introduction to the Comparative Study of Law*, Boston and Toronto: Little, Brown.
Merryman, J.H. (1985), *The Civil Law Tradition: An Introduction to the Legal Systems of Western Europe and Latin America*, 2nd edition, Stanford: Stanford University Press.
Pringsheim, F. (1935), 'The Inner Relationship Between English and Roman Law', *Cambridge Law Journal*, **5**, 347–65.
Rogowski, R. (1995), 'German Corporate Lawyers: Social Closure in Autopoietic Perspective', in Y. Dezalay and D. Sugarman (eds), *Professional Competition and Professional Power: Lawyers, Accountants and the Social Construction of Markets*, London: Routledge, pp.114–35.
Rogowski, R. (1996), 'The Art of Mirroring: Comparative Law and Social Theory', in G.P. Wilson and R. Rogowski (eds), *Challenges to European Legal Scholarship*, Aldershot: Elgar (forthcoming).
Rogowski, R. and T. Wilthagen (eds) (1994), *Reflexive Labour Law*, Deventer: Kluwer.
Teubner, G. (ed.) (1987), *Juridification of Social Spheres: A Comparative Analysis in the Areas of Labor, Corporate, Antitrust and Social Welfare Law*, Berlin/New York: de Gruyter.
Teubner, G. (1992), *Law as an Autopoietic System*, Oxford: Blackwell.
Watson, A. (1981), *The Making of the Civil Law*, Cambridge MA and London: Harvard University Press.
Watson, A. (1993), *Legal Transplants*, 2nd edition, Athens, Georgia: University of Georgia Press.
Zimmermann, R. (1993), 'Der europäische Charakter des englischen Rechts', *Zeitschrift für Europäisches Privatrecht*, **1**, **4–51**.

# Part I
# Legal Science and Legal Education in Civil Law

# [1]

# The Importance of Roman Law for Western Civilization and Western Legal Thought

by *Franz Wieacker**

## Part One: Ancient Roman Law

### I. Introduction

I have been asked to speak about the importance of ancient and medieval Roman law for western civilization and western legal thought. After a general introduction, my first lecture will deal with the relevant characteristics of ancient Roman law. The subject of the second lecture will be the forms in which these elements were adopted by western society and the continuing presence of these "roots" in the modern legal systems of the European-Atlantic world.

The large amount of material which has been handed down to us and which we encompass in the term "Roman law" forms a constituent part of the occidental world. It formed nations and legal systems and allowed them to become aware of their own identity. It provided the basis for the rational character of the systems and the legalism of the western nations. Further, even the very principle of settling social and economic conflicts not only by force, authority or compromise, but also by the application of general conceptual rules — which is *the* characteristic feature of western legal thought — became possible on the basis, and perhaps only on the basis, of Roman law, or what was thought to be Roman law. In reality, to use the fine words spoken in

* Emeritus Professor of Roman Law and [German] Civil Law, University of Göttingen, Federal Republic of Germany. The text of this article is taken from lectures given by Professor Wieacker at the Harvard Law School on April 8 and 9, 1980. Because the lectures are a synthesis of Professor Wieacker's works, it seemed best to leave the article in the lecture form in which it was given and not to provide a full complement of footnote support. The reader who wishes some further introduction in English to the material treated here might wish to consult H. JOLOWICZ & B. NICHOLAS, HISTORICAL INTRODUCTION TO THE STUDY OF ROMAN LAW (3d ed. 1972), for the Roman law, and W. ULLMANN, LAW AND POLITICS IN THE MIDDLE AGES (1975), for the medieval developments, both of which contain up-to-date bibliographies. For an elaboration of Professor Wieacker's ideas and references, the reader is referred to three of his works: VOM RÖMISHCEN RECHT (2d ed. 1961); ALLGEMEINE ZUSTÄNDE UND RECHTSZUSTÄNDE GEGEN ENDE DES WESTRÖMISCHEN REICHS (Ius Romanum Medii Aevi No. I, 2, a, 1963); PRIVATRECHTSGESCHICHTE DER NEUZEIT (2d ed. 1967).

honor of the famous European legal historian, Paul Koschaker, Roman law is a *vinculum iuris quo totiens occidens continetur* [a bond of law by which so often the West is held together, *ed.*].[1]

Although they developed along different lines, the two great legal systems of the Western world have this rational character in common. I am referring, of course, to a well-known dualism. On the one hand, there are the legal systems of the European continent and of Latin America. These systems are essentially characterized by the great codifications. In the first place, there are the Latin codes modeled after the Napoleonic codes. In the second place, there are the Central-European codes of Austria, Germany and Switzerland and their followers in other countries. Within the boundaries of the United States we find a well-known example of this legal system in the Code of Louisiana. On the other hand, there is the common law of the Anglo-American countries which, if you will allow me to speak as a continental legal historian, I regard as an historical unity. On the whole, this system is characterized by a unique court system and, despite the growing importance of statute law, by the dominance of case law based on the principle of the binding force of precedents.[2]

## II. THE RECEPTION OF ROMAN LAW

### A. *The Continental Systems*

Historically, the continental systems grew mainly from the medieval Roman law. The substantive rules of these systems largely follow those of Justinian's law. The medieval doctrine of *ius commune* allowed these rules to be applied directly and to supersede much of the original legal tradition of each nation. Even more important than this external reception was the adoption of the Bolognese legal method of the *studium civile*. This method established the basic characteristics of the continental judicial systems, *i.e.*, decision-making not on the basis of precedents but by way of subsuming a case under the terms of an abstractly formulated authoritative text or statute.

The reception of Roman law into the continental legal systems took place in the following ways:

First, the old, legally untrained jurors (*Schöffen*, *échevins*, *etc.*), comparable

1. *See* Wieacker, *Zur Aktualisierung des römischen Rechts*, in 1 L'EUROPA E IL DIRITTO ROMANO: STUDI IN MEMORIA DI PAOLO KOSCHAKER 532 (D. Giuffré ed. Milan 1954). [This paper presents Professor Wieacker's ideas with respect to the role of Roman law in the modern world. *See* Part Two, § IV of text, *infra*. *See also* F. WIEACKER, PRIVATRECHTSGESCHICHTE DER NEUZEIT 424 n.32 (2d ed. 1967). *Ed.*]

2. Here, for the sake of brevity, I must omit any reference to the Scandinavian legal system. This system occupies an independent position, in many respects, between the two principal western legal systems. Further, the well-known similarities between the two main systems, *i.e.*, the factors which make the code and the case law systems approximate each other, must also be neglected.

to the English jurymen, were gradually replaced by legally educated *doctores iuris civilis et canonici*. At the same time, these *doctores* became official servants of the sovereign in power.

Second, these new "oracles of law," who held key positions in both the judicial and administrative branches of government, gave practical effect to a peculiar conception of Justinian's law. The conception had already become ideologically predominant in the Holy Roman Empire and subsequently became predominant in the western European kingdoms by means of the fiction *superiorem non recognoscens imperator est in terra sua* [he who acknowledges no superior is emperor in his own land, *ed.*]. This conception was that the law of Justinian was *ius commune*, applicable everywhere in the absence of special regional sources of law (either traditional or statutory).

Third, the individual customs or statutes (*coutumes, ordonnances, Landrechte, Stadtrechte*) and, later, the regional or national codes were reformed in accordance with the Roman *ius commune*.

### B. *The Common Law Systems*

The substantial reception of Justinian's law and the unrestricted dominance of the academically-trained jurist appointed by a sovereign did not, with certain exceptions, occur in the Anglo-American system. Accordingly, I shall not recount at this point the well-known details of this important development on the European continent. For an American audience interested in the importance of Roman law for the *general* outlook of western legal thought, those elements of Roman law which were significant in the genesis of the Anglo-American legal system are more important. That the doctrines of the glossators and even those of pre-Bolognese medieval Roman law influenced the intellectual organization of English common law, and especially equity, has been known since Vinogradoff and has been confirmed by recent research.[3] Common law and civil law did not wholly part company until after the Tudor period; that is, not until after the Inns of Court had definitely prevailed over academic legal education in the preparation of barristers, sergeants-at-law and judges.

The tradition of medieval Roman law had the following effects in England and in the former English colonies, including the United States of America:

(1) In the twelfth century in England, such Italian scholars as Vacarius and, somewhat later, native English scholars, began teaching and using the legal literature of the first Bolognese glossators. The doctrines and teaching of Anglo-Norman law began to assume intellectually disciplined forms and concepts at the same time. Glanvill's *Tractatus de legibus et consuetudinibus regni*

3. P. VINOGRADOFF, ROMAN LAW IN MEDIEVAL EUROPE (1909, 3d ed. 1961). [For a survey of more recent work *see* Donahue, *The Civil Law in England*, 84 YALE L.J. 167 (1974). *Ed.*]

*Angliae*[4] and, especially, Bracton's *De legibus et consuetudinibus Angliae*[5] are works of learned men trained in medieval Roman law.

(2) Medieval *canon* law was a synthesis of ecclesiastical sources (such as Holy Scripture, the Fathers of the Church and the canons of ancient and medieval church councils) and of a medieval interpretation of Roman law. Canon law was applied in the medieval and early modern English church courts, whose wide jurisdiction included cases dealing with marriage, defamation, testaments and, in some periods, contracts. The chief and the members of the Court of Chancery were originally, and for a long time, clergymen. Consequently, many rules of equity which developed in this court can be traced back to the *aequitas canonica* and thereby, partly, if not completely, to Roman law.

(3) The separation of the Church of England from Rome diminished the importance of the ecclesiastical administration of justice. Similarly, the fierce reaction of the lawyers of the Inns of Court stopped a newly incipient romanization of the common law in the Tudor period. However, the Court of Admiralty, the Star Chamber and the ecclesiastical courts continued to apply the principles of the civil law (*i.e.*, a version of the *ius commune*) in decisions of maritime, penal and ecclesiastical matters. Civil law was also applied to questions of the conflict of laws and in certain other fields.

(4) The close contacts between the *Scots* law and the continental *ius commune*, which lasted beyond the Union of 1705, are of perhaps minor importance in this context. The same may be said with respect to the incorporation of such civil law jurisdictions as Quebec and the countries of Roman-Dutch law (such as the Cape Colony, Ceylon and British Guyana) into the British Empire and, later, the Commonwealth.

(5) On the other hand, a last wave of Roman law influenced the United States even more strongly than Blackstone's Great Britain and many countries of the European continent. I am referring to the enthusiastic acceptance in this country of the modern (*i.e.*, "secularized" and rational) form of the law of nature of the early Enlightenment period. This form of natural law was at the bottom of American constitutional theory and its concept of the law of nations and of general jurisprudence. The doctrines of Grotius, Pufendorf, Barbeyrac and others were adopted by Wise[6] and his followers. This philosophy was influential in Pennsylvania, Massachusetts and other colonies before and during the American Revolution to such an extent that the constitutional ideology of

---

4. R. DE GLANVILL, THE TREATISE ON THE LAWS AND CUSTOMS OF THE REALM OF ENGLAND COMMONLY CALLED GLANVILL (G. Hall trans. 1965).

5. H. DE BRACTON, ON THE LAWS AND CUSTOMS OF ENGLAND (G. Woodbine ed. S. Thorne trans. 1968).

6. [John Wise (1652-1725) was a New England Congregational clergyman and opponent of British colonial governor, Sir Edmund Andros; his works include: *The Churches' Quarrel Espoused* (1710), *A Vindication of the Government of New England Churches* (1717), and *A Word of Comfort to a Melancholy Country* (1721). *Ed.*]

this country may be considered to have grown out of it. This form of natural law was based on the moral theology and philosophy of the Middle Ages which had been transmitted by the late Spanish scholastics to Protestant north-western Europe where it merged with the new scientific theory of Galileo, Descartes and Hobbes. This law, however, remained basically Roman law — not so much in its medieval version but, rather, in the elegant humanist interpretation which the great French and Dutch jurists had given to it. Thus, to a continental observer, it seems that more Roman blood flows in the veins of the North American legal system than would be expected in light of the overpowering independence, vitality and progressiveness of this system.

Now we should examine the relevance that all of this has for us today to determine whether these historical developments enable us to understand modern law better. In order to do that, we should first consider the relevant characteristics of Roman law itself.

## III. PRIMARY AND SECONDARY EFFECTS OF ROMAN LAW

That we had to refer to "ancient" and "medieval" Roman law when we began suggests the necessary ambiguity of the expression "Roman law." I will briefly explain the meaning of these terms.

The term "ancient Roman law" refers to the law of the Roman city-state and, later, to that of the ancient Roman empire. That law was an elemental phenomenon; it was an historical reality of great vital power. Ancient Roman law was at one time the living law of a powerful community.

The term "medieval Roman law" (as well as all other forms of Roman law) refers to a tradition, *i.e.*, to the vital effects certain surviving facts, or authoritative texts, of antiquity had on the life, society and legal systems of the medieval and modern Western world. Whether these new societies understood these surviving elements in their "proper" sense is not important. "Prolific misunderstanding" is a typical and perhaps necessary factor in the process of appropriating another civilization.[7] What I am referring to is simply the distinction between two specific objects of historical writing. On the one side, there is the reality of the ancient Roman world. On the other side, there is the conception which the jurists, historians and philologists of successive epochs had of this reality. I will illustrate this with a simple example: The well-known maxim *princeps legibus solutus* (meaning the Roman emperor himself is not bound by the law) can have at least three different meanings. According to the Roman jurist Ulpian (approximately 220 A.D.), its originator, it meant that

7. Some modern German philosophers have proposed the suggestive term "*Wirkungsgschichte*" [roughly, "the history of effects," *ed.*] to describe those secondary effects of past events. But I shall not deal with the far-reaching implications of distinguishing, in this way, the primary existence and the secondary effects of historical phenomena in ontological, theological and even historical hermeneutics.

the emperor was exempt from a specific statute which disadvantaged unmarried or childless citizens.[8] In the *Pandects* of Justinian, three hundred years later, the statement acquired a more general meaning. There, it was placed under the general title *De legibus senatusque consultis et longa consuetudine.*[9] In this context, the statement should be understood to mean that the emperor is exempt from *all* statutes.[10] In the philosophy of European absolutism, this paroemia finally came to be the justification of the principle that the sovereign is not bound by law at all.

## IV. THE RELEVANT CHARACTERISTICS OF ANCIENT ROMAN LAW

The remainder of this part of my lecture will be devoted to *ancient* Roman law. I will restrict myself to those elements which came to have a lasting meaning for western civilization and western legal thought. The lasting effect Roman law had on world history may be explained by: (1) the incorporation of the Mediterranean ecumene into one empire, which survived spiritually in modern Europe; (2) the Roman concept of political power as a legal order; (3) the strict isolation of this legal order from its social and economic background; and (4) the control of legal decision-making by means of a consistent system of cognitive principles.

Roman law and Roman jurisprudence are products of an ancient city-state. No other ancient city-state, however, produced a positive legal science or a legal system of equivalent significance. The lasting effects of Roman law must, therefore, be the result of certain unique conditions that prevailed only in the *Roman* city-state — their *civitas* or *res publica,* as they called it.

### A. *The Autarchic Roman Polis*

The phenomenon of the ancient polis is principally confined to the occidental, Mediterranean cultures. The polis was Greek, Italo-Etruscan and western Semitic, *i.e.*, Phoenician (Tyre, Sidon, Arados, *etc.*) or Punic (Carthage, Utica, *etc.*). The archetype is the Greek polis, and Athens is the one we know best. To us, the polis is a remarkable and singular political organism. The polis was a basically agrarian community of landlords and peasants, cut off from the surrounding world by its city walls. Inside, there was generally a

8. These legal disadvantages were a part of Augustus's program of "Moral Rearmament." The emperor, due to obvious dynastic grounds of expediency, was impliedly exempt from this statute, according to Ulpian. It is only consistent that Ulpian added: "the wife of Caesar is, however, not exempted."

9. DIGEST OF JUSTINIAN 1.3.

10. At least Justinian's compilers are honest enough not to conceal the old, more restricted context of this statement. The compilers, in DIGEST OF JUSTINIAN 1.3.32, do cite the original source: *Ulpianus libro tredecimo ad legem Iuliam et Papiam, i.e.*, Ulpian's thirteenth book on the matrimonial statutes of Augustus.

temple of the city deity, a citadel (ἀκρόπολις, *arx*) and a market place (ἀγορά, *forum*). The polis was an autarchic unit in three ways: (1) with respect to religion, the polis was a sacred precinct for its deities, *i.e.*, Athena Promachos or Jupiter Optimus Maximus; (2) the relationship of the polis to the rest of the world was defined by the absence of foreign rule ( ἐλευθερία ) and by the freedom to lay down its own laws ( αὐτονομία ); and (3) the *internal* structure of the polis was determined by its quality as a community of free men, *i.e.*, men who, enjoying full political rights, were all subject to the same law ( ἰσονομία ). This principle did not exclude slavery, however, nor did it mean that there was no gradation of political rights according to economic status (*census*).

In the fully developed polis, the constitution of the city and the legal relations among the citizens ( νομος ἀστικός , *ius civile*) were based on statutes. These statutes could either be the result of an act of "codification" by a *nomothete* who had been nominated by the city and vested with extraordinary powers (such as Solon or the Roman *decemviri*), or it could be resolutions of the popular assemblies ( ἐκκλησία , *comitia*), as later became the rule. Similarly, leading officials ( ἄρχοντες , *magistratus*) were elected by voting assemblies. Important legal issues were also resolved directly by the citizens' assemblies. Other matters were presented to large juries, and cases of minor importance may have been decided by single jurors.

"Law" in the developed polis was not conceived of as a divine gift or an immemorial custom, but rather as a man-made, autonomous institution. This conception played an important role in the formation of western legal thought; it was the beginning of a notion of a state founded in the free will of its citizens.

The strongest impulse for the development of this conception came from the necessity of defense. Defense required a heavily armed infantry (φάλαγξ *classis*) which replaced — or, rather, pushed into the background — the old feudal cavalry. Consequently, this newly important infantry began to make political demands. As a result of these demands, the old tribal kingdoms, or feudal aristocracies, evolved into *poleis*.

### B. *The Roman Nobility and the Expansion of the Roman Polis*

The general structures of the Greek polis are also characteristic of the Roman *res publica* from the fourth century B.C. Of all the *poleis*, however, Rome had three distinguishing features which led to the uniqueness of Roman law in world history. One element was of an *external* nature: the military success which brought this polis alone from a hegemonial position in an Italic confederation to a position as the ruling power in the Mediterranean world. Without this achievement, Roman law would naturally have failed to have historical importance lasting into modern times; and the legal systems and the science of law in the West would not be what they are today.

A second element was the way in which the Roman *res publica* deviated from the regular model of the Greek polis. Economic and social changes in Greece frequently led to the development of democracy with full equality of all citizens. This development was cut off in Rome. On the other hand, unlike other great commercial city-states, such as Carthage or Massilia, the Roman *res publica* did not become, or remain, a closed oligarchy either. Both extremes were avoided by a happy compromise struck between the old patrician aristocracy and the rising upper stratum of the plebs. At first, the upper stratum of the plebs allied themselves with the economically endangered smaller landlords and with the landless population of the city. This alliance threatened to upset the old patrician state. But, the fusion of the patriciate and the leading plebean families resulted in the stabilization of a new aristocracy. This so-called *nobilitas* led Rome in the next two centuries to dominance in the Mediterranean world. At the same time, the establishment of the plebean tribunate and the integration of the *concilia plebis* into the constitutional framework, the democratization of the *census* and the popular election of the magistrates quieted the remaining lower stratum of the plebs. In this unusual, but very successful manner, "populistic" elements were blended with an old oligarchy. The magistrates were thus put under supervision, and the state was saved from usurpation by tyrants — a constant threat for most Greek *poleis*. On the other hand, the Roman nobility kept its ability to overcome internal and external setbacks — a typical virtue of a tradition-minded leading caste. The annual elections of the magistrates, who took seats in the Senate after finishing their term of office, brought about a constant "changing of the guard." At the same time, the Senate provided the *res publica* with a virtually inexhaustible reserve of experienced statesmen, military commanders and public administrators.

The third unique element of the Roman polis was the way in which this Roman nobility developed unprecedented methods of military, political and economic expansion during its classical period. A network of Roman and Latin settlements (*coloniae*) made possible the expansion of the city-state into vast regions. These settlements were independent in their sources of livelihood. With respect to the law, however, they remained sectors of the parent city, although they were geographically distant. Thus, the ground was laid for the urbanization and Romanization of the Iberian, Celtic, Germanic and Illyrian provinces which were to become the birthplaces of early medieval Europe.

### C. *The Unique Institutions of Roman Law*

The traditionalism, realism and authoritative attitude of the Roman nobility were the sources of the peculiarities of Roman law. Rome was the first polity to develop an independent and highly objective procedure to arbitrate social and economic conflicts. This development liberated the Roman legal system from archaic ritualism and, later, kept it free from the too-immediate impact of changing political and moral ideologies.

One should emphasize that this development is, perhaps, the primary Roman contribution to western legal thought. The Roman contribution consists principally in the development of highly objective methods of conflict-resolution, not in the discovery of the concept of law as such nor in the reduction of law to general conditions and qualities of justice. These latter developments are glorious achievements of the Greek spirit. The Greeks' discovery and refinement of the concept of law was, of course, known to the Roman jurists, and it did indeed influence Roman legal thought after the second century B.C. Through Roman legal texts, these Greek achievements had considerable effect on European legal thought, as well. But the singular contribution of Rome to legal culture did not consist of this. This point requires some explanation, brief though it must be, because it is not obvious:

(1) In contrast to the role legislation played in the Greek *poleis*, Roman legislation remained somewhat "underdeveloped." In times of constitutional crisis, legislation was used by the conflicting parties to advance their position or it was used as a means of effecting a compromise. In matters of social concern, legislation was intended to bring about reforms or merely to appease the masses. In the field of private law, legislation was of minor importance — fortunately, one should like to say. Thus, legal progress was protected from the intrigues of the nobility, the demagoguery of the tribunes or of their promoters and the emotions of the metropolitan masses which so often corrupted Greek statutes.

(2) In a similar manner, the Roman constitution succeeded in protecting the administration of civil justice from misuse for political purposes. Large juries, or even the *comitia* themselves, were competent to try only exceptional *civil* cases, those of special political or social importance. Despite the dangers inherent in having only men of the senatorial class mete out justice,[11] this system proved beneficial to the continuity and security of *private* law. The speeches of the great Attic orators and of Cicero are evidence of how dangerous the emotionalism and the persuasiveness of rhetoric would have been to the justice of a decision.

(3) The place of legislation and of trial by popular courts in the field of private law was taken by a uniquely Roman institution, the praetor. One of the annually elected magistrates, the praetor supervised the decision-making of private judges (*iudices privati*). The praetor had coercive power to enforce judicial measures, *i.e.*, to issue summonses or subpoenas, to appoint trial judges or to grant execution by a judgment creditor. The praetor did not,

11. Only men of the senatorial class had this responsibility prior to the crisis of the Republic, *i.e.*, in its last century.

however, hand down judgments himself. Instead, he appointed private judges and vested them with the authority to collect evidence and to decide the case in accordance with his instructions (*formulae*).[12] At the beginning of the praetor's year of office, he informed the public of his intentions and procedural programs by an edict.[13]

From the time of the later Republic, the praetor was no longer bound by statutory forms of action (*legis actiones*); he could devise procedural *formulae* for individual cases and include them in his general edict. Such measures were not restricted to the application of laws in force, but could be used to modify or replace existing law. When the praetor's successors adopted such innovations, as they did more often than not, the result was substantially the creation of new law (*ius honorarium*).

The tendency of these innovations was often similar to that of English equity. They were essentially progressive; like English equity, in contrast to the common law, the *ius honorarium* was likely to support ethical and technical change. As Max Weber observed, *Amtscharisma* (the charisma of an official) is more likely to tend toward social and moral innovation than traditionalistic judicature. Thus, the praetor eliminated, or reduced, the effect of antiquated rituals of the *ius civile.* He protected both minors and adults from cheating, intimidation or undue influence. He set up new ethical standards in *bonae fidei iudicia.* Similarly, he adapted the sluggish law of an agrarian tribal society to new needs of commerce. This development was necessitated by the advanced contract and credit system of the Hellenistic economy which Rome entered and finally absorbed after the third century B.C. Important innovations of the praetorian edicts were intended to serve the banking and credit system, a more highly specialized system of production and maritime commerce.

Although the praetor thus played an active part in "keeping the bloodstream in the body" of ancient Roman law, he was essentially uninterested in the intellectual and scientific development of law. Most praetors were ambitious competitors for the consulate, the highest office of the *res publica.* They were not, as a rule, legal experts, and some may have been legally illiterate. The experienced, and possibly able, clerks (*apparitores*) of the praetor's staff, who served beyond the one-year term of office, could not relieve the praetor from the burden of his creative tasks. Who was it, then, who showed the praetor the techniques by which he could realize his intentions? And especially, who suggested the innovative *formulae*? As one might expect, the responsibility for these advances belongs in large part to a group of legal experts. This brings us to the essence of Rome's contribution to all subse-

12. The formulae of the praetors have been compared to the Anglo-Saxon writs, in spite of essential differences in origins and functions.

13. This "edict" was known as the *edictum praetoris* or the so-called *edictum perpetuum.*

quent legal thought, *i.e.*, the *iuris consultus*, the professional Roman jurist — a phenomenon almost unknown to the Greek world.

(4) The Roman jurists were a unique type of legal functionary. They were neither legislators nor judges; neither advocates nor prosecutors. They performed their crucial tasks as advisers without being public officials; their expertise was not tainted by the receipt of a payment. They could not have played their role if they had not enjoyed great social and intellectual prestige because the development and the improvement of the private law was almost completely in their hands. The social prestige of the Republican jurists derived from their membership in the ruling class of the *nobilitas*; this also made them economically independent and allowed them to work gratis. Nevertheless, these activities were rewarding in that they were a means of obtaining the favor (*gratia*) of the voting population. Thus, their chances to be elected to the higher magistracies were improved and election further helped them to maintain their public influence. The professional authority of the Roman jurists came from their monopoly of information and technical expertise. They alone were endowed with the highly specialized knowledge necessary to command the formalistic and traditionalistic *ius civile*.[14]

(5) The legal "monopoly" of the Roman jurists can be traced back to their original membership in the body of pontiffs (*collegium pontificum*). The *pontifices* were at one time the guardians of all written tradition and ritual techniques. The pontiffs alone knew all the laws, the forms of "writs" and documents, the court calendar and the *responsa*[15] which their predecessors had rendered earlier. In a traditionalistic society like old Rome, the dread of error concerning sacred or legal matters made the pontiffs indispensable. As time went on, an increasing number of *nobiles* turned to the practice of giving legal advice without being members of the *collegium pontificum* and a large part of the prestige of the pontificate passed to them. In addition, their greater independence from the directives of the *pontifex maximus* gave this new group greater liberties and greater flexibility.

(6) The last characteristic feature of ancient Roman law is that new law was created by giving legal advice (*consilia, responsa*) in contrast to the European way of creating law by legislation and the Anglo-American way of doing it by judicial decision. In this extremely closed society, the public actions both of private persons and of magistrates required the constant social backing of political, religious or legal authority. One might, for example, consult an

---

14. The *ius civile* of the time of the Roman jurists was similar, in these respects, to the common law of bygone times — and maybe not only of bygone times.

15. [A technical term, virtually untranslatable, for authoritative opinions given by a pontiff or jurist. *Ed.*]

oracle. In legal matters, one consulted the oracles of the law (*oracula iuris*), the jurists, who offered counsel (*consilium*). The *consilium* was used to determine the appropriate form of action (*agere*) or the appropriate document for a transaction (*cavere*) or — in its noblest form — to frame a legal opinion (*respondere*) addressed to the praetor, a private judge (*iudex privatus*) or a client. By means of these advisory activities, the Roman jurist maintained constant contact with actual cases. The fact that legal development came out of actual cases makes ancient Roman law much more like Anglo-American law than the practice of deducing law from statutes (continental legalism) or from scientific legal concepts (as in the *Begriffsjurisprudenz* of German Pandectism).

(7) A unique quality of Roman jurisprudence is that it did not stop at a purely pragmatic and precise casuistry. On the contrary, the greatest achievement of the Roman jurists was their ability to "purify" the case of its accidental elements, of the *species facti* and, thus, to specify the essential legal problem as a *quaestio iuris*. The first occasion to do this was presented by the *disputatio fori, i.e.*, the discussion held by the older jurist, who had been asked for a *consilium*, with his apprentices. This later developed into legal instruction and was finally set down in a legal literature. Under these conditions, legal science and literature were molded out of their original raw material; they were derived from the simple nature of the *formulae* and *responsa* which had been honed by practical experience, sorted and recorded. In this way, the decisions of a new science were reduced to common denominators, and the literary presentation of its professional knowledge became rationalized. A process of intellectual reasoning and the evolution of general propositions had begun.

The part that *Greek* theory of the formation of scientific concepts and systems played in the evolution of Roman legal science is controversial. Many of us believe it was of considerable importance, but not *the* deciding impulse. However, I cannot go into more detail on this question. The modern jurist, though, should be heedful of Scylla and Charybdis. He should not, especially as a European professor, imagine Roman jurisprudence as the model of a systematic or even axiomatic theory — as the law-of-nature school or the *Pandektenwissenschaft* was, for example. Similarly, he should not see it as a merely pragmatic, unprincipled case law or believe that Roman decision-making was based only on free and creative intuition.

## V. CONCLUSION OF PART ONE

In summary, all the factors that contributed to the glory and uniqueness of Roman jurisprudence for ages to come were present in the *iuris consultus* of the late Republic; the characteristic institutions, norms and concepts of this legal system were already developed at that time. The further development of

Roman private law between the early imperial period and the Justinianic codification was only a consequential result of those inherent elements. Admittedly, the codification was a unique and enriching development which gloriously overshadowed the older material from which it was made. For our present purposes, however, a short outline of the later developments will suffice:

(1) Our knowledge of Roman law is based almost exclusively on the "classical" legal literature of the Principate (first to third centuries A.D.). As far as we can tell, this literature is far richer and on a higher intellectual level than were the lost works of the Republican era.

(2) Classical jurisprudence absorbed all the questions which had arisen in the time of the late Republic. These questions were categorized, and often adequately answered for the first time, in the classical era. These questions were also enriched by the emergence of new issues. Undeniably, Roman jurisprudence came to its height at this time. It would only be nostalgic snobbery to deny that the Roman jurisprudence now had come to its height — just as it would be wrong not to trace this climax back to its older origins.

(3) The greatest jurists took a direct part in governmental tasks and the central imperial administration of justice from the time of the great adopted emperors of the second century A.D. Thus, the whole empire was within their area of interest. Responsibilities such as these liberated the jurist from city-state prejudices. Consequently, their sense of lawfulness was allowed to develop freely, and they were disciplined to care for the welfare of their imperial subjects.

(4) In the same spirit, the jurists assisted the emperors in the development of a new administrative law for the empire. This body of *ius publicum novum* was institutionalized and made more humanitarian by these jurists — perhaps one of their greatest achievements. Through the medium of Justinian's codification, this *benigna interpretatio* gave the leaven of moral reason and common sense to the European *ius commune,* the *ius canonicum* and English equity.

(5) The survival of this great legacy was not prevented by the catastrophes of the later third century A.D. or by the Byzantine absolutism which began with Constantine the Great. To be sure, further imperial legislation became more of a manifestation of the woes of an empire which was under stress and partly dying — perhaps this legislation was the darkest and most oppressive legacy of ancient Roman law. This last epoch may boast, however, of one very different achievement: Byzantine legal science and the Justinianic codification which this new science made possible. Thus, the jurists of the Byzantine period rescued the bulk of Roman law and, in fact, they conveyed its most superior version, the Roman classical jurisprudence, to the new European era.

## Part Two: The Nature and Significance of Medieval Roman Law

### I. THE SECONDARY EFFECTS OF EARLIER CULTURES

#### A. *The Problem of Cultural Influence*

To aid our understanding of the effects of ancient Roman law on western civilization, let me offer a few preliminary thoughts on the ways in which an historian views the secondary effects of an earlier culture on a later one. Historians cannot avoid generalizing about this phenomenon. The innumerable social and psychological processes by which cultural structures are carried over from one era to another cannot be described individually. To discuss this phenomenon at all, we must systematize the ways in which it occurs. The simplest concepts, such as "influence" or "impact," are harmless but rather meaningless. For example, the proposition: "A has influenced B" means only that the fact "B" has been conditioned in some way by the fact "A." Equally harmless and meaningless is the metaphor of legal succession, *i.e.*, the proposition that the continental concept of the legal obligation is a Roman legacy. When the metaphor of biological descent is employed, the effect is more dangerous — implying that a new civilization can inherit characteristics from a parent civilization in the same way in which a child receives hereditary characteristics from its parents. In this case, the metaphor is ambiguous and misleading. In fact, individuals in a new civilization may be the biological descendants of individuals of the older civilization; but "the spirit wafts from where it wills" and may at times favor the sons of Hagar and not the legitimate children of Isaac.

When historians apply more complex patterns in their attempt to comprehend generally the relationships between two civilizations, the danger of unintended implication is even stronger. These dangers are evident in such metaphorical expressions as "a new culture *learns* from the parent culture"; or in speaking of the "continuity" or "survival" of an older cultural element; or in referring to the "renaissance" or the "revival" of past cultural hypostatizations in new cultures.[16] These three models of historical expression, should be discussed further so that the misunderstanding caused by their use can be better understood.

At first sight, the most realistic model for conceptualizing the relationship between temporally separate cultures appears to be that of "learning." In much the same way as a pupil learns behavioral patterns or acquires informa-

16. The term "reception" will not be used here as it frequently is used to describe the adoption of the Roman law of antiquity in southern Europe in the early Middle Ages or its adoption in northern Europe at a somewhat later time. I believe that the term "reception" is most properly confined to the adoption by one legal order of the *existing* order of a contemporary legal system, *e.g.*, Turkey's "reception" of the Swiss Civil Code.

tion by observing a teacher, "the" early Middle Ages are thought to be pupils of "the" late antiquity. Leaving aside the fact that no teacher living in late antiquity ever taught an individual pupil living in the Middle Ages, this idea seems quite appropriate when speaking, *e.g.*, of handicrafts, Roman horticulture or glass fabrication. Similarly, we may speak of learning when we refer to the adoption of the seven-day or the planetary week, the script, the form of legal deeds, and perhaps, even the simpler legal institutions of late antiquity, such as earnest money (*arra*) in a sale. The more complex a cultural phenomenon, however, the more its assimilation requires intellectual productiveness on the part of the "pupil," and the more unsatisfactory is this model of the simple transfer of information. The further developments in the Middle Ages of the Christology of late antiquity, or of the Neoplatonic teaching on categories, are two forbidding examples of extremely complex processes. No less complicated was the process of adopting a legal ideology or a legal scientific method.

When an historian speaks of *continuity* (or *survival*), he is postulating, rather arbitrarily, that a certain cultural factor has remained constant. Thus, the cultural factor is said to have retained its identity despite the flow of time. Whatever specific surviving element the historian chooses,[17] its identity with the past element is, at best, only an initial working hypothesis. Thus, one cannot simply claim that the Roman municipal constitution more or less survived in the form of similar (but not identical) constitutions in the early medieval cities; one must *prove* it.

Lastly, there is the concept of *rebirth*, *revival* or *renaissance*, so popular among cultural historians. Since the time of the Italian *rinascimento*, the sublime paradigm of the rebirth of those redeemed by Jesus Christ has given this image its very special splendor. At the same time, it is a most imprecise analogy. For the exact description of a very complex and diffuse interplay, it substitutes the mystery of the pentecostal miracle — the pouring forth of the Holy Spirit, so to speak. Nevertheless, the comparison certainly thrives, not only because of its inner nobility, but also in response to the palable experience of historians. The encounter between a new culture and an old one may indeed be characterized as such a phenomenon. Such an encounter may in fact lead to a real spiritual initiation or initial "ignition" through which productive structures or ideologies may catch fire through the contact with the remains of a past civilization.

Thus, "survival," "continuity," "revival," "renaissance" and even the

17. Sometimes the individuals of former cultures are considered the persevering element, when we speak, for example, of "Celtic" or "Iberian" continuity. At other times, the reference is to an objective phenomenon, when we speak, for example, of the continuity of the ancient form of a deed, or of the Roman municipal constitution, or, sometimes, even of the Roman law itself as a whole.

modest "learning" are not precise and documentable propositions concerning the interaction of social and psychological elements and effects. The historian cannot do without them, however, for two reasons. First, these models have a legitimate purpose; they provide working hypotheses, or tentative "sketches," for the explication of facts in the context of scientific research. Second, these models provide an indispensable means of communicating the results of research. The models should, however, remain as flexible as possible. Modern genetics may offer the most appropriate model for describing the means by which past elements are reproduced in a new civilization. As I understand it, genetics describes the passing of hereditary factors as a process of conveying information. Living beings are defined by a code — a biochemical matrix — according to which similar forms are reproduced. This pattern probably corresponds best to the legal historian's perception of the secondary effects of Roman law on the Middle Ages.

### B. *The Two Phases of Roman Law in the Middle Ages*

These complicated reflections were necessary because the continuing existence of ancient Roman law in the western societies represents an especially complex and ambiguous process of transference. Legal systems are all-encompassing, psychological, social and intellectual structures. Legal systems are complexes of several elements, including social customs and behavioral patterns, organized social institutions, techniques of using public power, moral or ideological values and intellectual processes of perception.

In order to give an overview of the secondary effects of ancient Roman law, it is best to treat these effects in two phases. First, in the Early Middle Ages (fifth to tenth centuries), we have the immediate, continuing existence of Roman legal principles and institutions. Second, in the High Middle Ages (from the eleventh century onwards), we have the rediscovery of classical Roman legal science by the southern European law faculties. The cognitive models of "learning" and "survival" can be said to belong to the first phase, while the term "renaissance" belongs to the second phase. The second phase, or renaissance, was followed in countries north of the Alps by the so-called "reception" of the reborn legal science.[18]

These two eras represent different degrees of intellectual maturity in western civilization. In the Early Middle Ages, western civilization was still incapable of expressing its own identity and ideals; it was restricted to assimilating disparate antique elements. After the revival of the eleventh century, however, western civilization had matured to the point where it was capable of congenial and creative confrontation with the legacy of Roman classical jurisprudence, because it had created its own theological philosophical and political ideology.

18. *See* note 16 *supra*.

## II. Roman Law in Early Medieval Europe

### A. *The First Western European States*

In western Europe, the earliest organizations resembling the modern state grew out of the collapse of the western Roman Empire: the Visigothic and Burgundian kingdoms within a still-existing Empire and the later and more promising Frankish kingdom in the northwestern territories of the former Empire. The Frankish Empire was also responsible for having forced the Roman inheritance upon the Germanic tribes of the European interior (such as the Alemannians, the Bavarians and, finally, the Saxons) and upon the western Slavic peoples. Later, the Franks exported the Roman inheritance to the Scandinavians as well. England — due to the high intellectual and spiritual standard of her clergy -- had her own special standing in this process.

These "states" were able to constitute themselves only by taking advantage of the surviving Roman administrative organization. The Empire from which they arose, however, was no longer the principate, the Empire which the *principes*, from the time of Augustus, had forged on the base of the old Roman Republic. Instead, the new European communities succeeded to the "dominate," the absolutistic and centralized monarchy which was shaped by the catastrophies of the third century and which ruled thereafter over a society in which horizontal class divisions were suppressed and vertical divisions enhanced.

A hierarchical and highly specialized bureaucracy was an instrument of constant tyrannical intervention by a thoroughly regimented state. The main purpose of the state had become the securing of the finances and military services necessary for its defense and, thus, the preservation of the bureaucracy itself. To accomplish these ends, the once-free tenants (*coloni*) were bound to their land, and the huge manorial estates were feudalized. All crafts which were relevant to the public interest were transformed into hereditary, compulsory guilds. Of greatest importance, the economic productivity of the wealthier classes in the cities, which was once the backbone of the Empire's welfare, was sacrificed to a ruthless system of taxes, services and requisitions (*munera publica*).

### B. *The Legal Literature Which Influenced Early Medieval Europe*

In order to survive, the new Roman-Germanic societies had to continue managing within the existing bureaucratic structures. These included the laws and decrees of the late Empire. This "immaterial baggage" had, however, shrunk considerably in the interim between the fall of the Empire and the establishment of the western kingdoms. By far, the most important legal sources in the Early Middle Ages were the enactments of the Byzantine emperors together with some relics or epitomes of elementary legal literature.

These epitomes included an excerpt from an elementary legal handbook dating from around 300 A.D. (the *Sententiae Pauli*); a crude adaptation of Gaius' famous textbook (the *Epitome Gai*); various late commentaries orignating from the elementary instruction of provincial functionaries (*interpretationes*); and, lastly, a few collections of specimen deeds.[19] The law contained in this meager assortment is referred to as "Roman vulgar law."

Nevertheless, the command of even these humble leftovers required the mastery of some basic intellectual skills. Included among these skills were reading and writing, the organization and preservation of documents, and the drafting of statutes, court decisions, protocols (*gesta, acta*), wills and contracts of sale. These skills could only be passed on to a new generation where antique elementary education, especially the *trivium* (grammar, logic and rhetoric), had been preserved. Only those who were taught in these schools were literate and, thus, capable of writing down the statutes, administrative acts and decisions that were necessary to establish an organizational framework for the new communities.

Thus, those who were literate possessed a monopoly of all those positions in government, secular and ecclesiastical administration and the administration of justice which required the ability to read and to write and to perform basic bureaucratic tasks. These literates, in other words, had the exclusive control of the drafting of laws and of all records concerning accounting, taxes and fees and control of all those transactions which required notarization either for reasons of expediency or because notarization was legally required. While the leading literates and functionaries were originally recruited from the class of Roman provincial landlords (*possessores*), most of whom had senatorial rank, these tasks were ultimately left almost entirely to the higher functionaries of the Church. These churchmen became the backbone of the new Roman-Germanic states after the extinction of paganism and Arianism.

### C. *Fundamental Roman Legal Concepts in Early Medieval Europe*

Of prime importance in this discussion are the ideas of law and state which were adopted in early medieval Europe along with the basic intellectual skills. These ideas were to play an essential role in the forming of western Europe.

One influential idea was the Roman concept of *public office* (in the sense of organized authority) with its corresponding functional competencies. The permanent administrative body, first established by the classical *principes*, had been enlarged by the absolute monarchy into a hypertrophic bureaucracy.

---

19. [Convenient editions of the *Sententiae Pauli* and the *Epitome Gai*, and some of the other works mentioned may be found in 2 FONTES IURIS ROMANI ANTEJUSTINIANI (J. Baviera ed. 1968). For the English-speaking reader the best edition of Gaius's *Institutes*, his famous textbook, is 1-2 THE INSTITUTES OF GAIUS (F. de Zulueta ed. 1953). *Ed.*]

The Germanic conception of office as a personal relationship between the vassal and the king left little room for either an objective concept of public office or for the consequent development of set competencies. Thus, the only models for the latter type of organization available to the early medieval states were to be found in the imperial administration or in the ecclesiastical office organized on similar lines.

A similar process took place with the concept of *statutory law.* The Germanic tribes did not originally perceive law as a volitional act of free men, as did the ancient city-states, or as an imperative act of the ruler, as did Rome under the emperors. To the Germanic tribes, law was conceived of as a body of unwritten customs and traditions. All written law in the Early Middle Ages, therefore, must have been based on the absolutistic notion of law developed in the late principate and the Byzantine monarchy. The Germanic kings, however, for the sake of their own tribesmen, formally maintained the idea that the laws were made by the great men of the realm (*proceres, etc.*) and only drafted and promulgated by the king's staff.

Beyond the ideas of public office and statute law, the Church made the Early Middle Ages conscious of a *universal concept of law.* For the Christians unified under the Roman Empire, the powerful tradition of *ius romanum* evidently existed above and beyond the old tribal laws and the decrees of the new rulers. This universal law was connected by Augustine with the idea of the *ius divinum*; it remained a powerful living idea and continued to guide the thoughts and public actions of the literate staffs of the new rulers.

The carryover of political, literary and legal traditions from late antiquity to the Early Middle Ages remained for a long time only a sign of *sur*vival and not a *re*vival. In many respects, what we refer to as the early medieval "states" were not much more than provinces which had outlived the fallen Empire. They were not new, original creations which had adopted the norms and institutions of a former world by their own free choice.

## III. Roman Law in the High Middle Ages and in Early Modern Europe

### A. *The Studium Civile*

The western world did not begin to comprehend its own "identity" before the eleventh century. This process of comprehension was brought about by the emergence of new ideologies among the ruling ecclesiastical elite. In the religious sector, this new ideology took shape in the reform movement of Cluny. In the political sector, the process occurred through the idea of *translatio* and *renovatio imperii.* Finally, in the intellectual sector, the new ideology followed the reception of the new Platonic and Aristotelian dialectics by the early scholastics. In the sphere of legal thinking, this process found expression in the rediscovery, in a spiritual more than a literal sense, of the great heritage of the Roman classical jurists which had been collected in Justinian's *Digest*, study of which was revived by the end of the eleventh century. The European science of law evolved from this rediscovery, and that science formed the basis of the legal systems of modern continental Europe.

The *studium civile* blossomed in Bologna around the beginning of the twelfth century. Soon afterwards, the phenomenon appeared in other Italian and French cities. One must ask, what led to this unique intellectual explosion?

One prerequisite to the establishment of the *studium civile* was a political ideology, the so-called "Rome-Idea." The "Rome-Idea" was expressed in three versions. One was the imperial idea of the Hohenstaufen emperors and their rivals among the monarchs of western Europe. A second was the curial concept of the reform popes after Cluny. A third was the national version of the Italian city republics. In all three forms, the "Rome-Idea" encouraged a general recognition of Justinian's law.

Also favoring the establishment of the *studium civile* was a new scholarly enthusiasm for the texts of antiquity. This scholarly enthusiasm had captured the scholastics and was echoed in the Latin literature of the High Middle Ages. Finally, there was the impact of economic expansion in northern Italy. This expansion required a rationalization of legal intercourse and legal conflicts which could be accomplished through rules which had been made more predictable by a professional systematization. Significantly, the *studium civile* was established in Bologna by order of the municipal authorities.

### B. *The First European Jurists*

Under these conditions, the instructional method of the liberal arts (*trivium*) which was used in schooling the clergy, the secular *consules* and *sindici*, the *defensores* and the notaries was now applied to Justinian's *Digest*. In so doing, the Bolognese fathers of legal science discovered a complete new spiritual world. They became aware of the unique, free and superior mastership of the great Roman jurists. One of the wonders of our civilization is that the Bolognese glossators responded to the challenge of the Roman jurists with an understanding of equal rank. Their understanding was not historical, but they showed the same ability to assimilate their material that the school of Chartres showed with Plato, or Thomas Aquinas showed with Aristotle. For the Bolognese jurists Justinian's *Digest* was not a mass of lifeless texts. They made the timeless problems the texts posed their own concern.

These glossators became Europe's first jurists in the strictest sense. They did not deal with social conflicts merely within the bounds of accepted tradition or the dictates of moral ideology. Instead, they dealt with social conflicts by *discussing* each case as an independent juridical problem, as only the

Roman jurists had done before.[20] Thenceforth, there was in Europe a third authority to rival the actual political powers and the spiritual authority of Holy Scripture and contemporary theology (including the works of the Fathers of the Church). This new authority independently claimed the right to settle conflicts between individuals, groups and public powers. The jurists' demand that matters of a public nature be under the rule of law remains a living principle today. *This* feature is more a characteristic of our Western world than it is of any other past or contemporary civilization.

These great accomplishments would have been unthinkable if the rediscovery of ancient Roman jurisprudence had remained the privilege of a few. In fact, hosts of professional jurists were taught by the law faculties of Italy, France and, later, of every major European country. After the twelfth century, the youth of the ruling classes and the clergy streamed to these faculties from every part of Europe. Eventually, even talented and ambitious commoners were admitted to study at these faculties. These law students returned home with a technical knowledge of administration, politics and diplomacy. Later, this knowledge was extended to the administration of justice.

North of the Alps at least, the diplomatic, political and administrative activities of these new professionals always preceded developments in the administration of civil justice. The jurists first attained their public positions by rising through the large administrative apparatus of the Church or that of the Holy Roman Empire, the western European kingdoms, the greater feudal territories or the larger cities. Only through these channels did they advance to key positions in the central courts of the sovereigns and eventually to the common and local courts. The unschooled decision-makers of the Estates — the prelates, knights and representatives of the cities — resisted the encroachment of the jurists for a long time. This resistance was due in part to political mistrust of the sovereign and in part to their own material interests in their financially lucrative privileges. However, as the political power of the Estates began to crumble, the jurists began to occupy these positions as well. They made advances even in places like northern France, the Netherlands, the cities of the German *Hansa* and in Switzerland: in short, in regions where national or local law had been maintained.

### C. *The Role of Ecclesiastical Legal Science*

To omit mention of the simultaneous development of an *ecceliastical* legal science would leave this outline incomplete. Until the Reformation, the Church was not only universal in Europe but was also by far Europe's largest

20. The exegesis of legally relevant texts by Rabinnic or Islamic scholars — which was in some ways similar — had confined itself to religious texts which originally did not belong to a specially *legal* subsystem.

institution. The Church, which had always been a pioneer in promoting more objective and rational decision-making, began organizing its scattered legal sources into a corpus of canon law. This work was done under the influence of, and in competition with, the masters of the *ius civile.* When great canonists ascended to the papal throne at the end of the twelfth century, they transformed the Church into a *legalistic* Church, a universal body vested with a central legislation, administration and jurisdiction. The system of codified ecclesiastical law occupied a parallel position to that of the *ius commune*, and the "canonist" paralleled the "legist."[21] Since ecclesiastical law also governed many secular claims, thereby serving to develop a complementary relationship between the *ius commune* and the *ius canonicum*, both legal systems were increasingly seen as expressions of one universal legal order, the *ius utrumque.*

D. *Later Developments in the Growth of European Law*

These developments led to an intensified legalization and rationalization of public life in Europe. The jurists in the service of the ruling powers were gradually able to supplant the use of violence in the settling of conflicts and to eliminate private or community feuds — something which the Church and the monarchs had never fully achieved by the earlier medieval peace movements (*treuga Dei Landfrieden, etc.*). Thus, the jurists prepared the ground for economic expansion and for the gradual humanization of the European modern age.

While I cannot discuss the brilliant history of legal science and the expansion of the learned Roman law in detail,[22] it is appropriate to mention the outstanding landmarks in the further history of this process. These would include: (1) the elegant jurisprudence of the French and Dutch Humanists; (2) the newer school of natural law which was greatly influenced by Roman law; and (3) the revival of ancient Roman law in Savigny's historical school and in Pandectism. In some parts of Europe, in many regions of Germany, for example, the direct application of Roman law did not terminate until 1900. Even today, however, Roman law is alive; the continental codifications are based so much on Roman law that interpretation of them would remain incomplete or superficial without recourse to the *Corpus Iuris.* For an American audience, these events on the continent are of less consequence. In the Anglo-American legal system the immediate influence of Roman law is restricted to a relatively small body of civil law.[23] Rather than continuing with a history of the specific influences of Roman law, I would like to comment in conclusion on the general outlook of contemporary western legal thought.

21. "Legist" was the term used by medieval churchmen in referring to an expert in Justinianic law.

22. Further discussion of the subsequent expansion of the schooled Roman law in modern times is omitted for the same reason I did not pursue the later development of antique Roman law earlier. *See* Part One, §§ IV, V of text, *supra.*

23. *See* Part One, § II.B of text, *supra.*

## IV. Roman Law in the Modern World

### A. *Modern Historical Consciousness*

In western, southern and central Europe, Roman law has always been a subject taught by our faculties of law because it provides the necessary background for interpreting our own civil law. But the present crisis in matters of historical consciousness has had negative effects on the study of Roman law. The reasons for that crisis are obvious. We have entered an era of greater control of nature and futurist social planning. The Atlantic-European civilization has been transformed into a world civilization of "older" and "younger" nations. Similarly, there is the educational explosion which has made it necessary for many nations to offer the opportunity of elementary and specialized education to millions of young people; this development has led to a critical questioning of classical education. The humanistic study of the ancient languages, the classical systems of philosophy, idealistic historiography and even classical Newtonian physics are undergoing a new evaluation. Roman law belongs to this classical tradition.

I will not elaborate, however, on this educational and social trend for two reasons. First, growing criticism of one-sided technical specialization everywhere has brought forth a stronger interest in history. Thus, apologies for Roman law which I found necessary ten years ago before German and other European audiences would sound anachronistic today. Second, an apology of this kind is of minor interest in this country where Roman law was never in force, and was therefore not cultivated in connection with law but in connection with the classics, because of its obvious relevance to the economic and social history of antiquity. Consequently, I will simply point out the value which the study of Roman law can have for the student and graduate.

### B. *The Uses of Roman Law in the Modern World*

In the continental countries, ancient and medieval law belongs to the "prehistory," so to speak, of current law. The knowledge of Roman law is often a prerequisite to a basic understanding of the legal norms in force. An understanding of Roman law is also important for the critical evaluation of present or proposed legislation. Indeed, the battle against the historical misunderstandings of older or contemporary legislators is frequently won by a better appreciation of the Roman legal sources. One need only think of how much the appreciation of the continental doctrine of unjust enrichment might be advanced by greater understanding of its Roman underpinnings.

These general reasons for studying Roman law do not directly apply to students of the Anglo-American legal system. Other considerations, however, of a more general nature make the knowledge of Roman law worthwhile to an American audience.

In certain matters, one must frequently rely on the terminology, definitions and norms of a basically Romanistic civil law. This is so with international business transactions, in the field of conflicts of law whenever foreign law is applied by courts as the *lex fori* and in questions of the unification of legal norms among countries of the Anglo-American and the continental legal orders. Due to the common fundamental principles of western legal thought, the terminology of Roman law still provides a universal language.[24] In a more technical sense, Roman law terms are also the general vocabulary for comparative law and for one of the major problems of conflicts of law, the problem of "characterization" of a legal norm or institute. This *ius commune*, moreover, often constitutes a common set of values in conflicts between citizens of different nations. Thus, in such situations, Roman law facilitates agreement in principle. Similarly, one should recall the great part the *ius commune* played in the development of modern public international law.[25] This code of communication has become even more important because of the modern trend toward unification of laws. The common language of Roman law has facilitated the attainment of a certain uniformity of statutes which, in turn, has become a decisive factor in the advancement of international organizations.

The utility of Roman law, however, is not restricted to its direct effects on the *content* of modern legal systems. There is another significant contribution of Roman law to the training of the law student, including those in America. I am referring to the "classical" law in its original form. The Roman jurists' exemplary method of decision-making still has relevance for the modern jurist.[26] The decision-making method of these old masters contributes to the appeal they can still have for the modern jurist. He can learn the Roman jurist's method of clearly distinguishing legal issues and making those issues precise — an exercise which is essential for the objectification of social and political conflicts. Similarly, he can try to develop their sure instinct for the reality and practicability of legal solutions. He can, moreover, observe how they arrived at new and elegant solutions through the disciplined use of legal imagination. Even today, nothing develops the ability to discover the underlying legal issue in statutes or precedents more than the study of the casuistry of the classical jurists. The exegesis of Roman legal texts, which is customary for many law students in my country, often fascinates my practical-minded students even more than those who are interested in legal history. To observe this has always been a very enlightening personal experience for me.

---

24. Roman law provides, in the words of Sir Henry Sumner Maine, a *lingua franca*. To use a more modern term, it is the key code to understanding among jurists all over the world.

25. The *ius commune* has played a great part in the development of modern public international law since the times of the Spaniards in the sixteenth century and of Selden, Grotius and others in the seventeenth century.

26. *See* Part One, § IV.C of text, *supra*.

There is yet one more way in which familiarity with classical Roman law is of value in the modern world. The decisions of the classical jurists are a touchstone for testing many issues affecting the general theory of law today. The high "specific density" of their concentrated situational analysis provides an ideal test. In this way, the most eminent achievements of Roman jurists enable us to verify propositions and models, *e.g.*, of "legal axioms," of "logical empiricism," of "realism," of the so-called *topica iuris* and of the *nouvelle rhétorique.* Above all, their achievements offer an ideal paradigm for the theory of decision-making and of legal reasoning which is debated so heatedly even in this country. I believe that it is this paradigm which could prevent the present debate in legal theory from degenerating into one-sided or sterile dogmatism. The talent of the classic Roman jurists for providing answers can still be put to use in our society today — not only for the contemplative researcher but especially for the practical jurist who is confronted with new tasks daily. *Fabula et de te narratur*; this old story also applies to us today.

# [2]

# THE ORIGINS OF WESTERN LEGAL SCIENCE †

*Harold J. Berman* *

*The late eleventh, twelfth, and thirteenth centuries were years of intense political, economic, and religious change. In this Article, Professor Berman argues that the period also witnessed a revolutionary transformation in the nature of Western law. Three elements — the growth of university law teaching, the rediscovery of the ancient Roman law texts, and the new dialectical method of interrelating cases and concepts and of harmonizing contradictory authorities — were at the root of that development. The result was the birth of a transnational legal science — a system whose basic postulates survived without serious challenge until the twentieth century.*

THE historian is always keenly aware of the danger of speaking about "origins." Wherever one starts in the past, one can find still earlier beginnings — a fact which may testify to the continuity of the entire history of the human race. In the famous words of Maitland's opening paragraph of Pollock and Maitland's *History of English Law*:

> Such is the unity of all history that anyone who endeavours to tell a piece of it must feel that his first sentence tears a seamless web. The oldest utterance of English law that has come down to us has Greek words in it: words such as *bishop, priest,* and *deacon.* If we search out the origins of Roman law we must study Babylon . . . . A statute of limitations must be set; but it must be arbitrary. The web must be rent . . . .[1]

---



* James Barr Ames Professor of Law, Harvard Law School. B.A. Dartmouth, 1938; M.A. (History) Yale, 1942; LL.B., Yale, 1947. This Article is part of a large work in progress, tentatively entitled *The Western Legal Tradition — Its Relation to the Great Revolutions of Western History and to the World Revolution of the 20th Century*. The scope of the entire work is briefly indicated in two lectures given by the author, *see* Berman, *The Religious Foundations of Western Law*, 24 CATH. U.L. REV. 490 (1975); Berman, *The Crisis of the Western Legal Tradition*, 9 CREIGHTON L. REV. 252 (1975). The present Article is adapted from the third chapter of the first volume, following a first chapter on European folklaw prior to the eleventh century and a second chapter on the birth of the Western legal tradition in the Papal Revolution of the late eleventh and early twelfth centuries (on the Papal Revolution, see also note 4 *infra*). The fourth chapter, on the theological sources of the Western legal tradition, will be published in a forthcoming issue of the *Puerto Rico Law Review* dedicated to Helen Silving. Subsequent chapters of the first volume will deal with the new system of canon law and the emerging systems of secular law (feudal, manorial, urban, mercantile, and royal) in the late eleventh, twelfth, and early thirteenth centuries. Special thanks are given to Peter Banos, Edward Gaffney, Grace Goodell, Barnabas Johnson, and Bostjan Zupancic for their valuable comments and suggestions in the preparation of the chapter from which this Article is adapted.

[1] 1 F. MAITLAND & F. POLLOCK, THE HISTORY OF ENGLISH LAW 1 (2d ed. 1959).

Despite this warning, I am prepared to argue that there *are* seams, there are new things under the sun, and where one starts is not necessarily arbitrary. More particularly, it is the thesis of this Article that at one time what we know today as a *legal system* did not exist among the peoples of Europe, that in the twelfth century and thereafter Western legal systems were created for the first time, and that the creation and early development of those legal systems was made possible, in part, by the fact that the first universities were also created in the twelfth century and in those universities law was studied and taught as a science, that is, as a distinct and coherent body of knowledge with its own methodology.

## I. Historical Context

The term *legal system* is used here to mean something more narrow and more specific than a *legal order*. There was, of course, a legal order in England and elsewhere in the West prior to the eleventh and twelfth centuries, in the sense that there were legally constituted authorities which applied law. Indeed, we know of no time in the history of the peoples of Western Europe when there was not a legal order in that sense: the earliest written records of their history are collections of laws, and Tacitus, writing in the first and second centuries A.D., describes Germanic assemblies acting as courts. Also, ecclesiastical authorities from early times declared laws ("canons") and established procedures for deciding cases. Lacking, however, in the secular sphere was a clear differentiation of law from social custom and from political and religious institutions generally. Similarly, the law of the Church was largely diffused in the whole life of the Church — in its theology, its moral precepts, its liturgy — and it, too, was primarily local and regional rather than centralized or enacted. In addition, secular and ecclesiastical law were intermingled with each other. No one had attempted to organize the prevailing laws and legal institutions into distinct structures. Very little of the law was in writing. There was no independent, integrated, developing body of legal principles and procedures, clearly differentiated from other processes of social organization, and consciously cultivated by a corps of persons specially trained for that task.

The relatively unsystematized character of legal regulation and the relatively undeveloped state of legal science in the West prior to the twelfth century were closely connected to the prevailing political, economic, and social conditions. These included the predominantly local character of tribal, village, and feudal communities; their relatively high degree of economic self-sufficiency; the fusion of authorities within each; the relative weakness of the political and economic control exercised by the central imperial and royal authorities; the essentially military and religious character of that control; and the relative strength of informal community bonds of kinship and soil and of military comradeship.[2]

In the late eleventh and twelfth and early thirteenth centuries, however, a fundamental change took place in Western Europe in the very nature of law both as a political institution and as an intellectual concept. Politically, there emerged, for the first time, strong central authorities whose control reached down, through delegated officials, from the center to the localities; partly in connection with that there also emerged a class of professional jurists, including professional judges and practicing lawyers. Intellectually. Western Europe experienced, at the same time, the creation of its first law schools, the writing of its first legal treatises, the conscious ordering of the huge mass of inherited legal materials, and the development of a concept of law as an autonomous, integrated, developing body of legal principles and procedures.

A combination of these two factors, the political and the intellectual, helped to produce modern Western legal systems, of which the first was the new canon law of the Roman Catholic Church.[3] On the background of the new canon law, and often in rivalry with it, the European kingdoms began to create their own new secular legal systems. At the same time, there emerged in many parts of Europe free cities, each with its own governmental and legal institutions, forming a new type of urban law. Also in these centuries feudal and manorial legal institutions underwent systematization, and a new system of mercantile law was developed to meet the needs of merchants engaged in intercity, interregional, and international trade. The emergence of systems of feudal law, manorial law, mercantile law, and urban law strongly indicates that not only political and intellectual but also social and economic factors were at work in producing what can only be called a revolutionary development of legal institutions.

[2] An excellent description of the English experience may be found in H.R. LOYN, ANGLO-SAXON ENGLAND AND THE NORMAN CONQUEST (1962).

[3] The phrase *ius novum*, "new law," was used to characterize the legislation promulgated by popes and Church councils from the late eleventh century on, as contrasted with the earlier canons of the Church collected and systematized by Gratian in about 1140, which were then for the first time called the *ius antiquum*. Gratian's treatise, discussed at pp. 921–26 *infra*, was considered authoritative and largely replaced the original sources. The "new system of canon law" referred to in the text included both the *ius novum* and the (new) *ius antiquum*.

In other words, the creation of modern legal systems in the late eleventh, twelfth, and early thirteenth centuries was not only an implementation of policies and theories of central elites, but also a response to social and economic changes "on the ground."

Religious factors were also at work. The creation of modern legal systems was, in the first instance, a response to a revolutionary change within the Church and in the relation of the Church to the secular authorities. And here the word "revolutionary" has all the modern connotations of class struggle and violence. In 1075, after some twenty-five years of agitation and propaganda by the papal party, Pope Gregory VII declared the political and legal supremacy of the papacy over the entire Western Church and the complete independence of the clergy from secular control. Gregory also asserted the ultimate supremacy of the Pope in secular matters, including the authority to depose emperors and kings. Increasingly these events have been recognized as constituting the Papal Revolution.[4] The

[4] The concept of the Papal Revolution as a fundamental break in the historical continuity of the Church, and as the first of the Great Revolutions of Western History, was pioneered by Eugen Rosenstock-Huessy in DIE EUROPÄISCHEN REVOLUTIONEN (1931, 3d ed. revised 1960) and in OUT OF REVOLUTION: THE AUTOBIOGRAPHY OF WESTERN MAN (1938). *See also* E. ROSENSTOCK-HUESSEY, THE DRIVING POWER OF WESTERN CIVILIZATION: THE CHRISTIAN REVOLUTION OF THE MIDDLE AGES (1949) (Preface by Karl W. Deutsch). Among Church historians, see also G. TELLENBACH, LIBERTAS: KIRCHE UND WELTORDNUNG IM ZEITALTER DES INVESTITURSTREITES (1936), translated with an introduction by R. F. Bennett under the title CHURCH, STATE AND CHRISTIAN SOCIETY AT THE TIME OF THE INVESTITURE CONTEST (reprinted as a Harper Torchbook 1970). Tellenbach uses the traditional terminology of "the Gregorian Reform" and "the Investiture Struggle," rather than "the Papal Revolution"; nevertheless, he states that Pope Gregory VII "stands at the greatest — from the spiritual point of view perhaps the only — turning point in the history of Catholic Christendom." *See id.* at 164 (Harper Torchbook 1970). In 2 D. KNOWLES & D. OBOLENSKY, THE MIDDLE AGES: THE CHRISTIAN CENTURIES 169 (1968), the authors state that in the course of the Gregorian Reform "there emerged in the West, for the first time, an organized class, the clergy or great body of clerks, tightly bound together under bishops who themselves were tied tightly to the bishop of Rome, with a law and interest that separated them from the laity, who were to occupy a lower place." "Speaking loosely," the same authors write, "it may be said that it was the Gregorian reform that finally separated the clergy from the laity as two divisions within the church. This separation was emphasized more and more, and in a short time 'the church' and 'churchman' came to stand for the clergy as opposed to the laity." *Id.* at 260. *See also* B. TIERNEY, THE CRISIS OF CHURCH AND STATE, 1050–1300, at 2, 33–34, 45–95 (1964); R. SOUTHERN, WESTERN SOCIETY AND THE CHURCH IN THE MIDDLE AGES (1970).

Among secular historians the significance of the Papal Revolution has been in part illuminated and in part obscured by the rediscovery of the "twelfth century" as the formative period of modern Western institutions, thought, art, etc. The English-language literature goes back to C.H. HASKINS, THE RENAISSANCE OF THE TWELFTH CENTURY (1927). *See also* M. CLAGGETT, G. POST, & R. REYNOLDS,

Emperor — Henry IV of Saxony — responded by military action. Civil war between the papal and imperial parties raged sporadically throughout Europe until 1122, when a final compromise was reached by a concordat signed in the German city of Worms. In England and Normandy, the Concordat of Bec in 1107 had provided a temporary respite, but the matter was not finally resolved there until the martyrdom of Archbishop Thomas Becket in 1170.

It was out of the explosive separation of the ecclesiastical and the secular polities that there emerged the modern Western legal tradition. I propose in this essay to tell one part of the story, namely the origins of Western legal science.

To say that law was taught and studied in the West as a distinct science, at a time when the prevailing legal orders were only beginning to be clearly differentiated from politics and religion, raises a number of questions. What did the first law teachers teach? How was it possible to teach law when the prevailing laws and legal institutions, both ecclesiastical and secular, were largely local and customary and largely merged in religious beliefs and practices and in political, economic, and social life generally?

The answer surely sounds curious to modern ears. The law that was first taught and studied systematically in the West was not the prevailing law; it was the law contained in an ancient manuscript which had come to light in an Italian library toward the end of the eleventh century. The manuscript reproduced the enormous collection of legal materials which had been compiled under the Roman Emperor Justinian in about 534 A.D. — over five centuries earlier.

The Roman law compiled under Justinian in Constantinople had at one time prevailed in the Western Roman Empire as well as the Eastern. In 476, however, the last of the Western Emperors was deposed, and even before then Roman civilization had been superseded in the West by the primitive, tribal civilization of the Goths, the Vandals, the Franks, the Saxons, and other Germanic

---

TWELFTH-CENTURY EUROPE AND THE FOUNDATIONS OF MODERN SOCIETY (1961); S. PACKARD, TWELFTH CENTURY EUROPE: AN INTERPRETIVE ESSAY (1973). In fact, the great events and movements of the twelfth century had their beginnings in the last part of the eleventh century — but not before.

Social and economic historians have also stressed the fundamental character of changes that occurred in Western Europe in the late 11th and 12th centuries, including the emergence of hundreds of chartered cities and towns, the rapid expansion of commerce, the development of new technology, especially in agriculture, the systematization of feudal relations and the spread of the manorial system. *See* M. BLOCH, FEUDAL SOCIETY (L.A. Manyon trans. 1961); R. LOPEZ, THE COMMERCIAL REVOLUTION OF THE MIDDLE AGES, 950–1350 (1971); H. PIRENNE, MEDIEVAL CITIES (1952); L. WHITE, MEDIEVAL TECHNOLOGY AND SOCIAL CHANGE (1961).

peoples. After the sixth century Roman law survived in the West only in fragments, although it continued to flourish as a system in the Eastern Empire, called Byzantium (including southern Italy). Some of its individual rules and concepts appear in the occasional enactments of Western ecclesiastical and secular authorities as well as in the customary law of the peoples inhabiting what we call today France and (northern) Italy. The Carolingian and post-Carolingian idea of the succession of the Frankish king to the authority of the Roman emperors also fostered the survival of individual maxims and rules of Roman law, especially some concerning imperial authority. But Roman law as such, that is, as a system, had no validity in Western Europe when Justinian's work was rediscovered in Italy. The texts had disappeared. There were no Western counterparts to the Roman magistrates (praetors), legal advisers (jurists), or advocates (orators). The prevailing legal institutions were largely Germanic and Frankish. Thus it was the legal system of an earlier civilization as recorded in a huge book or set of books that formed the object of Europe's first systematic legal studies.

Two other ingredients were also necessary to the creation of the Western legal tradition. One was the method of analysis and synthesis which was applied to the ancient legal texts — a method which in modern times has been called, somewhat disparagingly, "scholasticism." The second was the context in which the scholastic method was applied to the books of Roman law — namely, the context of the university.

These three elements — the rediscovery of the legal writings compiled under the Roman Emperor Justinian, the scholastic method of analyzing and synthesizing them, and the teaching of law in the universities of Europe — are at the root of the Western legal tradition. The Roman law gave all Europe (including England) its basic legal vocabulary. The scholastic method has remained the predominant mode of legal thought throughout the West to this day. The universities brought together legal scholars — teachers and students — from all over Europe; brought them in contact not only with each other but also with teachers and students of theology, medicine, and the liberal arts; and made of them a calling or, as we would say today, a profession.

In the following pages I shall consider the structure of the first — or at least the first historically important — Western law school, at Bologna; its curriculum and mode of teaching; the scholastic method of legal analysis and synthesis; and the ways in which the structure, curriculum, and method of analysis at

Bologna and other medieval universities formed the basis for the creation of a legal science.[5]

## II. The Law School at Bologna

The newly discovered texts of Roman law were copied and began to be studied in various cities of Italy and elsewhere at the end of the eleventh century. Students would come together and hire a teacher for a year to expound them; the legal form adopted was that of a partnership (in Roman law, *societas*) of professor and students. One teacher in particular, named Guarnerius but historically known as Irnerius (about 1055–1130), who taught at Bologna in northern Italy, gained preeminence, and students began flocking to him from all over Europe. Eventually, thousands came each year to him and to the other teachers who joined him. By about 1150 there were some ten to thirteen thousand law students in Bologna.

Being aliens, most of the students were in a precarious legal situation. Any alien might be liable, for example, for the debts of any of his fellow-countrymen. To protect themselves against such hazards, the students banded together in "nations," on the basis of their ethnic and geographical origin — the Franks, Picards, Provençals, Alemanns (Germans), Angles, Spaniards, and others — in all, some twenty or more nations. Finally, they united in two corporate bodies, or guilds, one comprising all students from north of the Alps (*ultramontanes*), the other those from south of the Alps (*cismontanes*). Each of the two groups was organized in the form of a *universitas* — a term of Roman law then given the meaning of an association with legal personality or, as we would say today, a corporation. The professors (*doctores*, or teachers) were not members of the student *universitas*.

The virtues of incorporation were obvious to the students of Bologna, teen-agers who by medieval standards were mature young men ready for an active political life. United, they could bargain effectively with the city government and also dominate the administration of the school. Bologna was the archetype of

[5] The best account in English of the law school at Bologna is 1 H. Rashdall, The Universities of Europe in the Middle Ages 87–267 (2d ed. F.M. Powicke & A.B. Emden 1936). The classical work on the subject remains 3 F. Savigny, Geschichte des Römischen Rechts im Mittelalter 137–419 (2d ed. 1834). An excellent short account is that of D. Knowles, The Evolution of Medieval Thought 153–84 (1962). An invaluable study not only of law teaching at Bologna but also of the transplantation of the Bologna system to other European universities is that of Helmut Coing in 1 Handbuch der Quellen und Literatur der neueren europäischen Privatrechtsgeschichte 39–128 (H. Coing ed. 1973).

the medieval student-controlled institution of higher learning — in contrast to the professorially controlled university that was founded a little later in Paris.[6]

The student *universitas*, or corporation, or guild, received from the city of Bologna a charter which permitted it to make contracts with the professors, to regulate the rents of student lodgings, to determine the kinds of courses to be taught and the material to be covered in each, to set the length of lectures and the number of holidays, to regulate prices for the rent and sale of books, etc. The professors were paid directly by the students in their respective classes. The student guild was also given wide civil and criminal jurisdiction over its members. Thus students were exempted from the civil disabilities of alienage — they acquired, in effect, an artificial citizenship of their own. The charter of Bologna provided that the student guild should be responsible for

> the cultivation of fraternal charity, mutual association and amity, the care of the sick and needy, the conduct of funerals and the extirpation of rancor and quarrels, the attendance and escort of our candidates for the doctorate to and from the place of examination, and the spiritual welfare of members.[7]

The professors formed their own association, the college of teachers (*collegium doctorum*), which had the right to examine and admit candidates for the doctorate — and to charge examination fees. Since the doctor's degree was in effect an admission into the teaching profession, the professors retained the power to determine the membership of their own guild — but that was about all. If the students felt that a professor was not fulfilling his teaching duties, they would boycott his classes and refuse to pay him. And if a lecture did not begin promptly when the opening bell rang, or if it concluded before the closing bell, or if the course of lectures was not covered by the end of the term, the professor was fined by the student guild.[8]

[6] Only much later was the name "university" given to all such institutions; in the twelfth century and thereafter, the term applied to the university in our sense, that is, the entire institution or enterprise, was *studium generale*, "general education," signifying education available generally.

[7] *Quoted in* 1 H. RASHDALL, *supra* note 5, at 159–60.

[8] These and other matters were governed by the University Statutes, which were adopted by the student council. Each "nation" elected two members of the student council, whose decisions were taken by majority vote. The Statutes regulated the economic affairs of the institution, including fees and salaries, cost of renting books, housing, conditions of moneylending, and the like; they also regulated both student and professional discipline, as well as many aspects of the curriculum itself. A committee of students, called Denouncers of Professors (*Denunciatores Doctorum*) was appointed by the Rector to report professorial irregu-

The source of student power was in part economic. The students — sons of wealthy families or else supported by foundations (usually monasteries) — brought a very large income to the city. If they were dissatisfied they could easily migrate, taking the professors with them. Since the dormitories, dining halls, and lecture halls were owned by the city or by local entrepreneurs rather than by the students, the departure of the students could cause a severe economic crisis. In later times the professors came to be paid by the city and were bound by oath to the city not to depart. With that there came a sharp decline in student control over the university.

The ecclesiastical hierarchy also played an important role in controlling legal education. Except in the Italian cities, education throughout Europe in the twelfth century was chartered and supervised by the ecclesiastical rather than by the secular authority. However, in 1219, more than a century after Bologna was founded, the Pope decreed that nobody at Bologna could be installed in the office of teaching (that is, should receive the degree of doctor) without being examined by, and without receiving the license of, the Archdeacon of Bologna. Thus, the doctors were deprived of their independent role in granting degrees, and the Church's *licentia docendi* — "license to teach" — was henceforth required in Italy as elsewhere. In many parts of Europe remote control of universities by bishops led to periodic student revolts.

Historically more significant than episcopal control of the universities, however, was their relative freedom from such control, as compared with preexisting educational institutions. Prior to the eleventh century, formal education in Europe was carried on almost exclusively in monasteries. In the eleventh and twelfth centuries, cathedral schools were formed and gradually achieved preeminence. The cathedral being the seat of the bishop, the cathedral school was under his immediate supervision, just as the monastic school was under the immediate supervision of the abbot. A teacher would hardly dare to contradict his bishop or his abbot. Bologna, on the other hand, was founded by Matilda, Duchess of Tuscany and friend of Pope Gregory VII; it was she who invited Irnerius to teach Roman law there. For over a hundred years, the teaching at Bologna was free of direct ecclesiastical control. There was, to be sure, substantial indirect pres-

larities. (The Rector himself was elected by the student council.) A major limitation placed on student self-government, however, was the requirement that the Statutes could be revised only once every twenty years, and in the interim changes could be made only by unanimous consent of the students and the professors. *See* 1 H. RASHDALL, *supra* note 5, at 176–97.

sure; Irnerius himself was apparently excommunicated because of his support of the imperial cause against the papacy. Yet in general, Bolognese jurists were free to support opposing views concerning the extent to which various provisions of Roman law justified imperial and papal claims. Meanwhile, in Paris in the early 1100's, Peter Abelard dared to contradict his bishop and to teach a "countercourse" against him. It was out of this confrontation that the University of Paris emerged in the twelfth century.[9] Thus the European universities established themselves from the beginning as educational institutions where professors were free to take opposing positions. This was in contrast to the earlier system, known since antiquity, under which each school had been dominated by a single teacher or a single theory.

The structure of legal education at Bologna was transplanted to the dozens of universities which sprang up throughout Europe in the twelfth and thirteenth centuries.[10] At Oxford, Vacarius, who had been trained at Bologna, taught Roman law in the mid-1100's, although apparently law faculties as such were established at Oxford and Cambridge only in the next century.

## III. The Curriculum and Mode of Teaching

What was taught from the beginning at Bologna was the manuscript of the Roman law compiled by Justinian's jurists in the sixth century. Indeed, it is likely that the law school was founded primarily for the purpose of studying that manuscript.

The manuscript consisted of four parts: (1) the *Code (Codex)*, comprising twelve books of ordinances and decisions of the Roman emperors before Justinian, (2) the *Novels (Novellae)*, containing the laws promulgated by Emperor Justinian

[9] *See generally id.* at 50–54, 275–78.

[10] North of the Alps, most universities, although they followed Bologna's law curriculum and mode of teaching, adopted the general type of organization that was initiated in Paris, where doctors and students from various faculties (theology, law, medicine, the arts) were embraced in a single body and were subject to a common head and a common government. Bologna in contrast did not at first embrace any faculty other than law, and when eventually other faculties formed there, there was no constitutional connection among them except that all students received their degrees from the same chancellor, the Archdeacon of Bologna. It should be noted further that Bologna, like the other universities throughout Europe that were founded thereafter, was a graduate school in the sense that most of the students had previously received an education in the liberal arts, usually at a monastic or cathedral school. Where, as at Paris, the liberal arts became a fourth university discipline, its study remained a prerequisite to the other three. The liberal arts were grammar, rhetoric, logic (or dialectics), arithmetic, geometry, astronomy, and music. The most important were the first three, called the Trivium, which were based chiefly on the Bible, the writings of the Church Fathers, and some parts of Plato, Aristotle, Cicero, and other Greek and Roman works.

himself, (3) the *Institutes* (*Institutiones*), a short textbook designed as an introduction for beginning law students, and (4) the *Digest* (*Digestum*), whose fifty books contained a multitude of extracts from the opinions of Roman jurists on a very wide variety of legal questions. In a modern English translation, the *Code* takes up 1,034 pages, the *Novels* 562 pages, the *Institutes* 173 pages, and the *Digest* 2,734 pages.[11]

While the outlook of the medieval European jurists — which will be discussed in the next section — dictated that they treat all these writings as a single body, the *Corpus Iuris Civilis* ("Body of Civil Law"), primary focus was placed on the *Digest* (also called the *Pandects* (*Pandectae*)). The *Digest* was a vast conglomeration of the opinions of Roman jurists concerning thousands of legal propositions relating not only to property, wills, contracts, torts, and other branches of what we today call civil law, but also to criminal law, constitutional law, and other branches of law governing the Roman citizen. It was "municipal" law (*ius civilis*, "the law of the city"), covering everything except "the law of nations" (*ius gentium*), which applied to non-Romans. The *Digest* was not a code in the modern sense; it did not attempt to provide a complete, self-contained, internally consistent, systematically arranged set of legal concepts, principles, and rules. It was only in the West, after the founding of the universities, that together with the *Code*, *Novels*, and *Institutes* it came to be called *Corpus Iuris Civilis* — "the body" of civil law.

The legal propositions which the *Digest* set forth were very often "holdings," as we would say today, in actual cases. Others were statements ("edicts") of magistrates, called praetors, of how they would rule in prospective cases. For example:

> The Praetor says, "If you or your slaves have forcibly deprived anyone of property which he had at that time, I will grant an action only for a year, but after the year has elapsed I will grant one with reference to what has [subsequently] come into the hands of him who dispossessed the complainant by force."[12]

Such propositions are then followed by quotations from opinions of various jurists. For example, concerning the statement of the praetor presented above, the jurist Ulpian is quoted as saying:

[11] *See* THE CIVIL LAW (S. Scott ed. 1932) (17 volumes). Manuscripts of the *Code* and the *Novellae* had survived in the West and the *Institutes of Gaius*, upon which the *Institutes of Justinian* was patterned, had also survived. The *Digest*, however, which was by far the most important of the four books, had completely disappeared.

[12] DIGEST 42.16 (Concerning the Interdict Against Violence and Armed Force), *translated in* 9 THE CIVIL LAW, *supra* note 11, at 308.

> This interdict was established for the benefit of a person who has been ejected by force, as it is perfectly just to come to his relief under such circumstances. This interdict was devised to enable him to recover possession . . . . This interdict does not have reference to all kinds of violence but only to such as issued against persons who are deprived of possession. It only relates to atrocious violence, and where the parties are deprived of the possession of soil, as, for instance, to a tract of land, or a building, but to nothing else . . . .[13]

Other jurists also comment on the same interdict — for example, Pomponius is quoted as saying: "If, however, you are ejected by armed force, you will be entitled to recover the land, even if you originally obtained possession of it either by force (*vi*), or clandestinely (*clam*), or under a precarious title (*precario*)."[14]

The Roman jurists, as John P. Dawson has written, directed most of their attention

> not to theoretical synthesis, but to the consistent and orderly treatment of individual cases . . . . Their whole impulse was toward economy, not only of language, but in ideas. Their assumptions were fixed, the main purposes of the social and political order were not to be called in question, the system of legal ideas was too well known to require much discussion. They were problem-solvers, working within the system and not called upon to solve the ultimate problems of mankind's needs and destiny. They worked case by case, with patience and acumen and profound respect for inherited tradition.[15]

Professor Dawson notes the Roman jurists' "intense concentration on specific cases," sometimes hypothetical but often drawn from actual litigation:

---

[13] *Id.*

[14] *Id.* at 316.

[15] J. Dawson, The Oracles of the Law 114–15 (1968). Professor Dawson adds: "Despite the long centuries that have intervened, despite our vastly different hopes for mankind and its future, we in the twentieth century can still profit from their work. Those who should feel the strongest affinity for them are persons trained in American case law." This statement should be read against the background of the transformation of Roman law in the late 11th and 12th centuries by the glossators, which is one of the principal subjects of this Article. The glossators were less interested in working "case by case" and more interested in solving "ultimate problems," although, being more or less confined to Justinian's texts, they usually did not philosophize as much as the canonists did. Professor Dawson's statement should also be read against the background of the crisis of the Western legal tradition in the twentieth century. It is very likely that persons trained in American case law *would* feel the strongest affinity for the classical Roman jurists quoted in Justinian's *Digest* — if they could only look away from American cases in order to read Justinian; but whether or not they *should* feel such an affinity is another matter.

> The cases are briefly stated, likewise the jurists' own conclusions. No elaborately reasoned justification was needed, for to persons outside the elite group the jurists' own authority was enough and those inside would understand the reasons well enough. There were many assumptions that were unspoken or merely hinted at and that have only been disclosed through centuries of later patient study. The primary task of the jurists as they conceived it was to provide solutions for cases that had arisen or might arise, testing and revising their central ideas by observing their effects on particular cases.[16]

Modern European law students, who study Roman law as it has been systematized by Western university professors since the twelfth century, sometimes find it hard to believe that the original texts were so intensely casuistic and untheoretical. They are able to show that *implicit* in the myriad of narrow rules and undefined general terms was a complex system of abstract concepts. It is this very conceptualism of Roman law that is held up by way of contrast to the alleged particularism and pragmatism of English and American law. But that is to view the Roman law of Justinian through the eyes of later European jurists; it is they who first drew the conceptual implications, who made a theory of contract law out of the particular types of Roman contracts, who defined the right of possession, who elaborated doctrines of justification for the use of force, and who, in general, systematized the older texts on the basis of broad principles and concepts.

The curriculum of the twelfth-century law school consisted in the first instance of the reading of the texts of the *Digest*. Since the text was very difficult, it would have to be explained. Therefore, after reading the text the teacher would "gloss" it, that is, interpret it, word by word, line by line. (*Glossa*, in Greek means both "tongue," or "language," and "unusual word.") The glosses were copied by the student between the lines of the text; as they became longer, they spilled over into the margins. Soon written glosses had authority almost equal to that of the glossed text itself.[17]

The glosses were of several kinds. Some (called *notabilia*) gave short summaries of the contents of the passage glossed. Others (nicknamed *brocardica*) were statements of broad legal rules (maxims) based on the part of the text that was being glossed. In addition, the teachers would annotate the text by

[16] *Id.* at 116–17.

[17] In about 1250, the *Glossa Ordinaria* of Accursius became the standard authoritative work on the *Digest* as a whole. Thereafter came the "post-glossators," or "commentators," with their "commentaries" on the texts and the glosses.

classifications called *distinctiones*: they would start with a general term or broad concept and then divide it into various subordinate species, which in turn would be subdivided and further subdivided, the writer "following these ramifications of sense and terminology into the most minute details."[18] Finally, in addition to making "distinctions," the teacher would pose *quaestiones*, testing a broad doctrine by its application to particular problems or "questions."[19]

In addition to the readings of the texts and the glosses, and the analysis of them through distinctions and questions, the curriculum at Bologna and other medieval law schools included the *disputatio*, which was a discussion of a question of law in the form of a dispute between two students under the guidance of a professor or else a dispute between professors and students. It has been compared to a modern moot court, but the questions were always questions of law, not actual or hypothetical fact situations.

As time went on, the law curriculum at Bologna, Paris, Oxford, and other universities of Europe expanded to include more than the Roman law contained in the *Corpus Iuris Civilis*. The principal new subject added in the latter half of the twelfth century was the newly developed canon law of the Church; in contrast to Roman law, canon law was current, prevailing law, replenished by decrees of Church councils and applied by ecclesiastical courts. Also as the secular legal systems of the cities, principalities, and kingdoms of Europe developed — usually under the guidance of jurists trained at Bologna or elsewhere — the curriculum was enriched by references to current problems of secular law. In analyzing the texts of Justinian, the professors would introduce legal questions of current practical significance and would analyze them in the light of the Roman texts as well as of the canon law.

Thus the revival of the study of the Roman law of an earlier time led to the analysis of current legal problems. Roman law

---

[18] P. VINOGRADOFF, ROMAN LAW IN MEDIEVAL EUROPE 59 (1968).

[19] The curriculum and the form of lectures, disputations, etc., were prescribed by the statutes of the university. There has survived the introduction to a lecture in which the professor states:

> First, I shall give you summaries of each title [of the *Digest*] before I proceed to the text. Second, I shall pose as well and as clearly and as explicitly as I can the examples of the individual laws [given in the title]. Third, I shall briefly repeat the text with a view to correcting it. Fourth, I shall briefly repeat the contents of the examples [of the laws]. Fifth, I shall solve the contradictions, adding general principles (commonly called *brocardica*) and distinctions or subtle and useful problems (*quaestiones*) with their solutions, so far as Divine Providence shall enable me. And if any law shall seem, by reason of its celebrity or difficulty, worthy of a Repetition, I shall reserve it for an evening Repetition.

Odofredus, *quoted in* 3 F. SAVIGNY, *supra* note 5, at 553.

served at first as an ideal law, a body of legal ideas, taken as a unified system; current legal problems, previously unclassified and inchoate, were analyzed in its terms and were judged by its standards. In a sense, Roman law played a role for the medieval legal mind similar to that which legal history played for the modern Anglo-American legal mind from the seventeenth to the early twentieth century. It gave a perspective for analyzing prevailing laws, and it provided ideals for testing the validity of prevailing laws. This is not to say that Roman law was thought to be something other than prevailing law. It prevailed, alongside the newer laws, and in a sense *over* them. But it had a fundamental quality which they lacked. The newer laws were in the flux of becoming; the rules of Roman law were present to be concorded.

## IV. The Scholastic Method of Analysis and Synthesis

Underlying the curriculum and the teaching methods of the law school at Bologna and of the other Western universities of the twelfth and thirteenth centuries was a new mode of analysis and synthesis, which later came to be called the scholastic method. This method, which was first fully developed in the early 1100's, both in law and in theology, presupposes the absolute authority of certain books which are to be comprehended as containing an integrated and completed body of doctrine. But, paradoxically, it also presupposes that there may be both gaps and contradictions within the text, and it sets as its main task the summation of the text, the closing of gaps within it, and the resolution of the contradictions. The method is called "dialectical," in that it seeks the reconciliation of opposites.[20]

Both in law and theology,[21] and later in philosophy, the scholastic mode of analysis and synthesis was promoted by the

[20] In the nineteenth and twentieth centuries, the concept of dialectic as a method of synthesis of opposites has been generally derived from Hegel via Marx. However, the method itself goes back to the early twelfth century, especially to the works of Abelard and Gratian. *See* notes 21, 65 *infra*.

[21] The relationship between jurisprudence and theology in the eleventh and twelfth centuries is the subject of a companion article, to be published in a forthcoming issue of the *Puerto Rico Law Review*. *See* note * *supra*. It needs to be said here, however, that at the very time Western jurists were beginning to create what they conceived to be a science of law, Western theologians were beginning to create what they conceived to be a science of theology. Indeed, Peter Abelard (1079–1142), who was the first to use the word "theology" in the modern sense of a systematic analysis of the evidence of divine revelation, *see* D. Knowles, The Evolution of Medieval Thought 126 (1962), was also one of the great pioneers of scholastic logic, and is sometimes called the father of scholasticism. Abelard sought by means of scholastic methods of analysis and synthesis to apply rational

method of teaching in the university, particularly the method of "glossing" the text and posing "questions" for disputation. "The principal books of law and theology were the natural outgrowth of university lectures." [22] In other words, science — scholarship — came from teaching, and not vice versa.

In law, the scholastic method took the form of analyzing and synthesizing the mass of doctrines, many of them in conflict with others, found in the law of Justinian as well as in the prevailing law and custom of ecclesiastical and secular authorities. As in the case of theology, the written text as a whole, the *Corpus Iuris Civilis*, like the Bible and the writings of the Church Fathers, was accepted as sacred, the embodiment of reason. But the emphasis on reconciliation of contradictions gave the twelfth-century Western jurist a greater freedom and flexibility in dealing with legal concepts and rules than his Roman predecessors had had. Like them, he was, to be sure, concerned, in Professor Dawson's words, with the "consistent and orderly treatment of individual cases." But he was also concerned, as they were not, with finding "elaborately reasoned justifications" and a "theoretical synthesis." [23] And in seeking justifications and synthesis, he often sacrificed the narrower kind of consistency which the Romans prized.

### A. The Relation of the Scholastic Method to Dialectical Reasoning in Greek Philosophy and in Roman Law

The method of the twelfth-century European jurists was a transformation of the methods of dialectical reasoning characteristic of ancient Greek philosophy and of classical and post-classical Roman law. "Dialectic," in Greek, means "conversa-

criteria for judging which revealed truths were of universal validity and which were of only relative validity. This was not, then, the kind of fundamentalism which takes every word of the text as being equally true under all circumstances; the whole is taken to be true, and within the whole the parts are assigned various shades of truth. Indeed, one of the most important books of Abelard, *Sic et Non* ("Yes and No"), documents by successive quotations a list of over 150 inconsistencies and discrepancies in the Bible and in the writings of the Church Fathers and other authorities, assuming them all to be true and leaving it to the reader to harmonize them. P. ABELARD, SIC ET NON: A CRITICAL EDITION (B. Boyer & R. McKeon eds. 1976). In the Prologue, Abelard indicates several possible ways of reconciling the contradictions (for example, the same words may have been used in different senses), but if not he himself, at least his followers, recognized that a mechanical reconciliation may be impossible and that the meaning of contradictory passages is often to be found only in the interconnections and purposes of the whole body of scriptural and patristic writings. *See* M. GRABMANN, 2 DIE GESCHICHTE DER SCHOLASTISCHEN METHODE 168–229 (1911).

[22] C. HASKINS, THE RISE OF UNIVERSITIES 53 (1923).

[23] J. DAWSON, *supra* note 15, at 116, 114.

tion" or "dialogue." Ancient Greek philosophers referred to the "art of conversation" (*tekhne dialektike*) as a method of reasoning; indeed, Plato viewed it as the only sure method of arriving at knowledge of the truth. The Socratic dialogues reported by Plato involved several basic "dialectical" techniques: (a) the refutation of an opponent's thesis by drawing from it, through a series of questions and answers, consequences that contradict it or that are otherwise unacceptable; (b) the deriving of a generalization — again, by questions and answers — from a series of true propositions about particular cases; (c) the definition of concepts by the techniques of distinction, that is, repeated analysis of a genus into its species and the species into their subspecies, and synthesis, that is, repeated collection of species into their genus and the genera into larger genera. Through such reasoning Plato sought to achieve sure knowledge of the nature of Goodness, Justice, Truth, Love, and other "Forms" existing, as he thought, in the universe.

Aristotle greatly refined Plato's concepts of dialectical reasoning. He distinguished, first, between reasoning from premises that are known to be necessarily true (such as "all men are mortal" or "fire burns") and reasoning from premises that are generally accepted, or propounded by experts, but are nevertheless debatable (such as "man is a political animal" or "philosophy is desirable as a branch of study"). Only the latter kind of reasoning is dialectical, according to Aristotle, and since its premises are disputable it is not capable of arriving at certainty but only at probabilities. The former kind of reasoning, on the other hand, called "apodictic," is alone capable of demonstrating necessary truths since only from indisputable premises can indisputable conclusions be drawn.

In both apodictic and dialectical reasoning, Aristotle said, either inductive or deductive logic may be applicable. Nevertheless, in Aristotle's view inductive logic is to be preferred in dialectical reasoning, since it is clearer and more convincing to most people, whereas in apodictic reasoning deductive logic is appropriate to certain kinds of science (*e.g.*, mathematics) but not to others (*e.g.*, biology). Inductive logic moves from experience either to certainty or to probability, by finding the common element in the particular cases that have been observed.[24]

The special distinguishing feature of dialectical reasoning, however, is not that it is partial to inductive logic, for, as Aristotle showed, apodictic reasoning also inclines toward the inductive method in many fields. Dialectical reasoning is dis-

[24] *See* ARISTOTLE, TOPICS, bk. I, ch. 1, 100a 25 to 100b 23, ch. 12, 105a 10–19, in THE BASIC WORKS OF ARISTOTLE 188, 198 (R. McKeon ed. 1941).

tinguished above all by the fact that it does not start with "propositions," that is, with declarative statements that must be either true or false, but rather with "problems," or "questions," about which people may differ, although ultimately the disputed question will be resolved conclusively by a proposition, or first principle, in favor of one side or the other if valid methods of dialectical reasoning are used.[25]

Aristotle's distinction between apodictic and dialectical reasoning was accepted by the Stoics of the third century B.C. and thereafter. However, the Stoics viewed dialectical reasoning not as a method of arriving at first principles but as a method of analyzing arguments and defining concepts by distinction and synthesis of genus and species. And they lacked Aristotle's overriding concern for systematic exposition; dialectics now became an independent discipline, not essentially different from logic but with strong elements also of rhetoric and grammar.

It was in its Stoic form, with the writings of Plato and Aristotle in the background, that Greek dialectics was imported into Rome in the republican period (second and first centuries B.C.). There it was taken up among the educated classes, including the jurists, who applied it for the first time to prevailing legal institutions.[26] However, the Roman jurists took an intensely

---

[25] *See* L. Wittgenstein, On Certainty (G.E.M. Anscombe & G.H. von Wright eds. 1969).

[26] The Greeks had never attempted such an application. The reasons for that are complex. The Greek cities did not experience the rise of a prestigious class of jurists entrusted with the development of law. Adjudication was by large popular assemblies, and those who argued before the assemblies practiced a mode of declamation that relied less on legal argument than on appeals to moral and political considerations. Moreover, the Greek philosophers did not recognize legal rules as starting points for reasoning. They professed an allegiance to a higher philosophical truth, attainable by observation and reason alone. *See* W. Kunkel, An Introduction to Roman Legal and Constitutional Law 98–103 (2d ed. J.M. Kelley trans. 1973); J. Dawson, *supra* note 15, at 114. Legal rules and decisions were, for them, not *authorities* to be accepted, or at least to be reckoned with, as embodiments of the community's sense of justice; they were, instead, merely *data* to be used, or not used, in constructing their own philosophical theories. Thus Greek philosophers would gladly debate questions concerning the nature of justice and whether a ruler should govern by law or by his own will, but they considered it unimportant to debate whether, for example, the law should give a remedy to an owner of goods against one who has bought them in good faith from another who had fraudulently persuaded the owner to part with them. When they did consider such questions of civil law, they generally treated them as matters of personal ethics. Conversely, questions of constitutional law were generally treated as matters of politics.

In Rome on the other hand, a prestigious class of jurists came into existence quite early. From the fifth century B.C. on, priests (pontiffs) kept records of various legal remedies ("actions") available for various causes. Thereafter there emerged the practice of electing each year praetors who, in the form of an annual

practical approach to law. Their importation of Greek dialectical reasoning, although it was the first scholarly inroad into Roman law, was not the intermarriage of Roman law with Greek philosophy that took place over a thousand years later in the universities of Western Europe. The Roman jurists refused to adopt the Hellenistic system of education; legal training continued to consist chiefly of very informal individual apprenticeship in the house of an older practitioner.

> The [Roman] jurisconsults did not discuss with their pupils basic conceptions like justice, law, or legal science, though to the Greeks these seemed problems of the highest, nay almost of sole importance. The student was plunged straight into practice, where he was faced with the ever-recurrent question: What, on the facts stated, ought to be done? [27]

Nevertheless, it was in this period — *before* the great flowering of so-called classical Roman law in the first to third centuries A.D. — that jurists first attempted systematically to classify Roman law into its various kinds (genera and species) and with precision to define general rules applicable to specific cases.

Perhaps the earliest example of the systematic application of dialectical reasoning to law was the treatise on *ius civile* by the Roman jurist Q. Mucius Scaevola (d. 82 B.C.).[28] In this work, which is said to have "laid the foundations not merely of Roman, but of European, jurisprudence," [29] civil law was classified into four main divisions: the law of inheritance, the law of persons, the law of things, and the law of obligations. Each of these was subdivided into two or three broad categories and the subdivisions themselves were further subdivided.[30] Under the various genera

edict, declared general rules of law applicable to private disputes, and who received individual complaints concerning violations of rights laid down in the edict. The praetor would transmit such a complaint to a judge (*iudex*), who was a layman, appointed by the praetor ad hoc, with instructions to hold a hearing and, upon proof of the facts alleged in the complaint, to grant a remedy. In addition to praetors and judges there existed a third group of laymen who participated in legal proceedings, the advocates (*oratores*), who argued before the judges. Finally, and ultimately most significant, there were the jurists (also called jurisconsults). These were the only professionals. It was their chief task to give legal advice — to praetors, to judges, to advocates, to litigants, to clients wishing to engage in legal transactions, and so forth. *See* W. KUNKEL, *supra* at 84–86, 95–124.

[27] F. SCHULZ, HISTORY OF ROMAN LEGAL SCIENCE 57–58 (1946).

[28] *See* F. SCHULZ, PRINCIPLES OF ROMAN LAW 53 (1936); P. STEIN, REGULAE IURIS 36 (1966).

[29] F. SCHULZ, *supra* note 27, at 94.

[30] *See id.* at 95. Inheritance was divided into testaments and intestate succession; persons into marriage, guardianship, free status, paternal power, and some others; things into possession and nonpossession; obligations into contracts and delicts. These were further subdivided: thus contracts were subdivided into real

and species, each characterized by its governing principles, legal materials were reproduced — above all, the decisions of praetors in particular cases, but also legislative enactments, authorities from older collections of documents, and also authorities from the oral tradition. The major task which the author set for himself was to present "definitions," as he called them,[31] that is, precise statements of the legal rules implicit in decisions of cases.

In the work of Q. Mucius Scaevola, and of his fellow jurists of the second and first centuries B.C., not only the classification system but also the method of arriving at the formulation of specific rules was dialectical in the broad Greek sense. Questions were posed, various answers of jurists were collected, the author's own solutions were offered. For example, an earlier jurist had summarized various decisions concerning the scope of the law of theft by saying that one who borrowed a horse was guilty of theft if he took it to a place other than that agreed when he received it or if he took it further than the place agreed. Q. Mucius Scaevola reviewed the same decisions, and others, and achieved a broader, and at the same time a more precise, formulation: whoever receives a thing for safekeeping and uses it, or receives it for use and uses it for a purpose other than that for which he receives it, is guilty of theft.[32] Here not only loans but deposits are included, and "thing" is substituted for "horse."

Professor Stein writes: "Following the Aristotelian techniques [Q. Mucius] saw his task as that of explaining what actually happened in legal proceedings." [33] He sought to achieve that task by subdivision of genera and species until he reached specific decisions which, having classified, he was able to explain by finding "a form of words which included all the relevant categories and excluded all others." [34] His aim, and that of other jurists who followed him, was, as Professor Stein has said, to declare the preexisting law and to define its precise limits.[35] One would not look to the Roman jurists of the republican period for a discussion of legal concepts; "indeed the notion of a concept was not found in their mental equipment." [36]

Subsequently, in the classical and postclassical periods, the Roman jurists refined and developed the dialectical techniques

contracts, purchase and sale, letting and hiring, and partnership, while delicts were subdivided into assault, theft, and damage to property.

[31] *See* P. STEIN, *supra* note 28, at 36.

[32] *See id.* at 45–46.

[33] *Id.* at 37.

[34] *Id.* at 41.

[35] *Id.* at 48.

[36] *Id.; see* Behrens, *Begriff und Definition in den Quellen*, 74 ZEITSCHRIFT DER SAVIGNY-STIFTUNG FUR RECHTSGESCHICHTE, ROMANISTISCHE ABTEILUNG 352 (1957).

that had been applied by their republican predecessors, without changing them fundamentally. There was a tendency toward somewhat greater abstraction. In the first part of the second century they began to speak expressly of "rules" (*regulae*), and not only of "definitions" (*definitiones*). The difference between the two terms is a subtle one. The "definitions" seem to have been more closely connected with the cases which they generalized. The "rules," though derived from cases, were capable of being considered separately. Sometimes they were collected in "books of rules" (*libri regularum*), which were especially useful to the numerous minor officials of the Empire. Also a few law schools were founded in this period, and although their orientation remained intensely practical, they undoubtedly contributed to a tendency to search for broader rules. Aristotelian concepts of the "nature" of a thing were used, for example, to summarize rules concerning what may be omitted from the express terms of agreements of purchase and sale: it was said that terms that "naturally belong" (*naturaliter insunt*) to the case require no express agreement.[37] However, only one kind of term was given as "naturally belonging" to all types of purchase and sale — namely, that the vendor had title. Various other specific "implied warranties" (as we would call them today) for individual types of purchase and sale were then listed — for example, that an animal is healthy, or that a slave is not in the habit of running away. Sometimes common rules were developed to govern diverse types of contracts, such as sales and leases. Only occasionally would Roman jurists go so far as to postulate broad principles that seemed to embrace the entire law. Thus Gaius, the great jurist and law teacher of the middle second century, wrote that agreements concluded "against the rules of the civil law" are invalid,[38] thereby implying, but only implying, what was first spelled out in the twelfth century by the scholastic jurists of the West: that the law forms a whole system, a whole "body."

This implication was also present in some very broad *regulae* which, when abstracted from the cases from which they were first generalized, have the form of succinct, epigrammatic statements of fundamental legal principles. In Justinian's *Digest* the concluding title 50.17, "Concerning various rules of the ancient law," collects 211 such broad rules. Examples are: "No one is considered to defraud those who know and consent," "In doubtful matters the more benevolent interpretations should always be preferred," "Good faith confers as much on a possessor as the truth, when-

[37] DIGEST 19.1.11.1.

[38] *Id.* at 2.14.28.

ever the law (*lex*) offers no impediment."[39] However, as Professor Stein has recently shown,[40] these "legal maxims," as they came to be called in the twelfth century, have a wholly different meaning when taken as abstract principles from that which they had in the context of the types of cases in which they were originally uttered and which are generally reproduced in the earlier parts of the *Digest* itself. Thus the first of the "rules" quoted above originally referred to the case of one who acquires something from a fraudulent debtor with the consent of the creditors: the creditors may not later claim that they were defrauded. The second originally referred to legacies: the "more benevolent interpretations" are those that are more benevolent to legatees. The third originally referred to the good faith possessor of another's slave: if the slave stole from another, the victim has an action against the possessor. In 530 A.D. Justinian issued a constitution clarifying the older law on the subject. This constitution is the *lex* which is obliquely referred to in the concluding phrase of the *regula*.

The collection of 211 bare statements of abstract "rules" was not intended by Justinian to deceive anyone into believing that they had a meaning independent of the concrete situations to which they were originally applied. The very first *regula* presented in title 50.17 makes this clear: the jurist Paul is quoted as having said, "A rule is something which briefly relates a matter. . . . [B]y means of a rule a short account of matters is passed on and . . . if it is inaccurate in any respect, it loses its effect." In other words, rules must not be considered outside the contexts of the cases which they summarize. This is also shown by the fact that each rule is preceded by a citation to its original context. Moreover, except that the first one belongs where it is, they are arranged entirely unsystematically, and some of them are contradictory to each other.[41] Justinian added the "*regulae* of the ancient law" partly, at least, as an ornamental index to his great collection. It is also likely that they were intended to be useful in argument, possibly as presumptions that could be used to shift the burden of proof. Finally, they served a didactic purpose as an aid to memory of the vast text. But no

[39] *Id.* at 50.17.145, .56, .136.

[40] *See* P. STEIN, *supra* note 28, at 118–23.

[41] Thus, according to DIGEST 50.17.67, "Whenever a sentence has two meanings, that should be accepted which is better adapted to the case," while according to DIGEST 50.17.114, "When words are ambiguous, their most probable and ordinary signification should be adopted." According to DIGEST 50.17.125, "Defendants are regarded with greater favor than plaintiffs," while according to DIGEST 50.17.126, "When a question arises with reference to the claims of two persons, the position of the possessor is preferable."

Roman jurist treated them as abstract principles. Indeed, the entire title 50.17 of the *Digest* must have demonstrated beyond a doubt to the Roman lawyers of Justinian's time the validity of the famous "rule" of Javolenus, also contained in title 50.17: "All rules [*definitiones*] in civil law are dangerous, for they are almost always capable of being distorted." That, too, was probably aimed at a specific "definition."[42]

The classical and postclassical Roman jurists thought of a legal rule as a generalization of the common elements of decisions in a restricted, specified class of cases. Only by thus limiting the scope of legal rules did they hope to achieve their objective of using Greek methods of classification and generalization as a rational basis for deciding cases. The Greeks had never attempted any such rationalization of legal decisions and rules. For them, dialectical reasoning was a technique for deriving valid philosophical conclusions — "propositions" — from agreed-upon premises. The Romans converted the Greek dialectic from an art of discovery (*ars inveniendi*) to an art of judging (*ars iudicandi*).

It is important to distinguish Roman legal casuistry from the legal casuistry of the later Western European jurists of the eleventh and twelfth centuries and thereafter, as well as from the "case method" of analysis characteristic of the English and American common law to this day. On the one hand, the Romans did not use cases in order to illustrate principles, or to test them by going back a step, so to speak, in order to see their applications. On the other hand, they reduced their cases to bare holdings, without treating them in their fullness — without discussing ambiguities or gaps in their fact situations, alternative formulations of the legal issues involved, and the like.[43] Max Weber undoubtedly went too far when he referred to the classical Roman jurists' use of rules as a "merely paratactic and visual association of the analogy."[44] Yet their failure to articulate the assumptions and deeper reasons on which the analogies were founded, indeed, their failure even to define the most important legal terms,[45] led to a narrowness, or woodenness, in case analysis — which is just what the Roman jurists wanted! When Cicero argued for a more complex systematization of the law, with clear definitions and abstract legal rules, the jurists "answered these strictures by

[42] *See* P. Stein, *supra* note 28, at 70.

[43] *See* T. Viehweg, Topik und Jurisprudenz 74–76 (5th ed. 1954).

[44] M. Weber, Kap. vii, § 1, at 395, *quoted in* F. Schulz, *supra* note 28, at 51–52; *see* 2 M. Weber, Economy and Society 787 (G. Roth & C. Wittich eds. 1968); T. Viehweg, *supra* note 43, at 46–61. *But see* P. Stein, *supra* note 28, at 74–89.

[45] F. Schulz, *supra* note 27, at 43–48.

polite silence."[46] They had no reason to try to transform the Roman genius for consistent adjudication into a philosophical system. They had every reason to be suspicious of the applicability of the higher ranges of Greek philosophy to the practical needs of adjudication.

The Western European jurists of the eleventh and twelfth centuries carried the Greek dialectic to a much higher level of abstraction. They attempted to systematize the rules into an integrated whole — not merely to define elements common to particular species of cases but also to synthesize the rules into principles and the principles themselves into an entire system, a "body" of law, or *corpus iuris*.

One of the techniques which the scholastic jurists used to achieve this objective was to treat the Roman *regulae*, found in title 50.17 of the *Digest* and elsewhere, as legal "maxims," that is, as independent principles of universal validity. The word "maxim" was drawn from Aristotelian terminology; it referred to a "maximum proposition," that is, a "universal." The sixth-century Roman writer Boethius, from whose Latin translations and commentaries Western scholars from the sixth to the mid-twelfth centuries learned their Aristotle, wrote that Aristotle postulated certain self-evident propositions, and that from these "maximum, that is, universal . . . propositions . . . the conclusions of syllogisms are drawn."[47] In the twelfth century, Peter Abelard, in his *Dialectica*, described such a maximum proposition as one that summarizes the meaning and the logic common to the particular propositions that are implied in it. For example, the propositions (a) that what may be said of a man may be said of an animal, (b) that what may be said of a rose may be said of a flower, (c) that what may be said of redness may be said of a color, and other similar propositions, are summarized in the "maxim" that what may be said of a species may be said of a genus. "The maxim," Abelard wrote, "contains and expresses the sense of all such consequences and demonstrates the mode of inference common to the antecedents."[48] In the same way, the jurists of Bologna, contemporaries of Abelard, adduced universal principles from the implications of particular instances. This was just the opposite of the older Roman concept of a rule as merely "a short account of matters"; now it was assumed that the whole law, the entire *ius*, could be adduced by synthesis from the common characteristics of specific types of cases.

---

[46] *Id.* at 65.

[47] *See* P. Stein, *supra* note 28, at 157.

[48] P. Abelard, Dialectica, cit. 263 (L.M. De Rijk ed. 1956), *quoted in* P. Stein, *supra* note 28, at 157–58.

It was this belief and this method that characterized the approach by which the scholastic jurists analyzed and synthesized the rediscovered texts of Justinian. This was Aristotelian dialectics — even before the translation of Aristotle's principal works on logic — carried over to law at a level of synthesis far higher than that of the Roman jurists whose writings were being studied.[49]

Yet there was another side to it. Aristotle had denied the "apodictic" character of dialectical reasoning. It could not achieve certainty because its premises were uncertain. The twelfth-century jurists of Western Europe, on the other hand, used the Aristotelian dialectic for the purpose of *demonstrating* what is true and what is just. They turned Aristotle on his head by conflating dialectical and apodictic reasoning and applying both to the analysis and synthesis of legal norms. In contrast to the earlier Roman jurists and the earlier Greek philosophers, they supposed that they could prove by reason the universal truth and universal justice of authoritative legal texts. For them, the edicts and *responsa* of Roman law, taken both individually and as a whole, constituted what they certainly had not constituted in the minds of the Roman lawyers themselves — a written natural law, a *ratio scripta*, to be taken, together with the Bible, the patristic writings, and the canons of the Church, as sacred. Since they were true and just, they could be reasoned from, apodictically, to discover new truth and justice. But since they contained gaps, ambiguities, and contradictions, they had to be reasoned from dialectically as well; that is, problems (*quaestiones*) had to be put, classifications and definitions made, opposing opinions stated, conflicts synthesized. The scholastics added another

[49] For example, whereas the Justinian texts made passing references to "the nature of a contract" in a very limited sense, as illistrated at p. 914 *supra*, the glossators debated whether the *naturalia* of a contract can be excluded by express agreement. In the fourteenth century Baldus developed an elaborate theory which distinguished between *substantialia*, *i.e.*, those elements of a contract which give it its "being," and without which it cannot exist (*e.g.*, in a contract of purchase and sale, the thing sold and the price), the *naturalia*, *i.e.*, those elements which are inferred from the contract and which may be altered by express terms, and the *accidentalia*, *i.e.*, those elements which derive solely from the express ordination of the parties. *See* BALDUS D.2, 14, 77. No. 1; *cf.* Gloss to *Extra naturam* D.2, 14, 7, 5; Coing, *Zum Einfluss der Philosophie des Aristoteles auf die Entwicklung des römischen Rechts*, 69 ZEITSCHRIFT DER SAVIGNY-STIFTUNG FÜR RECHTSGESCHICHTE, ROMANISTISCHE ABTEILUNG 24 (1952). Although he cites this passage from Baldus, Professor Coing does not in this essay distinguish medieval European from Byzantine legal reasoning but rather traces the influence of Aristotle as though it moved in a straight line.

A brilliant example of the way in which the glossators used a maxim to derive a wide variety of specific kinds of results may be found in G. OTTE, DIALEKTIK UND JURISPRUDENZ 214-15 (1971).

methodological "topic": where possible, legal maxims, the *brocardica*, were to be formulated as autonomous universal principles. Thus Aristotle's contradiction between dialectical reasoning and apodictic reasoning was itself resolved. The dialectical method became the scientific method in law — as it eventually became the scientific method in other branches of learning as well, including the natural sciences.

The scholastic jurists differed from the Greek philosophers not only in their belief that universal legal principles could be derived by reasoning from authoritative texts but also in their belief about the nature of such universal principles. Plato postulated that universals exist in nature — that the idea of justice or beauty, the idea of a triangle, the idea of color, the idea of a rose, and other general ideas in people's minds are imperfect reflections of "paradigms," or "forms," that exist in external reality. Aristotle accepted this "Realist" view of universal ideas, as it was later called in the West (today we would call it "Idealist"), although he modified it somewhat, distinguishing universals that are self-evident maxims, and that form starting points for apodictic reasoning, from universals of a dialectical nature that are only probably true. In the West, Christian philosophers had raised some questions concerning the "reality" of universals, but the first sharp and systematic attack on the Realist position was taken in the eleventh and twelfth centuries, above all by — again — Peter Abelard.[50] Abelard denied the external reality of the common characteristics that define a class of individual substances. He argued that only the individual substances exist outside the mind, and that universals are names (*nomina*) invented in the mind to express the similarities or relationships among individual things belonging to a class. Some "Nominalists" denied that universals have any meaning at all. Abelard, however, asserted that the names do have meaning, in that they characterize the individuals in the class, but that they do not "exist" except as they inhere in the individuals. Thus "goodness," or "society," or "color," or "rose," are not to be found either in the physical world or in some ideal world of forms. They are simply general qualities that the human intellect attributes to good acts, or to individual people living in social relations with each other, or to particular pigments or individual roses.

Nominalism played an indispensable role in the movement to systematize law; for Realism in the Platonic sense, however convincing or unconvincing it may be as metaphysics, was wholly alien to the effort of twelfth-century jurists to classify, divide,

[50] For a brief summary of Abelard's views, see 2 F. COPLESTON, A HISTORY OF PHILOSOPHY 170–72 (1962).

distinguish, interpret, generalize, synthesize, and harmonize the great mass of decisions, customs, canons, decrees, writs, laws, and other legal materials that constituted the legal orders of that time. To have postulated, in Platonic style, the external reality of justice, equality, consistency, procedural regularity, and other universal principles, and to have attempted to deduce from them specific legal rules and institutions, would have been a futile academic exercise. None of the emerging polities, ecclesiastical or secular, could have accepted or used such an abstract system. On the other hand, to have attempted to proceed by Aristotelian induction from the mass of existing legal institutions toward the same Platonic ideals would have also been misguided, since the existing legal institutions did not, in fact, necessarily imply those ideals.

What was needed was the Greek genius for classification and generalization but without the Greek belief that the classifications and generalizations reflect the realities of the external world — without, in short, Greek naturalism. In law, such naturalism could not go much beyond the casuistic *regulae* of the Roman jurists. The Nominalists, on the other hand, although they shared with the Realists (including Plato and Aristotle) a deep concern to establish general principles and to prove the validity of general concepts, nevertheless denied that such principles and concepts exist *as such*. For the Nominalists, universals are invented by the mind, by reason and will, and therefore can be revised by reason and will; at the same time, they inhere in the particulars that they characterize, and can therefore be tested by those particulars. Extreme Nominalism denies that "the whole is greater than the sum of its parts," but a more moderate Nominalism such as that of Abelard asserts that the whole is *in* the parts, holding them together, so that the parts taken in isolation from each other (rather than as "parts") are not as "great" as the parts taken in relation to each other. Thus the parts are not, strictly speaking, derived from the whole (deduction), nor is the whole, strictly speaking, derived from the parts (induction), but rather the whole *is* the parts interacting with each other. Therefore Nominalism was congenial to the systematizing and synthesizing of law; for in law there can be no such separation of the whole and the parts, the general and the particular, the form and the substance, the ends and the means, as is inherent in both Platonic and (though to a lesser extent) Aristotelian philosophy.

The paradoxes implicit in the combining of universals and particulars were closely related to the paradoxes implicit in the combining of apodictic and dialectical reasoning. Both were closely related, in turn, to the paradoxes implicit in the scholastic synthesis of faith and reason. The scholastic dialectic was more than a method of reasoning and more than a way of organizing thought. Its criteria were moral as well as intellectual; it was a way of testing justice and not only truth. Thus the scholastic antitheses included not only general versus special, object versus subject, argument versus reply, but also strict law versus dispensation in exceptional cases, precept versus counsel, absolute rule versus relative rule, justice versus mercy, divine law versus human law. These and similar "oppositions" were used as means of logical reconciliation of contradictory texts, but they were also used for shaping the legal institutions of both the Church and the secular society in such a way as to manifest alternate values. For God himself was conceived to be a God both of justice and of mercy, both of strict law and of equity. The paradoxes of divine justice were now for the first time systematically applied to human laws. Thus "scholasticism" was not only a method but a jurisprudence and a theology.

*B. The Application of the Scholastic Dialectic to Legal Science*

Probably the most striking single example of the role of the scholastic dialectic in the formation of Western legal science is the great treatise of the Bolognese monk Gratian,[51] written in about 1140 and entitled, characteristically, *A Concordance of Discordant Canons* (*Concordia Discordantium Canonum*). This work, which in a modern edition fills over 1400 printed pages,[52] was the first comprehensive and systematic legal treatise in the history of the West, and perhaps in the history of mankind — if by "comprehensive" is meant the attempt to embrace the entire law of a given polity, and if by "systematic" is meant the express effort to present that law as a single body, in which all the parts are viewed as interacting to form a whole.

Prior to the eleventh century, there had been no effort to collect all the laws of the Church into a single book or books, and in such partial collections as existed the laws (typically called *canones*, "rules") were arranged chronologically. Near the end of the eleventh century, Ivo, Bishop of Chartres, made a collection arranged not chronologically but according to various categories, although he only loosely adhered to his categories. He also included a large number of rules concerning homicide, theft, certain types of voluntary transactions, possession, adjudication, and

[51] What is known of Gratian's life is recounted in Kuttner, *The Father of the Science of Canon Law*, 1 JURIST 2 (1941).

[52] GRATIANUS, CONCORDIA DISCORDANTIUM CANONUM (DECRETUM), in 1 CORPUS IURIS CANONICI (E. Friedberg ed. 1879).

a variety of other matters.[53] Ivo was one of the first to set forth conflicting passages in the authorities and to suggest some standards by which they could be reconciled. Gratian built on Ivo's work. He also had before him the work of the glossators of the Roman law, above all his fellow citizen Irnerius.

Gratian, however, pursued a method of systematization different from that of any of his predecessors. Unlike the Romanists, he did not have a predetermined text but had to dig out for himself from many written sources the canons that he wished to systematize. He collected and analyzed approximately 3800 canonical texts, including many from early periods of Church history. He did not, however, group them according to the conventional categories of earlier canonical collections (ordination, marriage, penance, etc.) or of Roman law (persons, things, obligations, succession, crimes, etc.). His categories were, on the one hand, more comprehensive: the first third of his work was arranged in 150 "divisions" (*distinctiones*) analyzing and synthesizing authoritative statements concerning the nature of law, the various sources of law, the relationship between the different kinds of law, the jurisdiction of various offices within the Church, and so forth. On the other hand, Gratian's categories were also more functional than those that had previously been used in legal literature, for in the second part of his work he posed specific legal "questions," often in the form of complex cases, in the context of which he presented authorities pro and con, reconciled the contradictions where possible or else left them unresolved, offered generalizations, and sometimes sought to harmonize the generalizations.[54]

The best example of his more comprehensive method of analysis and synthesis is found in the first twenty "divisions" of the text, in which various kinds of law are identified (divine law, human law, natural law, the law of the Church, the law of princes, enacted law, customary law), and relationships among them are defined. Gratian did not, of course, invent these categories: the Roman jurists had adapted to their own use Aristotelian distinctions between natural law and positive law, universal law and national law, customary law and enacted law, and the distinction between divine and human law had always existed within the Church. But Gratian was the first to explore systematically the legal implications of these distinctions and to arrange the various

[53] Ivo died in 1116. In the Prologue to his *Decretum*, written about 1095, he stated that he was attempting to unite the ecclesiastical rules "into one body." 166 MIGNE PATROLOGIA LATINA col. 47.

[54] *See* S. KUTTNER, HARMONY FROM DISSONANCE: AN INTERPRETATION OF MEDIEVAL CANON LAW (1960).

sources of law in a hierarchical order. He started by interposing the concept of natural law between the concepts of divine law and human law. Divine law is the will of God reflected in revelation, especially the revelation of Holy Scripture. Natural law also reflects God's will; however, it is found both in divine revelation and in human reason and conscience. From this Gratian could conclude that "[t]he laws [*leges*] of princes [that is, of the secular authorities] ought not to prevail over natural law [*ius naturale*]." [55] Likewise ecclesiastical "laws" may not contravene natural "law." [56] "*Ius*," he wrote, is the genus, *lex* is a species of it." [57]

Gratian also concluded that, as a matter of natural law, "princes are bound by and shall live according to their laws." [58] This was a wholly new legal principle, unknown to the older law, whether Roman or Germanic. There were passages in the earlier texts to the effect that a good prince or emperor ought, as a moral matter, to observe his own laws, but it was uniformly stated that, as a matter of *law*, he was absolved from them.[59] Under the new theory, on the contrary, although the lawmaker could change the old laws in a lawful manner, he could not lawfully disregard them at will. This principle is one which cannot adequately be explained by positivist theories that derive law ultimately from the will of the sovereign.

Moreover, special laws (*leges*) and enactments (*constitutiones*) of princes were, according to Gratian, to be subordinate to ecclesiastical *leges* and *constitutiones*.[60] Further, customs (*consuetudines*), he wrote, must yield not only to natural law but also to enacted laws, whether secular or ecclesiastical.[61]

The theory that customs must yield to natural law was one of the greatest achievements of the canonists. When Gratian

---

[55] GRATIANUS, *supra* note 52, at Dist. IX, Pars. I, c.1.

[56] *Id.* at c.11.

[57] *Id.* at Dist. I, c.2.

[58] *Id.* at c.2.

[59] F. Schulz has argued strenously that such classical Roman law texts as "What has pleased the prince has the force of law" and "The prince is absolved from the laws" are to be construed narrowly, and that only in the postclassical period did the Emperor come to be above the laws generally. *See* Schultz, *Bracton on Kingship*, 60 ENG. HIST. REV. 136 (1945). Nevertheless, no statement of any Roman jurist claiming that the Emperor was bound by the laws has survived (or as Peter Banos has said, perhaps no jurist ever made such a statement and survived). The position taken in the text is supported, rather than refuted, by the provision of Justinian's *Codex* 1.14.4: "It is a statement worthy of the majesty of a reigning prince for him to profess to be subject to the laws; for Our authority is dependent upon that of the law."

[60] GRATIANUS, *supra* note 52, at Dist. X, c.1 & Pars. II.

[61] *Id.* at Dist. XI, Pars. I.

lived, most law in the West was customary law; that is, most legal norms were binding not because they had been promulgated by political authorities, whether ecclesiastical or secular, but because they were practiced and accepted as binding by the communities in which they prevailed. Enacted laws were relatively rare. Also, enacted laws were still justified, for the most part, as restatements of preexisting custom. The theory of Gratian and of his fellow canonists provided a basis for weeding out those customs that did not conform to reason and conscience. Elaborate criteria were developed to determine the validity of a custom: its long duration, its universality, its uniformity of application, its reasonableness, and the like — tests still used in the twentieth century. This meant that custom lost its sanctity; a custom might be binding or it might not.

Thus the canon lawyers "marked off," in the words of Gabriel Le Bras, "from the principles of eternal validity the variable elements of the law, which had been suggested by particular circumstances, whether of time, place, or persons, and enforcement of which other conditions might render unseasonable. This amounted to the recognition of the relativity of rules and provided a technical method of harmonizing contradictions."[62] Two contradictory rules could both be true if, in the words of Gratian's Prologue to the *Concordance of Discordant Canons*, they related to a law which was "variable," and the contradiction was due to a dispensation in a special case.

Gratian's emphasis on natural law and on reason was derived in part from Greek, and especially Stoic, philosophy. In addition, the newly rediscovered Roman law of Justinian had included many references to and remarks about natural law and equity, but had not developed those concepts into any sort of system. The sources of law were classified but they were not organized into a hierarchy or pattern. As we have seen, the Roman lawyers were not philosophers; the Greek philosophers were not lawyers. However, in the twelfth century the canonists and Romanists of Western Europe combined the Greek capacity for philosophy with the Roman capacity for law. In addition, they deepened the earlier concepts of reason and equity by adding to them Judaic and Christian concepts of conscience, which they related to mercy and love.

Moreover, the division between positive law and natural law was now for the first time specifically identified as a division between *lex*, that is, an enacted law, and *ius*, that is, the system of Justice, of Right. Not only princes and other secular authori-

[62] Le Bras, *Canon Law*, in THE LEGACY OF THE MIDDLE AGES 321, 326 (C.G. Crump & E.F. Jacob eds. 1926).

ties, but also ecclesiastics — popes, local councils, bishops — enacted individual *leges* and *constitutiones*, but the body of *ius*, whether the "body of Roman law" (*corpus iuris Romani*), as it now came to be called, or the new "body of canon law" (*corpus iuris canonici*), was sacred, and the validity of an enacted law depended on its conformity to the body of law as a whole, which in turn reflected the natural *ius* and the divine *ius*.

The subordination of positive law to natural law was reenforced by the dualism of secular and ecclesiastical law as well as by the coexistence of conflicting secular authorities. The Church claimed that secular laws which contradicted the law of the Church were invalid. Princes did not always yield to that claim. Nevertheless, they themselves made similar claims with respect to laws of competing secular authorities (feudal lords, city councils, and others) and occasionally also ecclesiastical authorities. Given plural legal systems, victims of unjust laws could run from one jurisdiction to another for relief in the name of reason and conscience!

The laws of the Church itself, as has already been indicated, were to be tested by their conformity to natural law. Gratian wrote: "Enactments [*constitutiones*], whether ecclesiastical or secular, if they are proved to be contrary to natural law, must be totally excluded."[63] However, only rarely was anyone in a position to say authoritatively that an ecclesiastical enactment was contrary to natural law, for the Pope was not only the supreme legislator in the Church but also the vicar and representative of Christ on earth. In the twelfth and thirteenth centuries, at least, most of the men who served as officials and judges and counselors of kings and emperors were clerics who owed at least half their allegiance to the Pope. Nevertheless, secular authorities did sometimes challenge ecclesiastical enactments on the ground that they were contrary to natural law.

The theory of the relativity of rules was thus based partly on the politics of competing legal systems. But it was also based partly, as I have tried to show in the preceding pages, on the scholastic dialectic, which provided a method for placing both customary laws and enacted laws within a larger theoretical framework of the nature and sources of law.

A good example of Gratian's second principal method of systematization — the analysis and synthesis of conflicting solutions to a particular legal "question" — is his discussion of whether priests should read profane literature.[64] After posing

[63] GRATIANUS, *supra* note 52, at Dist. IX, Pars. I, c.11.

[64] *See id.* at Dist. XXXVII, *translated in* A. NORTON, READINGS IN THE HISTORY OF EDUCATION 60–75 (AMS Press ed. 1971).

the problem, Gratian quotes the statement of Church Councils, Church Fathers, and others, as well as examples from scripture and Church history, tending to show that priests should not read profane literature, followed by similar authoritative statements and examples to the opposite effect. After each authoritative statement or example is given, Gratian introduces his own interpretation. Thus he starts with the pronouncement of the Carthaginian Council, "A bishop should not read the books of the heathen." His commentary notes that nothing is said about books of heretics, which may be read "carefully, either of necessity or for some special reason." The gloss comments further on the word "necessity," interpreting it as signifying that priests may read the books of heretics "in order that they may know how to speak correctly." A more significant gloss accompanying the statement of the question itself sums up the interpretation of all the authorities against reading profane literature: "pleasure alone seems to be forbidden." Ultimately Gratian offers his conclusion, "solving the contradiction" by stating that anyone (and not only priests) ought to learn profane knowledge not for pleasure but for instruction, in order that what is found therein may be turned to the use of sacred learning. Thus general principles and general concepts were used to synthesize opposing doctrines — not only to determine which of two opposing doctrines was wrong, but also to bring a new, third doctrine out of the conflict.[65]

[65] This is an example of the kind of synthesis referred to at note 20 *supra*. The simple choice of one of two contradictory solutions is characteristic of the philosophical method of Thomas Aquinas (late 13th century), who in that respect took a backward step. Another, even more striking example of synthesis of opposites, as contrasted with choice between them, is found in the development of legal standards for testing the legitimacy of the use of force. Both the Old Testament and the New Testament forbid killing. Yet both give examples in which the use of force is approved. Roman law, on the other hand, although it did not purport to lay down moral standards, contained the rule *"Vim vi repellere licet,"* "Force may be used to repel force." Like Roman legal rules generally, this was not conceived as embodying a general principle or concept but was limited to the specific types of situations in connection with which it was found, chiefly the rule of the Lex Aquilia that a man could use physical force to protect his property from seizure. The European jurists of the twelfth and thirteenth centuries converted the Roman law *regula* into a general principle, which they juxtaposed with the so-called pacifistic utterances of Jesus ("turn the other cheek"), and from the opposing maxims they developed a general concept of justification for the limited use of force applicable to a whole series of interrelated categories systematically set forth, such as force necessary to execute the law, to defend oneself, to defend another, to protect one's own property, to protect another's property. These principles were applied not only to civil and criminal law but also to political and theological questions concerning a "just war." *See* F.H. RUSSELL, THE JUST WAR IN THE MIDDLE AGES (1975).

This is a rather simple example of the scholastic technique of posing a *quaestio* relating to contradictory passages in an authoritative text, followed by a *propositio* stating authorities and reasons in support of one position, followed by an *oppositio*, stating authorities and reasons for the contrary view, and ending with a *solutio* (or *conclusio*) in which it is shown that the reasons given in the *oppositio* are not true or, alternatively, that the *propositio* must be qualified or abandoned in light of the *oppositio*. In fact, the scholastic method of posing "disputed questions" was usually much more complex.[66] The teacher or writer would often pose not one but a series of interconnected problems, one after the other. Arguments were then made on opposite sides, as though by a plaintiff and a defendant in a lawsuit. The pros and the cons would be "arranged in two battle fronts." [67] In support of each argument rules of law were cited; sometimes dozens of such *allegationes* were made to support a single argument pro or con. Most of the characteristic terms of the argument, as Hermann Kantorowicz has shown, were derived either from the available literature on Greek dialectics or from the Roman law texts of Justinian or from both.[68] What was wholly new, according to Kantorowicz, when the method was first invented by the jurists in the second quarter of the twelfth century,[69] was the putting together of all these terms in a highly complex structure resembling pleading and argumentation in difficult cases in court. The resemblance was not accidental. Kantorowicz, at least, believes that the style was first developed in litigation and then imitated in the classroom and in the literature — just as the style of the English Yearbooks of 1280–1535 was probably derived from student notes of arguments in cases in the king's courts.[70] That still leaves the question, why did argument in court take the form of a whole battery of positions pro and con, with multiple citations, intricate refutations, and complex syntheses? Surely an important part of the answer is that, again in Kantorowicz's words,

---

[66] *See* Kantorowicz, *The Quaestiones Disputatae of the Glossators*, 16 TIJDSCHRIFT VOOR RECHTSGESCHIEDENIS/REVUE D'HISTOIRE DU DROIT 5 (1939).

[67] *Id.* at 23.

[68] *Id.* at 55–56. Kantorowicz lists the following: *titulus, rubrica, summaria, exordium, casus, causa, materia, thema, ponere, queritur, questio, controversia, disputatio, actor, argumentum, decisio, definitio, determinatio, iudicium, sententia, responsum, distinctio, divisio, problema, solutio*, and others. *But see* Pringsheim, *Beryt und Bologna*, in FESTSCHRIFT FÜR OTTO LENEL 204, 252 (1921). Kantorowicz points out that Pringsheim errs in attributing many of these terms to the Roman law that developed in the East *after* the time of Justinian.

[69] Kantorowicz, *supra* note 66, at 1–6.

[70] *Id.* at 43.

> the *questiones disputatae* were the chief link between the written law of Justinian and its application in the contemporary courts of justice. Thus was developed the courage to draw audacious analogies, to handle far-flung principles of equity, to fill the *lacunae* of the law by intuition and imagination. Therefore, the historical importance of these questions as a dynamic factor in the adaptation of the Roman law to changed and everchanging views and conditions was great indeed.[71]

The same audacity, and the same techniques, were applied in adapting Biblical, patristic, and canonical principles to the new conditions of life.

In addition to elaborating general legal principles that underlie the rules applicable to concrete cases, the jurists of the twelfth and thirteenth centuries, both canonists and Romanists, also defined general concepts, such as the concept of representation, the concept of the corporation, the concept of jurisdiction, and the like. Here again, while the Roman law of Justinian provided the basic terminology and the Greek dialectics of Plato and Aristotle provided the basic method, the combination of the two — in a wholly different social context — produced something quite new. For example, the Roman jurists had laid down various rules under which a slave could act in behalf of his master, as his agent, and the master would be liable, but they offered no general definition of agency or of representation. Similarly, they had stated a variety of situations in which a group of people were to be treated as a collective unit, such as a *societas* ("partnership"), but they offered no general definition of group or corporate personality and they did not develop the idea of limited liability. Justinian's Roman law lacked even a general concept of contract; it provided for certain specific types of contracts, but they were not subordinated to a general concept of binding promises, so that an agreement which fell outside the types of contracts named by law was ipso facto not a contract.[72]

It would be wholly incorrect to say that there were no general concepts in the Roman law of the time of Justinian and before; on the contrary, Roman jurists eagerly discussed situations in which a contract would be void because of "mistake," situations in which the enforcement of an informal obligation was required by "good faith," and various other types of situations in which legal results involved a reference to concepts. Indeed, Roman law from early times was permeated by such concepts as "ownership," "possession," "delict," "fraud," "theft," and dozens of others. That was its great virtue. However, these concepts

[71] *Id.* at 5–6.

[72] *See* F. SCHULZ, *supra* note 28, at 43–44.

were not treated as ideas which underlay the rules and determined their applicability. They were not considered philosophically. The concepts of Roman law, like its numerous legal rules, were tied to specific types of situations. Roman law consisted of an intricate network of rules which was not presented as an intellectual system but rather as an elaborate mosaic of practical solutions to specific legal questions. Thus one may say that although there were concepts in Roman law, there was no concept of a concept.

In contrast, the European jurists who revived the study of Roman law in the eleventh and twelfth centuries set out to systematize and harmonize the huge network of Roman legal rules in terms both of general principles and of general concepts, using methods similar to those which their colleagues in theology employed to systematize and harmonize the Old and New Testaments, the writings of the Church Fathers, and other sacred texts. The jurists took as a starting point the concept of a legal concept and the principle that the law is principled.

The conceptualization of general legal terms, like the formulation of general principles underlying the legal rules, was closely related not only to the revived interest in Greek philosophy but also to contemporaneous developments in theology;[73] and both the philosophical and the theological aspects were closely related to the great changes in political, economic, and social life which constituted the Papal Revolution. Above all, it was the coexistence and competition of newly emerging centralized polities, ecclesiastical and secular, that made it important to articulate the principles underlying the rules and the concepts underlying the principles. The Church led the way. Thus the Church in the eleventh century was the first collective to call itself a corporation (*universitas*). The authority of bishops and priests, formerly derived solely from the sacrament of ordination, was now held to be derived also from jurisdiction: they were now for the first time appointed with the consent of the papacy ("by grace of God *and* of the Apostolic See") and could be removed only by the papacy. A bishop was now an official of the corporate Church. His "jurisdiction" included the power and duty to try cases in his court, under the rules of a universal body of procedural and substantive law, with an automatic right of appeal by the losing party to the papal curia.[74]

[73] There seems to be no published work that examines in detail the relation of legal reasoning to theological reasoning in the formative era of Western legal thought. Some excellent hints may be found in F. WIEACKER, PRIVATRECHTSGESCHICHTE DER NEUZEIT 54–56 (2d ed. 1967).

[74] In his *Dictatus papae* of 1075 Pope Gregory VII stated that the bishop of Rome alone (that is, without a synod) has the power to depose and reinstate

A similar process of conceptualization took place in the development of secular legal systems. The same terms, derived largely from Roman law, were used in the articulation of general principles and eventually in the formation of general concepts. The principles and concepts were then used as a basis for extrapolation of new applications. This development revolutionized the science of law. It meant that the validity of a legal rule could be proved by showing its organic consistency with the principles and concepts of the system as a whole.

## V. LAW AS THE FIRST MODERN WESTERN SCIENCE

The scholastic jurists created a legal *science* in the modern Western sense, rather than in the Platonic or Aristotelian senses. For Plato, "science" (*epistēmē*) was knowledge of the truth derived by deduction from the general to the particular. Although Aristotle recognized a whole series of separate and distinct sciences, all sharing in common the method of observation and hypothesis,[75] he nonetheless focused on finding the true cause or necessity that produces a certain substance or conclu-

---

bishops, that he alone has the power to issue new laws, that no general council may be called without his consent and no action of a general council may be considered canonical without his authority, and that the most important cases of every church may be appealed to the papal curia. The document is translated in B. TIERNEY, THE CRISIS OF CHURCH AND STATE 1050–1300, at 49–50 (1964).

Concepts of jurisdiction and of corporate personality also involved the concept of representation. The institution of agency, which had always existed in a rudimentary way, was now conceptualized in scholastic terms. The person represented was absent, yet he was also present in his representative. Thus the Pope was for the first time acting not only as one of Christ's agents but also as his unique deputy. At the same time he was now said to represent the Church as a corporate person. In that capacity he sent out "legates" to administer and adjudicate in his name. When an unordained, subordinate member of the clerical hierarchy, such as a subdeacon, was appointed by the Pope to be a legate to judge a bishop, for example, one may see the new concepts of representation, corporate personality, and jurisdiction working in combination with each other. *See* H. HOFMANN, REPRÄSENTATION (1974).

[75] Aristotle divided Platonic "science" into physics, biology, geometry, ethics, politics, metaphysics, and other sciences, each of which had "its own distinctive *archai* or 'principles' [literally, "beginnings"] and its own determinate subject matter," and each had its own method of investigation, "growing out of the subject-matter itself." J. RANDALL, ARISTOTLE 33, 54 (1960). Once the postulates, or first principles, of a science are given, its reasoning may proceed by the apodictic method of demonstration of scientific truths, rather than by the dialectical method of reasoning from disputable premises to probabilities. *See id.* at 162–65. Medicine was for Aristotle an "art" (*techne*) rather than a science, since it applies scientific truths but does not itself lead to the demonstration of such truths. Law, for Aristotle, was not even an "art" but was dissolved in ethics, politics, and rhetoric.

sion. Thus, for Aristotle the ultimate model of science was geometry.

For modern Western man, however, the very certitude of mathematics, the fact that it is based on its own inner logic rather than on fallible human observation, makes it appear more like a language or a philosophy than a science. A science in the modern Western sense, unlike Aristotelian science, focuses on formulating hypotheses that can serve as a basis for ordering phenomena in the world of time, and hence in the world of probabilities and predictions rather than certitudes and necessities. The legal science of the scholastic jurists was just that kind of science. It used a dialectical mode of establishing general legal principles by relating them to particulars in predication. It was not, to be sure, an "exact" science, like modern physics or chemistry, nor was it susceptible to the kind of laboratory experimentation that is characteristic of many (though not all) natural sciences, although it did (as I shall explain) utilize its own kinds of experimentation. Also it was concerned with constructing a system out of observed *social* phenomena — legal institutions — rather than observed phenomena of the world of matter. Nevertheless, like the natural sciences that developed in its wake, the new legal science combined empirical and theoretical methods.

A science, in the modern Western sense of the word, may be defined by three sets of criteria: (a) methodological criteria, (b) value criteria, and (c) sociological criteria. By all three sets of criteria, the legal science of the twelfth-century jurists of Western Europe was the father of the modern Western sciences.

### *A. Methodological Characteristics of Legal Science*

A science in the modern Western sense may be defined in methodological terms as: (a) an integrated body of knowledge (b) in which particular occurrences or phenomena are systematically explained (c) in terms of general principles or truths ("laws"), (d) knowledge of which (that is, of both the phenomena and the general principles) has been obtained by a combination of (i) observation, (ii) hypothesis, (iii) verification, and (iv) to the extent possible, experiment. However, (e) the scientific method of investigation and systematization, despite these common characteristics, is not the same for all sciences but must be specifically adapted to the particular kinds of occurrences or phenomena under investigation by each particular science.

By all the criteria listed above, the scholarly researches and writings of the Italian, French, English, German, and other jurists of the late eleventh, twelfth, and thirteenth centuries, both canonists and Romanists, constituted a science of law. The phenomena studied were the decisions, rules, customs, statutes, and other legal data promulgated by Church councils, popes, and bishops, as well as by emperors, kings, dukes, city magistrates, and other secular rulers, or found in Holy Scripture, the Roman law texts of Justinian, and other written sources. These legal materials were treated by the jurists as data to be observed, classified, and systematically explained in terms of general principles and general concepts or truths. The explanations were subjected to verification in terms of both logic and experience. To the extent that positive examples of their application could be adduced, and the effects measured, a kind of experimentation was also involved.

To take a specific example, the jurists observed that in all the various legal systems under examination the question arose whether one who was forcibly dispossessed of his goods has the right to take them back by force. One solution was reached by interpretation of the Roman law texts of Justinian, where it appears that the Roman praetor had decreed that one who has been forcibly dispossessed of his land (nothing is said about goods) may not take it back by force after a certain period of time has elapsed. The twelfth-century jurists concluded that the rule is equally applicable to goods, since the same purposes are involved in both classes of cases. Further, it had been laid down by certain Church councils and in individual ecclesiastical cases that a bishop forcibly ousted from his bishopric must not resort to force to recover it. A bishopric, it was noted by the twelfth-century jurists, includes not only rights in land but also rights in goods and, in addition, rights in perquisites — rights in rights ("choses-in-action")! Such instances gave rise not only to analogies but also to hypotheses. It appeared that underlying the various rules was a basic legal principle — nowhere stated in the law but now stated by the legal scientist to explain the law — that persons whose rights are violated are required to vindicate them by legal action rather than by "taking the law into their own hands." This was verified logically by the proposition that it is a basic purpose of law to provide an alternative to force as a means of settlement of disputes. It was further verified by experience, including experience of the circumstances that gave rise to the rule, namely, the disorder and injustice that existed when disputes over rights in land, goods, and choses-in-action were settled by a series of violent acts of dispossession first by one of the disputants and then by the other. Such experience reached the level of experimentation when the jurist was able to compare the consequences of diverse legal rules and of changes in legal rules. Rules that were considered unsatisfactory sometimes were amended or repealed or fell into disuse. Rules that were considered satisfactory were often continued. Such "experiments" lack the exactness of laboratory tests; yet they are a kind of social experimentation, a "laboratory of history" — what modern scientists would call "natural experiments." Using modern terminology we may say that experience, including the experience of applying rules in concrete cases, was viewed as a process of constant feedback concerning the validity both of the rules and of the general principles and concepts thought to underlie them.

The verification of general legal principles by logic and experience constituted legal science at its highest intellectual levels; usually, however, the legal scientist of the twelfth century, like his counterpart today, was concerned with what much later was called "legal dogmatics," that is, the systematic working out of the ramifications of legal rules, their interconnections, their application in specific types of situations. To go back to the example of forcible dispossession: once a principle was established forbidding a person to recapture his property by force, knotty questions arose concerning the remedy of the person forcibly dispossessed. May he be restored to possession even if he had previously taken possession by force, and even if the person now dispossessing him was the true owner? Are the remedies to be the same with respect to goods as with respect to land? Is there a time limit within which the victim of the dispossession may lawfully defend his rights by force ("hot pursuit")? Such questions were not viewed by the jurists primarily as moral or as political questions but rather as legal questions; they were questions to be resolved on the basis of the interpretation of legal authorities — decisions, rules, customs, statutes, scriptural texts, and the like, authoritatively laid down. The authoritative texts were taken as objectively given; no attempt was to be made to show that they were contrary to reason or that they were not useful or that they were historically conditioned. The jurist's task was to organize and make sense out of them. As I have tried to indicate, his methods of doing so were not essentially different from those later used by natural scientists to explore and synthesize other kinds of data.

### *B. Value Premises of Legal Science*

Although science, in the modern Western sense, has usually been defined only in methodological terms, there has been an increasing recognition that it must also be defined in terms of the attitudes, convictions, and fundamental purposes of those engaged in the scientific enterprise. One may, indeed, speak of a scientific code of values,[76] which includes (a) the scientists' obligation to conduct research with objectivity and integrity, and to evaluate their own and each other's work solely on the basis of universal standards of scientific merit; (b) the requirement that scientists adopt a position of doubt and of "organized skepticism" toward the certitude of their own and each other's premises and conclusions, together with a tolerance of new ideas until they are disproved and a willingness publicly to acknowledge error; and (c) a built-in assumption that science is an "open system," that it seeks "increasingly close approximations to the truth rather than final answers," and that "science cannot be frozen into a set of orthodox conceptions . . . but is an ever-changing body of ideas with varying degrees of plausibility." [77]

Many would doubt the likelihood, or even the possibility, that a "lawyer" could meet these three standards. His objectivity, integrity, and universality seem questionable, since he is called upon both by political and by private partisans to promote and justify their interests. Further, if he is to be skeptical of his own conclusions he may place difficulties in the way of their acceptance, and it is often part of his professional responsibility to persuade people to accept them. The same difficulty obstructs the conception of legal science as a body of ever-changing ideas: society itself seems to demand that law be something more than that. Finally, if we speak of science in the West during the period when not only the authority and the power of the papacy, but also its dogmatism, were at their height, it seems incredible that "lawyers" — even though they might have been legal scholars and not practitioners (in fact many of them were both) — or, indeed, any other pursuers of knowledge, could have had the disinterestedness and open-mindedness that is at the basis of the code of values of modern Western science.

These doubts raise fundamental questions concerning the freedom not only of legal science in the twelfth century but of any science in any society.[78] The scientific code of values is always precarious; it must always be defended against political and ideological pressures from without and from the prejudices and partisanship of scientists themselves. What is striking about the twelfth century is that at the very climax of the movement to centralize authority and power in the Church, and at the very time when

[76] *See* Cournand & Zuckerman, *The Code of Science: Analysis and Some Reflections on its Future*, 23 STUDIUM GENERALE 941, 945–61 (1970). I am indebted to Grace Goodell for calling this invaluable essay to my attention.

[77] *Id.* at 945.

[78] *See* Berman, *The "Right to Knowledge" in the Soviet Union*, 54 COLUM. L. REV. 749 (1954).

dogma itself first became legalized and heresy defined in terms of criminal disobedience,[79] there emerged the belief that the progress of science depends on the freedom of scientists to take opposing points of view on matters of scientific truth. It was presupposed, of course, that such dialectical reasoning from contradictory positions would result in a synthesis, and that the synthesis would correspond to authoritative declarations of the true faith; nevertheless, it was also presupposed that the dialectical reasoning must proceed scientifically or else it would be worthless. Thus at the same time that unorthodox doctrines were legally proscribed, and heretics who persisted in "disobedience" were put to death, the values of scientific objectivity, disinterestedness, organized skepticism, tolerance of error, openness to new scientific truths, and others, were not only proclaimed but given expression in the very form of the new sciences that then emerged.

Doubts concerning the capacity of "lawyers" to adhere to such values rest on several misconceptions. It is true, of course, that when a lawyer is an advocate for a party or cause, he must act as a partisan and not as a scientist. However, this role is an essential part of legal proceedings in which opposite points of view are presented to a tribunal charged with making a decision. Indeed, the legal proceedings themselves are, in one sense, scientific, since the contest is designed to bring before the tribunal all relevant considerations. In a trial, the court is supposed to decide the case "objectively," on the basis of "the evidence" presented on behalf of the disputants. Yet a trial, or legislative debate, or other such legal proceeding, has other characteristics that are quite unscientific. For one thing, the tribunal must act under the pressure of given time limits, whereas the scientist may wait indefinitely until he is ready to draw conclusions. Beyond that, the tribunal is a political body; it stands too close to community prejudices and pressures to maintain the kind of "distance" re-

[79] Heresy had been denounced by the Church from the first century on and it had been persecuted at various times both by secular and ecclesiastical authorities. However, it did not assume the character of a legal offense until the Papal Revolution established the Western Church as a legal entity. In the eleventh and twelfth centuries the inquisitional procedure was used for the first time to expose heresy as an ecclesiastical crime and the death penalty was for the first time made applicable to it. The gist of the offense was dissent from the dogmas of the Church. If the accused was willing to swear an oath to adhere to those dogmas, he was to be acquitted, although he was still subject to penances if he had sworn the oath only because of torture or other duress. Of course, if he persisted in heresy he remained liable to prosecution. *See generally* H. GRUNDMANN, KETZERGESCHICHTE DES MITTELALTERS (1963). Valuable documentary sources are given in English translation in R.I. MOORE, THE BIRTH OF POPULAR HERESY (1975) and J.B. RUSSELL, RELIGIOUS DISSENT IN THE MIDDLE AGES (1971).

quired of scientists. However, it is neither the "lawyer" nor the "tribunal" (whether it be a judicial or legislative or administrative body), but the law teacher and legal scholar who is asked to adhere to the scientific code of values. He, too, has difficulties in doing so — greater difficulties, perhaps, than scholars in fields that are more remote from everyday political, economic, and social life. Yet by the same token he may be more aware of the outside pressures upon him as well as of the inside pressures of his own passions and prejudices, and hence better able than others to resist them, or at least more sensitive to the precariousness of his own scientific freedom.

Ultimately, however, the extent to which the values of science, including legal science, are upheld depends not only on the determination and self-discipline of scientists themselves but also on social factors, including the legal institutions which safeguard those values. I shall discuss in the next section some of the social factors underlying the new legal science of twelfth-century Europe. My concern in this section, however, has been to show that the values themselves were implicit in the dialectical method of analysis and synthesis of legal problems created by the scholastic jurists of the eleventh and twelfth centuries. The intense concentration on contradictions in the law, on "dialectical problems," *quaestiones disputatae*, and the intense effort to reconcile them by legal principles and concepts on ascending levels of generalization — could only succeed, as a method, by adherence to the very values that characterize science itself: objectivity, integrity, universalism, skepticism, tolerance of error, humility, openness to new truth — and, I would add, a special time-sense that is associated with the coexistence of contradictories. Since it was believed that the whole of law was informed by a common purpose, a *ratio*, it was taken for granted that the paradoxes would ultimately be resolved; meanwhile, the corps of jurists would patiently cope with the uncertainties that the paradoxes created.

### *C. Sociological Criteria of Legal Science*

In addition to its methodology and its value premises, a science, in the modern Western sense of that word, must be defined in terms of sociological criteria. There are certain social preconditions that not only are indispensable to its existence but also help to form its character.[80] These include (a) the formation of scientific communities, usually coextensive with the various dis-

[80] *See* R. Merton, *Science and Democratic Social Structure*, in SOCIAL THEORY AND SOCIAL STRUCTURE 550–61 (1957).

ciplines, each of which has a collective responsibility for the conduct of research, the training of new recruits, the sharing of scientific knowledge, and the authentication of scientific accomplishments within the discipline and outside it; (b) the linking of the various scientific disciplines in larger scholarly communities, and especially in universities, whose members share a common concern for both the advancement of learning and the education of the young as well as a common implicit assumption that all branches of knowledge rest ultimately on the same foundations; and (c) the privileged social status of the communities of scientists, including a high degree of freedom of teaching and research, which is correlative to their high degree of responsibility to serve the cause of science itself, its methods, its values, and its social function.

That Western legal scholarship was, in the twelfth century, and still is, a collective enterprise, and that legal scholars did, and still do, form a community of shared interests and concerns will scarcely be seriously disputed. That legal scholars also formed, and still form, a profession, in the sense that the individual members have a public responsibility and are pledged to place the advancement of their discipline above their personal self-interest or profit, is perhaps only slightly less obvious. These truisms of Western historical experience may also be applicable to all sciences wherever and whenever they have existed. What is especially characteristic of Western science since the twelfth century, however, including legal science, is its close historical connection with the institution of the university; it was born in the university and the university bestowed upon it its precarious heritage of freedom of teaching and research.

Here is another key to the solution of the question why modern Western scientific concepts and scientific methods emerged in the late eleventh and early twelfth centuries. It was because the universities emerged then. This may seem simply to put the question back one step. But it does more; it removes the question from the realm of history of ideas to the realm of history of communities. The scientific methodology and the scientific values that I have described in the two preceding sections of this chapter, and that characterize what I have called "science in the modern Western sense," are to be explained *not* in terms of the unfolding of ideas in some Platonic or Hegelian sense, but as social responses to social needs. It takes more than the progressive translation of the works of Aristotle to explain why, in the year 1150, ten to thirteen thousand students from all over Europe could be found in the town of Bologna in northern Italy studying legal science.[81] They were there because society made it possible — indeed, made it urgent — that they be there; more than that, the social conditions that made it both possible and urgent also inevitably played a critical part in determining the nature of the legal science that they were there to study.

The scholastic dialectic, and consequently modern science, it is submitted, was produced by the contradictions in the historical situation of Western European society in the late eleventh and twelfth centuries, and by the overwhelming effort to resolve those contradictions and to forge a new synthesis. It was produced, in short, by the Papal Revolution. Surely that is true of the scholastic dialectic as it was applied in legal science. A learned profession of jurists emerged in Western Europe in response to the need to reconcile the conflicts that raged within the Church, between the Church and the secular authorities, and among and within the various secular polities. Formed primarily in the universities, the legal profession produced a science of law; that is, the jurists constituted a community in which that science was the expression of the community's reason for being. Through its legal science, the legal profession helped to solve the contradictions in the social and historical situation of Western Europe by solving the contradictions between that situation and the preexisting legal authorities. Legal science was, in the first instance, an institutionalization of the process of resolving social-political conflict by resolving conflicts in authoritative legal texts.

This can be demonstrated by reference to the principal social characteristics of Western legal science in its formative period in the late eleventh and twelfth centuries, especially as they were influenced by the universities.

In the *first* place, the universities helped to establish the transnational character of Western legal science. As David Knowles has written:

> For three hundred years, from 1050 to 1350, and above all in the century between 1070 and 1170, the whole of educated Europe formed a single and undifferentiated cultural unit. In the lands

[81] Historians of ideas sometimes turn things around the other way. *Cf.* A SCHOLASTIC MISCELLANY: ANSELM TO OCKHAM 27 (E. Fairweather ed. & trans. 1956) ("Indeed, the whole history of medieval thought can be organized in terms of the progressive rediscovery of Aristotle."). In fact the major works of the founding fathers both of the new theology and the new legal science, especially those of Abelard and Gratian, just antedated the translation of Aristotle's major works on logic. This is not to say that Aristotle's theories of logic, as they had been transmitted by Boethius in the sixth century, were unimportant. The question is: why did they suddenly acquire a new significance? Why was it suddenly so important that his major works be translated?

between Edinburgh and Palermo, Mainz or Lund and Toledo, a man of any city or village might go for education to any school, and become a prelate or an official in any church, court, or university (when these existed) from north to south, from east to west . . . . In this period a high proportion of the most celebrated writers, thinkers, and administrators gained greatest fame and accomplished the most significant part of their life's work far from the land of their birth and boyhood. Moreover, in the writings of many of them there is not a single characteristic of language, style, or thought to tell us whence they sprang. True, we are speaking only of a small educated minority, to which the land-owning aristocracy in general, many monarchs, and even some bishops, did not belong. The world of Church and State was often rent by schisms and wars, while the bulk of the population, fast rooted in the soil, knew nothing beyond the fields and woods of their small corner. But on the level of literature and thought there was one stock of words, forms, and thoughts from which all drew and in which all shared on an equality. If we possessed the written works without their authors' names we should not be able to assign them to any country or people . . . ."[82]

What Knowles writes of scholarship in general in that period was equally applicable to legal scholarship in the fields of canon and Roman law. These were disciplines without national boundaries. They were taught in the universities to law students gathered from all the countries of Europe. They all, of course, spoke Latin, which was the universal Western language not only of the law but also of teaching and scholarship and of worship and theology.

*Second*, in addition to giving legal scholarship a transnational character, the European universities helped to give the law itself a transnational vocabulary and method. The graduates of the university law schools went back to their own countries, or moved to other countries, where they served as ecclesiastical or lay judges, practicing lawyers, legal advisors to ecclesiastical, royal, and city authorities and to lords of manors, and as administrative officials of various kinds in both church and state. To the extent that they were involved with canon law, they could use

[82] D. KNOWLES, *supra* note 21, at 80–81. As Knowles writes, it was

the age of Lanfranc of Pavia, Bec, and Canterbury [Lanfranc was William the Conqueror's chief advisor and Archbishop of Canterbury]; of Anselm of Aosta, Bec, and Canterbury [Anselm succeeded his former teacher Lanfranc under William's successor]; of Vacarius [a famous professor of Roman law] of Lombardy, Canterbury, Oxford and York; of John of Salisbury, Paris, Benevento, Canterbury and Chartres [an intimate associate and counselor of kings, archbishops, and popes, "the most accomplished scholar and stylist of his age"]; . . . of Nicholas Brakespeare of St. Albans, France, Scandinavia and Rome [son of English peasants who became Pope Hadrian IV]; of Thomas of Aquina, Cologne, Paris and Naples . . . .

their university training directly; to the extent that they were concerned with secular law, they applied to it the vocabulary and the method of the Roman and canon law that they had studied.

*Third*, the legal method which was taught in the European universities was one which made possible the construction of legal systems out of preexisting diverse and contradictory customs and laws. The techniques of harmonizing contradictions, coupled with the belief in an ideal "body of law" (*corpus iuris*), made it possible to begin to synthesize canon law (*corpus iuris canonici*) and then feudal law, urban law, commercial law, and royal law.

*Fourth*, the universities exalted the role of the scholar — the scientist — in the shaping of the law. The law was to be found, in the first instance, in the ancient texts, and hence it was necessary to have a class of learned men who could explain the texts to those who wished to be introduced to their mysteries. The "doctor," that is, the university teacher, became the authoritative expositor of the "true rule." This, too, gave a universality to legal science that helped to overcome the contradictions of laws.

*Fifth*, the juxtaposition of law and other university disciplines — especially theology, medicine, and the liberal arts — also contributed a breadth to law studies that would otherwise have been lacking. The scholastic method was used in all the disciplines, and the subject matter of all the disciplines overlapped. Thus the law student was conscious that his profession was an integral part of the intellectual life of his time.

*Sixth*, law, though linked to other university disciplines, also was separate and distinct from them; it was no longer, as it had been before the rise of the universities, a branch of rhetoric, on the one hand, and of ethics and politics, on the other. In the Roman Empire, the autonomy of legal thought had been maintained by practitioners — especially, praetors and professional legal advisers; in Western Europe that autonomy was maintained by the universities.

*Seventh*, the fact that law was taught as a university discipline made it inevitable that legal doctrines would be criticized and evaluated in the light of general truths, and not merely studied as a craft or technique. Even apart from the universities, the Church had long taught that there was a divine law and a moral law by which all human law was to be tested and judged; but the university jurists added the concept of an ideal human law, the Roman law of Justinian's books, which — together with the Bible, the writings of the Church fathers, the decrees of Church councils and popes, and other sacred texts — provided basic legal principles and standards for criticizing and evaluating existing legal rules and institutions. These inspired writings of the past, and not what any lawgiver might say or do, provided the ultimate criteria of legality.

*Eighth*, the Western universities raised the analysis of law to the level of a science, as that word was understood in the twelfth to fifteenth centuries, by conceptualizing legal institutions and systematizing law as an integrated body of knowledge, so that the validity of legal rules could be demonstrated by their consistency with the system as a whole.

*Ninth*, the universities produced a professional class of lawyers, bound together by a common training and by the common task of guiding the legal activities of the Church and of the secular world of empires, kingdoms, cities, manors, and merchant and other guilds. The law students themselves, initially at least, formed a corporation, a guild, and although upon graduation they scattered to many countries, they remained bound together informally by their common training and their common task.

It is true that in England in the fourteenth century there grew up alongside the university law schools of Oxford and Cambridge a different mode of legal education, in the Inns of Court. Nevertheless, in England as in other countries of Europe the system of university law teaching established in the twelfth century had a profound influence on legal thought. It is also true both that the growth of nationalism in modern times has made inroads into the transnational character of Western legal education and that the links between law and other university disciplines have been substantially weakened. Yet something of the Bologna tradition, and something of the scholastic dialectic, survive nine centuries later — even in the law schools of America. Indeed, they have spread throughout the world. Only in the latter part of the twentieth century have they come to be seriously challenged.

## VI. Conclusion

I have discussed what may be called, from one point of view, the "formal" aspects of the Western legal tradition as it emerged in the late eleventh and twelfth centuries: its logic, its "topics," its style of reasoning, its levels of generalization, its techniques of interrelating particulars and universals, cases and concepts. I have tried to show that the new legal methodology was an essential part of the conscious systematization of law as an autonomous science, which, in turn, was an essential part of the creation of autonomous legal systems for the new polities that emerged from the Papal Revolution: the new church-state, the emerging secular kingdoms, the chartered cities and towns, the newly systematized feudal and manorial relationships, the translocal community of merchants. The emphasis on conflicting authoritative legal texts, and on their reconciliation by means of general principles and concepts, was a creative intellectual response to the felt need to reconcile the sharply conflicting elements that coexisted and competed within the structure of the society itself. To recognize the legitimacy of each of the contradictory elements — ecclesiastical and secular, royal and feudal, feudal and urban, urban and guild — and yet to recognize the structural unity of the total society — Europe, the West, Western Christendom — of which they were parts, and to find a genuine synthesis, that is, a way of dealing with the ambiguities and conflicts without destroying the autonomy of the factors that constituted them — that was the revolutionary challenge of the times. And that was the challenge which was confronted in legal science by the glossators and the canonists, just as it was confronted in the development of the new legal systems that were created with the help of that science.[83]

By the same token, however, the new Western legal science was much more than an intellectual achievement — much more, as was said earlier, than a method of reasoning or a method of organizing thought. Its criteria were moral as well as intellectual. The "form" expressed "substantive" values and policies.[84]

[83] My colleague Roberto Unger has attributed the emergence of the concept of law as an autonomous system in European history to the convergence of a theology of transcendence, a belief in group pluralism, and the idea of the liberal secular state. *See* R. UNGER, LAW IN MODERN SOCIETY: TOWARD A CRITICISM OF SOCIAL THEORY 66–76, 83–86, 176–81 (1976). There are some striking parallels between his analysis and the account given above, despite the sharp contrast between his more philosophical and this more historical interpretation. However, in dating the origins of the Western concept of an autonomous legal system from the 17th century, and in linking it with the emergence of a positivist political and legal theory, Professor Unger avoids the crucial questions of the political and legal character of the Church and the interrelations of church and state, questions which were central to Western political and legal thought from the late eleventh to the nineteenth centuries and which, in disguise, still haunt Western secular religions, including both liberalism and socialism. *See* H. BERMAN, THE INTERACTION OF LAW AND RELIGION (1974).

[84] A similar belief in the interdependence of form and substance in legal thought, but a different view of the nature of each, has been presented recently by my colleague Duncan Kennedy in his article, *Form and Substance in Private Law Adjudication*, 89 HARV. L. REV. 1685 (1976). Professor Kennedy asserts that in contemporary American private law adjudication all *forms* of law fall into two opposed categories, namely, "rules," which are relatively narrow and specific and are supposed to operate with objectivity and generality, and "standards," such as fairness, reasonableness, and due process, which are relatively broad and which permit persons and situations to be dealt with on an ad hoc basis. Professor

The reconciliation of opposing legal rules was part of a larger process of attempting to reconcile strict law and equity, justice and mercy, equality and freedom.

Above all, the effort to combine these conflicting norms and values was seen in the eleventh and twelfth centuries as part of an even more formidable reconciliation — the reconciliation of God and man. It was a new vision of his ultimate destiny, more than anything else, that first led Western man to put his faith in legal science.[85]

Kennedy further asserts that all *substantive goals* of law fall into two opposed categories, namely, "individualism," which he identifies with self-interest, party autonomy, reciprocity, etc., and "altruism," which he identifies with sharing, sacrifice, and communal involvement. To complete the circle Professor Kennedy asserts that a preference for legal argument cast in the form of rules is connected with the substantive goal of individualism, while a preference for legal argument cast in the form of standards is connected with the substantive goal of altruism. There is an overlap, he writes, but at "a deeper level . . . the individualist/formalist and the altruist/informalist operate from flatly contradictory visions of the universe." *Id.* at 1776. This analysis represents a sharp break with the traditional Western conception that conflicting rules and standards (as well as other conflicting forms of legal utterance, such as doctrines, concepts, and analogies) are ultimately reconcilable by the legal system as a whole. Similarly, it breaks with the traditional Western belief that conflicting purposes of law, including not only individualism and altruism but also other polar values (for example, diversity and unity, change and continuity, freedom and equality) are ultimately reconcilable within the values of the whole legal system. Moreover, it is a postulate of traditional Western legal thought that the extent to which a particular purpose of law is served by a particular legal form cannot be answered in the abstract but can only be answered in a historical context. In some societies (for example, Communist societies) and in some areas even of so-called private law (for example, community property law) the rules may be more altruistic and the standards more individualistic, in Professor Kennedy's sense of those words.

By reducing the framework of analysis to a series of dualisms, which are themselves ultimately reduced to a single dilemma, Professor Kennedy gives dramatic expression to a widespread skepticism regarding legal rules and a widespread faith in what may be called the "adhocracy" of decisions based on legal standards. Contemporary Western man finds it hard to believe in rules since he tends to view them in isolation from the entire system of which they are integral parts. He finds it easy to believe in values since he sees them unencumbered by the rules required for realizing them in various types of cases. This "antinomy of rules and values" has been exposed by Roberto Unger as a dead end of modern liberal thought. *See* R. UNGER, KNOWLEDGE AND POLITICS 88–100 (1975).

One purpose of exploring the origins of Western legal thought in the eleventh and twelfth centuries is to show, by implication, the contrast between the synthesizing legal science which is at the root of the 900-year-old Western legal tradition and the fragmenting jurisprudence that has become prominent, if not dominant, in the West in the twentieth century.

[85] As indicated in notes * & 21 *supra*, a companion article will deal more systematically with the relation of Western legal thought to theology.

# [3]

# Legal Education There and Here: A Comparison*

John Henry Merryman†

The examination of legal education in a society provides a window on its legal system. Here one sees the expression of basic attitudes about the law: what law is, what lawyers do, how the system operates or how it should operate. Through legal education the legal culture is transferred from generation to generation. Legal education allows us to glimpse the future of the society. Those who will man the legal system and will fill those positions of leadership in government and the private sector that seem to fall more frequently to lawyers, at least in Western societies, come out of the law schools. What they are taught and how it is taught to them profoundly affect their objectives and attitudes and the ways in which they will fill these social roles.

The same ideas can be put in a more sociological form. A legal system is a component part (a subsystem) of a social system, and the system of legal education is a component part (a sub-subsystem) of the legal system. The system and its subsystems are organically related and give meaning to each other. A change in any part resounds throughout the whole.

These considerations indicate both the importance and the difficulty of a comparison of systems of legal education. Such a comparison, if well done, throws light on much more than legal education; it tells us something essential and profound about legal systems and the societies in which they operate. But such a comparison requires, if it is to be useful and valid, that what is said about any system of legal education be put into legal and social context. It is difficult enough to do this for one's own society; to do it for all those in two great legal families—civil law and common law—goes beyond the limits of this Essay and the abilities of the author. The most one can hope to do is to suggest general points of contrast that seem to be significant and interesting and to indicate some of the ways in which these differences are related to legal systems and societies.

 I wish to thank Mauro Cappelletti, Thomas Ehrlich, Dietrich Andre Loeber, Inga Markovits, Max Rheinstein, and Robert B. Stevens for their advice and criticisms. An earlier version of this Article was delivered at the Seminar on Comparative Legal Education in Perugia, Italy, in October, 1973. I am indebted to Professor Alessandro Giuliani, who organized the Seminar, for his invaluable help and to the other participants in the seminar for their thoughtful comments.

† B.S. 1943, University of Portland; M.S. 1944, J.D. 1947, University of Notre Dame; LL.M. 1951, J.S.D. 1955, New York University. Sweitzer Professor of Law, Stanford University.

One difficulty is that there is no single system of legal education in civil law nations. Legal education in Italy is not exactly like legal education in Germany or in Ecuador. Generalizations that one might validly make about legal education in France simply do not apply in Spain or Mexico. In this brief Essay I shall of necessity deal in generalities that are, by their nature, only partially accurate for any civil law nation. In deriving these generalizations, I shall depend primarily on my personal contact with legal education and legal educators in several civil law jurisdictions[1] and on a certain amount of hearsay about others. Similarly, legal education is not uniform throughout the common law world. In particular, legal education in England and in the United States are in many ways strikingly different; English legal education often seems more like that in Europe than that in the United States. Here again one must generalize, and this Essay will do so by referring primarily to legal education in the United States.[2]

Even within the United States there are significant variations among law schools. In part these differences are explainable by the large number of schools and their wide distribution among 50 quasi-sovereign states, Puerto Rico, and the District of Columbia, but other factors, described below, are also at work. One result is a universe of legal education in which there are a relatively few "leading" law schools and an informal but generally understood declining rank order below them. The tone is set by the leading schools, where one finds the best students, the most eminent faculty, the largest libraries, the most influential law reviews, the richest curricula (and extracurricula), and the most generous supporting facilities. Most of the other schools try to emulate them, but at a certain point their ability to do so becomes so attenuated that only superficial resemblances remain. The substance of what goes on in the name of legal education at a leading school is accordingly quite different from what goes on at many lesser schools. In describing legal education in the United States I will focus on the objectives and methods of the leading schools. As a result, the picture of American legal education drawn here represents an ideal which only a few schools—possibly 10 or 12—approach. The remaining 200 or so depart more or less drastically from the model in practice, but it is significant that most of them accept that model, seek to conform to it, and regard their deviation from it as an undesirable condition.[3]

1. That contact has been most intensive and prolonged in Italy, over a period beginning in 1961 and continuing today, and in Chile from 1966 to 1969, as consultant to the Ford Foundation and the International Legal Center and as Director of the Stanford-Chile Seminar on Legal Education. Contact with legal education has been less intensive, but still direct and significant in Colombia, Costa Rica, France, Germany, Greece, Mexico, and Peru.

2. Much of what is said will also be applicable to some extent to legal education in Canada, Australia, and New Zealand, where there has been a significant tendency to adopt the main features of American legal education.

3. For additional discussions of legal education in the United States, *see* Currie, *The Materials of Law Study*, 8 J. LEGAL ED. 1 (1955); Stevens, *Law Schools and Law Students*, 59 VA. L. REV. 551

## I. Higher Education: Three Fundamental Differences

There are certain fundamental differences between the systems of higher education in the United States and those in most civil law countries, and these differences strongly affect the two systems of legal education. I will discuss three such fundamental differences, the first of which might be summed up in the terms "democracy" and "meritocracy." In a sense this first difference results from two major inconsistent forces in higher education: on the one hand there is a desire to make higher education available to everyone without distinction; on the other there is the desire to make the university a place in which academic merit is recognized and rewarded. One ideal leads to the conception of the mass university; the other to the university in which admission and advancement are controlled on the basis of academic aptitude and performance. It is my observation that universities in the civil law world lean in the democratic direction, while meritocracy is the dominant ideal in American universities.[4] This is not to say that merit is totally ignored or devalued in the civil law world, nor that American universities ignore democratic considerations; it is only to suggest a significant difference in emphasis.

Thus, the Faculty of Law at the University of Rome has 12,000 to 15,000 students, while the Stanford Law School has a student body of 450. The difference arises in part from the power of American law schools to exclude applicants on the basis of merit. In a single year Stanford Law School has received more than 3,000 applications for admission, and of these it can admit only 160 and still retain its present size. The principal determinants for admission are totally academic: the student's score on a nationally administered Law School Aptitude Test and the grades received by the student in his undergraduate university education. The American law school does not admit every applicant who meets certain minimum standards; every applicant is in competition with every other applicant for a limited number of spaces, and those with the highest academic qualifications are the ones chosen.

An enormous amount of administrative and faculty time is spent in re-

(1973); Stevens, *Two Cheers for 1870: The American Law School*, in 5 Perspectives in American History 405 (C. Fleming & B. Bailyn eds. 1951); Proceedings of Assn. of Am. L. Schools, 1971 Annual Meeting, Training for the Public Professions of the Law pt. 1, § 2 [hereinafter cited as The Carrington Report]. For a thoroughly disenchanted view *see* Kennedy, *How the Law School Fails: A Polemic*, 1 Yale Rev. L. & Soc. Action 71 (1970). For comparative discussions *see* C. Eisenmann, The University Teaching of Social Sciences: Law. (rev. ed. 1973); E. Schweinburg, Law Training in Continental Europe, Its Principles and Public Function (1954). Additional readings will be found in D. Djonovich, Legal Education: A Selective Bibliography (1970); and in C. Szladits, Bibliography of Foreign and Comparative Law (1955, 1962, 1968, Supps. 1970 & 1971).

4. On the increasingly meritocratic character of higher education in the United States, particularly in the professional schools, *see* C. Jencks & D. Riesman, The Academic Revolution ch. 1 (1968); Riesman, *Notes on Meritocracy*, Daedalus, June 1967, at 897–908.

viewing and evaluating applications for admission in the effort to select the best possible group of first-year students from the pool of applicants. It is common for students to apply to several law schools, since they have no certainty of being accepted at any of them. Because of the competition among law schools for the best students, and the desire of the best students to go to the more eminent schools, a student who is denied admission at Harvard or Yale or Stanford may be admitted to some less highly regarded school. Thus, there is a tendency for the academic quality of student bodies to be stratified according to the national reputations of the schools. The cycle is, to some extent, self-perpetuating, since one of the important factors in the reputation of a law school is the quality of its student body. Thus, although there is likely to be a place in some law school for almost any student, the best students go to the best schools and get the best legal education and move more easily into the best careers.

The situation in many civil law universities is entirely different. There anyone who has completed certain formal prerequisites and has survived a certain number of years of prior education is automatically admitted to the university and to the faculty of law.[5] In the post–World War II period of mounting affluence, rising expectations, the extension of public primary and secondary education to greater numbers of people, and the greater democratization of society in such nations, the old economic and social barriers to university education lost much of their effectiveness. Suddenly, great floods of students descended on universities with inadequate numbers of faculty and inadequate libraries, classrooms, and other physical facilities. This phenomenon provides a partial explanation of the student upheavals in Paris and other parts of Europe in 1968: too few universities with too few resources submerged by thousands of students. An adequate explanation of the situation of students in civil law universities would be extremely complex, but as this example shows, the democratic principle—the notion that the student is, at a certain stage of his education, entitled as of right to admission to the university—is an important component of it.

Even among those who favor academic meritocracy, there is wide recognition that it can compound social injustice. Many young people never reach the point of applying to or attending a university, or of applying to law school, out of economic or social disadvantage. One's performance on a Law School Aptitude Test and in an undergraduate university are, to some extent, functions of one's social and economic background. Even those who succeed in breaking out of the poverty cycle or surmounting the dis-

5. Of course, the flow of students to the civil law university is conditioned by factors that distinguish it from that in the United States: a more rigorous and demanding system of secondary education, and a socio-economic structure that have tended historically to limit access to the university to a relatively small group (or class) of the population.

advantages imposed on them by racial or social prejudice often begin with a serious handicap. They, unlike more wealthy, more fully assimilated competitors, may have had inferior primary and secondary educational experiences, and may have come from families in which there was little of the sort of intellectual stimulation—little opportunity to develop the kind of reflective minds and studious habits—that university education values. Even though reliance on merit as a criterion for admission to the university is not intended to be undemocratic, meritocracy can operate in an undemocratic way.

This problem has received much attention in the United States in recent years. Universities first attempted to provide enough money to enable poor students to attend their institutions (all of which charge tuition fees and the best of which charge very substantial fees. In most civil law universities, consistent with the democratic approach described above, tuition fees are extremely low and do not in themselves exclude many students). The stated ideal at this stage was that *qualified* students should not be excluded from attending the university by financial considerations. The next major step was an attempt to do something about the possible injustices concealed by the term "qualified." This was accomplished in part by such direct methods as discrimination in the admission process in favor of members of identifiable disadvantaged groups. A more fundamental attack on the same problem attempts to provide equality of opportunity through equal access to quality primary and secondary education and through elimination of poverty, discrimination, and social disadvantage. Some progress has been made, but the injustice inherent in a system of meritocracy in a society in which wealth and prior educational opportunity are unequally distributed is far from completely solved. The continued emphasis on quality itself limits the options; no law school has abandoned academic merit as the basic criterion of admission. Certain minor concessions are made, but most law schools still hope to meet their social obligation by admitting "qualified" minority students. The lack of emphasis on merit in civil law universities greatly reduces the significance of this problem.

A second distinguishing feature of higher education in the civil law world is the minor role played by private universities. Indeed, in most civil law nations private universities do not exist.[6] Instead, universities are maintained and are subject to control by the state, usually through the same ministry that has the responsibility for public elementary and secondary education. In the United States, on the contrary, both private and public uni-

6. By private I mean universities supported and maintained primarily by private funds, and not administered under the direct supervision of governmental officials. Private universities in the United States may, and do, seek grants from governmental as well as private sources to finance specific programs.

versities compete with each other for faculty and students, as well as for gifts and grants from individuals, corporations, foundations, and government sources. In this competition, the private universities occupy a position of leadership and have done so throughout the history of the nation. There are excellent and influential public universities, but as a general proposition the private universities set the standard for higher education.

Because the private university is not subject to anything but the most limited form of governmental supervision, it has more freedom to experiment, to innovate, and in general to progress. The autonomy of private universities leads in turn to greater freedom for public universities. Since the major private universities provide the leadership for all of higher education, the other universities, including the public ones, tend to emulate them. Any attempt to establish rigid control over the policies, faculty, curricula, and operations of public universities is met with the objection that such controls will put them at a disadvantage in the competition with private universities and lead in the end to deterioration of the public university. In this way, the autonomy of the private university helps to maintain the autonomy of the public university. The emphasis of the private university upon excellence—that is to say on meritocracy—makes it necessary for the public university to do the same. Otherwise it will lose out in the competition for students, faculty, funds, and prestige. These are powerful considerations.

In a number of civil law nations none but the most trivial reforms seems to be possible without ministerial, and sometimes legislative, action at the highest levels. Uniformity is the rule, so that policies adopted for one university extend to all. The notion of the dynamic university, constantly experimenting and progressing, does not exist. Nor does the notion of academic competition among universities, with each striving for leadership, for the best faculty and students, and for the most distinguished scholarship. Instead, one finds a relatively static and standardized university system.

A final major difference between American and civil law universities is the higher degree of self-consciousness in the United States about the objectives and methods of university education. This characteristic is particularly marked in the law schools. It is significant that a professional association (*The Association of American Law Schools*) and a professional journal (*The Journal of Legal Education* and its predecessor, *The American Law School Review*), concerned solely with legal education, its objectives, methods, and problems, have existed in the United States since the earliest years of the century. Only in common law law schools does one find continuous self-searching about what we are doing, why we are doing it, and how we might better do it. Most who teach in civil law universities are, by comparison, totally unconcerned with such issues. Questions about teaching objectives and methods are considered uninteresting or not open to discussion. One teaches as professors have always taught; one's purposes are the same purposes as they have always been; questions about such matters do not arise. In recent years, things have begun to change in a number of civil law jurisdictions,[7] but the trend is still uncommon.

An obsession with objectives and methods in legal education can easily become excessive, by diverting energy better directed toward other activities (such as scholarship) or problems (such as substantive questions). Still, one wonders about the vitality of a system in which such questions are not even asked. Society, after all, changes, and the legal system either changes with it or becomes increasingly archaic and irrelevant. In turn, the system of legal education either reflects the responses of the legal system to social change or degenerates into something artificial, useless, and perhaps even socially harmful. In a society undergoing substantial change, legal education should be in constant flux.[8]

## II. The Goals of Legal Education

The objectives of legal education in the two systems are vastly different. This can be shown through a few generalizations that oversimplify but may be sufficiently instructive to justify the risk. First, legal education in the civil law world is, at bottom, general education, not professional education. It is true that many civil law faculties include some instruction of a technical or professional nature, but courses of this kind typically are recent minor additions to a corpus that is fundamentally liberal in character and outlook. It is not anticipated that all, or even most, of those who attend the faculty of law will become advocates or judges or notaries. Law is merely one of the curricula available to undergraduate students.

This is one reason why legal education in civil law universities seems to

7. This trend is most prominent in Latin America, where a variety of programs for reform of legal education have been instituted. The most far-reaching is under way in Chile. All Chilean law faculties are involved in the reform, and their efforts are supported and coordinated through the interuniversity Instituto de Docencia y Investigaciones Juridicas in Santiago. The Instituto is in part an outgrowth of the Stanford-Chile Seminars on Legal Education. In Chile the principal directions of reform are: conversion to active teaching methods; appointment of full-time professors; building law libraries capable of supporting research; increasing the curricular demands on students; expanding the extracurriculum; encouraging empirical and socially responsive research.

Other significant reform efforts are going on in Peru, at the Pontifical Catholic University in Lima, and in Costa Rica. It is unclear whether related efforts at reform in Colombia and Brazil have had any significant effect on legal education in those countries.

8. One who believes that law is immutable will resist the suggestion that the objectives and methods of legal education need periodic reexamination. One who sees law primarily as a conservative, stabilizing social force will find it easier to believe that law is immutable. And one who is by nature or preference conservative will find it easier to see law as a conservative, stabilizing force. Accordingly it is not surprising that the pressure for reform of legal education in civil law countries, where it exists at all, tends to come more from the center or left than from the right.

us to be comparatively "nonprofessional" or "nontechnical." Any movement in the direction of technical or professional education is a movement away from the paradigm. Thus, instruction in civil law faculties is more abstract, more concerned with questions of philosophic than immediate practical importance, more removed from the solution of social problems. University legal education in England shares these characteristics; in this respect it is more like the legal education in the typical European or Latin American university than that in most American law schools. In England and on the Continent the professional side is taken care of after the university: in the *Referendarzeit*, or in apprenticeship with a solicitor, advocate, or notary, or in special advanced professional schools for administrators or judges.

In the United States, legal education is primarily professional education, with some admixture of nonprofessional elements. In part this difference is structural: here legal education is *graduate* education, something undertaken *after* completion of the undergraduate degree requirement. Law is not regularly taught in the university as a liberal or humane subject, or as a social science. One obvious disadvantage of such a system is that the great mass of undergraduates leave the university without any organized exposure to the legal system. Virtually no courses are available for the student who wishes to learn about the legal system, but does not want to spend the additional years in law school.[9]

Recent developments have tended to blur the distinction between liberal or nonprofessional—university legal education in the civil law world and professional legal education in the United States. The introduction of *travaux pratiques* (meetings with teaching assistants to discuss concrete cases as a supplement to the theoretical lectures given by the professor) in France and a number of Latin American universities is only one example of the many ways in which the purity of a liberal legal education is impaired in the civil law world. American law schools continue to demonstrate growing interest in the study of law from the perspectives of the social sciences and the humanities, not merely as desirable components of the education of professional lawyers but in and for themselves.

A second generalization about the objectives of legal education might be put as follows: In the civil law world the practicing lawyer or judge is seen as a technician, as the operator of a machine designed and built by others. In the United States, the practicing lawyer or judge is seen as a sort

9. There has been a good deal of concern about this lacuna and a variety of attempts to deal with it. Currently the tendency is for professors in the law schools to offer occasional undergraduate courses in law. No one is convinced that this satisfies the need, and in all probability more ambitious programs—perhaps even undergraduate majors in law—will soon appear.

of social engineer, as a person specially equipped to perceive and attempt to solve social problems. Lawyers in the United States gravitate toward positions of responsibility in government and the private sector. The advice they give frequently extends beyond technical legal questions to consideration of the broader consequences of alternative forms of action and to advice on how to anticipate and deal with such consequences. Lawyers are seen as key elements of social reform, as experts on making new social programs work.

In other words, the lawyer in the United States is seen as a kind of omnicompetent problem-solver, and the system of legal education, with the self-consciousness described above, earnestly tries to prepare him for this kind of social role. In civil law countries, even though lawyers tend to occupy the same positions in government and in the private sector as they do in the United States, there seems to be less general understanding of this fact and little interest in relating it to legal education. The professional lawyer is thought of as a technician who does important but uncreative and narrowly professional work. Such a view affects civil law legal education in two significant ways: it justifies the prejudice of law faculties who ignore professional training as beneath their dignity and prefer instead to emphasize law as a liberal study; it also reinforces the tendency to approach professional training, wherever it is carried out, as technical education.[10]

A third general difference can best be illustrated by a look at the character of legal scholarship in the two systems. In the civil law tradition, legal scholarship is pure and abstract, relatively unconcerned with the solution of concrete social problems or with the operation of legal institutions. The principal object of such scholarship is to build a theory or science of law. In its most extreme form such scholarship displays a detachment from society, people, and their problems that astonishes a common lawyer. On the common law side, we tend to think of the work of legal scholarship as another aspect of social engineering; it is our business as scholars to monitor the operating legal order, to criticize it, and to make recommendations for its improvement. Improvement, to us, means coping more adequately with concrete social problems. Our outlook is professional. These diverse attitudes, expressed in the form of legal scholarship, are also expressed in the content of legal education itself, since the scholars are, almost without exception, professors. In this way the minds of lawyers in the two systems are trained in ways that are fundamentally quite different.

10. Legal educators in the United States are accustomed to hearing from the practicing bar that law schools are too theoretical, too remote from practice. It all depends on the point of view. To a civil law professor our legal education looks much too pragmatic and professional, sadly weak on theory and "culture."

## III. Professors

One can also sharply contrast the role played by the law professor. The law professor in the United States generally spends his working time at the law school, in the classroom and in his office. His office there is his study; that is where he does his writing, prepares for class, and meets with students and colleagues. His presence there makes him more available to students and encourages faculty-student contact outside of class. The number of faculty, when compared to the number of students, produces a ratio that encourages small classes and a more personal relationship between professor and student than in the civil law counterpart.

The contrast with law faculties in civil law nations is striking. In most of them (Germany is a major exception), the concept of a full-time professor is relatively unfamiliar. The professor comes to the law school to deliver his lecture and leaves when it is finished. Outside of his actual time in class he is seldom seen at the school and he is not expected to be there. Confronted by an enormous number of students, it is almost impossible for the professor to become familiar with them, even if he had the time and the inclination. At the end of the class, both he and the student leave the university.

The American professor's continual presence at the law school deeply affects collegial life. It is easy to find a colleague to talk to about an interesting problem or to get an authoritative reaction to an idea. The situation permits spontaneity and informality, encourages collaboration in teaching and research, and offers easy accessibility to a wide range of interests and expertise. The result is a natural tendency toward "horizontal" or collegial, scholarly, and personal relationships that is lacking in many civil law universities. There one more typically finds a hierarchical or vertical pattern. At the top is the professor who occupies the chair. Arrayed beneath him are junior colleagues, assistants, and researchers. Communication habitually runs vertically within the *cathedra.*

The full-time nature of law teaching in America tends to produce a substantial number of professors who maintain little, if any, direct contact with the practice of law. In most civil law jurisdictions, however, professors carry on law practice or engage in other careers; teaching is viewed as an accessory activity. Stipends reflect this difference: in the United States law professors are paid enough to support themselves without the necessity for additional income. But in Chile and Italy, for example, the pay for university law teaching is low because it is anticipated that the professor will devote a major portion of his time to law practice or some other remunerative career. Indeed, in some civil law nations the position of professor in the faculty of law is more important for the prestige (and the additional business) it provides than for the professorial stipend.

The organization of civil and common law law schools is another area of substantial difference. The typical civil law university is composed of a group of "faculties." Each faculty, in turn, is a collection of "chairs" or "*cathedra*" occupied by senior professors. Occupancy of a *cathedra* in a law faculty carries with it the direction of an institute, with its own budget, staff rooms and library, and the right to a certain number of younger assistants interested in academic careers. The assistants help the professor in his teaching and research. Where the professor maintains an active professional practice, his academic assistants are also likely to be his junior law associates. If he is engaged in a political career, his academic assistants will be part of his political staff. The professor is expected to promote the interests of his assistants, particularly to assist them in their academic careers. This system makes the senior professor lord of a substantial domain and gives him great power over the lives of his assistants and his staff. Indeed it is common to speak of the professor as a "baron" and to complain (if one is an impatient young scholar with unfulfilled academic aspirations) of the "baronial system."

American law schools are organized in a different way. Professors do not have their own institutes or retinues of assistants. Libraries, research funds, secretarial assistance, and the like are centrally administered by a strong dean. It is only in the case of a special grant from a foundation or a government agency for a substantial research project to be carried on by an identified professor that the tendency toward creation of an institute appears. On the whole, such tendencies have been resisted. Although institutes or their equivalents occasionally appear in American law schools, they are generally regarded with suspicion. The habit of central administration by a strong dean, a quite different tradition of recruitment of law professors, the emphasis on collegiality within the law schools, a different approach to teaching and to scholarship, all reinforce the resistance of American law schools to the establishment of institutes.

## IV. Curricula and Teaching Methods

The curricula of American law schools typically include a few prescribed courses and a large number of electives covering a broad range of subject matters. By comparison, the curricula at civil law universities tend to be much more limited, both in the number and in the scope of courses offered, and tend to include few electives. In part this difference may follow from the fact that the civil law faculty is less oriented toward professional training, and therefore less concerned with providing opportunities to study the nuances of various professional specializations. Another possible explanation is the greater freedom of American law schools to innovate and to experiment, unrestricted by an official policy of conformity or by the necessity for prior governmental approval of proposed reforms. Still another reason might be that the culture of the civil law takes a narrower, more restricted view of the nature of law and of the function of the lawyer in society, so that the conceptual limits on what seems appropriate for a law faculty curriculum are narrower.

There is yet another, more fundamental, basis for the difference. It is the belief, still widely held in the civil law world, that law is a science. From this it follows that the purpose of legal education is to instruct the students in the elements of the science. Such an approach tends to be dogmatic. The truth is known by the professor and is communicated to the students. There are, of course, disputes among scholars, and on some points one can find two or more theories that are sufficiently significant to deserve mention. But on the whole, the general structure, the broad outlines, are thought to be established. There are recognized categories. The law is divided into agreed subdivisions, which are taught as courses. The area of doubt is so narrow as to be imperceptible. Blessed with such certainty, the civil law feels less need for innovation and experimentation.

One could develop a surprising number of possible conclusions from this observation about the relative richness of the curriculum and the relative availability to students of options in the two systems. What does it tell us about the extent to which students are perceived as responsible individuals, capable of choosing intelligently among a variety of optional courses? Is this persuasive evidence that the development of new legal problems, as a consequence of social change, is only dimly perceived within the faculties of law in civil law universities? Or is it in part a matter, again, of chairs and institutes? To establish a new course may mean establishing a new *cathedra*—a new group of baronies; this is a grave step, and its accomplishment in the complex and slow-moving bureaucracy of nationally administered systems of higher education is risky and laborious.

Whatever the reasons, the tendency is for curricula in law faculties in civil law jurisdictions to be much more limited, more traditional, less responsive to social change, and less tentative and searching. The tentative nature of much of what is taught in the American law school deserves an additional comment.

American law schools have, over the last three decades, drastically reduced the proportion of the 3-year curriculum that is prescribed and have given the student an increasing opportunity (and obligation) to decide for himself which courses to take among a large body of available elective offerings during the remaining 2 years or so of law school. In one sense this movement reflects a loss of certainty among American legal educators about the substance of a proper legal education. It is not clear to us that all students should be required to take trusts and estates, or labor law, or international business transactions. As the area of doubt increases, the area of certainty—indicated by the required part of the curriculum—contracts.

In the civil law world, the educational focus is primarily on substance; method is deemphasized. In the United States, we are of course concerned about what we teach; but the emphasis is less on what is taught and more on how it is taught. We are concerned about developing certain qualities in the student: skill in legal analysis, the ability to distinguish the relevant from the irrelevant, the ability to deal with a large mass of facts in an authoritative way, the ability to put together careful and persuasive arguments on any side of a legal question, the ability to think usefully and constructively about social problems and their solution. Of course the student needs to be familiar with the existing law before he can responsibly discuss its application to concrete social questions, but we see that as the easy part. Rather than devote valuable class time to discussing what the law is, we expect the students to be familiar with it through prior reading. We focus, instead, on how it does or does not work, on its implications, on the social reality out of which it grew, and so on.

Our objectives accordingly raise important questions of method. How can we prepare students to deal thoughtfully, responsibly, and usefully with the kinds of social problems that will come before them as they assume public and private positions of leadership? The traditional system of education in civil law universities obviously assumes a different function: The professor lectures; the students listen. That system is clearly designed to convey information to the student. The information is substantive knowledge. There is little concern with method of the sort that preoccupies American law teachers.

There is a commonly held, but quite incorrect, notion that a case system or case method is the dominant method of instruction in American universities. This notion is particularly popular among foreigners who discuss our legal education, although it is also held by a surprisingly large number of Americans. In fact, there is no case method. It is true that we study cases, among other things, in law schools; but it is not true that we study all cases for the same reasons or in the same ways. Nor do we study only cases; we also study statutory and administrative materials and have an immense doctrinal literature that is heavily used in teaching.

Those in civil law nations who think that all American law schools teach by the case method share a number of incorrect assumptions. One of the most common of these is that we study cases because that is where the law is found. The common law, so the reasoning goes, is based on the principle of stare decisis. The law grows out of the decision of cases. Accordingly, in the common law country one studies cases, just as in the civil law nations one studies codes, because they are the prime sources of law. There is some truth in this, but only a small amount. Actually, to read a case is a very inefficient way to learn a rule of law. If all one is seeking is the rule, it is much easier to read it in a hornbook, and indeed our students frequently do this.

A second, somewhat more sophisticated view held by a number of civil lawyers is that we read cases for reasons analogous to the assumptions of traditional continental legal science: that one can abstract legal principles from specific legal rules, extract even broader principles from those derived by the first level of abstraction, and, by continuing the process, eventually produce a "general theory of law." Applying this notion to the common law world, one would study cases as the basic unit, draw from individual cases the broader principles of which they are specific manifestations, and so on up the scale, thus producing a general theory of law. In either tradition the data one works with are the naturally occurring materials of the law: in the civil law world, primarily statutes; in the common law world, primarily cases. Actually there was a period in American scholarship when such a view was prominent. Professor Langdell used such ideas to justify introducing the study of cases at Harvard in the 1870's. To a certain extent the great treatises of Williston and Wigmore and the *Restatement of the Law* are representations of this point of view. More recently the project undertaken by Professor Schlesinger of Cornell and colleagues on the "common core of legal systems" has sought to apply similar reasoning in the field of comparative law. (It has stayed alive in comparative law only because that field has a European, rather than American, center of gravity and is still dominated by European ideas.) This "scientific" rationale for the study of cases, however, was rather convincingly destroyed by the legal realists.[11] In any event, legal science never had a very large following in the United States, and it is doubtful that the writers of the great treatises or the drafters of the *Restatement of the Law* perceived themselves as en-

11. The attacks of the realists on the *Restatement* provide one of the few examples in American legal literature of the sort of academic mayhem that is relatively common in Europe (and in nonlegal fields in the United States). *See, e.g.*, T. ARNOLD, THE SYMBOLS OF GOVERNMENT 25, 51 (1935); C. CLARK, REAL COVENANTS AND OTHER INTERESTS WHICH "RUN WITH THE LAND" (2d ed. 1947); Green, *The Torts Restatement*, 29 ILL. L. REV. 582 (1935); Lorenzen & Heilman, *The Restatement of the Conflict of Laws*, 83 U. PA. L. REV. 555 (1935); Patterson, *The Restatement of the Law of Contracts*, 33 COLUM. L. REV. 397 (1933); Radin, *Contract Obligation and the Human Will*, 43 COLUM. L. REV. 575 (1943); Sims, *The Law of Real Covenants: Exceptions to the Restatement of the Subject by the American Law Institute*, 30 CORNELL L.Q. 1 (1944); Yntema, *The Restatement of the Law of Conflict of Laws*, 36 COLUM. L. REV. 183 (1936). For more general expressions of antipathy toward the attitudes they saw represented in the *Restatement* and the great treatises, *see* J. FRANK, COURTS ON TRIAL (1949); L. GREEN, JUDGE AND JURY (1930); Llewellyn, *A Realistic Jurisprudence—The Next Step*, 30 COLUM. L. REV. 431 (1930); Llewellyn, *Some Realism about Realism—Responding to Dean Pound*, 44 HARV. L. REV. 1222 (1931).

gaged in what was essentially a 19th-century European scholarly movement. Accordingly, the "legal science" rationale for studying cases in American law schools does not today command much support. Even where something of the sort appears to exist, it is likely to go on totally without consciousness of its similarity to the much more sophisticated and articulated tradition of European legal science.

Why then do we study cases, if not to learn the rules of law or to build a general theory of law? There seem to be three important reasons. The first, and most important, is that the case is an example of the legal process at work. When one reads the case, as cases are reported in our tradition, one encounters the facts out of which the litigation arose, the way in which these facts were resolved into legal questions, the allegations and arguments of opposing counsel concerning their proper solution, and the way the court dealt with them to achieve a decision. One studies cases in order to become familiar with the process, to learn how the legal system operates. To refer to an earlier distinction, the emphasis is not on substance but on method.

It is true that cases reflect only part of the legal system at work.[12] That is why we also study legislative, administrative, and scholarly materials. Still, in the American system, the judge is the protagonist, the hero of our legal tradition. We perceive judicial activity to be central to the legal system, and accordingly we spend a great part of our effort in observing and learning from that process at work.

A second reason for studying cases in American law schools is that each case is a piece of social history. The study of judicial decisions for 3 years builds in the student a reservoir of familiarity with incidents in our social history, some great and far-reaching, some relatively modest. This gives the student a feeling of contact with the culture, of having seen the concrete social circumstances to which the law must respond. Frequently the parties are individuals with whom the student can identify and sympathize. It is easy to take a warm, personal interest in such cases, and to develop opinions as to the way the law operates. Was the result just? Should the legal system produce the kind of outcome that this case illustrates? What changes in the legal system should be made in order to prevent the recurrence of such results?

In many parts of the civil law world, that sort of case study is impossible or very difficult. Judicial decisions are published, if they are published at

12. It is also true that the cases are almost solely appellate cases in a system in which the parties are not entitled to review of the facts found in the trial. Accordingly, the facts stated in the opinion are those abstracted from real life by the parties, their counsel, and the trier of fact at the trial, further limited by the kind of trial record kept, the restrictions of the appellate process, the tactical decisions of the parties and their lawyers, and reduced further by the appellate judge in selecting the facts to be stated in his opinion. Still, despite these restrictions and distortions, the typical reported decision in the United States is much richer and fuller in facts than its civil law counterpart.

all, in a form that appears emasculated to an American lawyer: the facts are omitted or sharply reduced and the process of judgment is made to seem abstract, mechanical, and inhuman. The civil lawyer could respond that his system of reporting judicial decisions represents greater objectivity, provides less temptation to succumb to the human aspects of the case and to endanger the purity and objectivity of the law. (Whether such legal purity and objectivity are possible or desirable is another discourse that cannot be pursued here.) In response, the argument could be made that constant exposure to this sort of temptation as a law student may produce lawyers and judges who are less likely to succumb to its dangers and more likely to make intelligent use of the nuances and richness of social texture it provides in their professional careers.

We also study cases because they are difficult. They are difficult, first, because it takes a good deal of concentration to understand cases, to master them to the point at which informed discussion of them can begin. But there is another, more important kind of difficulty: it is the difficulty faced by the judge when the problem before him seems to provide no possibility of easy solution, when he is confronted by parties, both of whom can reasonably argue that justice is on their side. Often, in such cases, the law is unclear; there is no easy answer. Still, the judge must decide. It is good for students of the law to confront this difficulty early in their careers; they will have to live with it throughout their professional lives. At the extreme, a civil law legal education makes the student impatient with facts, unwilling to face disorder, unprepared for the encounter with the concrete. Ours immerses the student in such realities from the start.

The fundamental differences between the traditions of teaching can be reduced to two. First, American legal education assumes that the student has studied assigned material before the class. In the civil law world, it is assumed that the student has not studied in advance of class; indeed, the main purpose of the lecture is to instruct him, to transfer basic knowledge to him. Second, in the United States the student is expected to participate actively in class discussion. Again, the contrast with law schools in the civil law world is clear. There the student does not participate; he is a passive, receiving object. The professor talks; the student listens.

The two differences are obviously related; one cannot expect unprepared students to discuss complex legal materials with which they are unfamiliar. Accordingly, it is necessary that they have studied them in advance. Then, in the American classroom we ask questions to test their knowledge of the facts of the case, the content and purpose of the statute, or the argument made by the author of the article. Students are encouraged to take a critical view of what they have read; we ask them whether the outcome of a case would have changed if the facts were varied in certain ways; we ask them to discuss hypothetical cases, to suggest answers to hypothetical problems; we inquire whether the solution reached is a socially desirable one; and so on. The emphasis is on active participation in class by the students.

The reasons our methods differ so sharply relate to differences in university context and to divergences in attitude toward the objectives of legal education, the nature of legal scholarship, and the roles and functions of lawyers in the two systems. It bears repeating, however, that our objectives and methodology are not tied to judicial decisions. Our case law provides a rich, fascinating, and relevant body of study material, but equivalents or alternatives are certainly conceivable, and probably exist, in civil law nations. The active method does not necessarily presuppose the doctrine of stare decisis or the study of judicial decisions.

## V. Students

I now turn to a range of less profound, but still significant, differences between the two systems of legal education. One is the fact that our student bodies are, on the whole, much smaller. At the Stanford Law School we have a total of approximately 450 students. The Harvard Law School, which is considered large by our standards, has approximately 1,500 students. In the civil law world one typically finds much larger student bodies. The University of Rome, with 12,000 or more, is not the most extreme example. At some point (or points) on a continuum between 450 and 12,000 students, the human dynamics of the process of legal education drastically change. There are important qualitative differences between large and small law schools flowing from the simple fact of different student body size.

Another significant point is that American law students are expected to be full-time students; they are expected to devote their full energies to their studies and not to engage in any other significant enterprise for the 3 years of law school.[13] In a number of civil law jurisdictions, attendance at the university faculty of law is very much a part-time undertaking. The difference can be exaggerated and is, in the end, one of degree, but the expectations of the two traditions are really quite different: in the United

13. This generalization must be qualified in two ways. First, there are part-time law schools in the United States. They normally offer courses in the evening, and the student normally must attend for 4 or 5 years in order to acquire the law degree after completing his university education. *See generally,* Association of American Law Schools, The AALS Study of Part-Time Legal Education (1972).

Second, even in the regular full-time law school it is not unusual for a number of ostensibly full-time students to hold part-time jobs. *See* Stevens, *supra* note 3, at 589–90.

States, our expectation that the students will be full time makes it reasonable for us to make greater demands on, and to maintain higher expectations of, their performance. Students' lives are expected to center around the law school. They are expected to be there not only to attend classes but to prepare for them, to work in the law library, and to involve themselves in law review or the other paracurricular organizations that seem to grow up around our law schools. In civil law universities, there is no such assumption and consequently no basis for such expectation. Frequently, if only because of inadequate classroom facilities, it is not even anticipated that the students will regularly attend classes.

A third unique feature of our system is that it places great responsibility on the student. One sign of this greater responsibility is the student-run law review, a phenomenon that exists at over a hundred law schools in the United States. This is a legal periodical, normally quarterly, which is entirely edited and published, and partly written, by law students. The tradition is for such reviews to be independent, free of faculty authority. It seems important that these students have power consistent with the responsibility they bear. We encourage them, we cooperate with them, we respond to their requests for advice and assistance, but they make the editorial decisions.

Law review experience is still the most prestigious component of what has become, at many law schools, an extremely rich extracurriculum. The student may choose from a variety of activities: trial and appellate moot court, legal aid and civil rights organizations, environmental law societies, international law journals. Such institutions are also student-initiated and student-run. Professors help (when they are asked) and activities are subsidized by law school funds or by gifts or grants solicited by the students themselves from foundations or private donors. The extracurriculum is an extremely important part of legal education for a substantial number of students in American law schools. There is nothing remotely comparable to it in European law faculties.

## VI. Conclusion

The reader may have formed the impression by now that I consider legal education in the United States to be superior to that in most civil law universities.[14] That is a correct impression; ours is better. It is better because it has grander objectives; because it draws on the full time and energies of teacher and student; because it is concerned with human problems and their solution; because it engages students directly in the study and active discussion of such problems and of the process of their solution within the

14. Let me note that, as a comparative lawyer, I seldom make such judgments. On most qualitative comparisons between legal systems I would not even venture an opinion.

legal order; because it displays a higher opinion of the student and demands more of him; and because its conception of the work of the professional lawyer—and accordingly of the mission of legal education to prepare persons for that profession—is a much richer, more demanding, and more realistic one.

No one should infer from the preceding paragraph anything more than a judgment about a process and a tradition of legal education. It is not a judgment about people. The civil law world includes numbers of men and women of distinction and eminence who have somehow surmounted the barriers placed in their way by an inadequate and impoverished system of legal education. They are at least the equal, in every way, of the best of us. Conversely, many graduates of American law schools fail to justify the system. They lack scope, imagination, and the ability to deal productively with social problems. They are, and will always be, petty technicians. The wealth and the abundance of American legal education seem to have been wasted on them. No system of legal education can guarantee that the lawyers it produces will be great lawyers.

No one really knows how much effect education has on the student. One can always find instances of students who were apparently untouched by what would appear to be an enormously effective educational system. Others appear to surmount a weak legal education, to acquire in some mysterious way all those attributes that the system seemed to ignore or undervalue. Still, we must assume that education has some effect in a substantial number of cases. On that assumption, the common law education system seems to me to be more likely to produce the kind of lawyers society requires.

This does not mean, however, that American legal educators should be complacent. On the contrary, the real strength of the system in the past has rested on the fact that it was constantly under searching critical review by those responsible for it. The Carrington Report,[15] the Meyers Report,[16] and the Packer-Ehrlich Report[17] provide encouraging evidence that this tradition of critical self-examination is alive and well. The attitudes these studies express show no trace of complacency, no sense of superiority; the system is exposed as imperfect, in need of substantial reform. Since the authors are all law professors, they are in a position to do something: to change, to innovate, to abandon the field experiment, to take up the brilliant proposal. As law teachers they consciously bear the power and the responsi-

15. *Supra* note 3.

16. PROCEEDINGS, ASSN. OF AM. L. SCHOOLS, REPORT OF THE COMMITTEE ON CURRICULUM 7–38 (1968).

17. H. PACKER & T. EHRLICH, NEW DIRECTIONS IN LEGAL EDUCATION: A REPORT PREPARED FOR THE CARNEGIE COMMISSION ON HIGHER EDUCATION (1972).

bility to determine, and to re-determine, the form and substance of legal education. In civil law universities neither the power nor the responsibility is so consciously or conspicuously assumed by the law professors. On the contrary, most of them are unconcerned and uninterested. In the end, that may be the most significant difference of all.

# [4]

WILHELM KARL GECK

## The Reform of Legal Education in the Federal Republic of Germany

In the Federal Republic of Germany the system of legal education, notwithstanding its long and firmly established tradition, has been undergoing far-reaching changes in the last five years. As a matter of fact, there is more experimenting going on in legal education in the Federal Republic at present than in any other European state. Some of the German problems mentioned here may be recognizable as being American problems as well.

### I. Traditional Legal Training in Germany

#### 1) *Essentials*

For many decades legal education in West Germany and its predecessor, the German Reich, followed a rather uniform pattern. All persons preparing for a career as judge, public prosecutor, notary public and all members of the bar, whom I shall call attorneys at law, had to undergo the same legal training. Most higher civil servants and most lawyers in economic enterprises also had this same training. So did law professors, for whom there were, however, certain additional scholastic requirements.

Every prospective *Volljurist*, i.e. full-fledged jurist, first had to qualify for admission as a law student, usually after thirteen years of previous schooling. The studies at a law faculty comprised at least 3½ years. Although the student had to fulfill certain requirements, especially in practical courses concerned with the solving of cases, there were no intermediary examinations. One comprehensive written and oral state examination before a board of law professors and other jurists covered the whole of university studies (*Erstes Staatsexamen* or *Referendarexamen*).

The successful candidate was then admitted as legal trainee (*Referendar*) for 3½ years to learn the practical side of the law at various courts, under a public prosecutor, a practicing attorney and with some administrative authority. The trainee participated in the public sessions and the private deliberations of the courts and drafted a number

---

Wilhelm Karl Geck is Professor, University of the Saarland, Saarbrücken.

Annexes I-IV are an integral part of this study. Annex V contains bibliographical notes following the order of the text.

of decisions. In minor cases he would function as public prosecutor. He would also argue private law cases in court for the attorney under whom he was working or act as *pro deo* counsel in criminal cases. In the administrative agency he would, for instance, draft legal regulations or prepare administrative decisions. During this period the trainee was a state official. He received a stipend which used to be very low, but now amounts to 70% of a lower-court judge's salary. After these 3½ years, a second comprehensive state examination before a board composed of judges, public prosecutors, administrative officers and attorneys tested the practical ability of the trainee and qualified him for any of the careers mentioned, except a university professorship with its special scholastic requirements. Not until this second state examination (*Grosses Staatsexamen* or *Assessorexamen*) was a person considered *Volljurist*. But once a legal trainee had passed it, he was then qualified in any state of the Federal Republic for any legal career.

On 1 January 1975, there were between 84,000 and 85,000 active jurists with this background in the Federal Republic. 14,054 were career judges in federal or state service; 3,000, public prosecutors; 27,755, attorneys at law and notaries public. Higher civil servants with this training were estimated at about 29,000; managers and employees in economic enterprises, at about 10,000-11,000. There were some 520 law professors with tenure on the law faculties.

The professional requirements mentioned above were basically prescribed by federal statute. The details regulating state examinations and admission to these were however left to state statute and to the state cabinets or ministers of justice. By prescribing the requirements for admission to the first state examination, these authorities had an indirect but considerable influence on the curriculum of the law faculties, which had to offer at least the courses required for admission to the state examination. The legislatures' and the ministers' indirect influence on the curriculum did not touch the content or method of teaching (and research), the freedom of which is protected by the federal and the state constitutions. The practical training period before the second state examination was however directly regulated by state statute and the ministers of justice, and implemented by the latter.

In the Federal Republic there were no evening schools or correspondence courses at the university level. Law students had to register for courses of different kinds. Most courses were traditional lectures. However each student had to participate successfully in six or seven practical courses, solving cases which took him several weeks at home, and easier ones under classroom supervision. This solving of cases is a most important element of German legal education. These papers were graded with the help of assistants, and the cases discussed by the professor in charge. There were two obligatory practical courses, one each for beginners and for advanced students, in private law, public law and criminal law. The registration for seminars was usually optional. Here from five to twenty-five students delivered papers on advanced legal problems and discussed them with the possible purpose of learning the technique of writing a doctoral dissertation. With the exception of the elective seminars and a few hours devoted to writing classroom papers in the obligatory practical courses, the student was free to attend or not to attend classes. He was required however to spend a four to eight week period between semesters observing the work of a lower court, and—in some states—of an administrative authority.

*2) Criticism*

This system was subject to severe and widespread criticism. There was general agreement that the subject matter covered by the curriculum and—at least theoretically—by the first state examination had grown too vast. Parts of it seemed neither of any special didactic value nor of much practical relevance for the later career. This criticism was directed e.g. at Roman law as well as at details in the law of family relations, inheritance or civil procedure. On the other hand, curriculum and examination were blamed for the omission of subjects considered important for the proper application of the law. There was a special demand for sociology, but also for economics and some psychology. The wide span of subjects and the lack of individual guidance were mainly held responsible for the fact that the number of "drop outs" was considerable, and that the average study period up to the first state examination lasted ten semesters instead of the prescribed minimum of seven. To many, the traditional lectures by professors on subjects already covered by books seemed outdated, promoting a merely passive attitude and stifling creativity. Classes of 100 to 300, even in the practical courses, left the average student little chance for active participation. In law faculties ranging from 1,200 to 4,000 students, the individual felt lost in an amorphous mass. Largely for these reasons, from the fourth semester on, a large number of students spent more time in private cram courses or in correspondence courses of a "*Repetitor*" than in the university.

The first state examination was blamed mainly for covering the whole period of studies and too many subjects, and—in contrast to its avowed aims—for putting a premium on the mere technique of solving cases and perhaps on crammed knowledge. A deeper criticism aiming at the entire system will be dealt with later. The practical training was also bitterly criticized. 3½ years were considered too long. The time seemed divided into too many stations, most of which appeared too short for making the trainee really familiar with the practical legal problems and working techniques of any particular court, public prosecutor, attorney or administrative agency. Even in the practical training too much weight was put on passive learning and too little on independent decision-making. Some of the jurists to whom trainees were assigned were accused of not taking sufficient interest in their charges, or of giving them work inappropriate for their training.

Taken as a whole, this legal education with its minimum of 7½ years seemed to many observers too long and—at least in part—badly spent. The separation of theory and practice through the sharp division between the university and the practical training was a frequent subject of attack.

### 3) *Reforms*

Many years of discussion and entire libraries of reform literature finally led to great changes from the early 1970s on. Some changes were supposed to remedy faults, without however upsetting the system. First, after long deliberations in the faculties, the *Juristischer Fakultätentag* (the Conference of Law School Deans) suggested a drastic reduction of curriculum requirements for the first state examination. There were also the 1970 recommendations of the *Deutscher Juristentag* (the one organization of jurists from all legal occupations); and by the *Verband Deutscher Studentenschaften* (the nationwide student organization). On the basis of the various reform proposals, the Conference of the Ministers of Justice reached agreement on certain fundamentals. These were to be incorporated into state statutes or statutory orders which at the same time reflected any specific ideas of the states.

The number of obligatory subjects to be studied at the university during the legally prescribed minimum of 3½ years, and to be tested in the first state examination, was cut down considerably. Each student had however to add one group of elective subjects. Through this group he could follow his special interests, and thus gain a broader knowledge and a deeper understanding in a particular field. The compulsory and the elective subjects show certain variations from state to state. As one fairly typical example, I may refer to the subjects listed in § 11 of the Examination Regulations of my home state, the Saarland (see Annex I). They are a compromise between the principles agreed on by the Conference of Ministers of Justice and the suggestions of the law faculty of my university.

In theory, most professors favor a reduction of subject matter. Usually however, this reduction is to apply not to one's own "important" subjects but to the "unimportant" subjects taught by colleagues. Disregarding this, a considerable reduction of obligatory subjects was necessary, and the introduction of electives an improvement. I do however consider the treatment accorded to legal philosophy, German (not Roman) legal history and, to a lesser extent, legal sociology a great mistake. The examination requirements of all German states call for candidates who have the necessary knowledge and understanding of law, and can apply it with regard to its historical, social, economic, political and legal-philosophical background (see e.g. § 10 to Annex I). Disregarding their own principles in practice, the state examination requirements relegate the background subjects—legal philosophy, history and sociology—to the electives. Most states attempt to compensate by making admission to the first state examination dependent not only on the successful completion of the six or seven practical courses I have mentioned, but also on the successful completion of a course in one (!) of these background subjects [see e.g. § 13 (2) in Annex I]. But this, in my opinion, is not much more than a face-saving gesture. The demand for more economics was met by some states in a similar manner; the demands for psychology remain largely unheeded.

As to electives, it is clear that some groups of them are too large or not homogeneous. First experiences also indicate that many students seem to choose according to the most limited subject matter and the easiest grades. In my home state, group 3 (criminology, juvenile law and law and practice of prisons) is at present the most popular of the electives mentioned in Annex I. Group 4 (some special administrative law and the fundamentals of administrative practice and social security law) and group 5 (economic law, fundamentals of tax and budgetary law, of patent and copyright law) take second and third place. The situation in most other states seems similar. To some extent the students' preference for the easiest electives is understandable, as there already is a surplus of turnouts, and good grades can shorten the waiting period for admission to the overcrowded practical training. On the other hand, this practice defeats the very purpose of having electives.

As for teaching methods, there have also been certain changes. Some courses now include visits to courts, administrative agencies or prisons to show law in practice. For some time questions of the professor or students had helped to enliven the traditional lecture. Now, more than before, professors give their students mimeographed material in order to have a basis for discussions in place of mere lectures. This method however meets with certain obstacles. In the top law schools of the United States, the students' preparation for each hour in class works very well, as I know from my own experience as a student and teacher there. This is largely due to the fact that the final grade of the student depends on the sum of his grades in each class, and that the overall working load of the curriculum takes homework into consideration. In the West German law faculties neither condition exists. There the classload is still too heavy, particularly since the cases to be solved at home in the practical courses require a great deal of the students' time. There is no incentive in the form of grades for students to prepare for each class, as there is no individual course grading that counts in the final state examination. Besides, British or American case law probably lend themselves better to the case method than does the codified German statute law. In any event, the few case books that exist are still in the trial stage, so that most students would have to use the traditional textbooks. I myself have twice let the students decide in a course on public international law whether they wanted fewer class hours with discussion after individual home preparation or rather the lecture system, which did not require any student preparation. Both times more than two-thirds voted by secret ballot for the traditional lecture. There is a final factor which will keep the well-criticized lecture alive; on German law faculties there is now at best an average of 110-120 law students to one professor. As a result of the increasing student numbers and budgetary cuts everywhere the situation will worsen. Classes of more than 100 students are certainly not conducive to teaching by discussion.

In order to deepen their understanding of the lecture and to increase participation in discussions, the hundreds of students attending certain lectures have sometimes been divided into smaller units. Under the guidance of an assistant, they meet once or twice a week for additional training. Even though these groups comprise at least twenty to thirty students, they can—for lack of money—be made available only for a small number of lectures. In Saarbrücken, the lectures on fundamental rights and freedoms (Constitutional Law II), and on the general sections of both the criminal and civil codes are supplemented by these working groups. These workshops also attempt to bridge the gap between the somewhat abstract lecture and the application of the theoretical knowledge thus gained in practical cases. In other words, they are an introduction to the solution of cases in the practical courses. Wherever possible, the law faculties now divide the practical courses into parallel programs in order to give the individual student a better chance for active participation. Again, the limited staff is a hindrance. At my university we are, for reasons beyond our control, overstaffed in civil and criminal law, and thus able to have parallel practical courses in these fields, but not in our somewhat understaffed public law. The law faculties also have been trying to compete better with private cram courses, by initiating classes which aim at repetition and at simulation of the examination.

The time available for solving cases in class in the practical courses (*Klausuren*) is usually two hours. In order to prepare the students for the first state examination, which allots five hours per case, special case courses were introduced with five-hour cases graded with the help of assistants and afterwards analyzed by the professor. Frequently the cases solved here had been used by the same professor in a previous state examination. As stated before, the student has to solve at least one fairly complicated homework case in each of the practical courses. To prevent him from spending 3-6 weeks on it during the semester, and thus keeping him away from other courses, one of the two homework cases offered in each practical course has to be worked on between semesters. In a number of universities, the months between semesters are partially used for review courses, offered especially for examination candidates, and usually taught by the junior staff. These practices also help to face growing criticism that the overcrowded universities are empty during five months of the year, while unadmitted applicants are waiting for a place to study. All faculties now have student advisers. The faculties have also drawn up a study program that—if followed—qualifies the student for the first state examination after the required minimum of seven semesters. You'll find the study program of my law faculty as Annex II, and will undoubtedly notice the close connection to the examination requirements prescribed by the State Cabinet in Annex I. Finally, a new type of study book should be mentioned. The books (*Programmiertes Lernen*) (Programmed Learning) cut the subject matter into very small segments. They lead progressively from one statement to the next, with constantly interspersed questions, by which the students can check their knowledge of rules and—to some extent—their understanding of problems.

Most recent university statutes assign the universities the task of providing for contact studies, that is, continued education for graduates already engaged in a career. In practice, nothing much has yet been done about this, at least in the law faculties, as manpower is too short. Personally, I doubt that there is really much demand for such law courses except, say, in tax law for practicing attorneys, or short courses briefing practicing jurists on important statutory changes.

All these changes—as already indicated—left the heart of the system intact. Most important, the first state examination remained comprehensive, covering the whole period of studies. Now, as before, a doctorate can be obtained without additional formal courses. Admission is usually subject to an above-average grade in the first or second state examination. Requirements for the degree are a doctoral dissertation which usually takes 1½-2½ years and the passing of an oral examination. All in all, the present requirements are higher than at any time during the last 100 years and the number of doctorates conferred has dropped accordingly.

In spite of unquestionable improvements in the law faculties, the overall picture in legal training is far from bright. To a great extent this is due to a continuing student explosion which has no parallel in German history. In 1962, about 59,000 young people qualified for the university; in 1974, about 104,000 did. Most of them entered institutions of higher learning. In the winter of 1975/76 the universities and teachers' colleges had about 636,000 students. The upward trend was fostered by free tuition and aid for students of the lower financial brackets, provided they met certain minimal requirements. As for law, in 1953 there were about 12,000 law students; 1963, about 19,000; 1973 about 36,000; now there may be over 46,000. The hope that students would complete their studies in fewer semesters has still not been realized.

Although about half a dozen new law faculties were founded, a considerable number of new professorships created and the junior staff increased, these measures did not keep pace with the growing number of students. While I mentioned before that there is an average of one professor with tenure to about 110-120 students, in the law faculty of Münster there is a ratio of one to 200. By now, most if not all law faculties have a "*numerus clausus*," meaning that only a limited number of students is admitted each year. On complaints filed by rejected applicants, the administrative law courts supervise the implementation of the *numerus clausus* in order to make the faculties use their capacities to the fullest. As a matter of course, there is constant political pressure on the ministers of culture and the universities to raise the number of admissions, to increase the teaching load of the professors and to cut down on the so-called vacations, that is, the time traditionally reserved mainly for the private studies of the students and for the research of the professors. As the financial situation in the Federal Republic is getting bleaker and bleaker, these pressures will undoubtedly grow. The allocations for libraries and assistants have been cut drastically. Often chairs are deliberately kept vacant for long periods in order to save money. Consequently the newly introduced reforms are already greatly endangered. The anxiety of the students is also increasing. It is true that they can get more guidance than formerly; but on the other hand they feel like particles in a mass of fellow students larger than ever before, and are facing a competition which will be very tough compared with that of the last thirty years or so. In 1950 there were about 7,700 legal trainees. In 1975, there were about 14,300, to which about 1,300 young jurists involved in the practical part of single-phase training should be added (see part II infra); the figures for the beginning of 1976 are respectively 13,411 and 2,196. I believe it is partly due to the competitive situation that the great political unrest, which began in 1967 in the West German universities, has largely subsided. Now, in 1976, student leaders find it harder than before to activate their electorate for specific student purposes, not to mention general political goals which four years ago still brought student masses into the streets. However this may change again.

In summary, for lack of funds the prospects for effectively reforming the traditional study of law look rather bleak, even though reforms were clearly necessary and their implementation was on the whole feasible and not overly expensive. The criticism of the practical training period has also resulted in changes. The traditional training still aims at the all-round jurist, qualified for all legal careers. As in the universities, some specialization has been introduced, but on a limited scale. The prescribed 3½ years were shortened twice by federal statute and now stand at two years, not including the additional time needed for the examination. Instead of the many stations, there are only five stations now, each lasting at least three months. The training period takes place 1) at a court dealing with private law; 2) at a criminal court or under a public prosecutor; 3) at an administrative agency; 4) under an attorney at law and 5) at an elective station, which can be either one of the first four or another court of law, a legislative body, a notary public, a trade union, an economic enterprise, an international or foreign organization or any other agency offering appropriate legal training. The state ministers of justice, who are mainly responsible for the implementation of this training period, are trying to make it more effective. In some states, the practical training starts with a four-week intensive introductory course held by judges. During the later work with a court, public prosecutor or administrative agency, the trainees spend at least a few hours weekly in workshops under jurists whose other duties are lightened accordingly, at least theoretically. The main emphasis remains however on the trainee's doing the same type of work as the supervising jurist. Wherever possible, trainees are to be assigned only to those individuals who take a real interest in this task. However the steadily growing number of young jurists who have passed the first state examination causes bottlenecks in practical training. Candidates frequently face waiting periods of up to eight months, mainly depending on the training openings in courts and on their grades in the first state examination. In the future, waiting periods may grow even longer.

While predominant opinion still strongly favors practical training in principle, it is too early yet to judge the effectiveness of the new two-year form. Much depends on the trainees themselves and on the individuals to whom they are assigned. When practical training lasted for 3½ years, there was a great deal of dissatisfaction due to wasted time. Now complaints seem to grow that two years are really too short, and that the second state examination no longer produces the all-round jurist who can step into any field of legal practice. Some law faculties keenly feel one negative result of the changes. The greater demands on the trainees make it more difficult to work half-time as paid university assistants or on a doctoral dissertation, which better qualified trainees had frequently done.

As to the selective effects of the two state examinations, in 1973 about 20.5% of some 6,500 students failed the first one; in 1974 about 22% of 6,300 students did. In 1973 about 7% of some 4,300 trainees failed the second one, and in 1974 about 8% of some 5,500 did. In 1975, 25% of 5,780 students failed the first state examination, and 9.5% of 5,912 legal trainees the second. A fair number of failures however succeed in a second attempt after one or two additional semesters of preparation. In 1973, about 35% of the candidates received the lowest passing grade in the first examination; about 25% in the second. The corresponding figures for 1975 are 36% and 27%. The screening effect of the first examination is really much higher than indicated here. Among the many "drop outs" are numerous students who realize during the practical courses their slim prospects of passing. The second examination has always been less selective. At times in some states its screening effect was quite limited, since the usually lenient grades given in the training stations were counted towards the final examination grade. Due to negative experience, federal statute now prohibits their counting more than a third towards the final examination grade, and some states have meanwhile abandoned this practice altogether. There is little hope that the general examination average will rise soon. Due to the stricter *numerus clausus* in other fields, the new masses of law students include a disproportionate number of poorly-motivated or badly-qualified ones. In the long run the bleak professional prospects for jurists and the stiff competition may again lead to better achievements.

In concluding this sketch of the reforms of the traditional legal education, I want to underline one important aspect. The differences among the states still leave a broad common basis. This is important for legal unity in the Federal Republic and for the preservation of the *Volljurist* capable of changing from one legal occupation to another and from one state to the next.

## II. New Experimental Models

A number of critics were not aiming at mere parts of the present educational system, but at its roots. In order to make far-reaching experiments possible, the applicable federal statute was amended in 1971. § 5b of the *Deutsche Richtergesetz* authorized the states to combine university studies and practical training into one single unit or phase (*Einphasen-Ausbildung*), and to replace the first state examination either by an intermediary examination or by grades obtained during the course of studies. Four problems were considered paramount: a better interlocking of theory and practice, more emphasis on the social sciences, limitation of subject matter and specialization in some fields, and better adaptation of the examinations to the previous training. In contrast to some reformers, mostly of the political left, who wanted to abolish the practical training altogether, the federal statute required parts of this single-phase training to take place in a court, an administrative agency and under an attorney at law. On this basis most German states worked on the development of reform models. It is impossible and also unnecessary to describe all the various plans, some of which may never materialize. I can only mention in passing the models of Bielefeld, Hamburg, Hannover, Konstanz and Trier, I must limit myself to sketching two models which are also already functioning, and are probably best suited to illustrate the divergent trends of the innovations.

### 1. *The Augsburg Model*

The State of Bavaria, governed by the fairly conservative Christian Social Union, is experimenting with the Augsburg model. This model was designed mainly by a committee appointed by the Bavarian Ministry of Justice. The model has been in effect since 1971 in the University of Augsburg, which was founded in 1969. The Augsburg model aims to produce an improved version of the traditional type of jurist described in § 10 of Annex I. Therefore it retains more or less the same obligatory subject matter as the usual curriculum exemplified by Annex II. The Augsburg model tries however to meet the criticism that university studies are too isolated from practice and vice versa, and that the practical training is too technical. Augsburg is also concerned with the fact that law studies are generally fragmented into too many small particles.

For these reasons the 6½ year legal training is not divided along the traditional lines between university training before, and practical training after the first state examination, but into related units (see Annex III). First there is a basic study period of two years at the university. These two years are each divided not into the usual two semesters, but into three terms. The six terms of this basic study period are chiefly devoted to civil and criminal law, but also to the background subjects, legal philosophy, legal history, sociology and economics. These background subjects are obligatory. After basic study period I and a short introductory course under a practising jurist, the students are assigned to a court and public prosecutor for nine months' practical training in civil and criminal law. Next, for three terms, comes basic study period II, which emphasizes public law, especially constitutional and administrative law. This is followed by a six-month practical training period with an administrative agency. The idea behind this constant alternation between theory and practice is, of course, for the student to apply as soon as possible in real life the knowledge gained in school. During the following term at the university, the student is expected to integrate the various subject matters he has learned so far, to consider them in their connection to related disciplines and to prepare himself for the intermediary examination. As far as subject matter and methods are concerned, this examination does not really seem very different from the traditional first state examination, which consists of orals and solving cases. Those who have passed the intermediary examination will then specialize for three terms at the university in a field of their particular interest. The student chooses one out of four groups of elective studies oriented towards his later career: either the judicial branch, including the attorneys at law; or public administration; or finance and economics; or labor and social security. Plans for a fifth option with international law and supranational European law have not yet been realized. Next come two practical training periods, each lasting three months; the first, under an attorney at law; the second, in the trainee's particular field of interest. A final 6 weeks of integrated studies at the university is to be used for deepening special interests and for preparing for the second state examination. This differs from the traditional state examination mainly in one point: the intermediary examination counts as 25% of the final grade.

The Augsburg law faculty has also somewhat changed the usual arrangement of courses and teaching methods. Traditionally, courses on say constitutional or criminal law are spread over a whole semester for three hours weekly. Under the new system, constitutional law is taught only during the first three weeks of the term, but for four hours daily. The next three weeks are then dedicated to criminal law on the same intensified basis. After that, another subject follows. The block system has not proved completely satisfactory in practice. In this block system, the lecture is replaced as much as possible by work in small groups. In a course on constitutional law for instance, about half the class hours are used for lectures; the other half for small workshops with at most thirty-five students. The reaction of the students to work in small groups is very favorable. There is a liberal distribution of working material, especially designed for these courses, which partly takes the place of the traditional textbooks. The Augsburg law faculty employs a higher percentage of practicing jurists as part-time teachers than other universities. All these changes are only partial though. Thus, the traditional practical case-solving courses have been retained as one of the pillars of university education.

It is too early to pass final judgment on the Augsburg model. Some tentative conclusions are however possible. The fact that the background subjects, legal philosophy, legal history, as well as some legal sociology and economics, have been made obligatory compares favorably with the improved traditional models sketched above. Still, practical integration of these subjects into other legal studies as well as student interest in these subjects leave much to be desired. Augsburg allots the electives more time, but offers fewer types of them than does the traditional system in its new form. However, up to now the majority of students, professors, judges and other public officials seem to be fairly satisfied with the new arrangements. The requirements of basic study period I have a screening effect at an early stage. Within the first two years of study 30-35% of the students give up law or leave for other universities. In contrast to most other university cities in the Federal Republic, so far no private cram courses have been established in Augsburg. The official of the Bavarian Ministry of Justice who is mainly responsible for the planning of practical training has stated that most students who have finished the two year basic study period I and start as trainees at a court soon get used to the practical side of their work. He rates a minority as excellent, while he gives the majority a satisfactory rating in spite of a university preparation which is shorter than the traditional one. Discounting the "drop outs," the number of outright failures seems to be small. On the other hand, it seems very hard to get the students used to the daily homework and the constant preparation for classes.

Personally, I do not find this very surprising. The German law student—in contrast to the student of medicine or chemistry—is used to working when he pleases. More important, the incentives are lacking which, for instance, make the American law student bear his considerable daily working load: in Augsburg the student has to meet certain requirements to be admitted from one stage to the next. If he fails he will lose not one term but a whole year. Yet not all courses are graded individually and final success depends on the comprehensive intermediary examination and the second state examination. According to another observer, Augsburg represents a technocratic reform, and forces the formerly free student into a strait jacket. These critics maintain that there is no private cram school because the law faculty itself has taken this role over.

One thing is certain. The Augsburg model was planned for a professor/student ratio of one to forty. It is most unlikely that it will work under the average ratio of one professor to one hundred ten or twenty students. It is uncertain whether the present favorable ratio in Augsburg can be maintained. This is, on the one hand, probably a condition for successful experiment. On the other hand, Bavaria is—like all other German states—under great financial strain. This works against the "privileged" status of students at one single law faculty. It is even doubtful whether the four groups of elective studies after the intermediary examination will be offered consistently.

*2) The Bremen Model*

While the Augsburg model overhauled the traditional system, the Bremen model revolutionized it. The Bremen model is based largely on the work of the "*Loccumer Arbeitskreis*," a private group of university professors, assistants, legal trainees, students and one judge who had made himself a name fighting for reforms of the judiciary. Let me briefly describe the *Loccum* tenets.

The *Loccum* program aims at emancipation. First the jurist himself is to be emancipated. The law of an industrial state in the 20th century is not so much a decision by the legislature which a judge or administrator merely applies on the basis of scholarship, legal experience and common sense. Since modern statutory law with its many general clauses leaves more and more possibilities of application open, the modern judge or administrator develops from an interpreter of the law into the real law-giver. Present-day problems do not require a servant of the statute, but a social engineer who forms the law and who does it with a special goal, the emancipation of the people. Traditional legal education does not prepare one for this task. The customary methods of interpretation—considering the wording of a norm, its context within the system, the intent of the norm and its legal history—seem inadequate. They help to stabilize the existing social and economic system. In order to bring about the necessary emancipating changes as a social engineer, the jurist should put the greatest possible emphasis on the social and economic background of each case he has to decide. A broad basis in economics and sociology is the first condition for the new jurist. Also the teaching methods must be thoroughly changed. University education as well as practical training have mainly been a one-way street of communication, with information fed by the professor, judge, administrator, etc. to the student or legal trainee. This has also contributed to the production of jurists who are faithful members of the establishment. Examinations are still virtually initiation rites to the establishment, as they force the candidate to adapt himself to the ruling system. Legal education and examination disregard modern psychology, as they prevent the future jurist from developing himself free of repression and from working in cooperation with others. Moreover, the whole traditional system of legal education is oriented towards the judiciary career and not towards the other legal professions.

The authors of the *Loccum* program, starting from these premises, suggested the following main changes. As a system like Augsburg does not really abolish the traditional faults, the whole legal training should take place at the university but at a university quite different from the traditional one. The study of law should be arranged, not according to the system of the subject matter, like the different books of the civil code, but according to practical problems; for instance, from the conclusion of a sales contract to a law suit resulting from it, and on to a judgment and its execution. The studying should take place in small groups, using the experience of modern psychology. Instead of the repressive comprehensive examinations, the student should prove his qualification by work done in individual courses, and by writing a final research paper on a subject of his own choice. After five years, the university should award a diploma giving the same qualification as the second state examination.

These plans could not be realized entirely, as federal law, at the insistence largely of judges' and attorneys' associations, has stipulated that a part of the legal training take place in a court, in an administrative agency, and under an attorney at law. Otherwise, however, the *Loccum* concept is being followed fairly closely at the University of Bremen.

Bremen, the smallest state of the Federal Republic, is governed by a firm Social Democratic majority. The founding of the new university in 1971 was preceded by a number of crises. It is unique, in so far as all the governing councils in the university are composed of representatives of three groups on an equal basis. The first group comprises the teachers; the second, the students; and the third, the administrative and technical staff, from the head of the library to the charwomen. The Federal Constitutional Court has ruled that such a system of university government is unconstitutional. This system violates the freedom of teaching and research of the professors, who are—not in tenure or salary, but in the performance of research and teaching—largely dependent on the university councils in which they are but a minority. This court decision was however technically directed at the university statute of another state, and has so far not influenced the development of Bremen University. However law suits against the constitution of Bremen University are pending at both the Federal and the State Constitutional Court. Also § 38 of the federal *Hochschulrahmengesetz* of 26 January 1976, provides for an (at least) absolute majority of professors in university councils concerned with research, teaching and the calling of professors. As this federal statute permits no exemptions, Bremen will have to adapt its university system by January 1979.

Over the opposition of the judges' and attorneys' associations, the State Parliament of Bremen passed a statute on legal education. This statute was declared partially unconstitutional by the State Constitutional Court, mainly for leaving to other authorities decisions which under the constitution the legislature had to make itself.

Since April 1975, a new statute for the Bremen version of the single-phase education of the jurist has been in force. The aim of the training is to produce a jurist capable of practicing in a changing society under the rule of law and a democratic and social constitution. Through exemplary models and a critical understanding of scholarly methods, the prospective jurist is to gain the knowledge and the capability to learn which he will need in practice. Theory and practice must not be separated. Working in small groups is the preferred form of study and tutors are to play an important role.

This legal education is to last six years (see Annex IV). The first year is devoted to an integrated study of the social sciences. Law students have the same two courses as the students of economics and sociology. The first course deals with the position and activities of jurists and social science graduates in their professions and in society. The second one examines the structure of bourgeois society to the present day. Courses like this are chiefly supposed to teach the economic and social basis on which the legal order is founded, and which a lawyer has to take into consideration.

The specific legal training is divided into two phases, one of three and one of two years. During the first main period, three semesters are used for the main subject matter in private, labor, public, criminal and procedural law. This subject matter is of course so vast that the exemplary learning called for in the statute can only deal with very small segments of these fields. They are to be chosen according to their practical, social and systematic relevance. The law is always to be viewed in its social context and its methods are to be viewed critically. During the second part of the first main period, the student, after a one month introductory course, undergoes fifteen months of the same practical training as his fellows in Augsburg and those under the traditional model. Parallel to the practical training, there are to be complementary courses held jointly by professors and judges or other jurists in practice. Then the student goes back to the university for the second main period, devoted to specialization either in the fields of labor and economic law, or of public administration or social and criminal law. In his special field of interest, the student is to review critically the theories and methods he had become acquainted with earlier, to recognize the historical, social and political reasons for legal rules and decisions, and to work on suggestions and drafts for legal regulations and changes of existing regulations. The preferred working method in this stage is study by research, preferably on special projects of an interdisciplinary nature. Finally the student will take practical training for six months in his special field of interest.

The real dimension of the changes introduced here is not apparent from the statute alone, but must be gathered from the study program in law. I have not been able to obtain a complete study plan from Bremen, since parts of it, especially the second main period, still seem to be under discussion. However the catalogues of the last years, a report of the University on legal education in Bremen during the winter semester 1973/74 and the summer semester 1974, and the study plan for the winter semester 1975/76, in addition to the statutes already mentioned and the statutory order on law examinations, indicate that only a part of the legal subject matter taught at other law faculties has so far been dealt with in Bremen. Here the 1975 statute will probably effect some changes. Except for the final examination prescribed by federal statute, there are and will be no examinations in the traditional sense. Instead, the student can gain points for very different kinds of work during his studies. He can keep the minutes of a seminar session, deliver papers in the courses, write critical appraisals of books, articles or court decisions, or of the content or method of a course he is taking, make drafts of contracts or statutory regulations, as well as perform the traditional task of the law student in solving cases. Each contribution is graded either "passing" or "not passing"; there is no further differentiation. Work done in a group can be rated like individual work; however the individual contribution should be apparent. During the practical training, the trainee has to draft judgments, administrative regulations, etc. like everywhere else. The final examination already begins in the practical training as drafts of judgments, administrative rules, etc. are counted in the final result. In contrast to the traditional second state examination, the emphasis is not on the solving of practical cases. In Bremen, the central part of the final examination is a thesis and its defense and a discussion on a subject of the candidate's main field of interest. The candidate is entitled to suggest the subject of the thesis and three subjects for the oral discussion. The examining committee consists of two university teachers, two other jurists, one student and one legal trainee. The student and the legal trainee participate in the deliberations, but have no vote. Here, again, the work is graded only as "passing" or "not passing." An annex to the diploma contains the reasons for the decision of the examining committee.

The Bremen model is a theme of heated controversy. One observer has concluded that in Bremen sociology has taken the place which theology held in the Medieval Ages as the sole key to truth. He considers Marxism alone the basis for the social studies in the first year, and believes that typical individual themes used for discussion in Bremen would be considered by the traditional jurist as legitimate subjects for Marxist party schools, but not for public institutions funded by the taxpayer. Critics ask how a Bremen-trained judge can loyally apply the law after he has only been trained to change it. On the other hand, defenders of the Bremen model maintain that its law professors teach more or less the same legal subjects as other universities, but also give them an additional dimension.

I cannot make a final judgment of the Bremen model. It only began in the winter 1971/72. The second main period of the legal training has not even been put into practice yet. It is also not certain that the model, as practiced now, will be practiced in the same manner two years hence. Experimentation is the heart of the model. Constant changes are in accord with the Bremen statute providing for perpetual development. Still, I must make an attempt at a tentative evaluation. After having studied the catalogues of the last semesters, I have found that the actual legal program of the past did not cover the legal subject matter prescribed by the recent statute of 1975 or taught at the other German universities. Also it seems to me that the program for the integrated study of the social sciences used a mainly Marxist terminology. On the other hand, the description of the law courses pointed only occasionally into this direction and the terminology of the integrated study has recently changed.

Bremen has no law faculty in the usual sense; legal studies are organized as part of the social sciences. For the selection of professors, their endorsement of the Bremen model was an important criterion. The Bremen law professors have not been recruited from scholars who have qualified in the formal procedures customary for university professors in Germany (see, part III infra.). This was no accident, as the founders of Bremen University were bitterly opposed to these procedures. Thus it is logical that the scholarly achievements of candidates for a chair are, as a rule, still judged on the basis of their doctorates. Consequently the scholastic requirements would appear lower than those of the traditional law faculties. Politically, there is a noticeable tendency towards the very left. In one of the last elections for student representatives Marxist groups drew a vote of 87%. The Young Socialists, the student group of the governing Social Democratic Party, with about 12%, though on the left wing of the party is considered a rightist body at Bremen University.

It is however not my task and also out of place here to dissect the political preferences of the Bremen law teachers and students. It is perhaps worthwhile though to draw a few preliminary conclusions from the program in its present form, leaving aside the political issue as much as possible. Personally, I doubt very much that the two courses offered in the integrated study of the social sciences are worth a year. As far as the study of law proper is concerned, I am of the opinion that the catalogue of obligatory legal subjects under the modified traditional German model, as well as under the Augsburg model, can and should still be reduced. However I am sure that Bremen goes too far in this reduction. With a whole year devoted to a dubious integrated study of the social sciences, with the practical training prescribed by federal statute and with about the same degree of specialization as promoted in Augsburg, only 20 months remain for studying the basic core subjects of law. That is little more than three semesters. I believe it impossible to obtain the necessary knowledge and basis for practical training in so short a time. The next few years will tell. So far I tend to agree with one observer who said that the Bremen law student will learn to be critical of existing law and legal methods, but will not really know what he is critical of. I regret that Bremen as well as Augsburg offer small choice in electives compared with the more traditional law faculties. International law seems to have no place at all.

I am also skeptical of a legal education in the Federal Republic aiming mainly at the production of a social engineer with a one-sided, policy-oriented approach. Nowadays it is common knowledge that every judge, administrative officer, attorney, etc. participates to some extent in forming the law which he is called upon to apply. Still a basic difference remains between the making and the application of a statute. The requirements of our times do call for a jurist with appreciation of the law in its political, economic and social context. Yet the Federal Republic of Germany is a parliamentary democracy with equal rights for voters, with well-protected fundamental rights and freedoms, with courts supervising the executive and with constitutional courts supervising the legislatures. Even disregarding the question of one-sided political leanings, I doubt that such a state needs jurists who see themselves mainly as self-appointed legislators. I also expect that the Bremen law graduate will be facing grave difficulties in his career. The federal statute can and does make the Bremen qualification legally-equivalent to the second state examination. It cannot prevent the judiciary and the executive of other states and the executive of the Federal Republic itself, not to mention business enterprises and law firms, from giving preference to jurists trained in the more traditional manner or in a less controversial reform system like Augsburg. The abolishment of the usual examinations, called repressive; of grades, called misleading; the great influence of students and legal trainees in deciding about their own curriculum and methods of examination may offer only short-term advantages, if any. The dependence of the professors on the students and the nonprofessional staff can hardly fail to be reflected in the actual grading. Even in law faculties practicing less controversial reform models, students are leaving for other universities after a few semesters, out of fear for their later market value. In Bremen, as in Augsburg, such a transfer is virtually impossible in later semesters, whereas elsewhere such changes used to be fairly frequent and are still encouraged by the professors in faculties with the more traditional approach.

The difference between the jurist with the traditional training and the Bremen jurist is striking; and so is the difference between the Bremen and Augsburg jurist. One may well fear that the Bremen jurist on the one hand and the Augsburg or the traditional jurist on the other may in the long run not have much more in common than the name. There is one thing however that Bremen, Augsburg and all other reform models do have in common: a favorable ratio of professors to students. Early plans for the Bremen model envisaged a ratio of one professor to ten students; newer plans, of one to fifteen. Even if Bremen should have the 600 law students counted on for 1978/79, the professor-student ratio will probably still make Bremen the most expensive reform model in the Federal Republic.

Due to the student explosion and a financial squeeze not foreseen in the reform enthusiasm of the beginning 1970s, the future of a thoroughgoing reform of legal education in the Federal Republic is not at all bright. This is regrettable, since the reform movement, in spite of some inconsistencies and shortcomings, was overdue. It is also unfortunate that to date the traditional system has never been tried out under the same favorable conditions granted to the reform models. The wide ideological and technical differences between the models now practiced in the various German states prevent any prophesies of when and if there will be a return to an essentially uniform system of legal education, which is so important for the unity of the law and the jurists' freedom of professional movement. Certainly the cost factor will play a role in the decision.

The Conference of Ministers of Justice is at present constituting a central study group for the evaluation of legal training in the Federal Republic. This group is to compare the traditional training in its present forms and the various one-phase models in cooperation with local study groups on some law faculties and on some other institutions involved in legal training. Under present law the trial period for the new models is to end in 1981. It is possible that it will be extended to gain still more experience or due to lack of agreement on essentials.

## III. Legal Education and the Teaching Body

Since legal education in general largely depends on the law teachers, I will add a few remarks about the education and position of the West German law professor and junior staff.

Statutory law qualifies a full university professor *per se* for a position as judge or higher civil servant without the two normally required state examinations. In practice however the law professor has usually passed these two examinations with good grades, written a doctoral dissertation and worked as a professor's assistant. He then qualifies for a professorship (becoming a *Privatdozent*) in a formal procedure before a law faculty (*Habilitationsverfahren*). This requires an additional monograph (*Habilitationsschrift*) or a number of shorter but significant publications and a test-lecture before the faculty council. High ranking judges and other jurists who have excelled in their fields through practice and publications are sometimes called to a chair without these formal procedures. All this produces, on the whole, scholars well qualified in their special fields. Capability as a teacher has not usually played the role it should have. In fact, for a long time a German professor often considered himself a scholar who also taught, rather than an individual whose scholarly research and teaching were equally balanced. Recent developments have made it very difficult to retain this self-image; in the many fields with masses of students, it is impossible.

Traditionally, German professors are not promoted at their own university, but better their working conditions, as well as salaries, only when they receive a call from another faculty. Since such calls again depend more on scholarly writing than on success in teaching, some German professors are more interested in research and publication than in teaching.

The freedom of research and university teaching is protected by the federal and state constitutions. The full and associate professor has life tenure, i.e. to a retirement age of 65 or 68 years. Depending largely on the calls he has had, he has one or more assistants and a half or full-time secretary. The full professor's salary is at least equal to that of a judge presiding over a 3-judge senate in a court of appeals. In extremely rare cases, it could reach the salary of the presidents of the highest federal courts, with the exception of the Federal Constitutional Court. The majority of the professors are somewhere in between. They are better off than most attorneys, but earn much less than the stars in that field.

As a body the full professors formerly practically ruled the university; they also elected its head, usually for a term of one or two years. Only ten years ago—according to public opinion polls—the full professor enjoyed the highest social prestige in the Federal Republic. During the last years, this picture has changed considerably. Personally, I have always been of the opinion that place no. 1 on the prestige ladder was an exaggeration, as well as a danger. A university where the professors were next to God was not suited for performing the service functions expected in a modern democratic society. The overcrowding of universities, the 19th century attitudes of some professors, and growing Marxism among the students contributed to the student (and assistant) revolt beginning in 1967 and petering out towards the middle of the seventies. The student revolt brought considerable change. The governing bodies of the universities were henceforth composed of the representatives of different groups. In some states, the professors were in the minority and still are, since the judgment of the Federal Constitutional Court requiring a small majority of professors in questions of teaching and research has not yet been implemented everywhere. While a less conservative style and more democratic forms of organization have their advantages, the process of "democratization" has been carried to extremes. There are too many councils, sometimes with overlapping competences, in which too many unqualified people often carry too much weight. The new federal *Hochschulrahmengesetz* of 1976 will better the situation in some states but will not eliminate the numerous councils and the power struggle between the various groups. These intergroup fights make the university administration much more cumbersome and unduly burden the professors. The student explosion has also contributed towards changing the traditional *Einheit von Forschung und Lehre* (unity of research and teaching) gradually into an *Einheit von Lehre, Prufung und Verwaltung* (unity of teaching, examining and administration). Research is on the decline almost everywhere.

There has been some inflation of professors. Under the influence of democratization postulates and political pressure, the state authorities decided on wholesale promotions of members of the junior staff, who were frequently not fully qualified and now block these positions for better qualified candidates. The state authorities also conferred the title of professor on the teaching staff of other institutions of higher learning besides universities. In consequence, new statutory regulations have been passed which will greatly curtail the chances of future professors to improve their working conditions, as well as their salaries. The fact that we have no shortage of qualified candidates now, due to the glamor of the past, contributes to this development. Before long, the professorship will likely lose its attraction. The times when a judge of the highest federal court would gladly accept a professor's chair may already be over.

As professorial publications have a considerable influence on the practice of the judiciary and the executive, I have always regretted that many German law professors had no practical experience except for their time as legal trainee. Even so there are valuable contacts between theory and practice. The law qualifies the full university professor for all the legal careers I have mentioned, even if he has not taken the two state examinations. He may act occasionally as a defense counsel, but is not permitted to engage permanently in private law practice. Still, a number of professors are actively engaged in legal work outside the university, not to mention the ones who go into politics as parliamentarians or state or federal cabinet ministers. In some universities it is a tradition that one or more law professors act as part-time judge on a court of appeal, in civil, criminal or administrative law. They usually take on only a quarter of a regular judge's burden. Professors of constitutional or economic law are called upon to write advisory opinions on difficult legal questions, or to represent a party in procedures before a constitutional court. In many big legal battles before the Federal Constitutional Court there has been a small army of law professors. In several cases recently decided by the Constitutional Court of my home state, the Saarland, two public law professors of Saarland University served as legal adviser to the parties, and a third as a member of the Court. A fourth represented the state in a lawsuit before the Federal Constitutional Court. The law faculties have been very well represented on the Federal Constitutional Court during its first twenty years. At the moment, there are two full and two honorary professors among the sixteen judges.

In spite of the gradual decline of the professor's status, the title of honorary professor is still coveted. In most law faculties some judges, especially from courts of appeal, higher government executives, and attorneys at law teach on a part-time basis. Their incentive is often not money, but rather a liking for teaching, and the hope of being appointed an honorary professor after a few years of service.

Most professors have at some time or another worked as assistants. The assistants play an important role in the university. It is impossible for the professors alone to grade the numerous papers in the practical courses. The assistants do most of the teaching in smaller groups. If there is still time, they help the professors in their research. The full-time assistants have passed the second state examination, usually with well above average success. They have almost the same salary as a beginning judge of a lower court. For those assistants who later enter the judiciary or the higher administrative service, two years of university service may be counted toward obtaining life tenure. The full-time assistants are usually also working on their doctorates or on a monograph towards the *Habilitation*. Most part-time assistants are legal trainees. The surplus of jurists we anticipate will, it is hoped, provide the universities with a sufficient number of candidates qualified for a full-time assistantship. In a number of universities there is however a real dearth of qualified part-time assistants. Only a small percentage of the legal trainees is considered good enough, and not all of these are interested. Since the practical training has been condensed into only two years, it does not allow much time for other activities. Under the reform models, additional activities in the university seem well-nigh impossible. Fortunately there are always some young jurists starting out as judges or in the higher administrative service who are willing to take on temporary part-time positions correcting case work in the practical courses or teaching in the smaller groups. However, the present cuts in appropriations are keenly felt as regards university assistants as well as jurists in temporary part-time positions.

Some of the changes sketched in this article will not stand the test of time. Others may contribute towards bridging differences existing between legal education in the United States and the Federal Republic of Germany. One can only hope that those reform measures which are expedient will not be counteracted by the unlucky combination of the student avalanche and the cuts in manpower and material. At present the universities are in serious danger of becoming mass production mills which take in more and more law students and grind out worse and worse lawyers, many of whom will not even find a legal position. The consequences of such a development for legal research, the legal profession and law itself are all too obvious.

## *Annex I*

Excerpt from the Examination Regulations of the Saarland (prescribed by the state cabinet for the first legal examination)

§ 10 Purpose of the examination.

(1) The first legal state examination is to determine whether the candidate has achieved the objectives of his legal studies and is thus qualified for the practical legal training.

(2) The examination is to determine whether the candidate is able to comprehend and apply the law and whether he possesses the knowledge necessary for this purpose in the subjects of examination [see § 11(1)], as viewed from their historical, social, economic, political and legal-philosophical aspects.

§ 11 Examination subjects.

(1) Examination subjects include the obligatory subjects and one group of electives chosen by the candidate. Other legal fields may be examined only in connection with the examination subjects and only to test the candidate's understanding and working methods, but not his knowledge.

(2) Obligatory subjects are:

1. in private law: the general section of the private law code, law of obligations, real property and chattels, and the fundamentals of family law and inheritance law;
2. in commercial law: the law of the single merchant and the fundamentals of company law and securities;
3. in labor law: the employment contract and the fundamentals of collective labor law;
4. in criminal law: the general section and the specific section of the criminal law code;
5. in public law: constitutional law in its relationship to the general theory of the state and to international law, general section of administrative law, administrative procedure, police law, the law of municipal corporations, and the fundamentals of planning and zoning law;
6. in the law of court organization and procedure: fundamentals of court administration, of civil procedure (including bankruptcy, execution, and non-contentious procedure), fundamentals of criminal procedure, administrative law court and constitutional court procedure.

(3) Groups of electives are:

1. roman law, medieval legal history; recent private law history and recent constitutional law history;
2. legal philosophy, legal sociology and general theory of law;
3. criminology, juvenile law, law and practice of prisons ("*Strafvollzugskunde*");
4. fundamentals of administrative practice and of social secu-

rity law; from the special sections of administrative law: law of public servants, planning and zoning law, law of public roads;

5. economic law (including economic administrative law), fundamentals of tax and budgetary law, patent and copyright law;
6. public international law, law of international organizations, law of the European Communities;
7. comparative law, fundamentals of French law, private international law.

§ 13

. . . .

(2) The candidate must have participated during his legal studies in courses of all examination subjects [cf. § 11 (1)]. The candidate must also have participated in a course from elective group 1 or 2 [cf. § 11 (3)].

(3) The candidate must have participated regularly in at least one workshop for beginners.

(4) The candidate must have successfully completed
a) one practical course each for beginners and advanced students in private law, criminal law and public law;
b) an additional practical course (elective);
c) one economics course for jurists.
The successful participation in a seminar will be counted as an additional practical course (b).

. . . .

§ 15

(1) The candidate must have audited for four weeks each during the university vacations the proceedings in a court of first instance and in an administrative agency of town or county level in order to acquaint himself with the practical work of these authorities.

. . . .

## *Annex II*

University of the Saarland
Faculty of Law and Economics

### Study Program*
### For the Study of Law
### (as of April 1975)

#### I. General and Compulsory Courses

| *First Semester* | *Weekly hours* |
|---|---|
| Introduction to law | 3 |

* The following arrangement of studies is *recommended* for all law

| | Weekly hours |
|---|---|
| General section of the private law code | 4 |
| + Workshop (supplementing the lecture) | 2 |
| General section of the criminal law code | 4 |
| + Workshop (supplementing the lecture) | 2 |
| Constitutional law I (organization of the Federal Republic) | 3 |
| Introduction to economics (with graded tests) | 3 |
| | 21 |

*Second Semester*

| | |
|---|---|
| General section of law of obligations | 4 |
| Real property and chattels I | 3 |
| + Workshop on law of obligations and property | 2 |
| Special sections of the criminal law code | 4 |
| Criminal law: practical course for beginners | 2 |
| Constitutional law II (basic rights) | 3 |
| + Workshop (supplementing the lecture) | 2 |
| | 20 |

*Third Semester*

| | |
|---|---|
| Special sections of law of obligations I | 3 |
| Real property and chattels II | 3 |
| Private law: practical course for beginners | 2 |
| Constitutional law III (in its relationship to international law) | 2 |
| General theory of the state | 3 |
| Fundamentals of constitutional court procedures | 2 |
| Constitutional law: practical course for beginners | 2 |
| Fundamentals of court organization | 1 |
| | 18 |

*Fourth Semester*

| | |
|---|---|
| Special sections of law of obligations II | 2 |
| Fundamentals of family law | 3 |
| Fundamentals of inheritance law | 3 |
| Fundamentals of criminal procedure | 3 |
| Criminal law: practical course for advanced students | 2 |
| Special sections of administrative law | 4 |
| | 17 |

students. The program starts in the fall semester. The practical courses and the review courses are held in each semester; all other courses, once a year. Each semester a considerable number of additional optional courses not listed here, in particular seminars, is also offered. Students working for a doctorate must successfully complete two seminars.

| *Fifth Semester* | *Weekly hours* |
|---|---|
| Commercial law I | 1 |
| Labor law | 4 |
| Fundamentals of civil procedure | 4 |
| Private law: practical course for advanced students | 2 |
| General section of administrative law | 4 |
| Fundamentals of administrative law court procedures | 2 |
| | 19 |

| *Sixth Semester* | |
|---|---|
| Commercial law II | 3 |
| Commercial law III (fundamentals of securities) | 2 |
| Constitutional and administrative law: practical course for advanced students | 2 |
| Fundamentals of bankruptcy and execution | 3 |
| Fundamentals of non-contentious procedure | 1 |
| Elective courses (cf. II below) | 8 |
| | 19 |

| *Seventh Semester* | |
|---|---|
| Private law: elective practical course | 2 |
| Practical course preparing specifically for the written part of the first state examination | 4 |
| Review course in private law | 2 |
| Review course in criminal law | 2 |
| Review course in constitutional and administrative law | 2 |
| Elective courses (cf. II below) | 4 |
| | 16 |

*After the Seventh Semester (between semesters)*

Review course in private law, criminal law, constitutional law and administrative law = 60 hours

*During any semester*: in addition to the foregoing program
One elective course from group 1 or 2 (cf. II below)

## II. Elective Courses*

*Elective Group 1*

| *Sixth Semester* | *Weekly hours* |
|---|---|
| Roman law | 4 |
| Medieval legal history | 4 |

* The elective courses recommended for *all* students are marked with +. The students will have an opportunity in each elective group to write practice examination papers.

| *Seventh Semester* | *Weekly hours* |
|---|---|
| Recent private law history + | 2 |
| Recent constitutional law history + | 2 |
| *Elective Group 2* | |
| *Sixth Semester* | |
| Legal philosophy I + | 3 |
| Legal sociology I + | 3 |
| General theory of law I + | 2 |
| *Seventh Semester* | |
| Legal philosophy II | 1 |
| Legal sociology II | 1 |
| General theory of law II + | 2 |
| *Elective Group 3* | |
| *Sixth Semester* | |
| Criminology I | 4 |
| Juvenile law | 2 |
| Law and practice of prisons | 2 |
| *Seventh Semester* | |
| Criminology II | 4 |
| *Elective Group 4* | |
| *Sixth Semester* | |
| Fundamentals of administrative practice | 2 |
| Administrative law (special section)—subject matter not included in the obligatory administrative law courses | 4 |
| Fundamentals of social security | 2 |
| *Seventh Semester* | |
| Intensive study courses taken from the preceding electives | 4 |
| *Elective Group 5* | |
| *Sixth Semester* | |
| Economic law I (including economic administrative law) | 2 |
| Fundamentals of tax and budgetary law I | 2 |
| Patent and copyright law | 4 |
| *Seventh Semester* | |
| Economic law II (including economic administrative law) | 2 |
| Fundamentals of tax and budgetary law II | 2 |
| *Elective Group 6* | |
| *Sixth Semester* | |
| Public international law | 3 |

| | *Weekly hours* |
|---|---|
| Law of international organizations | 3 |
| Law of the European Communities | 3 |
| *Seventh Semester* | |
| Intensive study courses taken from the preceding electives (including one 2-hour seminar) | 3 |
| *Elective Group 7* | |
| *Sixth Semester* | |
| Comparative law | 3 |
| Fundamentals of French law I | 2 |
| Private international law | 3 |
| *Seventh Semester* | |
| Fundamentals of French law II | 3 |
| Intensive study courses taken from the preceding electives | 1 |

## *Annex III*

The Augsburg Model
(as of the academic year 1974/75) *

| Phase: | Duration: | Subject matter: |
|---|---|---|
| Basic studies I | 6 terms | Background subjects (e.g. economics and legal philosophy); private law, criminal law with related subjects |
| Practical training I (Judiciary) | 9 months | Practical work in private and criminal law |
| Basic studies II | 3 terms | Constitutional and administrative law with related subjects |
| Practical training II (Administration) | 6 months | Practical work in an administrative agency (county) |
| Integrated studies I | 1 term | Overall perspective and review of all previous subjects |
| Intermediary examination | 1½ months | written and oral tests (written tests consisting mainly of case-solving) |
| Specialized studies (= electives) | 3 terms | chosen according to personal interest out of four groups of subject matter |
| Practical training III (Attorney at law) | 3 months | participation in the daily work of a law practice |
| Practical training IV (elective) | 3 months | practical work in a court, administrative agency or under an attorney at law according to the trainee's special interest |
| Integrated studies II | 6 weeks | overall perspective and review |
| Second state examination | 3-4 months | written and oral test (written tests consisting mainly of case-solving) |

* Under the Augsburg Model the academic year is divided not in semesters but in three terms. The whole program is planned for 6½ years.

## *Annex IV*

The Bremen Model
(as of 18 April 1975)

| Phase: | Duration: | Subject matter: |
|---|---|---|
| Integrated study of the social sciences | 1 year | Courses: Jurists and social science graduates in their professions and in society. The structure of bourgeois society from the beginning of capitalism to the present day |
| Law studies: main period I | 3 years | |
| | 20 months | University studies: The main subject matter in private, labor, public, criminal and procedural law by exemplary method |
| | 1 month | Introductory course to the |
| | 15 months | Practical training in private, criminal, and administrative law at courts, an administrative agency and under an attorney at law |
| Law studies: main period II | 2 years | Specialization (in labor and economic law, or in public administration or in social and criminal law) |
| | 3 semesters | Studies at the university |
| | 6 months | Practical training |
| total | 6 years | |

## *Annex V*

It is impossible to give more than a few titles on the problems of German legal education and on the numerous reform proposals. The following titles will give access to the abundant material and publications existing on the subject.

For part I: The first important reform proposals can be found in *Die Ausbildung der deutschen Juristen—Darstellung, Kritik, Reform* by the *Arbeitskreis für Fragen der Juristenausbildung* (1960). The most important recent surveys on the traditional system of legal education, as well as many reform suggestions, are published in the *Verhandlungen des 48. Deutschen Juristentages* (1970). This conference was prepared by written reports of the President of the Bremen Court of Appeals, Dr. Richter, and of Professor Oehler (Vol. I, Part F, pp. F1-F212 and Vol.I, Part E, pp. E1-E157, and by oral reports of University Assistant Rinken (now Professor in Bremen) and the former Federal Judge Professor Mühl (Vol.II, Part P, pp. P7-P33 and pp. P35-P54). The discussion, in which the legal trainees played a particularly vocal part, covers about 265 pages (Vol.II, P55-P313). The resolutions are printed on P314-P316. The *Presse- und Informationszentrum des Deutschen Bundestages* has published excerpts from parliamentary debates and hearings in *Reform der Juristenausbildung* (1971). The Federal Cabinet has published a collection of reports on legal education in the various German states, which however concentrates on the practical training period: *Unterrichtung durch die Bundesregierung—Bericht über die Juristenausbildung in den Ländern* (Bundesrat Drucksache 321/75 of 5 May 1975). This report also contains interesting statistics. It is summarized in 53 *Deutsche Richterzeitung* 337-340 (1975). The most comprehensive as well as recent survey on legal education in all Western German universities is the *Fachstudienführer Rechtswissenschaft* by A. Kaufmann and E. Behrendt (1973 with a supplement, 1975). Recent descriptions of the careers open to jurists are the *Jura-Berufsreport 1973/74*, ed. by Henrich and Lambert (1973) and von Nieding, *Berufschancen für Juristen* (2nd ed. 1975). The neglect of background subjects and a certain provincialism of German legal education are criticized by Geck, "Die Lehre des Völkerrechts an den Universitäten in der Bundesrepublik Deutschland," 33 *Zeitschrift für ausländisches öffentliches Recht und Völkerrecht* 72 (1973). See also the reports of the "*Deutsche Gesellschaft für Völkerrecht*": 1971 *JZ* 544; 1973, 551; 1975, 409; 1975 *JuS* 542. For the procedures leading to a doctorate see Geck, *Promotionsordnungen und Grundgesetz* (2nd ed. 1969).

Under part II, some one-phase reform models were only mentioned. The monthly legal periodical "*JuS*" (*Juristische Schulung*) which gives special attention to the reforms of legal education, contains general surveys on the reforms and on one-phase models (1973 *JuS* 123 and 1974, 266) as well as special reports on the Hamburg Model (1970 *JuS* 482; 1973, 657; 1975, 815); on Hannover (1972 *JuS* 611; 1973, 191); and Hessen (1973 *JuS* 794 and 797; 1974, 131). The book *Neues Recht durch neue Richter? Der Streitum die Ausbildungsreform der Juristen*, ed. by Gutjahr-Löser deals extensively with one-phase models in Bremen and Augsburg, and more briefly with such models in Hessen and Nordrhein-Westfalen (1975). See for an extensive discussion of the one-phase model in Bielefeld, *Einstufige Juristenausbildung—Colloquium über die Entwicklung und Erprobung des Modells im Land Nordhein-Westfalen* (1974). The Augsburg Model is also depicted in 1971 *JuS* 550, and by the official formerly responsible for the practical legal education in the Bavarian Ministry of Justice, Dr. Niebler, now a judge on the Federal Constitutional Court (1975 *Bayerische Verwaltungsblätter* 153 and 1975 *JuS* 603).

As to the *Loccum* tenets see *Neue Juristenausbildung—Materialien des Loccumer Arbeitskreises zur Reform der Juristenausbildung*, ed. "Loccumer Arbeitskreis" (1970). Various authors have contributed to *Der neue Jurist—Materialien zur reformierten Juristenausbildung in Bremen*, eds. Benseler, Rasehorn, Wassermann (1973). The controversy on the Bremen Model is reflected in *Neues Recht durch neue Richter?* (supra), and in the articles of professors Rinken and Böhm 1974 *JuS* 538; 679, 818; 820) and of Court of Appeals President Richter (1973 *JZ* 356). The first rector of Bremen University, Professor von der Vring, has published *Hochschulreform in Bremen* (1975), which a (Christian Democrat) reviewer has called an honest documentation of a false policy, 6 *Hochschulpolitische Informationen* No. 13 at 11 (1975).

The decision of the Bremen State Constitutional Court of 23 September 1974 declaring the 1973 state statute on legal education partially unconstitutional is published in 1974 *NJW* 2223 and 1975 *Deutsches Verwaltungsblatt* 429 and summarized in 1975 *JuS* 65. It is criticized by Professor Heinz Wagner and Assistants Fangmann and Geulen of the Free University of Berlin in 1975 *JZ* 430. The revised version of the Bremen statute on legal education of 18 April 1975 appears in "Gesetzblatt der Freien Hansestadt Bremen" No.27 of 14 May 1975 at 245.

From a leftist point of view Leibfried has appraised the tendencies of one-phase legal education, *Kritische Justiz* 182 (1973). He comes to the conclusion that legal education has, after all, not changed very much. For a warning against the politicizing of legal education and the judiciary from a traditional vantage point see Dr. Ethel Behrendt (University Assistant in Munich) *Radikale Ausbildung—Radikalenausbildung?* (1974) and "Aufbruch in die Politische Aktion? Gefahren für das rechtsstaatliche Richteramt durch veränderte Ausbildung," 22 *Zeitschrift für Politik* 16 (1975).

For the student revolt mentioned in Part III see e.g. Rupp and Geck, *Die Stellung der Studenten in der Universität* (1968); also printed in 27 *Veröffentlichungen der Vereinigung der Deutschen Staatsrechtslehrer* 113, 143 and the subsequent discussion at 188 (1969); and, in English, the contribution by Geck on West Germany in the international symposium "Student Power in University Affairs," 17 *Am. J. Comp L.* 337 (1969), as well as H.H. Klein, *Demokratisierung der Universität?* (2nd ed. 1968). The important judgment of the Federal Constitutional Court of 29 May 1973, protecting academic freedom and guarding the university professors against the most extreme over-representation of other groups, follows largely along these same lines, 35 BVerfGE 79 (1974). Excerpts and comments can be found in many German legal periodicals. The federal statute providing for unified principles of university government, the *Hochschulrahmengesetz* of 26 January 1976 is printed in 1976 BGBl. I at 185 (29 January 1976). See also *Mitteilungen des Hochschulverbandes*, no. 3 at 124 (1975) and Hall, "Das Hochschulrahmengesetz (HRG)," 1976 *JuS* 267. The most recent presentation of German university law already includes the *Hochschulrahmengesetz*: Wolff and Bachof, *Verwaltungsrecht II (Organizations- und Dienstrecht)* (4th ed. 1976).

A distorted picture of the German professor (which partly motivated the structure of Bremen university) can be found in von der Vring (supra at 10). For contrast see Henrich (in Henrich-Lambert supra at 111); see also Rüthers, "Die rechtswissenschaftlichen Habilitationen in der Bundesrepublik zwischen 1945 und 1969," 1972 *JZ* 185. The gradual deterioration in working conditions of the professors can be seen in each number of the *Mitteilungen des Hochschulverbandes*. The federal statute, which will have a decisive negative impact on the salaries of university professors, is published in 1975 BGBl. I at 1173 (28 May 1975).

On legal education in some other states, see e.g., the reports in 1969 *JuS* (195 on the German Democratic Republic; 346 on Great Britain), 1971 *JuS* (49 on the United States), 1973 *JuS* (127 on the Soviet Union), 1974 *JuS* (748 on Ethiopia), and 1975 *JZ* (599 on the Soviet Union). There is a brief comparison on West German legal education with legal education in the United States, Great Britain and France by Oehler (supra at E 7). The article by Koch, "Neuere Entwicklungen in der englischen und amerikanischen Juristenausbildung," is useful also for the German point of view, 39 *RabelsZ* 197 (1975).

# [5]

# The French Legal Studies Curriculum: Its History and Relevance as a Model for Reform

Thomas E. Carbonneau*

## I. Introduction

Much like a fine wine of precious vintage, the legal studies curriculum in France took centuries to reach its point of maturity. By and large, it is a product of careful molding and enlightened experimentation, although some disparity exists between its theoretical promise and its actual implementation within the French university system. Moreover, its history is not without its share of ill-conceived hopes and retrogressive thinking. This article attempts to describe and analyze those events which fostered the historical metamorphosis of the French legal studies curriculum.

The predominance of a broad academic approach to law and the concomitant absence of a narrow "trade school" mentality in the French law schools might be attributed to the general organization of higher education in France.[1] The basic law degrees, the *licence* and the *maîtrise en droit*, are undergraduate degrees; students enter the university law program at the age of eighteen or nineteen after having obtained the *baccalauréat* (the French high school diploma).[2] A liberal arts approach to the study of law, consisting of a general introduction to the basic principles of

---

* Diplôme supérieur d'Etudes françaises 3e degré, University of Poitiers (1971); A.B. Bowdein College (1972); B.A. Oxford University (1975); J.D. University of Virginia (1978); M.A. Oxford University (1979); M.A. University of Virginia (1979); LL.M. Columbia University (1979). The author is a Jervey Fellow at the Parker School of Foreign and Comparative Law and is currently doing research in France.

[1] For a brilliant comparative discussion of French and U.S. legal education, see Deák, *French Legal Education and Some Reflections on Legal Education in the United States* [1939] Wisc. L. Rev. 473. It is the basic thesis of the late Professor Deák's article that U.S. legal education, with its obsessive concentration on preparing practitioners, could be modified on the basis of the French example. In his view, U.S. law schools place too little emphasis upon the lawyer's mission as a social engineer, and, as a result, produce highly skilled technicians rather than educated jurists: *ibid.*, 474, 479-80.

[2] For a general description of the French educational process as it relates to law studies, see, *e.g.*, Herzog, *Civil Procedure in France* (1967), 68-73, reprinted in Schlesinger, *Comparative Law* 3d ed. (1970), 95. Professor Herzog's discussion is valid as a description of the process before 1954.

juridical science with the choice of specialty deferred to the final two years of study, is more suitable for students who are relatively inexperienced and who lack prior university training. It also should be mentioned that since the end of the nineteenth century, legal education in France has been viewed as a general preparation for a career in fields other than law. In fact, only a very small proportion of French law graduates enter the legal profession,[3] and those who do are given practical training by way of either an apprenticeship program or further study in a specialized school.[4] The method of recruiting law professors and other teaching personnel is another factor contributing to a more academic legal education. As a general rule, educators have had little or no contact with the legal practitioner's world; they are selected by means of a rigorous and extremely competitive national examination after they have completed (or while they are completing) their doctoral research.[5]

One of the primary contentions of this article is that the fundamental character of French legal education, which emphasizes the educating of jurists as opposed to the training of lawyers, is the product of a set of factors which are deeply rooted in French history and are part of the basic intellectual assumptions of French culture. The *Faculté de droit* never was independent of the general university structure — it was one of the four constituting faculties of the university. Also, the original substance of the law curriculum was exclusively scholarly in character. Practical legal training was a post-university phenomenon, obtained by means of an apprentice-

[3] Professor deVries estimates that only some 20% of law students enter the legal profession, while the remaining 80% go into government service or business positions: deVries, *Foreign Law and The American Lawyer: An Introduction to Civil Law Method and Language* (1969), 75, n. 21.

[4] Those who do enter the legal profession either go into private practice as an *avocat, avoué*, or *notaire*, or enter the *magistrature* to work as judges or prosecutors. To enter the *magistrature*, a candidate must pass a very competitive examination. If successful, he enters the *Centre nationale d'Etudes judiciaires* for a three-year course of intensive study which is more narrow and technical in orientation than the basic legal studies program. To become an *avocat*, the law graduate must study for an additional year, pass the bar examination, and undergo a three- to five-year apprenticeship program. For an extensive discussion of this system, see Szladits, *European Legal Systems* (1976), 278 *et seq*. See also Tunc, *Modern Developments in the Preparation for the Bar in France* (1949-50) 2 J. Legal Educ. 71. For a description of recent changes in the legal profession, see Herzog & Herzog, *The Reform of the Legal Professions and of Legal Aid in France* (1973) 22 Int'l & Comp. L.Q. 462.

[5] See, *e.g.*, deVries, *supra*, note 3, 76-77.

ship program. The traditional academic character of French legal education was altered considerably by the deterioration of the law faculties in the eighteenth century and by the utilitarian orientation of the Napoleonic reforms. The twentieth century law faculties represent a reassertion of the early university character of the *Faculté de droit* as it has been redefined by new intellectual currents. It is the basic thesis of this paper that the French legal studies program provides a model for the long-overdue reform of North American legal education.

## II. The medieval law faculties

During the Middle Ages, the law faculties in France were known as *Facultés de droit civil et canonique.*[6] Despite their disparate historical origins, these university institutions proffered a uniform program of instruction consisting of lectures (given in Latin) on Roman civil law and canon law.[7] The case of the *Faculté de droit* of Paris, the most prestigious law faculty of the time, is illustrative: from the early thirteenth century until well into the seventeenth century, its curriculum was devoted entirely to instruction in the principles of canon law.[8]

A complex set of legal, political, and cultural factors militated against the establishment of a single legal system in France at this time.[9] As a consequence, national legislation was disunified and frequently disregarded.

At the close of the Middle Ages, the system of legal education in general began to fall into discredit.[10] Although some universities continued to offer the traditional program,[11] many abandoned law teaching altogether.[12] In those institutions in which some sort of legal instruction was maintained, the quality of the teaching de-

---

[6] See Bonnecase, *Qu'est-ce qu'une Faculté de Droit?* (1929), 52.

[7] See Allemès, *The System of Legal Education in France* [1929] J. Soc. Pub. Teachers L. 36. See also Bonnecase, *supra*, note 6, 41-54.

[8] See Bonnecase, *supra*, note 6, 55. The law faculty at the University of Paris was a faculty of canon law from November 16, 1219, date of the Bull of Pope Honorius II, until the issuance of the 1679 Edict.

[9] The monarchy had yet to triumph over the feudal structure, the Church and ecclesiastic courts were an obstacle to the application of a national law, and the country was divided into two different legal regions. See generally Bonnecase, *supra*, note 6, 41-56.

[10] See Allemès, *supra*, note 7, 36.

[11] Most notably the universities of Paris, Orléans, Bourges, Poitiers, and Rheims: *ibid.*

[12] *Ibid.*

teriorated considerably — professors often failed to appear for lectures.[13]

A quiet movement towards change in the legal system and in legal education eventually became apparent at several institutional levels. During the sixteenth century, a number of distinguished French legal scholars initiated a trend (at least a tacit one) favoring the integration of the national law into the law school curriculum.[14] The increasing power of the Royal Administration, which entailed the growing secularization of the State, augured well not only for French political and cultural unity but also for a unitary system of national law.[15] Progress in the legal area was being achieved and the mutation of historical forces was leading inevitably to the assertion of a political and legal system with a distinctively French personality. Such a development unquestionably required a revitalization and restructuring of legal education.

## III. Louis XIV's reform of legal education

Under Louis XIV, French legal education reached the first stage of its modern development. As an absolute monarch preoccupied with the centralization of all political power within his own hands, he invested the French legal system with sufficient force to give it a truly national dimension. From 1667 to 1673, the Royal Administration issued a series of ordinances dealing with, *inter alia*, French civil and criminal procedure and commercial law.[16] This new role of national French law brought about a renewed interest in the *Facultés de droit*.

In April 1679, a landmark date for French legal education, the King issued the celebrated Edict of Saint-Germain-en-Laye.[17] The

---

[13] *Ibid.*, 36-37.

[14] During the Middle Ages, some legal scholars already had written works on French law (most notably Pierre Defontaines, Philippe de Beaumanoir, and Jean Bouteiller). In the sixteenth century, the work on French law was led by Dumoulin with the help of Charondas, Loisel, and Guy-Coquille. It also should be noted that the *coutumes* eventually were recorded, which helped to strengthen the trend toward a unified legal system. For a detailed discussion of these points, see Bonnecase, *supra*, note 6, 63-67.

[15] *Ibid.*, 65.

[16] The dates and subject matter of the ordinances are as follows: civil procedure (1667); forests and water (1669); criminal procedure (1670); and land commerce (1673). For a general discussion of this legislation, see Bonnecase, *ibid.*

[17] L'Edit de Saint-Germain-en-Laye d'avril 1679, reprinted in Bonnecase, *ibid.*, 41-46. For a general discussion of the substance of the 1679 Edict, see also Allemès, *supra*, note 7, 36-37.

chief accomplishment of this document and two supplementary *Déclarations*, enacted in 1682[18] and 1690,[19] was to institute the teaching of French law in the *Facultés de droit*. The preamble of the 1679 Edict attributed the poor quality of judicial decisions and legal work generally to the insufficiency of legal instruction, and proposed to remedy the problem by regulating the principal components of legal education: the curriculum, the degree requirements, and the institutional status of students and professors.[20]

Regarding the curriculum, all universities with law faculties were required to reinstate the course offerings in both Roman civil law and canon law.[21] Those institutions which had abandoned law teaching entirely were ordered to re-establish their law faculties.[22] Moreover,

> afin de ne rien omettre de ce qui peut servir à la parfaite instruction de ceux qui entreront dans les chargers de judicature, nous voulons que le droit françois, contenu dans nos ordonnances et dans les coutumes, soit publiquement enseigné; et à cet effet, nous nommerons des professeurs qui expliqueront les principes de la jurisprudence françoise et qui en feront des leçons publiques, après que nous aurons donné les ordres nécessaires pour le rétablissement des Facultés de droit canonique et civil . . . .[23]

Under the provisions of the Edict, legal education consisted of three stages, each of which culminated in the conferral of a degree (the *bachelier, licence* and *doctorat*).[24] The Edict also contained stringent administrative requirements to assure that the degrees actually were earned by knowledgeable recipients. For example, the *licence* program, the basic law program, required three years of study.[25] During this period of time, the aspiring candidate had to attend at least two different classes each day and satisfy all the written work demanded of him by his professors.[26]

To ensure compliance with these standards, students underwent two separate registration procedures: a formal personal registration procedure four times a year and a less formal registration procedure every three months.[27] Moreover, favorable professorial recommenda-

[18] Déclaration du 6 août 1682, reprinted in Bonnecase, *ibid.*, 46-50.
[19] Déclaration du 17 novembre 1690, reprinted in Bonnecase, *ibid.*, 50-52, n. 1.
[20] *Supra*, note 17.
[21] *Ibid.*, arts. 1 and 2.
[22] *Ibid.*, art. 2.
[23] *Ibid.*, art. 14.
[24] *Ibid.*, arts. 7 and 8.
[25] *Ibid.*, art. 6.
[26] *Ibid.*
[27] *Ibid.*, art. 15.

tions were indispensable for graduation.[28] At the end of the third year, the candidate for the *licence* would sit a written examination, defend a thesis publicly, and pass a three-hour oral examination on both Roman civil law and canon law.[29] Upon successfully completing the examination process, furnishing evidence of his unfailing attendance at lectures, and with satisfactory testimonial letters in hand, the student would be awarded the *licence en droit*.[30]

As was mentioned earlier, the conduct of the law professors also had contributed to the degeneration of legal education. To guarantee a minimum level of quality law teaching, the 1679 Edict mandated that professors give their lectures in conformity with established schedules and be duly present at examination sessions.[31] Anyone giving a law lecture who was not *bona fide* a professor of law would be fined and stripped of all past and future degrees. Those persons taking lessons from unaccredited teachers also would be sanctioned.[32] Finally, law professors who excused students from established degree requirements or furnished them with false letters of reference would be dismissed and the students involved would lose their diplomas and would be unable to acquire any other degree.[33]

The two subsequent *Déclarations* provided for the practical implementation of the 1679 Edict. As a result of the recommendations made by the *Facultés de droit* of several universities, the *Déclarations* contained a number of additions to the original reorganization program. For instance, they provided for the appointment of *docteurs agrégés* to help the law professors cope with their increased workload, laid down guidelines by which these assistants would be selected, and defined the scope of their responsibilities.[34] The most

[28] *Ibid.*, art. 6.

[29] *Ibid.*, art. 7.

[30] For a description of the requirements for the initial and terminal degrees, see *ibid.*, arts. 7 and 8.

[31] *Ibid.*, arts. 10 and 11.

[32] *Ibid.*, art. 5.

[33] *Ibid.*, art. 12.

[34] *Supra*, note 18, arts. 2-8. Four criteria were established for the appointment to the position of *docteur agrégé*. The candidate had to be at least thirty years of age, hold a doctorate in law, receive two-thirds of the vote of the faculty, and be chosen from among aspiring teachers of law, *avocats*, or judges: *ibid.*, art. 9. It is worth noting that highly qualified auxiliary personnel continue to be used in contemporary law faculties. For a discussion of the modern practice, see Eisenmann, *The University Teaching of Social Sciences: Law* (1973), 74. Under art. 19 of the 1682 *Déclaration*, the position of professor of law could be obtained only by way of a formal competition

significant part of the *Déclarations* pertained to the newly created position of *professeur royal de droit français*. While it was clear from the substance of the 1679 Edict that the Royal Administration attached substantial importance to the teaching of the national law in the law faculties, the implementing legislation appeared to set the occupants of the Chair of French Law somewhat apart from their colleagues and to give them an inferior rank in the institutional hierarchy. The 1682 *Déclaration* stated, on the one hand, that the professors of French law

> seront du corps des dites Facultés, et auront voix délibérative dans toutes les assemblées et séances entre le plus ancien et second professeur. . .[35]

while adding, on the other hand,

> sans qu'il puisse devenir doyen ni participer aux gages et émoluments des dits professeurs.[36]

The *professeur royal du droit français* was indeed an oddity in the halls of the tradition-bound law faculties. Not only was he the sole faculty member to carry the title of *professeur royal*, teach in the French language, and reflect upon a "living" corpus of legal doctrine, but he was poorly paid and generally disliked by his fellow professors, who deemed him to be an outsider.[37] Despite the inadequate remuneration and other drawbacks, a significant amount of prestige accompanied the appointment to the royal professorship. The text of the 1682 *Déclaration* explicitly stated that the King himself would fill any vacancies by choosing a successor from a list of three candidates submitted by the bar.[38] In order to appear on the list, a candidate had to have been an *avocat* or a member of the judiciary for at least ten years.[39] Finally, in order to solidify

---

and nomination process. Art. 20 prohibited a professor of law from simultaneously holding a position in private practice or in the judiciary. These features are still part of the modern process.

[35] *Ibid.*, art. 11.

[36] *Ibid.*

[37] See Bonnecase, *supra*, note 6, 63. The *professeur royal de droit français* received some compensation directly from his students; in order to receive his degree, a candidate for the *licence* had to obtain a testimonial letter from the professor of French law, for which letter he paid the professor a small fee. See Déclaration du 6 août 1682, *supra*, note 18, art. 13.

[38] *Supra*, note 18, art. 15.

[39] *Ibid.* One U.S. foreign law scholar (deVries, *supra*, note 3) has stated that the criterion of professional experience for the selection of the *professeur royal* represented a "recognition of the need for maintaining a close relationship between the academic world and that of the practitioners": *ibid.*, 73. It seems that this claim is somewhat exaggerated; it would be more accurate to interpret the requirement for practical experience as one con-

the place of French law in the law faculty curriculum, the Royal Administration proclaimed that all prospective *avocats* must take at least one course in French law during their three years of study.[40]

The reforms of the Sun King, however, were no more than a starting point in the development of a modern legal studies curriculum. During the eighteenth century, the attempt to revitalize legal education proved at times to be ineffective.[41] Roman civil law and canon law continued to dominate the curriculum; Latin was still the principal language of lectures and examinations; the former were poorly attended and the latter too easy to give legal education credibility.[42] In a word, prior to the French Revolution, it had become clear that, despite the integration of national French law into the law school curriculum and the revival of the system generally, the reforms of the late seventeenth century had failed to offset the decline of legal education. The *Facultés de droit* were content to see their task as the preparation of practitioners who, quite paradoxically, were trained in classical oratory, and, thanks to the force of blind tradition, received the major part of their substantive education in the precepts of Roman civil law and canon law.[43]

## IV. The revolutionary ideology: legal education as civic instruction

In the aftermath of the Revolution, many universities closed their doors.[44] A few years thereafter, the Republican Convention enacted legislation establishing the *Ecoles centrales* to replace the former system of higher education.[45] Since previous republican legislation had made the professions open to all without

---

ditioned by practical necessity. Since legal education until this time had been relegated to instruction in Roman civil law and canon law, only practitioners and judges, who had received their legal training through apprenticeships to members of the *Ordre des avocats* (the bar), were qualified to speak authoritatively on the state of French judicial doctrine. In any event, the requirement certainly did not establish a close affinity of a permanent duration between the academic world and that of the practitioners.

[40] *Ibid.*, art. 13.

[41] See Allemès, *supra*, note 7, 38.

[42] See Valeur, *Deux conceptions de l'enseignement juridique* (1928), 16.

[43] *Ibid.*

[44] See generally Bonnecase, *supra*, note 6, 72-80.

[45] By the provisions of the Décret de la Convention du 15 septembre 1793, the Republican Convention abolished not only the existing institutions of secondary education, but also "les collèges de plein exercice et les Facultés de théologie, de médecine, des arts et de droit". Although this decree was repealed on the following day, subsequent legislation — the Loi du 7 ventôse an III (25 février 1795) which was never applied and which was re-

regard to formal qualifications, and also had eliminated the bar,[46] law teaching apparently was of minor importance to the legislators.

Within the framework of the *Ecoles centrales*, one professor, who held the Chair of Legislation, was responsible for the entire curriculum of legal education in each school.[47] His mission, as described by a proponent of the new system, essentially consisted in imparting a sense of civic values to his students:

> [L]e cours de législation n'est point destiné à former de profonds jurisconsultes pas plus que des hommes consommés dans l'économie politique ou dans la science du gouvernement, ou dans celles de négociations, mais à donner aux jeunes gens les sains principes de la morale privée et publique, avec les développements nécessaires pour en faire des citoyens vertueux et éclairés sur leurs intérêts et sur ceux de leur pays... .[48]

In practice, the substance of the one course in legislation varied with the individual discretion of the professor who taught it. Some confined their attention to the provisions of revolutionary legislation; others lectured on the principles of natural law, or on a combined program of natural law and a special subject; still others taught a survey course in civil law. Although the professors apparently took their responsibilities seriously, the structure of the course did not allow for more than the most basic sort of teaching. With some striking exceptions, most lectures were poorly attended and the course itself gradually ceased to have any impact upon or importance in the educational process.[49]

Rather late in this period, the private efforts of a few legal scholars demonstrated unequivocally that legal education transcended its base purpose of training practitioners and instilling a rudi-

---

placed by the Loi du 3 brummaire an IV (25 octobre 1795) on the organization of public education — had the same effect. These statutes replaced the previous university system with the *Ecoles centrales*, the purpose of which was to provide teaching in the sciences, the arts, and letters. For the texts of these legislative documents, see Bonnecase, *ibid.*, 81-88.

[46] See Law of March 2, 1791 (freedom of access to all professions) and the Laws of September 11, 1790 and March 6-26, 1791 (suppression of the bar) in Allemès, *supra*, note 7, 37.

[47] See Bonnecase, *supra*, note 6, 88.

[48] Circulaire du ministre de l'Intérieur en date du 5e jour complémentaire de l'an VII aux professeurs de législation: *ibid.*, 89.

[49] *Ibid.*, 91-93. It should be noted that in addition to the creation of the Chair of Legislation at the *Ecoles centrales*, the revolutionary government had maintained a Chair of *Droit de la nature des gens* at the *Collège de France*, the only institution of the *Ancien régime* to find favor with the republican government. Although the occupant held a position of high prestige, he proffered little guidance for the renovation of legal studies. For a detailed discussion of this point, see Bonnecase, *ibid.*, 94-98.

mentary sense of moral and civic responsibility; it could constitute an authentic area of intellectual inquiry and fulfil the vital professional needs of society. These scholars founded the *Académie de législation* and the *Université de jurisprudence*, which began operating in 1802 and 1803 and offered a comprehensive program of law teaching.[50] The *Académie*, for example, had twelve chairs of law. It offered courses in a wide variety of legal topics, from private French law through natural and international law and Roman law to a course in logic, morality and eloquence; its curriculum even included a course in medical-legal problems. In fact, this curriculum contained the basic elements of what French legal education was to become in the twentieth century.[51] However, these imaginative innovations remained the private offspring of a few men, and, as such, could not and did not have an important influence upon public legal education. Moreover, in historical terms, they came late — too close to the age of the Napoleonic reform of French legal education to be other than an isolated instance of truly exemplary law teaching.

### V. The Napoleonic Charter on legal education

Under Napoleon, the evolution of French legal education reached the second stage of its modern development — a critically decisive stage which was to leave a firm imprint on legal education, one characterized by an emphasis on practical pedagogy. The need for a bar and a judiciary and Napoleon's personal predilections made the newly reinstituted law schools a training ground for practitioners. The law of May 1, 1802, a document pertaining to public education generally, announced, *inter alia*, that the old law faculties would be re-established in the form of ten *Ecoles de droit*, each having no more than four professors.[52] The law of March 13, 1804 and the decree of September 21, 1804,[53] which related specifically

[50] The *Académie* benefited from better leadership and, as a consequence, offered a program of instruction in law which was quantitatively and qualitatively superior. The *Université* curriculum consisted only of six courses on basic legal subjects. Moreover, its faculty was reputed to be less gifted and conscientious than its counterpart at the *Académie*. For a detailed discussion of both institutions, see Bonnecase, *ibid.*, 95-98.

[51] *Ibid.*

[52] Loi du 11 floréal an X sur l'instruction publique, reprinted in Bonnecase, *ibid.*, 100-4.

[53] Loi de 22 ventôse an XII relative aux Ecoles de droit; Décret du 4e jour complémentaire an XII concernant l'organisation des Ecoles de droit: *ibid.*, 104-14. For a general discussion of this legislation, see Allemès, *supra*, note 7, 39.

to law teaching and which constituted the Napoleonic Charter on legal education, made the provisions of the 1802 law a reality.

Despite dissenting views appealing for a broad vision of legal education,[54] the spirit of utilitarianism dominated the 1804 legislative enactments, which ratified the view that the *Ecoles de droit* should function as professional "trade schools".[55] According to the Charter, education in the law schools would be restricted to the texts of the codes and the principles of private French law. The professors would teach private law by dictating their comments on the codal provisions to their students. Such courses as the philosophy of law, legal history, and natural law were not included in the curriculum.[56]

---

[54] See Bonnecase, *ibid.*, 115-22.

[55] Termed "écoles professionnelles" or "écoles spéciales": *ibid.*, 114.

[56] See Bonnecase, *ibid.*, 114-15, 123-25. In large measure, this system of legal instruction reflected Napoleon's personal views; he was averse to scholars and philosophers generally since they needed independence in order to function. Also, he believed that schools of higher education should respond to and perform a limited and well-defined task. This view was premised on his idea that all cultural learning should be completed at the secondary education level. The law of March 13, 1804 had given a limited place to the study of public law, and had defined the study of legal philosophy as the study of natural law and the rights of man, with legal history consisting of the study of Roman law in its relation to civil law. The implementing provisions of the decree of September 21, 1804 were even more restrictive — they further confined the place of public law and eliminated the study of legal philosophy and history entirely. The ordinance of March 24, 1819 represented a slight improvement; it created a number of chairs in the neglected areas of law. Many of its provisions, however, were either never implemented or implemented only half-heartedly. In fact, some were tacitly abrogated by the ordinance of September 6, 1822. See Bonnecase, *ibid.*, 126-27. See also Allemès, *supra*, note 7, 40.

The law curriculum at this time no longer included canon law; Roman law was taught only in its relation to French law. Major emphasis was placed on private French law as contained in the codes. The compulsory subjects in the law faculties were: French civil law, French public law, Criminal Law, Criminal Procedure, Civil Procedure, and Civil Law in relation to Public Administration. The entire process of legal education was dominated by the imperial spirit, and the insistence on a single professional mold was accentuated by the influence of codification on French legal scholarship. The codes were seen as definitive and immutable works; this attitude gave rise to a casuistic tendency to give the codal texts primacy over legal principles and fostered a belief in mechanical jurisprudence. Scholarship was further marked by the narrow professional spirit of the Napoleonic Charter. Rather than engage in a scientific inquiry into legal phenomena, scholars became preoccupied by the exegetical method, contriving semantic arguments on the basis of the codal provisions. Legal teaching and scholarship at this time and until the last decades of the nineteenth century confirmed

Opposition to the Napoleonic method of educating lawyers began as early as 1819. A number of scholars, taking exception to the idea that the simple memorization and the logical and grammatical analysis of the code provisions could produce educated lawyers, inveighed against its vocational orientation and its lack of a scientific base.[57] They insisted upon the need to foster a higher form of jurisprudential activity, opining that the fundamental purpose of legal education was to endow the students with a humanistic understanding of the law. In their view, this objective could be achieved only by incorporating courses in legal history and philosophy into the curriculum.[58] These criticisms laid the groundwork for a third stage in the evolution of French legal education, one with a historical personality that was less well-defined than the two previous stages, but which would give French legal education its modern character.

## VI. The movement toward a hybrid legal curriculum: social science and the law

In 1838, in response to the mounting dissatisfaction with the legal education process, de Salvandy, the then *ministre de l'Instruction publique*, appointed a committee on legal studies.[59] It recommended that the current curriculum be expanded by supplementing the exegetical commentary on private law with courses in public law, political economy, comparative legislation, and legal history and philosophy. The intention of the committee was to infuse law teaching with a comprehensive social scientific perspective which could account for legal phenomena accurately and give the law faculties an authentic university and academic status.[60] The political

a commonly held impression of the law, namely, that it was "un ensemble de règles arbitraires mises en oeuvre par un art de chicane": Valeur, *supra*, note 42, 17-21.

[57] *E.g.*, Athanase Jourdan, the founder of the journal *La Thémis* (1819); Lherbette in his book *Introduction à l'étude philosophique de droit* (1819); and Lerminier in his book *Introduction Générale à l'Histoire du Droit* (1829). All these scholars lamented the fact that the study of law had been reduced to a sort of vocational training; they unanimously called for a higher form of jurisprudential inquiry based upon philosophic and historical considerations. See Bonnecase, *supra*, note 6, 130-35.

[58] Klimrath was the principal advocate of the historical study of law. He promulgated his views in 1833 in his doctoral dissertation, stating that an incomplete and superficial education, based upon routine learning and rote memorization, constituted misguided science and could lead only to short-sighted ideas and narrow bias. See Bonnecase, *ibid.*, 135-37.

[59] *Ibid.*, 139.

[60] *Ibid.*, 140-41.

instability of the times, however, did not permit that objective to be realized.[61]

The next serious attempt to revamp legal studies in France came in 1872 upon the initiative of another *ministre de l'Instruction publique,* Jules Simon, who also appointed a committee to evaluate the substance and structure of legal education.[62] By comparison, the recommendations of this committee were much more modest, representing at best a perfunctory attempt to achieve fundamental reform. For example, to integrate a social scientific perspective into the current curriculum, the committee confined itself to proposing that two new courses be added to the *licence* program, namely, a course in political economy and a general introductory course to the study of law (which included a survey of natural law principles and legal history as well as a treatment of the organization of public institutions). These courses represented the only part of the de Salvandy committee recommendations that were retained by the Simon committee.[63] The Simon committee, however, appeared to be more sensitive to the new educational needs generated by the practical development of the legal system; in a more forceful way, it advocated that courses in criminal and administrative law be incorporated into the curriculum. In effect, these reforms relegated a social scientific inquiry into law to the doctoral research level.[64]

Accordingly, during the first three-quarters of the nineteenth century, the spirit of the law of March 13, 1804 (emphasizing private law, the code provisions, and practical training) dominated the process of French legal education. In the last two decades of the century, however, the criticisms voiced throughout the century began to have their effect: the narrow professional mentality was beginning to erode and to give way to the social scientific vision of the legal education and law teaching.[65] In the closing years of

[61] *Ibid.,* 142-46.

[62] La Commission des études de Droit chargée de rechercher et de proposer les mesures propres à réorganiser l'enseignement du Droit en France: see *ibid.,* 150.

[63] *Ibid.,* 152.

[64] *Ibid.,* 152-53.

[65] The decree of December 28, 1878 rendered the teaching of political economy obligatory in all law faculties. It would be taught for three hours a week during the entire second year. The decree of December 31, 1879 re-established the Chair of Constitutional Law at the University of Paris law faculty. Only doctoral students, however, were permitted to take the course. The decree of December 28, 1880 introduced two new courses in the basic law curriculum: a course in the general history of French public and private law for first year students and a course in private international law for third year students. See Valeur, *supra,* note 42, 39-40.

the century, courses in political science and political economy became an integral part of the curriculum of the law faculties. The pedagogical *raison d'être* of the *Facultés de droit* gradually was being reassessed:[66] while not abdicating their responsibility as centres of professional learning, the law faculties also recognized their status as university institutions —"des établissements de haute culture intellectuelle et de recherche scientifique".[67]

## VII. French legal education during the first half of the twentieth century

At the beginning of the twentieth century, French legal education, while remaining faithful to certain traditional features of its past, had advanced considerably in its substantive curriculum. The most salient of the traditional characteristics that persisted into the modern era was the method of law teaching by way of the formal lecture.[68] The preference for this pedagogical method — allowing for little, if any, student participation — inhered in the nature of the French legal system and educational process. Despite the integration of French law into the law school curriculum to supplement the more academic subjects, case law in the French civil law system never occupied the central position that it has in common law countries.[69] At least in theory, *jurisprudence* is not recognized in the French system as on an equal footing with statutory

[66] The ministerial circular of January 12, 1889 stated:

"[L]a licence en droit, l'économie politique exceptée, semble avoir été surtout considérée comme une préparation professionnelle au barreau et à la magistrature. Là est sans doute une de ses fonctions essentielles: mais ce n'est pas la seule; il ne faut pas oublier que, parmi nos licenciés en droit, un très grand nombre ne se destinent ni à la magistrature ni au barreau, mais aux fonctions administratives et politiques et aux carrières commerciales et industrielles". Cited in Valeur, *supra*, note 42, 45.

[67] Duguit, *Le droit constitutionnel et la sociologie* (1889) 18 Revue internationale de l'Enseignement 484, cited in Valeur, *supra*, note 42, 23.

[68] For a detailed description of the French law teaching method, see Valeur, *supra*, note 42, ch. 4.

[69] Some French scholars, however, did attempt to introduce the study of case law as a supplement to the lecture course (based on a treatise). An effort was made in this direction by Professor Henri Capitant in his book *Les grands arrêts de la jurisprudence civile* which was published in 1927 and revised in 1934. This book was reviewed by Deák (1934-35) 9 Tul. L. Rev. 149 and by Wigmore, *The Case-Study System in Continental Law Schools* (1930-31) 25 Ill. L. Rev. 579. For a discussion of the case method in civil law countries, see Deák, *The Place of the "Case" in the Common and the Civil Law* (1933-34) 8 Tul. L. Rev. 337. The case method, however, still occupies a distinctly secondary position in French law teaching.

and customary law.[70] Moreover, since the principles of French law were codified in the early nineteenth century, the lecture format, already widely used to explain the precepts of Roman civil law and canon law, was tailor-made for the elucidation of the theoretical implications of the general legal principles in the codal provisions.[71] The less adversarial character of the legal system and the diversity of the career orientation of the law students also favored the continued use of the lecture method. Finally, the expansion of the curriculum to include social scientific courses reinforced the use of the lecture method. Despite the consistency in teaching methodology, the substance of the curriculum and the purpose of law teaching had been altered: law was envisioned not only as a technical apparatus for the resolution of disputes, but as an historical entity with profound philosophic underpinnings interacting with social and political phenomena.

Following the example set by Louis XIV and Napoleon, legal education in France continued to be the responsibility of the State-controlled universities, with the government acting as ultimate arbiter in all matters and setting a uniform educational policy for all the law faculties.[72] Throughout the first half of the twentieth century, the course offerings at the *Facultés de droit* not only were uniform, but also remained fairly constant. In 1905, a government decree[73] provided that the three-year *licence* program would consist of the following set of courses:

| *First Year* | *Second Year* | *Third Year* |
|---|---|---|
| Roman Law | Civil Law | Civil Law |
| Civil Law | Criminal Law | Commercial Law |
| Political Economy | Administrative Law | Civil Procedure |
| General History of French Law | Political Economy | Private International Law |
| Constitutional Law* | One Elective* | Industrial Legislation |
| | | Two Electives |

* Indicates a one semester course, all other courses were two semesters long.

[70] See Szladits, *supra*, note 4, 188.

[71] deVries, *supra*, note 3, 78: "... French legal reasoning appears to start with a highly generalized proposition of law to which the facts are then fitted, rather than to begin with a detailed examination of the facts followed by application of a narrowly formulated rule".

[72] *Ibid.*, 73.

[73] Décret relatif à la licence en droit, J.O., 3 août 1905.

The entire three year curriculum consisted mainly of required courses. It achieved its diversity in the intertwining of basic law courses and social science courses. It required students to attend approximately fifteen hours of lectures per week and to sit for year-end examinations.

Subsequent legislation, enacted in 1922, modified the curriculum only slightly.[74] The law of October 30, 1940,[75] however, provided for more substantial change by requiring all law students to attend weekly sessions devoted to individual practical work on the subject matter of one of the lecture courses. Regular attendance at these *conférences et travaux pratiques* was a prerequisite to sitting for examinations, and the student's performance at these sessions was a factor in the faculty's total evaluation of his work.[76] The purpose of introducing this additional requirement was to bridge the gap between students and professors, between the virtual absence of student participation and a more individualized forum to cultivate opinions and views, and, finally, between theoretical analysis and its application to practical problems. Without question, it was a welcome addition to a system (however much enlightened it had become by the cross-breeding of the strictly legal and the social scientific) which had been impersonal, abstract, and overly theoretical.[77]

---

[74] Décret du 2 août 1922 modifiant le régime des études et des examens en vue de la licence en droit, J.O., 5 août 1922. The changes consisted in slightly modifying the title of the courses in constitutional law; eliminating the second year elective course and adding Roman Law to replace it; and substituting a course in fiscal legislation for the course in industrial legislation in the third year curriculum. For a critical account of French legal education around this time, see Bullington, *Legal Education in France* (1925-26) 4 Tex. L. Rev. 461. In addition to summarizing the workings of the system, the author decries the fact that too little attention is given to practical matters in the French law faculties and that the lectures are often boring and tedious: *ibid.*, 467-69.

[75] Loi du 30 octobre 1940 faisant obligation aux étudiants des facultés de droit d'assister aux conférences et travaux pratiques, J.O. 22 novembre 1940.

[76] *Ibid.*, art. 4.

[77] For a comparative account of continental and U.S. legal education at about this time, see Riesenfeld, *A Comparison of Continental and American Legal Education* (1937-38) 36 Mich. L. Rev. 31. Although the author focuses upon the German and the Italian processes, his study contains significant insights into the continental system as a whole. In particular he notes (at p. 47) that "[t]he aim of the university law school [in Europe] is not to give the most useful technical training, but to give the most complete and thorough picture of the basic ideas of the legal system and the difficulties of certain basic legal institutions and concepts, and above all to develop

The most significant re-evaluation of French legal studies during this period came in 1954, again in the form of a government decree.[78] The preamble of this document stated unequivocally that the time had come to realign the structure and organization of legal education to enable it to respond to changes in society, namely the growth of public law and social legislation, the surfacing of new economic theories, and the growing diversity of career options open to law faculty graduates. The reshaping of the curriculum was to be guided by the two-fold mission that had been entrusted to the *Facultés de droit*: to provide students with a general but solid social science background through a hybrid teaching of law and political economy, and to prepare them to engage in professional activity in their chosen career field.

To accomplish this objective, the Decree of March 27, 1954 lengthened the program of legal studies for the *licence* to four years, divided it into two cycles — a general and a specialized cycle — and placed a renewed emphasis upon the weekly *travaux pratiques*. The rationale behind the additional year of study was to provide students with a more complete education, thereby eliminating the previous practice of pursuing advanced studies at the doctoral level. The first cycle consisted of a general program of required courses; in the final two years, in addition to a limited common program, students would specialize in one of three sections — either private law or public law and political science or political economy — and would take the courses corresponding to their choice of specialty. Finally, during each year of the *licence* program, the students were required to take two one-and-a-half hour sessions of *travaux pratiques* each week and to write a final examination each year.[79] The 1954 law curriculum consisted of the following courses:

'legal grasp' ". He also maintains (at p. 52) that "[i]n Europe the whole attitude is more critical ... . Greater influence is exerted by theoretical, deductive considerations in dealing with legal problems, the effort to rationalize, to work out fundamental principles, to maintain harmony of the whole. ... Nobody on the continent would bother to raise for lengthy discussion each year the question about what the holding of Slade's case really was".

[78] Décret du 27 mars 1954, D.1954.141, modifying the program of study and examinations in law. The reforms were implemented under the provisions of Décret du 23 octobre 1954, D.1954.432.

[79] For a discussion of the 1954 reforms in French legal education, see Dainow, *Revision of Legal Education in France: A Four-Year Law Program* (1954-55) 7 J. Legal Ed. 495; Tunc, *New Developments in Legal Education in France* (1955) 4 Am. J. Comp. L. 419.

| FIRST CYCLE | |
|---|---|
| **First Year** | **Second Year** |
| Judicial Institutions & Civil Law<br>History of Institutions & Societal Facts<br>Political Economy<br>Constitutional Law & Political Institutions<br>International Institutions*<br>Financial Institutions* | Civil Law<br>History of Institutions & Societal Facts<br>Political Economy<br>Administrative Law<br>Labor Law*<br>Criminology & General Criminal Law* |
| **SECOND CYCLE** | |
| *All Sections:* Commercial Law & Social Security* | |
| **Third Year** | **Fourth Year** |
| *Private Law Section* | |
| Civil Law<br>Criminal Law*<br>Civil Procedure*<br>Criminal Procedure*<br>Roman Law & Old French Law* | Commercial Law<br>Civil Law<br>Private International Law*<br>Roman Law & Old French Law*<br>Elective Course(s) |
| *Public Law & Political Science Section* | |
| Political Science Methodology*<br>Advanced Public International Law*<br>Fiscal Science & Techniques*<br>History of Political Ideas*<br>Civil Procedure*<br>Criminal Procedure*<br>Fluctuations in Economic Activity* | Important Administrative Departments & National Enterprises<br>Colonial Law*<br>Public Liberties*<br>Private International Law*<br>Financial Economics*<br>Elective Course(s) |
| *Political Economics Section* | |
| Fluctuations in Economic Activity*<br>History of Economic Thought & Analysis of Contemporary Theories*<br>Statistics & Methods of Economic Observation*<br>Fiscal Science & Techniques*<br>History of Political Ideas* | Economic Systems & Structures<br>Economic Geography*<br>International Economic Relations*<br>Business Management & Accounting*<br>Financial Economics*<br>Elective Course(s) |
| * Indicates a one-semester course; all other courses are two semesters long. | |
| Course work in each year of the program is supplemented by three hours of *travaux pratiques* each week. While attendance at course lectures is optional, it is compulsory for the *travaux pratiques*. | |

The 1954 reform shows that the theory underlying the organization of the French legal studies curriculum had grown increasingly sophisticated. The *Facultés de droit* were capable of functioning both as *bona fide* academic institutions dispensing a broad education in law and as professional schools providing a substantial (albeit theoretical) preparation for business, government, and legal careers. State control over higher education, however, was to have a pernicious consequence. Although the centralization of educational policy in the national government provided for a nationally uniform curriculum and guaranteed the worth of national diplomas, it did not allow the regional universities to determine their own educational policies and prevented them from dealing effectively with their particular problems. Rigid government control also had the effect of supporting and maintaining a strict hierarchy of authority in which students and faculty had little or no place. The lack of autonomy from government supervision, combined with student alienation and mounting dissatisfaction, gave rise to a final episode in the modern development of the French legal studies curriculum.

## VIII. The present curriculum

Prior to the May 1968 student riots, the French national government had been the chief architect of French educational policy. In matters relating to higher education, for example, the Ministry of National Education not only set university budgetary requirements and the procedures governing the recruitment of professors, but also established the substance of the university curricula for degree programs. Opposition to this rigid hierarchical system manifested itself in violence, which gave rise to an almost immediate legislative response. On November 12, 1968, the French Parliament unanimously enacted a statute, entitled the *Loi d'orientation de l'enseignement supérieur*,[80] which provided for faculty and student participation in the administration and management of the universities. More importantly for purposes of the present analysis, the 1968 statute gave the universities some measure of autonomy vis-à-vis the national government in matters concerning the curriculum and pedagogical organization.

Under the provisions of the 1968 statute, the universities acquired the right to establish their teaching activities, their research pro-

[80] Loi no 68-978 du 12 novembre 1968, D.1968.317. For a detailed commentary on the consequences of the statute on the system of French higher education generally, see Carreau, *Toward "Student Power" in France?* (1969) 17 Am. J. Comp. L. 359.

grams, their pedagogical methods, their examination procedures, and the status of their teaching personnel.[81] Moreover, by granting the universities the benefit of a moral personality and financial autonomy[82] and by creating a network of elected university and regional advisory councils on educational matters,[83] the statute further reduced the previously all-encompassing authority of the Ministry of National Education, and in effect made university curricula the fruit of a partnership between the Ministry and the individual universities. While the national government retained the discretion to set mandatory requirements for conferring nationally-recognized degrees,[84] the universities were free to determine the distribution of these requirements and to supplement them with their own requirements and a broad range of electives.[85] The administrative restructuring of the system of French higher education — its "decentralization" — did not alter, however, the basic pattern of French legal studies: the basic degree course remains a four-year program consisting of two principal "cycles" or stages of study.[86]

The first two-year cycle essentially is a period of general orientation to the study of law; students achieve a limited concentration (or major) in an academic department only in the second year. Upon completing this first cycle, students are awarded a general studies degree, called the *Diplôme d'Etudes Universitaires Générales, mention Droit* (D.E.U.G.), which corresponds to an associate degree with specialization in law. During the second two-year cycle, students must concentrate in one of the departments providing instruction in law. For example, a senior law student may take the majority of his courses in the program designed by the departments of commercial law, political science, or economics. At the end of the third year, students receive a *licence en droit*, the equivalent of a B.A. in law; at the end of the fourth year, they are granted a *maîtrise en droit*, an M.A. in law, which, for all practical purposes, has become the basic French law degree. The weekly work load of French law students during each year of study normally amounts to twenty class hours, consisting approximately of fifteen hours of university lecture courses (*cours magistraux*), three hours

[81] *Ibid.*, art. 19.
[82] *Ibid.*, art. 3.
[83] *Ibid.*, arts. 8 and 9.
[84] *Ibid.*, art. 20.
[85] *Ibid.*, art. 19.
[86] See French Cultural Services, *Higher Education in France* (1977), 20-22.

of directed study classes (*travaux dirigés*), a one-hour introductory course to professional practices, and a weekly language seminar.[87]

Although the basic pattern of legal studies in France is unchanged, the sharing of power instituted by the 1968 statute in matters of curriculum policy has accentuated the already marked tendency of French universities to teach law in an interdisciplinary fashion. As with the 1954 legal studies curriculum, the interdisciplinary perspective is present at the initial stage of study and continues, despite the specialization, into the final years of the program. Although the Ministry of National Education still determines nearly half of the substantive content of the legal studies curriculum, even these core courses foster the interdisciplinary objective. The remainder of the curriculum consists of university and departmental requirements as well as electives and it is here that the impact of the decentralization of educational policy is most pronounced.[88] The French law student is confronted with a plethora of course packages and electives both within and without the area of chosen concentration. This allows the student to move from one social science perspective to another, from an initial introduction to a more advanced consideration, and provides for a well-rounded legal education with courses from allied or more remote academic disciplines. It also is worth noting that the required program includes courses in public or private international law as well as comparative law.

This brief description, of course, does not do justice to the originality of the legal studies curriculum in each of the French universities. This study will focus upon the program that is being administered at the University of Paris I (Panthéon-Sorbonne), a university long recognized as one of the most distinguished centers for the study of law in France. Although its legal studies curriculum probably is more exemplary than it is representative of the programs offered at other French universities, Paris I provides a forceful illustration of the educational and intellectual advantages that can be derived from the interdisciplinary study of law.[89]

At Paris I, five Teaching and Research Units (departments) provide instruction in law: the Departments of Public Administration

---

[87] *Ibid.*

[88] *Ibid.*, 20-21.

[89] For the description of the legal studies curriculum at the University of Paris I, the author has used a catalogue entitled *Université de Paris I Panthéon Sorbonne, Licence et Maîtrise en Droit* (1977-78), 9-18, 29-58. The tables presented in the text are summaries of the content of the booklet, but have been reorganized considerably.

and Domestic Public Law; Commercial Law; Development and International, European and Comparative Studies (Law Section); Political Science; and Labor and Social Studies. For both administrative and academic purposes, entering law students are required to select tentatively one Teaching and Research Unit as their major department. During the first two years of the program, the student's choice of a major area of academic concentration is of relatively minor importance and, in fact, can be changed from one year to the next; it does, however, become binding during the last two years of study when a final orientation in legal studies is chosen.

First year law students at Paris I are required to take three year-long university lecture courses, entitled Political Institutions and Constitutional Law, General Introduction to Civil Law, and Economics, and a one-semester departmental course. For those students who have registered as majors in the Department of Political Science, the departmental requirement is satisfied by taking Political Science: The Sociology of Politics; students in the other departments must take History of Law and of Institutions. The program of elective courses also is administered on a departmental basis. Students registered in the Departments of Public Administration and Domestic Public Law, Commercial Law, and Labor and Social Studies may satisfy their elective requirements by taking three of the following courses: International Relations; Political Science: The Sociology of Politics; The History of Political Doctrines — 19th and 20th Centuries; or Sociology and Social Psychology. Students in these departments, however, also have the possibility of fulfilling their three credit elective requirement by taking certain specified courses in other university departments. For example, they may take a purely historical elective component, consisting of Introduction to the Historical Sciences and Survey of Contemporary History, or the three-credit course General Philosophy and the History of Philosophy; or offerings in art, such as Introduction to the Art of Modern Times, Introduction to Contemporary Art, and Introduction to Cinematographic Studies; or business-related electives, namely, Statistics, Mathematics, and National Accounting. Students from the Department of Development and International, European and Comparative Studies and the Department of Political Science choose their electives from a similarly diverse list of courses, although the distribution of these electives caters more to the particular interests of these departments.

In addition to the foregoing program, first year law students at Paris I are required to take three hours of directed studies classes (the *travaux dirigés*) each week. These classes are intended to provide students with individual instruction on the subject matter covered in the basic curriculum. For example, all students must take the two directed studies classes in Political Institutions and Constitutional Law, and Introduction to Law and Civil Law. The choice of the third directed studies class again depends upon the student's major concentration. Students who are registered in the Departments of Public Administration and Domestic Public Law, Commercial Law, or Labor and Social Studies, may select between a directed studies class in Economics or History of Law and of Institutions, while students in the Department of Development and International, European and Comparative Studies and in the Department of Political Science may choose between Economics or, respectively, International Relations or Political Science as their third directed studies class.

By the second year of the D.E.U.G. program, law students at Paris I begin to work more closely within the framework of the program administered by their major department. Although the elective and inter-departmental offerings are reduced significantly during the second year, the curricula established by the individual departments, while promoting specialized study in a given social science discipline relating to the law, incorporate a sufficient diversity of courses to maintain a full-fledged interdisciplinary character. It is also during this final year of the D.E.U.G. program that law students at Paris I receive weekly instruction on the more practical aspects of professional life and work. The table below summarizes the basic second year course requirements in two of the five departments. While one program is more traditional in character than the other, they both reflect an unfailing commitment to the interdisciplinary study of law.

| | Department of Commercial Law | Department of Development and International, European and Comparative Studies |
|---|---|---|
| University Lectures: | Criminal Law<br>Civil Law II | Contemporary Economic Problems<br>Political Organizations<br>or<br>Criminal Law |
| Professional Practices: | Corporate Accounting | Organizations and Relations (International Orientation) |
| Directed Studies Class: | Commercial Law<br>Civil Law | Commercial Law<br>Administrative Law and Institutions |

The organization of the second year D.E.U.G. program around the departmental structure foreshadows the type of specialization law students engage in during the second cycle of the legal studies program. The candidates for the *licence* and the *maîtrise* have chosen a definite area of concentration; as a consequence, in their final two years of study, they are obliged to take the specialized program established by their major department. Specialization entails a drastic reduction in elective offerings and inter-departmental distribution requirements. These limitations, however, are counterbalanced by the interdisciplinary character of individual departmental programs. The table below provides a description of both the *licence* and the *maîtrise* curricula in the Department of Commercial Law and the Department of Development and International, European and Comparative Studies. It should be noted that the *maîtrise* program is divided into two semesters in which special concentration is achieved in the second semester in the form of a certificate program.

| LICENCE | | |
|---|---|---|
| | Department of Commercial Law | Department of Development and International, European and Comparative Studies |
| University Lectures | Labor Law<br>Civil Law<br>Suretyship<br>Family Law<br>Commercial Law<br>Negotiable Instruments<br>Bankruptcy<br>Public International Law I<br>Private International Law<br>Administrative Law I | Public International Law<br>Private International Law<br>Labor Law<br>Administrative Law I<br>Commercial Law<br>Major Legal Systems and<br>Anglo-American Law<br>or<br>German Law |
| Directed Studies Classes | Three from among:<br>Labor Law<br>Suretyships<br>Family Law<br>Negotiable Instruments<br>Bankruptcy | Three from among:<br>Public International Law<br>Private Internatonal Law<br>Major Legal Systems and<br>Anglo-American Law<br>or<br>German Law |

| | | |
|---|---|---|
| Electives | One from among:<br>The History of Business<br>Company Organization and Financial Management<br>Public Liberties<br>Criminal Procedure<br>Major Legal Systems<br>Insurance Law<br>Private Judicial Law | One from among:<br>Public Liberties<br>Economic Politics<br>Administrative Law II<br>Introduction to EEC Law<br>Civil Law<br>Suretyship<br>or<br>Family Law |
| **MAÎTRISE** | | |
| | Dept of Commercial Law | Dept of Development & Int'l, European & Comparative Studies |
| *First Semester*<br>University Lectures | Commercial Law<br>Taxation<br>Private International Law<br>Civil Family Law | International Commercial Law<br>Public International Economic Law<br>Private International Law |
| Directed Studies Classes | Commercial Law<br>Taxation | International Commercial Law<br>Public International Economic Law |
| Electives | (None) | Two from among:<br>The Sociology of International Relations<br>Foreign Administrative Institutions<br>Comparative Labor Law<br>Seminar in German Law |
| *Second Semester* | *Certificate in International Business Matters* | *Certificate in the Law of International Life* |
| University Lectures | International Commercial Law<br>European Commercial Law<br>European Organizations | European Organizations<br>European Commercial Law |
| Directed Studies Classes | International Commercial Law | European Organizations |

| | | |
|---|---|---|
| Electives | * | Two from among:<br>Oil Law<br>Middle East Oil Politics<br>Maritime Law<br>Computer Programming and International Relations<br>International Law of Development |
| | *Certificate in Domestic Business Matters* | *Certificate in Anglo-American Law* |
| University Lectures | Commercial Criminal Law<br>Banking & the Stock Market<br>European Commercial Law | U.S. Company Law<br>Contract Law in Common Law Countries and Private International Law<br>English Company Law<br>Seminar in Anglo-American Law |
| Directed Studies Classes | European Commercial Law | (none) |
| Electives | * | (none) |
| | *Certificate in Management* | *Certificate in European Institutions & Law* |
| University Lectures | Commercial Management<br>Financial Management<br>Banking & the Stock Market | EEC Institutional Law<br>European Commercial Law<br>EEC Economic Problems |
| Directed Studies Classes | Financial Management | EEC Institutional Law<br>European Commercial Law |
| Electives | * | One from among:<br>European Social Legislation (includes a directed studies class)<br>European Tax & Finance Law** |

* In addition to the certificate program, all students in the Department of Commercial Law must take two electives from among Remedies, History of Private Law, English Company Law, European Social Legislation, Insurance Law, Industrial Property, Management Supervision, and Special Criminal Law.

** The Department of Development and International, European and Comparative Studies also offers Certificates in African Law and Economics and Third World Studies. Considerations of space did not allow for a description of these two additional certificate programs.

When compared to the legal studies curriculum established by national government decree in 1954, the current program at the University of Paris I represents a considerable advance in the social scientific interdisciplinary methodology. While law students are nurtured in a particular departmental discipline, the initial phases of the program and the continuing diversity of both the required and elective curricula oblige them constantly to perceive the law as a multi-faceted phenomenon with political, economic, and social ramifications. The university, in its capacity as an academic institution whose fundamental mission (according to the language of the 1968 statute) is to provide for the elaboration and transmission of knowledge, the development of research and the training of men,[90] is concerned that students understand the law in its full dimension: its origins and interrelationships with society as well as its actual elements in a more narrow vocational and technical sense. The principal question emerging from this description of the evolution and present status of the legal studies curriculum in France is whether its theoretical promise and appeal can be transcribed — either wholly or in part — into the reality of the French legal education process. Do students emerge from the program of study with a firm intellectual understanding of the law? Does the program cater to their interests and needs or is it more a reflection of the academic proclivities of their professors? Is such a curriculum operable within the framework of the French university system?

## IX. The value of the French legal studies curriculum as a comparative model

In actual practice, the French legal studies curriculum suffers from a number of drawbacks which, although they do not undermine its status as a model of substantive legal instruction, call into serious question the pedagogical worth of some aspects of the French university system.[91] On the one hand, these flaws are endemic to any educational system which places so much importance upon strictly academic values and establishes so clear a demarcation between the world of ideas and the realm of existing fact. Rightly or wrongly, the French university appears to function prin-

[90] Loi du 12 novembre 1968, art. 1.

[91] In describing the characteristics and the operation of the French university system, the author has relied on his own experience at the University of Paris and the University of Tours. He wishes to express his gratitude to Professor John M. Kernochan, Professor William J. Bridge, Antoine N. Paszkiewicz, Esq., and Ms Marie-Annick Fédéli, a fourth year

cipally upon its own momentum. Academic inquiry becomes meaningful in itself; knowledge is prized exclusively for its own sake and perhaps at the expense of other human endeavors. Accordingly, despite statutory language and government policies proclaiming educational egalitarianism and the need to have the universities respond to the immediate needs of society, the French universities have held fast to an elitist tradition, envisioning themselves primarily as breeding grounds for academic vocations.

On the other hand, the deficiencies that attend the legal studies (or any other) curriculum within the setting of the French university system stem from the fact that higher education in France is "part of a nationally uniform system of free, secular, public education"[92] which is funded rather parsimoniously by the national government.

law student at the University of Paris, for their comments and observations on their experience in the French legal studies program. See also Hauser & Hauser, *The Study of Law in France: A Student's View* in Harvard Law School Bulletin, vol. 10, no. 4 (Feb. 1959).

[92] deVries, *supra*, note 3, 72. Because of its public character, tuition and fees at the French university are minimal, rarely exceeding more than $50 a year; room and board costs are subsidized heavily by the State. The "open admissions" policy was instituted in France primarily for political reasons, to assuage critics who assailed selectivity as elitist and undemocratic; it is not a policy which reflects a purely pedagogical design. Although the open admission policy admittedly equalized access to higher education, it also created a more subtle form of post-admission selectivity, engendering, for example, a 50% attrition rate during the initial years of professional studies. A few years ago, the then Minister of National Education, Joseph Fontanet, recognized that the open admission policy had particularly brutal consequences, essentially eliminating after a few years of study many of those students whose expectations had been raised unjustifiably and whose investment of their time and effort in a program of study for which they were unsuited and unprepared went to naught. Most of the teaching personnel do not have offices or secretarial support. Libraries lack sufficient space to accommodate students, library hours are inconvenient, and it is difficult to get books and almost impossible to take them out. A sense of participation in the life of an academic community or a willingness to engage in extracurricular activities are unknown in the majority of French universities. These general conditions of university life promote an attitude of indifference and cynicism, not only among students, but also among the teaching staff. While students focus their attention almost exclusively upon getting a passing grade on examinations, professors, who usually can rely upon the job security guaranteed by their status as civil servants, minimize their pedagogical roles and devote their time and energy to research or other personal pursuits. Finally, in direct contradiction to the open admissions policy, the French university system remains hierarchical and elitist in character, catering primarily to the needs and interests of a small minority of academically-inclined students who aspire to enter the teaching profession.

An alternative to this system in the form of private universities has yet to be proposed; in light of the commonly-held attitude in France that the government bears full responsibility for the educational needs of the country, it is unlikely to be forthcoming in the future. Admission to the French universities is open to any high school student who has obtained his *baccalauréat*. The exceedingly large numbers of students generated by this admissions policy, combined with inadequate government funding, leads to overcrowding and generally inadequate facilities for both students and professors, especially in the large metropolitan areas.[93]

As with other university programs, the university lecture courses in law may be attended by anywhere from five hundred to a thousand registered students. Professors deliver formal lectures, presenting a view of the law which is not only didactic, but also dogmatic in character. Clearly, the size of the courses discourages both formal and informal contacts between students and professors; the method of presentation prohibits any attempt to question the fundamental principles of the law, the memorization of which usually is the key to success in the final examination. Moreover, students often complain that the basic instruction is too erudite and theoretical to be of any value to them when they leave the university. For many French law professors, the lecture is an art form, the substance of which responds to a detached analytical imperative and is delivered in an elegant and impeccably articulated French. By his training and personal predilections, the French law professor avoids the practitioner's perspective; he weaves a web of theoretical abstractions that is destined to inspire those few members of his anonymous audience who aspire to follow in his footsteps.

The more individualized group instruction proffered by the directed studies classes was meant to remedy the impersonal and theoretical character of the lecture method of instruction. These weekly sessions were designed to provide students with an opportunity to apply the knowledge they acquired in lectures to existing legal problems. The actual operation of the directed studies classes, however, appears to deviate from this statement of purpose. In keeping with the training they have received and with the precedent set by the professors they wish to emulate, the graduate instructors, who conduct these sessions under the general supervision of a law professor, devote their teaching efforts to expounding upon funda-

[93] See Herzog, *supra*, note 2, 69.

mental legal principles rather than encouraging students to develop a critical perspective upon the law. Often, the analysis of the practical legal problem is relegated to a hurried treatment in the closing minutes of the sessions. Paradoxically, the professors, who have established themselves as educators, have the least amount of contact with students, while the graduate instructors, who have just begun to teach, have the most direct influence upon the students' education.

This brief summary of the deficiencies of the French university system does not compromise the substantive intĕgrity of the French legal studies curriculum or undercut its viability as a comparative model, especially in regard to a system which has the benefit of more adequate educational funding. The independence of the curriculum from external pressure exerted by the bar, its grouping together of a number of social science disciplines, and its provision for guided specialization in a given area during the final years of study are features which could provide an illuminating and profitable comparative perspective upon the more focused, vocational orientation of the North American law school curriculum. Needless to say, the substantive differences between the French and North American legal studies curricula are radical in character. One could argue that any extensive comparison between the two programs would be misleading and false, on the ground that the French legal studies curriculum finds its closest analogue in the North American undergraduate program, in which students are exposed to a diversified liberal arts perspective and choose a particular field of concentration in their final years of study. In the final analysis, the law program in French universities is an undergraduate course of study, established for students who lack any previous university training and fixed professional goals.

In contradistinction to the French curriculum, the program of courses in North American law schools represents graduate-level study designed to inculcate, in students with well-defined career ambitions, certain professional values and basic skills that are deemed requisite to the practice of law. In the majority of North American law schools, faculty time and institutional resources devoted to an interdisciplinary treatment of the law are frills around a basic core curriculum of traditional law courses. The study of law in North America is a serious practical business. In fact, some law professors feel obliged to engage in several years of actual law practice, in lieu of graduate legal study, before seeking academic positions. Moreover, in order not to disappoint student expectations, law professors focus the substance of their courses upon "real world" legal problems and disregard the more esoteric aspects of their subject matter.

All these differences, however, discount the fact that the French and North American legal studies curricula share a common pedagogical goal: to give students an understanding of the law. They merely represent different ways of achieving this same goal; each of them inevitably falls victim to the deficiencies of its particular methodology. The French system has attempted (albeit with minimal success) to introduce more practical instruction in its curriculum through the directed studies classes and the survey courses in professional practices. North American law schools have established distinguished reputations for training legal practitioners, although they have been under increasing pressure to do so more effectively and with greater sophistication. It is undeniable that a professional school with a vocational mission must give its students high quality, intensive training in the basic skills that are indispensable to the exercise of their future profession. Quite possibly, the most efficacious way of fulfilling that mission is to retain the traditional first year format, possibly supplementing it with a more elaborate clinical writing program. The North American system, however, appears to have been guilty of a lack of commitment in those areas where the French system has engaged in excesses. In the opinion of this writer, North American law schools have failed to maintain a sufficient autonomy from the practical demands of the bar and consequently have neglected to assert fully their academic character and establish a viable law teacher training component in their curricula.

Much ink has flowed over the question of what is to be done with the curriculum after law students have been through the rigors of the first year of law school. In recent years, there has been a growing trend favoring the complete elimination of the second and third years of study and the reintroduction of a form of apprenticeship program. Many of the proponents of this abbreviated legal studies program stress the strength of character and personality that can be gained from actual experience and maintain, with some accuracy, that senior law students who aspire to practice law are really only impatiently putting in their time after the first year of study. Such a position, however, unjustifiably belittles the academic status of law schools and even more unjustifiably discounts the fact that the law has an intellectual life of its own.

Proposals for the reformulation of the North American legal studies curriculum should take into account the fact that the law schools are university institutions which, although they have a strong commitment to professional endeavor, also have the responsibility of furthering the pursuit of knowledge and preserving intellectual traditions and of acting as the impartial and independent repositories of ideas. Any abridgement of the length of the current curriculum would work a considerable disservice not only upon the academic status of law schools but also upon the social standing of the legal profession itself. Although the present second and third year curricula are defective in many respects, the answer is not to eliminate them, but rather to refurbish them so that they can be made to provide students with greater stimulation. In this way, the advanced curriculum could satisfy the need for improved legal services and provide a means by which law schools could lay claim to an authentic academic and intellectual status as university institutions. It is precisely in this area that certain features of the French model — the history of its vacillation between practical and academic instruction, its adoption and continued use of an interdisciplinary social scientific approach, its emphasis upon academic values and the training of professors, and finally, its program of guided specialization in the concluding years of study — can be particularly instructive to institutions with more adequate financial resources and physical facilities to deploy its principal ideas.

This article seeks to advance the general idea that the quality of North American legal education could be enhanced considerably by transforming the second and third year curriculum into a three-tier system of areas of concentration, with a common first year program (closely akin to the current program at most law schools) assuring a basic uniformity of legal training. The first track of the advanced curriculum would be in keeping with the substance of the curriculum that is being offered presently; it would consist of basic core courses in corporate law, commercial law, evidence, conflicts of laws, a few required courses in legal history and philosophy, and a fairly elaborate clinical program in such subjects as trial advocacy and negotiations. The second track would represent a hybrid program, combining strictly legal courses with interdisciplinary offerings, and would act as an intermediary between the first and the third options. It would appeal to students who are interested primarily in practising law, but who also wish to spend some of their time in law school exploring the law from a less practical perspective. The third track would be designed for students who intend to become teachers of the law. Although they would take courses in a certain area of the substantive law, their time would be devoted primarily to an interdisciplinary consideration of the law, ultimately preparing them to engage in graduate legal study and professional research. The content of their program would focus upon philosophy, economics, political science, and sociology, as these disciplines relate to law.

Admittedly, the foregoing description only provides the skeletal structure of a potential program, the details of which would require more thought and extensive planning. Nonetheless, it is submitted that the general idea of a three-tier advanced curriculum, based upon the French model, could be of immense use and benefit to North American law schools. It would enable them not only to respond more effectively to a multiplicity of social needs and student expectations, but also (and more importantly) to give more breathing room to the intellectual side of the law. The institution of such a program would be the beginning of a response to Professor Auerbach's description of his short-lived experience in a North American legal education program:

> After so many years spent learning what to think it was a relief to be told that I was learning how to think. The experience was paradoxical: the more I learned how to think like a lawyer the less I wanted to become one. Legal education was designed to evade precisely those questions which, in my naiveté, I believed that lawyers should contemplate: Is it just? Is it fair? If not, how can law be utilized to make it so?[94]

---

[94] Auerbach, *Unequal Justice* (1976), ix.

# Part II
# Codification and Statutory Law

[6]

MICHIGAN LAW REVIEW

VOL. 38 APRIL, 1940 No. 6

# THE CODIFICATION OF THE FRENCH CUSTOMS

*John P. Dawson* *

A RENEWED attack on central problems of English legal history can gain fresh perspective from the history of French law. France and England entered the later middle ages with a common fund of legal and political institutions. Much of the area that was to be included in modern France was united with England under a common sovereign; political institutions were shaped by the same basic forces into similar forms of feudal organization; private law was largely composed of unformulated popular custom, remarkably similar even in detail. As early as the thirteenth century the tendencies toward divergence, both in law and government, had made themselves apparent. But we have even now no connected account of the processes by which this divergence occurred, or of the numerous parallels that persisted in later history. We know the main stages of political development by which in England a feudal monarchy was slowly transformed into a constitutional, parliamentary democracy and in France similar institutions had been molded by the eighteenth century into a centralized, bureaucratic state. As to private law, we know the methods by which the common law was constructed; and in France we know the end result, how six hundred years of continuous development were climaxed by the Napoleonic Code of 1804. The rest of the story must be filled in from scattered sources.

Only one chapter in this long narrative can be recounted here. The objective is to concentrate on one critical phase in a long development, the eighty years of the sixteenth century in which the customs of northern France were codified. The choice may be justified in part because the process of codification was itself inherently interesting, involving as it did the creation of some special legislative machinery, largely subject to popular control. More important is the light that may

* Professor of Law, University of Michigan Law School; B.A., J.D., Michigan; D.Phil., Oxford.—*Ed.*

be thrown on the condition and content of French private law at this intermediate stage in its history. Likewise important were the effects of the codifications, incomplete and unsystematic as they were, on the later development of French private law. Incidentally involved are some central questions as to the relations between the political sovereign and private law, questions with which English law has been much concerned at various stages of its history. And finally, in any study of sixteenth century developments, it is difficult to avoid some reference to events in Germany, where local custom proved inadequate in this critical period and was rapidly submerged in the "reception" of Roman law.

## THE CONDITION OF FRENCH PRIVATE LAW AT THE YEAR 1500

The condition of French customary law at the start of the sixteenth century suggests the reasons why codification was attempted. Approximately two-thirds of the area included in modern France was governed by rules which still rested largely in oral tradition.[1] Attempts had been made earlier to formulate the customs of particular districts, through private treatises that enjoyed a high authority and, more rarely, through official or semi-official codification.[2] Judicial experience in ap-

[1] The division between the *pays de coutumes* and the *pays de droit écrit* is familiar, and it is only with the districts governed by customary law that this article is concerned. The *pays de droit écrit* was a large and prosperous area, the northern limit of which included the district surrounding Bordeaux, and passed along the northern border of Périgord and Limousin, then north of Lyons, ending on the east in the region of Geneva. The survival of Roman law throughout this area hampered the growth of local customary law, and official codifications were less common. But the contrast between *pays de coutumes* and *pays de droit écrit* should not be exaggerated. There appeared in the *pays de droit écrit* some important legal institutions comparable to those of the *pays de coutumes*. Caillemer, "Les Idées Coutumières et la Renaissance du Droit Romain dans le Sud-Est de la France," ESSAYS IN LEGAL HISTORY, ed. Vinogradoff, 174 (1913). In some districts, particularly in the southwest, codifications appeared in the sixteenth century. Furthermore, the reception of Roman law in this area was selective, with a high degree of adaptation to local conditions, as is suggested in the interesting biography by OURLIAC, ETIENNE BERTRAND (1937). When one considers that Roman law had high persuasive authority even in the *pays de coutumes*, it appears that the difference between the two areas cannot be described as more than an important difference of degree. 2 CHÉNON, HISTOIRE GÉNÉRALE DU DROIT FRANÇAIS 331-334 (1929).

[2] Of private compilations, the most important were the Coutumes de Beauvaisis, by Phillipe de Beaumanoir (finished in 1283); the Etablissements de Saint Louis (about 1272); the coutumiers of Normandy (1194-1220 and 1254-1258); the coutumier of Berry (about 1312); and the custom of Brittany (1312-1325). 1 CHÉNON, HISTOIRE GÉNÉRALE DU DROIT FRANÇAIS 553-562 (1926).

Official or semi-official publications appeared in Anjou and Maine as early as 1246, and fragments of the custom of Vexin Français in 1235. There are records of publications in Anjou (1411); in Poitou (1417); and in Berry (1450). 1 BRISSAUD, COURS D'HISTOIRE GÉNÉRALE DU DROIT FRANÇAIS 362, note 2 (1904).

plying customary law had produced an increasing volume of "notorious and approved" customs, of which the courts in effect took judicial notice.[3] For purposes of litigation, however, it was still necessary in most instances to employ the procedure of local inquest, the *enquête par turbe,* in which inhabitants of the particular district would testify to their recollection of local practices. This reliance on lay testimony in the formulation of legal rules had not precluded the development of a professional class of trained lawyers, whose influence was steadily increasing. But in the absence of a system of judicial reporting, the expansion and doctrinal development of customary law could not proceed without some more permanent and reliable statement than local inquests supplied.

Confusion was increased by the divergences between customs in different districts and the growth of local variations. The Parlement of Paris and its provincial counterparts,[4] unlike the central courts in England, had not fused the great mass of customary rules into a unified "common law," whose supremacy over local custom was constantly extended. It is true that the main institutions of the *pays de coutumes* revealed a basic similarity, but in matters of detail there were numerous and important discrepancies. Even within particular districts local variations appeared, particularly in the northeast of France, where the codifications were to reveal a rich growth of highly localized customs.[5] Both as to general customs, extending throughout whole dis-

[3] PISSARD, LA CONNAISSANCE ET LA PREUVE DES COUTUMES 70-74 (1910); 1 CHÉNON, HISTOIRE GÉNÉRALE DU DROIT FRANÇAIS 493-494 (1926).

[4] The organization of provincial Parlements, modeled on the Parlement of Paris and exercising similar powers as appellate courts of last resort, had commenced with the Parlement of Normandy, whose independence dates from 1315 though the title of Parlement was not assumed until later. During the fifteenth century were organized the Parlements of Toulouse, Grenoble, Bordeaux, Dijon, and Provence. Between 1515 and 1775 eight other Parlements were organized, of which the most important was the Parlement of Brittany. 1 CHÉNON, HISTOIRE GÉNÉRALE DU DROIT FRANÇAIS 875-879 (1926); 2 ibid., 500-504 (1929). The Parlement of Paris retained, however, its predominant influence. If one excepts the provinces of Normandy and Brittany, each of which had its own Parlement, the jurisdiction of the Parlement of Paris can be described as almost coextensive with the limits of the *pays de coutumes,* extending to the south even into the *pays de droit écrit.*

[5] It has been estimated that at the end of the *Ancien Régime* there were 65 general customs and about 300 local customs. 2 CHÉNON, HISTOIRE GÉNÉRALE DU DROIT FRANÇAIS 322 (1929). Even these terms are relative. The customs of Normandy and Brittany had the widest geographical scope, and local variants were few and unimportant. To the northeast the customs were centered in the municipalities and the process of codification was enormously complicated by claims of local autonomy from numerous small communities. Between these two extremes there was a wide range of variation. It should not be forgotten that the process of codification itself drastically reduced the number of local customs, and that at the year 1500 the situation was far more confused than it was in 1789.

tricts, and local variants, uncertainty prevailed as to the territorial limits within which they applied. Such multiplicity and diversity were not necessarily fatal, as events later proved. But they greatly retarded the processes of adjustment to new social and economic conditions in a century of rapid and fundamental change.

If these processes of adjustment could not be accelerated, French law might readily have followed the same course as German customary law. Indeed, a contemporary observer, surveying the legal systems of France and Germany at about the year 1500, would have seen important differences but many striking similarities. In both areas the law consisted largely of custom, unformulated, vernacular, and localized to a high degree. The study of Roman law, continuous among educated classes since at least the thirteenth century, had supplied a background of ideas, which were used increasingly to interpret and supplement local customary rules. Both in France and in Germany a "reception" was in process. How far it would be carried would not depend on the will of a royal legislator nor on the degree of popular attachment to ancient legal institutions. The preservation of native elements in either country would depend on how well the legal system as a whole could be made to function in the expanding society of the sixteenth century.

The organization of the imperial *Kammergericht* in 1495 is usually taken to mark the beginning in Germany of the "reception" of Roman law. The importance of this event has frequently been exaggerated. The "reception" of Roman law in Germany was in fact an immensely complicated process, occupying more than a century, prepared for long in advance, more complete in some areas than in others. Dates are significant only as marking stages in a continuous development, whose main tendencies were revealed only in retrospect. It seems unlikely that political agencies or political motives played an active part, and a political authority as feeble as that of the emperor was scarcely equipped to undertake a fundamental reform of German private law.[6] If one could look to political leadership to initiate and conduct a "reception," there was available in France an instrument far more effective than the German *Kammergericht*. The *Grand Conseil*, a judicial branch of the

[6] The disintegration of political authority in Germany was reflected in the limited appellate jurisdiction of the imperial *Kammergericht*. The dilatoriness and ineffectiveness of its procedure provided further handicaps, as is pointed out by Stölzel in a book review, 47 KRITISCHE VIERTELJAHRSSCHRIFT FÜR GESETZGEBUNG UND RECHTSWISSENSCHAFT, pt. 2, p. 1 at 25-46 (1907). In German literature the conventional accounts of the reception attribute the influence of the *Kammergericht* very largely to the personal prestige of its membership, giving added impetus to forces that were already strongly at work.

Privy Council, was organized on a permanent basis in 1497, only two years after the organization of the *Kammergericht* in Germany.[7] With a developed procedure and extensive powers of appellate review,[8] the *Grand Conseil* was far better prepared than the German *Kammergericht* to assume leadership in the reform of private law.

Analogies between France and Germany can easily be pushed too far. In the first place, no evidence has been found in original or secondary sources that the French *Grand Conseil* conceived its mission to be the development or reform of private law. It remained primarily an instrument of royal policy, fully competent in private litigation but confining its functions to a general supervision of the administration of justice and the advancement of political objectives of the Crown.[9] The causes of this abstention of course lie deeper. The French monarchy had suceeded long before in establishing an efficient centralized court system, with trained personnel. A professional class of lawyers had had long experience in the analysis and application of French

[7] The separation from the *Curia Regis* of a definitely judicial branch, the Parlement of Paris, occurred in France toward the end of the thirteenth century. But the council around the king, as in England, retained judicial functions which it exercised occasionally through the fourteenth and fifteenth centuries. During the reign of Louis XI (1461-1483) there was a rapid development, though the records tell extraordinarily little of the process. After 1483 a series of continuous registers reveal that the judicial branch of the Privy Council had become a fully organized court of justice. 1 VALOIS, INVENTAIRE DES ARRETS DU CONSEIL D'ETAT (Règne de Henri IV), Introduction, xxvi-xxix (1886). Its position was finally consolidated by an edict of Charles VII in 1497, confirmed by his successor the following year. 21 ORDONNANCES DES ROIS DE FRANCE 4, 56. The edict of 1497 provided that the *Grand Conseil* should be a *cour souveraine*, with authority throughout the kingdom, that its presiding officer should be the chancellor, and that it should consist of 17 councillors, in addition to masters of requests.

[8] Access to the *Grand Conseil* was available either through ordinary appeal, the procedure on which the jurisdiction of the Parlements usually depended, or by way of *évocation*, an exceptional proceeding which involved an exercise of royal power to intervene in ordinary litigation. In either case it was clear that the jurisdiction of the lower court was completely superseded and the *Grand Conseil* was free to dispose of the case on the merits.

[9] Evidence in support of this conclusion cannot be given here. It rests in part on an examination of the register of the *Grand Conseil*, starting Dec. 21, 1497, and continuing through June 16, 1502. ARCHIVES NATIONALES, V[5] 1042. Abundant evidence to the same effect is found in the secondary sources of the sixteenth and seventeenth centuries. Supervision over the administration of justice was confined to cases of jurisdictional dispute between the various Parlements and claims of partiality (the so-called *récusations de juges*) which opened a wide avenue for intervention. In its later history the *Grand Conseil* was much concerned with the enforcement of the king's ecclesiastical policy and with disputes concerning royal finances. See further, 2 CHÉNON, HISTOIRE GÉNÉRALE DU DROIT FRANÇAIS 531-533 (1929).

Similar questions arise as to the functions and objectives of the new judicial branch of the Privy Council which emerged toward the end of the sixteenth century

customary law. Legal doctrine had become articulate, through published treatises and professional tradition.[10] A continuous development of French law through existing agencies was possible, if materials already available could be sifted and redefined. That desperate need for *doctrine*, for a rational and plausible explanation of concrete results, which played so large a part in Germany,[11] was not felt in the same degree. The French "reception" could be selective because the technical development of French customary law had already reached a higher level and was to be still further stimulated by the process of codification.

## THE ORGANIZATION OF MACHINERY

The impulse toward codification of the customs came in the first instance from the king. In a celebrated ordinance of 1454 Charles VII ordered that the customs, usages and rules of practice of every district in the kingdom were to be reduced to writing by the local inhabitants, brought before the king, and examined by his Council or by the Parlement with a view to publication.[12] The response was disappointing.

and which survived under the title of *Conseil Privé* till the end of the *Ancien Régime*, exercising most of the functions which had been assigned to the *Grand Conseil* a century earlier. A study of the original registers of the *Conseil Privé* for the first six months of 1601 (ARCHIVES NATIONALES, $V^6$ 1172-1173) confirms the evidence from secondary sources and indicates that the *Conseil Privé* did not undertake the active and systematic improvement of private law. The *Conseil Privé*, like the *Grand Conseil*, was a fully organized court with a permanent personnel, an elaborate procedure, and unquestioned power to supersede the ordinary courts. In spite of the range and variety of its activities, the *Conseil Privé* remained essentially a branch of the central executive.

[10] Even private and unofficial compilations of customary law could provide a bulwark against the tide of Roman doctrine, as is suggested by the history of Saxon law, whose independence can be traced very largely to the influence of a private treatise, the *Sachenspiegel*. SCHRÖDER-VON KÜNSBERG, LEHRBUCH DER DEUTSCHEN RECHTSGESCHICHTE 873 (1922). Similar compilations had appeared in France as early as the thirteenth century and continued to exert a widespread influence. Above, note 2.

[11] This is not the place to undertake an answer to the much debated question of the causes of the German "reception." In any movement of opinion on so extensive a scale the causes were necessarily complex. But there was surely significance, whether as symptom or as cause, in that insatiable public demand for crude popularized restatements of Roman doctrine, a major phenomenon of the sixteenth century. 1 STINTZING, GESCHICHTE DER DEUTSCHEN RECHTSWISSENSCHAFT 77-84 (1880). A similar need for more sophisticated doctrine must have played some part in the increasing resort to arbitration before Romanist doctors and in the consultations of the doctors by the lay judges of the popular courts. Ibid., 53-54.

[12] Ordonnance de Montils-les-Tours of April, 1453, art. 125. 9 RECUEIL GÉNÉRAL DES ANCIENNES LOIS FRANÇAISES 252-253 (1825): "ordonnons, et décernons, déclairons et statuons que les coustumes, usages et stiles de tous les pays de nostre royaume, soyent rédigez et mis en escrit, accordez par les coustumiers, praticiens et gens de chascun desdiz pays de nostre royaume, lesquelz coustumes, usages et stiles ainsi accordez seront mis et escritz en livres, lesquelz seront apportez par-devers nous, pour les faire veior et visiter par les gens de nostre grand conseil, ou de nostre parlement et par nous les décréter et conformer. . . ."

The only result was the official publication of the custom of Burgundy under the authority, not of the king, but of the Duke of Burgundy.[13]

The initiative was more vigorously assumed by Louis XI (1461-1483), the son of Charles VII. The *Memoirs of Phillipe de Commynes* reveal the king's interest in the project and suggest a much more ambitious plan to unify the divergent local customs into a single authoritative text.[14] A personal letter from the king discloses his plan for a systematic comparison of French customs with those of Italy,[15] and by letters patent in 1481 he instructed local officials to proceed at once with the preparation of texts, which were to be approved and authorized by the king.[16] This exhortation had as its only result the drafting of preliminary texts in four districts.[17] After the death of Louis XI similar pressure was exerted by his successor, with the result that meetings were held in at least ten districts for the purpose of drawing up

[13] 1 BRISSAUD, COURS D'HISTOIRE DU DROIT FRANÇAIS 363 (1904); 2 BOURDOT DE RICHEBOURG, NOUVEAU COUTUMIER GÉNÉRAL 1193 (1724) (hereafter cited simply as DE RICHEBOURG).

[14] 2 MÉMOIRES DE PHILLIPE DE COMMYNES, Mandrot ed., bk. 6, c. 5, p. 37 (1903): "Des à ceste heure là [i.e., after the battle of Guinegate in 1479] delibera de traicter paix avecques ce duc d'Autriche. . . . Aussi desiroit fort que en ce royaume l'on usast d'une coustume et d'ung poys et d'une mesure, et que toutes ces coustumes fussent mises en francoys en ung beau livre, pour éviter la cautelle et la pillerye des advocatz, qui est si grande en ce royaulme que en aultre elle n'est semblable. . . ."

That royal officials actively prosecuted the project is indicated by a financial record of 1480, which recites a payment to Pierre Chappon, *clerc*, for a voyage made for the purpose of transmitting the royal command to local officials throughout the kingdom, directing them to send copies of the local customs to the king "pour en faire une coustume nouvelle." Published by L. Delisle, 18 NOUVELLE REVUE HISTORIQUE DE DROIT FRANÇAIS ET ÉTRANGER 555 (1894).

[15] "Mons[r] du Bouchaige, vous savez bien le desir que j'ay de donner ordre aus coustumes, au fait de la justice et de la police du royaume. Et pour ce faire, il est besoing d'avoir la manière et les coustumes des autres pais. Je vous prie que vous envoiez querir devers vous le petit Fleurentin, pour savoir les coustumes de Fleurance et de Venize, et le faictes jurer de tenir la chose secrète, afin qu'il vous dye mieulx et qu'il le mette bien par escript." Letter of Aug. 5, 1481, in 9 LETTRES DE LOUIS XI, ed. Vaesen and Charavay, 59-60 (1905). I am indebted to M. Olivier Martin for calling my attention to this letter.

[16] Letters to the *baillis* of Vermandois and Sens, dated Aug. 18, 1481. 1 VARIN, ARCHIVES LÉGISLATIVES DE LA VILLE DE REIMS 651-652 (1890). I am indebted to M. Olivier Martin for this reference also.

[17] Meetings for this purpose were held in 1481 in Vermandois—1 VARIN, ARCHIVES LÉGISLATIVES DE LA VILLE DE REIMS 654 (1890); Troyes—3 DE RICHEBOURG 267; and Berry—KLIMRATH, ÉTUDES SUR LES COUTUMES 6 (1847). In Poitou there was apparently a text drawn up in this period, for Dumoulin refers to some customs of Poitou that had been printed in 1486. 4 DE RICHEBOURG 775, note a.

or revising preliminary texts.[18] None of these texts, however, was officially published. The work of codification was at a standstill.

The main obstacle was the inaction of the central government. It had clearly been contemplated by Louis XI that the texts should be reviewed by his own Council before publication.[19] Letters of Charles VIII in 1493 had merely provided that royal commissioners would collect them and carry them before the king.[20] In 1496 a commission of judges of the Parlement of Paris was appointed, to study the texts and report its opinion on any difficulties they might contain. Its report was then to be examined by a larger commission, presided over by the first president of the Parlement.[21] This machinery was soon found to be unworkable, chiefly because the members of the Parlement were fully engrossed with the ordinary judicial business of the court.[22]

Behind these problems of procedure there still lay undecided a fundamental problem of French public law. Where, in the last analysis, did the power reside to declare, and possibly to modify, the customs? Reliance on the local inquest for proof of customary law in ordinary litigation might suggest a principle of local autonomy. On the other hand, the king's power to amend or abrogate customary law had frequently been exercised in the late middle ages,[23] and in the customary

[18] Troyes in April, 1493-4—3 DE RICHEBOURG 267; Nivernais from June 23 to July 10, 1490—Boucomont, "Le Coustumier des Pays de Nivernoys et Donzioys," 21 NOUVELLE REVUE HISTORIQUE DE DROIT FRANÇAIS ET ÉTRANGER 770 at 770-771, 820 (1897); Chaumont in April, 1493-4—3 DE RICHEBOURG 371; Ponthieu in January, 1494-5—1 ibid., 81; Lorris-Montargis in 1493—3 ibid., 829, note; Sens in March, 1495-6—3 ibid., 484, note; Boulenois in 1493-4—1 ibid., 40; Melun in 1494-5—KLIMRATH, ÉTUDES SUR LES COUTUMES 7 (1847); Amiens—ibid.; and Clermont en Beauvaisis in 1496—Testaud, "La Coutume du Comté de Clermont-en-Beauvaisis," 27 NOUVELLE REVUE HISTORIQUE DE DROIT FRANÇAIS ET ÉTRANGER 250 ff. (1903).

[19] In the letters patent of Aug. 18, 1481 (cited above, note 16), the royal officials named in the letters were ordered to have the customs of their districts reduced to writing and sent before "the members of our *Grand Conseil*, wherever it may be."

[20] Letters of Jan. 28, 1493. 3 DE RICHEBOURG 267.

[21] The appointments were made on Jan. 19, 1495-6, according to the recital in letters of March 15, 1497-8. 4 DE RICHEBOURG 639.

[22] Letters of March 15, 1497-8, 4 DE RICHEBOURG 639: "If it were necessary to observe the said formality of communicating with one of the presidents and others of our judges, it would be very difficult to put an end to the task, in view of the great and continual burdens on our said court."

[23] The customs of Toulouse were drawn up by local officers and sent to the royal council in 1283. The council approved all but 20, placing in the margin opposite the rejected articles *non placet* or *deliberabimus*. LANGLOIS, LE RÈGNE DE PHILIPPE III, p. 292 (1887).

The *Olim*, reports of cases decided by the Parlement of Paris in the late thirteenth and early fourteenth centuries, contain several examples of customs abolished by the king's authority. 1 LES OLIM 530, no. 12; 1 ibid., 497, no. 19; 1 ibid., 562, nos. 12, 13; 1 ibid., 563, no. 14; 2 ibid., 163, no. 28.

regions of Belgium a similar power was reserved by the Holy Roman Emperor through the sixteenth and seventeenth centuries.[24] The decline of representative institutions in France had already invested the king with independent legislative authority, which was being exercised on a constantly wider scale.[25] In the early meetings of local assemblies in France there seems to have been serious uncertainty as to their relations with the central government. It is true that the preparation of preliminary texts was from the first entrusted to the population of each district.[26] But where dispute arose within a local assembly as to what the custom was,[27] or where a desire appeared to change an unjust or obsolete rule,[28] it was common for the estates to appeal to the king.

[24] In the Belgian publications it was usual to insert a clause reserving to the Emperor the right to "change, correct, modify, and reform, restrict and interpret the said customs and usages whenever this is found by us in our said Council to be expedient and necessary to do." 1 DE RICHEBOURG 366, 343, 276, 257, 254, 729, 952, etc. The same reservation was made by the Duke of Burgundy in the publication of the custom of Burgundy in 1570. 2 ibid., 1181. See also, 1 BRISSAUD, COURS D'HISTOIRE DU DROIT FRANÇAIS 364 (1904).

[25] 1 CHÉNON, HISTOIRE GÉNÉRALE DU DROIT FRANÇAIS 524-531 (1926); 2 ibid., 345-350 (1929).

[26] This procedure was clearly proposed by the ordinance of 1454 (above, note 12) and by the royal letters of Jan. 28, 1493-4 to the *bailli* of Troyes: "We order and direct you . . . that . . . after calling together our own attorneys and solicitors, clerks and other officers, and members of the clergy, nobles, bourgeois, and persons familiar with the customs, of good reputation and renown, in sufficient numbers, and after taking from them their solemn oath . . . you inquire and cause to be inquired well and diligently of and concerning the truth and effect of the said customs. . . ." 3 DE RICHEBOURG 267-268. Similarly in letters of March 15, 1497-8. 4 ibid. 638.

[27] At Chaumont in 1494 an article concerning appeals from manorial courts was disputed in the assembly and a note added: "let the King and his Council provide in this matter, as he shall think proper." 3 DE RICHEBOURG 378.

At Reims in 1507 an article on the seisin of executors was attacked by persons demanding its reformation, but the estates could not agree. A note at the end says: "And therefore, may it please the King our lord and his noble and prudent Council, to provide concerning this at his pleasure." 1 VARIN, ARCHIVES LÉGISLATIVES DE LA VILLE DE REIMS 681-682 (1890).

At Peronne in 1507 there were two articles referred to the disposition of the royal commissioners. 2 DE RICHEBOURG 599, 619. At Auxerre in 1506 a large number of disputed articles were "remitted to the members of the Court [i.e., the Parlement of Paris] and others having power to draw up, decree and determine the said customs." 3 ibid. 591.

[28] Especially in the meetings in Boulenois in 1495. For example, article 82, allowing subleases, was left with this suggestion: "It would be desirable and expedient, if this is the pleasure of the King, that our said lord decree, ordain, and provide that from now on in the future all leases and rents be created and acknowledged in the courts of the feudal lords." 1 DE RICHEBOURG 34. Article 95, under which some lords had been taking double rents from sublessees, was left with the comment: "And since this last usage has seemed to many experienced persons to be a right usurped by

Finally, in 1498, the important decision was reached that the customs should be published before local representative assemblies in each district, by vote of their membership. There is no evidence that this decision was dictated by a broad principle of local autonomy in matters of private law. Some such principle might perhaps have been formulated if local control had been directly challenged. It is impossible to say whether local particularism could have withstood a determined effort by the central administration to deprive local communities of effective influence. In fact, no such effort was made. The newly established *Grand Conseil*, to which the local assemblies had occasionally appealed, had directed its attention toward larger affairs of state. Even the judges of the Parlement who had been expressly commissioned by the king were too much occupied with the ordinary judicial business of the court.[29] The letters patent of 1498 in which the final decision was announced explain this important concession in terms of greater convenience in the preparation of texts and the high evidentiary value of testimony by local residents.[30]

The effect of this decision was not to eliminate the king's sanction entirely. An essential part in the machinery of publication was the group of royal commissioners, especially delegated by the king for the

superior authority . . . to provide for and remedy these matters, it is and would be expedient that the pleasure of the King be to decree and provide which of the above mentioned methods be followed . . . in order that it be done and practiced hereafter in accordance with the decree and order of our said lord." Similarly with article 98, concerning the feudal dues exacted of widows after the deaths of their husbands. 1 ibid., 35.

The same phenomenon appeared at Chaumont in 1494. 3 ibid., 376-377.

[29] See the royal letters of March 15, 1497-8, quoted above, note 22.

[30] Letters of March 15, 1497-8 (4 DE RICHEBOURG 638): "It would be a great circuity to communicate first with members of the said Court and then assemble the members of the three estates, to see what had been decided and in what matters difference and disagreement might thereafter arise, which would then have to be reported back to us; in view also of the fact that there is no more clear and evident proof of the custom than that which is made by the common agreement and consent of the said estates."

One could, perhaps, spell out of this recital the assumption that the vote of the local assemblies should be decisive except where "difference and disagreement" appeared, so that royal interference would in any event be narrowly restricted. On the whole it does seem unlikely that anyone at this stage seriously considered the unification or fundamental reform of customary law through royal legislation. On the other hand, the extent of local autonomy and the methods by which it should be maintained were still wholly undefined. In this state of confusion, expediency pointed toward an abdication in favor of the local assemblies. Expediency here can be taken to include a fundamental indifference of the central administration toward the issues raised by strictly private-law disputes, so long as the revenues or political authority of the Crown were not involved.

purpose of presiding over and directing the last stages of publication.[31] An indispensable formality was the final promulgation in the king's name in the presence of the three estates of the district.[32] As a result, then, of this ingenious compromise, a legislative instrument was created which enlisted royal authority for the authentication of the final text but which reserved to local assemblies the essential control over the legislative process.

Eight years later the formal publications began. The customs of Melun, Ponthieu, and Sens were officially published in 1506 by royal commissioners in the presence of local assemblies. The period from 1507 through 1510 was one of vigorous and fruitful activity. The customs of fourteen districts, mostly in the north central area, were reduced to writing and formally published. The culminating point was publication of the custom of Paris in 1510. During the next decade the movement shifted to the south and west, penetrating even into the *pays de droit écrit* with publications in the district surrounding Bordeaux. From 1521 through 1552 the work progressed more slowly, though the important customs of Nivernais, Berry, and Brittany were published in this period. Then, under the leadership of Christophe de Thou, first president of the Parlement of Paris, the campaign was vigorously resumed. At the death of de Thou in 1582 substantially all the customs of the *pays de coutumes* had been formally published.[33]

[31] From the outset in 1506 the actual work of publication was done by a group of two or three royal commissioners, who attended meetings of the local estates in each district. As late as Sept. 18, 1509 (3 DE RICHEBOURG 410-411) royal letters patent refer to a larger central commission with undefined powers of review, but there is no evidence that this commission participated actively at any time and after 1509 it wholly disappears.

[32] See, for example, the comment of Bourdot de Richebourg, in his note to the 1509 custom of Orléans: "la rédaction d'une Coutume étant considerée comme un cas Royal, le peuple ne pouvant en France se faire de Loix sans l'autorité du Roy." 3 DE RICHEBOURG 735.

After publication it was usual for the final text to be reported back to the Parlement for official registration, but Louët refers to a decision of the Parlement of Paris on Sept. 7, 1571, holding that even this formality was not essential, since the customs took effect from the moment of their publication before the local estates. LOUËT, RECEUIL D'AUCUNS NOTABLE ARRETS, ed. Brodeau, C, c. 20 (1650).

[33] The only important publications not completed at his death were the publication of the custom of Normandy in 1583 and the "reformation" the same year of the custom of Orléans, which had been first published in 1509. The reformation of the custom of Orléans, which was completed in 1583 on the basis of plans made by de Thou before his death, was to rank with the reformation of the custom of Paris (in 1580) in the range of its influence. It will be recalled that the reformed custom of Orléans later provided the basis for Pothier's great treatise on French private law.

During the seventeenth century a few scattered publications occurred, but the

More important, the machinery of publication had been employed for the revision and clarification of customs already published in the early years of the century. This last program of reform must be more fully described in a later section. Attention will be directed first to a problem of procedure which caused difficulty at the outset and might have threatened the success of the whole enterprise.

## THE TREATMENT OF DISPUTED ARTICLES

Even after the responsibility for declaring their own customs had been delegated to the inhabitants of each locality, there remained the danger of dispute within the local assemblies themselves. The solution first proposed for such cases was the reservation of disputed articles for later action by the king. The royal commissioners were also given discretion to fix the text by vote of "the larger and wiser part,"[84] but in the early publications this discretion was sparingly exercised and numerous articles were withheld from publication entirely.[85]

The inconvenience of this expedient was clear enough. Even if the disputed article should remain in the official text, as frequently hap-

customs involved were of minor importance. Bouhier in the eighteenth century listed the customs of four districts that had not as yet been published. 1 BOUHIER, LES COUTUMES DU DUCHÉ DE BOURGOGNE 173 (1742) (Observations sur la Coutume du Duché de Bourgogne, c. I, no. 4). The custom of one district was not promulgated until 1787. LEBRUN, LA COUTUME 76, note 1 (1932).

[84] Letters of March 15, 1496-7 (4 DE RICHEBOURG 639-640): "If any difference and disagreement arise, as to which the said estates cannot agree, the said difficulties, differences and disagreements shall be drawn up and put into writing together with the causes of their said differences, to be ordered and ended by us, the remainder of the said customs to be entirely published. . . . And nevertheless if on making the said publication certain difficulties arise concerning some articles of the said customs, we . . . have given and give you . . . power and authority to determine them with the consent in all cases of the said three estates in each *baillage*, *sénéchaussée* and jurisdiction, or of the larger and wiser part thereof." Similar provisions appear in the letters of Sept. 2, 1497 (3 ibid., 428) and regularly in the royal letters of the sixteenth century.

The phrase "maior et sanoir pars" was a canonist formula, important in the church's theory of collective action. 3 GIERKE, DAS DEUTSCHE GENOSSENSCHAFTSRECHT 324-327 (1881); Gierke, "Über die Geschichte des Majoritätsprinzips," ESSAYS IN LEGAL HISTORY, ed. Vinogradoff, 312 (1913).

[85] Four articles in Bourbonnais in 1500—3 DE RICHEBOURG 1207; general reservation of all articles on which there had been dispute at Ponthieu in 1506—1 ibid., 103; and Amiens—1 ibid., 137; three articles at Melun in 1506—3 ibid., 431-432; eight articles at Sens in 1506—3 ibid., 485-496; ten articles in Touraine in 1507—4 ibid., 634; three articles in Maine in 1508—4 ibid., 522-529; three articles at Meaux in 1509—3 ibid., 407-410; and three at Chaumont in 1509—3 ibid., 366, 367, 369. Dispute over the burden of proof as to the liability of land to rents and other burdens caused the reservation of articles on that subject in three places: Vitry, 3 ibid., 332; Troyes, 3 ibid., 261; and Chaumont, 3 ibid., 367.

pened, it could have no legal effect without further action by some outside agency. In the meantime the older mode of proof through local inquest was the only means of ascertaining the custom for purposes of litigation. In effect, all the advantages of codification would be lost if large sections of the customary texts were to be expressly excepted from publication.

As early as September, 1497, the royal letters began to specify that disputed questions should be referred, not to the king or his Council, but to the Parlement whose officers conducted the publication.[36] This solution of the difficulty proved to be ineffective. The press of judicial business prevented the Parlements from intervening on their own initiative to dispose of the questions reserved.[37] The burden of litigating such disputes was placed on interested parties, and it was rarely that self-interest was sufficiently strong for private individuals to initiate judicial proceedings and prosecute them through to final decree.

There are records of two cases in which the Parlement of Paris was induced through private litigation to exercise the powers reserved to it by royal commissioners. Of these the most celebrated was the dispute arising in the 1510 publication of the custom of Paris over the feudal dues claimed to be payable on the grant or repurchase of a rent charge. As a result of debates between the clergy and the representatives of Paris merchants, the commissioners had ordered provisionally that the articles requiring payment of such feudal dues should stand, with the privilege of appeal to the Parlement of Paris reserved to the Paris merchants. The essential functions of the rent charge in the credit system of the sixteenth century gave the dispute more than passing importance. For lawyers, engaged in an effort to reconstruct the theory and extend the usefulness of the *rente constituée*, the technical problems involved were vital. The appeal by the *Prévôt des Marchands* was not prosecuted before the Parlement until 1556. Decision was delayed by the *évocation* of the case by the king to his Privy Coun-

[36] The letters of March 15, 1497, had ordered a reference back "before us and the members of the *Grand Conseil* or such Commissioners as we shall appoint, to be by them decided and determined as they shall think fit." 4 DE RICHEBOURG 640. Reference back to the Parlement was substituted in the letters of Sept. 2, 1497—3 ibid., 428; March 4, 1505, 4 ibid., 640; and generally in the later publications. The exceptional resort to the Privy Council in the customs of Brittany and Normandy is referred to below, note 40.

[37] The only instance reported where the Parlement acted on its own initiative in reviewing the disputes within the local assemblies was in the custom of Berry (1539), where a number of questions were settled by formal decree. 3 DE RICHEBOURG 990-994.

cil. Finally, after the Privy Council had remitted the dispute to the Parlement for its decision, the court decreed on May 10, 1557, that the articles provisionally inserted should be struck out and three new articles substituted in their place.[38]

In spite of the results achieved in this and in one other instance,[39] it soon appeared that reference back to the Parlement had failed as a device for fixing the form of disputed rules. In most of the publications there was no other agency competent or, if competent, willing to intervene in matters of local private law.[40] The remaining alternative was to expand and perfect the functions of the local assemblies as legislative institutions. The expedients adopted for this purpose were chiefly two: (1) an increasing reliance on professional lawyers, and (2) a development of the principle of majority rule.

Lawyers had been prominent in the publications from the very first, not only in preparing preliminary texts[41] but in testifying as to

[38] The decree is reproduced in 3 DE RICHEBOURG 5, note a; JOUY, ARRESTS DE RÈGLEMENT 315 (1752); and FILHOL, LE PREMIER PRÉSIDENT CHRISTOFLE DE THOU ET LA RÉFORMATION DES COUTUMES 271-272 (1937). A full account of the legal and economic background is given by FILHOL, op. cit. 249-290.

[39] Another well-known case of the Parlement's intervention was the dispute in the publication at Blois in 1523, concerning the unusually large fine demanded by the land-owning classes for all mutations of tenants. The commissioners had ordered that the article incorporating this alleged privilege "shall remain as custom provisionally, without prejudice to the opposition of the members of the said third estate." 3 DE RICHEBOURG 1108. After an appeal by the third estate, in which Dumoulin appeared as counsel, the article was ordered stricken from the text and it was provided that the landlords at Blois prove their rights by whatever private documents they might have. 3 ibid., 1055, note c. There is a full discussion of the case in the commentary of Dumoulin on the Custom of Paris, art. 76 of the new custom, gl. 1, nos. 12-31. 1 DUMOULIN, OPERA 719 (1681).

A similar dispute between nobles and clergy, on the one hand, and third estate, on the other, arising in the custom of Vitry in 1509, became involved in litigation in 1612. The court ordered the parties to the particular case to secure a final decision of the controversy within one year, the article provisionally fixed to take effect in the meantime. De Richebourg asserts that no further steps were taken, so that the article remained in force. 3 DE RICHEBOURG 332, note.

[40] There was a reservation in favor of the Privy Council of the right to settle disputed articles in the 1539 publication of the custom of Brittany, 4 DE RICHEBOURG 333, and four articles were referred back accordingly, but apparently no further steps were taken. 4 ibid., 358. Quite exceptionally, the Privy Council intervened in the custom of Normandy (1583) to reject 15 articles as prejudicial to the rights of the king. 4 ibid., 127.

[41] As at Reims in 1481, 1 VARIN, ARCHIVES LÉGISLATIVES DE LA VILLE DE REIMS 652 (1890), and at Amiens in 1507, 1 DE RICHEBOURG 114. Evidence of similar activity by local lawyers appears abundantly in the later publications. See below, note 94.

the state of local law[42] and in influencing lay opinion.[43] In the later publications the assemblies themselves were composed predominantly of lawyers, appearing as authorized representatives of persons entitled to attend.[44] It was natural that the royal commissioners, in debates over rules that were often technical, should give great weight to the testimony of local lawyers, even against the protest of strong minority groups of laymen.[45] It seems hardly too much to say that the extraordinary efficiency of the later publications was chiefly due to the silent conquest by a professional class of the local popular assemblies. As time went on the reports of the debates become more meager; the methods by which agreement was reached are increasingly obscure. But the appearance of unanimity which the later publications frequently present may be traced to a body of professional opinion which filtered into the local assemblies through their altered personnel.

The principle of majority rule had been admitted to a limited extent from the outset. Even in the early publications the royal commissioners had been willing to overrule small minorities when the opinion of the great majority was clear.[46] At first this power was ex-

[42] Bourbonnais, 1493—3 DE RICHEBOURG 1208; Paris, 1506—Martin, "De L'Ancienne Coutume de Paris," 42 NOUVELLE REVUE HISTORIQUE DE DROIT FRANÇAIS ET ÉTRANGER 192 at 212, 216, 218, 219 (1918). At Troyes in 1494 they are seen testifying unanimously against certain nobles and clergy who sought to defend their manorial jurisdictions against royal encroachment. 3 DE RICHEBOURG 269. In Anjou in 1508 the diversity of views among the lawyers as to the form of an existing rule led the commissioners to withhold it from publication. 4 ibid., 593.

[43] For example, at Amiens in 1507 a large group of lawyers persuaded the majority that the old requirements of attendance by the vassal at the lord's court were "too rigorous." 1 DE RICHEBOURG 131.

[44] The *procès-verbaux* of the commissioners regularly include a full list of the persons attending the local assemblies. The lists in the later publications indicate a high percentage of lawyers appearing as *procureurs*, particularly on behalf of the nobles and clergy. In many instances lawyers are listed as appearing in their own right.

[45] For example, at Paris in 1510 "most of the clergy and nobility" claimed that tenants of land in the city owed the same fine for non-payment of rent as those outside the city. The "practiciens," however, swore that the exception in favor of the lands in the city (incorporated in article 62) was *coutume notoire* and it was accordingly allowed to remain. 3 DE RICHEBOURG 21-22. Two articles at Orléans in 1509 were settled over the opposition of the nobles when the "collèges des avocats, procureurs, et praticiens" came to the support of the clergy and third estate. 3 DE RICHEBOURG 769-770. Similarly at Vitry in 1509. 3 ibid., 334.

The reliance on the testimony of lawyers became very marked in the publications after 1520. For example in Bourbonnais (1521), articles 318, 319, 340, 342, 434, 479, and the chapter on *Batards et Aubains*; La Marche (1521), articles 62, 99, 123, 136, 175, 222, 230, 234, and 315; Blois (1523), articles 11, 20, 21, 33, 105, 109, 182, 183, and 258; and so on.

[46] In Touraine in 1507 the objection of one noble to article 1 of the chapter

ercised with the greatest caution, but before long the commissioners resorted to an expedient which preserved the rights of disaffected minorities and yet went far toward definitive formulation of a binding text. They began to adopt provisionally the rule for which a majority could be found, and reserve to those who objected the right to appeal to the Parlement.[47] The advantage of this device was obvious. It placed minorities in the position of appealing against a settled text, which in the meantime would be fully operative.[48] A second consequence of this procedure must have been to emphasize the legislative powers of the local assemblies, in fixing provisionally, by vote of a majority, which one of several competing rules should govern them in the future.[49]

## LEGISLATIVE REFORM BY THE LOCAL ASSEMBLIES

In the popular assemblies of the early fifteenth century, meeting perhaps for the first time to declare their customs, there appeared a strong feeling that certain rules of immemorial custom were unjust or inequitable. The slow evolution of French customary law had proceeded with little stimulus from direct legislation. The available agencies for conscious reform and adaptation could not keep pace with the social transformations of the fifteenth century. It was inevitable that a widening gap should appear between contemporary opinion and a body of customary rules which bore the deep imprint of their medieval origin. The difficulty came in finding a procedure by which such con-

"De Banc de Vin" and those of four or five nobles to article 2 of the chapter "Des Droits du Seigneur Chatellain" were overruled. 4 DE RICHEBOURG 632-633. At Sens in 1506, article 245 was allowed to remain against the opposition of an archbishop and a bishop. 3 ibid., 501, note f.

The power expressly conferred by the king to fix the text by vote of *la plus grande et saine partie* has already been referred to, above, note 34.

[47] In Anjou (1508), articles 40 and 222; Troyes (1509), article 74; Meaux (1509), article 39; Orléans (1509), articles 29, 36, 37, and 38. Similar dispositions of disputed articles in the customs of Paris (1510) and Blois (1523) have already been referred to, above, notes 38 and 39.

[48] Dumoulin, note to the *procès-verbal* of the custom of Paris (3 DE RICHEBOURG 26, note d): "Partant les articles accordez par la plus grand'-partie des Estats, et mis au Coustumier sont gardez pour coustume, nonobstant la litispendence de l'opposition et appel de la moindre partie. Et ainsi en usons."

[49] In later publications it was even admitted at times that the vote of two of the three estates could prevail over the other, as at Auxerre in 1561, where the nobles and clergy established a disputed article over the objection of the third estate. 3 DE RICHEBOURG 629. Compare the note of Dumoulin to the custom of Montfort (1556), where he attacked the clergy for not supporting a reform proposed by the third estate, "car deux Etats eussent fait la plus grande part et conséquemment la loy." 3 ibid., 153, note d.

victions, however widely held, could be translated into an effective program of legislative reform.

The first impulse of the local assemblies was to invoke the aid of the king.[50] No response to this appeal was immediately forthcoming. It was not until the machinery of publication was organized in 1498 that a sanction was by implication provided. When publication before local assemblies was ordered, the estates soon took advantage of their opportunity. As early as 1506 the estates at Paris went so far in their preliminary meetings as to recommend specific changes in existing custom.[51] In other districts the initiative was assumed in the same way by the local assemblies, and some of the changes so proposed were included in the published texts.[52]

These first steps must have been made easier by the fact that it was difficult to draw a sharp distinction between legislation in the sense of making new law and mere codification or publication of existing custom. As the effort to compile the customs in an orderly form revealed uncertainties and gaps in local tradition, these gaps could be filled without formal legislative action. Furthermore, even in areas as to which tradition had crystallized, the necessity for verbal formulation must have impelled a new precision of thought and given sharper contours to the experience expressed, often in colloquial language, by the early texts.

Nevertheless, the evidence of systematic innovation is not long in appearing. The *procès-verbaux* of the commissioners began to distinguish between "ancient custom" and custom that should be observed in the future. In one of the earliest publications, in 1506, proposed articles were rejected as "too rigorous and contrary to reason and equity."[53] In Touraine in 1507 a large number of articles underwent minor change and several were entirely recast.[54] Very soon these ex-

[50] Above, notes 27 and 28.

[51] M. Olivier Martin, "De L'Ancienne Coutume de Paris," 42 NOUVELLE REVUE HISTORIQUE DE DROIT FRANÇAIS ET ÉTRANGER 192 at 218, 220 (1918).

[52] Maine, art. 98, on the right of collateral relatives to the guardianship of minors, 4 DE RICHEBOURG 523; Chartres, article allowing representation by children of their deceased parents, 3 ibid., 731; Vitry, art. 2; Orléans, art. 1.

[53] Melun, arts. 38 and 39, on the feudal dues required from relatives after exercise of the *retrait lignager*. 3 DE RICHEBOURG 430. In the same publication three other changes from the preliminary text were voted by the local estates, though with no indication whether these changes constituted a departure from existing custom. 3 ibid., 430-431.

[54] 4 DE RICHEBOURG 631-637.

amples were imitated in other districts.[55] Almost without conscious claim and certainly without resistance from the agents of the king, the estates were establishing their right to legislate in the promulgation of their own customs. It is true that in 1510 and on two occasions in 1521, royal commissioners refused to publish new customary rules without express authorization from the king.[56] But in later publications the scruples of the commissioners were anticipated by an authorization in advance of any changes agreed upon at final publication.[57]

As early as 1508 the increasingly legislative powers of the local estates were thrown into relief by the commissioners themselves, in their attempts to persuade the estates to modify objectionable rules. One customary institution of which the commissioners were especially critical was the system of guardians for infant nobles. The right to guardianship belonged first to the parent of the infant, and then to his nearest adult relative. Its most undesirable feature was the incidental right to all the personalty of the infant, and to the revenue of his realty. Whatever justification there may have been in feudal society for this privilege, it seemed anomalous and unfair at the beginning of the sixteenth century. Both the *garde* of ascendants and the *bail* of collateral relatives were vigorously attacked by the commissioners as "contrary to reason and equity."[58] They succeeded in most places in wiping out the *bail* of collateral relatives entirely.[59] They attempted to persuade the estates that the *garde* of ascendants should be restricted to the infant's

[55] Examples are too numerous for exhaustive citation. See, for example, the customs of Anjou, 4 DE RICHEBOURG 591; Chaumont, 3 ibid., 366; Orléans, 3 ibid., 769; Troyes, 3 ibid., 260-262; Paris, 3 ibid., 20.

[56] In Auvergne in 1510 the new articles voted by the estates were remitted by the commissioners "to the pleasure of the King our said lord and of the said Court," and were subsequently confirmed by a decree of the Parlement of Paris on March 1, 1510-1511. 4 DE RICHEBOURG 1223, 1226. In LaMarche and Bourbonnais in 1521 the reservation was in favor of the king alone, and the result was the grant of royal letters expressly confirming all alterations and additions by the estates. 4 ibid., 1146; 3 ibid., 1303.

[57] In Nivernais, 1534, 3 DE RICHEBOURG 1165; Brittany, 1539, 4 ibid., 333; and generally in the later publications. But in the custom of Berry, which was an independent dukedom like Auvergne, LaMarche, and Bourbonnais, special letters were issued after the publications, ratifying the changes made. 3 ibid., 988.

[58] Maine, 1508, 4 DE RICHEBOURG 523. Similar arguments of the commissioners are reproduced in the *procès-verbaux* in Anjou (1508), art. 85; at Chaumont (1509), art. 11; Troyes (1509), arts. 15 and 16; Paris (1510), art. 99.

[59] Maine, art. 98; Chartres, art. 108; Dreux, art. 98; Anjou, art. 85; Vitry, art. 64; Troyes, arts. 15 and 16; Chaumont, art. 11; Meaux, art. 147; Orléans, art. 38, depriving collateral relatives of the right to profits; Paris, art. 99.

father and mother,[60] and usually obtained consent to a clause providing that the *garde* should cease on the guardian's remarriage.[61]

For the alteration of another common rule such promptings from the commissioners were unnecessary. This was the rule of intestate succession which denied to children the right to the intestate shares of their deceased parents, a rule which had appeared in medieval England[62] and which must be explained by the need in feudal society of an able bodied adult to perform the military services of the fief.[63] By the sixteenth century this explanation had been forgotten. The desire to alter the rule was stimulated by the fact that the legislation of the late Roman empire had admitted representation in the direct line of succession, and in one case in the collateral line.[64] In preliminary meetings the estates of at least one district had spontaneously declared their dislike of the rule.[65] It was allowed to pass as accepted custom in the first publications,[66] but by 1508 the estates began to vote for its abolition. The right of representation was regularly introduced in successions in the direct line, and usually in the collateral line as well within limited degrees.[67]

The system of community property, established quite generally through northern France during the fourteenth century, commonly carried with it a right of survivorship. Though no desire appeared to attack the system of community property as a whole, an effort was consistently made to protect the children of the marriage in the event of remarriage by the surviving spouse.[68] Likewise in cases of testate

[60] This limitation was introduced in Maine, art. 98, at Chaumont, art. 104, at Troyes, art. 15, and Meaux, art. 147, but in other districts the right of guardianship was preserved to grandparents.

[61] For example, at Paris, 3 DE RICHEBOURG 22; CHARTRES, art. 104; Anjou, art. 85; Troyes, art. 16; Meaux, art. 152.

[62] 2 POLLOCK AND MAITLAND, HISTORY OF ENGLISH LAW, 2d ed., 283-286 (1911).

[63] 1 BRISSAUD, HISTOIRE DU DROIT PRIVÉ 600-601 (1904).

[64] Nov. 127, c. 1; Nov. 118, c. 3.

[65] At Chaumont in 1494—3 DE RICHEBOURG 376-377. At Chartres in 1508 (art. 93) the change had been made in the preliminary meeting and the commissioners simply overruled the objections of three nobles. 3 ibid., 731.

[66] Melun, art. 100; Sens, art. 72; Amiens, art. 37.

[67] Chartres, art. 93; Troyes, art. 92; Vitry, art. 66; Chaumont, art. 79; Meaux, art. 41; Paris, art. 133. In all of these, representation was introduced in the direct line, and in all except the customs of Meaux and Paris, in the collateral line as well, to include the children of a deceased brother.

[68] Anjou (1508), art. 283; Meaux (1509), art. 49; Chaumont (1509), art. 6; Vitry (1509), art. 74; Troyes (1509), art. 11; Paris (1510), arts. 116 and 131. In the four instances last referred to, the *procès-verbaux* of the commissioners recite

succession there was a strong tendency to extend the powers of the testamentary executor and free him from control by the heir.[69] Formalities required for the execution of wills were made more strict and the wide variations in different districts were reduced to something like a uniform style.[70] The system of *retrait lignager* and the right of primogeniture were somewhat modified, though here as elsewhere the object was not so much a basic revision of established institutions as the removal of injustice in some of their details.[71]

When the work of publication was resumed in the third decade of the sixteenth century, no basic change was introduced in the machinery of publication, but the significant step was taken of making a formal

at length the arguments by which they persuaded the estates to introduce the changes in question.

The effort to protect children of a first marriage against the effects of a parent's remarriage was also extended to the case of mutual gifts made inter vivos which included a similar right of survivorship in the event of the death of one spouse. Anjou, art. 321; Maine, art. 334; Chartres, art. 87; Dreux, art. 75; Vitry, art. 113; Troyes, art. 85; Meaux, art. 23; Paris, art. 155. Only at Troyes was there definite evidence that the changes were actively advocated by the commissioners.

[69] The testator's heir was quite commonly deprived of the privilege of administering the will and the executor given seisin for a year and a day. Anjou, art. 274; Maine, art. 291; Vitry, art. 105; Meaux, arts. 34 and 35. In many places new articles were introduced, increasing the amount of property to which the executor was entitled, and allowing him new powers of charging other property for the purpose of carrying out the testamentary intent. Maine, art. 291; Anjou, art. 274; Vitry, arts. 106 and 107; Meaux, art. 38; Chaumont, arts. 89, 90, and 91; Troyes, arts. 98, 99, and 100; Paris, art. 95.

[70] Vitry, art. 102; Troyes, art. 97; Paris, art. 96. In Maine (art. 292) the old requirements were somewhat stiffened, and at Chartres and Dreux new articles on the subject were added (arts. 90 and 80 respectively). At Troyes and Paris the *procès-verbaux* indicate that the commissioners took the initiative in urging such modifications.

[71] The *retrait lignager*, by which relatives of a transferor of "family" land were allowed to repurchase the land at the price paid by the transferee, had been so favorably treated in the custom of Paris that purchasers had been seriously prejudiced. In the preliminary meeting some restriction of this privilege was demanded, a large number of persons declaring that in its existing form "the said custom is not good and is not to be tolerated." Martin, "De L'Ancienne Coutume de Paris," 42 NOUVELLE REVUE HISTORIQUE DE DROIT FRANÇAIS ET ÉTRANGER 192 at 220 (1918). At final publication the recommended change was adopted (art. 181). On the other hand, the commissioners themselves persuaded the estates in other districts to protect relatives against secret transfers, of which actual notice might not be received until after the year's period of limitation had expired. Troyes, art. 145; Vitry, art. 126; Chaumont, art. 112.

The chief modification proposed by the commissioners in the rules as to primogeniture lay in the direction of enlarging the share of later-born children, where local customs showed undue preference for the first-born. Maine, arts. 238 and 239—4 DE RICHEBOURG 524; Anjou, arts. 226, 230—4 ibid., 592. In other places, however, the rights of the first-born were simply defined with greater precision, as at Troyes, art. 14.

record of innovations.[72] It became increasingly clear that this machinery was being employed for the deliberate change of customary law, both in its content and formal expression.

Then in the second half of the sixteenth century there appeared a new movement more obviously devoted to a program of legal reform. Customs that had already been published in the early part of the century were now to be republished by the same procedure, through vote of the local assemblies.[73] The period of the "reformations" begins with the custom of Sens, which had been first published in 1506.[74] A group of local lawyers conceived the plan of republishing the custom with the avowed purpose of reforming rules which they considered unjust.[75] After drawing up a new text they addressed themselves to the king and in the year 1555 secured the appointment as commissioners of Christopher de Thou, one of the presidents (later first president) of the Parlement of Paris, and two other judges.[76] The following year the same commissioners were ordered to publish four other customs not as yet published, and to republish two others whose *procès-verbaux* had

[72] At Bourbonnais in 1521 the royal commissioners explained to the local assembly how convenient it would be in future litigation to have a clear distinction between older custom and newly formulated rules. 3 DE RICHEBOURG 1287. In publications of 1521, 1534, and 1556 the commissioners required an oath of the estates that they would inform the commissioners which articles were new and which ones old. 4 ibid., 1137; 3 ibid., 1180; 2 ibid., 553. The *procès-verbaux* in the second half of the century come to consist almost exclusively of a careful record of innovations.

[73] A detailed account of this later stage has become unnecessary since the appearance of the admirable study by FILHOL, LE PREMIER PRÉSIDENT CHRISTOFLE DE THOU ET LA RÉFORMATION DES COUTUMES (1937) (hereafter cited as DE THOU). The material for the present article was collected some time before its appearance, but the general conclusions here suggested are very similar to his. The only important omission in Filhol's work is an account of the history and procedure of the publications before the advent of de Thou. An effort is made here to supply this omission and to state some conclusions of interest to American readers.

[74] The loss of the *procès-verbal* of the 1506 publication is the reason given in royal letters authorizing republication. 3 DE RICHEBOURG 530. This pretext was at least plausible, since the *procès-verbal* often contained important information concerning the procedure and circumstances of publication.

It should be added that there had been one prior instance in 1521 of a republication, in the custom of Bourbonnais, which had been published hastily and uncritically in 1500. The royal letters ordering republication had given two reasons—the omission of numerous customs from the official text and the failure of the commissioners to add the usual prohibition of attempts to prove customs inconsistent with the text. 3 ibid., 1283-1284.

[75] Their project is described by Jean Penon, one of the local lawyers who participated, in his subsequent edition of the custom of Sens, pp. 2b-3a (1556). I am indebted to M. Oliver Martin for this reference, which also appears in FILHOL, DE THOU, 41, note 4 (1937).

[76] Letters of Aug. 17, 1555. 3 DE RICHEBOURG 530.

been lost.[77] A recent reorganization of the Parlement of Paris had given de Thou leisure for the prosecution of the enterprise.[78] It was no doubt at his instigation that new letters patent were issued in 1558, authorizing the commissioners to reform not only the customs in which uncertainties remained after final publication, but also those containing "unjust and unreasonable" rules.[79]

The number of customs actually reformed by the commissioners was not great. The outbreak of the religious wars a few years later retarded their work. But the publications of all kinds in this period totalled fifteen,[80] and the wide experience they gave was incorporated in the crowning achievement of all, the reformation of the custom of Paris in 1580. Furthermore, the fruits of this crusade cannot be measured merely through the number of customs published. In every one of them may be found the marks of de Thou's well-conceived program of reform, which is testified to by one of his lawyer contemporaries.[81] The result of his labors was to consolidate the triumph through most of northern France of the legal doctrine emanating from the Parlement of Paris.

Many reforms of this period followed the lines that had been marked out in the earliest publications. The extension of the right of children to represent their parents in intestate succession was one of the declared objects of de Thou's campaign.[82] In the publications over which he presided this change was almost automatic.[83] The right of guardianship over infant nobles was restricted or else wiped out entirely.[84] Restrictions on the effect of survivorship between married

[77] Letters of Aug. 19, 1556. 2 DE RICHEBOURG 539.

[78] 2 PASQUIER, OEUVRES 186 (1723) (Letters, bk. 7, no. 10).

[79] Letters of Feb. 12, 1558. 2 DE RICHEBOURG 642.

[80] Within the jurisdiction of the Parlement of Paris there were seven republications: Sens (1555), Touraine (1559), Poitou (1559), Melun (1561), Amiens (1567), Paris (1580), and Orléans (1583); and eight new publications: Montfort (1556), Vermandois (1556), Mantes (1556) Étampes (1556), Dourdan (1556), Grand Perche (1558), Auxerre (1561), and Peronne (1567). In addition there was a republication in 1580 of the custom of Brittany, by other commissioners.

[81] 2 PASQUIER, OEUVRES 186 (1723).

[82] The refusal of representation was mentioned as the chief example of the "harsh, inequitable, and unreasonable" customs that were to be eliminated, in the royal letters of Feb. 12, 1558, with which the period of extensive reformation really opens. 2 DE RICHEBOURG 642. The extension of representation was described as a principal object of the reformations in Jean Penon's edition of the custom of Sens, p. 3a (1556), and in 2 PASQUIER, OEUVRES 186 (1723).

[83] This phase of the reformations is studied in detail by FILHOL, DE THOU 223-248 (1937).

[84] Collateral relatives were deprived of the right of guardianship at Sens, 3 DE

persons were commonly inserted for the protection of children of the marriage.[85] Uniform requirements for the formal execution of wills were introduced in most of the customs,[86] and the institutions of the *retrait lignager* and primogeniture were regulated in detail.[87]

Various other changes reflected the dominant professional opinion of the period. The widow's option to take either legal or contractual dower was usually restricted.[88] The widespread antagonism toward the

RICHEBOURG 556, and Reims, art. 328. At Peronne (art. 225), collateral relatives were denied the right to the profits of non-noble land. At Amiens in 1567, however, the articles allowing collateral relatives to take guardianship and keep profits were allowed to stand (arts. 126 and 130). Grandparents were denied the right to guardianship at Valois, art. 72; Clermont, art. 173; Senlis, art. 152; and Noyon, 2 ibid., 576.

Forfeiture of guardianship on remarriage was provided for at Montargis—3 ibid., 868; Valois, art. 67; Senlis, art. 152; Sens, art. 156; Mante, art. 180; Reims, art. 332; Grand Perche, art. 168; Melun, art. 286; Peronne, art. 230.

At Chalons in 1556 (art. 10), guardianship was eliminated entirely.

[85] The right of the survivor to community movables was cut off entirely in the event there were children of the marriage or of any other, at Sens, art. 83, and Montfort, art. 133. In other places the less drastic step was taken of declaring the survivor's rights forfeited on remarriage: Chalons, art. 35; Reims, art. 293; Touraine, art. 319; Melun, art. 218.

In the analogous case of mutual gifts between married persons, clauses were added in some places making them entirely void where there were children alive: Sens, art. 122; Mante, art. 147; Montfort, art. 149; Laon, arts. 47 and 48; Ribemont, art. 48; Grand Perche, art. 94; Touraine, art. 243; Melun, art. 226; Auxerre, art. 222; Amiens, art. 106.

[86] Clermont, art. 140, and Valois, art. 170 (slight variations); Sens, art. 69; Mante, art. 153; Étampes, art. 107; Auxerre, art. 226; Montfort, art. 86; Dourdan, art. 104; Laon, art. 58; Chalons, art. 67; Reims, art. 289; Saint Quentin, art. 21; Grand Perche, art. 122; Touraine, art. 332; Melun, arts. 244 and 245; Amiens, art. 55; Peronne, art. 162; Paris, art. 289; Orléans, art. 289 (slight variation).

[87] The problem of priority between two or more relatives seeking to exercise the *retrait* was provided for in the customs of Grand Perche, art. 181; Noyon, art. 35; and Reims, art. 190. Formalities required for the exercise of the *retrait* were modified in favor of the relatives at Reims, art. 200. Attempts to defeat the rights of relatives through simulated or secret transactions were provided against at Orléans, art. 384; Melun, art. 130; Noyon, art. 34; and Paris, art. 132. At the same time some effort was made to prevent the *retrait* from interfering unduly with liberty of commerce, by requirements of prompt payment by relatives to ejected purchasers. Étampes, arts. 173 and 175; Chalons, art. 232; Melun, art. 153 and 155; Auxerre, arts. 183 and 184.

In most districts the rules of primogeniture were simply defined with greater precision, but the commissioners undertook to ensure more adequate provision for later-born children in those districts along the eastern border where privileges of the first-born seemed excessive. For example, Ribemont—2 DE RICHEBOURG 580; Saint Quentin, 2 ibid., 577; Amiens, 1 ibid., 312.

[88] Senlis, art. 185; Valois, art. 107; Laon, arts. 34 and 35; Saint Quentin—2 DE RICHEBOURG 579; Auxerre, art. 213; Melun, art. 238; Peronne, art. 142.

fiscal privileges of the nobility showed itself in numerous changes, though no attempt was made to undermine the main sources of power of the feudal aristocracy.[89] The developing theories of the jurists were reflected in some important changes in the law of rents.[90]

The radicalism of these and many other reforms should not be exaggerated. It is clear that their objects were at once to liberalize and to unify the divergent details of the various customs. Though the influence of Roman law can be traced at certain points,[91] the result of the later publications was to preserve the essential principles of customary law through organization and perfection in detail. The fact that the primary responsibility was entrusted to local assemblies made it certain that reform when it came would be moderate in scope and sympathetic in spirit.

## THE POWERS OF THE ROYAL COMMISSIONERS

The most remarkable fact in all the publications was the self-restraint of the royal commissioners. In the period ending in 1510 the burden of directing the publications fell largely on Thibault Baillet, president of the Parlement of Paris. On most of the questions debated before him he and his assistants were known to have strong opinions. The *procès-verbaux* reveal that these opinions were advanced freely and sometimes vigorously, with all the authority that the commissioners' position might lend. But they observed in good faith the king's instruction to publish the custom according to the vote in the local assemblies. There is no trace in the earlier period of a single rule incorporated in a final text against the will of a clear majority in the estates.[92]

[89] The observations of FILHOL, DE THOU 152-158 (1937), on this subject are excellent.

[90] An extended review of doctrinal developments, and their effects on the reformation of the customs, will be found in FILHOL, DE THOU 290 (1937).

[91] Though Roman law was frequently referred to as authority for the extension of representation in intestate succession, the chief instance of direct borrowing from Roman law is the introduction of the *légitime*, which provided a restriction on gifts by parents for the protection of the intestate shares of their children. See, for example, Noyon—2 DE RICHEBOURG 576; Laon, art. 51; Peronne, art. 111; Auxerre, art. 219.

[92] The debate in 1508 concerning article 454 of the custom of Maine is typical. This article provided a general exemption of minors from rules of prescription. The *procès-verbal* records the remonstrances of the commissioners, to which the estates replied "that such was the custom of the district . . . saying that the said article must be observed and followed." It accordingly remained. 4 DE RICHEBOURG 526. The same result was reached in both Maine and Anjou on another customary rule to which the commissioners objected—4 ibid., 527 and 595; at Vitry—3 ibid. 331; Troyes—3 ibid., 257; and Bourbonnais—3 ibid., 1291, 1292.

In the later period the work of the commissioners is shrouded in greater obscurity, as the *procès-verbaux* grew more brief. At the same time, evidence from contemporary sources indicates that their personal influence was in fact increasing.[93] While the preliminary texts were still prepared, as a rule, by local lawyers,[94] the commissioners assumed a broader control over the drafting of the final texts, after debate had revealed the wishes of the local assemblies.[95] To this control over

[93] CHOPPIN, COMMENTARY ON THE CUSTOM OF ANJOU (part 3, qu. 3, note 1) expressly declares that the recently reformed customs represented "the product of changes by the commissioners and laws pronounced by their decision, rather than ancient institutions of the districts."

Dumoulin, with his usual self-effacement, did not hesitate to charge Lizet, the chief commissioner at the publication in Berry (1539), with borrowing from Dumoulin's own writings: "Lizet took this from my writings and added it." 2 DUMOULIN, LES COUSTUMES GÉNÉRALES ET PARTICULIERES DE FRANCE 336 (1635) (Coustumes de Berry, tit. 12, "Prescriptions," art. 4). In another place, "This view of mine was imitated by Lizet at this point." Ibid., p. 333 (tit. 9, "Executions," art. 83). Again, "This is the inequitable addition of Pierre Lizet." Ibid., p. 319 (tit. 5, "Fiefs," art. 19).

Coquille in his commentary on the custom of Nivernois describes the commissioners in Berry (1539) and at Blois (1523) as the "authors" of those customs, and in general rates the customs as to their persuasive authority according to the reputations of the commissioners who presided over their publication. COQUILLE, LA COUSTUME DE NIVERNOIS 305, 324, 3-4 (1646).

[94] There is affirmative evidence to this effect in Brittany in 1539—4 DE RICHEBOURG 336; at Sens in 1555—3 ibid., 547; at Laon, Noyon, Saint Quentin, Ribemont and Coucy in 1556—2 ibid., 553; Étampes in 1556—3 ibid., 108; Grand Perche in 1558—3 ibid., 662; Melun in 1561—3 ibid., 466; Paris in 1580—3 ibid., 75; and at Orléans in 1583—3 ibid., 817. See further the summaries by FILHOL, DE THOU 291-298 (1937).

On the other hand, in Berry in 1539 the preliminary proceedings were directed by the royal commissioners and were quite exhaustive. 3 ibid., 974, 979. At Mante in 1556 the commissioners drew up a new text themselves at the request of the estates. 3 ibid. 201. In Burgundy in 1570, the preparation of a text was entrusted to judges of the Parlement of Burgundy, who showed the greatest freedom in adding to, modifying, and interpreting the existing custom. 1 BOUHIER, LES COUTUMES DU DUCHÉ DE BOURGOGNE 34-72 (1742) (Procès verbal des conférences). In Brittany the commissioners for the reformation of 1580 were also drawn from the provincial Parlement, and also deliberated separately before presenting a reformed text to the estates general. 4 DE RICHEBOURG 422. The same was true in Normandy, in the publication of 1583. 4 ibid., 111-113.

[95] In several districts the *procès-verbaux* expressly refer to a power conferred on the commissioners to alter the arrangement and improve the language of the articles agreed upon by the estates. Vermandois—2 DE RICHEBOURG 553; Amiens—1 ibid., 210; Brittany—4 ibid., 338; Grand Perche—3 ibid., 662. An incident at Peronne in 1567 suggests that the commissioners may occasionally have used this power to eliminate articles of which they disapproved, but which had passed their first reading in the assembly without opposition or debate. The article involved in this instance contained a provision in the law of rents, which was consistently eliminated in other publications

phraseology and arrangement may undoubtedly be attributed the marked improvements in draftsmanship that appear in the later publications. Furthermore, the prestige of their high office and their experience in directing debate must have given the commissioners increasing influence over the decisions of the assemblies on matters of substance. Representatives of the highest court in France and spokesmen for the most enlightened professional opinion of the period, they possessed a unique opportunity to impress their views on the legislative product. It seems unlikely that most of the changes made in the later publications could have been produced by spontaneous demand from within the local assemblies. The issues involved were frequently technical; the changes made were too numerous and too uniform to be explained in terms of deeply-rooted popular conviction. In effect, the local assemblies, under the skillful guidance of the commissioners, had become a passive but willing instrument in a program of moderate reform.

In the last analysis, however, there were limits to the influence that the commissioners could exert. Formal assent of the local assemblies was still required, even for changes that the commissioners themselves had suggested.[96] When a clear majority remained unconvinced by tactful argument and persuasion the commissioners were compelled to give way. It is remarkable that direct conflict between the commissioners and the local assemblies was so rare. But where such conflict could not be avoided, there was no longer any doubt that the will of the estates would prevail.[97]

and which quietly disappeared at Peronne between first and final reading. FILHOL, DE THOU 284-285 (1937). It may be inferred that the commissioners were responsible. How commonly such devices were resorted to it is impossible to say.

[96] Compare the protracted litigation over an article in the custom of Amiens, reformed in 1567. A considerable part of the membership of the local estates at Amiens appealed to the Parlement of Paris, attacking the procedure of the commissioners in various respects but emphasizing particularly the absence of any real consent by the estates to many of the changes made. The objections were finally overruled by the Parlement of Paris, de Thou himself presiding. The whole incident is described in detail by FILHOL, DE THOU 94-121 (1937), with the conclusion that in substance the appellants were attempting to assert that "une disposition coutumière nouvelle ne devait pas seulement avoir été consentie, mais qu'elle devait en outre être désirée." A distinction as subtle as this the Parlement felt itself free to reject.

[97] In the publication of the custom of Chalons, in 1556, delegates from the estates met with the royal commissioners and agreed on a new text, with the exception of two articles which the commissioners proposed to modify. The delegates reported back to the estates, which then instructed the delegates to insist upon the articles in their existing form. The commissioners capitulated. The incident is reported in the BULLETIN HISTORIQUE DU COMTÉ DES TRAVAUX HISTORIQUES ET SCIENTIFIQUES 139-143 (1887), and is discussed by FILHOL, DE THOU 84-86 (1937).

THE POPULAR ORIGIN OF THE CUSTOMS

From the whole process of publication there emerged a principle of public law which strangely contradicted the main conclusions of French political theory. During the sixteenth century, and still more in the seventeenth, the movement of French political thought was increasingly toward the recognition of royal absolutism. It was impelled in this direction by the irresistible growth of royal power, the steady development of a central bureaucracy, and the pressure of Roman law conceptions of political authority. Among the many currents of opinion that swept across this confused and turbulent age, one single stream pursued an independent and divergent course. The relations of royal power to the private law of the customs could be divorced in men's minds from the broader issues of policy which provided the main material for political debate. In the private law of the customs the expanding political authority of the king was restrained by a strict requirement of popular consent, expressed through representative institutions; the tendency toward centralization of political functions was reversed in favor of complete local autonomy.

Approval by local representative assemblies had been from the first an essential element in the process of codifying the customs. Royal sanction remained, it is true, an indispensable formality; the expert guidance and technical skill of the royal commissioners exerted increasing influence in fact; but the formal vote of local assemblies was the essential medium for translating the custom of the neighborhood into codified "law." The machinery of publication functioned throughout on this assumption. Royal letters at times made this assumption explicit.[98] There is no evidence that the king attempted personally to interfere with or control the free decision of local assemblies, but where such interference was suspected the assemblies did not hesitate to resist.[99]

[98] Letters of Sept. 18, 1555, addressed to local officers at Sens and directing the convocation of the estates for republication of the customs of Sens: "And since, as you know, this cannot and should not be done except in the presence of the three estates of the said *baillage*. . . ."

[99] The estates general in Brittany in 1539 showed themselves extremely suspicious of proposals for changing the customs, and demanded full time to examine the tentative draft submitted to them, since "by the said proposed text the ancient custom may have been somewhat changed, and this would be to alter their form and manner of living, which must not be done unless the members of the said three estates have seen the said text and have had adequate time to deliberate concerning it." After three days had been given them for the purpose, they demanded still a longer time, and it was only after assurances that "the King did not wish or intend to change their customs in any respect" that they were satisfied. 4 DE RICHEBOURG 337, 339.

The requirement of popular consent was enforced under unusual circumstances in the region of Calais. After the reconquest of Calais from the English in 1558, the mayor and chief burgesses of the city supplicated the king to authorize the adoption of the custom of Paris as the law of the district. The king, by letters of May 18, 1571, granted their request, but the Parlement of Paris refused to register his letters until the three estates of the whole district had been assembled, had heard the custom of Paris read aloud, and had agreed to adopt it. Ten years later this procedure was followed in detail, and the custom finally published in 1581.[100]

Theoretical implications were drawn in even broader terms by legal writers of the sixteenth century. Coquille, the author of an important commentary on the custom of Nivernais, expressed a view that was widely held when he derived the validity of customary law from the will of the people, expressed through their representatives in the local estates.[101] A well-known writer on Roman law relied on the popular origin of the French customs in denying the ruler any power of interpretation and assigning a monopoly of this function to organized courts of justice.[102] Even more extreme was the assertion sometimes made that royal legislation was wholly ineffective in areas regulated by customary law.[103]

[100] The incident is described in the royal letters of March 22, 1583, published in 1 DE RICHEBOURG 18-19.

[101] COQUILLE, QUESTIONS, RESPONSES, ET MEDITATIONS SUR LES COUTUMES, no. 1: "Le premier mouvement et vie de ce droit civil est en la volonté des états de provinces. Le roi, en autorisant et confirmant ces coutumes, y attribue la vie extérieurement, qui est la manutention et exercice de ce droict. . . . Les commissaires ordonnés par le roi pour presider ces assemblées d'états, les ont autorisées, en y inspirant la puissance de loi. Mais, en effect, c'est le peuple qui fait la loi." For similar expressions by sixteenth century lawyers, see FILHOL, DE THOU 68-71 (1937).

Such explanations of customary law were of course no novelty in continental thinking, which was deeply penetrated with the *consensus utentium* theories of Roman and canon law. The expressions by French writers of the sixteenth century seem, however, to be less influenced by these theories than by the immediate and familiar experience with the process of publication.

[102] CONNANUS, COMMENTARIORIUM IURIS CIVILIS, bk. 1, c. 11, p. 47 (1724), after discussing the power of interpretation conceded to the sovereign by Roman law texts: "These things are to be done before and by the prince, unless the law is of a kind that did not emanate from him or his predecessors and is not in his control, such as the laws of the regions of France that we call customs; these can and must be interpreted by the judges. . . . For it is not our practice to consult the king concerning all the private controversies that present difficulty, as the Romans formerly were accustomed to do. In these matters the authority of the Parlement and of all the judges is supreme, and from the judges the appeal is to the Parlement; from the Parlement no one can appeal, not even to the king."

[103] This is most vigorously asserted by Dumoulin in his note to the custom of

These main conclusions seem all the more striking when one contrasts developments in France with those in the customary lands of Belgium. In Belgian publications local assemblies were employed, as in France, for proof and even for modification of customary law, but their role was far more restricted and passive, and the sovereign retained far wider powers of interpretation and correction.[104]

On some of the matters for which the customs at first purported to provide, French political authority refused to accept the principle of popular control. The regulation of weights and measures, which the king was attempting to extend on a national scale, was thus eliminated from some of the texts.[105] Rules of judicial procedure were likewise considered inappropriate subjects for inclusion in the published texts,[106]

Maine, art. 447, concerning the period of limitation on actions for rescission of contracts. After stating that an ordinance of Louis XII, issued in 1512, was not intended to override a custom to the contrary, Dumoulin says: "The custom indeed was not only sanctioned thus in perpetuity by the three estates of the district, but it was enrolled at the Parlement of Paris, and from their authority the good king Louis XII could not, and did not wish or intend to derogate." 2 DUMOULIN, LES COUSTUMES GENERALES ET PARTICULIERES DE FRANCE 156 (1635). But notes of Brodeau, a seventeenth century writer, following this and a similar annotation by Dumoulin to the custom of Anjou, reveal that the royal ordinance in question was in fact in force in both districts. 4 DE RICHEBOURG 511-512, note h, 575, note d.

In his notes to other customs Dumoulin adopted wholly inconsistent positions, sometimes admitting and sometimes denying that royal ordinances were effective in abrogating customary rules. 3 ibid., 845, note e, 851, note b, 1239, note a; 1 ibid., 147, note a. That Dumoulin had some support in judicial decision for his denial of effect to royal ordinances is indicated by a decree of the Parlement of Paris reported in 1 BRILLON, DICTIONNAIRE DES ARRETS 565, no. 57 (1711): "On January 26, 1593, the Parlement meeting in the city of Tours, the First President de Harlay said that he had pronounced a decree on January 19, 1591, by which it was decided that when there is an ordinance contrary to the custom, the custom is to be followed; before that time the opinion of the bar had been to the contrary."

The nobility in the convocation of the Estates General at Blois in 1576 asserted the same principle as to the superiority of custom over royal legislation. FILHOL, DE THOU 76 (1937). That this principle proved impossible to maintain in the seventeenth century is indicated by the strong language of LOUËT, RECUEIL D'AUCUNS NOTABLES ARRESTS, ed. Brodeau, D, c. 25 (1650). The whole subject is discussed by LEBRUN, LA COUTUME 105-109 (1932).

[104] Hirschauer, "La Rédaction des Coutumes d'Artois," 42 NOUVELLE REVUE HISTORIQUE DE DROIT FRANÇAIS ET ÉTRANGER 43 at 63 (1918).

[105] Touraine in 1507—4 DE RICHEBOURG 701; Reims in 1556—2 ibid., 572.

[106] Touraine in 1507—4 DE RICHEBOURG 637; Paris in 1510—3 ibid., 25; Amiens in 1508—1 ibid., 219. The whole subject of judicial procedure was eventually regulated by the great ordinance of 1667, which applied throughout the kingdom.

and the same attitude occasionally appears as to the law of crimes.[107] In the early publications the texts were allowed to include rules for the limitation of actions in certain special cases, but such provisions disappeared when royal legislation had supplied the deficiency.[108] In the course of time these distinctions were drawn with increasing clearness, and the local assemblies left free to legislate only in matters that lay within the broad area of private substantive law.

With popular legislation thus restricted in scope, the central administration detected no threat to its supremacy. On the contrary, complete freedom of action for the local assemblies entailed some obvious advantages. For the primary and limited purpose of proving existing custom, local assemblies were by far the most efficient instrument. Even when the local estates undertook direct legislative reform, their many adjustments in detail brought private law into closer conformity with prevailing beliefs in the community. It seems unlikely that royal officials ever desired to secure more than this, or that they were greatly concerned over the methods by which the adjustments were accomplished. A comprehensive reform of private law involved enormous difficulties. So long as administrative functions or royal revenues were not affected, the central administration was strictly neutral on most of the issues involved in private law disputes. It should not be surprising that so wide an area was left for the activities of the local assemblies and that the principle of popular control was so readily conceded.

The popular origin of customary law was obscured in later history. The very process of codification, in which the theory of popular consent was most vigorously asserted, transformed the working materials of French law and gave a tremendous impetus to doctrinal elaboration. Through effective cooperation of courts and theoretical writers, French customary law was rapidly withdrawn from direct popular control and enmeshed in all the complications of an elaborate legal technique.

[107] In Touraine in 1507, six articles prescribing the penalties for certain crimes were rejected and it was ordered "that the penalties for delicts mentioned in the said article will be remitted to the discretion of the judges, to be decided by their consciences according to royal ordinances and written reason." 4 DE RICHEBOURG 701. The whole distinction between rules of private law, appropriate for inclusion in the texts of the customs, and rules of "police" or general administration, is further discussed by FILHOL, DE THOU 71-77 (1937).

[108] Such provisions appear in the customs of Paris in 1510 (art. 199), Meaux (art. 64), Troyes (arts. 200-201), and in Chaumont (art. 119), in several instances at the suggestion of the commissioners themselves. After the royal ordinance of 1510 on the subject, such articles disappear from the texts of the customs, except at Bourbonnais in 1521, where the commissioners refused to publish a provision covering the subject which had been inserted in the preliminary text. 3 DE RICHEBOURG 1288.

This is not the place to describe the methods by which French law was further developed during the rest of the *Ancien Regime*. It is enough to say that these processes of growth and refinement did not require direct participation by political agencies or political authority. To one familiar with English law it seems remarkable that French private law should have depended so little, throughout its history, on political authority as a source of innovation and reform. Though constitutional restraints on royal power were one by one abandoned, French private law remained essentially free from direct influence or control by the political sovereign. But this is another and a longer story.

## EFFECTS OF THE CODIFICATIONS

The profound effects of the codifications can be measured by reviewing briefly the condition of French private law at the year 1600. Before the end of the sixteenth century, substantially all the customs of the *pays de coutumes* had been codified. The customs of eight districts, including the custom of Paris, had been republished with important revisions and technical improvements. The local inquest as a method of proving custom had for practical purposes disappeared,[109] and in its place was substituted a formal text, carefully prepared, fully authenticated, and invested with the force of law. The mass of local customs had been sifted, their geographical scope determined, their relations to provincial customs defined. Though diversity and variation still remained, the resulting confusion was greatly reduced. French lawyers were at last supplied with material that responded to close analysis and systematic treatment.

The result was an outburst of creative energy that makes the French sixteenth century one of the decisive periods of legal history, comparable to the age of Bracton in England and the period of the

[109] The royal legislation through which the procedure of publication was organized clearly contemplated the total abolition of the *enquête par turbe*. Often the royal commissioners, in the final stages of publication, expressly prohibited proof of any customs deviating from the pubished texts and for a time these prohibitions were reinforced by formal decrees to the same effect by the Parlement of Paris. Before long, however, the older practice was re-established, and the *enquête par turbe* held admissible (1) where a new custom had developed since the publication of the text and (2) where the published text *omitted* an existing custom. On the whole, however, resort to the *enquête par turbe* was extremely rare after the customs were published and the official texts were assumed to be authoritative both in theoretical discussion and court decision. By royal ordinance of 1667 the *enquête par turbe* were finally abolished, the last vestigial remnant being the certificates of local practitioners that occasionally appeared in the eighteenth century. The whole subject is admirably discussed by PISSARD, LA CONNAISSANCE ET LA PREUVE DES COUTUMES 165-186 (1910).

classical jurists under the earlier Roman empire. Among the personalities that played an active part, the leading place was unanimously conceded to Charles Dumoulin, whose commentary on the custom of Paris was published in 1539.[110] His work was carried on and supplemented by Guy Coquille, commentator of the custom of Nivernais, René Chopin, Bertrand d'Argentré, and the group of humanist lawyers that were centered around the Parlement of Paris. Christopher de Thou, first president of the Parlement of Paris and the leader in the program of reformation of the customs, had intimate personal and professional relations with this group and impressed their views at many points on the texts of the reformed customs.[111] The decisions of the Parlement, which rapidly became a primary and authoritative source of new legal rules, likewise reflected to a remarkable extent the conclusions of Dumoulin and other contemporary writers.

The intense activity of the sixteenth century was followed by a period of assimilation and organization. Through the seventeenth and eighteenth centuries a doctrinal structure, increasingly elaborate, was built around the framework of the codified texts. As this process continued, the basic similarities of the customs became increasingly clear. Out of divergent details it became possible to construct a system of general ideas, a "common law" of the customs, which could not displace the codified texts but which could be used to supplement and interpret them. Though influenced at many points by concepts derived from Roman law, the "common law" of the customs was in the main composed of native elements. The model employed for this construction of legal theory was the custom of Paris, particularly after the reformation of 1580 to which the best legal intelligence of the capital had been devoted. A by-product of the codifications, the "common law" of the customs enabled a trained legal profession to continue the processes of reform and unification that the codifications began.[112]

The codification of the customs likewise had important effects in

[110] An adequate study of Dumoulin is much to be desired. Even in French the fullest account of his life and achievements is that of Brodeau, published in the 1681 edition of the collected works of Dumoulin. For Anglo-American readers, interest would chiefly lie in a comparison of Dumoulin with Coke, the only English lawyer with whom Dumoulin can be compared in the depth and pervasiveness of his influence.

[111] The relations between de Thou and Dumoulin are further discussed by FILHOL, DE THOU 38-39, 170-174, 178-180 (1937).

[112] See the interesting study by Professor Meynial, "Sur le Rôle Joué, etc.," 7 REVUE GÉNÉRALE DU DROIT, DE LA LÉGISLATION ET DE LA JURISPRUDENCE 326, 446 (1903). Concerned particularly with specific problems of the law of succession, this study contains some penetrating remarks of general application.

fixing the content of French private law and restricting the influence on the customs of lay practices and laymen's beliefs.[113] The processes of growth and adaptation were in effect entrusted to the conscious control of a professional class, whose methods and attitudes acquired decisive importance. A narrow and technical approach to the codified customs would have rendered them wholly inadequate to meet the needs of a developing society. It was fortunate that the customs were interpreted in a progressive spirit, by lawyers who were faithful to French tradition but whose minds were alive to the needs of their own time.

There was ample room for expansion. As codes of private law, the published texts were, to modern eyes, extremely incomplete. The 1510 custom of Paris, for example, comprised 199 articles; the reformed custom of 1580, only 362. Many of these were extremely brief, supplying the main outlines of a system of private law but refraining from specification in detail. In still another sense the customs were incomplete. The areas of law which they purported to regulate were essentially those which reflected the needs of a medieval society. They contained abundant provisions as to land tenure, including leaseholds and rents, a law of intestate succession, a family law that was primarily concerned with property rights of husband and wife, a law of gifts and testaments. As to other branches of private law, especially the field of contract, the customs were silent altogether. The "gaps" left to be filled by legal theory and court decision included large areas in which the needs of the future would be most strongly felt.

The codification of the customs did not by any means eliminate the influence of Roman law. The abbreviated language of the published texts was read against a broader background of general ideas, of which Roman law continued to supply important elements. The existence of this body of ideas was frequently suggested in the process of publication, when proposed articles were stricken from the texts and their contents left for regulation by general rules of law.[114] Such areas

[113] Compare note 109, supra, as to the limited operation of the *enquête par turbe* after publication of the official texts.

[114] Even in the early publications there were numerous articles withdrawn from the formal texts and "remis à droit." This occurred at Troyes in 1494 as to an article on the right of nobles to seize land to which the possessor could not prove his title—3 DE RICHEBOURG 276-277; in Touraine in 1507 (article defining the offenses which would lead to forfeiture of a fief and another article on the punishment to be administered to notaries for falsification of documents)—4 ibid., 637; in Anjou in 1508 (article on the right of the wife to claim lands descended to her during her marriage)—4 ibid., 595; at Orléans in 1509 (on the liability of the heir for debts)—3 ibid., 770; Troyes (on the right to take execution for rent due)—3 ibid., 261;

as the law of contract, which were entirely omitted from most of the texts, were constructed by courts and lawyers from Roman law materials. Nor was the infiltration of Roman law confined to the gaps left by imperfections and omissions in the published texts. The thinking of French lawyers was deeply penetrated by concepts, methods, and points of view derived from Roman law. The process of penetration had begun long before the sixteenth century; it continued through the period of the codifications; in the later period of technical elaboration the influence of Roman law was if anything increased.[115]

The conflict between national law and alien doctrine provides a leading theme for modern legal historians, particularly the historians of English and German law. Read in terms of such conflict, the legal history of the sixteenth century takes on added elements of drama and taps reserves of accumulated emotion.[116] Even for English and German

and Vitry (on the liability of the feudal lord for rents after confiscation of the fief)—3 ibid., 332.

Sometimes this "droit" appeared clearly as "droit romain," as at Mantes (1556), where provisions concerning the rights of tutors (art. 184) were "remis à la disposition du droit escrit." But it sometimes took the name of "droit commun," as at Dunois (1523), where the right of clergy to alienate church property was involved—3 ibid., 1115; at Melun in 1561, involving rules of prescription—3 ibid., 472; and Auxerre (1506), art. 146—3 ibid., 577.

In some places the reference to Roman law appeared in the official texts themselves, as in the 1506 custom of Sens, art. 260: "L'usage touchant les usucapions & prescriptions en autres choses consonne à la disposition du droit écrit: & partant n'y eschet poser aucune coustume." Similarly, custom of Amiens (1567), art. 139.

115 The whole subject of the relation of customary law and Roman law is admirably discussed in the monograph of MARTIN, LA COUTUME DE PARIS, TRAIT D'UNION ENTRE LE DROIT ROMAIN ET LES LÉGISLATIONS MODERNES (1925).

116 This deliberate heightening of dramatic effects may be seen best in the famous essay of Maitland, "English Law and the Renaissance," 1 SELECT ESSAYS IN ANGLO-AMERICAN LEGAL HISTORY 168 (1907). Maitland reveals his own bias when he says (p. 175): "We have all of us been nationalists of late. Cosmopolitanism can afford to await its turn." His argument may be attacked on several grounds. In spite of the caution with which his evidence is analyzed, Maitland may be charged with exaggerating greatly the "danger" of a reception in England in the sixteenth century. Furthermore, he apparently shares the conviction of German historians, so frequently expressed in German literature, that a large-scale reception of Roman law would necessarily be a "national tragedy." As to German law, it is easy to understand the modern German reaction against excessive Romanization. Perhaps an outsider may be permitted to suggest that the real "tragedy" of the German reception lay not so much in the triumph of more sophisticated legal ideas, but in the lack of selectivity, greatly aggravated by the sterile scholasticism to which the methods of the civilians degenerated. As to English law, it would seem that there might have been an enormous gain if the infection had spread across the Channel in the sixteenth century, as it did in the thirteenth century and again in the eighteenth.

Maitland's final explanation of the main course of English development gives a

law it would seem that this reading of history involves an intrusion of modern ideas, which at the time had scarcely begun to emerge. In French law it would certainly be a mistake to attribute the codification movement to a developed spirit of nationalism, reacting against the importation of foreign doctrine. It is true that the codifications gave new form and a new precision to French customary law at a critical stage of its history and thereby preserved its essential elements; it is probably true that the codifications were inspired by a conscious desire to organize and perfect the existing legal system and prevent disruption of existing social adjustments. But it would no doubt have surprised many persons if they had been told that this effort to restate and consolidate existing materials involved a conflict of systems or ideologies. It was everywhere assumed that French customary law had much to learn from the Roman law of the sixteenth century, with its large accretions of medieval and post-medieval experience. The resort to Roman law doctrines was throughout selective and discriminating. Where there were differences of opinion as to the permissible limits of direct borrowing, they related chiefly to matters of detail.[117] French lawyers in the end were successful in adapting to their practical needs the immense learning and complex technique that had been built around the Roman texts. This process of adaptation occurred concurrently with an effort to preserve and perfect a highly localized system of popular law. Their success in harmonizing these diverse elements suggests that a middle course was still open in the sixteenth century between the sweep-

large place to the formal instruction in English law conducted through the Inns of Court. But it should be pointed out that the continuity of French law was preserved without the benefit, till the latter part of the seventeenth century, of any organized instruction in "national" law. While it cannot be denied that "Taught law is tough law," one may doubt whether the Inns of Court provide the main clue to English insularity.

[117] For example, Coquille, in a celebrated passage, referred to a difference of opinion between Christopher de Thou and Pierre Lizet as to the extent to which Roman law should be used as a model in the publication of the customs. COQUILLE, LA COUSTUME DE NIVERNOIS 2 (1646). Lizet had preceded de Thou as first president of the Parlement of Paris and had presided over the publication of the custom of Berry in 1539. This difference of opinion is testified to in other sources, and it appears likely that it led to some differences in results both in judicial decision and in the provisions of the published texts. Indeed it has been urged that the program of publication conducted by de Thou was part of a general movement which was favorable to the development of a national system and which aimed at restricting the influence of Roman law. FILHOL, DE THOU 125-140 (1937). The evidence in support of this thesis, however, suggests at most a difference in emphasis and a dispute over matters of detail, rather than a radical and thoroughgoing conflict of ideas.

ing reception of Roman law that occurred in Germany and the exclusiveness and insularity of English law.

The codification of the French customs represents merely one stage in a continuous development. Like the more comprehensive codification accomplished under Napoleon, it left open many avenues for growth and change, as new pressures and new ethical standards emerged in French society. Like the Napoleonic codification, however, it altered radically the formal sources of private law and gave a new direction to basic tendencies. Coming at a critical point in French legal history, the codification of the customs marks the point at which French law clearly diverged from the other great legal systems of Europe, to pursue its own independent course. Though the texts were restricted in scope and in language often crude, the completion of the task was in itself a considerable achievement. At a later stage another and more sweeping reformulation was still to be necessary, in order to unify French law and adjust it to the needs of a modern society. But the codification of the customs prepared the way for the great codification of the early nineteenth century, both by preserving the main elements of the customary systems and by supplying a more tractable material for the skilled legal technicians of the intervening centuries. In this sense it may be said that the codification of the customs provided an essential bridge across the wide gulf between medieval and modern law.

# [7]

## COURTS AND CODES IN ENGLAND, FRANCE AND SOVIET RUSSIA

BERNARD RUDDEN*

Stanley Kowalski was a true civilian. For him life's difficulties were lightened because, as he frequently insisted, "In the State of Louisiana we have the Napoleonic Code."[1] Professor Lawson, on the other hand, is a true comparativist who has wisely observed that "it is not . . . at all necessarily the mark of Civil Law systems that they are or should be codified, or of Common Law systems that they are or should not. Nor is there any profound difference between codified and uncodified systems as such. Like nature, law knows no sharp divisions between species."[2]

It is the purpose of this paper to draw some comparisons of the role of the courts, the style of judgment, and the place of civil legislation in England, France and the RSFSR. The words "role" and "style" are meant to cover, not merely the constitutional position and verbal skills of the judges, but also their consciousness of their own function, and of the creative nature of their activity; and the extent to which this is made explicit by the tribunals themselves. For reasons of space, I shall focus largely on the higher courts and on questions of private law. Furthermore, the method will be to describe what appear to be the distinctive traits of English law and to show the differences; and to suggest that, in terms of the role and style of the courts, the English and French systems are the extremes, with that of Soviet Russia falling in between.

### THE INSTITUTIONAL STRUCTURE

Of the three countries, England's particular features are that there are no comprehensive codes and that the judges overtly make the law. Of course in some fields—those, for instance, of sale of goods or bills of exchange—there is virtual codification; but the basic topics of property and obligations are not to be found in the statute book. Indeed, on the part of the legislature, there is a pronounced aversion to deal with them. Thus the Law Reform (Frustrated Contracts) Act of 1943 begins, "When a contract . . . has become . . . frustrated" without attempting to define the notion; and section 1 of the Misrepresentation Act of 1967 begins by tin-

---

* Fellow of Oriel College, University of Oxford. B.A. 1956, M.A. 1960, University of Cambridge; Ph.D. 1965, University of Wales; Solicitor 1959.

1 Tennessee Williams, A Streetcar Named Desire, Act I, Scene 2.

2 F. H. Lawson, A Common Lawyer Looks at the Civil Law 52 (1953). What this paper owes to all of Lawson's work will be obvious, as is its debt to J. Dawson, The Oracles of the Law (1968).

kering about with basic rules which, in any rational Civil Code, would have been set out at the start. Furthermore, even in property, that area where English law—as Lawson has so brilliantly demonstrated[3]—is both the most conceptual and the most subject to enactments, the latter never attempt to define the basic notions, clear though they be.

English judges have, from time to time, denied that they make law and have spoken of it as if it were something there which could, with sufficient learning, assiduity, and insight, be descried and brought forth to the people. This view is no longer popular; and, even if it were, it would be true that the courts are a source of law whether they make it or find it. The best argument for this is simply the absence of any other source for those basic concepts mentioned above: on them there are no statutes; but there is law aplenty. The creative function of English courts is, of course, strengthened by the doctrine of precedent by which courts are bound as to the law by the decisions of superior tribunals with only the House of Lords being free to overrule itself.[4]

There is one further point about the English system which might be taken to be of merely procedural significance but has, in fact, a great effect on both substantive law and the role of the courts. In order to appeal to the House of Lords *leave* is needed;[5] the highest court deals with only 30-40 cases a year and so has time enough to devote to its law-making function. Thus it will not hesitate to consider facts, and inferences therefrom, at much greater length than its Continental counterparts; it will decide, for instance, what one word in a contract between two private parties means—a role that both the French and the USSR Supreme Courts would be loth to undertake. One perhaps unfortunate result of this is that many propositions of fact tend to become elevated into rules of law.

The French constitutional structure is quite different. Firstly, there is the great *Code Napoléon* whose task, in the words of Portalis, one of its draftsmen, was "to fix, in broad perspective, the general maxims of the law; to lay down principles rich in consequences, and not to descend into the details of questions which may arise on each topic."[6] Those details, he said, were to be dealt with by judge and jurist.

---

[3] F. H. Lawson, The Rational Strength of English Law (1951); F. H. Lawson, An Introduction to the Law of Property (1958).

[4] Statement of Lord Gardiner, L.C., [1966] 3 All E.R. 77.

[5] Administration of Justice (Appeals) Act 1934, 24 & 25 Geo. 5, c. 40, § 1; Administration of Justice Act 1969, ch. 58, Pt. II.

[6] Portalis, *Discours Préliminaire*, in 1 P. Fenet, Recueil Complet des travaux préparatoires du Code civil 464 *et seq.* (1830).

The courts, however, may not make law. This prohibition stems from the doctrine of separation of powers and finds formal expression in article 5 of the Code: "Judges are forbidden to decide the cases submitted to them by laying down general rules." (*Il est défendu aux juges de prononcer par voie de disposition générale et réglementaire sur les causes qui leur sont soumises.*) We shall consider later how far the Supreme Court—the *Cour de Cassation* —obeys this rule, but meanwhile it should be said that the tribunal never, of course, openly admits to flouting it, and that the majority of French jurists still hold the view that the court is not a source of law.[7]

It follows from the constitutional position of the French courts that there can be no formal doctrine of precedent. The *Cour de Cassation* is not bound by its own decisions and no lower court is strictly bound by those of a superior; indeed, a lower court to whom the *Cour de Cassation* has remitted a case on the grounds that the previous decision got the law wrong is not, the first time, bound by the Supreme Court's ruling.

The final preliminary point to be made is that, provided the motion alleges a misapplication or misunderstanding of law, no leave is needed to bring the case before the *Cour de Cassation.* The result is that that Court—sitting in six chambers—deals with, not 40, but over 4,000 cases a year. The effects of this pressure are manifold; they reinforce the French judges' natural inclination to terseness; they leave no time for a contemplation of past decisions or an analysis of policy choices; and they are one cause of the Supreme Court's resolute refusal to deal with issues of fact.

The Soviet system falls midway between these positions. As in France there are codes: Basic Principles enacted at the Federal level and then expanded into the Codes of the constituent Republics.[8] Further, as in France, there is no express or implied grant of law-making power to the courts. It is perfectly clear that a single decision or even a series thereof, does not formally bind other

[7] For the debate see F. Gény, Méthode d'interprétation et sources en droit privé positif Nos. 46 *et seq.* (2d ed. La. State L. Inst. transl. 1963); Waline, *Le pouvoir normatif de la jurisprudence*, in 2 La Technique et les principes de droit public: études en l'honneur de G. Scelle, 613 *et seq.* (1950); Maury, *Observations sur la jurisprudence en tant que source de droit* in 1 Le Droit Privé français au milieu du XXe siècle: études offertes à Georges Ripert 28-50 (1950); Esmein, *La jurisprudence et la loi* [1952] Rev. trim. dr. civ., 17 *et seq.*; Boulanger, Jurisprudence, [1950] Encyclopédie Dalloz, (Civil III) 17 *et seq.*; G. Ripert, Les forces créatrices du droit (1955).

[8] For our purposes the main statutes are: Basic Principles of Civil Legislation of the U.S.S.R., 1962; and the R.S.F.S.R. 1964 Grazh. Kod. (Civil Code). Translations may be found in Law in Eastern Europe (Leyden) No. 7, 1963, and No. 11, 1966.

courts in like cases; although a ruling on appeal or protest will bind the lower court in the particular instance.

The Soviet codes, however—especially those of the 1920's—were far from perfect, and the courts soon found themselves confronted with situations that cried out for judicial remedy but were not provided for by statute. Examples will be given later to show that the Supreme Court filled the gaps in the Code, that their decisions were then treated virtually as if part of the Code, and that they were later enacted as such with no discernible difference to their actual operation.

The Full Bench of the Supreme Courts of the USSR and RSFSR come nearer to the English system in two other ways. Firstly, unlike the *Cour de Cassation*, they are protected against a flood of appeals, since proceedings may be initiated before them only by superior officials of the judiciary or Procuracy and not by any private litigant. Secondly they are given power to issue "guiding explanations"—pronouncements based, not on the facts of one particular case, but from a survey of judicial practice in particular areas.[9] There is the usual dispute among jurists as to the normative effect of these utterances but the quasi-official authority of the journal *Soviet State and Law* asserts that "guiding explanations are normative by their general character and are law-creating."[10] Moreover—and more importantly—the Supreme Courts, whether or not they have normative power, *act as if they do*.

## Judicial Method

Torstein Eckhoff has pointed out that "[t]he characteristic features of judicial decision-making are to a considerable extent conditioned by the *professional training of judges*. Belonging to a profession makes for dependence in the sense that the person concerned is left to rely upon the body of theory and the ways of handling problems in which he is trained. Dependence on a field of learning which one masters is, however, usually not felt as a constraint, but as a source of satisfaction and strength."[11]

---

[9] U.S.S.R. Supreme Court Act 1957 art. 9; R.S.F.S.R. Court Organisation Act 1960. The power was formally given in 1938.

[10] O iuridicheskoi prirode rukovodiashchikh ukazanii plenuma VS SSSR, 1956 Sovetskoe Gosudarstvo i Pravo [hereinafter cited as S.G.P.] 8 13. Other main articles are by: V. Kaminskaia, 1948 S.G.P. 6 33; I. Tishkevitch, 1955 S.G.P. 6 29; N. Zeider, 1958 Pravovedenie 2 79; A. Kats, 1964 Pravovedenie 2 87; V. Akimov, 1969 Pravovedenie 3 110; S. Polenina 1969 S.G.P. 4 49; A. Pigolkin, 1970 S.G.P. 3 49 [hereinafter cited as Pigolkin]; K. Komissarov 1971 S.G.P. 3 71; V. Tolstoi, 1971 S.G.P. 10 37; S. Alekseev & I. Diuriagin, 1972 Pravovedenie 2 25; V. Lazarev, 1973 S.G.P. 2 20.

[11] Eckhoff, *Impartiality, Separation of Powers and Judicial Independence*, 9 Scandinavian Studies 11, 32-33 (1965) [hereinafter cited as Eckhoff].

To this I would add that, not only is the individual judge conditioned by his background, but that the decades, or even centuries, of a traditional training, of particular methods of recruitment, even of the physical characteristics of the place where the job is done, create a corpus of professional habits and assumptions which affects judicial method and, through it, the legal order, and does so all the more strongly for being so rarely made articulate.

Nowadays the word "court"—at least to a lawyer—may mean either the institution or the place; but in the latter sense it conveys the idea of a room—indeed in the United States one speaks of "the court room." But, even as descriptive of a place—in England a relatively modern usage—a glance at its earlier connotations may assist both comprehension and comparison. The typical *court* of the English system—there is one still in Oxford—is not a room but a box. At one end, slightly elevated, is, quite literally, a *bench* for the judges; in front of that, a large table; and, surrounding the table on three sides, is a kind of wooden wall or—and the sight will be familiar to anyone who has visited an English pub—a *bar*.

A brief contemplation of this structure explains a great deal about the common law. In the first place it is small; and one recalls that, until the last century, when the courts sat in Westminster Hall, the picture was not one of several rooms but of one large hall with boxes by each pillar. Secondly the nearness of the *bench* and the table makes it clear that rhetoric, or oratory, would have been quite inappropriate. It was a place for argument of course; but by way of conversation, not set speeches; and nothing was easier—in physical and spatial terms—than for the judge to interrupt the advocate, or for counsel sitting on opposite sides of the table to conduct their case through a discussion with each other and with the Bench. This facility combines with the effect of recruiting judges from the bar—so that the move is only one of a couple of yards—and with the court's awareness of its creative role to produce the distinctive features of the common law style: the four dialogues.

*First dialogue: Bench and Bar*

The fact that the process of arriving at a decision involves argument and discussion among the judges and advocates leaves its mark on judicial style. Far from being Olympian, detached, "the mouth that enunciates the words of the Law" (in Montesqieu's phrase[12]) the judge is forced to come to terms, openly and explicitly, with the views of counsel; to present, in short, his own assessment

[12] L'Esprit des Lois, Tome I, Livre XI. ch. VI (1842).

of them and, where necessary, his counter-argument. Virtually any reported judgment will contain such phrases as "in deference to the argument of counsel for the plaintiff" or "counsel for the defendant sought to persuade me . . ." and the like. Thus the judge is led to see his own role as not altogether different in kind from that of the bar. His final task is to decide, but as, on the way, he has to deal with the arguments advanced, it is clear on the surface of the judgment that there was a choice as to the result. And further, since the bar know him as a man who was once one of them, they know his strengths and weaknesses; and he knows that they know. He can thus admit his role as judge and yet retain a certain detachment which enables him to assess both his own contribution and that of counsel. Thus Sachs, L.J., after spending years as a judge of the Queen's Bench Division, found himself, after his elevation to the Court of Appeal, faced with a Chancery action. His judgment includes the following passage:

> There is, however, a further matter to which I would advert with the natural diffidence of one who has for the first time entered the hallowed fields of trusts and powers, of uncertainties, and of perpetuities, and has incidentally found roaming there one no less than the Attorney-General seeking to achieve on the construction of a short document the one result which could be manifestly contrary to the legitimate intentions of the dead man and also contrary to the interests and wishes of each and every one of all others concerned.[13]

*Second dialogue: among the Bench*

At first instance a judge sits alone, but in any higher court there will be more than one judge. The usual practice, at any rate in non-criminal cases, is for each to give judgment. It is thus possible—even when all members of the court agree on the result—to discern differences of approach and argument. This is facilitated when the Court takes time for consideration for then draft judgments are circulated; but—as is common in the Court of Appeal—even when judgment is delivered as soon as counsel have concluded their arguments the judges who speak after the first are able to comment on, and differ from, their colleagues. For instance: "I agree that this appeal should be allowed although the legal route which has led me to this conclusion is not at all points identical with that traversed by the Master of the Rolls. After all, that is the beauty of the common law; it is a maze and not a motorway."[14]

---

[13] Re Leek, [1968] 2 W. L. R. 1385, 1396 (C.A. 1967).

[14] Morris v. C.W. Martin & Sons Ltd., [1966] 1 Q.B. 716, 730 (C.A. 1965) (Diplock, L.J.).

If a diversity of approaches to the same result is a commonplace of English law, the presence of the dissenting judgment is even more striking. Its author will analyse, dissect, and attempt to refute the arguments of the majority; so the court, far from being unanimous, anonymous, laconic and poker-faced is visibly displayed as divided. The dissent may vary from the courteously devastating: "[For the majority] to proceed thus does not accord with my conception of the proper administration of justice,"[15] to the wryly baffled as where MacKinnon, L.J., on the construction of a difficult statute, confesses:

> [H]aving once more groped my way about that chaos of verbal darkness . . . I have come to the conclusion, with all becoming diffidence, that the [lower] court judge was wrong in this case. My diffidence is increased by finding that my brother Luxmoore has groped his way to the contrary conclusion.[16]

The dissenting judgment has two main effects. Firstly it makes it perfectly clear to the world that the court had a choice; that it was not a matter of fitting facts to law and getting that answer as from a slot-machine. Secondly it highlights those areas of the law which are developing and uncertain. It is no accident that those parts of private law in which the lower courts of France and the USSR most frequently diverge from the decisions of the Supreme Courts—in the field of automobile and industrial injuries—are precisely those in which the House of Lords is likely to be divided 3-2.

The judicial candour of the dialogue among the judges has never seemed alien to the common law. In the civil tradition of both France and Russia it has been strongly opposed. Thus Odilon Barrot argued: "It would, no doubt, be possible to compel each judge to state his reasons. This would make each judge responsible . . . but would entail the serious disadvantage of reducing the weight of the decision by revealing to the public the diversity of opinions that went to make up that decision."[17]

*Third dialogue: with the past*

The English judge converses with the dead. He has to, for several reasons. As there are in general no codes, the law is what his predecessors have laid down; and the rule of precedent obliges him to come to terms, in public, with arguments from the past. While the *Cour de Cassation* or the USSR Supreme Court can

15 Bedson v. Bedson, [1965] 2 Q.B. 666, 698-99 (C.A.) (Russell, L.J.).

16 Winchester Court, Ltd. v. Miller, [1944] K.B. 734, 744 (C.A.)

17 De L'organisation judiciaire en France 69, *quoted by* S. Kucherov, Courts, Lawyers and Trials Under the Last Three Tsars 39 (1953).

reverse itself completely on a fundamental issue without ever admitting this, the House of Lords in such a situation would feel bound to analyse and evaluate the older decision, to accord it respect and to overrule it only by producing compelling reasons.

The most frequent instance, of course, is not of overruling but of extending, refining, and applying. Virtually every tort case of the present day contains a reference to Lord Atkin's speech, forty-two years ago, in *Donoghue v. Stevenson.*[18] Lord Diplock has recently paused, as it were, in the middle of deciding a case, to give an analysis of this type of dialogue. "[T]he judicial development of the law of negligence rightly proceeds by seeking first to identify the relevant characteristics that are common to the kinds of conduct . . . involved in the case for decision and the kinds of conduct . . . which have been held in previous decisions of the courts to give rise to a duty of care . . . . The choice to extend [liability] is given effect to by redefining . . . in more general terms. . . ." His Lordship then describes the decisions of his predecessors Ashurst, J., Blackburn, J., Willes, J., and Lord Atkin—in cases spanning a century and a half—as "landmarks in the common law . . . instances . . . where the cumulative experience of judges has led to a restatement in wide general terms of characteristics of conduct and relationships which give rise to legal liability."[19]

*Fourth dialogue: with the future*

Because the English judge—especially of an appellate court—knows that his judgment will be cited as authority in arguments yet to come, he must be conscious of the effect of today's case on tomorrow. He will, in consequence, often adopt the approach: if I decide this way, what will be the likely effect on future conduct in this sphere. For instance, in imposing liability on a council whose building inspector had carelessly certified a privately-built house as safe, and where the plaintiff was the second purchaser, Lord Denning candidly admits "This case is entirely novel. . . . It seems to me that it is a question of policy which we, as judges, have to decide. . . . I ask: If liability were imposed on the council, would it have an adverse effect on the work? Would it . . . hold up work unnecessarily? . . . I see no danger. If liability is imposed on the council, it would tend, I think, to make them do their work better, rather than worse. In some cases the law has drawn the line [because] . . . if no limit were set there would be no end to the money payable. But I see no such reason here for limiting dam-

[18] [1932] A.C. 562.
[19] Dorset Yacht Co. v. Home Office, [1970] A.C. 1004, 1058-59.

ages. . . . Finally I ask myself: If we permit this new action, are we opening the door too much? Will it lead to a flood of cases . . . ?"[20]

In contrast to the features just described, the judgments of the *Cour de Cassation* and—though to a lesser extent—of the Soviet Supreme Court are terse, addressed to the one issue, and apparently, as it were, instantaneous; they hold few echoes from the past and do not set out to reverberate into the future. In both countries the judges, from the beginning of their professional training, form a separate career-group from that of the bar, becoming at first something the equivalent of the American judge's "clerk," then taking a seat on one of the lower or provincial tribunals and so working up. The effect of this separate training interacts with the constitutional role of the courts as will be shown later.

Thus the four dialogues described above leave no traces on a French or Soviet law report. There is, however, one relationship of which the common law knows little: that with the public power. In France its representative is the Procurator-General of the Republic, with his staff of advocates-general. Technically, theirs is a judicial office—the *magistrature debout* as opposed to that *du siège* and there is some career movement between the two branches; but the *parquet*—so called because their table used to stand on the floor at a lower level than that of the *bench*—does not have the same guarantee against removal as do the judges proper. The corps derives from a long tradition of independence; it is not a watchdog of State—as opposed to individual—interests but, according to the traditional formula was "instituted to watch over the observance of statutes and decrees, see that judgments and decisions are enforced, and defend the interests of the incapable and of charitable bodies."[21] Thus the Procurator-General or his staff act as a kind of institutionalised *amicus curiae* and, as such, intervene in all kinds of civil actions the outcome of which can have no possible political or public significance. It is in their submissions to the Court that one finds the features so familiar to a common-law judgment: a review of previous cases and of academic opinion; a discussion of policy factors such as insurance; and observations on the possible future effect of the course proposed. But the Court is in no way bound by these submissions; and, whether they are adopted or rejected, the judgment will usually do so without counter-argument.

In the USSR the name is the same—Prokuror-General—and his office was, in fact, copied from the French.[22] His functions are far wider than those of his French counterpart but, for our pur-

20 Dutton v. Bognor Regis U.D.C., [1972] I Q.B. 373, 397-98 (C.A. 1971).
21 Vincent, Procédure civile No. 177 *et seq.* (1969).
22 G. Morgan, Soviet Administrative Legality (1962).

poses, his important powers are those of taking a case *proprio motu* by way of "protest" to a higher court for reconsideration, and of presenting his submissions to the tribunal. Unfortunately these are rarely published, but one comes across many cases of his acting as a watchdog on behalf of individual parties and of his asking the court—not always, of course, with success—to think again.

### JUDICIAL STYLE

In the style of judgments as reported are to be found reflections of the constitutional position of the courts; of their relationship with other bodies; of their role as presented by academic writers; and of the judges' training, selection and self-awareness. It is the actual words used by the judge which set the tone of the system and reveal the nature of law as a social institution. The point is best made by extracts.

#### *An English style: from* Gray v. Barr (1971)[23]

> LORD DENNING, M.R. Mr. and Mrs. Barr have a prosperous business at Tooting in ladies' blouses, which they run together. In 1965 they bought a country home at Warlingham. About a quarter of a mile away there was a farmer and his wife, Mr. and Mrs. James Gray, of Farleigh Court Farm. The Barrs had three boys. The Grays had a boy and a girl. On Guy Fawkes day the Barrs had a bonfire party for the children and the Grays brought their children to it. The families became friends. But the results were disastrous. Mr. Gray and Mrs. Barr fell in love with one another. By May 1966, Mr. Gray had become so infatuated with Mrs. Barr that he wanted to make his life with her. He left the farm and his wife and children—all without a word—and went out to New Zealand. He gave Mrs. Barr £240 to buy her ticket out to join him. But, before she went out there, Mr. Gray's father told him that he must come back for the sake of the farm. So, in October 1966, he returned to England and ran the farm. But he still kept seeing Mrs. Barr. So much so that Mrs. Gray could not stand it any longer. She separated from him. He bought her a house in Edenbridge, 15 miles away. She had the children there with her. Mr. Gray entered into a deed of maintenance providing for her and the children. He stayed on alone in the farmhouse running the farm, but no doubt still seeing Mrs. Barr. In May 1967, he took Mrs. Barr to Scotland for a week's holiday. When they came back Mrs. Barr went to her mother's for three days and then returned home to her husband. At first she told him that she wanted to stay with him, but also that she still loved Mr. Gray. But on Tuesday evening Mr. and Mrs. Barr went out to dinner at the country club and then she told him to his great delight that she did not love Mr. Gray

[23] [1971] 2 Q.B. 554, 564-65 (C.A.).

any more and was coming back to live with him, Mr. Barr. They went back to their home hand in hand.

Now comes a tragic sequence of events. Mr. Barr went into the kitchen of his house to make up the boiler, and afterwards to the lavatory. His wife, he thought, had gone upstairs. But when he went up to join her, she was gone. He looked everywhere for her, but could not find her. He thought that she must have gone back to Mr. Gray. He got out the car and drove first towards her mother's and then back to Mr. Gray's farm. He drove in the gates, but turned round and went back again to his own house. He asked his cousin who was there: "Have you found Ethel?" She said, "No." Mr. Barr by this time was in a terrible state. He was crying and praying at the same time. He thought that his wife must have gone to Mr. Gray at the farm. He went to the dining room and picked up his shotgun. (He had bought it from Mr. Gray six months earlier.) His cousin said to him: "You don't need that, Bill." He said nothing. He took up a handful of cartridges and loaded two of them. He asked his cousin to come with him. She would not. He went out with the loaded gun. He drove up to the farm. He got out of the car, leaving the engine running. He opened the front door. There at the head of the stairs he saw Mr. Gray. Mr. Gray said: "Come in, Bill." He called out: "Is Ethel here, Jim?" Mr. Gray said: "No, she is not." Mr. Barr said: "I want to see for myself." He went up the stairs, holding the gun at the port. He was determined to see into the bedroom. But Mr. Gray stood in the way. He said: "Put that bloody thing down and get out." Exactly what happened next is not clear. Two shots went off. The first went up through the ceiling. The second killed Mr. Gray.

It was all a mistake. Mrs. Barr was not in the bedroom. She was not even in the farmhouse. She was lying in the woods 100 yards from her home, unconscious, having taken an overdose of sleeping tablets. She had attempted to commit suicide. She was found early next morning, taken to hospital, and recovered in three weeks. She and her husband are now together again, with their family and their business.

A literary critic might well classify this as the style of Simenon. The sentences are short, the words simple and, if possible, monosyllabic. Facts are given—the ladies' blouses or the bonfire party, for instance—which are quite irrelevant to the legal issues involved but whose mention is revealing: they build up the impression that the judge, far from being a detached, Olympian figure is acutely conscious of his role in helping out in the aftermath of a very human affair. The structure of the paragraphs is deliberately dramatic: "Mrs. Barr was not in the bedroom. She was not even in the farmhouse. She was lying in the woods. . . ." There is an important sense in which this shows the judge as involved, even as enjoying the story; *not* as a mere spectator, there for the thrill, but as a judge who perceives—and reveals—that it is in the sad tangles of human life that the law is secreted.

This section is headed "*an* English style" since there are as many different versions as there are men on the bench. Unlike their Continental brethren the English judges make no attempt to write a "judicial" prose in the sense of one accepted medium. Lord Denning, M.R. is perhaps unusual in his treatment of facts and in his candour as to the legal choices open to him—the latter is shown in the earlier extract. One weapon he never uses is irony; but to his brethren it often comes naturally as a handy tool of argument. A judgment of Megarry, J., for instance, will be studded with such phrases as: "This may be the law; it might even be equity; but it is indisputably remarkable."[24]

But, whatever the individual differences of formulation, it is generally true that the English style is closely tied to—and indeed relishes—the facts; that it uses exaggeration, irony, and other devices to make its point; that it accepts the need to meet and rebut argument; and that it is candid as to the options open.

*The French Style:* Cour de Cassation 1.12.69[25]

> THE COURT;—On the single ground:—Whereas it appears from the findings of the judgment complained of that Sandrock, being near to a collision between the automobile of Veidt and the moped of Martin, in the course whereof the latter's engine caught fire, attempted to put out the flames with an extinguisher but was wounded when the petrol tank exploded;—Whereas it is complained that the court of appeal ordered Martin to compensate the damage caused to Sandrock on the ground that a rescue contract had been formed between the parties, but there can be no agreement without the consent of the parties and the judgment did not mention that of the victim;—But whereas the court of appeal did not have to find the express consent of the victim since, when an offer is made in his exclusive interest, the offeree is presumed to have accepted it; that having, within their sovereign power, concluded that a rescue contract had been formed between Sandrock and Martin the judges of appeal were quite right to hold that the victim was obliged to compensate the damages sustained by one who lent assistance through benevolence; therefore the ground cannot be accepted; For these reasons, reject.

The French style is evident from the very beginning of the report. The case is referred to by its date and, although the parties' names are reported, it is not by them that the judgment will be remembered. It is "THE COURT" and not a single judge which is

[24] Re Figgis, [1969] 1 Ch. 123, 149 (1968).
[25] D.S.1970.422, note by Puech.

presented as speaking. Its whole judgment is cast in one sentence, and this is true of all French judgments no matter how lengthy the facts or how complex the law. This verbal style is at once a symptom and a technique. It is a reflex of the precept of article 5 forbidding the judge to lay down general rules and of the whole tradition that it is for the legislature and not the courts to make law; so, by expressing the judgment in that particular grammatical form, an impression is given that all is an easy deduction from the principles of enacted law.

The very act of decision implies a choice; but the French grammatical technique enables the judge to conceal this. If one looks at this particular case in the round, certain policy considerations appear. It is in the interests of accident victims that they should receive help; and of rescuers that they should be indemnified against risks. Were the decision to go the other way there is a danger that, in future emergencies, prudent passers-by will emulate the Priest and the Levite. The defendant is insured. An action in tort might lie but there are problems of proving fault; whereas by construing a contract—"I offer to help you if you recompense any injury I sustain"—the plaintiff wins with, presumably, some influence on future behaviour in like situations. But the only hint of this that appears in the judgment is in the final reference to the kind of moral considerations associated with the word "benevolence." Other particular omissions may be noted. Firstly, the failure to cite an article of the Code. The trouble here is that the only relevant rule is that of article 1108 which requires *consent* as an essential condition for the validity of an agreement. Clearly the defendant's case was based on this; but the second omission is of any argument in rebuttal. Indeed—and thirdly—the Court, in saying that acceptance is "presumed" appears to be acting in flat defiance of article 5, though this is not even remotely acknowledged. And finally one notes the absence of any findings as to the behaviour of the automobile driver, whose role in responsibility is not discussed at all; and that there is no discussion of the general policy considerations outlined above.

There are many other examples of the French style of handling injury. When Madame Dehen picked up a bottle in a supermarket and was injured by its explosion before reaching the check-out the choice was clearly between tort—which might involve questions of fault—and sale, under which liability is strict. The Court of Cassation devotes one phrase to the issue: "the liability of [defendant] to the victim could only be contractual."[26] In another recent case the defendant bloodbank supplied blood to a hospital which gave

[26] Cass. civ., Oct. 20, 1964, D.S. 1965.62.

the plaintiff patient a transfusion. The blood turned out to be infected with syphilis. The lower court's finding of fault—sufficient for the tort action in which the case was brought—was doubtful, as, had the blood been checked by the defendant, the incubating disease would not have been discovered. The Court of Cassation noted this but averred that "it is for [this] Court to *restore their true character to the legal relationships deduced* from the facts found by the judge . . ." and found a contract (with strict liability) for the benefit of the third party, the plaintiff.[27]

This paper is not concerned with the results of such cases but with their style of expression. It will be seen from the three examples given that the language is of assertion. not of argument. But more than this, it is existential and descriptive, not normative and prescriptive. The supermarket's liability "can only be" contractual; the Court of Cassation *restores* relationships to their *true* character. It is a clear example of Eckhoff's observation that "expressions associated with knowledge and perception (*e.g.*, 'examine' 'see' 'find' and 'is') occur much more frequently than do expressions associated with evaluation, preference and choice."[28]

*The Soviet Style: RSFSR Supreme Court Plenum 28.6.26*[29]

> The principle of mixed liability is unknown to the Civil Code. Life, however, creates circumstances of harm arising which are significantly more complex than those provided for by law. In many cases it would be quite wrong to place responsibility in full on the tortfeasor, while in others it would be no less mistaken that he should be entirely exonerated from liability. Particular difficulties in judicial practice have arisen when, along with the gross negligence of the victim, there occur equally gross carelessness, indifference and so on on the part of the tortfeasor. For instance the court in this case finds that the victim was in a state of intoxication at the moment the damage (injury) was caused but at the same time the railroad employees failed to observe the rules on sounding a warning whistle, cutting speed and so on. In such cases the courts have ordinarily either ignored the victim's gross negligence and imposed liability for the injury in full on the railroad or [other defendant] or have denied the victim any redress.
>
> The Court considers the application of the principle of mixed liability necessary in such cases. Its essence is the following: in so far as the harm is caused by the incorrect, careless or negligent actions of both tortfeasor and victim,

[27] Cass. civ., Dec. 17, 1954, D. 1955.269, note by Rodière (emphasis added).
[28] Eckhoff, *supra* note 11, at 19.
[29] Sbornik raz'iasnenii Verkhovnogo Suda R.S.F.S.R. 149 (Stuchka ed. 1931) [hereinafter cited as Stuchka].

the liability for the damage must be 'mixed' that is it must be placed equally, or in some proportion, upon both.

It will be seen that the Soviet style falls between the personal and idiosyncratic judgments of the common law and the elegant austerity of the French. This is partly due to the institutional role of the court. In the extract above, while it is dealing with a particular fact situation, it takes the opportunity to review similar cases. It freely admits its creative role and that the Code is insufficient to cope with life's problems. Homely illustrations are given and the remedy is laid down in simple language. The style is, admittedly, largely that of officialdom (and the phrase "mixed liability" might displease a purist) but the tone is that of a tribunal admitting the existence of problems, acknowledging the possibility of different solutions, and buttressing its proposed remedy, if not by formal argument, at least by example and by an appeal to common sense.

The extract was taken from a case of the 1920's because that was the heyday of the Supreme Court's creative power. In several other situations it reproached lower courts with taking a "formal" stand on the words of the statute—perhaps its most striking creation in this field was to broaden the tort law for industrial injuries. The relevant statute permitted such an action—for the excess of earnings lost over social security payments—only where the employer was guilty of "a *criminal* act or omission"[30] but the Supreme Court simply read the word as "negligent."[31] Similarly, in rescue cases involving State property and injury to the rescuer, the Court invented liability in defiance of what it again referred to as a "formalist" position.[32]

If the Soviet higher courts appear less creative today, one reason is that they did their work so well that many of their earlier decisions have simply been elevated into articles of the more recent civil codes.

## The Paradox of Precedent

Within the common law world, the English have been the high priests of precedent. But, as any lawyer knows, even the strictest doctrine leaves a good deal of leeway; and it is within this leeway and through the tensions between a perfect theory and a developing society that the new law grows.

---

[30] R.S.F.S.R. 1922 Grazh. Kod. (Civil Code) § 413(2).

[31] Decisions of June 9, 1924 and July 18, 1927, reported in Stuchka, *supra* note 29, at 174, 176.

[32] Pigolkin, *supra* note 10, at 56.

The vital effect of the extreme English position, however, when taken with the institutional position of the courts, the training of the judges, and the role of the bar, is that any higher tribunal is forced, openly and in public, to come to terms with itself both past and future. Precisely because Blackburn, J., or Lord Atkin were making law, today's judge must reckon with them; precisely because he is making law, he must look to his successors. The paradox is that a constitutional system which gives great power to the judges finds it necessary, by a doctrine of precedent, to make responsible the exercise of that power; while a system which denies the creative role of the judge sets him free to legislate. This cannot, however, be shown by any one facet in isolation; it emerges only from a consideration of all the elements discussed above.

The "legislative" power of the French judges can be demonstrated easily. The following case—translated in full—deals with the issue of enforcing injunctions. The problem is that there is no power to commit for contempt; that article 1142 declares that *damages* is the remedy for breach of a duty to act or refrain; and that they may not exceed the loss sustained and (in appropriate cases) profit foregone by the plaintiff. The case turns on the legality of the *astreinte*—a monetary penalty fixed by the court for noncompliance and payable to the plaintiff even though far in excess of his loss.

> THE COURT;—On the single ground in its two branches:—Whereas it is complained that the judgment under attack, in assessing the total of an *astreinte* ordered earlier to ensure performance of an obligation to act, took into consideration the culpable resistance of the debtor without taking into account the damage caused to the creditor by the delay in performance, while, according to the motion, the judge who assesses an *astreinte* is bound not to exceed the total damage, a finding as to which is indispensable to justify the order;—
>
> But whereas, in deciding that the provisional *astreinte*, a measure of constraint entirely distinct from damages and, in the final analysis, nothing more than a means of overcoming resistance to the execution of a court order, is not designed to compensate the damage caused by the delay and is normally assessed in terms of the gravity of the fault of the recalcitrant debtor and of his means, the court of appeal, whose judgment is reasoned, has legally justified its decision; For these reasons, reject.[33]

Once again the points of comparison are obvious. The Court discusses no facts. In fact the defendant was carrying on an indus-

[33] Cass. civ., Oct. 20, 1959, D. 1959.537, note by Holleaux. The decision has now been codified into Law No. 72-626 of July 5, 1972; D.S.L. 1972.361.

trial process and was presumably committing some sort of nuisance, the profits of which exceeded his neighbour's loss. No article of the Code is cited—none could be—and the one article to the contrary (1142), far from being distinguished, is not even mentioned. Counsel's arguments are not met. Only six years previously the same court—though in a different fact situation—had announced precisely the contrary rule of law.[34] And finally the Court gives no thought to the future: what is to be done where the defendant is not making that extra profit?

Thus the Court of Cassation can act more decisively and more boldly—not less—than the English court. The case just quoted is perhaps peculiar to France; but one cannot envisage the English judiciary construing supermarkets, bloodbanks, or accident rescues as contractual situations so as to make it easier for the plaintiff.

Once again, the Soviet court occupies an intermediate position. Compared with an English report its style is dull; compared with the French it is helpful. For instance, the interminable litigation in the latter country on the strict liability of a *"gardien"* was largely obviated in the USSR by a guiding explanation as to what is meant by the "guardian" (*vladelets*) of a source of increased hazard. Thus the driver, the machinist and the like do not fall within the category; nor is one who proves that the source left his control through no fault of his own but through the illegal act of a third party; in that case the latter is strictly liable.[35]

A 1971 case demonstrates that the Federal Supreme Court is still anxious to get things right. The plaintiff's eye was injured by a splinter of metal while he was working on a vice. The Court undertakes a fairly full review of the facts and directs a finding for him, saying "[r]egardless of the experience and qualifications of the worker, the creation . . . of conditions enabling him to carry out his work in safety is the job of the administration, which is required also to check the workers' observance of technical safety regulations, including the use of protective measures . . . when jobs are being simultaneously carried out in one place the benches should have safety grids. . . ."[36] At first sight there may seem nothing unusual in this review of the facts. But nowhere does the Court mention a date or an article of the Code. In fact the decision is a reversal of that of the RSFSR Supreme Court taken *ten years earlier* which had denied recovery on the ground that the plaintiff's own experience should have made him wear goggles.[37] Thus we find,

34 Cass. civ., Feb. 27, 1953, S. 1953.I.196.

35 Decree of U.S.S.R. Sup. Ct. Plenum of 23.10.1963, Sbornik postanovlenii plenuma Verkhovnogo Suda 1924-70, 109 (1970).

36 U.S.S.R. Sup. Ct. Bull. 311 (1971).

37 R.S.F.S.R. Sup. Ct. Bull. 42 (1961).

in 1971, the Plenum of the Federal court interpreting, *sub silentio*, a Civil Code then repealed; so that the plaintiff's justice, though long delayed, was not, in the end, denied.

## CONCLUSION

In attempting a brief comparison of the judicial method of three countries I have tried to emphasise the interrelationship of many factors: the position in constitutional theory, the training and background of the bench, the demands made on judges, and the way in which they see their role. It seems that the systems all require some area of tension within which the judges can act. In England this is provided by the play of precedent; in France by the way in which the courts pay literal lip-service to their restrictions and, by the very style so imposed, free themselves from the Code. In the USSR the fecund tensions come from several sides. The Federal Principles of Civil Law, for instance, give the *plan* as one of the sources of civil rights and duties. Further, there is a potential creative conflict between article 88 al.4—"Harm caused by lawful acts must be compensated only in cases provided for by statute"—and article 5 al.2: "In exercising rights . . . citizens . . . must . . . respect the rules of socialist cohabitation and the moral principles of a society which is building communism."

The final point is merely a tentative suggestion. The Soviet system is seen by the judges as developing and responsive to change and so as part of a process. The striking contrast is between English and French law and lies in the attitude to *time*. Thus in substantive law the classic preoccupations of the civilians have been —following an old tradition—the law of sale and—in modern times —that of tort. But both of these are, by and large, instantaneous incidents which produce their results here and now. The *typical* creations of the common law are the estate and the trust. The former welds the notion of time into its concept of "ownership"— "for an estate in the land is a time in the land, or land for a time, and there are diversities of estates which are no more than diversities of time. . . ."[38] The trust, likewise, is an institution designed to endure and within whose temporal structure the concepts of estate and fund can interlock.

A similar point may be made about legal method. The French judgment—like the contract of sale—appears as instantaneous, new-minted; it no tomorrow has, nor yesterday. The English judge seems to feel that his role this morning is no bar to a conversation with his predecessors nor is it without relevance to the future; and

[38] Walsingham's Case, 2 Plowden 547, 556 (1579) (Barham).

he must accept both the facilities *and the limits* of that position. It was suggested that a helpful insight into the common law might be afforded by imagining the judge in the box described above. But the point is that it is the same box.

# [8]

## 23

## THE ATTRACTION OF THE CIVIL LAW IN POST-REVOLUTIONARY AMERICA

AT the present time the interest of historians and publicists of American law appears to be focused particularly on what Roscoe Pound dubbed "the formative era of American law"[1] and Charles M. Haar has recently hailed as "the Golden Age of American law,"[2] that is, roughly the period from the Revolution to the Civil War. Throughout this period, but especially in its middle decades, a determined effort was made by a succession of zealots to introduce into the United States the institutions and methods of the civil law, if not as a substitute for, at least as a supplement to, those of the common law. The advantages of the civil law were trumpeted from Massachusetts to South Carolina with almost crusading enthusiasm.

This propaganda campaign failed to achieve its objects and is now largely overlooked. But in the middle of the nineteenth century it seemed to at least one perspicacious observer that it was succeeding. In 1856, Sir Henry Maine observed that it was incorrect to regard America as belonging to the common-law camp:

> During many years after the severance of the United States from the mother-country, the new States . . . did all of them assume as the standard of decision for the Courts, in cases not provided for by legislation, either the Common law of England, or the Common law as transformed by early New England statutes into something closely resembling the Custom of London. But this adherence to a single model ceased about 1825.[3]

---

* Visiting Professor, University of Virginia School of Law; Professor of Jurisprudence, University of Aberdeen. B.A., 1949, LL.B., 1950, M.A., 1951, Cambridge University; Ph.D., 1955, Aberdeen.

1 POUND, THE FORMATIVE ERA OF AMERICAN LAW (1938).

2 THE GOLDEN AGE OF AMERICAN LAW (Haar ed. 1965). See generally MILLER, THE LIFE OF THE MIND IN AMERICA 164-71 (1965) (specifically devoted to the civil law).

3 MAINE, *Roman Law and Legal Education*, in VILLAGE-COMMUNITIES IN THE EAST AND WEST 330, 359-60 (3d ed. 1876), originally published in CAMBRIDGE ESSAYS (1856).

Thereafter, said Maine, it was the Code of Louisiana, not the common law of England, which the newest American states were taking for the substratum of their laws. He concluded that the Roman law was "fast becoming the *lingua franca* of universal jurisprudence," since its jural conceptions underlay "the legal systems of nearly all Europe and of a great part of America."[4]

Maine had no doubt an exaggerated impression of the influence of the civil law in the United States, just as he was probably inaccurate in stating that, in the period immediately following the Revolution, new states automatically adopted the English common law. Yet there is considerable evidence of civil-law influence. It was particularly strong in the areas of legal education and commercial and maritime law, and at times it permeated other parts of the law as well. The present study is an attempt to document the extent of that influence.

## I.

Even in the colonial period[5] the traditional preparation for a legal career included a study of the law of nature and of nations, and of moral philosophy generally. The works on these topics in fact contained much civil-law material. The substance of the law contained in Justinian's *Digest* and *Institutes*, in contrast with its defective arrangement, was considered in the seventeenth and eighteenth centuries to be *ratio scripta*, reason in writing, and as near to perfection as juristic ingenuity could be expected to attain.[6] The standard treatises on the law of nature and of nations were Grotius' *De iure belli ac pacis* (1625), Pufendorf's *De iure naturae et gentium* (1672), Heineccius' *Elementa iuris naturae et gentium* (1737), and Burlamaqui's *Principes du droit naturel* (1747). All these works adopted the position that Roman law, though no longer authoritative by reason of the (Holy Roman) Empire (*ratione Imperii*), should still be followed in the empire of reason (*imperio Rationis*). It is important to remember that they were all available in English translations. There were a number of translations of Grotius and Pufendorf early in the eighteenth century, Nugent's translation of Burlamaqui appeared in 1748, and Turnbull's translation of Heineccius was published in London in 1763. Burlamaqui

[4] *Id.* at 361.

[5] For the earlier period see Radin, *The Rivalry of Common-Law and Civil Law Ideas in the American Colonies*, in 2 NEW YORK UNIVERSITY SCHOOL OF LAW, LAW—A CENTURY OF PROGRESS 404 (1937).

[6] Stein, *Elegance in Law*, 77 L.Q. REV. 242, 252 (1961).

proved so popular in America that editions of Nugent's version were published in Boston in 1792, in Cambridge, Mass. in 1807, in Philadelphia in 1823 and 1830, and in Columbus, Ohio in 1859. Thus it is unnecessary to attribute prodigious linguistic feats to those who claim familiarity with the natural-law writers.

Many works on moral philosophy contained similar material. A widely read *Introduction* to the subject was that of Francis Hutcheson, who became professor of moral philosophy at the University of Glasgow in 1729.[7] He divided his course into two parts, "ethicks" and "knowledge of the law of nature," and under the latter head he dealt with "the doctrine of private rights or the laws obtaining in natural liberty," which look very like the rights set out in contemporary treatises on the civil law. Many of the leading eighteenth century works on moral philosophy were produced by Scots, and of course Scotland was, and is, a civil-law country. Several of the most influential college teachers of colonial America were Scotsmen who had received their education in Scotland, such as Jefferson's beloved William Small at William and Mary and the formidable John Witherspoon at Princeton.

Grotius and Pufendorf figure prominently in the curriculum for law students drawn up in 1756 by William Smith (1728-1793), later Chief Justice of New York.[8] They were class texts at Princeton when James Madison was a student there under Witherspoon in 1769-1771,[9] and they were studied by James Kent "in huge folios" when he was preparing for the study of law in 1781-1782.[10] Hutcheson's *Introduction* appears in a course of preliminary reading for prospective lawyers recommended by Thomas Jefferson.[11] In his autobiography, written in 1802, John Adams claimed to have told his master in law, Jeremiah Gridley, in 1758 that he had read Burlamaqui and Heineccius in Turnbull's translation,[12] but this was impossible since the latter work was not published until five years later.

Whatever works on natural law Adams studied, his knowledge of the civil law was not confined to second-hand learning derived from such works. Even before meeting Gridley he had procured from the

---

[7] HUTCHESON, INTRODUCTION TO MORAL PHILOSOPHY (1747); see Stein, *The General Notions of Contract and Property in Eighteenth Century Scottish Thought*, 8 JURID. REV. (n.s.) 1, 2 (1963).

[8] See HAMLIN, LEGAL EDUCATION IN COLONIAL NEW YORK 197-98 (1939).

[9] See 1 BRANT, JAMES MADISON—THE VIRGINIA REVOLUTIONIST 76 (1941).

[10] W. KENT, MEMOIRS AND LETTERS OF JAMES KENT, LL.D. 19 (1898).

[11] See 1 RANDALL, THE LIFE OF THOMAS JEFFERSON 54 (1858).

[12] 3 ADAMS, DIARY AND AUTOBIOGRAPHY 271 (Butterfield ed. 1961).

Harvard College library a copy of Vinnius' commentary on Justinian's *Institutes*, a work first published in 1646 and recommended by Lord Mansfield[13] as suitable for beginners. Adams' motive was frankly a desire to get ahead of his fellows and draw attention to himself by an exhibition of learning—a form of "one-upmanship."

> Let me read with Attention, Deliberation, Distinction. Let me admire with Knowledge. . . . Few of my Contemporary Beginners, in the Study of the Law, have the Resolution, to aim at much Knowledge in the Civil Law. Let me therefore distinguish my self from them, by the Study of the Civil Law, in its native languages, those of Greece and Rome. I shall gain the Consideration and perhaps favour of Mr. Gridley and Mr. Pratt by this means.[14]

When Adams met Gridley a few weeks later, Gridley provided him with a better reason for studying the civil law; whereas a lawyer in England could specialize, a lawyer in America could not. The latter "must study common Law and civil Law, and natural Law, and Admiralty Law, and must do the duty of a Counsellor, a Lawyer, an Attorney, a sollicitor, and even of a scrivener, so that the Difficulties of the Profession are much greater here than in England."[15] In Gridley's view the value of the civil law was that it provided a ground plan of the legal system as a whole, and thus enabled the lawyer to get his bearings as he switched from one matter to another. This is shown by the fact that he lent Adams Van Muyden's commentary on the *Institutes*, a more elementary work than that of Vinnius. Adams noted that it was designed to "explain the technical Terms of the civil Law, and to settle the Divisions and Distributions of the civil Law." He observed, "this is the first Thing a student ought to aim at, viz. distinct Ideas under the terms and a clear apprehension of the Divisions and Distributions of the science."[16]

In eighteenth century eyes the civil law was associated with order, clarity and coherence. The most popular work was probably Jean Domat's *The Civil Laws in their Natural Order* (1689-1694), in which the material of Justinian's *Corpus Iuris* was set out in the rational order advocated by the natural-law school, that is, as a series of logical deductions from a number of self-evident premises. William Strahan's

13 Fifoot, Lord Mansfield 29 (1936).

14 1 Adams, *op. cit. supra* note 12, at 44-45.

15 *Id.* at 55.

16 *Id.* at 56.

translation from the French appeared in 1722 and enjoyed a considerable vogue in America. The best of the civilian works written originally in English was Thomas Wood's *A New Institute of the Imperial or Civil Law*, first published in 1704. These works were the principal sources of information in English on the civil law as a whole until 1798, when Arthur Browne (1756-1805), of Trinity College, Dublin, published his lectures as *A Compendious View of the Civil Law and of the Law of the Admiralty*. The second edition in two volumes appeared in 1802, and according to Thomas Cooper, it was "commonly used among the bar in this Country . . . ."[17] Browne was the son of Marmaduke Browne, one of the original fellows of Rhode Island College, and had received part of his own education at Harvard. His lectures attempted to follow the method and order of Blackstone's *Commentaries*, so that the familiarity of its arrangement would entice the student of the common law to learn something of the civil law.

## II.

Immediately after the Revolution, there was a widespread feeling that efforts should be made to develop a particular American jurisprudence, which would not be just a slavish imitator of the English common law, but would be eclectic—selecting the best principles and methods from whatever system they might be found in. One of the first manifestations of this idea was the establishment of a course of lectures on law in the College of Philadelphia, and the appointment of James Wilson (1742-1798), Associate Justice of the Supreme Court and one of the signers of the Declaration of Independence, to deliver them in 1790-1792. Wilson was born and brought up in Scotland, and had attended the University of St. Andrews. In his inaugural lecture he urged that "the *foundation*, at least, of a separate, an unbiased, and an independent law education should be laid in the United States."[18] He was concerned that this education should be based on a sound metaphysical foundation which recognized an objective moral order and the principles of natural law. This he derived largely from the Scottish common-sense school of philosophers. It was natural that a Scot, with

[17] Cooper, Justinian's Institutes 670 (Philadelphia 1812). An American edition of Browne's *Civil Law* was published in New York in 1840.

[18] Smith, James Wilson—Founding Father 312 (1956). See also Leavelle, *James Wilson and the Relation of the Scottish Metaphysics to American Political Thought*, 57 Pol. Sci. Q. 394 (1942). The lectures are published in *The Works of James Wilson* (Andrews ed. 1896).

no particular love for English institutions, should wish to make American law more independent of the English common law, and he made much use of the natural law to give his exposition of American law a more rational structure.

A year or two after Wilson's lectures at Philadelphia, James Kent gave the first law lectures at Columbia College. Kent too felt the attraction of the civil law and particularly the French writers on commercial law, to whom he had been introduced by Alexander Hamilton.[19] (Hamilton had a fluent command of French, which he had learned as a boy in the West Indies). Kent's lectures were only given for a couple of years,[20] and he was then appointed to the New York bench, where he continued his civil-law studies. Like Adams, he used them to put himself "one up" on his colleagues: "I made much use of the *Corpus Juris*, and as the judges (Livingston excepted) knew nothing of French or civil law, I had immense advantage over them."[21]

In a few years, however, Kent had succeeded in educating his fellow judges to some degree, and discussions of comparative law occurred not uncommonly in their opinions. In *Vandenheuvel v. United Insurance Co.*,[22] in 1801, the issue was whether the sentence of a foreign court of admiralty, condemning certain property as prize, was conclusive evidence as to the character of the property. Judge Radcliff quoted Grotius and Vattel, who seemed to support the rule followed by the English courts that the court's decision was conclusive. He then observed,

> [I]n France, the law is undoubtedly otherwise settled. . . . [citing Emerigon, Valin and Roccus] [T]he authorities on which they proceed, in cases of new impression, would merit great attention and respect; but, independent of the circumstance that they impose no obligations on our courts, I think they do not comport with the sound interpretation of the contract, nor with the system of our jurisprudence. The English courts, on questions of commercial law, are to be regarded as at least equally enlightened and correct.[23]

19 See W. Kent, *op. cit. supra* note 10, at 318.

20 Columbia University Foundation for Research in Legal History, A History of the School of Law—Columbia University 11-18 (1955).

21 W. Kent, *op. cit. supra* note 10, at 117.

22 2 Johns. Cas. 127 (N.Y. Sup. Ct. 1801), *rev'd*, 2 Johns. Cas. 451, 457 (N.Y. 1802).

23 *Id.* at 139-40.

Judge Benson gave an even more elaborate account of the civil law authorities, including Perezius' *Praelectiones in Codicem* (1695). Kent himself concentrated on the English authorities and noted that they were in accord with the law of nations, as discussed by Grotius, Vattel, Martens and Erskine's *Institute of the Law of Scotland* (1773). He commented, "nor do I think that the English decisions, since the year 1776, are to be thrown *wholly* out of view, although they are confessedly of no binding authority,"[24] and concluded, "whatever opinion may be entertained, as to the justice or policy of the rule, is not to the purpose. Our duty is *jus dicere, non jus dare* [to declare the law, not to make the law]."[25]

In many cases, however, the law had to be made by the judges, and in New York at least, they adopted a policy of eclecticism, considering the common-law and civil-law authorities respectively and then choosing one rather than the other. At first the preference would be based on whichever was better adapted to the particular case; but gradually as a body of peculiarly American jurisprudence grew up, the test was which doctrine was best adapted to the ethos of that system.

When he became Chancellor of New York, Kent had increased opportunities to use his judicial opinions as occasions for comparative legal studies. The typical form of his judgments is illustrated by *Underhill v. Van Cortlandt*,[26] in 1817, concerning the validity of an umpire's award. He first discussed the English cases on the subject, observing that "the *English* law on the subject of awards has, as I apprehend, been adopted very universally in this country."[27] Then he continued, "nor is this general doctrine, on the subject of awards, peculiar to the *English* law, or to the courts in this country, which have followed its jurisprudence. We find in the civil law the conclusiveness of awards asserted as strongly as in any of the *English* decisions."[28] Kent then quoted various passages from Justinian's *Digest* and *Institutes*, and Vinnius' *Commentary*, and concluded, "this award would be declared binding by *Vinnius*, sitting under the civil law; it must be equally so under the law of this country."[29]

24 *Id.* at 146.
25 *Id.* at 147.
26 2 Johns. Ch. R. 339 (N.Y. Ch. 1817), *rev'd*, 17 Johns. R. 405 (N.Y. Ct. App. 1819).
27 *Id.* at 367.
28 *Id.* at 368.
29 *Id.* at 369.

Immediately after the Revolution, there was so little local authority in many areas of the law, that the American courts could have incorporated much civil law into their systems with little opposition. There was considerable distrust of the common law as an English product and a corresponding sympathy for things French. There could well have been a reception of civil law into America corresponding to the French "Reception," which was a gradual process whereby Roman law was deliberately incorporated into French law in cases where the local customary law was deficient.

An interesting example of appeal to Roman law almost as a sort of higher law occurs in the *cause célèbre* known as *The Batture at New Orleans* (a *batture* is the land created by the alluvion of a river). The question was whether the owner of land adjacent to the Mississippi River could deal with the beach between the river and his land as his own when the beach was continually increasing in size by the alluvion of the river. The local court, basing its decision mainly on French and Spanish authority, held that the beach was the private property of the riparian owner (who was, in fact, Edward Livingston, the future draftsman of the Louisiana Civil Code). But the latter's activities, in attempting to breach the *batture* with a canal from the river to his land, alarmed the public, who feared damage to the levees and consequential flooding. The Governor referred the matter to Washington, and President Jefferson ordered that further work on the *batture* be stopped. This order was enforced by a marshal with a *posse comitatus*, despite a court injunction obtained by Livingston.

In 1812 Jefferson published a long memorandum justifying his order.[30] He dealt first with the law to be applied and referred to the French and Spanish customary laws, which he called "feudal." He then went on,

> But as circumstances changed, and civilization and commerce advanced, abundance of new cases and questions arose, for which the simple and unwritten laws of feudalism had made no provision. At the same time, they had at hand the legal system of a nation highly civilized, a system carried to a degree of conformity

[30] JEFFERSON, THE BATTURE AT NEW ORLEANS (1810), reprinted in 5 AMERICAN L.J. 1 (1814) and in 18 THE WRITINGS OF THOMAS JEFFERSON 1 (Lipscomb memorial ed. 1904). For a brief account, see Montgomery, *Thomas Jefferson, Admirer and User of Roman Law*, SYNTELEIA V. ARANGIO-RUIZ 170 (1964).

with natural reason attained by no other. The study of this system too was become the favorite of the age, and, offering ready and reasonable solutions of all the new cases presenting themselves, was recurred to by a common consent and practice; not indeed as laws, formally established by the legislator of the country, but as a RATIO SCRIPTA, the dictate, in all cases, of that sound reason which should constitute the law of every country.[31]

Jefferson's argument, supported by abundant citations from the *Digest* and *Insitutes*, was subtle and acute. Roman law, he argued, gave alluvion only to the riparian owners of an *ager* (which, he held, means rural property), and not to the owners of urban property. Thus, "were this question to be decided by the Roman law, the conversion of the farm into a fauxbourg of the city passed to the public all the riparian rights attached to it while a rural possession and among these the right of alluvion."[32] Jefferson then offered an alternative argument, to the effect that the *batture* was not in fact an alluvion at all. It was to be regarded as the bank of a public river, and the owner of the adjacent land had no right, under Roman law, to engage in activities which might prove injurious to the public. He concluded,

> We see, then, that the Roman law not only forbade every species of construction or work on the bed, beach or bank of a sea or river, without regular permission from the proper officer, but even annuls the permission after it is given, if, in event, the work proves injurious . . . [and] does not common sense, the foundation of all authorities, of the laws themselves, and of their construction, declare it impossible that Mr. Livingston, a single individual, should have a lawful right to drown the city of New Orleans, or to injure, or change, of his own authority, the course or current of a river which is to give outlet to the productions of two-thirds of the whole area of the United States?[33]

The matter was eventually settled by Congress.[34]

31 18 THE WRITINGS OF THOMAS JEFFERSON 34-35 (Lipscomb memorial ed. 1904).

32 *Id.* at 65.

33 *Id.* at 92. For other opinions on the case see Du Ponceau, *A Review*, 4 AMERICAN L.J. 517 (1813); Livingston, *Examination of the Title of the United States to the Land Called The Batture*, 2 AMERICAN L.J. 307 (1809).

34 Act of March 3, 1807, ch. 46, 2 Stat. 445; see also Act of March 2, 1805, ch. 26, 2 Stat. 324.

## III.

The branch of substantive law in which the common law offered least to the new nation was commercial law. At the time of the Revolution, the radical decisions of Lord Mansfield in this field had hardly made themselves felt in America. It was therefore particularly in this branch of the law that American jurists turned for guidance to the leading French writers on the civil law. Among them the outstanding figure was that of Robert Joseph Pothier (1699-1772). His main work in this field was the *Treatise on Obligations* published in 1761, but he also wrote separate monographs on the individual mercantile contracts. His works were noted not only for the accuracy and completeness of the subject matter, but also for their clarity and systematic arrangement. Pothier was the most distinguished civilian of his time. Two other French jurists, who were frequently cited with him by American writers, were Balthazard Marie Emérigon (1716-1785) and René Josué Valin (1695-1765). Their reputations were the result of having produced specialist works of high authority—Emérigon's treatise on insurance, *Traité des assurances*, published in Marseilles in 1783 and Valin's commentary on Louis XIV's *Ordonnance de la marine* of 1681, published in 1756.

The first English translation of Pothier's *Treatise on Obligations* was published in New Bern, North Carolina, in 1802. It was the work of François Xavier Martin (1762-1846), who was born in Marseilles and arrived in North Carolina from the French West Indies during the Revolution. He studied English and law and set up as a printer and publisher, an occupation which he continued after his admission to the North Carolina bar in 1789. His firm of Martin and Ogden published the translation without mentioning the translator's name, but it is recognized as the work of Martin. Indeed it was said that he had the French text propped up on the type case and translated it directly into English type in his composing stick.[35]

Martin's translation of Pothier is less well-known than that of the English barrister, William David Evans, which was published in 1806. The two translators must have been in correspondence with each other, for in the same year that Martin's translation appeared, his firm also published—contemporaneously with publishers in Liverpool—Evans' *Essays on the Action for Money Had and Received, on the Law of Insurances, and on the Law of Bills of Exchange and Promissory Notes.*

[35] Howe, Studies in the Civil Law 348-49 (1896).

In the preface, Evans explained that the work was not "a professional exercise of the law" but a delineation of the principles of jurisprudence connected with mercantile transactions "as a matter of general science." He also mentioned that he had so frequently resorted to Pothier's *Treatise on Obligations* that he had attempted an adaptation of it to the English law and hoped to submit it to the public before long. Evans' translation, published in 1806 in England, was reissued in Philadelphia in 1826.

Peter Stephen Du Ponceau (1760-1844), another Frenchman who provided translations of civilian literature, was an almost exact contemporary of Martin and came to this country at the same time. He had learned English as a boy in France and came to America as secretary to Baron von Steuben. After the Revolutionary War he settled in Philadelphia and practiced as a lawyer. In 1797 his translation of a leading work on the conflict of laws, Ulric Huber's *De Conflictu Legum*, was published in the third volume of Dallas' *Supreme Court Reports.*[36]

Translations of the classical continental treatises of mercantile, and more especially maritime law, became quite common in the first two decades of the nineteenth century. In 1806, William Johnson of New York published *The Maritime Law of Europe* by Domenico Alberto Azuni. This work originally appeared in 1795 in Italian under the title *Sistema universale dei principi del diritto maritimo dell' Europa*, and was thereafter speedily translated into a French version (1797), from which Johnson's translation was made. Three years later Joseph Reed Ingersoll published in Philadelphia an edition, with notes, of a much older work, *A Manual of Maritime Law*, translated from the Latin of Roccus (Francesco Rocci), first published in Naples in 1655.

The same year (1809) John Elihu Hall (1783-1829) published in Baltimore *The Practice and Jurisdiction of the Court of Admiralty*. The work was in three parts: first, an historical examination of the civil jurisdiction of admiralty; second, a translation of Francis Clerke's classic *Praxis Curiae Admiralitatis*, first published in 1679; and third, a collection of precedents. Hall's enthusiasm for translations was not exhausted by his labors with Clerke. The previous year he had founded *The American Law Journal*, of which six volumes appeared between 1808 and 1817. In the preface to Volume 1, he emphasized the diffi-

[36] See Emory v. Grenough, 3 U.S. (3 Dall.) 369, 370 (1797); Nadelmann, *Peter Stephen Du Ponceau*, 24 PA. B.A.Q. 248 (1953).

culties caused by the differences between the various state laws, and expressed the hope that the *Journal*, by helping to remove the inconveniences caused by such differences, "may, in time, comprise the rudiments of a complete system of American jurisprudence."

Hall observed that "the foundation of the maritime and commercial law of *Europe*" was provided by certain titles in Justinian's *Digest*, and he proceeded to include translations of these titles in successive volumes of the *Journal*.[37]

In addition to these titles from the *Digest*, Hall published a translation of the first forty-three chapters of another fundamental source of maritime law, the *Consolato del mare*.[38] As a separate publication Hall issued in 1811 a translation of Emérigon's *An Essay on Maritime Loans* with notes and an appendix, in which he reprinted the *Digest* titles 14.1, 14.2 and 22.2, together with title 4.33 from Justinian's *Code*, on maritime loans, and the relevant section of the *Ordonnance de la Marine*. The motto of the work was taken from Juvenal,[39] *Gallia causidicos docuit facunda Britannos*. (Eloquent France has taught British pleaders.) In this book Hall announced that he expected to publish a translation of Emérigon's major work on insurance, generally considered to be the best book on the subject, but he appears not to have been able to carry out his plan. In the same year Hall stated that he had already completed a translation of Hubner's treatise on the right of searching and seizing neutral vessels, which also was never published.

In the field of international law, which, like maritime law, had a pronounced civil law content, there was a corresponding progression from translations of short elementary manuals to versions of more elaborate and more authoritative texts. Already in 1795, the Radical journalist William Cobbett published in Philadelphia a *Summary of*

[37] Volume 1, at 491 contained *Digest* 4.9 concerning the responsibility of mariners, innkeepers and stablekeepers. Volume 2 contained two titles, the short *Digest* 47.5 on the action for theft against mariners, innkeepers and stablekeepers, at 250, and *Digest* 14.1 concerning the responsibility of shipowners for the acts of the shipmaster, and the so-called *actio exercitoria*, at 462. Volume 3, at 14, had *Digest* 14.2 on the Rhodian Law concerning jettison, and, at 151, *Digest* 22.2 on maritime loans, with title 3.5 of the French Ordinance of the Marine by way of comparison.

[38] See *Il Consolato Del Mare, The Judicial Order of Proceedings before the Consular Court*, 2 American L.J. 383 (Hall transl. 1809); *Il Consolato Del Mare, The Judicial Order of Proceedings Before the Consular Court*, 3 American L. J. 1 (Hall transl. 1810); *Of Cases of Recapture, Translated from the Consolato del Mare*, 4 American L.J. 299 (Hall transl. 1813).

[39] Satires, 15.111.

*the Law of Nations*, translated from Martens' *Précis de droit des gens*, published in 1788. This work was designed as an introductory course for prospective diplomats. The following year there appeared in New York the first American edition of the classic of international law, *The Law of Nations*, by the Swiss Emerich Vattel, which had first appeared in French in 1758. New American editions of Vattel came out regularly during the first half of the nineteenth century: in Northampton, Massachusetts, 1805 and 1820; and in Philadelphia, 1817, 1829, 1835, 1844, and 1849.

In 1809, William Duane of Philadelphia produced his own sketch of *The Law of Nations* and the following year Hall published in volume 3 of the *Journal* the first book of Cornelius van Bynkershoek's *Quaestiones Iuris Publici*, translated by Peter Du Ponceau under the title of *A Treatise on the Law of War*.[40] In his preface, the translator held up the Dutch Republic as a model which the United States should emulate, observing that Holland "has proved to the world, that the republican spirit of commerce, and the honourable pursuits of industrious enterprise are not incompatible with any of those more brilliant attainments by which nations as well as individuals are raised to celebrity."[41]

The translations of continental treatises, sponsored or carried out by Hall, made a lasting contribution to American jurisprudence, though their impact may not have been as great as he hoped. His credo was stated quite simply. "[H]owever the annals of our domestic jurisprudence might fail in the contribution of materials, we should be at no loss. The legal lore of former ages and foreign nations is an abundant treasury, to which the scientific lawyer can always resort for those abstract principles of right which are applicable at all times and in all places."[42]

## IV.

The flow of translations was interrupted by the War of 1812 and its aftermath, and afterwards the emphasis of civil-law interest in the United States shifted. Henceforth it focused on the method rather than the substance of the civil law. This trend is reflected particularly in the pages of the *North American Review*, which was founded in

40 VAN BYNKERSHOEK, A TREATISE ON THE LAW OF WAR (Du Ponceau transl.), in 3 AMERICAN L.J. (1810).

41 *Id.* at xi.

42 Hall, *Advertisement to the First Volume of the Second Series*, 4 AMERICAN L.J. 1 (1813).

Boston in 1815 by William Tudor, Jr., and edited in quick succession by Tudor, Willard Phillips, Edward Everett and Jared Sparks, all of whom had strong legal interests.[43]

The *Review* tended to be Harvard-oriented and its policy in legal matters was influenced to some extent by Joseph Story (1779-1845) who had become Associate Justice of the United States Supreme Court in 1811.[44] In a review[45] of W. Frick's translation of *Laws of the Sea* by the German scholar F. J. Jacobsen, which was published in Baltimore in 1818, Story compared the achievements in commercial jurisprudence of Lord Mansfield in England with those of his contemporaries Pothier and Emérigon in France. What was wanted, he noted, was a synthesizing genius who would naturalize the work of these great innovators in the same forum. Kent led the way:

> To the honour of America, there is one man, once a chief justice, and now a chancellor, (need we name him?) whose acknowledged learning has taught us how much judicial judgments may be enriched by the manly sense of Pothier, and the acute investigation of Emerigon. . . . [W]e trust that it is no idle dream to anticipate, that the next age of the law will find our accomplished lawyers consulting the continental jurists with the same familiarity, with which we now cite Blackstone and Marshall.[46]

When considering the state of the law in 1821, Story pointed out that the jurisprudence of the twenty-three common-law states was "perpetually receding farther and farther from the common standard. . . . and the conflict of opinion upon general questions of law in the rival jurisdictions of the different states will not be less distressing to the philosophical jurists, than to the practical lawyer."[47] Furthermore,

> The mass of the law is, to be sure, accumulating with an almost incredible rapidity, and with this accumulation, the labor of students as well as professors, is seriously augmenting. It is impossible

[43] Note, 1 MASS. L.Q. 319, 322 (1916).

[44] See Dowd, *Justice Joseph Story: A Study of the Legal Philosophy of a Jeffersonian Judge*, 18 VAND. L. REV. 643 (1965); Pound, *The Place of Judge Story in the Making of American Law*, 48 AM. L. REV. 676 (1914).

[45] Story, Book Review, 7 NORTH AMERICAN REV. 323 (1818).

[46] *Id.* at 343. All contributions to the *Review* were anonymous, but an *Index* giving the authors of articles in volumes 1-125 (1815-1877) was published by William Cushing at Cambridge, Mass., 1878. It has, however, been overlooked by some historians. See, *e.g.*, AUMANN, THE CHANGING AMERICAN LEGAL SYSTEM 102, 124, 125, 153 (1940).

[47] Story, *Address to the Suffolk Bar*, 1 AMERICAN JURIST 1, 13-14 (1829).

> not to look without some discouragement upon the ponderous volumes, which the next half century will add to the groaning shelves of our jurists. The habits of generalization, which will be acquired and perfected by the liberal studies, which I have ventured to recommend, will do something to avert the fearful calamity, which threatens us, of being buried alive, not in the catacombs, but in the labyrinths of the law.[48]

The moral was clear. The multiplicity of jurisdictions and the mass of judicial opinions they produced required a concentration on general principles which would constitute a unifying element to counteract the centrifugal tendencies which he had so graphically described. Elsewhere, Story pointed to another factor which supported such a search for principles, namely the lack of specialization in the legal profession in America. In words recalling Gridley's advice to Adams, he said, "in England, the profession is broken up into distinct classes. . . . In America all this is different. The same gentleman acts, or may act, . . . in all these different capacities" (proctor, advocate, solicitor, barrister, attorney, conveyancer and special pleader). As a result the American lawyer may not be as exact as his English counterpart, "but a survey of the whole structure of the law conducts him to large and elevated views."

> He knows too, that in the American courts there is no disposition to discourage the study of foreign jurisprudence. . . . What we mean to assert is, that the general tendency of our system is to excite an ambition for such studies and attainments, and that the genius of the profession is perpetually attracted in its researches and reasonings to those general principles, which constitute the philosophy of the law.[49]

The source from which such principles were to be derived was obvious.

> Where shall we find such ample general principles to guide us in new and difficult cases, as in that venerable deposite of the learning and labors of the jurists of the ancient world, the Institutes and Pandects of Justinian. The whole continental jurisprudence rests upon this broad foundation of Roman wisdom; and the English common law, churlish and harsh as was its feudal education, has condescended silently to borrow many of its best principles from

48 *Id.* at 31.

49 Story, Book Review, 20 North American Rev. 47, 69 (1825).

> this enlightened code. . . . The law of contracts and personalty, of trusts and legacies, and charities, in England, have been formed into life by the soft solicitudes and devotion of her own neglected professors of the civil law.[50]

Story was optimistic about the prospects for a large infusion of civilian principles into America.

> There is no country on earth, which has more to gain than ours, by the thorough study of foreign jurisprudence. We can have no difficulty in adopting in new cases such principles of the maritime and civil law as are adapted to our own wants, and commend themselves by their intrinsic convenience and equity. Let us not vainly imagine, that we have unlocked and exhausted all the stores of judicial wisdom and policy. Our jurisprudence is young and flexible, but it has withal a masculine character, which may be refined and exalted by the study of the best models of antiquity.[51]

Whether the civil law would make the impact which Story expected depended on legal education. A deep knowledge of the civil law would probably always, he realized, be restricted to the more ambitious lawyers, who were not satisfied with being mere practitioners. For in his review[52] of Nathan Dane's *Digest of American Law* (1824), which included substantial extracts from the civil law, he asked:

> Can it then be doubted, that an incorporation of such of the civil law principles, as are illustrative of the common law, into an Abridgment, is of great value to students, and especially to those, who wish to acquire philosophical views of jurisprudence, and aspire to something beyond the reach of an ordinary attorney?[53]

Edward Everett was more vehement in his suggestions that legal education be reformed to take more account of the civil law. He edited the *Review* from 1820 to 1824. Having just returned from Göttingen, where he was the first American to receive the Ph.D. degree, he was naturally interested in Jefferson's proposals for the new University of Virginia, and submitted them to a detailed critique in the *Review*. Law, he observed, was taught on the continent of Europe in univer-

[50] Story, *Address to the Suffolk Bar*, 1 AMERICAN JURIST 1, 13-14 (1829).
[51] *Ibid.*
[52] Story, Book Review, 23 NORTH AMERICAN REV. 1 (1826).
[53] *Id.* at 24.

sities, whereas in England it was taught in private, "much as with us, and it is a fair question which is the best method, and which is best adapted for America." The forms of practice must admittedly be learned in the office or the court. But the bulk of our law, like the civil law, is to be learned from books. The main difference between the two systems is the lack of system in the common law, and this makes it all the more necessary to pursue the study with all the artificial aids of the academic method.

> Are not the multitude of books, the want of a digested system of the whole law, the confusion and obscurity of some of the most important treatises, and the want of reference of the whole to one grand plan of law study, are not these so many obvious reasons why an attempt should be made to supply, in the manner of learning, that method, which is wanting in the records of the science itself, and to give that symmetry to our legal education, which characterizes the writings of the continental jurists, so highly to their advantage in comparison with ours? . . . Besides our common law, which might, for the reasons we have hinted, we think, be advantageously studied in the academic method; there is the civil law, which it would do us no harm to know something of. Our law is not yet built up. Nolumus leges Angliae mutari[54] is not our principle. We will have the law of America to be changed, where it is unjust, or obscure, or wavering, or defective. It is our duty to resort to all the sources which are open to us, for the means of healing these defects, where they exist. The civil law is the richest of these sources, and ought to be studied by all, who have the perfection and honour of our jurisprudence at heart. . . . Under the circumstances, it would surely add much to the perfection of our law-studies, did we revert to the practice of our fathers before the Revolution, who, we are well informed, acquainted themselves at least with the contents of Domat.[55]

If Jefferson had had his way in the appointment of the first professor of law at the University of Virginia, there would have been a better chance of Everett's hopes being fulfilled there. For the appointment was originally given to Thomas Cooper, an accomplished civilian who

54 "We do not wish the laws of England to be changed"—the reply of the barons at Merton in 1236 to the suggestion that the canon law principle of legitimation by subsequent marriage be introduced into English law.

55 Everett, Book Review, 10 NORTH AMERICAN REV. 115, 129-30 (1820).

had already published a translation of Justinian's *Institutes*, with extensive notes (Philadelphia, 1812). But Cooper was a notorious freethinker, and clerical opposition to his appointment forced Jefferson to withdraw it.[56]

Once the hare was started, it was pursued with vigour. In the next volume of the *Review*, appeared a learned article entitled *On The Study of The Civil Law*, written by Caleb Cushing,[57] who was then aged twenty. He opened with a comment on the political implications of the civil law. "The civil law is frequently stigmatized, in the books which now form the basis of our legal education, as being in the highest degree unjust and arbitrary."[58] On the other hand, it is a system

> which is esteemed the perfection of written reason by so many enlightened nations, and which is the fountain of all the most admirable legal doctrines and maxims that pervade the continent of Europe. Republics in abundance, and those of the most jealous spirit of freedom, have made it their model and their text-book: how, then, can its principles be so completely and dangerously despotical?[59]

Apart from its intrinsic value, the civil law provides a standard of comparison.

> [I]t is by comparison of our rules and practice with those of foreigners, that we become fully sensible of what is defective or excellent, and therefore of what is to be cherished and upheld, or to be disapproved and abolished in our institutions. Nothing more inevitably checks improvement than a jealous or contemptuous rejection of foreign, and an over weening admiration of domestic habits, customs, and principles.[60]

Cushing then detailed a number of particular advantages in the study of the civil law: it includes "many things relative to personal rights, which are of special usefulness in this nation," such as the distinction between alien and citizen, the status of corporate bodies and the rules

---

[56] Curiously, the first professor of ancient languages at Virginia, George Long, was known in his later career as a Roman lawyer and became Reader in jurisprudence and civil law to the Middle Temple in London.

[57] Cushing, *On The Study of the Civil Law*, 11 NORTH AMERICAN REV. 407 (1820).

[58] *Ibid.*

[59] *Ibid.*

[60] *Id.* at 408.

on "involuntary servitude."[61] The rules and methods of chancery proceedings "are in fact close imitations of the civil law. . . . Therefore it is apparent that we must study the civil law in order to be capable of proceeding with any credit in chancery causes."[62] International law is little else but civil law. "All the modern writers on this extensive subject are to be considered little else than civilians, or expositors of that system, from which almost all our notions of natural justice are immediately deduced. Whoever is ambitious of the character and rank of a statesman must therefore unavoidably become a civilian."[63] The federal structure of the United States provides many problems "of which the common law never conceived, and for which it of course contains no provision. We have therefore constant occasion for applying the rules of the civil law concerning international intercourse."[64] Lastly the civil law is the origin of the mercantile and maritime law "which now regulates our most important affairs, as a commercial people."[65] Mansfield's great success was due as much to his knowledge of civil law as to his ability. "[F]or, without disparaging his unerring acuteness, his close, systematic reasoning, or his vigorous intellect, it is apparent that he had drunk deeply in the streams which flowed from the imperial constitutions of Justinian."[66]

Cushing's powerful conclusion deserves quotation in full:

> The common, civil, and customary law of Europe have each precisely the same force with us in this branch; that is, our courts study them all, and adopt from them whatever is most applicable to our situation, and whatever is on the whole just and expedient, without considering either of course obligatory. If Mansfield, Scott, or Ellenborough, is cited with deference or praise, so likewise are Bynkershoek, Valen, Cleirac, Pothier, and Emerigon. The authority of a decision or opinion, emanating from either of these sources, is rested on exactly the same foundation, viz. its intrinsic excellence. And if we seek instruction on mercantile law from jurists in England, why not seek it from their masters on the continent of Europe? Why do we not go to the fountain-head? Why do we content ourselves with second-hand information? In fact all

[61] *Id.* at 408-09.
[62] *Id.* at 410.
[63] *Ibid.*
[64] *Ibid.*
[65] *Id.* at 411.
[66] *Id.* at 412.

> eminent lawyers in this country sooner or later find it necessary to study the law books of the continent; but such a course ought to be more early and universal, the continental law ought to be made an important, it might almost be said the most important, branch of elementary legal education.[67]

This plea for more consultation of the continental civilians was not, perhaps, entirely disinterested. For, when he wrote it, Cushing had in the press a translation of Pothier's *Maritime Contracts of Letting to Hire* which appeared in Boston in 1820. Henry Wheaton welcomed it in the *Review*[68] with an exhaustive discussion of Pothier's life and work, in which he echoed the current refrain. The value of the translation for the legal profession lay in the fact that

> the law of contracts is necessarily the same, or very nearly the same, in every civilized and commercial country; since it depends not so much upon positive institution, as upon general principles applicable to human conduct in an advanced stage of society. The common law of England, and the commercial jurisprudence of Europe, have been largely indebted to the civil code for these principles, which were first invented by the Roman jurisconsults, and have been subsequently applied to the new relations, to which the vast increase of maritime commerce in modern times has given rise.[69]

The enthusiasm generated by this propaganda for the civil law was infectious. A new legal periodical, launched at New Haven in 1822, bore the title *The United States Law Journal and Civilian's Magazine*, and contained in the first issue a translation of Dupuy's *Historical Sketch of Roman Law*. Caleb Cushing welcomed it in a rather condescending note in the *North American Review*.[70] Expressing his pleasure at seeing "springing up in different parts of our native land, writers of inquisitive minds, sterling sense, deep science, and patriotic sentiment," he felt bound, however, to warn them "not . . . to rest contented with drawing all our law from the troubled fountains of transatlantic jurisprudence."[71] Unhappily, the *Civilian's Magazine* folded up after two issues.

67 *Ibid.*
68 Wheaton, Book Review, 13 NORTH AMERICAN REV. 1 (1821).
69 *Id.* at 2.
70 Cushing, Book Review, 16 NORTH AMERICAN REV. 181 (1823).
71 *Ibid.*

## V.

Though its impact on the legal practitioners was disappointing, the campaign for civil law had more success in the field of legal education. There the leading figures saw in the civil law the source of that academic method of legal study which they hoped would replace the traditional practical learning. It would give form and structure to the law, and would counteract the tendencies which were leading to the fragmentization of American law. Peter Du Ponceau, the translator of Huber and Bynkershoek, became provost of the Law Academy at Philadelphia in 1821. In his inaugural address, he urged the practical importance of the civil law in America where "the administration of the civil and the common Law is committed to the same Judges; and the same body of jurists is called upon to practise both."[72] As he put it in his *Dissertation on the Jurisdiction of the Courts of the United States* in 1824,

> general jurisprudence is a part of the common law, but its rules and principles are not exclusively to be found in common law writers. That science ought to be studied, particularly in this country, where a light is to be held to the judiciaries of twenty-four different States. Whence is this light to proceed, but from the writings and discussions of liberal and learned jurists?[73]

The most sustained use of the civil law as an educational medium was made by David Hoffman (1784-1854), who was born in Baltimore and was professor of law in the University of Maryland from 1816 to 1836. His most interesting work is his *A Course of Legal Study*, published in Baltimore in 1817, and republished in a greatly enlarged form in 1836. In urging the study of Roman law, Hoffman, who acquired a doctorate in law from Göttingen, stressed particularly the extensive borrowings which the English common law had made, without acknowledgment, from the civil law. The point was that a knowledge of the civil law was necessary for a proper understanding of the common law itself, and if even the English had turned to the civil law for guidance when they found no authority in their own system, Americans should do so more readily and openly.

---

[72] Du Ponceau, A Dissertation on the Jurisdiction of the Courts of the United States 169, 181 (1824).

[73] *Id.* at 126. An excerpt of the *Dissertation* is reprinted in The Legal Mind in America 107 (Miller ed. 1962).

> For it is unquestionable that there are large departments of our jurisprudence, in which, (in the absence of more authoritative law,) we may, and ought to resort to the Civil Law for light, for instruction and for authority. . . . [H]aving sprung from the Roman code, we are bound *'in casibus omissis,'* (and so we have done by long usage) to resort for illustration and authority, to the pages of the Digest and Code, in the same manner, and with the same view, as we at present resort to the modern British authorities on innumerable other subjects. In our courts of Admiralty and maritime jurisdiction, also, and in our courts of Equity, on various subjects, as likewise in the law of Contracts, of Executors, of Bailments, Legacies, Presumptions, Accession, Confusion, Extinguishment, Set-Off, &c. &c. we should appeal to the Civil Law, with as much confidence that we were resorting to an authoritative source, (when our own special provisions have failed,) as we now do to the reports of decisions in Westminster Hall, on the law of bills of exchange, policies of insurance, or charter parties.[74]

Hoffman suggested that a process of gradual modification of the law by the adoption of civilian solutions had in fact been going on. "The truth is, that the numerous departures of the American law, which have taken place since the middle of the last century, from the law of our forefathers, have been little else than so many approximations to the Roman code."[75] The same plea for a comparative, critical approach to law, was made in Hoffman's lectures, published in 1829 under the title *Legal Outlines*. Peter Cruise, reviewing that work in the *North American Review*, remarked how, in reading it, he had been "impressed with new convictions of the importance of natural jurisprudence."[76] "[I]t is certain," he opined, "that this salutary process of modification and change will be retarded in proportion as the lawyer confines himself to his indigenous jurisprudence."[77]

The Harvard Law School which began operating effectively in the 1820's exhibited the same tendency. The moving spirit was Chief Justice Isaac Parker of Massachusetts, who became Royall Professor of Law in 1816. In his inaugural address, he spoke of the conception of law held by the "galaxy of jurists, chiefly sons of Harvard," who arose

74 2 Hoffman, A Course of Legal Study 508 (2d ed. 1836).

75 *Id.* at 518.

76 Cruise, Book Review, 30 North American Rev. 135, 139 (1830).

77 *Id.* at 142.

after the Revolutionary War. "[T]he law as understood and administered by them, was a comprehensive system of human wisdom, derived from the nature of man in his social and civil state, and founded on the *everlasting basis* of natural justice and moral philosophy."[78] An account of the "flourishing state" of the school which appeared in the *American Jurist*, a new Boston law magazine, in 1830, shows that the course of study included a section on civil law, in which the famous account of Roman law in the forty-fourth chapter of Gibbon's *Roman Empire*, Justinian's *Institutes*, Pothier's *Treatise on Obligations*, selected titles from Domat's *Civil Law* and Browne's *Civil Law* were all prescribed.[79]

In his address at the dedication of the Dane Law College at Harvard in 1832, President Josiah Quincy echoed Hoffman's assertion of the unacknowledged debt of the common law to Roman law.

> It is an admitted fact, that a great proportion of the boasted wisdom of the English common law, was acquired by a silent transfer into it of the wisdom of the Roman law, through the medium of the courts of justice, and that thereby the English law was "raised from its original state of rudeness and imperfection."[80]

This process, he pointed out, was the result of the introduction of the academic study of law in the universities.

Hoffman's programme for the development of American law called for detailed studies of particular topics, in which the common law and civil law reached different solutions, and a comparison of the advantages and disadvantages of each. An example of such a study is Gulian C. Verplanck's *Essay on the Doctrine of Contracts*, published in New York in 1825. The occasion of the work was a case arising out of the situation immediately after the signing of the Treaty of Ghent ending the War of 1812. A certain merchant in New Orleans learned about the treaty before the news became public and bought a quantity of tobacco, at the low price prevailing, from a merchant who had not heard the news. It was held that he was not bound to communicate the information. Verplanck set out the respective common-law and civil-law rules concerning concealment, error and inadequate price, and dis-

[78] Inaugural Address by the Hon. Isaac Parker, in the Chapel of Harvard University, 1816, in 3 NORTH AMERICAN REV. 11, 18 (1816).

[79] *The Law Institution of Harvard University*, 4 AMERICAN JURIST 217 (1830).

[80] Address by President Josiah Quincy of Harvard University, Dedication of Dane Law College, at Harvard University, Oct. 23, 1832, in THE LEGAL MIND IN AMERICA 206-07 (Miller ed. 1962).

cussed how far positive law, in administering justice between man and man, varied from the strict honesty and good faith required by conscience. His conclusion was clear:

> No more practical or beneficial innovation can be made in our civil jurisprudence, than that of introducing the civil law rules of implied warranty of quality and kind. This should not be done piecemeal, as has occasionally been heretofore attempted, or in insulated decisions which only create confusion;—It should be done thoroughly and upon principle.
>
> The odious maxim of *Caveat Emptor* with all its trains of absurdities and contradictions, should be for ever expelled from our courts.
>
> In this reform there need be nothing wild or theoretical, or experimental. All the light that can be given by long experience, by venerable authority, by judicial wisdom, is at our command. We have but to borrow from the ancient civil law, from the more modern law of Germany, France, Holland, Scotland, and Louisiana, from the English equity, from our own insurance law, those principles and rules which have grown out of the practical experience of many centuries.[81]

Henry Wheaton welcomed Verplanck's work in the *North American Review*,[82] approved its civilian learning and showed its relation to the movement to codify the law. He was not prepared to express an opinion on the wisdom of codification but commented:

> But supposing it to be expedient, an essential preliminary to its execution would seem to be a careful examination of the present system of law and equity, in order to ascertain upon what foundations it rests, how far its different parts are reconcilable with the principles of natural justice and the dictates of reason and conscience, how far they depend upon positive institution and the mere authority of adjudged cases, and whether they can be arranged into a consistent whole, suited to the wants and adapted to promote the welfare of a highly civilized and commercial society.
>
> Such appears to be the object of the Essay before us.[83]

The main fruit of the academic revival in legal education is found

81 VERPLANCK, AN ESSAY ON THE DOCTRINE OF CONTRACTS 217 (1825).

82 Wheaton, Book Review, 22 NORTH AMERICAN REV. 253 (1826).

83 *Id.* at 258.

in the great commentaries of Kent and Story. They stem from their authors' experiences as professors of law at Columbia and at Harvard, and bear out Maitland's dictum that "taught law is tough law." As has been noted, both scholars were enthusiastic civilians, and their work shows traces of their partiality for the civil law. Both regarded David Hoffman as their guide and forerunner.

Having retired from the bench, Kent resumed his law professorship at Columbia in February 1824 and gave three series of lectures.[84] Thereafter he concentrated on his great *Commentaries on American Law*, which appeared in four volumes from 1826 to 1830. In discussing the sources of municipal law, Kent pointed out that the value of the civil law is not to be found in public law.

> In every thing which concerns civil and political liberty, it cannot be compared with the free spirit of the English and American common law. But upon subjects relating to private rights and personal contracts, and the duties which flow from them, there is no system of law in which principles are investigated with more good sense, or declared and enforced with more accurate and impartial justice.[85]

The *Commentaries* displayed the broad sweep of American law for the first time, and provoked much speculation on its particular character. One of the most thoughtful reviews was by Hugh Swinton Legaré (1797-1843). After studying law for three years in his home state of South Carolina, Legaré spent two years in Europe, studying languages in Paris and law in Edinburgh. In 1827 he was one of the founders of the *Southern Review*, a counterblast to the *North American Review*, on whose form and style its own were obviously modelled. His review of the first two volumes of Kent's *Commentaries* appeared in 1828.[86]

Legaré opened by remarking that after independence the American people could no longer import their opinions ready-made "by balefuls" from England. They were "compelled by the very novelty of their situation to think for themselves." In politics they were confident of their success. "If anything is taken for granted in this country, as a truth better established than all others, it is that in matters of government

[84] COLUMBIA UNIVERSITY FOUNDATION FOR RESEARCH IN LEGAL HISTORY, A HISTORY OF THE SCHOOL OF LAW—COLUMBIA UNIVERSITY 11-18 (1955).

[85] 1 KENT, COMMENTARIES ON AMERICAN LAW 507 (1826).

[86] Legaré, Book Review, 2 SOUTHERN REV. 72 (1828), reprinted in 2 WRITINGS OF HUGH SWINTON LEGARÉ 102 (1845).

we have found the philosopher's stone—and are now in possession of an infallible secret to make men free and happy, and to keep them so for ever, even in spite of themselves." This, suggested Legaré, is "not only an error, but a most pernicious error. [N]o constitution in the world is worth a straw but public opinion and national character. . . . [N]o general principles in politics—except such as are too general to be of much practical utility—can be safely depended upon in the administration of affairs."[87]

While politics can "scarcely aspire to the dignity of a science at all," law, by contrast, is "at once the most exact and the most complicated of the moral sciences." The separation from England took place at a very critical juncture, from the standpoint of legal development. The modernization of the law at the hands of Hardwicke and Mansfield was still in a state of progress and improvement. Many important decisions were still to be made. As a result American courts had the opportunity of considering many matters after they had been disposed of in England and of accepting or rejecting the English solutions. In helping them to reach a judgment upon such matters of new impression, they could have recourse to the writings of the civilians. These are manifestly of vast utility. For, aside from matters of coincidence and similarity between legal systems, "there is a tendency to a gradual abolition of merely technical rules and arbitrary institutions, and to the adoption in their stead of such as are more simple and rational, and of more universal application."[88] Legaré here referred to the Roman notion of the *ius gentium* as the body of institutions, "which are so manifestly reasonable and proper, or so agreeable to the general condition and exigencies of society, as to have found their way into every system of laws."[89] In an advanced state of society, he noted, a very large portion of every system of jurisprudence is *juris gentium*, as each body of law approximates more and more to the standard of what natural reason has laid down among all peoples. Comparison suggests that the substantive similarities are far more numerous than the peculiarities.

> Thus, by our law, the most solemn contract is in the shape of a sealed writing—by the civil, it was a verbal stipulation. So far there is a wide difference between them; but for one question that arises about the *form* of a covenant, there will be, at least, a hun-

---

[87] 2 Writings of Hugh Swinton Legaré 103-04 (1845).

[88] *Id.* at 107.

[89] *Id.* at 108.

> dred involving principles of universal application; as to the meaning of the parties, the extent to which their responsibility goes, the effect of fraud, mistake or duress, the rights and liability of sureties, &c. In all such matters, the writings of the Civilians are a never-failing source of light and instruction, and we have no hesitation in saying that, in many most important enquiries, we have derived, in the course of our own experience, much greater assistance from Voet and Cujacius, or Domat and Pothier, than from our own books.[90]

While eschewing a comparison of the respective merits of the civil and common laws, Legaré expressed the view that "the civil law will be found, in general, to study a refined equity more than the policy of society, whereas the common law seldom departs from its stern maxim, that a private injury is better than a public inconvenience."[91]

It is not, however, so much in its substance that the civil law is superior to the common law as in its form. For it has a clear advantage in the manner in which it has been expounded and illustrated.

> In comparing what the Civilians have written upon any subjects that have been treated of by English text writers, or discussed in the English courts, it is, we think, impossible not to be struck with the superiority of their truly elegant and philosophical style of analysis and exposition. Their whole arrangement and method—the division of the matter into its natural parts, the classification of it under the proper predicaments, the discussion of principles, the deduction of consequences and corollaries—every thing, in short, is more luminous and systematic—every thing savors more of a regular and exact science. Even Blackstone . . . admits that before his time "the theoretical, elementary parts of the law had received a very moderate share of cultivation". . . . There is, in spite of all the pompous eulogies that have been passed upon . . . [the *Commentaries*], a great deal of justness in Horne Tooke's remark, that "it is a good gentleman's law book, clear, but not deep."[92]

None of the other elementary writers of the common law are any better:

---

90 *Id.* at 109.
91 *Id.* at 110.
92 *Ibid.*

> They are mere *pragmatici*—who treat their subjects in a strictly technical manner, and whose whole system of logic consists of a case in point. They seem to dread nothing more than generalization, or the stating a proposition in the form of a theorem. They string together cases from which it is often difficult to extract any distinct, general principle, and which are determined to be analogous, or otherwise, by circumstances comparatively immaterial. Let any one reflect upon the confusion into which the courts of England were betrayed in their attempts to reconcile the necessity of words of perpetuity to carry the fee in a will, with the rule that the intention shall govern, and the figure which a digest of these decisions makes as part of a scientific system![93]

As he warmed to the charge, Legaré became more vehement and concluded that common-law jurisprudence gives the impression of "a mass of irregularities and incoherencies, which consists rather in particular usages and occasional decisions, than in immutable principles, or in consequences deduced immediately from the rules of natural justice."[94]

It was significant, he pointed out, that at one time the same complaints were made about the civil law. Indeed the excellencies which characterize the writings of the civilians "do not arise out of anything in the nature of that law, but solely from the preparatory discipline and general intellectual habits of its professors," who have been in effect philosophers.

> There are among the Civilians those who have pushed this love of systematic arrangement and close rigorous logic so far, as to emulate the reasonings of the geometricans. Thus, Puffendorf made his debut in the learned world by a work, entitled 'Elements of Natural Law, according to a Mathematical Order.' Heineccius also, who has been pronounced by a high authority, the first of elementary writers, adopts the same precise method in his popular commentaries upon the Digest and the Institutes. His way is to begin with a definition, which is made as comprehensive as possible. He then proceeds to deduce from it, what he calls *axiomata*, or clear, indisputable propositions. These he again applies to more complicated questions, and runs them down to all their consequences, with wonderful exactness and logical connections.[95]

93 *Id.* at 111.
94 *Id.* at 112.
95 *Id.* at 114.

Following the Scottish philosopher Dugald Stewart, whom he had no doubt heard in Edinburgh, Legaré affirmed his conception of the legal system as a logically consistent whole.

> In all other sciences, the propositions, which we attempt to establish, express *facts*, real or supposed, whereas in mathematics (and we may add, in jurisprudence also) the propositions which we demonstrate, only assert a connection between certain suppositions and certain consequences. The premises which we proceed upon are altogether arbitrary—we frame our definitions at will and reason from them. . . . Our reasonings, therefore, in mathematics and in law, are directed to objects essentially different from those of the other sciences—not to ascertain *truths* with respect to real existences, but to trace the logical filiation of consequences which follow from an arbitrary hypothesis, and, if, from this hypothesis we reason with precision, the evidence of the result is of course irresistible.[96]

Could American law be made more rational and systematic? Legaré concluded with an expression of cautious optimism.

> It is true that, owing to something in the state of public opinion here, or the uncertainty of popular elections, the bench in America is not always as ably filled as it might be, and our books of reports, along with much learning and ability, are often encumbered with disgraceful trash—with truisms pompously elaborated, or with exhibitions of deplorable ignorance. We are disposed to think, that our lawyers, although they sometimes excel the English in the discussion of great principles and of new points, are not, however, so *thorough-paced* in their profession, so familiar with 'the file,' as they. . . . But this evil will be corrected in the progress of things: and, in the mean time, the character, which is already stamped upon the profession in this country, of liberal, and enlarged and philosophical enquiry, holds out to us the most encouraging prospects of future excellence.[97]

## VI.

The 1820's and 1830's were the hey-day of the civil law in the United States. The publication of Edward Livingston's Civil Code for Louisi-

[96] *Id.* at 115.
[97] *Id.* at 117.

ana in 1825 seemed to assert its ascendancy and to presage an extension of its influence among the common-law states. Yet by 1850, it had probably ceased to be a real force in the development of American law. Why?

Various reasons may be suggested. First, the most zealous champions of the civil law were members of the legal establishment, and the older of them tended to be Federalists and Whigs in their politics. Story and Kent had held high judicial office, Everett became Secretary of State, Caleb Cushing and Hugh Legaré both became Attorney General of the United States. Their enthusiasm for the civil law never permeated down to the humdrum practitioner of the law. Indeed it probably seemed to him to be one of the characteristics which marked them off from the likes of him. When he did think about more general aspects of the law than those which occurred in his daily practice, it was to public law and politics that the average American lawyer turned his mind rather than to the law of private rights. Once he had mastered the details of the latter, he preferred not to see it changed. So appeals to the civil law as "the principal source from which we may derive means of improving this department of legislation and jurisprudence in our country"[98] tended to leave him cold. He had no burning desire to improve the law of private rights.

Secondly, the intellectual leaders of the legal profession themselves turned away from the civil law as a means for developing American law. The more philosophically inclined among them, those who had earlier been attracted by the broad principles and systematic arrangement of the civil law, were now thinking in terms of codification of the law. They drew their inspiration from the ideas of Jeremy Bentham[99] rather than of Justinian, and their model was the *Code Napoleon* rather than the *Digest*.

Those whose tastes were more classical and "liberal," in the contemporary sense, were now less interested in the civil law as expounded by Domat and Pothier than in the law of the classical Roman jurists, seen as a manifestation of the culture of antiquity. The historical school of jurists, led by the Germans, Hugo and Savigny, had turned the attention of scholars to the more antiquarian aspects of Roman law. In 1817 Niebuhr discovered in the Cathedral Library of Verona a manuscript of the *Institutes* of Gaius. The discovery was hailed as the first great

98 Follen, *Law School at Cambridge*, 36 North American Rev. 395, 417 (1833).

99 See Everett, *Bentham in the United States of America*, in Jeremy Bentham and the Law 185 (Keeton & Schwartzenberger eds. 1948).

triumph of the historical school. The *Institutes* were the only complete work of a classical jurist which was transmitted directly and not merely through excerpts in Justinian's compilation. Edward Everett commented on the discovery in the *North American Review* in 1821.[100] He noted that even before the publication of the manuscript, its discovery "was frequently pronounced to promise an *era* in the study of Roman law, and to exceed in importance any other which had been made, since that of the manuscript of the Pandects." But he doubted its practical importance. "We are apprehensive, however, when we reflect on the mass of Roman law condensed into the Corpus Juris, and contained in the Jurisprudentia Antejustinianea, as well as on the mutilated and illegible state in which the Verona manuscript appears to exist; that, though single questions of learned jurisprudence may receive light from the discovery, yet no new point of great practical moment will be disclosed."[101]

By the 1840's, however, the historical school was winning. The study of Roman law had become part of gentlemanly learning; it was motivated by "elegance" rather than "utility."[102] In 1841, a New Orleans lawyer, Gustavus Schmidt, founded the *Louisiana Law Journal* which seems to have been inspired by Savigny. In the course of its single year of life, the new review contained a discussion of Savigny's *Treatise on Possession*, and a number of purely historical items, including an *Outline of the History of the Roman Law*, by Schmidt himself.[103] A copy of the first issue was sent to the aged Kent, who acknowledged it in an illuminating letter.

> I admire the Roman law, but I am too old (by the way I am 78 this day), or too dull, or too much disciplined in the English common law, to relish greatly the metaphysical theories and philological *minutiae* of the German Philosophers and Jurists. . . . I am tired of everlasting Commentaries on Roman law and Roman early History. Life is too short, and we have too much to learn and put in practice this side of the Atlantic to enter deeply into such kind of researches. As far as concerns my own private study and amusement, I would not give one cent for any new, laborious, profound and prolix German Commentator on Virgil, Horace, Juve-

100 Everett, Book Review, 12 NORTH AMERICAN REV. 385 (1821).
101 *Id.* at 392.
102 Jolowicz, *Utility and Elegance in Civil Law Studies*, 65 L.Q. REV. 322 (1949).
103 LA. L.J., Apr. 1842, p. 109.

nal, Livy or Tacitus, because my relish for them is sufficiently strong, glowing and accurate for all the useful purposes for which I study them. So I find sufficient in the texts of the Institutes and the Pandects for all the illustration of the principles of the Roman jurisprudence that I care for. . . .[104]

Thereafter the study of Roman law declined in the United States. There were sporadic bursts of interest, mainly in the South, such as *The Use and Authority of Roman Jurisprudence in the Law Concerning Real Estate*, published by James M. Walker in Charleston, South Carolina, in 1850. But otherwise references to it were antiquarian in tone. It is significant that Luther Cushing's Harvard lectures on Roman law,[105] though they solemnly listed a number of practical benefits to be derived from its study, dealt almost exclusively with the external history of the institutions of Roman law and hardly at all with its substance.

[104] *Id.*, Aug. 1841, p. 158.

[105] Cushing, An Introduction to the Study of the Roman Law (1854).

# Part III
# The Civil Code and Statutory Interpretation

# [9]

## STATUTORY INTERPRETATION—CIVILIAN STYLE

KONRAD ZWEIGERT* AND HANS-JÜRGEN PUTTFARKEN**

### INTRODUCTION

Interpretation is necessitated by darkness of language, juridical interpretation by ambiguity of language destined to determine legal decisions. Such language may be contained in a private juridical act—a contract or a will—or in a rule of law—case law, customary law, or statute. The need for interpretation in both categories follows from its being pronounced by human beings. Law as well as private legal transactions aim at resolving past or present conflicts, and at avoiding or regulating future conflicts. Even man's ability to make a clear statement of facts which have already happened is limited; and his inability to presage future events is genuinely human. Therefore, man can set up a legal order only for such future conflicts which he knows from experience are likely to arise, or which he is able to imagine. But experience and imagination do not match the inventiveness of reality. At the root of the problem of interpretation we thus find man's limited ability for exact statements and his inability of genuine prophecy. Whereas in these cases the ambiguity of legal language is unintentional, there may be instances where it is calculated—usually, where the legislator does not have a solution for a problem known to him, and therefore relies on courts and professors to find it in the course of time.

The problem of interpreting private juridical acts has by and large been mastered by civil law doctrine and practice. Also, the interpretation of law has almost always been mastered with much common sense—in practice. However, we cannot claim in good faith that we have developed an adequate doctrine of interpretation, that we have been able to reduce the results of practice to a consistent and rational system of rules or methods of interpretation, in spite of an important body of literature in this field.[1] It would seem as

---

* Dr. iur; Professor of Law, University of Hamburg; Director, Max-Planck-Institut für ausländisches und internationales Privatrecht.

** M.C.L., Michigan; Research Associate, Max-Planck-Institut für ausländisches und internationales Privatrecht.

[1] *Cf.* the works of Emilio Betti, *Ergänzende Rechtsfortbildung als Aufgabe der richterlichen Gesetzesauslegung*, Festschrift für Leo Raape 379 (1948); Interpretazione della legge e degli atti giuridici (1949); *Zur Grundlegung einer allgemeinen Auslegungslehre*, 2 Festschrift für Ernst Rabel 79 (1954); Teoria generale della interpretazione, (1955); *Di Problematik der Auslegung in der Rechtswissenschaft*, Festschrift für Karl Engisch 205 (1969). In Germany, probably the most influential studies have been by Theodor Viehweg, Topik und Jurisprudenz (1953), and Josef Esser, Grundsatz und Norm in der richterlichen Fortbildung des Privatrechts, Rechtsvergleichende

if from a certain point, juridical interpretation defies all attempts to put it into a system, that there are moments of artistic inspiration which are beyond rationalization. Max Weber has stated in his sociology of the law[2] not only that making law and finding law shift between the rational and the irrational in the course of their historical development but also that any actual way of interpretation has its strata of rational and irrational ("charismatic") elements that are difficult to disentangle. However, this must not lead us to the conclusion—which would be "pure" according to Kelsen's pure theory of law[3]—but inadequate for jurisprudence, being a "non-exact" social science—that the science of law could only find the "gaps" in the law but would be incompetent to fill them.[4] This would be the end of all rational legal thinking. The task of methodology is to find the rational elements in the processes of interpretation, to extend if possible the field of the rational, and to draw the line toward the irrational. That there is such a line, and that "the basically non-mechanical nature of the judicial process"[5] involves a substantial influence of common sense which is beyond rationalization is most probable, but this fact must not discourage us from further scrutiny. Such is the background for the present discussion of legal interpretation.

## Statutory Interpretation in Civil Law and in Common Law

A caveat for the common law lawyer seems called for at this point. Up to now, we have discussed legal interpretation in general terms, and have included all three of the main traditional sources of law, *i.e.*, statutory law, customary law, and case law. The scope of this paper is limited to statutory interpretation, for the present civil law methods of legal interpretation have been developed almost exclusively for statutory law. Except for part of Germany where "Roman Common Law" was in force until the enactment of the Civil Code (*Bürgerliches Gesetzbuch*) in 1900, most of Western Europe—those countries which we usually refer to as "civil law

Beiträge zur Rechtsquellen-und Interpretationslehre (1956). For a most recent and comprehensive survey of the problem, *cf.* K. Larenz, Methodenlehre der Rechtswissenschaft 291, 341 (2d rev. ed. 1969).

[2] Wirtschaft und Gesellschaft, (3d ed. 1947), II. Halbband 387, 394, In English—Max Weber, On Law in Economy and Society 41, 59, 63 (M. Rheinstein ed., M. Rheinstein & E. Shils transl. 1954).

[3] *Cf. H. Kelsen, Was ist die Reine Rechtslehre?*, in: Demokratie und Rechtsstaat, Festgabe für Giacometti 143, 150 (1953). Kelsen would certainly not have accepted this phrasing; however, his fundamental contra-distinction of interpretation by the law-applying authority and interpretation by legal science would seem to mean exactly this.

[4] *Cf.* Betti, *Ergänzende Rechtsfortbildung, supra* note 1, at 380.

[5] von Mehren, *The Judicial Process in the United States and Germany*, I Festschrift für Ernst Rabel 77 (1954).

systems"—has had codified law for at least a century.[6] Customary law, which in the civil law terminology does not mean law made by judges, but law arising from common usage prior to any judicial recognition, has become virtually negligible; the methods of finding and applying it are well-settled in theory, and almost irrelevant as a practical matter.[7]

Case law, *i.e.*, judge-made law, presents quite the opposite picture: it is of manifest practical importance in today's civil law systems, and yet the problems of its methodology and of integrating it into a system which basically remains one of codified law have not been resolved, nor even generally recognized as one of the greatest issues of present civil law jurisprudence.[8] We shall revert to this point later.

The core of my caveat is to warn the reader not to equate and compare prematurely civil law methods of statutory interpretation with common law rules or "maxims" of statutory interpretation. The common law rules were developed for "special statutes," *i.e.*, statutes passed by the legislature to cope with urgent problems of the day, and limited to such single problems. This was at a time when legislation was regarded as exceptional and was applied strictly and narrowly by the courts so as to confine it to the cases which it expressly covered. One observer remarked of the English courts in 1882 that some of their rules of statutory interpretation "cannot well be accounted for except upon the theory that Parliament generally changes the law for the worse, and that the business of the judge is to keep the mischief of its interference within the narrowest possible bounds."[9] We do not mean to say that this is still the attitude prevailing among common law judges; however, rules once established have a strong tendency to persist, and so it is the civil law jurist's impression of the common law rules of statutory interpretation that they tend more toward restricting than toward extending the scope of application of a statute.[10]

The civil law pattern is quite different: Our rules of interpreta-

[6] *E.g.*, the Prussian General Code—*Preussisches Allgemeines Landrecht* (1794); the French *Code Civil* (1804); and the Austrian General Civil Code —*Allgemeines Bürgerliches Gesetzbuch* (1811). The French and Austrian codes are still in force today.

[7] [*See* accompanying article by Dean Rodriguez Ramos, 44 Tul. L. Rev. 723 (1970). Ed.] *Cf.* § 293 of the German Code of Civil Procedure of 1877, which does not require the courts to know customary law ex officio, and authorizes them to request evidence in order to ascertain the existence of a rule of customary law.

[8] *Cf.* accompanying article by Judge Tate, 44 Tul. L. Rev. 673 (1970). [Ed.]

[9] F. Pollock, Essays in Jurisprudence and Ethics 85 (1882).

[10] *Cf.* Stone, *The Common Law in the United States*, 50 Harv. L. Rev. 4, 12, 13 (1936).

tion have been developed mainly for the construction of codes. This does not mean to say that we do not have "special statutes" in the sense outlined above, or that they are of lesser importance than in common law systems. Quite to the contrary: it would seem to be a fair estimate that the volume of special statute law by far exceeds the volume of code law, and that cases decided under special statutes outnumber the cases decided under code rules. However, traditional civil law jurisprudence has focused mainly, if not exclusively, on the codes, and all civilian methodology including legal interpretation is, basically, code methodology. There are several reasons for this. First, a code usually contains, either in a separate part or implied in other provisions throughout the whole text, the "general part," *i.e.*, the basic rules and the basic philosophy of its specific area of law, and such general problems have always been the greater challenge for legal thinking. Secondly, when codes were first enacted, they were a new phenomenon in the history of law, and this fact alone probably attracted vast energies of legal thinking. Thirdly, special statutes are normally of more recent origin than the codes, they are more specific, their language more up to date,[11] their legislative intention less obscured by the lapse of time, and so they need less interpretation. Fourthly, a code regulates a whole area of law—such as private law, commercial law, or criminal law—and considering its coverage, is fairly short and concise.[12] Normally, its language is general and very abstract, giving rise to a large amount of statutory construction.

This last point is the basic reason that civil law rules of statutory interpretation show a pronounced tendency toward extending

---

[11] Although the fact should be noted that *e.g.*, the German Civil Code, although difficult in some areas to understand even for a trained lawyer, is a masterpiece of exactness and clarity in its carefully defined terminology, as compared to some more recent examples of careless and hasty draftsmanship. The French *Code Civil*, on the other hand, is easier to understand and more popular in its language but at times lacks the scientific precision of the German Code. For a brief outline of the differences, and the reasons for the differences, in these two most important civil law codes, see F. Lawson, A Common Lawyer Looks at the Civil Law 52 (1955).

[12] The German Civil Code in its original text had 2385 sections, the French Civil Code 2281, both covering the entire field of traditional private law. The German Commercial Code numbers 460 sections, excluding the Fourth Book on maritime law, while the United States Uniform Commercial Code numbers some 400 sections, and covers a much wider field than the German Code. The only notable exception was the Prussian Code of 1794 which attempted—and by necessity failed—to pre-regulate in minute detail each and any case which life could possibly bring up. It had some 17,000 sections, with the result that it was never really appreciated as long as it was in force. It is today only, in historical retrospective, that we regard it as a piece of good legislation containing some surprisingly modern ideas of law. Some of its provisions, although no longer in force technically, are still being applied today as rules of customary law.

the scope of application of a statute rather than toward restricting it, a tendency reinforced by the fact that even the more specialized parts of a code are not kept up to date by the legislature. If a code provision, taken at face value, thus ceases to conform to today's standards of law and social order, its meaning has to be changed by reinterpretation; or, as an alternative remedy, some other code provision has to be extended beyond its original scope; or some "general principle" has to be concocted from a number of statutory rules, and applied instead of a provision that has become obsolete. In general, the civil law judge enjoys—or perhaps, suffers—much greater freedom in interpreting statutory or code provisions than the common law judge.

As for special statutes, we apply the same rules of interpretation as for code law, perhaps with some slight modifications. The dichotomy of case law and statute law, the mistrust of legislation which was, in particular, the mark of the English common law of the nineteenth century, could not possibly have developed in a civil law system. Technically speaking, codes are statutes like any special statute, and they have never been regarded as anything fundamentally different. It may even be said that at times, civil law judges have submitted to legislative authority to a greater extent than was becoming to the law.

For the purpose of comparison—which would be a worthwhile task but cannot be fully accomplished in the framework of this short paper—it should be obvious that the common law rules of statutory interpretation are in no way equivalent to the civil law methods of code interpretation. It has become a truism that comparative law has to be functional; *i.e.*, only such legal institutions may be compared which, in different legal systems, play the same practical part in the whole of the judicial process. The mere fact of showing the same flag—"interpretation"—is an insufficient basis for comparison; it may be dangerously misleading or, at best, fruitless.

A code is, in the definition of section 1-104 of the Uniform Commercial Code, "a general act intended as a unified coverage of its subject matter";[13] its common law counterpart would not be any single statute but rather the whole body of case authority pertaining to the entire field of law which in a civil law system is covered

[13] A civil law code should not be confused with the general American usage of the term "code," the most notable example of which is the United States Code. Such American codes are, in the words of an American observer, "ordered collections of separately enacted statutes rather than unitary codes enacted as such." Farnsworth, An Introduction to the Legal System of the United States 71 (1963).

by a code. The proper object of comparison for the civil law methods of code interpretation is not the common law system of statutory interpretation but rather the methods of legal reasoning from precedents, the techniques of case law, the ways of distinguishing cases, of determining holdings and dicta, of ascertaining the *ratio decidendi* of previous cases, and thus finally distilling the rule of law applicable to the issues of a present case. It is submitted that this comparison of two apparently disparate legal techniques would yield the most striking similarities between the common law and civil law systems.

STANDARDS OF INTERPRETATION: HISTORICAL VS. ACTUALIZING

It is in the process of application of law that a lawyer—judge, attorney, or professor—encounters the problem of interpretation. Interpretation is necessary if finding the law for a certain set of facts does not work without friction, be it that a rule of law which appears to have some relation to the facts is ambiguous as to whether it is really applicable, or that the whole body of law does not yield a rule applicable to this specific case. Since in all modern systems of law a judge must not refuse to decide a case because he cannot find a rule applicable to it, he has to resort to interpretation in order to clear the doubts or fill the gaps in the law.[14]

So the central problem of interpretation is to search for meaning where words are ambiguous or incomplete—meaning, that is, which can serve as the *ratio decidendi* for an actual case. How to solve this problem has been an age-old controversy of civil law jurisprudence: is this *ratio decidendi*—or, as we say in the terminology of codified law, *ratio legis*—to be ascertained by historical or by actualizing methods? More specifically, should the judge look to the meaning which the historic "legislator" intended a specific rule of law to have or which he would have given it had he known the present case? Or, on the contrary, does the judge have the authority, and consequently the obligation, to apply different, actual standards of interpretation, with the result that the law, and every rule of it, would lead a life of its own, cut loose from the original intention of the historic legislator and given its meaning by the judge? Arguments against the historical method are plentiful, and it may fairly be said that modern jurisprudence tends toward actualizing interpretation. Is it not, as we may ask following a Canadian observer, too fallacious, at the very basis of the historical method of interpretation, "to assume that the author of ambiguous words had any definite intention as to their mean-

[14] *See* accompanying article by Dean Rodriguez Ramos, 44 Tul. L. Rev. 720 (1970). [Ed.]

ing? If he was aware of the ambiguity, then surely the assumption should be that he was being deliberately ambiguous. If he was not aware of the ambiguity, then the assumption is patently ridiculous."[15]

Fascinating as this argument would appear, it seems to be a little too abstract in itself—or maybe it is only correct as to the typical common law statute and the problems of interpretation arising therefrom. It does not give due regard to the necessary abstractness of civil law code provisions which to a large extent accounts for the necessity of statutory construction in civil law systems. Here, the "legislative intention" may very well have been clear, but for the sake of conciseness of the code it had to be framed in abstract rather than specific language.

There are other arguments against an historical method of interpretation. First, every case which presents an issue of statutory interpretation is a case of today, *i.e.*, an actual conflict of interests. However, facts and values of society and standards of social behavior change in the course of time, and they do so at an ever-increasing rate. Value judgments made by the historic legislator may have lost their basis and, consequently, their validity under the social conditions of today. Were the judge to decide a case on an historical interpretation of a statute, the law would be petrified in the value judgments of the historic legislator. It has been suggested that in order to avoid this petrification the proper test would be to ask what the historic legislator would have decided had he known the present set of facts. But this would mean imposing on the judge a "divinatorial" interpretation which would be more uncertain and less rational than any actualizing method of interpretation, and would also run the risk that "mistakes in the formation of the legislative command—which lies in the past—would be regarded as absolutely binding, and would be transferred upon the judicial interpretation if such mistakes had, presumably, arisen in legislating on the problems at issue."[16]

The second argument against the historical interpretation is that it is difficult, if not impossible, to ascertain the legislative intention. The modern legislator is an anonymous entity comprising a plurality of persons and a plurality of intentions. A realistic approach, if possible at all, has to depart from the assumption that only the draftsmen in the executive agencies and those very few members of the legislative branch who seconded a bill in the committees and on the floor may possibly have had a clear picture of the legislative intention of a dubious statute. The Supreme Court of

[15] Kilgour, *The Rule Against the Use of Legislative History*, 30 Canadian Bar Review 769, 771-72 (1952).
[16] Betti, *Ergänzende Rechtsfortbildung*, *supra* note 1, at 389.

the United States has in fact ruled that "utterances of only such persons who have actually and not merely constructively influenced the passage of a bill, and only such utterances which unequivocally demonstrate the position taken by the legislature"[17] may be admitted as evidence of legislative will.[18]

But even this approach would seem to be arbitrary. Substituting for the "intention of the legislator" the intentions of a few specialists—staff of the agencies and members of the legislative committees—could hardly be reconciled with the objectivity of the law. Even for most lawyers, and definitely for the average citizen for whose conduct and transactions the law is supposed to be the guide, such "intentions" are unknown and, even if recorded, are not easily accessible. They have the text of the law to rely on, and for them, its interpretation by legislative intention is even more an *ex post facto* interpretation by the courts than would be its interpretation by any other method. Historical interpretation overlooks the fact that statements of intention by drafters, members of the legislature, etc., have not been enacted into the law.

On a more philosophical basis, the necessity of actualizing rather than historical interpretation has been worked out by German jurisprudence, and has been epitomized in an almost classical form by one of the most famous German jurists of this century, Gustav Radbruch:

> The Will of the State which speaks through the law, and through the law alone, is as foreign to its creators as it is for its succeeding interpreters, and their belief to have expressed in the statute a certain idea of the law cannot prevail over the interpreter's finding a different meaning in it. It is nothing but the contents of the law itself that are decisive . . . . The intention of the legislator speaking through the law is not the intention of the draftsman, not an idea once conceived, not a definite fact of history; it is subject to constant development, answering to new demands and new questions with new meanings of which the drafter of the law could not possibly have known. The history of a legal concept does not come to an end when it is reduced to a statute, nor is the ensuing history of its different interpretations a sequence of misunderstandings; on the contrary, the successive plurality of equally valid interpretations unfolds, beyond any prediction of the author, the fertility of the concept which is being appropriated anew and in different form by every new generation.[19]

---

[17] Silving, *A Plea for a Law of Interpretation*, 98 U. Penn. L. Rev. 499, 506 (1950).

[18] *E.g.*, United States v. United Mine Workers, 330 U.S. 258, 276 (1947); Chicago, M., St. P. & P. R.R. v. Acme Fast Freight, 336 U.S. 465 (1949).

[19] Radbruch, Einführung in die Rechtswissenschaft (9. Auflage 1958), besorgt von Konrad Zweigert, 243 (author's translation).

This certainly does not mean that the intention of the historic legislator is without any importance whatsover. It cannot possibly be binding either. If a legal rule in the course of its development has been subject to a change of meaning by different interpretations, we cannot today start interpreting it as if it had never been interpreted before; we cannot totally disregard history. The "legislative materials" may at least serve as a starting point; they may yield aspects of interpretation which are still valid today, and they may be most important as additional support for an interpretation based on actual criteria if the result of such interpretation coincides with the intention of the historic legislator. An absolute ban on the use of legislative history, which seems to be the rule in England and Canada,[20] would therefore seem to be out of place.

It is another result of this historical development of different meanings of a legal rule that there is a proportion between the age of the rule and the weight of its "legislative intention": as for a recent statute, there is a presumption that its meaning as intended by its draftsmen in the legislature should be its actual meaning;[21] however, the older a statute, the more legitimate is a method of interpretation which frees itself from the ideas of the historic legislator and attempts to find its meaning from different criteria based on the conditions of today.

### THE PLAIN MEANING RULE VS. REASONING BY ANALOGY

The perimeter of the field of interpretation in traditional jurisprudence is marked by the plain meaning rule on the one hand, and reasoning by analogy on the other. The plain meaning rule—in civil law jurisprudence usually referred to under its French term *sens clair*—hardly needs to be explained to the common law jurist; it is the equivalent of the old common doctrine and has much the same meaning: "Where the statute is 'clear,' 'plain,' and 'unambiguous' on its face, so that taken by itself it is fairly susceptible of only one construction, that construction must be given to it and any inquiry into the purposes, background, or legislative history of the statute is foreclosed."[22] Although this rule supposedly derives from Justinian's Digest—*cum in verbis nulla ambiguitas est, non debet admitti voluntatis quaestio*[23]—it has fallen into almost com-

[20] Maxwell on the interpretation of Statutes 26 (11th ed. Wilson & Galpin 1962); *cf.* Kilgour, *supra* note 15, at 770.

[21] *Cf.* one of the first judgments of the German Federal Constitutional Court, 1 BVerfGE 127, 130 (1952).

[22] Farnsworth, *supra* note 13, at 72.

[23] Paulus, D.32.25.1. The fact should be noted that in its original context, this maxim refers to the interpretation of a will rather than of a statute; a fine example of interpreting into a text a meaning which by its plain words it was not intended to have.

plete disfavor in civil law jurisprudence. Even the most authoritative, and, with due respect, most conservative, treatise on German civil law gives a strongly worded warning against applying the plain meaning rule.[24] However, in practice it does reappear now and then,[25] and when it does, it usually meets with severe criticism.

The basic argument against the plain meaning rule is the self-contradicting assumption that an "unambiguous" meaning would render an interpretation superfluous, "for that unambiguity is . . . in itself a result of interpretation."[26] Language is "plain" only if its meaning is plain; if not, the language is ambiguous. So in reality, it is the meaning, and the meaning only which we examine; whether or not we regard a statute as having a plain meaning is a result of our interpretation of the statute. Deciding a case on the basis of the plain meaning of a rule is, in terms of logic, a tautology; psychologically speaking, it is hypocrisy, for the judge who renders judgment on this ground pretends to give a reason for his decision, when actually he gives none.[27]

The concept most unfamiliar to common law practice seems to be that of analogy[28]—unfamiliar, of course, only insofar as statutes

---

[24] L. Enneccerus — H. Nipperdey, 1 Lehrbuch des bürgerlichen Rechts, Allgemeiner Teil, part 1, 333 (15th ed. 1959).

[25] One most recent example is a judgment by the Federal Supreme Court, Fifth Senate for Criminal Matters, applying to a Nazi criminal case a provision of the Criminal Code (sec. 50, sub. 3 StGB) introduced by a law the main purpose of which was to take traffic violations out of the ambit of the Criminal Code and turn them into administrative offences (Introductory Act of the Law of Administrative Offences of 24 May 1968, BGBl. I, 503). The legislative intention was clear in that this provision was plainly not intended to cover this case; by the time the judgment was rendered it was obvious that the wording of the statute was due to a gross oversight of the draftsmen in the Ministry of Justice and of the members of the Parliamentary Committee. The Court applied it nevertheless on the ground that by its words it did cover the case, and flatly refused to look to its legislative history for interpretation. The result was that prosecution of the crime was statute-barred which it would not have been under the prior law. Judgment of 20 May 1969, Neue Jur. Wochenschrift 1181 (1969). *But cf. id.* at 1725, where the Court seems to back up from the consequences of its previous judgment by a closer distinction of the facts.

[26] A. Wach, I Handbuch des deutschen Civil prozessrechts 268 (1885).

[27] *Cf.* Y. Esser, Die Interpretation im Recht, 7 Studium Generale 372, 375, 378 (1954).

[28] [*See* C. J. Morrow, quoted in accompanying article by Judge Tate, 44 Tul. L. Rev. 675 (1970). Ed.] Even an author who is so well experienced in foreign legal systems as Professor Farnsworth seems to misunderstand it when, after stating this fact, he gives two classes of cases as exceptional examples of common law courts applying the principle of analogy: illegality of a contract, the making or performance of which violates a statute even if the statute does not expressly make the contract void or confers a right of recovery upon the injured party; and, secondly, negligence as a matter of law if conduct injuring another party was in violation of a statute. Farnsworth,

are concerned, for analogy of previous court decisions would appear to be the most important element of case law reasoning. The reason for this unfamiliarity is the traditional common law tendency, the simplest expression of which is the plain meaning rule, toward restricting the field of application of a statute as far as possible. Reasoning by analogy is the greatest possible contrast: the plain meaning rule limits the application of a statute to those cases which it covers by its plain words; analogy extends its application to cases which it plainly does not cover. For this reason, analogy has in traditional civil law doctrine been regarded as something fundamentally different from interpretation:[29] interpretation means implementing the law, analogy means supplementing it.

It is submitted that the opposite is true, that statutory construction by analogy is but one special technique of interpretation, that it raises the same problems, and that the same rules and methods apply. Disregarding for the moment the somewhat more realistic arguments of modern jurisprudence, this result follows from the classical concepts themselves. For analogy, like almost every other maxim of interpretation, finds its counterpart in the *argumentum e contrario*. Analogy means, in short, that one or more statutory provisions are stripped of their non-essential parts, and in this "purified" form are applied to cases which are different, but not essentially different, from the cases regulated in the statute or statutes.[30] However, if a statute is "intended" to be restricted to cases expressly covered by it, its application by analogy to other cases, however similar they may be, is prohibited. This is usually expressed in the form of an *argumentum e contrario*: since of all apparently similar cases, the legislator regulated only one specific case, he intended all others to be excluded from this regulation—an argument which seems fatally similar to the common law maxim *expressio unius est exclusio alterius*. It is obvious that as a matter of logic, analogy and *argumentum e contrario* are functionally anal-

*supra* note 13, at 78. No civil law jurist would regard these as being based on statutory analogy. Nor can we agree with Professor Farnsworth's contention that in Hoisting Engine Sales Co. v. Hart, 142 N.E. 342 (N.Y. 1923), the court found a warranty in the lease of a derrick, on the ground that the transaction was analogous to a sale. Farnsworth, *supra* note 13, at 78. It would appear that this judgment was based on the typical common law reason that the facts of the case were analogous to those of a number of previous decisions finding implied warranties in non-sale cases. The court did not find it necessary to consider the point "that the hiring of a chattel should be assimilated to the sale of goods and that section 96 of the Personal Property Law [*i.e.*, § 15, Uniform Sales Act] applies . . . ." This would indeed have been statutory analogy.

29 Enneccerus-Nipperdey, *supra* note 24, at 340. Admittedly, however, quite often the distinction between (extensive) interpretation and analogy will remain doubtful.

30 *Id.*

ogous and that, therefore, they can only serve as forms of expressing a decision rather than as reasons for a decision. How then do we find out whether or not a statute does permit its extension by analogy, which are the "essential" parts of it, and which cases are similar to the one decided by the statute? By interpretation, obviously; and the bromide of analogy simply vanishes from our eyes. To determine whether or not a statute is susceptible of analogous application, and if so, to what cases, is a matter of interpreting the statute by all the usual methods and rules of interpretation.

## "Judicial Legislation"

Conspicuously lacking in civil law jurisprudence is a methodology of the judicial development of the law, a methodology which would analyze, rationalize, and systematize the specific role of the judge in the process of finding and making law. From a common law point of view this must be the most astounding feature of civil law. One need not even go so far as to say that in reality the volition of the judge is the decisive final element in every possible case, although this would be a worthwhile argument to make. It has in its favor the fact that the trial judge has a monopoly on the ascertaining of facts, and is therefore able to "preformulate" them so as to render either logically impossible or unavoidable a certain application of the law.[31] It is beyond the scope of this paper to deal with these basic facts of every legal system; we are merely concerned with the resulting wording, the resulting text of the law. However, considering the vagueness of all rules of interpretation and the freedom of decision which in reality they give to the judge, it is obvious that even within these limits there is an important element of "judicial legislation." If civilian courts, over the course of centuries, adapted the meaning of a statutory rule to the social conditions of the time, its wording having remained unchanged, civil law jurisprudence would still by all means attempt to bring such adaptation under the heading of "interpretation" and thus "application" of the original statute. If this same adaptation were effected by legislative enactment of a new statute, nobody would doubt that this was legislation and consequently, "making" law.

There are instances of code provisions, notably in the French *Code Civil*, which is the oldest of the most important codes still in force today, whose present meaning is the exact opposite of their original legislative intention.[32] Hardly an unexpected result, as we

---

[31] *Cf.* Esser *supra* note 27, at 373; Scheuerle, *Finale Subsumtionen—Studien über Tricks und Schleichwege in der Rechtsanwendung*, 167 Archiv für die civilistische Praxis 305 (1967).

[32] Two famous examples: (1) The assured purpose of arts. 1119 and 1120 of the *Code Civil* was to deny recognition to third party rights in con-

may be tempted to say upon comparing the conditions of 1804 to those of 1970. However, this is still "interpretation." For most areas of the law, the provisions of our codes have been implemented, clarified, concretized, extended, restricted, modernized—*i.e.*, "interpreted"—by chains of subsequent court decisions; the more important a code provision, the greater the number of decisions. Indeed, the importance of a provision may itself be the result of its continuous and consistent judicial application. Is it really necessary to remark that the weight of consistent previous decisions may be much more important for the decision of a present case than the statute itself? Although the rule of stare decisis is not generally recognized in any civil law system,[33] our courts' attitude toward their own previous decisions is pretty much the same; and the higher a court, the greater will be its reluctance to overrule its own decisions.[34]

Nothing could be more incorrect than the still existing assumption that in civil law, there is a clear-cut code provision from which, by simply applying the rules of logic, the decision of a case could be deduced: "In the Continental law we start with the principles and the cases are mere applications of them."[35] The present meaning of most of our code provisions is simply unintelligible without knowing the whole body of pertinent case authority, and it is with utter disbelief that we look at this remark by an English observer: "Compared with this English law of torts which is like a gnarled old oak full of roughness and irregularities and with some of its branches rather decaying, the French law of torts is a simple and

tract. Today, the rule deriving from these very two sections is that recognition is normal, non-recognition exceptional. *Cf.* F. Lawson, *supra* note 11, at 56. (2) Art. 1384(1) of the *Code Civil*, originally regarded as a mere preface to the following sections, today serves as basis of a comprehensive system of strict liability for damages caused by property (*choses inanimées*) including automobiles. *Cf.* Ripert-Boulanger, 2 Traité de droit civil d'après le traité de Planiol 390 (1957); Zajtay, Begriff, *System und Präjudiz in den kontinentalen Rechten und im Common Law*, 165 Archiv für die civilistische Praxis 97 (1965); 43 Tul. L. Rev. 907 (1969).

33 *Quaere*: whether this so frequently repeated statement should not, in a more thorough analysis, be given its proper qualification? *Cf., e.g.*, sec. 546, sub. 2 clause 2 of the German Code of Civil Procedure requiring a Court of Appeals always to admit "Revision" (appeal of law) to the Federal Supreme Court if its own judgment deviates from a Supreme Court decision; and sections 136-138 Gerichtsverfassungsgesetz (Court Organization Law) providing for special procedures if one Senate of the Supreme Court intends to deviate from a prior judgment of another Senate.

34 For the different civil law systems see Germann, Präjudizien als Rechtsquelle 11 (1960); R. David-H. de Vries, The French Legal System 113 (1958); Meijers, *Case Law and Codified Systems of Private Law*, 33 J. Comp. Leg. & Intl'l L. (3d ser.) 8 (1950).

35 Walton, *Delictual Responsibility in the modern Civil Law (more particularly in the French law) as compared with the English Law of Torts*, II, 2 Mémoires de l'Académie internationale de droit comparé 445, 454 (1934).

coherent system."[36] It may well be that this image appears from the very few tort provisions of the *Code Civil*, but to believe that they represent the present state of the law means taking the curtain for the stage.[37]

With a certain amount of good faith, innovation through judicial interpretation might still be brought under the heading of code law. But even so, there are large areas of *pure* case law in the civil law systems. It would be too much to analyze this in detail here; the law of conflict of laws is but one example which in the *Code Civil* is almost totally unregulated, and which in Germany has found a very fragmentary regulation in the Introductory Act of the Civil Code. Another famous, although temporary, example was the German law of family relations from 1953 to 1958. Under article 3(2) of the Basic Law,[38] "Men and Women are equal before the law," and by specific provision of article 117 of the Basic Law, every previous rule of law which was contrary to this principle automatically ceased to be valid as of April 1, 1953. Since Parliament did not pass new laws until that date our judges found themselves alone without any legislative guidelines except the Basic Law itself to rely on. They managed to get along perfectly, and within a few years, up to the enactment of new family relations laws in 1958, established a smoothly operating case law system covering this field; and it is a widespread feeling that this was better than the new statutory laws which replaced it.

It should be obvious from all this that in civil law systems the judiciary has as important and as dominant a part in the process of "law in action" as in any common law system.[39] It would seem to us that a common law observer who knows not only our codes but also the practice of our courts should come to the conclusion that except for theoretical concepts, civil law is very similar to

[36] *Id.* at 453.

[37] To what extent civilian courts are prepared to go may be illustrated through a German example. Section 253 of the BGB provides, in unambiguous terms, that unless a statute expressly provides otherwise, no money award shall be given for injuries causing nonfinancial loss. The only express exceptions are section 847 BGB (pain and suffering) and section 1300 BGB (breach of promise to marry). But in right of privacy and defamation cases, the Federal Supreme Court has plainly overruled section 253 without even attempting to "adapt" or "re-interpret" it. The leading case, "Herrenreiter," 26 BGHZ 349 (1958), like some of the nastier common law judgments, did not even mention the provision which was being overruled, although the issue must have been considered. The court hinted at section 253 only in expressly overruling a precedent which had held that section 253 forbade recovery of monetary compensation for nonfinancial loss under the law of torts.

[38] The Basic Law is the Constitution of the Federal Republic of Germany.

[39] *See* accompanying article by Judge Tate, 44 Tul. L. Rev. 673 (1970). [Ed.]

common law.[40] However, as for the doctrine and theory of civil law, the mainstream of jurisprudence has constantly refused to recognize the true extent of judicial law-making;[41] it has not succeeded nor even—with a few notable exceptions[42]—attempted to reduce this to a consistent and logical system, to analyze its processes, and to establish rational and controllable criteria of decision. Instead, it has tried and is still trying to declare as "law" rules of interpretation which in reality are no more than methods of arguing, "rules of art," and thus to justify every present rule of law pronounced and applied by our judges by some higher authority: common will, legislative intention of a historic legislator who may have lived a century ago, "idea of the law" or whatever there may be found — "juridical superstition reduced to a system."[43]

## CONCLUSION

The greatest issue for any jurisprudence today is to determine rational criteria for judicial decision, whether based on statutes or on case authority, in a society which is changing at an ever-increasing rate. As yet, this task has not been accomplished. It would seem that toward this end, civil law and common law could learn a great deal from each other. The amount of statutory law and the number of civil-law type codes will certainly increase in all common law systems. The Uniform Commercial Code, for example, is, by all standards of civil law, an excellent piece of legislation. It may be expected that in the course of putting it into practice, American judges will encounter exactly the same problems which European courts have faced in interpreting their codes. It might be helpful to draw upon the European experience in statutory interpretation. On the other hand, it almost goes without

[40] *See* J. Dawson, The Oracles of the Law 432 (1968).

[41] As for this point, we cannot agree with Professor Dawson's statement that "among theoretical writers, the issue whether judges can and do make law is no longer seriously debated." Dawson, *supra* note 40, at 495. It would seem to us that most writers cannot help admitting that in cases like Herrenreiter, 26 BGHZ 349, the law is made by judges, simply because they cannot totally disregard plain facts; nonetheless, they seem to feel quite uneasy about accommodating these facts into traditional doctrine. The "unchallenged leadership" of the judiciary in law and doctrine which Professor Dawson has so impressively and accurately described would not appear from any of the treatises on the "General Part," on methodology, or on legal philosophy. The prevailing view, in our opinion, is still represented by the flat statement of Enneccerus-Nipperdey that "Precedents ('Rechtsprechung') as such are not a source of law." Enneccerus-Nipperdey, *supra* note 24, at 275.

[42] Principally, Y. Esser's monumental analysis, Grundsatz und Norm in der richterlichen Fortbildung des Privatrechts, *supra* note 1.

[43] A. Hägerström, I Der römische Obligationsbegriff im Lichte der allgemeinen römischen Rechtsanschauung (1927) (foreword at III).

saying that the common law experience in case law methods will be most valuable in finding our proper approach to a civilian case-law system. This change will require on both sides men like the one whose memory we are honoring here—Professor C. J. Morrow—who, exposed to the influences, values and techniques of both civil law and common law, and, sometimes, to the fight between the two systems, contributed to the mutual understanding of both, for their common benefit.

# [10]

## THE WEST GERMAN CIVIL CODE, ITS ORIGIN AND ITS CONTRACT PROVISIONS

ROBERT A. RIEGERT*

The statutory provisions of German contract law are in what is for American jurists the most novel and difficult part of the German Civil Code (Bürgerliches Gesetzbuch, or BGB) : the first two books. An understanding of these provisions and their organization helps to illuminate the entire code. Although articles have been already written in English about German Civil law,[1] much of the literature breaks the Code into isolated pieces of a jig-saw puzzle, making the Code difficult to use and difficult to fix in one's memory. To indicate how the various pieces fit together,[2] this essay first surveys

---

* Visiting Associate Professor of Law, Southern Methodist University. B.S., University of Cincinnati, 1948; LL.B., Harvard, 1953; J.U.D., University of Heidelberg, 1966. The author wishes to thank the following German scholars who were helpful in the preparation of this article: Professor Hermann Weitnauer of the University of Heidelberg; Dr. Axel Flessner of the Hamburg Max Planck Institute for Foreign and International Private Law; Professor Werner Lorenz of the University of Munich; and Professor Karl Nastelski, recently retired Senatspräsident of the German Supreme Court. The views expressed are, however, the sole responsibility of the author.

1 Professor Charles Szladits of the Parker School of Foreign and Comparative Law of Columbia University lists more than 300 items written in English which relate to the subject of this article in his Bibliography of Foreign and Comparative Law (1911). Although many of these are brief and twenty percent of them may be repetitions, some are of great value. A number of articles have appeared since the cut-off date of the last Szladits volume; they can be found in the Index to Legal Periodicals. The most useful German literature is the following: J. von Staudinger, Kommentar zum Bürgerlichen Gesetzbuch und dem Einführungsgesetz (an elaborate eleven volume commentary on the Civil Code, founded in 1898 and now in the 11th edition, the one cited here), the various parts being written by different authors. Here, Staudinger is cited to the volume, the name of the work, the name of the author, the section, and the part, *e.g.*, 1 Stau/Brändl § 24,—pt. II. The same method applies to a five volume leading textbook set by L. Enneccerus, Lehrbuch des Bürgenlichen Rechts (1952). The abbreviation Enn/Nip stands for Enneccerus/Nipperdey. K. Larenz, Allgemeiner Teil des Deutschen Bürgerlichen Rechts (1967) [hereinafter cited as Larenz AT]. K. Larenz, Lehrbuch des Schuldrechts (vol. 1, 10th ed. 1970; vol. 2, 7th ed. 1965) [hereinafter cited as Larenz SR] is probably the leading textbook for the law of obligations which does not belong to a set. F. Wieacker, Privatrechtsgeschichte der Neuzeit unter Besonderer Berücksichtigung der Deutschen Entwichlung (2d ed. 1967) [hereinafter cited as Wieacker] is a leading work on the history of German private law in modern times. O. Palandt, Bürgerliches Gesetzbuch (29th ed. 1970) [hereinafter cited as Palandt] is a concise one volume commentary.

2 *See generally* E. Cohn, 1 Manual of German Law (1968) [hereinafter cited as Cohn]; K. Ryan, An Introduction to the Civil Law (1962). Cohn's continental approach, as well as the use of English law instead of American law for comparisons with German law, makes his book less readable as a textbook for Americans. Ryan's book contrasts French versus German solutions of several problems. A presentation of the principles of the BGB can be found in E. Schuster, *Principles of German Law* (1907) [hereinafter cited as Schuster]. It follows the arrangement of the Code but does deviate occasionally to achieve clarity. Rather than translate, it interprets the Code's provisions.

the whole BGB. The second part then discusses the doctrines of German contract law differing most from American counterparts.

## General Principles of German Law

### *The German Private Law Prior to the BGB*

Before the BGB took effect on January 1, 1900, the private law of Germany was regulated by the local states, as it is in the United States today. In 1815, when the Germanic States threw off the Napoleonic rule, they formed a loose union called the Germanic Federation. The legislative Bundesrat could not pass laws binding on the citizens, but it could obligate with varying degrees of effectiveness the individual states to adopt the proposed laws. For example, the German General Negotiable Instruments Law of 1848 and the German General Commercial Law of 1861[3] are traceable to the early Bundesrat. Not until 1873, two years after the more reluctant of the German princes had finally joined in forming the "Second Empire," was authority to draft a civil code given to the Federal Government by a constitutional amendment.

At this time, Germany had more than twenty states, each with authority to determine its own private law. Four main systems of civil law were in force: the Roman common law, the Prussian Code of 1794, the French Code of 1804, and the Saxon Code of 1863.

The most important antecedent of German civil law was undoubtedly the Roman common law, or more simply "the common law" (das gemeine Recht). At one time it was subsidiary authority in all parts of Germany and by the end of the nineteenth century still covered about 33 percent of the German population.[4] As compiled by Justinian's jurists in Constantinople between 530 and 534 A.D., the Roman law consisted of three parts to which a fourth was later added. Part one, the Institutions, was intended as an official elementary textbook for students.[5] It contains a description of the law in a style similar to the better West "hornbooks." The second part, called Pandects or Digests, contains quotations from writings of thirty-nine leading Roman jurists. It resembles in some ways West's digests. The quotations are arranged in an order (or lack of order) taken from a document issued each year by the new chief legal officers of Rome, the Praetors.[6] The Digests are unclear and contain many contradictions.[7] The third part of Justinian's

The advantages of Schuster's book are the length (seven hundred pages) and the detail; the disadvantages are that it is outdated on many points and that only a few copies still exist.

3 1 Enn/Nip, *supra* note 1, at 24.

4 I Stau/Brändl, *supra* note 1, at 2.

5 B. Nicholas, An Introduction to Roman Law 41 (1962) [hereinafter cited as Nicholas].

6 *Id.* at 21, 43. The document was known as the Edict.

7 *Id.* at 43. Scott, who obtained his knowledge of the digests by translating them, writes:

compilation, the Codex, has the decrees of Roman emperors. A fourth part, called the Novels, consisting of later decrees, completes the work known as the *Corpus Iuris Civilis.*

When the Roman law was "received" into Germany—a process which lasted from about 1400 to 1600[8]—it was accepted only as a "reserve" law, to be used when there was no other state or local law applicable.[9] Why it was received and whether it should have been received are questions which have interested historians ever since. The German emperors conceived of themselves as the descendants of the Roman emperors and desired to accept the Code as part of their inheritance. Furthermore, there was a practical need for the Code. German law suffered from procedural defects and was mostly unwritten. Changing from medieval to modern social conditions would have required substantial innovations in the old German law whether the Roman law had been adopted or not.[10] The Roman law had been rendered palatable by the glossators (1100-1250), whose notes written in the textual margins provided cross references and reconciliations,[11] and by the commentators (1250-1500), who adapted the ancient law to solve medieval problems.[12] The revised law was further modified by use and acquired in the second half of the 18th Century the name *usus modernus pandectarum,* meaning "the modern digest." Legal doctrines relating to contracts for the benefit of third parties and to offers for rewards were among those developed at this time.[13] Although Justinian had ordered that the Institutions, the Digests, and the Codex were to be of equal force,[14] the Digests were the most important in the Mid-

> The arrangement of the Digest is defective and lacks the method and convenience of reference which should characterize a work of this description. Notwithstanding the avowed intention of the Emperor that such imperfections would be avoided, it abounds in repetitions, contradictions and irreconcilable statements—often occurring within a few pages of one another—which are the cause of infinite perplexity and annoyance. Despite its claim to condensation it is still far too diffuse, and, by means of intelligent revision could be greatly abridged without detracting in any respect from its value, to the infinite advantage of those desirous of familiarizing themselves with its contents.

1 Civil Law 17-18 (S. Scott transl. 1932) [hereinafter cited as Scott].

8 1 Continental Legal History Series 333 (1912) [hereinafter cited as CLHS].

9 1 CLHS, *supra* note 8, at 339; 1 Enn/Nip, *supra* note 1, at 13. The extent to which the Roman law became effective varied with the place and changed with time. Usually, if a party relied upon a glossed text, there was a presumption in favor of its validity; the burden of proof that it had not been received or had been derogated from was on the other party. Wieacker, *supra* note 1, at 205-08.

10 *Cf.* P. Vinogradoff, Roman Law in Medieval Europe 119 (1968) [hereinafter cited as Vinogradoff].

11 1 CLHF, *supra* note 8, at 137; 1 Enn/Nip, *supra* note 1, at 59.

12 Nicholas, *supra* note 5, at 47; 1 CLHS, *supra* note 8, at 142; 1 Enn/Nip, *supra* note 1, at 60.

13 1 Enn/Nip, *supra* note 1, at 23.

14 1 Enn/Nip, *supra* note 1, at 18. For further information on the Roman law and the Roman law in Germany, *see* Nicholas, *supra* note 6; R. Sohm, The Institutes; a Textbook of the History and System of Roman Private Law (3d

dle Ages, because of their wealth of detailed rules, because of the intellectual challenge presented by their lack of order, and because of the possibility of finding authority for either side of many questions due to their contradictions.

As might be expected, government by a multiplicity of state and local laws with the Roman common law in reserve did not prove satisfactory. In 1746 Frederick II (the Great) of Prussia instructed his Grand Chancellor von Cocceji to devise a code to replace "that law which is written in Latin and has been compiled without system or order."[15] The von Cocceji draft was rejected and a new start was made in 1780 with von Carmer as Grand Chancellor. Known as the Prussian General Land Law, the Prussian Code containing 17,000 paragraphs was published in 1794. Although often unnecessarily complicated with detail, parts of it are sound and understandable.[16] The detail accounts for the Prussian Code's failure to achieve greater success. Also, it was written in the spirit of the age immediately preceding the French Revolution but was to be applied in the subsequent different social milieu. In parts of Germany it had only subsidiary validity similar to that of the Roman common law. If some of its provisions proved undesirable, the political subdivision often did not attempt to improve them. Instead local provisions were enacted to take precedence over the Prussian Code sections. Nevertheless, at the time of the adoption of the BGB the Prussian Code had partly primary, partly subsidiary, validity over 43 percent of the German population.[17]

The French Civil Code was primary law for 17 percent of the German population.[18] Its first book on persons includes some public law on citizenship. The second book has the law of things. The third entitled "Of the Different Modes of Acquiring Property" contains, according to Professor Rheinstein, "a hodgepodge of such hetero-

ed. Ledlie transl. 1907) [hereinafter cited as Sohm]; 1 CLHS, *supra* note 8, at 333-451; Vinogradoff, *supra* note 10 (a short classical account); 6 H. Coing, "Römisches Recht in Deutschland" 1 Ius Romanum Medii Aevi (1964) (an exhaustive work).

15 1 Enn/Nip, *supra* note 1, at 26.

16 Perhaps its best known provisions are sections 74 and 75 of the introductory part dealing with state liability. In 1953, in an action against a municipality by a child suffering from a smallpox vaccination required by law, the German Supreme Court reiterated the fact that the principle of section 75 had developed into a principle of German common law. Anyone who had been compelled to sacrifice his rights or advantages for the common good was entitled to reimbursement by the state. After extending the coverage of the doctrine to bodily injury, the Court ruled in favor of the child. Judgment of February 19, 1953, 9 BGHZ 83, 84. For details of the development of the doctrine, *see* 1 E. Fortsthoff, Lehrbuch des Verwaltungsrechts § 17 (8th ed. 1961).

Evidence of the breadth of the Prussian Code's influence is the reference to a Prussian Code rule by the French Code draftsmen, A. von Mehren, Civil Law System 530-31 (1957).

17 1 Stau/Brändl, *supra* note 1, at 2.

18 *Id.* at 3.

geneous topics as torts, sales, matrimonial property rights, wills, mortgages, the statute of limitations, the general rules on contracts, etc."[19] It is hardly a model of ideal organization.

Though valid for only about 7 percent of the German population,[20] the Saxon Code of 1863 became the organizational model for the BGB except that the book on things in the Saxon Code came before instead of after the book on obligations. The draftsmen of the BGB paid particular attention to both the Prussian and the Saxon Codes.[21]

*The Drafting of the BGB*

Against this background a committee was appointed in 1873 to determine the plan and method to be used in drafting a German civil code. The committee cautioned against assigning the task to the Ministry of Justice. Instead the committee favored a special commission. It is not untypical of German procedure that three commissions—rather than one—were eventually appointed, and twenty-two years elapsed before the Code was finally adopted.[22] The most important commission was the first one appointed in 1874 which worked thirteen years before completing its draft. Consisting of six judges, three higher civil servants, and two professors, the commission assigned each of the five major parts of the proposed code to one of its members. Although the entire commission met only once a year during this period, the five draftsmen met weekly. In this way, the commission worked for six years before the preliminary draft was finished. Unfortunately, the draftsman assigned to obligations died before his book was completed. To fill the breach, the commission substituted a draft known as the "Dresdner Entwurf," a Code accepted as a German General Law of Obligations by the German Confederation the day before the Confederation was dissolved.[23]

The commission as a whole commenced work in 1881 and worked until 1887. The draft, together with a five-volume condensed version

19 Rheinstein, *The Approach to German Law*, 34 Ind. L.J. 546, 550 (1959).

20 1 Stau/Brändl, *supra* note 1, at 3.

21 Larenz, *Some Comments on the Austrian, German, and Swiss Legal Systems, with Particular Reference to the Law of Contracts*, in 1 Formation of Contracts 254 (S. Schlesinger ed. 1968) [hereinafter cited as Schlesinger]. It is likely that our knowledge of European legal history will be greatly increased by the work of the Max Planck Institute for European Legal History which was founded in 1964. *See* Riegert, *Max Planck Institute for European Legal History*, 22 Sw. L.J. 397 (1968).

22 In the case of the Prussian code, two commissions and 44 years were necessary. A major reform in German substantive criminal law was undertaken at the turn of the century. After the work of numerous commissions, the first stage of this reform was finally adopted in 1969.

23 1 Enn/Nip, *supra* note 1, at 31.

of the explanatory notes, was published in 1888.[24] Professor Windscheid, the author of what was the leading text on the Pandects, was a member of the commission and his influence on the final product was pervasive. There were charges that the 1887 draft was "Windscheid's book with additions."[25] Those Germans who favored the reception of the Roman law praised the draft, while those who rejected the reception criticized it. A third group, who called for more consideration for the less privileged in society, also joined the opposition.[26]

The Ministry of Justice compiled six volumes of systematically organized criticism of the first draft.[27] A second commission of ten regular members, apparently all jurists, together with twelve laymen to be consulted on special questions was appointed in 1890.[28] The commission made substantial changes to suit the critics of the prior draft, and the new 1895 draft was sent to the Bundesrat where the sixth book on private international law was suppressed; however, several of its provisions were put in the introductory law.[29]

In the end, what Max Rheinstein could say about the civil law was true of the BGB codification process:

> The traditional consistency of the Civil Law is due not only to its professorial origin, but, during the last one hundred and fifty years or so, also to the very active role that has been played in its development by governments and their bureaucratic civil servants. Where legislative needs are constantly watched and laws drafted by highly trained governmental specialists more inner consistency can be achieved than in law that grows haphazardly from case to case. There are many problems which but rarely come to judicial decision at all, and in innumerable cases the outcome is determined not so much by judicial considerations of long range consistency as by the accidental circumstances of personality, the equities of an individual case, or advocatorial skill.[30]

---

24 1 CLHS, *supra* note 8, at 448. These few pages written by Professor Ernst Freund provide the best analysis of the BGB drafting process.

25 6 Harv. L. Rev. 317, 318 (1893). The leading critic was O. von Gierke, Der Entwurf eines Bürgerlichen Gesetzbuches und das Deutsche Recht (1888-89).

26 A. Menger, Das Bürgerliche Recht und die Besitzlosen Volksklassen (1891).

27 1 Enn/Nip, *supra* note 1, at 33.

28 *Id.* at 34.

29 Higgins, *The Making of the German Civil Code*, 6 J. Comp. Leg. 95, 102 (new ser. 1905) [hereinafter cited as Higgins]. Professor Freund believed the provisions on private international law were the first codification of conflicts law. Freund, *The New German Civil Code*, 13 Harv. L. Rev. 627, 630 (1900).

30 Rheinstein, *Common Law and Civil Law: An Elementary Comparison*, 22 Rev. Jur. U.P.R. 90, 103 (1952) [hereinafter cited as Rheinstein].

*Description of the BGB*

The BGB consists of five books. The first states general principles of law to be used in the remaining specific parts. The second contains the law of obligations, covering contracts, unjust enrichment, and torts. The third book is on property, the fourth on family law, and the last on inheritance. Smithers makes an appraisal of the BGB similar to that which many American jurists might make today after a first reading: "One is much impressed upon a cursory reading of the whole work by the scope of its general divisions, absence of repetition, and omission of provisions relating to public law and judicial procedure noticeable in other great codes. Some groupings of subjects, however, seem illogical and confusing."[31] Further on Smithers continues: "Sales [sections 481-515[32]] under which minute regulations concerning price, quality, acceptance, deceit, recision and damages for breach of contract are given so carefully, would seem to be too much the subject of definition to be permanent. The general principles of vendor and vendee as announced are a composite of the Roman law, the ancient customary laws established at cattle markets and the demands of modern commerce."[33]

One of the outstanding features of the third book on property is the efficient and inexpensive land registration system which it and the Land Registration Regulation (Grundbuchordnung) provide. The system and its precursor, the Prussian "Eigentumsgesetz," have worked well for nearly a century. German property law does not know the doctrine of market overt, but the BGB goes a small step in that direction. If an owner entrusts his property to someone who sells it to a bona fide purchaser, the purchaser gets good title; but if the owner's property was lost or stolen, the purchaser does not get good title.[34] Another interesting feature of the third book is the failure to provide for a security interest in personal property which is in the possession of the debtor. The need was so great, however, that the courts were willing to permit such a security interest despite the Code.[35]

---

31 Smithers, *The German Civil Code (Part II)*, 51 Am. L. Register 14 (1903) [hereinafter cited as Smithers]. Schmidt writes in *The German Abstract Approach to Law*, 9 Scandinavian Studies in Law 133, 134 (1965) [hereinafter cited as Schmidt] that he has "found some features of German legal thinking strange and artificial and therefore difficult to understand."

32 The provisions cited apply to the sale of named types of livestock.

33 Smithers, *supra* note 31, at 18-19.

34 BGB §§ 932-35. The Uniform Commercial Code § 2-403(2) adopts the BGB rule to the extent that the owner has entrusted his property to a merchant who trades in goods of that kind and who sells the property in the ordinary course of his business.

35 Palandt, *supra* note 1, at 7B(b)bb vor § 929.

Although much of the BGB has been relatively free from amendments,[36] the fourth book on family law has been altered extensively. Some sections relating directly to marriage and divorce were taken out of the BGB and are now regulated by a separate statute.[37] Of the family law provisions retained in the BGB, the most extensive changes were made in 1957 to reflect the West German Constitution's provision for the equality of men and women. Under the present provisions, if the husband and wife do not contract for a special marital property arrangement, all property acquired before and after marriage remains separate. The net gains are usually but not always divided at the time the marriage ends.[38] The parties have broad powers to regulate the marital property arrangements by contract; they can make or change such a contract even after the marriage.[39] Additional revisions in the law during 1961 revamped the legitimacy, control, and adoption of children.[40]

With regard to the last book on inheritance, Smithers says: "This part of the work is the most logical in its order and most consistent in its provisions."[41] The German law of inheritance differs from the American law as to who the heirs are; also title vests directly in the German heirs.[42]

Scholars say that the first two books contain more Roman law, the remaining books more German law.[43] While the last three books do contain mainly law of German origin, the Roman origin of the first two books is less clear. The Roman elements influenced the organizational structure and the substantive rules of pandect law, some of which were taken over into the BGB;[44] however, attempts to trace doctrines back to their ancient origins may sometimes lead to

---

[36] In the first eighteen years that it was in use, only six paragraphs were altered. Since World War II, the changes have come faster, but no important changes were made in the provisions regulating basic contract law. Probably the most important change in the first three books was a revision of the rent law, one of the special types of contract law. See the table preceding the BGB in H. Schönfelder, Deutsche Gesetze.

[37] The marriage law (Ehegesetz) of February 20, 1946.

[38] BGB § 1363. The provisions regulating the Zugewinngemeischaft are BGB §§ 1363-90. *See* Cohn, *supra* note 2, at 236-40.

[39] BGB § 1408. The provisions relating to contractual marital property are BGB §§ 1408-1518. *See* Cohn, *supra* note 2, at 240-41.

[40] See the table preceding the BGB in H. Schönfelder, Deutsche Gesetze. A law recently passed improves the position of illegitimate children. Law of August 19, 1969, [1969] BGBl I 1243.

[41] Smithers, *supra* note 31, at 28. The eighteen pages of the second part of Mr. Smithers's article present a readable description of the major features of the Code. A somewhat more detailed article is Schuster, *The German Civil Code,* 1 J. Soc. Comp. Leg. 191 (old ser. 1897).

[42] For a description of the German law of inheritance, see Cohn, *supra* note 2, at 257-93.

[43] 1 Stau/Brändl, *supra* note 1, at pt. 18 before § 1.

[44] *See* text at notes 5-14 *supra.*

unworkable interpretations.[45] Indeed, the movement back to the "pure" Roman law led by Savigny helped to bring an end to the applicability of pandect law in Germany.[46]

Even though each of the civil law countries adopted the Roman law, the widespread belief in the similarity of the countries' substantive laws is without basis in fact.[47] Max Rheinstein believes any likeness among the laws of these countries is due to the uniformity of conditions in the countries and the fact that two or three codes served as models for all the countries rather than due to any common observation of Roman law.[48] One must remember that the Roman law solution for many problems varied during its thousand years of existence. Also, because of contradictions, the digests can often give support to both sides of debatable questions. Professor Schlesinger quotes with apparent approval the statement of the late Reginald Parker that the majority of the private "legal institutions" of any civil law country are of non-Roman origin.[49] Wieacker writes that the basic concepts of the BGB, including the juridical act, declaration of will, the contract or agreement (Vertrag), and impossibility of performance, were the product of the jurisprudence of reason developed during the 1600 to 1800 period[50] and were not the product of the Roman law.[51]

One characteristic of civil law codification stressed by Professor Rheinstein is the solicitude which governmental bureaucracy showed for the middle classes and, in the twentieth century, for the proletariat.[52] The BGB, however, has taken up only a moderate amount of this solicitude. As Wieacker said, the BGB did not match the protection given workers by Bismark's social security laws, because the BGB was primarily geared to the views of bourgeois society.[53]

The language of the Code, even apart from its abstract structure,[54] has been criticized as being artificial and less understandable

[45] 1 Stau/Brändl, *supra* note 1, at pt. 17 before § 1.

[46] Higgins says that Savigny's return to the "bed-rock of ancient classical authority" meant a reintroduction of the classical Roman Law and that the world had changed since those days. This return to the text of Justinian and to an unworkable law gave the Germanists an advantage. Higgins, *supra* note 29, at 99.

[47] "Despite their long exposure to ideas derived from Roman law, each of the 'civil law' systems is the product of independent, conscious choices." Dawson, *Specific Performance in France and Germany*, 57 Mich. L. Rev. 495, 525 (1959).

[48] Rheinstein, *supra* note 30, at 93.

[49] R. Schlesinger, Comparative Law 173 (3d ed. 1970).

[50] Wieacker, *supra* note 1, at 249.

[51] Wieacker, *supra* note 1, at 374-75.

[52] Rheinstein, *supra* note 30, at 105.

[53] Wieacker, *supra* note 1, at 481.

[54] *See* text at notes 68-76 *infra*.

than that of the Swiss Code.[55] An occasional use of chain references, one section referring to another which in turn refers to a third, creates considerable difficulty in some instances.[56]

In evaluations of the BGB, discussion of its solutions to substantive problems seems, in recent times at least, to have been pushed into the background behind criticisms of its abstractness and its complexity, perhaps because the courts have supplied workable solutions to substantive problems in cases where the Code did not.[57] The Code's complexity probably aided the drafters in their task of writing a code acceptable to all parts of the Empire. The Code is so complex that only a relatively small percentage of the population was able to understand it. Such complexity, when combined with the "general clauses" like section 242,[58] makes the Code more plastic in the expert hands of the judges of the German Supreme Court than had, until recently at least, been generally realized.

The BGB contains few if any direct contradictions, little if any repetition, and it certainly does not suffer from lack of organization. It is not as long and detailed as the Prussian Code was. The BGB draftsmen produced a code which does not have the defects common to other codes of the time. Whether this was enough to make it the great Code it has often been proclaimed to be is an open question.[59]

Application of the Code has revealed a number of oversights. The general contract law of the Code only provides express remedies for two types of breach: for cases where performance is tardy and for cases where it has become impossible. Other forms of breach, such as failure to use due care, have been placed by scholars and the courts under the title "positive violation of contract." For these defaults, there is still dispute over which section of the Code justifies the imposition of remedies.[60]

Another oversight is found in section 325 which, taken literally,

---

55 Larenz AT, *supra* note 1, at § 1, pt. IV.

56 The first draft was worse in this respect. *Cf.* Wieacker, *supra* note 1, at 470-71. Examples are section 651 which is said to be a round trip ticket through the BGB and section 467 which refers to a series of sections including 292, 347 (which in turn refers to 987), 818, 819, and 820.

57 *See* text at notes 152-67, 274-91 *infra.*

58 This section requires an obligor to perform with good faith. Other examples of general clauses are sections 138, 157, and 826. Through the use of general terms, they give the courts an opportunity to exert considerable influence on the law. *Cf.* Wieacker, *supra* note 1, at 476-77.

59 Schuster, *supra* note 2, at iii, calls it "the most perfect attempt to systematize the whole of the private law of a country." Maitland is often quoted for the remark that the Code is "the most carefully considered statement of a nation's laws that the world has ever seen." O. Gierke, Political Theories of the Middle Age xvii (transl. Maitland 1900).

60 1 Larenz SR, *supra* note 1, at § 24, pt. I. *See* text at notes 234-47 *infra.*

would permit a party to rescind a breached contract but would not permit him to obtain damages unless he himself has performed. In many situations it is more efficient to grant damages without requiring the innocent party to perform, so the courts have allowed such relief despite section 325.[61] Section 275 speaks of impossibility and inability, but just five sections later the Code uses the word "impossibility" alone when both concepts are intended.[62] The wording of section 119 permits avoidance of a contract for a mistake relating to corporeal property, although there is no reason for excluding incorporeal property; consequently, the courts have refused to exclude incorporeal property.[63]

The Code represents a considerable achievement. Nevertheless, the Code's reputation for superhuman perfection is a myth, as these and other errors and inconsistencies reveal.

Parts of the Code have been copied by a number of other countries. The English version of the Thai Code[64] follows in some sections almost verbatim Wang's 1907 translation of the BGB. The present codes of Japan and the Republic of China show that numerous sections are from the BGB with some rephrasing and some rearrangement. The BGB has influenced the codes of several other countries, including Greece, Brazil, and Peru.[65] These countries were probably influenced favorably by the flexibility of the BGB.[66] Their choice of the BGB can also in part be explained by the small number of alternatives available. That these countries relied on another code like the BGB is evidence of the difficulty in drafting a new civil code.[67]

### *The Abstract Structure of the BGB*

#### The Abstraction of the Juridical Act

When the German scholars began to analyze the disorganized digests, they tried to systematize the material. Whether they were copying the method of the natural scientists or following the in-

---

61 1 Larenz SR, *supra* note 1, at § 22, pt. IIb.

62 Because section 275 equates impossibility with inability, some scholars argue that there is no inconsistency; however, the implication is that the equating in section 275 is limited to section 275.

63 The courts overlook the omission. Larenz AT, *supra* note 1, at § 26, pt. II.

64 Civil and Commercial Code, Books I-VI (Yamali & Ratanawichit 1962). The first section in the Thai code's book on obligations is extracted from the first section of the BGB's book on obligations.

65 Wieacker, *supra* note 1, at 484-86.

66 *Cf. id.* at 485.

67 The American experience with civil codes is just beginning to be fully evaluated. *See* Fisch, *The Dakota Civil Code: Notes for an Uncelebrated Centennial*, 43 N.D.L. Rev. 485 (1967); Fisch, *The Dakota Civil Code, More Notes for an Uncelebrated Centennial*, 45 N.D.L. Rev. 9 (1968).

fluence of natural law,[68] the pandectists wrote textbooks from the random mass of legal rules by segregating the most general principles and by progressively moving to the more specific. The result of abstraction was to collect in the first book some general principles for use in two or more of the following books.

The General Part of the pandectists' textbooks appears to have originated with Gustav Hugo in 1789.[69] Arnold Heise, a Professor in Göttingen, very likely copied it in 1807 for his pandects lectures.[70] The practice culminated with Windscheid's three-volume book in the latter half of the nineteenth century.[71] Because the organization of the BGB follows the pattern of a pandect textbook, scholars called the 1888 draft of the BGB the "Little Windscheid."[72] The major area of law suffering most from this abstract organization is contracts.

The concept of the juridical act illustrates abstraction in the BGB. What do offer, notice of rescission, and consent to adoption have in common? These are examples of juridical acts (Rechtsgeschäft); each is an act with *intent* to achieve legal consequences.[73] The rules governing juridical acts are in the first book of the BGB, because they are general principles of the Code applicable to all of the specific books. They are not only applicable to the law of obligations found in the second book but also to property, family, and inheritance law found in the later books of the Code.

---

[68] Both were suggested by Schmidt as explanations for the abstraction phenomenon. Schmidt, *supra* note 31, at 137-40.

[69] A. Schwarz, *Zur Entstehung des Modernen Pandectensystems*, in 42 Zeitschrift der Savignystiftung 578, 581 (1921) [hereinafter cited as Schwarz]; Schmidt, *supra* note 31, at 137.

[70] A. Heise, Grundriss eines Systems des Gemeinen Civilrechts (1st ed. 1807, 2d ed. 1816). Schwarz, *supra* note 69, at 581, with whom Schmidt, *supra* note 31, at 137, agrees, says that Hugo devised but later abandoned the general part. Therefore, he argues the present use goes back to Heise's first edition. In his second edition, Heise says that he follows Hugo's practice of putting an asterisk before Latin words not used by the Romans but used in the middle ages. If Heise copied one practice from Hugo, he more than likely copied another, so the better argument is that the present practice began with Hugo. *See generally* Schwarz, *supra* note 69.

[71] Until some years after the turn of the century, German courses in Roman Law were limited to the history of Roman law, pandect law, and the Institutes. Based on the Digests instead of the Institutes, the pandect law was the Roman law as applied in Germany during the nineteenth century. The course on the Institutes was originally an introductory course based on Justinian's first book. Those who taught the course never developed a general part as did the pandect teachers; instead they continued to follow the organizational plan of Justinian's Institutes: Book I, Persons; Book II, Things, broken down to include what we call property as well as obligations; Book III, Family Law and the Law of Inheritance; and Book IV, Procedure. *See* Sohm, *supra* note 14; Scott, *supra* note 7.

[72] Schmidt, *supra* note 31, at 137.

[73] The term "juridical act" is sometimes used in a more specific sense to describe an entire legal transaction.

In the textbooks, the rules on juridical acts were not quite so abstract. Besides stating them in his general part, Heise repeated them in his outline on obligations.[74] Even the Windscheid fifth edition, current during the later drafting of the BGB, contained in its section on obligations a set of rules to govern mistake, acceptance by silence, and the time a valid acceptance became effective.[75] By moving to the General Part all such rules on juridical acts, the BGB draftsmen intensified abstraction one more degree.

Should all actions falling within the theoretical classification of juridical acts be treated identically despite their differences? Should a person be able to rescind a transfer of property or a marriage as easily as he can an unexecuted purchase contract? No, the demands of real life will not permit the law to apply the same rules of rescission to all the diverse situations in which juridical acts play a part. Abstraction was carried too far here. To rectify the problem, the drafters of the original statute had to include exceptions to these general rules; these exceptions appear in the Code's more specific provisions. Many more exceptions were added later by the courts.[76]

Intertwining of Torts and Contracts and Other Abstractions of Book Two

The principle of abstraction in the BGB is not limited to the first book; it has been extensively applied to the inner organization of the second book on obligations. Because the book regulates contracts, unjust enrichment, and torts, the book begins with principles of law common to all three subjects and then proceeds to special provisions for each. The general provisions make up 133 sections or about 22 percent of the book; 57 sections or about 9.3 percent of the book apply generally and exclusively to contracts, and 370 sections or 62 percent of the book apply to special types of contracts, for example, sales, lease, and employment;[77] 11 sections or about 1.8 percent of the book are specific provisions on unjust enrichment, and only 31 sections or about 5 percent are specific provisions on torts.

Until recently German tort law appeared to be neglected. About twenty years ago, however, it seems to have awakened and since

[74] The subjects of force, fear, deceit and mistake have by coincidence almost exactly the same paragraph numbers as they have in the BGB.

[75] 2 B. Windscheid, Lehrbuch des Pandektenrechts §§ 306–07, 309 (5th ed. 1879).

[76] Larenz describes the statutory and court-made exceptions as the standard way of correcting provisions drawn too broadly. I Larenz SR, *supra* note 1, at § 3. *See also* text at notes 267-73 *infra*.

[77] Several of the debtor relationships included here, like quasi contract and partnership, would not ordinarily be considered as falling within a strict definition of contract.

then it has been the area of German obligations receiving the most attention.[78] Still, the lack of both a jury and the all-or-nothing contributory negligence rule has made the German tort a less exciting game than the American tort.

Although the intertwining of torts and contracts appears at first glance to have resulted only in very limited difficulties,[79] more careful investigation shows that some of the abstraction problems of the second book result from the attempt to deal not only with torts and contracts but also with unjust enrichment and related areas as a single subject. Professor Larenz criticizes the organization of the second book by pointing out how little these areas have in common: they are different *forms* of obligations.[80] The relationships and facts leading up to tort and contract obligations differ completely. If the resulting obligation alone were a sufficient reason for including both torts and contracts in book two, many other concepts should be included than now are. The first (1887) draft of the second book recognized this problem, so the draft was more functionally organized according to the origin of the obligation (contract, tort, or unjust enrichment). The unjustified criticism of that draft by von Bähr probably led to the extreme form of abstraction the book now has.[81]

If, as some scholars suggest, the presence of tort components in the contract law causes a minimum of direct difficulty, it is because torts and contracts are separated out by abstraction. There are three separate levels of provisions dealing with what Americans might call remedies and what the Germans call "disturbances in performance." The first level[82] applies to all obligations; it contains the only general provisions regulating "remedies" for unilateral obligations, such as contracts in which only one side is bound, and for obligations arising out of torts or unjust enrichment. The second level[83] applies only to contracts, the third only to special types of contracts (sale, work, bailment) and other particular types of obligations (torts, unjust enrichment).

The heterogeneous subject matter and the levels of abstractions are not the only causes of difficulty in the remedy provisions of the

78 The most important contribution to the development of tort law in the past twenty years is von Caemmerer, *Wandlungen des Deliktsrechts* in "Hundert Jahre deutsches Rechtsleben" Festschrift zum 100-Jähringen Bestehen des Deutschen Juristentages 49-136 (1960).

79 *E.g.*, sections 249-54, prescribing damages, and section 276, describing the amount of fault necessary to establish liability. These principles are applicable to both torts and contracts.

80 Larenz, *supra* note 1, at § 1.

81 II Stau/Weber, *supra* note 1, pt. Z1 before § 241.

82 BGB §§ 275-304.

83 Particularly BGB §§ 323-27.

second book. The use of the impossibility provisions to solve the problems of breach of contract is also a substantial cause of difficulty. The result is that the first and second levels and their interrelation compose one of the most complicated areas of the BGB. The provisions are not clear. Furthermore, they produce some unworkable rules of substantive law, the effects of which can only be avoided by complicated methods of interpretation.[84]

The Disadvantage of Abstraction

Although bad substantive rules of law are not dictated by abstractions, bad rules may be an indirect result. Abstractions make it difficult for statutory draftsmen to foresee the full effect of their work. As Wieacker suggests, when a particular legal problem is obscured by the abstractness of the statute, a poor solution is all too often the result.[85] The abstract concepts and system of the BGB on one side and social and economic values on the other are two different processes of reasoning which may naturally reach opposite results. The judges' sporadic switches from one approach to the other decreases public confidence in the legal system.[86] The dichotomy of approach has the added disadvantage of making civil law jurists do double work, first by thinking through the social end of the problem, second by recognizing the codal solution. Must these two approaches produce different results? Perhaps not, although they frequently do.

An average, even a well-educated, layman is not able to understand the BGB. The American lawyer trying for the first time to solve a contract problem under the BGB is like a hypothetical purchaser of a General Electric stove who discovers that the instruction manual covers all appliances General Electric manufactures and that he must work his way through six levels of abstraction in order to learn how to operate his stove.[87] This disadvantage of abstraction has been emphasized in numerous comparisons between the BGB and the Swiss Civil Code of 1907.[88] The Swiss, whose Code was completed about ten years after the final draft of the BGB, refused to follow the abstraction principle to the extent the

---

84 *See* 2 K. Zweigert & H. Kötz, Einführung in die Rechtsvergleichung auf dem Gebiet des Privatrechts 193 (1969) [hereinafter cited as Zweigert & Kötz].

85 Wieacker, *supra* note 1, at 476.

86 *Cf.* 1 Larenz SR, *supra* note 1, at vi.

87 Wieacker, *supra* note 1, at 475, adds, "[t]he situation is not a happy one."

88 The Swiss Code went into force January 1, 1912. Literature comparing the German and Swiss Codes is listed in R. Gmür, Das Schweizerische Zivilgesetzbuch verglichen mit dem Deutschen Bürgerlichen Gesetzlbuch 11 (1965). The present Swiss Code of Obligations, a revision of the Swiss Code of Obligations of 1881, is technically the fifth book of the Swiss Civil Code. Because the paragraphs are separately numbered, Obligations is often cited as if it were a separate code.

Germans did.[89] The Swiss Code has neither a general part at the beginning nor a general part within obligations.[90]

Schmidt voices a related objection when he writes: "Whether one considers the Swedish alternative preferable or not must depend on one's opinion as to the instructive effect of the Scandinavian idea that legislators should deal with ordinary cases before concerning themselves with those which seldom occur."[91] Additionally, the drafters should have defined key words in the Code. If maximum precision is a recognized goal of legal communication, that end is not achieved by the use of ambiguous terms. The BGB fosters ambiguity when it omits a definition of phrases like "juridical act" and "contract."

Finally, the BGB does not consistently follow the principle of abstraction. While the central theme of the second book is the result the law gives to certain events, the central theme of the fourth and fifth books is functional.[92] Family law and inheritance law consist of obligations and property relationships, so they could be abstracted into books two and three. Alternatively, the functional principle of books four and five could be followed in the earlier books by splitting book two on obligations into two books, one on contracts and one on torts.

The Dispute as to Whether the BGB is Too Abstract

The dispute concerning the abstraction in the BGB has been a long one.[93] Max Rheinstein and Ernst Rabel have led the defense, Rheinstein arguing that abstraction facilitates analysis,[94] conserves thought, and provides a rule for peculiar cases,[95] Rabel

[89] If the Swiss had opted for abstraction, they would not have been able to limit themselves to generally understandable terminology. Wieacker, *supra* note 1, at 492, says: "According to an almost unanimous well founded opinion the language [of the Swiss Code] is a model of clarity, pithiness, and general understandability. . . ."

[90] For an explanation of the redactor's reasons, see E. Huber, Erläuterungen zum Vorentwurf eines Schweizerischen Zivilgesetzbuches 22 (1915).

[91] Schmidt, *supra* note 31, at 149. Schmidt suggests that the structure of the Code may present a question of emphasis:

> It is a part of the technique of the German Code that the general principles are presented with great emphasis. Possibly this may lead the judge to attach greater weight to the general than to the specific. In his administration of the law he will be more formal and not so inclined as the judges of some other countries to consider the circumstances of the case.

*Id.* at 156.

[92] *Cf.* Schuster, *supra* note 2, at 6. Schwarz, *supra* note 69, at 579. At 579, n.5 he lists German articles criticizing the organizational system of the pandect textbooks and of the BGB.

[93] *See* note 88 *supra*.

[94] Rheinstein, *The Approach to German Law*, 34 Ind. L. Rev. 546, 548 (1959).

[95] *Id.* at 552. An extensive comparative study on the formation of contracts

agreeing with the BGB's selection in the choice between "advice to the lawyer" versus "information to the common intelligent man."[96] The BGB probably better satisfies the needs of the scholar who devotes his life to legal study than it satisfies the needs of a layman, or perhaps even of the jurist who does not constantly work with the BGB. The structure of the BGB had its origin in the pandectists' scholarly analysis of the digests.[97] However, the Code is not the place to publish a scholarly analysis. The price—namely, the Code's incomprehensibility to the neophyte—is too high. The Code should have been written with the aim of making it as understandable as possible for the persons subject to it. Analysis can be made outside the Code in the legal literature.

A measure of the investment that must be made in the BGB before one is able to interpret and apply it properly is the time required for a law student to acquire competence. The German bar requires a minimum of three and a half years of university study plus two and a half years internship. German jurists usually say that only after a student has completed his training and has had an additional year of experience is he fully competent to work with the BGB. Thus a total of seven years is necessary. Although other factors influence the length of this period, the complexity of the BGB is probably the most important.

Rheinstein may be correct when he says that the abstract structure tends to assure the availability of a rule for peculiar cases; but the drafters did not focus their attention sufficiently on the unusual cases, so their rule may not represent a satisfactory solution to the real-life problem. Consequently, Rheinstein believes the availability of the BGB's general rule does not free the court from the duty to determine whether the transaction is so unusual that an exception to the general rule ought to be made. As Larenz points out, the courts may more easily arrive at a satisfactory solution by an analogy to particular rules rather than by limiting a general rule which provides an unacceptable solution.[98]

One may be led to question whether the broader and more abstract thinking of the BGB is not really something higher and better than that of the common law (if we were only able to master the abstraction). Repeated examination seems to give a negative an-

seems to indicate that the abstract formulations of the BGB provide solutions for more cases than the less abstract Swiss and Austrian law. *See* the Austrian, German, Swiss Reports in Schlesinger, *supra* note 21.

96 Rabel, *Private Laws of Western Civilization*, 10 La. L. Rev. 265, 273 (1950).

97 *See* text at notes 3-21 *supra*.

98 2 K. Larenz, Methodenlehre der Rechtswissenschaft 221 (2d ed. 1969) [hereinafter cited as Larenz MR].

swer. The differences between the more abstract concepts and the less abstract concepts, which are included within the more abstract concepts, are so great as to inhibit extensive use of the more abstract concepts. To use effectively the more abstract concepts, one must refer to the differences of the included subgroups, whereupon the thinking immediately becomes less abstract.

On balance, the anti-abstractionists have the stronger position, Larenz who emphasizes the needless complexity created by six levels of abstraction,[99] Huber who suggests that the BGB attempts to abstract rules which can not properly be abstracted,[100] and Zweigert and Kötz who conclude that the academic achievement represented by the juridical act is overestimated. Too much abstraction lends an ordered appearance but an irregular impact; it fails to provide examples and goals necessary to resolve social conflicts.[101] Many German attorneys are not enthusiastic about the BGB, although few genuinely dislike it. At a time when there were plans to replace both the Austrian and German codes, the Austrian lawyers were more reluctant to depart from the Austrian Code of 1811 than the German lawyers were to depart from the BGB.[102]

The Possibility of a New Code

If the organizational form of the BGB is not an efficient one, what should be done about it? The passage of a new code would sacrifice the time, effort, and analysis invested in the BGB.

Nonetheless, during the period 1935 to 1945 an attempt was made to replace the BGB. As a first step, the central government reorganized legal education along functional lines.[103] In 1937 the well-known German legal scholar and Undersecretary of Justice, Dr. Franz Schlegelberger, published a lecture, "Farewell to the BGB."[104] Work on a new code was officially begun on May 13, 1939, in the Academy of German Law. Although the Academy admitted as members only National Socialist jurists, the stated intent of the code drafters was to consider all schools of thought and to develop a code of lasting value.[105] Those who disapproved of this project tend to dismiss it as being purely politically oriented,[106] because

99 1 Larenz SR, *supra* note 1, at § 3.

100 *See id.*

101 2 Zweigert & Kötz, *supra* note 84, at 5.

102 J. Hedemann, Das Volksgesetzbuch der Deutschen 11 (1941) [hereinafter cited as Hedemann].

103 Wieacker, *supra* note 1, at 555.

104 Hedemann, *supra* note 102, at 19.

105 *Id.* at 2.

106 Cohn criticizes it because it began with: "Supreme Law is the welfare of the German people." Cohn, *German Legal Science Today*, 2 Int. & Comp. L.Q. 169, 179 (1953). However, many early English law books began with similar mottos; for example, Gerard Malynes' famous work, The Ancient Law-Merchant (1636), bears the motto "*Salus Populi, suprema Lex esto.*"

some of the members of the Academy were primarily interested in promoting National Socialist aims. Nevertheless, many of those who worked on the new code and supported it, especially in its early stages of development, were striving to produce a better written and more easily understandable code; they were willing to accept some National Socialist thought as unavoidable concomitant.[107]

The new code was to omit the general part even though it had been a source of praise for German legal scholarship from beyond the German borders.[108] Contracts and torts were apparently to be separated more than they are now, but they were to remain enclosed in a single book entitled "Contracts and Liability."[109] The contracts section was to have prevented the use of contracts as a means of "exploiting the poor" and was to have encouraged economic "development by fair competition."[110] Because of its connection with the Hitler regime, the movement died with his downfall. All serious attempts to replace the BGB appear to have died with it.

Probably the leading alternative to the abstract organizational structure of the BGB is the "model" organization. The lawmaker writes into the statute solutions to a number of basic problems, to serve as a paradigm for the courts' use in solving other problems. Most American statutes would probably fall into this class.[111]

There is, however, no indication that the BGB will be replaced. Many agree with Wieacker and Schwarz that the once vaunted General Part of the BGB is superfluous if not harmful,[112] but they will not scrap the BGB and the seventy years of judicature built around it. Whether the result of conscious decision or the accidental turn of events, the BGB remains in force. Efforts to replace the BGB having proved futile, the trend now seems to be to turn to the

---

107 *Cf.* Wieacker, *supra* note 1, at 536. The amount of by-product they were willing to accept seems to have increased as the war and the code project progressed. See the draft of the first book of the proposed code in J. Hedemann, H. Lehmann, & W. Siebert, Volksgesetzbuch Grundregeln und Buch 1 (1942) [hereinafter cited as Draft I].

108 The draft of the first part of the proposed code did away with anything resembling the general part of the present code. Draft I, *supra* note 107.

109 *Id.* at 6.

110 *Id.* at 12f.

111 Larenz is the leading advocate of this method in Germany. Larenz MR, *supra* note 98, at 423-50. *See also* Larenz AT, *supra* note 1, at § 1, pt. IV, where three prototypes of the statutory style are discussed.

The Swiss code follows the "example" system as far as agreements are concerned. The Code of Obligations regulates the making, interpretation, and validity of contracts. Section 7 of the Civil Code then provides that the general provisions of the Code of Obligations on contracts are also applicable to other civil relationships. *See* J. Williams, Swiss Civil Code (1925).

112 Wieacker, *supra* note 1, at 488.

aid of law students and laymen by writing more easily understandable textbooks organized along functional lines.[113]

Concluding Comments

There are abstractions in the first book of the BGB similar to those of American law. They will cause the American lawyer little difficulty. For example, the principles of agency, as taught in the United States, affect contracts, transfers of property, and municipal law. Prescription (or statutes of limitation) is another topic rationally abstracted. Both agency and prescription are abstracted into the BGB's General Part.

Some abstraction is necessary in any legal system; only when abstraction is carried to excess does its disadvantage begin to outweigh its advantage. Because the BGB went too far, the satisfactory operation of the Code is probably due more to the decisions of the judges on the German Supreme Court than to the statute itself. Their decisions have produced an excellent body of civil law which a more literal, less sophisticated reading of the Code would not have. One of the not wholly intended but important functions of the BGB may have been to conceal the large role that judges play in law making at a time when German thought would have been less willing to permit them this role than it would be today.

*Legal Areas Covered*

The Introductory Law (Einführungsgesetz or EGBGB) is not a part of the BGB; it is a separate law "introducing" the BGB. Despite its title, the EGBGB contains some important substantive provisions, for example, those relating to private international law and those reserving some rights to the states. Certain questions relating to mining, to hunting and fishing, to land, and even to servants, were reserved to the states by the Introductory Law.[114] Other statutes contain provisions which are neither part of the Introductory Law, nor of the BGB. The statute setting up the land registry office[115] and the statutes regulating the limited absolute liability

[113] Staudinger's commentary begins its treatment of the book of obligations with a two hundred page introduction and contains other commentaries throughout the book, all of which are to some extent organized in a functional way. Although Larenz's textbook on the law of obligations follows in general the form of the Code, the author makes a special attempt to bridge the gap between the abstract formulations of the BGB and actual problems. See the preface to the first edition, reprinted in later editions. 1 Larenz SR, *supra* note 1. The widely used Alpmann-Schmidt Repetitor Series is considerably more functional in its organization than the Code. One of Germany's leading legal publishing houses has recently begun publication of a series of pocket books written for laymen, each of which deals with a functional area of the law.

[114] EGBGB §§ 55-152.

[115] GBO.

of automobile owners[116] are outside the BGB; but these laws are so closely related to the BGB that they are often considered in studies of the BGB.

Other important subjects of private law are considered to be special areas and are not taken up in the study of the BGB. One of these is the Commercial Code (Handelsgesetzbuch or HGB), which sets out special rules for use when one or sometimes both parties to a transaction are merchants. Although the HGB contains a substantial number of provisions relating to particular types of mercantile transactions—transactions undertaken by commission brokers, freight forwarders, or warehousemen—the number of its provisions relating to commercial sales is small,[117] because some of the substantive provisions of the old Commercial Code of 1861 were taken over by the BGB to form general law.[118] Section two of the Introductory Law to the HGB stipulates that the rules of the BGB will apply in commercial matters so far as the HGB fails to provide different rules.

The law relating to some of the leading German forms of business organizations have been taken out of the HGB, these forms of business being regulated by separate statutes. The law of negotiable instruments, insurance law, and labor law are also regulated by separate statutes.[119] As Schmidt points out, after passage of the BGB the Germans seem to have preferred laws organized along functional lines.[120]

Further excluded are questions of public law (legal conflicts between the state *qua* state and a citizen). Many Germans regard these questions as fundamentally different from questions of private law (legal conflicts between private citizens). As the more powerful German states became exempt from the judicial jurisdiction of the old Empire, their rulers sometimes refused to assign jurisdiction of public law questions to any court. Commencing with the example set by Baden in 1863, most states eventually created special courts competent only to deal with questions of public law.[121] Although the division between public and private law is still entrenched in Germany, it is beginning to come under serious attack.[122]

---

116 StVG §§ 7-20.

117 *See* HGB §§ 343-82. A merchant is not entitled to get an agreed forfeiture reduced, whereas a non-merchant may under some circumstances. BGB § 343. *See* HGB § 348.

118 1 E. Rabel, Das Recht des Warenkaufs 32 (1936). *Cf.* A. Baumbach & K. Duden, Handelsgesetzbuch 3 (17th ed. 1966).

119 1 Enn/Nip, *supra* note 1, at 2.

120 Schmidt, *supra* note 31, at 153-54.

121 Forsthoff, Lehrbuch des Verwaltungsrechts § 25 (8th ed. 1961).

122 Professor Martin Bullinger of Freiburg recently wrote a book addressed to the problem. M. Bullinger, Öffentliches Recht und Privatrecht (1968),

By far the most important social legislation of the Federal Republic is outside the BGB. For example, the Job Protection Law (Kündigungsschutzgesetz) of 1951[123] provides with some exceptions that an employee who is over the age of eighteen and who has been continuously employed by an enterprise for more than six months cannot be discharged unless the discharge is socially justifiable. A discharge is not socially justifiable unless the employee was at fault or unless the state of the business urgently requires that the employee be discharged. The employer has the burden of proof; usually the labor courts require a high standard of proof.[124]

Other German laws require a minimum of fifteen working days as a paid vacation for all employees under the age of thirty-five and eighteen days for those over thirty-five.[125] Mothers are relieved from work with pay for six weeks before and six weeks after birth.[126] There is an elaborate system of social security, including not only medical insurance but also continuance of pay for sick employees.[127]

*The Importance of Precedent*

The way the BGB functions in practice depends largely on the place of precedent in German law. No longer acceptable is the old theoretical statement that there is no system of stare decisis.[128] Ernst Rabel, who had been the head of a leading comparative law institute in Germany before emigrating to the United States, wrote: "So far as practice is concerned, one must look for the difference between the German . . . and American systems of precedent with a magnifying glass."[129] The German lower courts are not bound to follow precedent set by the Supreme Court, but the judges do follow precedent as often as American lower court judges do. Certainty in the law can only be achieved where there is respect for precedent. All judges dislike reversals, and a German judge may suffer the additional sting of slower promotion if he too often fails to respect

*reviewed*, Rüfner, 2 Mod. L. & Soc'y, 8, 9 (1969). He comes to the conclusion that the dichotomy is more the result of historical accident than of fundamental difference in subject matter.

123 BGBl. I S. 1317.

124 When the employer seeks to reduce his working force as a result of economic conditions, a discharge of an employee is still not justifiable if the employer did not give due regard for the social considerations in the choice of the employee to be discharged.

125 Bundesurlaubsgesetz 1963 BGBl. I S. 2.

126 Mutterschutzgesetz 1952 BGBl. I S. 69.

127 Exceptions are made in some cases for employees in executive positions or other employees with large salaries.

128 *See* Enn/Nip, *supra* note 1, at 167-69 (1952).

129 16 E. Rabel, Deutsches und Amerikanisches Recht, Rabels Zeitschrift für Ausländisches und Internationales Privatrecht 340, 345 (1951) [hereinafter cited as Rabel].

higher court decisions. To prompt change, the lower court may merely include in an opinion that follows the precedent of the Supreme Court all the reasons for deciding the other way. In such cases the Supreme Court will reconsider its position and may change its previous ruling.

More evidence of the importance of precedent in the German system can be found in the statute regulating the structure of the Supreme Court for Civil and Criminal Matters. If one Senate of the Supreme Court wants to deviate from a precedent set by another Senate, unless it can secure the consent of that Senate, it must call upon a "Great Senate" (consisting of the President of the Court and eight judges from various senates) to decide the dispute.[130]

Widely publicized was the German notary who disregarded prior decisions of the Supreme Court and was held liable to his client for damages.[131] Professor Weitnauer of the University of Heidelberg believes that precedent has become so important in German civil law that "the section numbers of the Code are often only systematic places where one files and later finds the results of judge-made law."[132]

The view that there is a fundamental difference between civil and common-law countries in the use of precedent may have arisen by a comparison of the practice in England, where the force of precedent is stronger than in the United States,[133] with the practice in France, where the force of precedent is substantially weaker than in Germany.[134] Just as all common-law countries do not have the same strong respect for precedent, likewise not all civil law coun-

130 § 136 Gerichtsverfassungsgesetz. That part of the rule allowing permission of the other Senate is not in the statute; it evolved as a means to avoid, when possible, the inconvenience of calling upon the Great Senate.

131 Rabel, *supra* note 129, at 345.

132 Letter from Professor Weitnauer to R. Riegert, April 27, 1970.

133 Not until 1966 did the British House of Lords decide not to be absolutely bound by precedents, although the Lords still regard the "use of precedent as an indispensable foundation on which to decide what is the law and its application to individual cases." Note, [1966] 3 All E. R. 77 (Lords).

134 This sometimes makes it difficult to tell what the French law on a particular point is. *See, e.g.*, A. von Mehren, The Civil Law System 483 (1957) [hereinafter cited as von Mehren CLS]. Professor Schlesinger points out that "[a] comparison between codified and case law systems shows that both have their strong points;" that "either system can be perfectly workable;" that "[in] France, a civil law country, there are practically no code provisions dealing with offer and acceptance;" and that "the decisions of the Cour de Cassation are reported in such a way that the reader is not reliably informed of either the facts or the reasoning of the Court. Perhaps, partly as a result of their semi-secret nature, the decisions of the Cour de Cassation have not obtained the same authoritative status which is the hallmark of the decisions of courts of last resort in some of the other civil law systems . . . ." 1 Schlesinger, *supra* note 21, at 54.

tries ignore precedent. For example, in Spain precedent becomes formally binding on the lower courts when the highest court has decided the same way in more than one case.[135] Thus Germany does follow precedent and, among civil law countries, Germany is not unique.

*Method of Interpretation of the BGB*[136]

Although the practice may be sometimes more conservative, German theory admits the possibility of reaching results contrary to the plain words of a statute when the dictates of justice and the needs of daily life require. Dr. Brändl, then a judge of the highest court of Bavaria, wrote:

> Interpretation in a narrow sense is the determination of the meaning of an existing statutory provision . . . . In cases in which the statute and customary law are silent, or seem to be silent . . . *or interpretation leads to obviously unacceptable results,* a suitable practical result must nonetheless be found. This is law development, supplementary and changing law development, finding the law beyond the statute and to a certain extent *contrary to the statute* if one identifies the statute with the literal meaning of its words, but a statute does not require blind obedience but thinking obedience; an evaluating legal method may find that even an interpretation which goes contrary to the literal meaning of the statute is covered by the intent of the law maker.[137]

Dr. Brändl then discusses in some detail interpretation in the narrow sense, as well as "supplementary law finding," such as analogy and argument *e contrario*. He proceeds with a description of the various German schools of thought, including the "free-law" school, the sociological method, and the similar but independently treated "jurisprudence of interests."[138] Then he concludes:

> The difference in method has not proven as important in the practical application of the law (by the courts and otherwise) as the polemic writings might have led one to believe . . . . The judges always take pains to find some kind of support for their decisions in the statutes . . . . Despite all their emphasis on fidelity to the statutes, the courts today are considerably more independent of the statute . . . . The decisons of the highest courts contain words from the

[135] R. Schlesinger, Comparative Law, Cases, Text, Materials 194 (3d ed. 1970) [hereinafter cited as Schlesinger CL].

[136] German writers have devoted considerable attention to problems of statutory interpretation. For example, Professor Larenz wrote a textbook on legal method. The first third of this book traces the historical development of the various theories; the remainder analyzes the theories. Larenz MR, *supra* note 98. 1 Stau/Brändl, *supra* note 1, at pt. 54-82 before § 1, contains a short seventeen page description of German theories which is followed here.

[137] 1 Stau/Brändl, *supra* note 1, at pt. 54 before § 1 (emphasis added).

[138] *Id.* at pt. 54-79 before § 1.

vocabulary of all of the various schools of statutory interpretation.[139]

A Senatspräsident of the German Supreme Court said that strict constructionists are rare in Germany today. The general tendency is to attempt to reach a just result in individual cases, either by interpreting or by appropriately filling in statutory interstices. Perhaps one could say that the statutory interpretation of German judges is neither more literal nor more liberal than would be expected of American judges if they had an integrated, detailed statute like the BGB to interpret.

The German Civil Code contains a number of so-called "general clauses" providing a statutory basis for the courts to deviate from the literal words of the code. But the broad effect given to the leading clause, section 242,[140] is itself due to interpretation. Some judges prefer to reach the desired result, if possible, without the use of general clauses, and some professors discourage their students from using the general clauses in solving problems. These judges believe the use of section 242 is tantamount to an admission that the result was not required by more specific provisions of the statute, so the responsibility for the decision is placed too squarely on the shoulders of the judges. Nonetheless, section 242 has played an important role in German court decisions and legal writings.[141]

*The Role of Academic Writings*

In the nineteenth century German law was governed by academic writers.[142] This is no longer true, although their position is still stronger than that of academic writers in the United States. The change was due not only to the enactment of the Code but also to the creation of a supreme court with broad geographical jurisdiction.[143]

Legal literature serves a different purpose in the Federal Republic than in the United States. Instead of explaining the law

---

139 *Id.* at pt. 79 before § 1.

140 Section 242 provides that a debtor is obligated to make performance in the way that good faith (more literally, fidelity and trust) and established custom require. The courts have extended it beyond the law of obligations to literally all areas of the law and have extended the duty it imposes also to the creditor. 2 Stau/Weber, *supra* note 1, at § 242, pt. A27-A107.

141 2 Stau/Weber, *supra* note 1, at § 242, contains 1400 large pages of small type digesting cases and legal writings which cite BGB § 242. *See generally* text at notes 128-35 *supra*; von Mehren CLS, *supra* note 134 ch. 16; Zweigert & Puttfarken, *Statutory Interpretation—Civilian Style*, 44 Tul. L. Rev. 704 (1970); Address by Professor Rheinstein, *The Struggle Between Equity and Stability in the Law of Post-war Germany*, 1936 Proceedings of the Forty-Second Annual Meeting of the Iowa State Bar Association at 67.

142 Cohn, *German Legal Science Today*, 2 Int'l & Comp. L.Q. 169, 186 (1953).

143 *Cf.* Schlesinger CL, *supra* note 135, at 247-49.

as the courts have interpreted it and then making suggestions for its improvement as many American and a few German text writers do, many German text writers are so busy attempting to develop new law that they often pay less attention to the courts' interpretation of the law than American authors do. Indeed, civil lawyers respect the views of the legal writers as a separate source of law, even if the views of the legal writers differ from those of the courts. In one extreme example, a writer stated a proposition of law, picked a particular set of facts to illustrate his point, and added in parenthesis that the German Supreme Constitutional Court had decided that case differently.[144] This is what surprises Americans most: the German scholar's method of presenting his own views as undisputed facts and only thereafter presenting the different views of the courts.

These Germans believe an encyclopedic condensation of judicial decisions is unworthy of scholars; they prefer the innovative function, that of advancing new ideas and of describing the historical development of legal doctrines. The pressure to come up with new ideas may be too great in view of the fact that the majority of important, relevant, and well-founded ideas have already been advanced by others. The need today may be not so much for new ideas but for recognition and support of certain of the older ideas. Overemphasis on innovation leads to unsound ideas and detracts from existing sound ideas, although evidence of this is more common in German public law than private law. That many German writers use a doctrinal as opposed to a social-fact approach[145] decreases the probability that they will find lasting solutions to practical problems.

Of the three steps sometimes associated with scientific work, the gathering of information, the formation of a hypothesis, and the verification of the hypothesis, the second step is obviously the one emphasized most by German writers. To formulate a theory, the writer will usually gather information only from law books; evaluation and verification of proposed solutions are often left to the readers and to the courts.

Other criticisms of German scholarship have been made from time to time but seem to be of limited validity. Rabel criticized the "scholastic excesses" and "hair splitting."[146] Nussbaum, of the Berlin and later of the Columbia law faculty, deplored the waste of "tremendous amounts of intellectual effort" on subjects, "the practical importance of which is not of enough value to cover the cost

[144] T. Maunz, Deutsches Staatsrecht 234 (10th ed. 1961).

[145] The German movement to go outside the "pure law" to sociology and economics is now gaining momentum. *See* Riegert, Book Review, 2 Mod. L. & Soc'y 144 (1969).

[146] Rabel, *supra* note 129, at 340, 348.

of printing the material dealing with them."[147] On the other hand, problems of no practical importance sometimes suddenly acquire such importance. In those cases the judges appreciate what has been written. Most of the one hundred and four judges of the German Supreme Court, while differing in their opinions of individual authors, find the literature useful; and they are well satisfied with it. The judges always attempt to study the relevant literature although they often do not cite it in their opinions.

A study in detail of the views of the leading authors on the BGB is virtually a lifetime task. In addition to Larenz there are a number of other scholars, such as Esser, Fikentscher, Flume, and Blomeyer,[148] who write on the problems of obligations. Then there are the earlier scholars still read and quoted. Each of the commentaries, Palandt, Staudinger, Erman, Reichsgerichtsrätekommentar, and Soergel-Siebert is the combined work of several authors. Many practitioners in the lower courts work almost exclusively with the one volume commentary by Palandt, so their reading is delimited. Many students and lawyers, who are seeking to obtain only an elementary knowledge of the law, find much of the literature useless for their purposes.[149] Much of the literature is written by experts principally for other experts. The students and non-specialists complain, while specialists express satisfaction or praise.

### *Civil Procedure*

German civil procedure contains some fascinating differences from its American counterpart. In a very real sense there are no civil trials in Germany; what would be the trial in the United States is divided into segments and spread over a long period of time. One of the three judges of the competent chamber of the court of general jurisdiction[150] listens to witnesses in the judge's office. The names of the witnesses are suggested to the court by the parties, but they do not become witnesses of the parties; instead, they are the witnesses of the court.

---

[147] A. Nussbaum, Die Rechtstatsachenforschung 18, 25 in Nussbaum, Die Rechtstatsachenforschung (Rehbinder ed. 1968).

[148] Some of the texts and authors which enjoy a particularly good reputation at the German Supreme Court are: Enneccerus, Kipp, and Wolff for their series on the entire BGB; Esser, Larenz, and Fikentscher for the law of obligations; Westermann and Baur on the law of things; Gernhuber on family law; and Lange on the law of inheritance.

[149] To satisfy the students' needs, there has been a proliferation of mimeographed materials put out by established tutors (Repetitors). For example, the functionally organized Alpmann-Schmidt courses have brief hypothetical cases, often modified versions of leading cases, with alternative answers and references to the authorities.

[150] Cases in which the amount in controversy is more than $375 are usually within the competence of the Landgericht, a three-judge court. When the amount in controversy is less, the case is handled by the Amtsgericht, a single-judge court.

The Supreme Court for Civil and Criminal Matters consists of 104 judges divided into ten civil and five criminal senates, each consisting of six or seven judges who sit in groups of five. The jurisdiction of the civil senates is divided according to subject matter. The seventh and eighth civil senates divide between them the specific contracts mentioned in the BGB; the sixth civil senate is responsible for tort cases. Although appeals are limited to questions of law, facts are sometimes considered on the theory that the conclusion of facts is as a matter of law not supported by the evidence.

Aside from the special court for constitutional law, there are separate court systems in the Federal Republic for general administrative law, for labor law, for tax law, and for social insurance law, in addition to the regular court system for civil and criminal matters. Arbitration, especially between big business firms, plays a larger role in Germany than it does in the United States. The courts are willing to enforce the arbitration awards.[151]

## Illustrative Principles of Contract Law

### *Introduction*

This purview of German contract law begins with two Code principles which have not worked, the principle of no liability without subjective fault and the principle of specific performance as a standard remedy. Social and economic forces dictated different rules from the ones broadly proclaimed by the two general principles. The legislature made exceptions to them in the more detailed parts of the Code and the courts stretched the exceptions and developed new ones by various means of judicial interpretation.

### *The "Responsibility" Doctrine: No Liability for Non-performance of a Contract Without Subjective Fault.*

Leistungsstörungen (breach of contract) is approached in German law from the standpoint of impossibility and delay. With or without fault of the obligor, the performance has either been delayed or performance has become impossible.[152] According to section 276, an obligor is only "responsible" for willful default and negligence;[153] and negligence is defined as lack of ordinary care.[154] That

[151] For further information on German civil procedure, see Kaplan, von Mehren, & Schaefer, *Phases of German Civil Procedure*, 71 Harv. L. Rev. 1193, 1443 (1958); Kaplan, *Civil Procedure—Reflections on the Comparison of Systems*, 9 Buffalo L. Rev. 409 (1960); 2 British Foreign Office, Manual of German Law pt. IV (1952).

[152] Zweigert and Kötz quote with approval Titze: that the BGB in taking up the impossibility teachings of the [Roman] common law, entered upon "an unhappy legacy sine beneficio inventarii." Zweigert & Kötz, *supra* note 84, at 193. *See also id.* at 216-19.

[153] The section does not use the word "only"; it lists "wilful default" and "negligence."

[154] In determining the standard of care required by section 276 the courts

an obligor is liable only for subjective fault is reiterated by Larenz: "unless there is a special statutory provision or unless the contract provides otherwise, the obligor is only responsible for willful default or negligence. This means, according to the majority opinion, that he must answer for his own fault and only for his own fault."[155] The definition of "responsible" in section 276 is used, for example, by section 280. By section 280 the obligor is required to compensate the obligee for any damage arising from nonperformance if performance has become impossible as the result of a circumstance for which the obligor is "responsible." Suppose the obligor promised to transfer title to the obligee but has in the meantime transferred it to a third person; performance has become impossible for the obligor as a result of something for which he is "responsible," namely because of his willful alienation of the object of sale. Likewise if the obligor has delayed performance past the time it was due, sections 284 through 286 make the obligor liable for any damage caused by a delay for which he was "responsible."

Sections 323 through 326 handle this problem at the next higher level of abstraction: the level of bilateral contracts. When *A* fails innocently to perform a bilateral contract, *B* has no claim against *A*; but *A* loses his right to *B*'s performance. If *B* has already performed and *A*'s failure to perform was without fault, *B* can only recover through unjust enrichment what he has given *A*. If *A* is no longer enriched, *B* may not recover at all.[156] In short, the rule excuses an obligor who is not at fault and places the risk of "no fault" breach on the obligee.[157] The innocently defaulting obligor may occasionally not have to return what he has received from the obligee.

A general rule placing the risk of no fault breach on the obligee is probably workable. In the ordinary case, a more efficient rule would put the loss caused by "no fault" nonperformance on the person who has contracted to produce the performance. The question is whether the promisor contracts only to act without fault in attempting to perform or whether he guarantees performance. Section 276 opts for the former, but the exceptions introduced elsewhere in the Code and by the courts cut away virtually the entire

are willing to consider the age, profession, education, and social circle of the defendant, but otherwise the courts have refused to consider his personal qualities on the theory that the statute sets an objective standard. Palandt, *supra* note 1, at § 276, pt. 4b.

[155] 1 Larenz SR, *supra* note 1, at § 20, pt. I.

[156] There are additional restrictions to unjust enrichment actions. BGB § 812.

[157] Only the main line of the statute is followed here. Such important questions as partial impossibility and subrogation are omitted so as not to cloud the central thought.

rule of section 276 so far as the nonperformance of contracts is concerned.

Section 279, the most important part of these exceptions, eats away more than half the rule. It provides that if the obligation is for the delivery of goods described by species and if performance is objectively possible, the obligor is responsible for his failure to perform even though he is not subjectively at fault. This section is the basis for the important and much more extensive rule that the obligor is always responsible for inadequate financial resources;[158] or, as the German law students memorize, a person is "required to have money." The courts have extended section 279 to a contract for something not described by species. Thus, if an obligor is unable to perform his contract due to lack of funds, he is held liable without fault regardless of whether the contract requires him to deliver a thing described by species or a unique chattel. The extension of section 279, although contrary to the statutory language, has been received with general approval.[159]

A second important qualification to the rule of no liability without personal fault is that the rule is not *jus cogens*; the parties can provide in the contract for liability without such fault. More erosion flows from the special part of the book on obligations. For example, the seller of a claim or other legal right is liable in case of its nonexistence regardless of personal fault;[160] the seller of defective goods is held liable without fault for some types of damage if the goods do not have the warranted quality;[161] a lessor is liable for defects in leased objects.[162] Other arguments have been devised to extend liability. An artist who undertakes to restore a picture but instead damages it because the restoration is beyond his ability could be held liable for his negligence (1) in entering the contract[163] or (2) for failure to meet the standard of care expected of artists.[164] Even without subjective fault, the artist may be responsible through the court's use of an objective standard to measure fault.

With these exceptions to section 276, German decisions look like the results in American decisions, particularly since American law excuses performance for impossibility. Only the syllogisms used by American and German courts differ: the Germans requiring fault but making exceptions, the Americans simply never asking about

158 1 Larenz SR, *supra* note 1, at § 21, pt. Id.

159 *Id.* Larenz cites two cases: Judgment of Feb. 8, 1911, 75 RGZ 337; Judgment of Jan. 3, 1911, 75 RGZ 106; 1 J. Esser, Schuldrect § 33, pt. IV (1960) [hereinafter cited as Esser]; Palandt, *supra* note 1, at § 279.

160 BGB § 437.

161 BGB § 463.

162 BGB § 537.

163 1 Larenz SR, *supra* note 1, § 20, pt. III.

164 *See* note 154, *supra*.

fault. One important difference is that Germany will not allow consequential damages unless fault is proven. If *A* buys a diseased cow and the disease spreads to *A*'s herd, *A* cannot recover for the damage to his herd unless he can show *B* either knew or should have known of the disease.[165] Even here, the courts have some discretion. Lack of fault is an affirmative defense, so the burden is on the breaching defendant.[166] The courts can set the standard so high in appropriate cases that the defendant has little chance of carrying his burden.

Although the German courts have in general refused to use the principle of section 276 to excuse obligors from liability for non-fault nonperformance on an individual basis, they have, on the other hand, been "judicial activists" in excusing debtors from performance when a changed situation has resulted in making performance substantially more difficult for a *class* of debtors, such as when the circumstance is war or extreme inflation. Why the courts are unwilling to aid the obligors in the one case and willing to aid them in the other is uncertain. Perhaps the reason is that an adjudication of well-known issues affecting many contracts is more important than an adjudication of issues affecting one contract.[167]

*Specific Performance*

The German Civil Code designates performance as the ordinary remedy and damages as the extraordinary remedy. "By virtue of an obligation the obligee is entitled to claim performance from the obligor. The performance may consist of a forebearance."[168] The principle is not limited to contract law; it is applicable to the full spectrum of German obligations, including those arising out of torts. Section 249 provides: "A person who is bound to make compensation [*e.g.*, for a tort[169]] shall bring about the condition which would exist if the circumstance making him liable to compensate had not occurred."[170] The next sentence in the section gives the injured party an option to avoid the rule: "If compensation is required to be made for injury to a person or damage to a thing, the creditor may

165 K. Zweigert, *Aspects of the German Law of Sale* in *Some Comparative Aspects of the Law Relating to Sale of Goods*, Int'l & Comp. L.Q. Supp. Pub. No. 9 at 3 (1964).

166 The rule is derived from an analogy to BGB § 282.

167 *See also* Zweigert & Kötz, *supra* note 84, at 191-93.

168 BGB § 241. The old German law tried to solve the problem of contract breach by treating it as a crime. A law suit for damages or performance was therefore unknown. 1 Larenz SR, *supra* note 1, at § 2, pt. III. The classical Roman law did not give an action for specific performance, but the law of the later empire did. Szladits, *The Concept of Specific Performance in Civil Law*, 4 Am. J. Comp. L. 208 (1955) [hereinafter cited as Szladits].

169 BGB § 823.

170 For a discussion of the use of section 249, see Szladits, *supra* note 168, at 224.

demand, instead of restitution in kind, the sum of money necessary to effect such restitution." Alternatively, the injured party can set a period for performance after the expiration of which he can get money damages.[171] When restitution in kind is impossible, disproportionately difficult, or insufficient to compensate the obligee, the court may award money damages.[172]

The Code of Civil Procedure of 1877 regulates the execution of judgments. A judgment for the delivery of a chattel or real estate is excuted by an officer's seizing the property and giving it to the obligee.[173] The Code of Civil Procedure also contains some rules which might more properly be classified as substantive. Where a party is ordered to do what could also be done by a third person and the party fails to do it, the court may authorize the third party's performance at the obligor's cost.[174] If performance depends solely on the will of the obligor, the court may compel the obligor by threat or imposition of fine or imprisonment to perform the act, but the court may not compel performance of agreements to marry or to live with one's spouse or to perform personal services.[175] An obligor's declaration required by a judgment (as when a judgment transfers land) is treated as made when the judgment becomes final.[176]

Suppose the obligee does not want specific performance; how can he get damages? First, if performance has become impossible as the result of the obligor's fault, such as when the obligor negligently destroyed the object of a sales contract or conveyed title to a third person, the obligee can obtain money damages.[177] Second, where performance is still possible in a bilateral contract, section 326 I provides that the obligee must give the obligor a reasonable additional period to perform, informing him that if he fails to perform by the end of the period, the obligee will refuse to accept performance; if the obligor does not perform by the end of the period, the obligee is entitled to damages or to rescission of the contract.[178] Third, if the performance is useless (of "no interest") to the obligee as a result of the delay, the obligee may sue for damages or for rescission immediately under section 326 II.

One of the reasons that the statute contemplates a "grace period" is to encourage performance when it still has some utility; also the

---

[171] BGB § 250.
[172] *Id.* at § 251.
[173] ZPO §§ 883, 885.
[174] *Id.* at § 887.
[175] *Id.* at § 888.
[176] *Id.* at § 894.
[177] *See* BGB §§ 280, 325.
[178] *See* text at note 59 *supra*, on oversights in the BGB.

"grace period" avoids the harsh penalty of a money judgment.[179] Therefore, the obligee is not excused from setting a "grace period" unless his loss of "interest" on the exchange has been caused by the obligor's delay, as for example the tender of seasonal goods after the season has ended.[180] The "grace period" can be omitted if the parties expressly or impliedly agreed in the contract[181] or if the obligor earnestly refused to perform.[182]

In "one-sided" contracts[183] the rules are the same as for bilateral contracts when the obligee has lost his "interest" in the performance as a result of a delay caused by the obligor's fault.[184] If someone promised gratuitously to lend his car to his nephew for a wedding trip and failed to provide the car until the honeymoon was over, the nephew could sue for damages despite a later tender of the car. When the obligor is entitled to a "grace period," unlike the obligee of a bilateral contract the obligee of a unilateral contract must obtain a judgment before the grace period can be set; then the obligee must wait until the period expires to get another judgment, this time for damages. However, if the court does not believe the obligor will comply with the order for specific performance,[185] the court can grant damages to the obligee contingent upon the obligor's failure to perform.[186]

Even though specific performance is theoretically the more readily available remedy under the German Civil Code, social and economic elements have led in Germany—as they led in the common law countries—to a different result. A buyer of chattels or services usually cannot wait for a judgment of specific performance. His demands are more pressing, so he will ordinarily purchase the chattels or the services elsewhere and rely on the remedy of damages to recoup his losses.

Thus, specific performance is another area of the German Code starting with a principle dramatically different from American law, but in practice this difference is not apparent. "[I]n the majority of cases, the creditor will sue for damages, and the practical importance and superior number of actions for damages may obscure the importance and pre-eminence of the claim for specific per-

179 *Cf.* 2 1c Stau/Werner, *supra* note 1, at § 326, pt. 171.

180 *Id.* at pt. 172.

181 *Id.* at pt. 180.

182 *Id.* at pt. 184.

183 "One-sided" contracts include *inter alia* promises to make a gift or promises to carry out a mandate.

184 BGB § 286.

185 ZPO § 259. *Cf.* 2 1c Stau/Werner, *supra* note 1, at § 283, pt. 23.

186 Also, county courts (Amtsgerichte) may grant contingent awards in all judgments for specific performance.

formance."[187] In both the United States and Germany specific performance is limited—by the courts or the petitions of the plaintiffs—to correcting defaults for sales of real property or unique chattels. For the rest of the cases, damages are the usual remedy.[188] There are some circumstances, however, in which the German right to specific performance produces a drastically different result from that produced in common-law countries, for example, in times of unstable currency or shortages or rationing of goods.

Drafts of the Uniform Law for the International Sale of Goods found on the question of specific performance the contrasts too great between the civil law and the common law to be resolved with a uniform law.[189] An early draft provided that the buyer could get specific performance (1) if specific performance were available in the municipal courts, (2) if a cover purchase were contrary to commercial practice, or (3) if the buyer met unreasonable difficulty in attempting to make a cover purchase.[190] The 1964 Hague Draft of the Law on the International Sale of Goods states: "[t]he buyer shall not be entitled to require performance of the contract by the seller, if it is in conformity with usage and reasonably possible for the buyer to purchase goods to replace those to which the contract relates."[191]

*Consideration and Form*

Although the German Civil Code does not use a word analogous to the common law's "consideration" or the French law's "cause," the results achieved under the Code are usually the same as those which would be achieved by the American doctrine of consideration. Under the German Code a promise without consideration is a gift, and section 518 provides that a promise to make a gift is not enforceable unless it has been made by judicial or notarial contract. Specifically, the donor must appear before a judge or a notary (who is always a lawyer) and make a declaration orally. After reducing the declaration to writing, the judge or notary reads the declaration back to the donor, lets the donor sign, and then the judge or notary authenticates and retains the original copy.

187 Szladits, *supra* note 168, at 221.

188 Uniform Commercial Code § 2-716(1) provides: "Specific performance may be decreed where the goods are unique or in other proper circumstances."

189 *Cf.* Rabel, *A Draft of an International Law of Sales*, 5 U. Chi. L. Rev. 543, 559 (1938).

190 Uniform Law on the International Sale of Goods, Art. 24. *See* 9 Rabel, *supra* note 129, at 15.

191 Uniform Law on the International Sale of Goods, Art. 25, *reprinted in* 13 Am. J. Comp. L. 460 (1964). *See generally*, Dawson, *Specific Performance in France and Germany*, 57 Mich. L. Rev. 495, 525-32 (1969); Neitzel, *Specific Performance, Injunctions, and Damages in the German Law*, 22 Harv. L. Rev. 161 (1909); Szladits, *supra* note 168, at 220-28. *See also* Zweigert & Kötz, *supra* note 84, at 162-69, 177-86.

To illustrate how German and American law reach the same destination by different routes, we can consider an uncle's promise to give his nephew a car for his next birthday. The promise is unenforceable in American law because there is no consideration; and the promise is unenforceable in German law because it is a gift without the requisite form. If the nephew had promised to purchase a car from his uncle, the uncle's promise would be enforceable in American law because there was consideration; and the promise is enforceable in German law because the nephew's counterpromise of payment removed the uncle's promise from the gift category and obviated the need for the special formalities required by German law for gifts.

On some questions the BGB does produce answers different from American law. Most of these areas of difference result from section 516's definition of a gift as being made "out of one's property." A service is probably not "out of one's property," so a gratuitous promise to perform a service is binding even though made orally without a writing. If an uncle makes a seriously intended promise to polish his nephew's car on his nephew's next birthday, he would not be bound in American law[192] but would be bound in German law.[193] Likewise, a promise to lend someone real or personal property is probably not a gift "out of one's property," so the promise requires no formalities to be enforceable.[194]

Borderline cases, such as cases involving "past consideration" or moral obligations, present special difficulty to German as well as American courts. To American courts the question is one of consideration, and to German courts the question is one of deciding if the transaction is a gift. The two systems do not agree on the disposition of several cases. Promises to fulfill an obligation contracted while the obligor is a minor and promises to pay an obligation when the statute of limitations has run are generally enforceable in American law but not in German law;[195] however,

---

[192] Of course, the promise may be enforceable under American law if the promisee has relied to his detriment. Restatement of Contracts § 90 (1932).

[193] However, this is by no means certain for two reasons. First, German scholars are divided on the question. Some contend that the donor is making a gift "out of his property," namely, the compensation he would otherwise receive for polishing a car. Larenz, who believes this is not a "gift" under German law, lists three scholars who agree with him and three who disagree. 2 Larenz SR, *supra* note 1, at § 43, pt. I. Second, section 671 provides that a person who accepts the obligation may withdraw without liability if he does so in time to permit the obligee to make other arrangements or if the obligor has an "important [personal] reason" for revoking. *See* Palandt, *supra* note 1, at § 662.

[194] This too is disputed. 2 Larenz SR, *supra* note 1, at § 43, pt. I. Also, according to section 605, the lender may cancel the loan if, as the result of an unexpected circumstance, he needs the thing himself.

[195] Von Mehren, *Civil-Law Analogues to Consideration: An Exercise in*

the promise of a bankrupt debtor to pay a released or discharged debt is enforceable in both systems.[196]

The essential function of consideration has been to separate the transactions involving exchanges from those involving gifts. Arrangements for exchanges are vital to the economy of any nation. Promises to make gifts are of such marginal utility that society hesitates to enforce them unless the parties express their interest in some special form, such as an authenticated document. Where the parties do not take the additional steps for a gift, the court machinery is reserved for the transactions of greater utility: contracts involving exchanges. Both the consideration required to make contracts enforceable and the formalities required for a gift protect promisors of gifts from their own indiscretion.[197]

Promises to hold open an offer for a stated period of time, often to permit the offeree to investigate the proposed transaction, were often ruled unenforceable under the common law because of lack of consideration or formality. Sections 145 and 148 of the German Civil Code make offers irrevocable for a period of time sufficient for the offeree to reply unless the offer expressly states a period of time. Then the offer remains irrevocable for that period of time. The Uniform Commercial Code makes a cautious start in this direction, so far as the purchase or sale of goods by a merchant is concerned, by making his written "firm offers" binding for a maximum period of ninety days.[198]

On the issue of modification without consideration, the common law suffers from the English decision, *Foakes v. Beer*.[199] Dr. Foakes

*Comparative Analysis*, 72 Harv. L. Rev. 1009, 1033 (1959) [hereinafter cited as von Mehren].

[196] *Id.*

[197] Chlores, *The Doctrine of Consideration and the Reform of the Law of Contract, A Comparative Analysis*, 17 Int'l & Comp. L.Q. 137, 140 (1968) [hereinafter cited as Chlores], rejects the utility of requiring consideration. Von Mehren, *supra* note 195, at 1016, lists "four general interrelated concerns" which lead the French, German, and common-law systems to treat a given transaction as unenforceable:

> There is a concern for evidentiary security, a desire to protect both the individual citizen and the courts against manufactured evidence and difficulties resulting from insufficiencies in the available proof. The individual must be safeguarded against his own rashness and the importuning of others. The enforceable obligation needs to be marked off or signalized so as to insure an awareness on the individual's part that his action may have legal significance and to simplify the administration of justice. Finally, there is unwillingness to enforce transaction types considered suspect or of marginal value.

*See also* Fuller, *Consideration and Form*, 41 Colum. L. Rev. 799 (1941) (upon which Professor von Mehren's analysis is in part based).

[198] Uniform Commercial Code § 2-205. If the promise to hold the offer open is on a form supplied by the offeree, the form must be separately signed by the offeree.

[199] 9 App. Cas. 605 (1884).

failed to make his payment on a note owed to Mrs. Beer. She promised to forgive the interest if Dr. Foakes paid immediately. Dr. Foakes complied, but thereafter Mrs. Beer sued him for the interest. An uncertain House of Lords held for Mrs. Beer, finding no consideration to support Mrs. Beer's forgiveness of interest. The German Civil Code has never known the rule of *Foakes v. Beer*. Contract modifications are valid without consideration unless they can be struck down for duress[200] or unconscionability.[201] The German approach seems preferable to that of *Foakes v. Beer*. Even the party agreeing to settle for a fractional amount of the obligation obtains several advantages: without the burden of a lawsuit he may receive his money faster than he otherwise would; he may avoid the risk of losing his entire claim in bankruptcy proceeding; and he may acquire access to assets of the debtor's friends who may be willing to come forward if they know that settlement for a fractional part of the debt will be binding. Apparently concluding that the German rule is better than the common-law rule, the Uniform Commercial Code permits the discharge without consideration of a claim or right arising from a breach of contract.[202]

Just as German law differs from common-law consideration, German law also differs from French cause.[203] Section 1108 of the French Civil Code provides that an obligation must have a licit "cause" to be enforceable. The requirement of cause is ordinarily satisfied not only by what would satisfy the requirement of consideration, but also by "past consideration," a moral obligation, or an intent to make a gift.[204] Sections 931 and 932 of the French Civil Code[205] are stricter than BGB section 518 I because the French require a promise of a gift to be made by a notarial act

200 BGB § 123.

201 *Id.* at § 138.

202 Uniform Commercial Code § 1-107 states:

> Any claim or right arising out of an alleged breach can be discharged in whole or in part without consideration by a written waiver or renunciation signed and delivered by the aggrieved party.

*See also* Uniform Commercial Code § 2-209(1).

203 Excellent analyses are available on the civil law counterparts of consideration. *See* Chlores, *supra* note 197; Zweigert & Kötz, *supra* note 84, at 41-60, 71-83; Lorenzen, *Causa and Consideration in the Law of Contracts*, 28 Yale L.J. 621 (1919); Mason, *The Utility of Consideration—A Comparative View*, 41 Colum. L. Rev. 825 (1941); Schiller, *The Counterpart of Consideration in Foreign Legal Systems* in N.Y. Law Revision Comm'n 2d Ann. Rep. 103 (1936); Sharp, *Pacta Sunt Servanda*, 41 Colum. L. Rev. 783 (1941); Von Mehren, *supra* note 195 (approaching the ,problem from the perspective of purpose instead of doctrine he presents the best analysis).

204 Chlores, *supra* note 197, at 146.

205 C. Civ. art. 931 (1935) provides:

> All transactions constituting inter vivos gifts are to be carried out before notaries and embodied in the form of an ordinary contract. An original copy shall remain with the notary; if these things are not done, the gift is void.

and to be accepted by a notarial act. To liberate donations, the French courts developed the theory of a feigned sale.[206] The theory was never accepted in Germany, because section 117 II of the BGB calls for the court to see the substance of a transaction through the disguised form.

Section 1341 of the French Civil Code functions like a statute of frauds by prohibiting oral testimony to prove a contract involving an amount in excess of ten dollars. The French courts have been able to circumvent this rule by liberally interpreting section 1347 of the French Civil Code, which permits oral proof where there are indicia of written proof.[207] If the contract is commercial, the French courts give a liberal reading to section 109 of the French Commercial Code, permitting oral testimony and the introduction of the parties' books when "the court considers that this form of proof should be admitted." The German Code does not set a general limit on the amount for an oral contract. It does, however, have three different forms from which to choose in appropriate circumstances. First, the simple written form of section 126 is necessary for the following transactions: to give an assignee a right against the debtor unless the creditor informs the debtor of the assignment in writing;[208] to establish a right to annuity;[209] and to establish or to recognize an abstract obligation.[210] Section 129's form of simple signature notarization may be required by the debtor to acknowledge payments of a promissory note when the original note is unavailable for cancellation.[211] Either a judicial or notarial contract is required for promises to make a gift "out of one's property" and for promises[212] to convey real property.[213]

*Frustration*

Frustration of contract is probably better and more extensively discussed in English than any other problem of German contract law. The BGB does not contain any rules to govern frustration. After the BGB took effect in 1900 the courts tried to solve the problem by extending the term impossibility to include economic futility.[214] A second doctrine, also successfully used to handle cases of frustration, was distilled from the principle underlying

---

206 Von Mehren, *supra* note 195, at 1060.
207 *Id.* at 1058-59.
208 BGB § 410.
209 Provided a higher form is not required. *Id.* at § 761.
210 *Id.* at §§ 780-81.
211 *Id.* at § 371.
212 *Id.* at § 518.
213 *Id.* at § 313.
214 Judgment of Feb. 23, 1904, 57 RGZ 116. Cohn, *Frustration of Contract in German Law*, 28 J. Comp. Leg. 15, 17 (3d series 1946) [hereinafter cited as Cohn].

sections 723 and 626. These sections provide that any party to an employment or partnership contract may terminate the contract contrary to its express terms at any time "for an important reason." Through a liberal method of codal interpretation, the courts have applied the principle to all contracts in which the obligor's performance lasts over a long period of time. Under some circumstances a contract's loss of its economic utility may be considered "an important reason."[215]

During the period of inflation after World War I, the courts protected obligors by holding that a performance is "impossible" if it would cause the obligor to be insolvent. Thereafter, the doctrine was extended temporarily to aid an obligor when no single obligation, but the aggregate of all his obligations, would result in insolvency. To rely on the doctrine of impossibility to solve the problems of frustrated contracts presented a number of difficulties. Theoretically, performance was not impossible but rather the value of counterperformance had deteriorated. The all-or-nothing result of the impossibility doctrine[216] gave the court no latitude; the court either released the obligor, throwing the entire loss on the other party, or the court enforced the contract, leaving the entire loss on the obligor.[217] This was out of tune with the usual German practice to divide the loss when there is no reason to place the entire loss on one or the other party.[218]

An opportunity for change came in 1920 when a lessor promised to supply steam to his lessee. The price of steam had risen so much that the steam cost more than the lessee's rent. Neither party wanted the lease as a whole to be cancelled. So instead of proceeding solely with the impossibility doctrine, the Supreme Court resorted to the good faith principle of sections 242 and 157[219] and suggested that the "basis of the contract" had ceased. Implicitly, the court said that the burden imposed on the lessor was beyond the limit of sacrifice, so the obligee breached good faith to insist on performance. Then the court proceeded to revise, rather than to terminate, the contract.[220]

---

215 Cohn, *supra* note 214, at 17-18.

216 Cohn, *supra* note 214, at 18.

217 The approach of sections 723 and 626 also restricts the court's freedom.

218 *Cf.* § 254, requiring the loss to be apportioned if the injured party was at fault, even though his only fault was his failure to mitigate the loss or his failure to call the other party's attention to the possibility of an unusually serious injury.

219 Two years earlier in Judgment of Oct. 15, 1918, 94 RGZ 46, the Court also rested a decision on sections 242 and 157.

220 Judgment of Sept. 21, 1920, 100 RGZ 129. A version of the basis-of-the-contract doctrine, based in part on the older "*clausula rebus sic stantibus*," had been suggested by Professor Windscheid in 1852. Then, the doctrine was advocated by Professor Oertmann in a book published in 1921. These academic contributions influenced the courts' adoption of the doctrine. *See* Cohn, *supra* note 214, at 20.

The cases now solved by the basis-of-the-contract theory fall principally into two groups: disturbed equivalency and loss of purpose.[221] Subsumed under the first heading are cases where subsequent developments upset the economic equivalence between performance and counterperformance. A "gross imbalance" is necessary, such that an "informed person could no longer consider the one performance an exchange for the other."[222] In one case, a contract for the sale of cotton was adjusted under the basis-of-the-contract doctrine, although the adjustment amounted to only 13 percent of the contract price.[223] But usually, a greater discrepancy is required. The explanation of the cotton case probably lies in the fact that the wholesale markup of cotton is quite small, so 13 percent was a relatively large amount. Under the second heading are the cases where the objective purpose of the contract becomes frustrated. Suppose someone leases a building with the idea of forging automobile parts; subsequently, the state forbids manufacturing in that section of town.[224] The purpose of the contract is frustrated. In many instances these cases also result in a disturbance of the equality of the performances although the disturbance might not be large enough to permit revision or rescission.

Sometimes the courts use principles that they are not sure they want to espouse permanently; these principles are not enunciated clearly. Perhaps the test most often applied (although not always expressly) is whether it would be a breach of good faith for the obligee to insist on full performance. The test is often expressed by the German word "Zumutbarkeit," which is in essence a test of "reasonableness." The obligor is not held to strict performance if such performance is unreasonable.

Since the beginning of World War II the legislature has enacted "contract help" or "judicial-contract-help" laws permitting a judge to adjust contracts affected by changed circumstances. The first important judicial-contract-help ordinance was passed in November, 1939.[225] Similar legislation was passed in various German states after World War II, all of which legislation was succeeded by the Federal Contract-Help-Law of 1952.[226] This law is applicable only to contracts made before the German currency reform of 1948. Where another law and section 242 overlap, the Supreme Court has stated that the obligor may seek relief under section 242 "only if

221 *See* 1 Larenz SR, *supra* note 1, at § 21, pt. II.
222 *Id.*
223 Judgment of June 18, 1927, 117 RGZ 284, 286.
224 1 Larenz SR, *supra* note 1, at § 21, pt. II.
225 *Id.* at pt. III.
226 BGBl I 198. The English passed a similar statute permitting a division of losses resulting from frustrated contracts under certain circumstances in 1943. *See* Law Reform (Frustrated Contracts) Act of 1943, 6 & 7 Geo. 6, c. 40 §§ 1-3.

the facts of his case are not governed by the contract-help law or if he seeks a remedy which goes beyond that provided for in the statute."[227]

The German Courts are more willing to grant relief in frustration cases than the courts of the United States, France,[228] and England.[229] Schlesinger believes American Courts afford the unfortunate party some relief, because equity may refuse specific performance and common-law juries may be prone to consider all the circumstances in fixing the amount of damages.[230]

Larenz opposes the liberal trend in Germany[231] except during times of economic chaos. Although admitting strict adherence to the contract may be harsh, he believes the economy will thrive only if the obligee's expectations are not disappointed.[232] The answer to his argument is history; the German economy continues to be healthy. The milder contract enforcement policy of German courts has prevented the destruction of numerous enterprises, so on balance the policy may have strengthened rather than weakened the economy.[233]

*Positive Contract Violation: A Gap in the Law*

In 1902, after the German Civil Code was in force for almost two years, Staub[234] pointed out that the Code did not provide a remedy for some breaches of contract.[235] The Code divides breaches into two groups: (1) when performance is impossible, as when the seller conveys the object of sale to a third party and (2) when performance is still possible but overdue. The authors of the BGB believed these provisions covered all possible violations of obliga-

---

227 Judgment of Feb. 12, 1952, 2 BGHZ 150. *See also* Judgment of Feb. 4, 1952, 5 BGHZ 301, 302.

228 *Cf.* Aubrey, *Frustration Reconsideration—Some Comparative Aspects*, 12 Int'l & Comp. L.Q. 1165, 1177 (1963) [hereinafter cited as Aubrey].

229 *See* the illustrations of early decisions of British courts in L. Fuller & R. Braucher, Basic Contract Law (1964).

230 Schlesinger, *supra* note 135, at 513.

231 1 Larenz SR, *supra* note 1, at § 21, pts. I-III.

232 1 Larenz SR, *supra* note 1, at § 20, pt. II.

233 *See* R. Gottschalf, Impossibility of Performance in Contracts 128-35 (1938); K. Larenz, Geschäftsgrundlage und Vertragserfüllung (2d ed. 1957); Zweigert & Kötz, *supra* note 76, at 221-31, 235-41; Aubrey, *supra* note 228; Cohn, *supra* note 214; Drachsler, *Frustration of Contract: Comparative Law Aspects of Remedies in Cases of Supervening Illegality*, 3 N.Y.L.F. 50, 70-77 (1957); Hay, *Frustration and Its Solution in German Law*, 10 Am. J. Comp. L. 345 (1961); Comment, *Commercial Frustration: A Comparative Study*, 7 Tex. Int'l L.F. 275 (1967). *See generally* United States v. Wegematic Corp., 360 F.2d 674 (2d Cir. 1966); Uniform Commercial Code § 2-615.

234 Staub, Die Positiven Vertragsverletzungen (1904) [hereinafter cited as Staub].

235 Staub asserted that there was a "huge hole" in the law. 2 1c Stau/Werner, *supra* note 1, at pt. 52 before §§ 275-92.

tions.[236] There are, however, several breaches not falling within either group. Probably the most obvious and the most important is defective performance, the obligor performing promptly but causing consequential damage. For example, the seller delivers contaminated oats which kill the buyer's cattle.[237] The BGB expressly redresses the bad feed, but the BGB does not stipulate a remedy for the dead cattle.[238] Staub named these breaches "positive contract violations";[239] the courts created a cause of action.

Gradually, the category broadened to reach all damages not covered by the remedies for impossibility or delay.[240] When an obligor violates an implied duty of care owed to his obligee (for example, a roofer's apprentice negligently discards a match which sets the roof on fire[241]) and even when a party violates an implied duty not to compete (for example, a lessor rents his bakery and then he opens another bakery across the street[242]), the breaches are positive contract violations; and so are a single defective installment,[243] anticipatory breach of contract,[244] and the act of an agent in excess of his authority.

The roofer whose apprentice negligently burned down the house could be handled by the American but not the German law of torts. Section 831 of the BGB excuses the principal from liability for the torts of his agents if he used adequate care in selecting and supervising them; section 278, on the other hand, holds the principal liable for defects in his performance caused by the intentional or negligent acts of his agents regardless of the care he used in selecting and in supervising them. Thus, whether the court finds the action to be *ex delicto* or *ex contractu* often determines the outcome, and the courts have stretched the *ex contractu* action very far to reach, inside the framework of the BGB, the same result as is reached by American courts: holding a principal liable for the torts of his agent done within the scope of employment.

A debate rages over the theoretical basis for allowing any recovery when the breach is a positive contract violation. At first,

236 1 Larenz SR, *supra* note 1, at § 24, pt. 1.

237 Judgment of July 9, 1907, 66 RGZ 289.

238 1 Larenz SR, *supra* note 1, at § 24, pt. 1.

239 The name is criticized for two reasons. First, "positive" is a misnomer, because the doctrine applies to active and passive breaches. Second, the term "contract" is inaccurate, because other obligations such as torts are included within the doctrine's scope.

240 1 Larenz SR, *supra* note 1, § 24, pt. 1.

241 *Id.*

242 *Id.*

243 For example, a brewery under a year contract supplies one load of bad beer and thereby alienates an innkeeper's customers. Judgment of Mar. 6, 1903, 54 RGZ 102.

244 2 1c Stau/Werner, *supra* note 1, at pt. 54 before §§ 275-92.

the Supreme Court relied on section 276[245] to define when an obligor is "responsible" (at fault); but section 276 is only a definition, one that specifies no penalty for the fault. Sections 280 and 325 spell out the consequences for impossibility of performance, and sections 286 and 326 the consequences for delay in performance. Where are the paragraphs attaching the consequences to other violations of obligations? A second and widely accepted theory answers that sections 280, 325, 286 and 326 are only illustrations of the ubiquitous codal principle that an obligor is liable for all breaches of his contract duties caused by his fault. A third theory falls back on section 242: "[T]he debtor is bound to effect performance according to the requirements of good faith, ordinary usage being taken into consideration." The German Supreme Court accepted this theory in 1953 and said that the right of action given for positive violation of a bilateral contract corresponds to the rights given in section 325 (impossibility) and section 326 (delay) but that the cause of action's real basis is section 242.[246] The uncertainty as to the theory on which the cause of action is based seems in no way to have diminished the certainty that such a cause of action exists.

The obligations whose breach leads to the granting of these actions are usually classified in German law as only secondary obligations, as for example obligations arising out of defective performance or the failure to exercise the required care for the safety of the other party. Nonetheless, relief includes not only the primary German remedy of restitution in kind but also, by analogy to the remedies provided for other breaches in the BGB, rescission or money damages.[247]

### *Unilateral Mistake*[248]

#### Avoidance Sought Before Contract Performed

The BGB contains what for Americans are some surprising provisions regarding unilateral mistake. Under section 119 a person may avoid a contract (or any declaration of will) for three different categories of unilateral mistake. As a pre-condition to avoidance the court must find that he would not have made the

[245] Judgment of June 13, 1902, 52 RGZ 18; Judgment of Dec. 19, 1902, 53 RGZ 200; Judgment of Nov. 29, 1922, 106 RGZ 22.

[246] Judgment of Nov. 29, 1957, 11 BGHZ 80, 84.

[247] 1 Larenz SR, *supra* note 1, at § 24, pt. I; 2 1c Stau/Werner, *supra* note 1, at pt. 56–58 before §§ 275–92. *See generally* A. Blomeyer, Allgemeines Schuldrecht 158–63 (1969); 1 Larenz SR, *supra* note 1, at § 24, pt. I; Palandt, *supra* note 1, at § 276; Staub, *supra* note 234; Zweigert & Kötz, *supra* note 84, at 195-97.

[248] *See* generally Larenz AT, *supra* note 1, at § 26, pt. II; Palandt, *supra* note 1, at § 119; 1 Stau/Coing, *supra* note 1, at pt. 35 before § 104, § 119, § 142 pt. 2; Zweigert & Kötz, *supra* note 84, at 96-100, 102-109; Holstein, *Vices of Consent in the Law of Contracts*, 13 Tul. L. Rev. 362 (1939); Sabbath, *Effects of Mistake in Contracts*, 13 Int'l & Comp. L.Q. 798 (1964).

declaration had he known the correct facts.[249] That the obligor be without negligence is *not* a requirement, and declarations of will can be avoided by the obligor regardless of whether the other party had reason to know of the mistake.

After the obligor learns of the mistake he must immediately make a reasonable effort to give the other party notice. Ordinarily, no special form of notice is required, but the intent to avoid must be clear. If the other party is unavailable, the notice should be forwarded to him where it will reach him the quickest.[250] Such notice is effective when he receives it.[251]

The German system operates successfully with this rule excusing performance because section 122[252] requires a party taking advantage of unilateral mistake to reimburse the other party for reliance damages. The other party gets his expenses, so he only loses his profit. Reliance damages cannot exceed the contract price.[253] If the obligee knew of the obligor's mistake[254] or if the obligee caused the mistake,[255] reliance damages are disallowed.

The first of three classes of unilateral mistake is a mistake in making a declaration, as for example when one party makes a typographical error or a slip of the tongue. The second class is comprised of cases in which the declarant intended to say or write the words he used, but he did not understand their meaning and therefore did not intend the content of his declaration. An example is the case of a person who sells his restaurant, saying "Einrichtung" and thinking "Einrichtung" includes only the fixtures when in fact the term includes the furniture. He is entitled to avoid his declaration because he did not intend its content. The words he used did not correspond to the mental picture he had of the deal he thought he was making. Cases in which a contract is concluded with the wrong Schmidt, the wrong object being purchased or sold, usually belong to one of the first two classes.

The third class involves mistakes about a characteristic of a person or thing. To be covered under section 119, the characteristic must be "considered important in ordinary dealings."[256] Important qualities of persons include age, sex, professional knowledge, and

---

249 BGB § 119.

250 *Id.* at § 121. The right of avoidance is barred if thirty years have elapsed since the declaration of intention.

251 *Id.* at § 130.

252 *Id.* at § 122. The duty to make compensation does not arise if the person injured knew or should have known that the declaration was voidable.

253 *Id.* at § 122 (1).

254 *Id.* at § 122 (2).

255 Judgment of Feb. 25, 1913, 81 RGZ 395.

256 A more common translation of the statute uses the word "essential" instead of "important," but "important" is a more accurate translation of the German term "wesentlich."

ability; important characteristics of things include form, color, and chemical structure, the genuineness of a painting, or the zoning of a lot. Which characteristic is important in each case depends on the transaction involved. In credit transactions a buyer's wealth and credit rating are "important characteristics;" for cash sales, they are not. Value alone is not an "important characteristic" under section 119.[257]

Aside from whether a mistake satisfies section 119, scholars disagree as to which class the mistake belongs.[258] If a person or thing is described by one of its characteristics and a mistake is made, does the mistake belong in one of the first two classes or in the third class?[259] Of course, if the scholars admit the mistake belongs in one of the three classes, then the discussion of class is purely academic,[260] because avoidance of the contract is possible under all three classes.

Numerous mistakes are not excuses for avoiding contracts.[261] A person contracts to buy a car, not realizing he is ineligible to obtain a driver's license; a merchant orders a particular product, forgetting he has an oversupply stored in the back of his warehouse. These mistakes are said to be *mere* mistakes in motive.[262]

A common mistake causing theoretical difficulty is a mistake by the seller in calculating the sales price. The Supreme Court has refused to consider the price an "important quality" of the product even when the correct price is obvious, as for example in the sale of silver bullion. An error in calculations has been held to be a mistake in the content of the declaration as long as the calculation was discussed during the contract negotiations or was known to the other party.[263] The rule is consistent with the German principle of giving the mistaken party relief from an error related objectively

257 2 Larenz AT, *supra* note 1, at § 26.

258 *See* Stau/Coing, *supra* note 1, at § 119, pts. 1d, 11-34c, 52-55.

259 Larenz AT, *supra* note 1, at § 26, pt. II.

260 *See* Stau/Coing, *supra* note 1, at § 119, pt. 52b; Larenz AT, *supra* note 1, at § 26, pt. II. The fact that a dispute is academic does not make it any less serious.

261 Related, but less important, sections of the BGB are 116 (on secret reservations); 117 (on pretended transactions) and 118 (on declarations made in jest). Section 123 permits avoidance for fraud or duress; the avoidance may be made anytime within a year after knowledge of the pertinent facts have been obtained, instead of "without culpable delay" as required by section 119; and there is no liability for reliance damages. Section 120 provides that incorrectly transmitted declarations of will may be avoided when the conditions in section 119 are met.

262 An error on an "important characteristic" of a person or thing is also a mistake of motive, but it excuses performance because of the specific statutory provision in section 119.

263 *See* Larenz AT, *supra* note 1, at § 26, pt. II; Stau/Coing, *supra* note 1, at § 119, pt. 53.

to the subject matter of the transaction; yet the rule tends to prevent abuse by granting relief only when the other party had some opportunity to know how the calculations were made.[264]

Section 119 cuts a wide swath. Not only contracts which are based upon declarations of will but also all declarations of will can be avoided under section 119. A tenant who has given his landlord notice of his intent to terminate the lease can avoid the notice if he made a section 119 mistake, but he must compensate the landlord for reliance losses. One declaration of will cannot be avoided by a unilateral mistake: the marriage vow.[265] A few provisions, such as those relating to the acceptance or rejection of an inheritance, require a special form for the avoidance.[266]

American jurists, who stress the need for security of transactions, might expect the German courts to have whittled down the rule of section 119. Instead, insofar as attempts to avoid contracts before they are performed, the rule usually is literally enforced.

The ease with which a party can escape an executory contract in Germany tends on the one hand to render contracts less useful, because they are less reliable. On the other hand, the ease of escape has the advantage of making contracts less dangerous, so people are more willing to enter contracts. Finally, by permitting a promisor to avoid an obligation he never intended, the Code makes the contract less an instrument for exploiting the unwary.

Avoidance Sought After Contract Has Been Performed.

Although the wording of section 119 makes no distinction between executory and performed contracts, the courts have been encouraged by the legal literature to make the distinction when a petitioner seeks to rescind a completed contract, theorizing that the performance is something separate from the agreement,[267] the courts argue that there is no mistake involved in the transfer: the party intends to transfer that which he transfers. Although this argument is of doubtful validity—it would be equally applicable to an attempt to make the underlying contract indestructible—it reaches the result demanded by social and economic conditions. Property transfers made in the execution of contracts for the sale of goods can usually not be rescinded under section 119, although the contract might have been voidable under this section while still executory.

[264] *Id.*
[265] Larenz AT, *supra* note 1, at § 26, pt. II.
[266] *Id.*; BGB §§ 1945, 1955.
[267] This is what is known as the *abstraction principle* in German law. It is to be distinguished from the abstract *method* that the Code uses to present rules of law.

The courts have made one exception. If the transfer of property occurs simultaneously with the agreement, they will strike down the transfer as well as the contract.[268] No social purpose appears to be served by making a sale voidable if the transfer is made at the time of the agreement, but not voidable if made a few hours later. In both cases the actual avoidance may be made at a much later time; the problem of restoring the parties to *status quo ante contractu* is exactly the same.

In most cases it will not matter whether a transfer made on the basis of an avoided contract is considered to fall within the direct reach of section 119. Section 812 requires a person to return something he holds without "legal cause."[269] Once the contract for exchange is avoided, the buyer loses his "legal cause" to have the goods, so the court can force him to return them.[270]

Social and economic conditions will not permit labor contracts, insofar as they have been performed, to be avoided; a person's labor cannot be returned to him. The courts have found a way to prevent avoidance with regard to the executed part of the contract but do permit termination immediately upon discovery of a section 119 mistake.[271] Similarly, contracts to participate in business associations can only be rescinded prospectively.[272] Negotiable instruments cannot be voided, because the need for free circulation demands that a trader have confidence in a bill valid on its face.[273]

In summation, for performed contracts the easy avoidance provided in section 119 often runs counter to the need for security in transactions. The need for security is greater for performed contracts than for executory contracts. The method of limiting the application of section 119 to completed contracts illuminates the process of legal development in a code system.

*Culpa in Contrahendo*[274]

When parties begin contractual negotiations, they owe to each other a duty of care, protection, and information. An intentional

---

[268] Judgment of Oct. 18, 1907, 66 RGZ 385.

[269] "Legal cause" is so obscure a concept that it gives the court wide latitude. *See* Ehmann, *Über den Begriff des rechtlichen Grundes im Sinne des § 812 BGB*, 1969 Neue Juristiche Wochenschrift 398.

[270] Stau/Coing, *supra* note 1, at § 104. The most important limitation to section 812 is section 818(3), saying a transferee need not return anything if he is not enriched. Larenz AT, *supra* note 1, at § 26, pt. II.

[271] *See* Larenz AT, *supra* note 1, at § 26, pt. II.

[272] *Id.*

[273] *Id.*

[274] The material here is drawn principally from 2 1c Stau/Werner, *supra* note 1; 2 1b Stau/Weber, *supra* note 1; 1 Larenz SR, *supra* note 1, at § 9; Kessler & Fine, *Culpa in Contrahendo, Bargaining in Good Faith and Freedom of Contract: A Comparative Study*, 77 Harv. L. Rev. 401 (1964) [hereinafter cited as Kessler].

or negligent breach of this duty gives the other party a right to recover so-called reliance or negative damages, to be put in the position he would be in if the other party had not breached his duty.[275] This doctrine of culpa in contrahendo has two histories in German law, one before the adoption of the BGB and one after.

In those parts of Germany where the Roman common law was persuasive before the BGB passed, a subjective, meeting-of-the-minds theory of contract formation was prevalent. A buyer who ordered 100 pounds when he only intended to order 10 was not liable to reimburse the seller for transporting the rejected merchandise, because there had been no genuine meeting of the minds. To correct this and other defects of the subjective theory, Rudolf von Jhering suggested in 1861 the theory of liability for fault while making an agreement: culpa in contrahendo.[276] In parts of Germany the doctrine was codified by the Prussian General Land Law, requiring a person to exercise the same degree of care in negotiating a contract as in performing it.

Although some elements of the doctrine were codified in several segments of the BGB, the doctrine as a whole was not transplanted to the new Code. Scholars at first assumed that only those applications of the doctrine specifically included had become part of the new law, that the general doctrine had not.

In a 1911 case the Supreme Court disagreed. The plaintiff, after purchasing several items in one department of a store, entered the linoleum department. During negotiations, she was injured by falling linoleum as a result of negligence of an employee. Because the clerk had insufficient assets, the plaintiff sued the store. *Ex delicto*, section 831 only holds the principal liable for the acts of his agent when the principal was negligent in hiring or supervising the agent.[277] *Ex contractu*, section 278 only holds the principal responsible for the employee's defective performance of the principal's contractual obligation to the buyer;[278] here the plaintiff had not yet bought anything in the linoleum department. Nevertheless, the Court said a special relationship between the buyer and seller began with negotiations, imposing on the principal (through his agent) the duty to refrain from injuring the health or property of the buyer.[279] In a later case, the Supreme Court said the relationship started as soon as the buyer entered the store.[280] Additionally, the Court has held that when a potential customer is injured in restaurants, stores, and hotels, the burden of proof is on the proprietor

275 1 Larenz SR, *supra* note 1, at § 9, pt. IV.
276 Kessler, *supra* note 274, at 401.
277 *See* text at note 244 *supra*.
278 *Id.*
279 Judgment of Dec. 7, 1911, 78 RGZ 239.
280 1962 Neue Juristische Wochenschrift 31.

to show lack of fault once an improper situation is shown to have existed.[281]

Culpa in contrahendo reaches beyond personal injury. Neither party may, without incurring liability, mislead the other party as to the likelihood of reaching an agreement. Corollarially, a party must promptly inform the other of a decision not to enter the contract.[282] A musician was told by an opera company that its increased budget would be approved and that he would be hired. The opera company knew that the musician was considering giving up his old job so as to be available for the new one. He quit his job, but the budget was not approved. The Supreme Court allowed partial recovery of his reliance damages, reducing the award, because the Court also thought he was at fault.[283] Similarly, if an owner of a house sold it and failed to inform another prospective buyer, the prospective buyer could recoup the cost of a long trip to see the house.[284]

Culpa in contrahendo even reaches cases where one party did not inform the other party of disadvantages inherent in the contract. Thus, a German agent who sells car insurance to a Turkish student must explain that the insurance is invalid in Turkey, at least if he knows the student is planning a trip to Turkey with the car.[285] Where the seller knew that the buyer's shop was too small to house the seller's machine and failed to tell him, the buyer was able to recoup his losses from the seller under the doctrine of culpa in contrahendo.[286] The Supreme Court has also attempted to extend the doctrine to cases where the required form of the contract has not been observed. The Court refused to abrogate the defense of the statute of frauds, but the Court made the defending party put the innocent party in as good a position as he would have been in if he had not relied on the contract. For example, the Court may require the seller to furnish the buyer with a house equivalent to the one the buyer did not get because of the statute of frauds.[287]

A search for the statutory basis of the culpa in contrahendo doctrine provides an illuminating example of the judicial process of

---

281 *Id.* To reverse the burden of proof for *culpa in contrahendo* is unique. In ordinary tort cases, section 823 *et seq.* leaves the burden with the injured party.

282 Stau/Weber, *supra* note 1, at § 242, pt. A 418.

283 Judgment of June 7, 1963 (Supreme Labor Court), 1964 Juristen Zeitung 325. *See* BGB § 254, permitting division of damages.

284 1 Larenz SR, *supra* note 1, at § 9, pt. I.

285 Judgment of June 20, 1963, 40 BGHZ 23.

286 1962 Neue Juristische Wochenschrift 1196. For other illustrations, see Stau/Werner, *supra* note 1, at § 276, pt. 33; Stau/Weber, *supra* note 1, at § 242, pt. A 418.

287 1965 Neue Juristische Wochenschrift 812.

lawmaking in a code system. Flexible interpretation permitted the courts to reach a socially desirable conclusion without express codal authority. Various theories were advanced to support the doctrine: that liability is based on the later contract (hardly convincing if no contract is concluded) and that liability is based on an implied in fact or implied in law contract.[288] The most generally accepted theory induces the doctrine from several abbreviated appearances in the Code, including sections 179, 307, 309, 463, 523 (1), 524 (1), 600, 637, and 694.[289] Some writers also add to this list section 122, which allows reliance damages in some cases of invalid contracts; others reject section 122, because the section goes further than culpa in contrahendo. Section 122 orders payment of reliance damages even where the defendant was not at fault; by contrast, culpa in contrahendo always requires fault.[290] The question of how best to establish a theoretical foundation for culpa in contrahendo has become less important, for the doctrine has become customary law.[291] Besides, even though scholars disagree on the foundation of the doctrine, they unamimously approve the result.[292]

*Acceptance Effective on Arrival and Related Rules*[293]

Special problems arise in the formation of a contract when the parties are not face to face at the time an agreement is reached. Under the German Code an acceptance is not effective when dispatched but is effective on arrival.[294] Unless otherwise specified in the offer, an offer is irrevocable;[295] but it is effective only for a period long enough to permit prompt acceptance.

The German rules produce results similar to those produced by American law. In both systems the offeror can revoke the offer so long as his revocation arrives at the same time or prior to the offer. Thereafter, the American offer remains revocable until it lapses or is accepted. The German offer is irrevocable, but it lapses by operation of law in a relatively short period. If the acceptance is mailed immediately after receipt of the offer, in both systems

[288] 2 Enn/Lehman Schuldrecht, *supra* note 1, at § 43, pt. III at 191; Stau/Werner, *supra* note 1, at § 276, pt. 30.

[289] Stau/Werner, *supra* note 1, pt. 99 before § 275.

[290] 1 Larenz SR, *supra* note 1, at § 9, pt. I.

[291] Stau/Werner, *supra* note 1, at pt. 99 before § 275.

[292] *Id.* For some American doctrines serving purposes similar to culpa in contrahendo, see Kessler, *supra* note 274.

[293] *See generally* Schlesinger, *supra* note 21; Zweigert & Kötz, *supra* note 84, at 31-35, 38-41; Macneil, *Time of Acceptance: Too Many Problems for a Single Rule*, 112 U. Pa. L. Rev. 947 (1964); Nussbaum, *Comparative Aspects of the Anglo-American Offer-and-Acceptance Doctrine*, 36 Colum. L. Rev. 920 (1936) [hereinafter cited as Nussbaum].

[294] BGB § 130. The effectiveness of a declaration of acceptance is not ordinarily affected by the declarant's death or incapacity.

[295] *Id.* at §§ 145-48.

the offeree can be confident of a contract: in German law, because the offeror can't revoke the offer until a reasonable time for the acceptance has run; in American law, because the posting of an acceptance completes the contractual formation.[296]

A combination of the German "arrival" rule and the American "revocable" rule would give the offeror an unfair advantage. The offeror could "veto" the acceptance by revoking the acceptance before it arrived; the offeree would not be certain of a contract until he received a verification from the offeror.[297] German offerors can get the advantage by marking their offers "ohne obligato" (without obligation). This permits the first party to treat his proposal as a mere invitation to negotiate, so the second party's "acceptance" becomes an offer the first party can accept or reject.[298] The only protection the second party has is the first party's duty to notify him within a reasonable time of a decision not to enter the contract. Silence by the first party creates a binding contract.

The offeree can turn the advantage around by requiring the offeror to make the offer irrevocable for a specified period of time, a stipulation which is enforceable even if the offeree gave no consideration.[299] Even if the offeree cannot convince the offeror to make the offer irrevocable for a specified period, the offeree still has an opportunity to speculate at the offeror's expense. An acceptance can be avoided if a revocation of acceptance arrives before the acceptance. For example, a buyer mails an acceptance of an offer to sell a house. That afternoon, he finds a better house elsewhere. In the evening he can by telephone or by telegraph revoke his acceptance of the first house. The seller's protection derives only from a stipulation in the offer that acceptances are binding when posted.

If a posted acceptance goes astray, American and German opinions differ. Under the American system an acceptance is valid when mailed, so a receipt is unnecessary. As a result, the offeror is bound by the contract even though he did not receive the original acceptance.[300] Under German law the loss falls on the offeree. With-

---

[296] Williston favored the "arrival" rule. 1 S. Williston, A Treatise on the Law of Contracts § 81 (1936). Nussbaum, *supra* note 293, at 920, says Langdell, Page, and Pollack "more or less disapproved of the [dispatch] rule."

[297] It has been suggested that an offeree accept by registered mail to be in a position to prove arrival. Larenz, *When Acceptance Becomes Effective*, in 1 Formation of Contracts 1464, 1472 (R. Schlesinger ed. 1968).

[298] BGB § 145.

[299] *Id.* at §§ 145-48. The Uniform Commercial Code § 2-205 takes a step in that direction.

[300] This is the rule, at least in theory; in practice, the courts juggle the technical rules by finding either an unauthorized means of transmission or that the offeror required arrival of the acceptance. *See* Macneil, *supra* note 293, at 963-72.

out receipt of the acceptance[301] the offeror is free.[302] If an acceptance arrives late due to the delay in transmission, the acceptance is effective unless the offeror promptly notifies the offeree of the late arrival.[303] Macneil suggests the problem is a prime opportunity to divide the loss, for neither party is responsible.[304] Evidently, the courts believe the accompanying complication and uncertainty outweigh the justice to be derived from Macneil's proposal.

In summary, the BGB, unlike the common law, makes offers irrevocable until the offeree has time to accept. Acceptance becomes effective when received by the offeror. Both of these rules can be varied by the offer to satisfy the parties' needs and desires.

*Conclusion*

The BGB's abstraction has its disadvantages. A negligent unilateral mistake may justify rescission of an unexecuted sales contract more readily than rescission of an executed adoption. What may be an appropriate remedy for torts is frequently inappropriate for contracts. On the other hand, the commingling of contracts and torts makes German contract law less rigid than common-law contract law.

Where the abstract system of the BGB produced an unworkable rule, the courts have usually created a workable rule. The demands of society for particular results in particular cases do not necessarily change with the crossing of international borders; and the German courts have proved themselves as attentive to those demands as their common-law counterparts. This judicial manipulation multiplies the complexity of what was originally a complicated document. Concomitantly, this method of interpretation accounts in large part for the Code's success.

[301] For the general rules governing what constitutes "arrival," see Schlesinger, *supra* note 297, at 1467.
[302] *See* BGB § 130.
[303] *Id.* at § 149.
[304] Macneil, *supra* note 293, at 963-72.

# [11]

## METHODOLOGY OF THE CIVIL LAW IN FRANCE

ANDRÉ TUNC*

Even assuming one could forget history, it would be self-evident that French law and Louisiana law have much in common. Both give preeminence to statute among the sources of law and, more precisely, to a civil code, the cornerstone of the law.

When two countries are miles apart, however, it would be surprising if their common principles were not applied in different manners. The legal systems of Louisiana, Quebec, and France, all inherited from a common tradition, are comparable to children of one family, with deep common features of character, but each with his own personality. All members of the family should be grateful to the Louisiana branch for its accomplishments in maintaining the ties which connect us.[1] Indeed, the idea of a renaissance of the civilian tradition is especially justified as we celebrate the sesquicentennial anniversary of the Louisiana Civil Code of 1825.[2] As a modest contribution to this renaissance, a study of the methodology of the civil law in France may be of interest.

Portalis' excellent *Discours préliminaire*,[3] which so admirably explains the thought of the drafters of the *Code civil*, suggests that the French concept of the law rests on three fundamental principles: A code ought to be complete in its field; it ought to be drafted in relatively general principles

* Professor of Law, University of Paris I. Honorary Member, Council of the Louisiana State Law Institute.

1 Justice Barham, late of the Louisiana Supreme Court, has pointed out that serious efforts are made to expose Louisiana lawyers to French law and doctrine. Barham, *Methodology of the Civil Law in Louisiana*, 50 Tul. L. Rev. 474 (1976) [hereinafter cited as Barham]. Of particular note are the efforts of the *Tulane Law Review*, the Louisiana State Law Institute, the Tulane Institute of Comparative Law, the Institute of Civil Law Studies, and the John Tucker and Bailey Lectures. Professor Joseph Dainow also has recently published an excellent book that should further tighten the bonds of civilian systems: The Role of Judicial Decisions and Doctrine in Civil Law and in Mixed Jurisdictions (J. Dainow ed. 1974) [hereinafter cited as Judicial Decisions].

2 *See* Barham, *A Renaissance of the Civilian Tradition in Louisiana*, in Judicial Decisions, *supra* note 1, at 38.

3 P. Fenet, Recueil complet des travaux préparatoires du code civil 463 (1827) [hereinafter cited as Fenet]. *See* 1 J. Locré, La législation civile, commerciale et criminelle de la français 243 (1827) [hereinafter cited as Locré]. *See also* Tunc, *The Grand Outlines of the Code*, in The Code Napoléon and the Common-Law World 19 (B. Schwartz ed. 1956).

rather than in detailed rules; and it ought at the same time to fit them together logically as a coherent whole and to be based on experience. To some extent these principles have proven capable of actual materialization, but inevitably circumstances have sometimes made it necessary to depart from them. Thus, the idea that the *Code* should be complete has occasionally been compromised by amendments and complements of the legislature itself. The framing of the *Code* in relatively general principles permits a discussion of our courts and our case law, and the need for logic and experience in the elaboration of legal rules prompts a consideration of the role of doctrine.

## THE *CODE* AND THE LEGISLATOR

It is perfectly true that the *Code* was nearly complete in the field it was intended to cover. Although it was only one of the five Napoleonic Codes, together with the Commercial Code, the Code of Civil Procedure, the Penal Code, and the Code of Criminal Procedure, it governed nearly all the relations which belong to the *droit civil.* During the 19th century, it was necessary, practically speaking, to complete it on only one point, mineral rights, which were the subject of an 1810 statute.

This is not to say that the 1804 *Code* would, in its original form, still be capable of governing private relations in contemporary society. The legislature had to amend and supplement it by separate statutes which, although very rare during the 19th century, multiplied with the social changes following World Wars I and II.

After World War II, many felt the need to revise entirely the *Code civil*. A commission was appointed to that end, under the chairmanship of the late Dean Julliot de la Morandière, with Roger Houin as secretary general, but the work could not be achieved. A piecemeal modernization of the *Code* is being realized, however, more or less continuously and systematically; the main matters covered by the *Code* are revised one after the other, and entire chapters of the *Code* are replaced by modern provisions.

In the process of amending the *Code* or supplementing it by separate statutes, a leading role is played by the Ministry of Justice and, more precisely, by the Division of Civil Affairs and of the Seal. It is this Division, composed of judges, that bears the main responsibility for permanently revising the law. It suggests corrections of archaisms or gaps and requests the Minister of Justice to submit to Parliament more satisfactory legislation. This Division drafts the necessary bills, sometimes on the advice of a commission appointed by itself or with the cooperation of a professor of law. Dean Jean Carbonnier has recently been the instigator of the most important reforms in the field of *droit civil.*

Despite the efforts toward modernization, the command of the *Code* over *droit civil* is more and more incomplete. Mainly during the last 50 years, numerous statutes have been passed which have not been incorporated into the *Code*. This phenomenon is not attributable to lack of diligence on the part of the legislature, but rather to a recognition that the provisions are in many respects different from the ones which are in the *Code*. First, a number of them do not have the generality of application which is traditionally considered a characteristic feature of the law. They relate to only a category of citizens (such as ex-servicemen, deported or repatriated persons, small traders, craftsmen, or economically weak persons). Many of them, furthermore, do not express those relatively general principles upon which Portalis wanted a code to be built. They are regulatory in nature and sometimes set forth extremely minute rules. By the same token, they are often short-lived; the regulations they contain have to be adjusted to new economic factors or new relations between the various social groups concerned. A typical case on this point has been the regulation of the various categories of lease: residential, commercial, and agricultural. In their very purpose, finally, these statutes differ from the law contained in the codes. The latter is usually conservative in character, restating the contemporary social relations; the new type of law is more aggressive, and it is meant to be progressive, to build a future hopefully better than the present. This aim explains both the narrow coverage and the short life of the rules. Some jurists have deplored this new type of legislation and have painted a sinister picture of the decline of law.[4] But who can lament "the majestic impartiality of law, which equally forbids the rich and the poor to sleep under bridges, to beg in the streets, and to steal bread."[5]

[4] G. Ripert, *Le déclin du droit*, in Etudes sur la législation contemporaine (1949).

[5] A. France, Le lys rouge 118 (1894) (translation by author).

In order to restore statutory law to its traditional prestige by clearing it of temporary rules, the 1958 Constitution circumscribed its field. It expressely provided that certain matters are of a regulatory character and are under the jurisdiction of the executive acting by decree. In *droit civil* matters, article 34 states: "[S]tatute determines rules governing nationality, personal status and capacity, matrimonial regimes, decedents' estates, gifts and wills [and] the fundamental principles . . . of property, property rights, civil and commercial obligations."[6] One will notice that in the latter matters, statute only determines fundamental principles, leaving it to the executive to determine the details of questions which may arise. Such apportionment of legal rules between statute and decree lightens, and thus should accelerate, the work of Parliament, and at the same time enlarges the field where swift action is possible by decree. It presents, however, the drawback of creating on a single matter a duality of provisions, which complicates the discovery of the applicable rule.

The executive has not undertaken a general consolidation of either the extra-*Code* statutes or the decrees. On the other hand, mainly in the last 25 years, a number of specialized codes have been promulgated, and they constitute a consolidation of the statutes, decrees, and rules which govern a given matter. The Forest Code, Rural Code, Labor Code, Social Security Code, Wheat Code, Wine Code, and Cinematography Code are but a few examples. Furthermore, the inconveniences which could result from the scattering of legal rules are largely alleviated by the initiative of a private publisher. The Dalloz firm yearly publishes a new edition of the *Code civil*, including not only the updated provisions of the *Code*, but also, under each article, a summary of the main cases which have applied or construed it and a reproduction of the related statutes that are not officially incorporated into the *Code*. Dalloz also frequently publishes new editions of the other official codes and compiles, under the name of topical codes, various statutes, decrees, and rules which relate to given matters, such as corporations or leases.

## THE *CODE* AND THE JUDGE

One of the most remarkable passages of the *Discours préliminaire* describes what will be the role of the courts in a codified system of law.

[6] Law of Oct. 5, 1958, [1958] J.O. 9151.

> The task of statutory law is to express in broad terms the general maxims of the law, to settle principles fertile in consequences, and not to go down in the details of questions which may arise in every matter. It is the task of judges and lawyers, engrained with the general spirit of the law, to conduct the application of those principles .... There is a science for legislators as there is one for the judges; and one is not similar to the other. The legislator's science consists in finding in every matter the principles most favorable to a general rule; the judge's science is to make such principles operative, to ramify them, to extend them by a wise and reasoned application to given cases.[7]

It is amazing that a man could so intelligently foresee what would be the respective roles of the *Code* and the judge.

The typical French judge markedly differs from his American colleague, even from his Louisiana counterpart.[8] The French judge spends his whole professional life on the bench. Upon leaving law school, he takes an examination for entry into the National School for the Bench (*École Nationale de la Magistrature*). If he succeeds, he devotes, at the school or under its control, 2 years to theoretical and practical studies and to periods of practical instruction. Although he may be only 25 years old, he may then be appointed as a judge to a court of first instance. His hope is to be promoted to one of the 31 courts of appeal and later on to the Court of Cassation. The latter, after various reforms, is now composed of six chambers: three civil, one commercial, one social, and one penal. It includes more than 100 judges at the summit of their careers. Working with them may be found 20 referendary judges (*conseillers référendaires*), who are younger judges whose value has already been appreciated. Their task is to prepare the cases entrusted to them and to sit in an advisory capacity in the chamber to which they are assigned.

The role of judicial decisions as conceived by Portalis appears threefold: (1) To clarify the meaning of the rules in the various circumstances which are submitted to the judge (in that respect, Portalis, and Planiol a century later, could say that the judge is the legislator of concrete cases); (2) to clarify

[7] Fenet, *supra* note 3, at 470. *See* Locré, *supra* note 3, at 258. *See also* O. Kahn-Freund, C. Lévy & B. Rudden, A Sourcebook on French Law 73 (1973) [hereinafter cited as Sourcebook]. On the conceptualism of French law see the excellent developments of F. H. Lawson, A Common Lawyer Looks at the Civil Law 62-81 (1953).

[8] Barham, *supra* note 1, at 483.

what is obscure in the law and to fill its gaps;[9] (3) to adjust law to the evolution of the society and, to the extent possible based on the existing texts, to provide against the inadequacy of the law in the face of contemporary problems.

Portalis had perfectly seen that judicial decisions should not be isolated, but should be integrated in order to form a body of law, the jurisprudence. In all civilized nations one can observe the formation of a layer of maxims, judicial decisions, and doctrine which is clarified by practice and by the clash of views expressed in judicial debates. This dimension of the law gains depth daily and has always been regarded as the true supplement of legislation. Experience has shown how correct Portalis was in his conception of the role of the judge, who has accomplished the threefold task which had been assigned to him.

First, one can see that the judges have been able, since 1804, to apply the rules of the *Code civil* to millions of individual cases submitted to them without significant difficulty. Whatever the respect due Justice Holmes, therefore, experience contradicts his famous statement: "General propositions do not decide concrete cases." That statement seems self-evident, but it is not substantiated by the facts, and it unfortunately infuses into thousands of common law attorneys a completely unfounded distrust of codification.

More often than not, however, the relative generality of the rule given by the *Code* left it to the courts to settle a number of questions, and the judges readily shouldered this responsibility. It is striking to consider in the Dalloz edition of the *Code civil* the articles which have not recently been amended or to consider editions of the *Code* prior to the amendments. The summaries of cases following such articles demonstrate that the text left to the courts four or five questions unsettled, but that these questions have been solved once and for all, for the most part during the 19th century.

At this point the author wishes to dissent from an idea generally accepted in France and abroad: that of *jurisprudence constante*. A solution may, of course, have been repeatedly stated by the Court of Cassation, but in the large

[9] "Experience will progressively fill the gaps that we leave. Codes are made only with time. But, properly speaking, they are not made." Fenet, *supra* note 3, at 476. *See* Locré, *supra* note 3, at 266.

majority of instances, when a question of law is clearly put to the court, the answer given in a first decision may be regarded as finally established. Case law, it is true, results from a gradual process based on experience and the clash of views expressed in judicial debates. Generally, it is only at the level of the courts of first instance and courts of appeal that conflicting decisions may be found. Once the Court of Cassation has spoken, it normally will be obeyed. One may even wonder whether, practically speaking, in most fields of law, the authority of a precedent of the Court of Cassation, while not reaching the level of that of an English precedent, is not greater than the authority of an American decision.

Wherever the *Code* has permitted, the judges have also fulfilled their task of modernizing law, often in a very innovative manner, but open to correction of possible excesses. Thus, the courts have developed a law of unjust enrichment[10] and a doctrine of abuse of right.[11] Moreover, in sheer disregard of a clear *Code* article, article 1165,[12] they have allowed stipulation on behalf of a third party and elaborated the rules which should govern it.[13] As early as 1911, judges imposed on the common carrier a duty to provide for the safety of the passengers.[14] They later clarified the limits of this duty and extended it, with variations adjusting it to the particular situation, to a number of other persons and enterprises.[15] One can also find an example of judicial creativeness in the development of the law of redhibition.[16] In fact, on the basis of provisions purely

[10] *See* M. Amos & F. Walton, Introduction to French Law 219 (3d ed. F.H. Lawson, A.E. Anton & L. Neville Brown 1967) [hereinafter cited as Amos & Walton]; 6 C. Aubry & C. Rau, Droit civil français § 442 (7. éd. P. Esmein & A. Ponsard 1975) [hereinafter cited as Aubry & Rau]; 4 J. Carbonnier, Droit civil 443 (7. éd. 1972) [hereinafter cited as Carbonnier]; J. Dawson, Unjust Enrichment 92 (1951); 2 G. Marty & P. Raynaud, Droit civil 309 (1962) [hereinafter cited as Marty & Raynaud]; 2 H., L. & J. Mazeaud, Leçons de droit civil 731 (5. éd. M. de Juglart 1973) [hereinafter cited as Mazeaud]; B. Starck, Droit civil: obligations 679 (1972) [hereinafter cited as Starck].

[11] *See* Aubry & Rau, *supra* note 10, § 444, nos. 366 *et seq.*; Carbonnier, *supra* note 10, at 339, 346; Marty & Raynaud, *supra* note 10, at 411; Mazeaud, *supra* note 10, at 422; 1 H. & L. Mazeaud & A. Tunc, Traité théorique et pratique de la responsabilité civile, nos. 547 *et seq.* (6. éd. 1965) [hereinafter cited as Traité théorique]; Starck, *supra* note 10, at 125; Mayrand, *Abuse of Rights in France and Quebec*, 34 La. L. Rev. 993 (1974).

[12] C. civ. art. 1165.

[13] *See* Sourcebook, *supra* note 7, ch. 6; Amos & Walton, *supra* note 10, at 175.

[14] Cass. civ., Nov. 21, 1911, D. 1913.I.249, note by Sarrut; Traité théorique, *supra* note 11, no. 154.

[15] Traité théorique, *supra* note 11, nos. 151 *et seq.*

[16] *See* Barham, *Redhibition: A Comparative Comment*, 49 Tul. L. Rev. 376 (1975) [hereinafter cited as *Redhibition*].

intended for the benefit of a buyer disappointed by the thing bought,[17] the courts have developed a very modern law of products liability, effectively protecting the last consumer and the "innocent bystander."[18]

In their desire to respond to current needs, the courts have sometimes been astonishingly bold. An excellent example is the theory of liability for damage caused by things.[19] The first paragraph of article 1384 of our *Code civil*,[20] like article 2317[21] of yours, is a text which is unique in that it is devoid of all meaning and is a purely stylistic effort at a smooth transition. Our courts, however, have used its final words, similar to those of the first sentence of your article 2317,[22] "or of the things which we have in our custody," to build a general liability for damage caused by things. This liability is of paramount importance since it governs all accidental damage, with the exception of industrial accident damage. This was a courageous endeavour. But was it entirely successful, or would it perhaps have been wiser to alert the legislature to its responsibilities and leave with it the task of passing a law of traffic accidents? Various opinions have been expressed on the question,[23] but in any event, it must be recognized that the case law built on *Code civil* article 1384[24] is a highly exceptional phenomenon, which is by no means typical of the relations between statutory law and courts in a codified system of law. This case law is a purely judge-made law, so detached from the *Code* that it has been compared to a pyramid built on a pinhead. Its free evolutions, sometimes surprising or contradictory, are more characteristic of the common law than of the jurisprudence of courts applying a code.

Whatever the value of French judges, their methods of work may not be the best. For example, the French decision is

---

17 C. civ. arts. 1641-46.

18 *See* Malinvaud, *La responsabilité civile du vendeur à raison des vices de la chose*, J.C.P. 1968.I.2153; Overstake, *La responsabilité du fabricant de produits dangereux*, [1972] Rev. trim. dr. civ. 485; Université de Paris I, La responsabilité des fabricants et distributeurs (C. Gavalda éd. 1975).

19 For an account of this theory see Stone, *Liability for Damage Caused by Things*, 11 Int'l Encycl. Comp. L., ch. 5, ¶¶ 24-28, at 6-8 (1970).

20 "One is responsible, not only for the damage occasioned by his own act, but for that which is caused by the act of persons for whom he is answerable, or of things which he has in his custody." C. civ. art. 1384.

21 La. Civil Code art. 2317 (1870).

22 *Id.*

23 A collection of doctrinal opinions is found in Tunc, *Louisiana Tort Law at the Crossroads*, 48 Tul. L. Rev. 1111, 1111 n.4, 1119-20 (1974).

24 C. civ. art. 1384.

anonymous, carrying neither dissent nor concurring opinion. This simplicity may have more drawbacks than advantages.[25] The decisions of the Court of Cassation are usually extremely short and drafted in a very abstract style, and a decision contrary to a full line of cases may be rendered without explanation.[26] The typical decision is a pure syllogism: Whereas ... (a general rule); whereas the court below has decided that ... and thus correctly (or incorrectly) applied the law; now, therefore, maintain (or quash) the decision. If the general rule expressed by the Court of Cassation is a reproduction of an article of the *Code* or of some other statutory provision, the decision is unquestionable. Often, however, the rule is a creation of the court, which never explains why it states a certain rule. Perhaps because the deductive approach does not make it easy, that court rarely takes the trouble even to clarify the precise meaning and scope of the rule. It remains for the commentators and the lower courts to monitor how the rule is used in further decisions and to ascertain the meaning, scope, and, perhaps, the justification for the rule.[27] Recently, Mr. Adolphe Touffait, *Procureur Général près la Cour de Cassation*, and this author have published a plea for a more explicit drafting of judicial decisions, especially those of the Court of Cassation.[28] Unfortunately, the suggestion has thus far met more skepticism or opposition than enthusiasm.

Another point of concern is the number of decisions made by the Court of Cassation—presently between 6,000 and 6,500 every year in civil matters. It seems difficult to prevent the magnitude of decisions from decreasing the value of each as well as their cohesion and, thus, the clarity of the whole law. French lawyers currently have the feeling that every citizen is entitled to submit to the Court of Cassation a point of law successively adjudicated by a court of first instance and a court of appeal. They forget that the task of a supreme court is to clarify the law, to adjust it to contemporary needs and thoughts, and that it should be freed from all cases which do

[25] *See* Barham, *supra* note 1, at 485.

[26] Justifiable surprise at this practice has been expressed in *Redhibition*, *supra* note 16, at 377.

[27] This is a function without parallel in the United States. The *Procureur Général près la Cour de Cassation*, who is the highest judge, at par with the *Premier Président* (comparable to a United States Chief Justice), is the head of *Le Ministère Public*, a section of the judiciary which is in charge of the state interests and the public interest before the courts.

[28] Touffait & Tunc, *Pour une motivation plus explicite des décisions de justice, notamment de celles de la cour de cassation*, [1974] Rev. trim. dr. civ. 487.

not permit it to fulfill this task. It is suggested that quantity harms quality and authority, and that it would be important to give preeminence to the latter by lightening the workload of the court.

THE *CODE* AND THE DOCTRINE

If there is a sentence which a French lawyer has great difficulty in understanding, it is Holmes' famous saying: "The life of the law has not been logic: it has been experience."[29] It is questionable whether the opposition between logic and experience has any justification. Exact sciences are equally based on experience and on logic. To deny that the world is governed by rules making a coherent whole would amount to asserting that it is chaotic, an unduly sinister view.

It was clear for the drafters of the *Code civil* that law has to be founded on experience. A striking maxim has already been quoted: "Codes are made only with time. But, properly speaking, they are not made."[30] They are a collective, progressive, and more or less noninstitutional creation. Portalis explained at length his thoughts on the subject:

> Laws are not pure acts of will; they are acts of wisdom, of justice, and of reason. The legislator does not so much exercise a power as he fulfills a sacred trust. One ought never to forget that laws are made for men, not men for laws; that they must be adapted to the character, to the habits, to the situation of the people for whom they are drafted; that one ought to be wary of innovations in matters of legislation, for if it is possible, in a new institution, to calculate the merits that theory may promise us, it is not possible to know all the disadvantages, which only experience will reveal; that the good ought to be kept if the better is dubious; that in correcting abuses, one must also foresee the dangers of the correction itself; that it would be absurd to indulge in absolute ideas of perfection in matters capable of a relative value only.[31]

Portalis additionally wrote, as if echoing Jefferson's words: "He governs badly who governs too much."[32] He also wrote: "We have too much indulged, in recent times, in changes and reforms; if in matters of institutions and laws the periods of

[29] O.W. Holmes, The Common Law 1 (1881).
[30] Fenet, *supra* note 3, at 476. *See* Locré, *supra* note 3, at 266.
[31] Fenet, *supra* note 3, at 466-67. *See* Locré, *supra* note 3, at 254-55.
[32] Fenet, *supra* note 3, at 514. *See* Locré, *supra* note 3, at 307.

ignorance witness abuses, the periods of philosophy and enlightenment too often witness excesses."[33]

It was clear for the drafters of the *Code*, therefore, that if law can and ought to influence manners, it ought to be strongly grounded on experience. For them, however, a code ought also to constitute a logical whole, not as a matter of aesthetics, but to insure the capability of governing the whole system of social relations. As perfectly seen by Dean Roscoe Pound, articles of a code are not only rules of law, but also sources of law as well.[34] That is to say, the judge does not merely apply the articles or draw consequences from them by deduction. If the need arises, he first proceeds by induction. On the basis of a number of articles, he sets out a more general rule and then from the latter draws consequences. This two-way process had been foreseen by Portalis: "The decision, in most of the cases, is less the application of a clear provision than the combination of a number of provisions, which lead to the decision more than they express it."[35] Only to the extent that the various provisions of the *Code* constitute a coherent whole can this method be successful.

To assert the necessity for an interwoven body of law, as was done by the drafters of the *Code*, leads to an admission of the importance of legal doctrine. It has often been remarked that the common law is a judge-made law, whereas codified law is a law of law teachers. The judge (of course, he can also be an author or teacher) goes from case to case, usually in most diverse matters. Conversely, the author stands well back and concentrates on a certain subject, perhaps a narrow one. By spending the necessary time to study its statutory, judicial, practical, and doctrinal aspects, he is in a much better position to arrive at a synthetic view of the matter.

Although the *Code civil* is largely inspired by doctrinal writings (especially those of Domat and Pothier), it is well known that its authority during more than the first half of the 19th century insured the absolute and exclusive rule of its literal provisions. Doctrine was reduced to exegesis,[36] and in the law schools, the *Code civil*, not the *droit civil*, was taught.

[33] Fenet, *supra* note 3, at 482. *See* Locré, *supra* note 3, at 272.
[34] Pound, *The Theory of Judicial Decision*, 36 Harv. L. Rev. 641, 647 (1923).
[35] Fenet, *supra* note 3, at 476. *See* Locré, *supra* note 3, at 265.
[36] *See* 1 G. Marty & P. Raynaud, Droit civil: Introduction générale à l'étude du droit, no. 75 (2. éd. 1972) [hereinafter cited as Introduction].

The provisions of the *Code* were studied, one after the other, in strict chronological order. Even around 1900, for example, a teacher who wanted to discuss the second paragraph of an article before the first one devoted the first quarter of his lesson to explain his audacity and apologize for it, while underlining that, for a statement of the rule of law, the order chosen by the drafters of the *Code* was the proper one.

Notwithstanding the efforts of a number of strong personalities, only the second half of the century, more particularly its last quarter, saw doctrine emerge in a significant role. Labbé, among others, paid attention to judicial decisions and devoted to some of them excellent commentaries in annotations reproduced in the *Sirey* reports. Aubry and Rau, starting in 1838, undertook the translation of a treatise on the French *Code civil* and inserted in it a wider and wider personal contribution. Their fourth edition, in eight volumes published from 1869 to 1879, constitutes a model of French legal classicism in which statutory law and case law are used together in an architectural construction which, if not yet enriched by sociology, is not deprived of realism. Some authors, among them Saleilles, explained that fidelity to the *Code* ought to be fidelity to the spirit of its drafters. This contemplated, he explained, the will to elaborate a law filling contemporary needs on the basis of existing provisions, even though the original meaning of the provisions must be disregarded. Saleilles explained his philosophy by the formula, "Beyond the Civil Code, but through the Civil Code,"[37] and introduced comparative law as a normal and stimulating ingredient of legal thought. A few years later, at the turn of the century, François Gény, systematically reexamining the sources of the law and the methodology of codified law, recommended free scientific research.[38] Saleilles, in 1899, summed up Gény's philosophy by a famous formula to which he finally gave his support: "Through the Civil Code, but beyond the Civil Code."[39] It was the door to the 20th century.

Today, the role of the doctrine is very widely recognized. Doctrinal writings comment on statutory law and judicial

[37] *See* Tucker, *Au-delà* du code civil, mais par le code civil, 34 La. L. Rev. 957 (1974).

[38] F. Gény, Méthode d'interprétation et sources en droit privé positif (2. éd. 1919) [hereinafter cited as Gény].

[39] Saleilles, *Préface* to Gény, *supra* note 38, at xxv; *cf.* Introduction, *supra* note 36, no. 76.

decisions in order to clarify them, to give of them a systematic view without which there would be no law. Of equal importance, however, is the purpose of guiding the courts and, more broadly, the lawgivers. In fact, doctrine could easily assign to itself a prophetic function.

It is now clear that doctrine must drink from all sources: codes, statutes, judicial decisions, practice and usages, sociological data, and teachings of comparative law. A remarkable example of this broad approach is Dean Jean Carbonnier's handbook.[40] After stating positive law, the author conducts research on "the questions"; he examines, for instance, the historical, psychological, and sociological aspects of the matter, the legislative policy and legal theory, and finally the judicial practice.

Doctrine takes various forms. The great general treatises of *droit civil* can no longer follow the law in its swift evolutions. It is remarkable, however, that Aubry and Rau's treatise is still edited by André Ponsard, formerly a professor of law and presently a member of the Court of Cassation.[41] Subject to this exception, the great treatises of *droit civil* are now replaced by *répertoires*, particularly *Dalloz*, and *Juris-Classeur Périodique*. These publications state what the law is more than they comment on it in a doctrinal manner. Although primarily written for students, *droit civil* handbooks, on the other hand, often remain doctrinal writings in the full meaning of the expression. The various problems which arise in the fields of *droit civil* and civil procedure are covered in the excellent *Revue trimestrielle de droit civil*. The first part, consisting of articles and a bibliography listing most books and articles on *droit civil* and related matters, is followed by a review of case law, where all important decisions are summarized and discussed in commentaries, usually from one to three pages in length. The *Revue trimestrielle*, furthermore, notices the laws of a number of other nations and provinces where French is spoken (*e.g.*, Belgium, Switzerland, and Quebec) and reviews French and Community legislation.

One of the most original and lively forms of doctrine is probably found in the law reports. Whether *Recueil Dalloz Sirey* or *La Semaine Juridique*, the weekly report opens by one

---

[40] Carbonnier, *supra* note 10.
[41] *See* Aubry & Rau, *supra* note 10.

or two relatively short articles, then reproduces selected judicial decisions with annotations written by the judge of a high court, perhaps a member of the Court of Cassation, some other practitioner, or, more commonly, a professor of law.

It is currently said that the authority of doctrine in France is without parallel abroad. The comparison, as a matter of fact, is not an easy one. Doctrine seems, for instance, to receive great attention from American and English judges. In France the impact on the Court of Cassation of some doctrinal writers has been striking. Aubry and Rau's treatise[42] has been the court's bible for decades. More than a century after its first edition, it still enjoys great authority. Authors such as Georges Ripert and, even more, Henri Capitant have very often been followed by the court. Do present judges, burdened by a heavy caseload, find the time to pay the same attention to doctrinal writings? Do not some of them look with a smile (let us set aside the idea of contempt) at what is produced by "the makers of systems"? Is there not a certain irritation on their part (hopefully not a resentment) toward those who, in commenting upon their decisions, cannot always fully approve them? Certainly, doctrine exercises a certain influence, if only through lawyers who study doctrinal writings in order to find arguments in support of their cases and then expressly refer to such writings. One may fear, however, that relationships between judges and authors are not as fruitful as they could be. The judges, as earlier mentioned, are somewhat inundated by the cases. The authors have to deal with decisions which are very short, at least when made by the Court of Cassation, and they have to guess at the justification and scope of the holdings. This quite obviously does not facilitate the contribution that they would wish to bring to the fabric of the law. The cooperation of judges, lawyers, and academicians in the improvement of the law is certainly greater in Louisiana than in France, and I hope that the picture painted by Mr. Justice Barham[43] will inspire us in that direction.

## CONCLUSION

Such are the main currents of thought underlying the methodology of the civil law in France. The rich material collected in Professor Joseph Dainow's book[44] or, alterna-

[42] *Id.*
[43] Barham, *supra* note 1.
[44] Judicial Decisions, *supra* note 1.

tively, in René David's *Le droit français*[45] provides a fertile ground for further exploration of this area. This report is merely an introduction to further discussion and questioning.

[45] 2 R. David, Le droit français (1960).

[12]

THE

MODERN LAW REVIEW

**Volume 50 January 1987 No. 1**

# TAKING CIVIL CODES LESS SERIOUSLY

WHEN it was announced that I would have the honour and pleasure of giving this lecture a quick look at the formidable list of my predecessors showed that you have only rarely taken the risk of inviting a foreign lawyer. This was undoubtediy wise. Not only is a foreign lawyer who ventures into English law bound sooner or later to fall into error, but he will expect you to forgive him and kindly put him right when he does so. Not only is he apt to rush in where local angels fear to tread, but courtesy may require you to call his views original and refreshing when they are heretical or bizarre. Sure to blunder though I am, I think I cannot go too far astray if I start with a text by Lord Wilberforce. In a speech he made during the debate on the bill that was to become the Law Commissions Act he said:

> "By presenting to the courts legislation drafted in a simple way by definition of principles, we may restore to the judges what they may have lost for many years to their great regret; the task of interpreting law according to statements of principle, rather than by painfully hacking their way through the jungles of detailed and intricate legislation. So I believe that a process of codification, intelligently carried out, will revive the spirit of the Common Law rather than militate against it."[1]

Charged "to take and keep under review all the law . . . with a view to its systematic development and reform"—rather a daunting task—the Law Commission nailed the flag of codification to the mast and set a straight course, or so it seemed, to a law where everything, in Baudelaire's words, is "*ordre et beauté, luxe, calme et volupté.*" Eight years later, Lord Gardiner, who had blessed the ship at launching, asked Her Majesty's Government about its present position. Lord Hailsham, then Lord Chancellor, had to admit that her speed had slowed down considerably,[2] and in 1980, her captain, Sir Michael Kerr, the immediate past chairman of the Law Commission, finally, though I think without much regret, pronounced her a total loss. The Law Commission, he said, is to

[1] H.L.Deb., Vol. 264, cols. 1175–1176 (April 1, 1965).

[2] See Hahlo, "Codifying the Common Law: Protracted Gestation" (1975) 38 M.L.R. 23, 26.

continue work on interstitial legislation on selected topics of the law where reform appears particularly desirable. But codification of the law of contract and of landlord and tenant had in his view "no prospect of realisation" and "may well be unattainable in this country."[3]

It is probably safe to say, therefore, that codification is a dead issue in England today, and as there seem to be few mourners around I do not intend to offer my condolences or attempt a resuscitation. But it is worth noting that epitaphs have been written by various members of the English and Scottish Law Commissions, perhaps to get rid of a guilt complex. They give reasons for the demise of the codification projects.[4] On some of those reasons I have little to say. It was argued, for example, that even if a draft code were produced it would be impossible to deal with it satisfactorily in Parliament. Not only would a code lack the political appeal needed to win the necessary legislative time, but the present parliamentary process of scrutinising bills clause by clause and line by line is simply not devised to cope with a project of this magnitude.[5] Even a draft code which was desirable on the merits would come under heavy fire from the legal profession who would regard it "as a more or less transparent attack upon the foundations of a system which it cherishes."[6] The gut feeling that the law should be left in the safe hands of judges rather than entrusted to legislation penned by maladroit law reformers is certainly a most powerful influence both in England and on the Continent, and it certainly helps to make the life of the law reformer more interesting, but a rational argument it is not.

What loomed large in the codification debate were arguments drawn from what were believed to be the main characteristics of codes in civil law countries. No reference was ever made to the great and increasing use of codification that common law jurisdictions have made and are making. Instead, the standard argument proceeded in three steps. First, it was assumed implicitly that codification in England would be more or less tantamount to what it is on the Continent. Secondly, Continental codes were described as being based on a number of distinctive and uniform characteristics. Thirdly, it was concluded that legislation in England following this pattern would be alien not only to English legislative practice but also to the spirit of the common law. While it is not for me to say whether this conclusion is right I would like to make a few comments about the assumptions on which it was based, and in particular to discuss the special attributes that have been ascribed to the Continental codes. "Codes" said Harry Lawson, "are not

3 Kerr, "Law Reform in Changing Times" (1980) 96 L.Q.R. 515, 527, 528.

4 Kerr, *op. cit.*; Anton, "Obstacles to Codification" (1982) Jurid.Rev. 15; North, "Problems of Codification in a Common Law System" (1982) 46 *Rabels Zeitschrift* 490.

5 See Kerr, *op. cit* pp.531–533; Anton, *op. cit.* pp.28–30; North, *op. cit.* pp.507–508.

6 Anton, *op. cit.* p.23.

monsters,"[7] and Professor Tallon has added that, at any rate, "they can be trained."[8] I agree. But having followed the debate in England on the pros and cons of codification I think it might be useful to indicate some of the principal ways in which the training process can be helped.

To the common lawyer the most characteristic feature of a Continental code seems to be its propensity for generalised statements of principle. Codification in the civil law sense is described as involving the "legislative formulation of a series of general rules in particular areas of the law which are then left to the courts to work out and apply in the infinitely varying situations which come before them.[9] Similarly, it was said in the Renton Report on *The Preparation of Legislation* that the deliberate aim of European codes is "to confine the statement of terms to principles of wide application, and to practise a deliberate restraint in the proliferation of detailed rules."[10] A historical authority often cited to support this statement is Portalis, one of the four draftsmen of the French Civil Code, who did indeed declare that:

> "the task of legislation is to determine the general maxims of the law, taking a large view of the matter. It must establish principles rich in implications rather than descend into the details of every question which might possibly arise. . . . There is a legislative skill as well as a judicial skill, and the two are quite distinct. The skill of the legislator is to discover the principles in each area which must conduce to the common weal; the skill of the judge is to put these principles into action, and to extend them to particular circumstances by wise and reasoned application."[11]

As an example of this style of legislation the reader is normally referred to articles 1382–86 of the French Civil Code which purport to cover virtually the whole of French tort law in a handful of majestic, if trivial propositions. To adopt this style of legislation in England, so the argument continues, would be in clear conflict with what Sir Michael Kerr called "a basic and apparently ineradicable feature of our constitutional philosophy" which requires all English legislation to be based on the premise "that every statute must, so far as possible, seek to cover every foreseeable situation" and which is opposed to provisions expressed in general language that "would leave unacceptably wide powers of interpretation and application to the judges"[12] and would therefore

[7] Lawson, "A Common Lawyer Looks at Codification" in *Selected Essays I: Many Laws* (1977), p.48.

[8] "Codification and Consolidation of the Law at the Present Time" (1979) 14 Israel L.Rev. 1, 12.

[9] Kerr, *op. cit.* p.528.

[10] Cmnd. 6053 (1975), para. 51.

[11] Fenet, *Recueil complet de travaux préparatoires du Code civil* (1836), pp.470, 475, transl. Weir, in Zweigert and Kötz, *An Introduction to Comparative Law* (1977), Vol. I, p.82.

[12] Kerr, *op. cit.* pp.527–528.

alter the traditional balance of power between Parliament on the one hand and the judiciary on the other.

Before I turn to the alleged generality of Continental codes I would like to raise the question whether it can really be said that English statutes invariably "seek to cover every foreseeable situation" or are "customarily drafted with almost mathematical precision, the object (not always attained) being in effect to provide a complete answer to virtually every question that can arise."[13] It would seem safe to say that the signs pointing in the opposite direction are already on the wall. In his inaugural lecture at Oxford in 1978[14] Professor Atiyah suggested that this country was already moving to an era when a great deal of strict law is being replaced by discretions of one kind or another. The proliferation of these discretions appeared to him to arise "at least in part from the realisation that legislation, even when fleshed out by detailed subordinate legislation, simply cannot anticipate and provide for the great variety of cases which are likely to arise, and that Parliament therefore prefers to proceed in partnership with the judiciary."[15] Even for a civilian observer it is not difficult to point out a few examples of this type of legislation. Thus, the Unfair Contract Terms Act 1977 abounds with provisions under which the validity of an exemption clause depends on a "reasonableness test." This test which has been said to stand "at the centre of the strategy of the Act"[16] requires the judge to decide whether the term in question "shall have been a fair and reasonable one to be included having regard to the circumstances which were, or ought reasonably to have been, known to or in the contemplation of the parties when the contract was made."[17] This is language at least as broad and general as the text used in the German Standard Terms Act 1976 which is the German counterpart of the English Act.[18] True, Schedule 2 of the Unfair Contract Terms Act sets out "guidelines" directing the judge's attention to certain circumstances he must consider in determining whether certain clauses satisfy the reasonableness test. But these "guidelines" are fairly broad and general themselves, and it is not easy—at least for a civilian observer—to understand why there is a need for them at all. No one in England seems to object to the judges using vague and indeterminate concepts and particularising them as cases come up so long as these concepts are common law concepts created by the judges themselves, as when a judge in an action for damages for

[13] Sir Charles David, Legal Adviser to the House of Commons Select Committee on European Secondary Legislation, submitting evidence to the Renton Committee: Cmnd. 6053, para. 52.

[14] *From Principles to Pragmatism* (1978).

[15] Atiyah, "Common Law and Statute Law" (1985) 48 M.L.R. 1, 5.

[16] Cheshire and Fifoot's *Law of Contract* (10th ed. Furmston, 1981), p.163.

[17] s.11(1).

[18] See Sandrock, "The Standard Terms Act 1976 of West Germany" (1978) 26 Am.J.Comp.L. 551 (with a translation of the Act by Nina Galston).

negligence decides whether the defendant's conduct has been that of a reasonable man who took reasonable care to avoid an unreasonable risk of causing injury to others. But when it comes to legislation, the parliamentary draftsman, if he can be persuaded to use a broad term like "reasonable", seems to be under an irresistible urge to teach the judge a lesson on what "reasonable" really means, and while the words commonly used for that purpose are no doubt well-meant they exude, at least to a Continental lawyer, a somewhat condescending and pedagogical flavour.

Another example of general language in an English statute is section 33 of the Limitation Act 1980. It confers on the judge a broad power to "disapply" time-limits for actions in respect of personal injury and death if it appears to him that it would be "equitable" to do so. I will spare you the many words used by the parliamentary draftsman in section 33(3) to tell the judge what factors he ought to consider in determining whether or not it is "equitable" to disapply the time-limits. At any rate, the discretion vested in the judge is so wide that a similar statutory rule would, in this particular field of the law, be unacceptable to German lawyers and, I believe, to lawyers from other Continental countries as well.

My last example is the Employment Protection Act 1978. It provides in section 54(1) that "every employee shall have the right not to be unfairly dismissed by his employer." Section 56(3) instructs the industrial tribunal that "the determination of the question whether the dismissal was fair or unfair . . . shall depend on whether . . . the employer acted reasonably or unreasonably in treating it as a sufficient reason for dismissing the employee; and that question shall be determined in accordance with equity and the substantial merits of the case." Does this add one ounce of substance to the general principle?

Not only does it seem to be an overstatement to say that every English statute seeks to cover every foreseeable situation, but one can also question the corollary that general statements of legal principle are known only to civil law systems. Conceded, English common lawyers are somewhat reluctant to lay them down in statutory form. But this does not mean that they do not exist. True, a case law system is usually seen as being casuistic in the sense that it is bound to work from specific situations that have been adjudicated in precedents. But it is still not true that precedents are at odds or incompatible with general principles. As Professor Lawson once noted, "English law contains a number of doctrines of great breadth which are more powerful than any of the decisions on which they are based or in which they are applied."[19] Common law judges are as anxious as their civil law brethren to present their decisions as being necessarily required by some rule of a scope broader than that of a single case. Case law is

[19] F. H. Lawson, "Further Reflexions on Codification" in *Selected Essays II: The Comparison* (1977), p.96.

not, I think, a mere "wilderness of single instances." What gives it its own internal consistency and systematic quality is the fact that the driving force behind the development of the law is the gradual emergence of some general principle which enables the judge to say whether and why two cases are, or are not, alike and how, if a new case comes up, "the inclusionary or exclusionary axe is to fall."[20] Both in England and in Germany, contracts may be void on grounds of public policy, assignees take subject to equities, and agreements can be terminated because of a fundamental breach. General propositions of this sort may not decide concrete cases, either in a civil law system where such principles are sometimes codified, or in the common law where they are not. But what they do achieve in both systems is that they help to organise legal thinking, to allow the formation of clusters of similar cases, to make the law manageable and findable, and to provide a language in which a meaningful discourse between lawyers can take place. It follows that if there is no major operational difference between the use to which general principles are put in a code law and in a case law then it is difficult to see why the mere enactment of such principles would alter the balance of power between Parliament and the judges and thus violate basic tenets of British constitutional philosophy.

Perhaps I can give an illustration by referring to Article 328 of the German Civil Code, one of those provisions that would probably be described in this country as typical of a Continental code in that it leaves "unacceptably wide powers of interpretation and application to the judges." According to this Article, one may by contract so bargain for performance to a third party that the third party directly acquires the right to demand performance. The Article then goes on to say that if the contract contains no express provision, the judge must take all the circumstances into account, especially the purpose of the contract, in order to determine whether the third party is to acquire such a right or is merely an incidental beneficiary. In England one starts from the general judge-made principle "that only a person who is a party to a contract can sue on it" and that "English law knows nothing of a *ius quaesitum tertio* arising by way of contract."[21] But there are a number of exceptions to this principle, of which some are statutory and others judge-made, to the effect that a third party may enforce a contract to which he is a stranger if he can bring himself within the definition of an undisclosed principal or a beneficiary under a trust. It is of no interest here whether the approach of German law is preferable or its development more orderly. The question is rather: Would the balance of power between Parliament and the judges be altered if the German rule were introduced in England

[20] Stoljar, "Codification and the Common Law" in *Problems of Codification* (1977) p.8.

[21] *Dunlop* v. *Selfridge* [1915] A.C. 847, 853 (Lord Haldane).

by way of statute? I do not believe so. In both countries judges operate under fairly broad principles, and in both countries the practitioner must eventually look at the precedents in order to find out what a court is likely to say in a difficult case.

Let us now look a little more closely at the assertion often made in England that rules in Continental codes are always expressed in terms of general principle and rarely spell out the precise way in which the law is to apply in differing circumstances. It often seems to be overlooked that the codes differ markedly *inter se* in regard to their style of drafting. Admittedly, the rules and principles of the French Civil Code, loose-textured as they are, in many cases appear to the reader today to do no more than indicate the general direction which development was to take. But the French at the time had really no alternative but to adopt this style of legislation. Since Napoleon had given the Code's drafters only a couple of months to do the job they could not but turn to the then available textbooks, such as those by Domat and Pothier, which had summed up the teaching of the past in a compendious and accessible, though fairly general and abstract, form. True, the modern student may be appalled at the simplistic way in which the Code treats the law of tort. But it must not be forgotten that compensation for accidents simply was not a problem of any major social significance at the end of the eighteenth century, and that a code can hardly be more inventive and sophisticated than the collected legal experience existing at the time it is drafted. The Swiss Civil Code of 1907 has its own characteristic features including a strong tendency to make extensive use of broad and sweeping terms. But again this is largely attributable to the particular circumstances in Switzerland in the 1890s. There was a general conviction, understandable at the time, but somewhat starry-eyed from the modern viewpoint, that the Code, in the words of its main draftsman Eugen Huber, "must speak in popular ideas" and that "the man of reason who has thought about his times and their needs should have the feeling, as he reads it, that the statute speaks to him from the heart."[22] The open texture of the Swiss Code was also necessitated by the fact that the judges of most lower Swiss courts, like English magistrates, were and still are, laymen without legal training who would have had a hard time working with a more closely-knit, technically refined statute. Finally, since the Code had to be ratified by 25 cantonal jurisdictions and there was always the risk that a popular referendum might be called to defeat it, a statute with intelligible and seemingly lucid rules was believed to be more readily acceptable than one characterised by rigour, precision and technical complexity.

As regards the German Civil Code of 1900, on the other hand, it would be rather misleading to say that it lays down the law in

[22] Zweigert and Kötz, *op. cit.* pp.170–172. See also von Overbeck, "The Role of the Judge under the Swiss Civil Code," in *Problems of Codification, op. cit., supra*, n. 20, pp.135 *et seq.*

general principles. In language, method and structure it is the child of the deep, exact, and abstract learning of the German Pandectist School which, by means of a long and wearisome process of classification and systematic analysis, had distilled precise concepts and institutions from the *rudis indigestaque moles* of the then existing case and statute law. Among the Englishmen who were impressed by this approach was John Austin who said that going from England to Germany to study law felt like escaping "from the empire of chaos and darkness to a world that seems by comparison the region of order and light."[23] On this basis the drafters of the Code were able to state the law in terms of interlocking concepts, principles, and rules which are clear-cut and expressed in a language which, despite its complex syntax and rather Gothic cumbrousness, is consistent and free from ambiguity. Swiss authors compared the German Code to its Swiss counterpart and came to the conclusion that it might be described as "the legal calculating machine *par excellence*"[24] and "perhaps the code of private law with the most precise and logical legal language of all time."[25] At any rate, fairly little play was left in the machine, and whatever the vices and virtues of the German Civil Code are, excessive generality and vagueness are not among them.

This brief survey shows not only that there are considerable differences between the Continental codes but that the legislative style adopted in each country is the result of the particular political, historical and social circumstances existing where and when the codes were drafted. The same conditions do not exist in England today, and it would seem highly misleading therefore to derive neat arguments, either for or against codification in England, from the characteristics of codes produced in other countries, at other times, and for other reasons.

In one respect, however, foreign codification experience may be of some assistance. It may show that once the decision has been taken to reform and develop a certain area of the law by statute, different levels of generality, or particularisation, are available to the draftsman. Choosing between them may well be one of the more difficult policy problems in the art of legislative drafting. Much depends on the subject-matter to be regulated. Property law is a field in which precise and clear rules are both desirable and possible. It is no surprise that the rules of the German Civil Code on the law of real property are every bit as specific and detailed as those of the Law of Property Act 1925. The situation is different in those areas where everybody will agree that more flexibility is needed, as in the law of tort and contract. But what is the proper

[23] *Lectures on Jurisprudence* (5th ed., 1885), p.58.

[24] A. B. Schwarz, *Das Schweizerische Zivilgesetzbuch in der ausländischen Rechtsentwicklung* (1950), p.8.

[25] Gmür, *Das Schweizerische Zivilgesetzbuch verglichen mit dem deutschen BGB* (1965), p.143.

degree of flexibility? When the tort rules of the German Civil Code were being drafted it was a long time before a decision could be reached on whether to adopt the casuistry of the special types of delictual liability inherited from Roman law or rather follow the French example and include in the Code a general rule imposing liability in damages whenever harm was unlawfully caused by somebody's negligent conduct. In the end, the majority concluded that the French solution would give German judges a discretion believed to be inconsistent with "the dominant conception among German people regarding the position of the judge."[26] A compromise solution representing a middle point between the extremes was therefore adopted.[27] A similar problem arises where the death of a person causes economic loss to a third party: when may the third party sue the tortfeasor for damages? The French Civil Code says nothing on the problem and leaves it to the judges to sort things out. In Switzerland some legislative guidance is given by Article 45 of the Code of Obligations which provides that compensation must be paid to a third party who by the death has lost his or her "provider." "Provider" is interpreted to mean anybody who has in fact provided support for the plaintiff or would have provided it in the normal course of events. Occasionally, there is a difficult case such as the surviving partner of an informal union. These difficulties the Swiss drafters were prepared to accept. Not so in Germany, where the Code provides that a third party can claim damages only if the deceased "was actually or potentially bound by law to support him."[28] This clearly precludes a recovery by stepchildren, fiancées, *de facto* spouses, or brothers or sisters of the deceased. This leads to very unsatisfactory results in some cases, but it undoubtedly makes for certainty and foreseeability of the law.

So—and many other examples might be given—the draftsman must not only find some passage or other between the Scylla of vague generalities and the Charybdis of mathematical precision. He must do more. He must steer the best course available by finding language that strikes an apt balance between certainty and flexibility and facilitates the orderly development of the law without unduly fettering judicial creativity. This is a difficult task, and English draftsmen do not seem to have been very good at it. In his remarkable study comparing the legislative techniques of various Continental countries and the United Kingdom, Sir William Dale has argued the case for a style of draftsmanship that would be guided by determination to seek the general priniciple, to express it, and to follow up in an orderly and logical development, with

[26] *Protokolle der Kommission für die 2. Lesung des Entwurfs des BGB*, Vol. II (1898), p.571.

[27] For details see Zweigert and Kötz, *op. cit.*, Vol. II, pp.264 *et seq.*; Horn, Kötz and Leser, *German Private and Commercial Law: An Introduction* (1982), pp.146 *et seq.*

[28] Art. 844(2), German Civil Code.

such detail, illuminating and not obscuring the principle, as the circumstances require.[29] Similarly, the Renton Committee came to the conclusion that the adoption of what it called the "'general principle' approach" would lead to greater simplicity and clarity. But tax law, industrial safety legislation, and building regulations must aim at a most precise enunciation of rights and duties, even at the expense of simplicity and clarity. In the law of contract and tort, on the other hand, and in commercial law and other more traditional areas of the common law, the statute, call it a code or not, can often do no more than lay down guiding principles lest the vitality and flexibility needed in these fields be lost.

Let us now look at another feature ascribed to Continental codes that has been used in this country as an *argumentum in terrorem* in the codification debate. It has been said that a special characteristic of a code is that within its field it is the exclusive, authoritative, and comprehensive source of the law, and that the judges must accordingly wipe out their knowledge of prior law and concentrate on the statutory words. A judge working with a code has indeed been likened to somebody who has been told he could walk about more or less as he liked in a room, but could not go outside.[30] On the other hand, the central assumption of the English legal system is that statutes are best regarded as derogations from a common law which continues to be in force in so far as it is consistent with the statute and is freely resorted to whenever there is, or appears to be, a gap or an ambiguity in it. This difference in philosophy has been described as "the crucial obstacle to codification," and it has been said that if a code on the Continental model were enacted in England, this would "alter the hierarchy of its sources of law and in consequence would strike at the heart of its principles of legal reasoning."[31] I think all of this needs to be reconsidered.

Frederick Pollock once observed that most English lawyers seemed to share the conviction that "Parliament generally changes the law for the worse, and that the business of the judge is to keep the mischief of its interference within the narrowest possible bounds."[32] There are indeed many cases in which statutes, particularly if they sought to protect some social interest or to advance some social policy, were narrowly construed so that the judges were able to fall back on the rules of the common law which they felt were more congenial. Whether this is still true today I do not know. I was impressed, though, by the remarks made by Professor Atiyah in the last Chorley lecture when he said that the relationship between common law and statute law may be changing and that statutes, rather than being construed narrowly at

[29] *Legislative Drafting: A New Approach* (1977), p.335.
[30] F. H. Lawson, *The Rational Strength of English Law* (1951), p.21.
[31] Anton, *op. cit.*, pp.19 and 23. See also Diamond, "Codification of the Law of Contract" (1968) 31 M.L.R. 375.
[32] Pollock, *Essays on Jurisprudence and Ethics* (1882), p.85.

all costs, are now sometimes used by the courts as analogies in the development of the common law.[33]

As regards the civil law, it is an overstatement to say that a code is always completely self-contained and therefore excludes all reference to any source of law other than itself. It is unrealistic to expect that lawyers trained under pre-code law can be prevented from going back to it if the code is silent, if its language is not clear or if the words used in it had previously acquired a technical meaning. A brief look at the German cases decided after the Civil Code had come into force proves that extensive use was made by the courts not only of the materials compiled by the drafting commissions but also of pre-Code cases.[34] When Lord Campbell visited Paris as a young barrister in 1819 he wrote a letter saying that if one attended the Palais de Justice one

> "would find the advocates and judges, in the discharge of their duty, necessarily referring to the Civil Law, to the *droit coutumier* before the Revolution, to the works of Daguesseau and Pothier, and to a body of recent decided cases little less bulky than the Reports which load the shelves of an English lawyer."[35]

Recourse to pre-Code cases has nowadays become very rare in Germany, much rarer even than references in this country to cases decided before the turn of the century. But there is no reason in principle why it should not be done in an appropriate case. Indeed all codes, partly from age, partly from the intention of their draftsmen, partly from mere oversight, leave wide gaps which cannot be filled by the available statutory rules. True, Continental judges are more inclined than English judges to develop a new rule by using legislative texts as the basis for an analogy or an argument *e contrario*. There is something to be said for the view that in many cases in the civil law statutory provisions have been used much as precedents are used in the common law, as the materials of argument in decision-making. But this does not detract from the fact that in many fields of the law judicial decisions are based on rules that are not contained, and do not even lie buried, in any code language. While passing reference to one or more code articles will be made, in nearly all cases what really happens is that methods similar to those of the common law are used to fill gaps, settle doubts and develop new rules. This is most obvious in the law of contract and torts where all codes, though some more than others, have wisely refrained from over-particularisation and where consequently the operative value of the codal rules is limited.

[33] Atiyah, *op. cit., supra*, n. 15, pp.25 *et seq.*

[34] See the exhaustive study by T. Honsell, *Historische Argumente im Zivilrecht* (1982), pp.108 *et seq.*, pp.116 *et seq.*

[35] *Life of Lord Campbell*, Vol. I (1881), p.363. I take this quotation from Lawson, "An English Lawyer's Reflexions on the Code civil" in *Selected Essays II: The Comparison* (1977), p.42.

Let me illustrate this by the way German courts have treated standard form contracts. It had long been realised that most of the text on printed forms was not read and, if read, seldom understood by the signers, and that this made nonsense of the usual tests of mutual assent. In the middle 1950s the courts came to the conclusion that the traditional technique of construing ambiguous clauses *contra proferentem* was not sufficient.

So they started to subject standard form contracts to severe scrutiny, striking out terms found to be oppressive, unexpected, or one-sided. This was a very bold step indeed. But the proper limits of judicial activism need not concern us here. What is of interest here is that no article in the Civil Code could serve in any way as a statutory basis for the newly created judicial power. Admittedly, the courts invoked Article 242 of the Code; and the fact that this was believed necessary shows that there is some truth in the statement that in the civil law judges generally do not feel safe until they have moored their ship to some statutory wharf. But this is often a largely ritual operation and so it was here, for Article 242 only provides that contracts are to be performed in the manner required by good faith. On this basis, if basis it can be called, a considerable body of case law grew up, and guidelines for testing the fairness of such clauses were developed. Academic writers gave a helping hand, and while Article 242 was gradually lapsing into benign neglect, they were busy lining up the cases in series, comparing and contrasting them, matching results against reasons given, and limiting the scope of decisions by imagining the effects of adding or subtracting particular facts. To a large extent, the subsequent legislation of 1976 simply enacted the rules and principles laid down by the courts, including a broad clause in Article 9 of the Act which says that standard terms are invalid when they unfairly disadvantage the customer. Needless to say, the courts have always felt free to use the pre-1976 cases to flesh out the skeletal rule of Article 9, and nobody has ever argued that the new Act is "self-contained" in the sense that recourse to the old cases is forbidden. For these reasons the thesis that, within their fields, codes are the exclusive source of the law does not do justice to the way in which the law is developed in a code jurisdiction, nor is it plausible to forge from this thesis an argument against codification in England. Codification may well be unattainable in this country, but the view that a well-drafted code would inevitably sound the death-knell of established techniques of developing the law by way of an orderly process of reasoning from case to case is quite unproven.

The vices sometimes ascribed to codification may therefore not be quite as harmful as suspected. Nor are its virtues as shining as the authors of the Law Commissions Act may have believed. Even on the Continent the idea of codification has lost much of its lustre in recent years. It has now become quite fashionable to talk about the crisis, or the demise, of the civil codes, and when Professor Irti of Rome diagnosed a process of what he called "decodification" he coined a catchword now used by many authors.[36] In their view, the rapid changes in the political, social and technological conditions of our time have led to detailed special legislation designed to further specific social objectives which are alien to the basic philosophy of the codes. They predict that this legislation will gradually supersede the codes and transform them into bodies of mere residual law to be resorted to only if no more specific provision can be found. Noted German authors have called the idea of codification a romantic anachronism since the demands and pressures on legislatures today to counteract specific social and economic ills have reached such a degree as to foreclose their undertaking any recasting or rewriting of code provisions on a more general and systematic basis in a attempt to keep them in touch with current needs.[37] This has been opposed by other writers,[38] and although the debate is largely academic it does occasionally have some practical importance. Thus, when the Bill which was to become the German Standard Terms Act was being debated, some authors including myself argued the case for incorporating the new rules into the Civil Code, on the ground that this would keep the Code in tune with present notions of contractual fairness and thus help to prevent its contract rules from gradually decaying into obsolescence. These arguments were unavailing. It was said that the new rules were not yet tested and should be given a trial run before they were admitted to the hallowed precincts of the Civil Code. The Federal Ministry of Justice also wanted to see quick results in view of the approaching elections, and there is no doubt that it would have taken time to fit the new rules into the existing Code structure. Finally, the Ministry may have believed that it would be easier to get Parliamentary approval for a special Bill sailing under the proud flag of consumer protection than for a number of amendments to scattered Code provisions that would look unattractively like mere tinkering.

But the passing of the Standard Terms Act may well have marked the turn of the tide. There now seems to be a growing awareness in Germany that, while the modern trend in favour of special legislation is to some extent inevitable, it nevertheless has its price. A special Act may be the only solution if a particular social problem cannot be solved without imposing administrative or

---

[36] *L'età della codificazione* (Milano 1979), also published in (1978) *Diritto a società*, pp.613 *et seq*. But see also De Cupis, *À proposito de codice e decodificazione* (1979 II) *Rivista di diritto civile*, pp.47 *et seq*.; Sacco, "La codification, forme dépassée de législation?" in *Rapports nationaux italiens au XIe Congrès International de Droit Comparé à Caracas 1982* (Milano 1982), pp.85 *et seq*.

[37] Kübler, "Kodifikation und Demokratie" (1969) *Juristenzeitung* 645; Esser, "Gesetzesrationalität im Kodifikationszeitalter und heute" in Vogel and Esser, *100 Jahre oberste deutsche Justizbehörde* (Tübingen 1977), pp.13 *et seq*.

[38] See K. Schmidt, *Die Zukunft der Kodifikationsidee* (Heidelberg 1985).

criminal sanctions at the same time, since adminstrative, criminal or procedural law cannot be grafted on to a Civil Code. On the other hand, there are good reasons for keeping the code up-to-date by means of amendment or revision if one possibly can rather than enacting special legislation. These are not of course the reasons that used to be given in the early days of codification, when a code was said to be a symbol of national identity or of social or political reform, or to help the legal education of the citizenry. The case for reforming the law by revising the code is based strictly on operational and technical grounds. The argument is that special legislation tends to be prolix and verbose and to introduce byzantine distinctions and technical details which later turn out to be not only unnecessary but actually harmful in opening up new areas of dispute. A code, on the other hand, stands for the ideas of internal economy and discipline, so codification tends to keep the law manageable, orderly, accessible and teachable without depriving it of the needed flexibility. At the same time it acts as a check on the legislature's propensity to rush off into special enactments whenever desired, instead of first asking whether the new proposals might not be fitted into the existing structure or expressed in existing terms. For these reasons, the routine work of legal practice and adjudication may arguably be easier in a system with a code than in a system rife with ill-coordinated special statutes. Having a civil code may also reduce the expense of providing legal services. This point was made nearly 50 years ago by Karl Llewellyn, the leading author of the American Uniform Commercial Code, and a master of both the common law and German law. "No one," he said,

> "who has never seen a puzzled Continental lawyer turn to his little library and then turn out at least a workable understanding of his problem within half an hour will really grasp what the availability of the working leads packed into a systematic Code can do to cheapen the rendering of respectably adequate legal service."[39]

You will have guessed on which side of the German debate my own sympathies lie. But this does not mean that it has been my intention to win you over to the codificationist camp. I would rather submit that the whole question whether or not codification is a sensible course to take in the reform and restatement of English law misses the point and that it was counterproductive to have put it on the agenda of the Law Commission. Perhaps because of its Benthamite ring, the word "codification" seems to mesmerise common lawyers into believing that their whole legal system with its characteristic feature of being still predominantly case law is to be swept away at a stroke and replaced by what is sometimes described as the vague generalities, sometimes as the

[39] "The Bar's Troubles, and Poultices—and Cures?" (1938) 5 *Law and Contemporary Problems* 104, 118.

rigorous inflexibility of legislation on the Continental model. Closer analysis reveals that the fears of those committed to maintaining tradition for its own sake are as unfounded as the hopes staked on codification by the aficionados of drastic change. Codes are no monsters, and Professor Lawson was basically right when he said that "the adoption of a code is not likely to do anyone any harm.[40] I would nevertheless suggest that the debate in this country on the vices and virtues of Continental codification leads nowhere and only obscures the more basic problem which confronts English law and any other law. It is the problem of finding an acceptable compromise between the complementary values of experience and order. Case law stands for experience, and there is no question that case law forms an indispensable component of any legal system. But there is no doubt either that if case law is left to its own erratic course it may lead, in the civil law just as in the common law, to an unwieldy, shapeless mass of legal results. So there is a need for order, form, and structure. How this order is to be achieved is a question for which each legal system must find its own solution tailored to its own needs. Order can be provided by a good textbook, by a Restatement of the law in the American sense, and of course by legislation. To what extent such legislation turns out to resemble a Continental code is a question I would leave to law professors once it has been enacted. As the English mathematician G. H. Hardy once said, "if the Archbishop of Canterbury says he believes in God, that's all in the way of business." But if a comparative lawyer tells you that the Continental codes with their specific characteristics, their weaknesses and their strength, provide little help for the solution of the problems of law reform in England today, you can take it he means what he says.

HEIN KÖTZ*

[40] *Op. cit.* n. 7, p.48.

* Professor, University of Hamburg; Director, Max-Planck-Institute for Foreign and Private International Law. This was the fifteenth Chorley Lecture delivered at the London School of Economics on June 4, 1986. I am grateful to Tony Weir for commenting on the text.

# Part IV
# Constitutional Law and Judicial Review

# [13]

# Lecture

# Constitutional Jurisdiction in Western Germany*

Dr. Ernst Benda**

## I. Introduction

The institutionalization of a constitutional jurisdiction in Germany was certainly influenced by the ideas and lessons from American constitutional experience. The political philosophy of "limited government" and the understanding of constitution as "fundamental law" developed in American revolutionary thinking and affirmed by the Supreme Court in *Marbury v. Madison*[1] were fundamental issues of the Basic Law Creating Process. Yet constitutional review has its own historical roots in Germany and was not — as for example in Italy or Japan — a brand new experience.

Constitutional review in Germany can be traced back to the Reichskammergericht of 500 years ago, which was the supreme court of the Holy Roman Empire. Very important for the constitutional jurisdiction of our days was the Frankfort democratic constitution of 1849, which — however — never entered into force. Here the idea of constitutional review was clearly expressed; statutes enacted by the German diet were to be reviewed against the constitution.

During the Weimar period the wording of the constitution of 1918 only provided for constitutional review to settle constitutional disputes within separate states or between the states and the fed-

* Text of Christopher Emmet Lecture, presented September 23, 1980 at the University Club in New York, under the auspices of the American Council on Germany. The Council is a non-profit, non-governmental organization that seeks to improve understanding between the United States and the Federal Republic of Germany.

** Der Präsident des Bundesverfassungsgerichts (President of the Constitutional Court of the Federal Republic of Germany).

1. 5 U.S. (1 Cranch) 137 (1803).

eracy; it was not possible to bring a constitutional complaint before the Staatsgerichtshof, the Reich constitutional court.[2] The situation was quite similar to that of the *Marbury* decision of 1803: the constitution itself did not expressly entrust the Court with the judicial review, but there was an atmosphere, created by precedents — or perhaps one should say quasi-precedents — and legal theory, to which the idea of judicial review could be very reasonably adapted.

All the vast powers and competences of the Federal Constitutional Court or FCC, however, find their secure foundation in the provisions of the Basic Law (*Grundgesetz*). Today there is no quarrel about that. This does not mean that the fundamental problem inherent in the idea of constitutional jurisdiction itself is no longer discussed.

The FCC has two chambers (senates), each composed of eight judges. The senates are independent of each other; each senate acts as the FCC. There is no appeal to the plenum by the litigants. But if one senate, in deciding a legal question, disagrees with the opinion of the other senate the question has to be referred to the plenum of the Court. In spite of the character of the FCC as a "twin court" the uniformity of constitutional law can be maintained.

The FCC, apart from being a judicial organ, participates in the exercise of the supreme power of the State. The status of the FCC is not inferior to that of the Federal President, the Bundestag, the Bundesrat or the Federal Government. Or, as our former Federal President, Walter Scheel, once put it:

> Each of these constitutional organs is the highest representative of the State, seen from a certain point of view: the Bundestag, in as much as the State conceives itself as a parliamentary democracy; the Bundesrat, insofar as the Federal Republic considers itself as a federal State; the Federal Government, in as much as the State is a politically active unity; the FCC, in as much as the State understands itself as a State governed by the rule of law, and the Federal President because he represents the

2. *See* T. MAUNZ, B. SCHMIDT-BLEIBTREU, F. KLEIN, G. ULSAMER, BUNDESVERFASSUNGSGERICHTSGESETZ, at Vorbemerkung 12 (1980).

whole State in all its functions and capacities.

## II. The Court as "Supreme Guardian of the Constitution"

To be the "Supreme Guardian of the Constitution" means duty and power for the FCC at the same time.

The powers of the FCC to fill this guardianship role are extensive. One may differentiate between four kinds of competences which signify at the same time the four major facets of constitutional jurisdiction in the Federal Republic.

### A. *Determination of the Hierarchy of Legal Norms*

The first is the determination of the hierarchy of legal norms, at the top of which stands the Constitution followed by other federal law which is superior to state law including the state constitutions.

Concrete and abstract judicial review serve this purpose.[3] The first may arise out of an ordinary litigation before any court. If a court considers unconstitutional a statute the validity of which is relevant to its forthcoming decision, the proceedings must be stayed and a decision sought from the FCC.

An example of *concrete judicial review* in recent times is the ruling on Divorce Law and the Division of Property subsequent to divorce.[4] On February 28 this year, the First Senate announced a wide-ranging decision which confirmed in essence the constitutionality of several provisions questioned by a number of Family Courts in Germany. The Court held that the Basic Law does not prevent the legislature from changing the basis for the grounds for divorce from a fault to a no-fault principle. It further held that the Legislature was not acting *ultra vires* in presuming that a marriage is dissolved in the non-legal sense after a three-year separation of the partners. Yet the Court was split four to four over the hardship clause by which one of the partners could oppose divorce on special material or non-material grounds within a five-year period. Such sharply split rulings are not a common occurrence and I gather they happen more frequently in the United States, with the Supreme Court publishing a number of concurring and dissenting opinions. In this particular case the FCC also had to examine whether the basic principle of dividing property and pension

3. Grundgesetz art. 93, par. 1(2); Law of Feb. 3, 1971, §§ 13(6), (11), [1971] Bundesgesetzblatt, Teil I [BGB1] 105 [hereinafter cited as BVerfGG [section]].

4. Judgement of Feb. 28, 1980, Bundesverfassungsgericht, 52 BVerfGE 257.

claims between divorced spouses violated the protection of private property pursuant to Art. 14 of the Basic Law.

Insofar as the law on division of property curtailed the actual and expected pension claims of the party obligated to transfer property pursuant to statute, the Court held that such curtailment is legitimated by Art. 6 (which protects marriage and family) and Art. 3 (on equality). Additionally, the Court held that it was not unconstitutional for the division of such claims not to take the relative fault of the divorced spouses into account.

Concerning *abstract judicial review*, the FCC may, at the request of the Federal Government, of a Land Government, or of one third of the Bundestag members, be seized in case of differences of opinion or doubts of the formal and material compatibility of federal law or state law with the constitution, or of the compatibility of Land law with other federal law.

As an example of abstract judicial review I would cite the case where nearly 200 deputies of the Bundestag belonging to the Christian Democratic Party contended the incompatibility of the Abortion Reform Act of 1974 with the Basic Law.[5] Under the Act, termination of pregnancy was no longer punishable during the first 12 weeks after conception; destruction of the fetus was permissible after that period if warranted on medical and eugenic grounds prior to the twenty-second week of pregnancy. The situation was thus adverse to that of the United States where, at the time of the Supreme Court's decisions in *Wade*[6] and *Bolton*,[7] the majority of state abortion laws were restrictive in the sense of legalizing abortion only on medical grounds. In 1975, the FCC — after eight months of deliberations — invalidated the relevant provision of the Abortion Reform Act. The Court invoked Art. 2, paragraph 2 of the Basic Law which says: "Everyone shall have the right to life and to the inviolability of his person," which is, in the understanding of the Senate, a fundamental or objective value decision. Human life, the Court argued, begins no later than 13 days after conception and is a continuous process which cannot be divided sharply into various stages. The majority of the Senate confirmed the obligation of the State to protect the unborn life even by penal sanctions. The Court admitted that this requirement is directed in the first instance to the legislature; yet it is the Court's duty to

5. Judgement of Feb. 25, 1975, Bundesverfassungsgericht, 39 BVerfGE 1.
6. Roe v. Wade, 410 U.S. 113 (1973).
7. Doe v. Bolton, 410 U.S. 179 (1973).

examine whether the legislature has fulfilled this task. I have to stress that there was a well-founded dissenting opinion of two judges who held the Abortion Reform Act to be in conformity with the Basic Law. They argued that the majority finding reversed the function of fundamental rights. In the opinion of the dissenting judges the question was not *whether* but *how* the value of human life is to be protected; this, they remarked, was a matter of legislative responsibility.

### B. *Protection of Federalism*

The second facet of constitutional jurisdiction is the protection of federalism. Today, this concept is in danger. There is a clearly perceptible tendency to "dry up" the Laender[8] in favour of the federal State. Reasons for this development can be found in the trend to a life more uniform than ever, the overall interdependencies, and last but not least the lack of financial means. But it is worthwhile to defend federalism; it is one of our fundamental principles of the Basic Law the importance of which lies in the vertical separation of powers as well as in the guarantee of the cultural identity and autonomy of the Laender; the checks and balances resulting from the consent or suspensive veto of the Bundesrat, our "Senate" or Second Chamber, are essential guarantees of individual freedom.

The Basic Law has recognized the FCC as umpire in those constitutional controversies arising out of differences of opinion on the rights and duties of the Federacy and the Laender, particularly in the execution of federal law by the Laender and in the exercise of federal supervision.[9] I think that in recent times the FCC has done a good deal of work in this respect. From a theoretical point of view one may observe that constitutional review in the United States as well as in Germany started from this arbiter function in order to hold the balance between the small entities and the Federacy.

### C. *Organstreit*

The separation of powers is also ensured by another procedure, the so-called Organstreit, disputes between constitutional organs of the Federal Republic necessitating an interpretation of the

8. Laender are the West German analogs of American States.
9. GRUNDGESETZ art. 93, par. 1(3); BVerfGG § 13(7).

Basic Law.[10]

*D. Protection of Human Rights*

The fourth facet is the protection of human rights. The Basic Law has provided for this purpose a special instrument, the constitutional complaint.[11] Any person who claims that one of his basic rights has been violated by public authority may file a complaint of unconstitutionality. As a rule, the FCC may be seized of such a matter only after all legal remedies have been exhausted.

Review of constitutional complaints forms the major part of the Court's activity. In recent years there have been 2500 to 3000 constitutional complaints yearly, of which less than two per cent have been successful. The numbers reflect the public's growing consciousness of human rights violations as well as their high esteem for and confidence in our Constitutional Court. Furthermore, one must take into account that the decisions of the Court on matters of constitutional complaints have an importance far exceeding the individual cases. They give signals to the Executive, the Legislature and the Judiciary and determine their future activities.

I should also like to point out that the Federal Constitutional Court may, either *ex officio* or upon application, issue interim orders if this is urgently necessary to prevent any serious harm or injury, the imminent use of force, or on any other important ground for the public good.[12] Cases of this nature occur frequently within the scope of constitutional complaints, for instance in disputes over family affairs or as concerns the law relating to aliens, but they also turn up in the abstract sense when the Court has to determine whether legislation is consistent with the Constitution. One such instance was the interim order applied for by the Bavarian government in 1972 in an attempt to prevent the entry into force of the Treaty on Basic Relations between the Federal Republic of Germany and the German Democratic Republic.[13]

Two spectacular applications for interim orders were submitted in 1977 during the Schleyer kidnapping affair but were rejected by the Court. As you may recall, Hanns Martin Schleyer, Chairman of the German Employers' Association, was abducted by terrorists in September 1977. The kidnappers demanded the release

10. GRUNDGESETZ art. 93, par. 1(1); BVerfGG § 13(5).
11. GRUNDGESETZ art. 93, par. 1(4a); BVerfGG § 13(8a).
12. BVerfGG § 32.
13. Decision of June 4, 1973, Bundesverfassungsgericht, 35 BVerfGE 193 (order not granted).

of 11 terrorists who were serving sentence or being held in custody pending trial. They were able to redouble their pressure on the authorities as a result of the simultaneous hijacking of a Lufthansa aircraft, whose crew and passengers were held hostage but were subsequently freed by force in Mogadishu. Because of the attempted blackmail by the Schleyer kidnappers and the danger of conspiratory activities by terrorists in collusion with their lawyers, Parliament authorized the Government, through the Land Minister of Justice, to suspend contacts among the terrorists in prison and between them and persons outside. This also included written and oral communication with defense counsel. This "Anti-contact Act" was challenged by defending lawyers who sought interim orders. The Federal Constitutional Court, weighing the merits of both arguments, concluded that there was no middle course between the unhampered defense of the accused and the necessity to sever contact between them and counsel. It considered that there was reason to suspect that an unchecked flow of information from the prison inmates to persons outside via their lawyers might obstruct the efforts to solve the kidnapping case and endanger the lives of other persons. The Second Senate of the Federal Constitutional Court therefore refused to issue an interim order.[14]

Shortly afterwards the First Senate was asked to issue such an order by Herr Schleyer's son. He applied on the ground that the Government's refusal to accept the kidnappers' demands prejudiced the protection of human life which is guaranteed by the Basic Law. The State, he said, could not maintain that it was protecting a right of higher value because no right could be of higher value than life itself. The Senate rejected the application on the ground that although the State was in principle obliged to protect human life it was up to the organs of the State to decide how they should effectively meet that obligation, choosing the most expedient means.[15] The Court held that the Basic Law made it incumbent on the State to protect not only the individual but the community as a whole, that the competent authorities had to be in a position to react appropriately to the circumstances of the individual case. Nor, the argument ran, did the Constitution stipulate that the authorities be required to adopt a specific means because otherwise the State's reaction in a given situation would be predictable for terrorists. The Court therefore emphasized that it

14. Decision of Oct. 4, 1977, Bundesverfassungsgericht, 46 BVerfGE 1.
15. Judgement of Oct. 16, 1977, Bundesverfassungsgericht, 46 BVerfGE 160.

could not prescribe the decision the authorities had to take.

*E. Additional Competences of the Court*

One of the further competences of the Federal Constitutional Court which ought to be mentioned here is that it can declare political parties to be unconstitutional.[16] Thus, pursuant to applications filed by the Federal Government, the FCC declared two parties unconstitutional: in 1952 the neo-nazi Socialist Reich Party[17] and in 1956 the Communist Party.[18] Since that time the question of applying for a declaration of unconstitutionality in respect of the right-wing extremist National Democratic Party and the KPD, the Communist Party, has played a certain role in German politics but it has diminished in the course of time as the polls did not evince a greater fear for our democracy through the existence of these small parties.

*F. An Example: The Ruling on the Co-Determination Act*

Having explained some of the functions and competences of the FCC, I would like to add a few remarks on the Court's ruling on the German Co-determination Act last year.[19] I know that American business circles have expressed scepticism whether German co-determination would work in practice. I cannot dwell on this aspect here but would like to explain the Court's reasoning.

Some 20 companies and employers' associations had filed a constitutional complaint. They argued that the Co-determination Act of May 4, 1976, violated the shareholders' right of private property, the right to freely choose one's profession, and the freedom of collective bargaining between the two sides of industry.

Essentially, the Court held that the Co-determination Act did not yet establish "full parity" of owner and labor representatives on the Board of Directors as the complainants had claimed. It found that the owner side falling within the scope of the law still exercised a little more influence within the corporate structure of an enterprise falling under the Co-determination Act. The Court held that the voting provisions allowing the chairman to cast a vote in cases of deadlock favored the ownership side, giving them a small "overparity". The central argument of the ruling perhaps is

16. GRUNDGESETZ art. 21, par. 2; BVerfGG § 13(2).
17. Judgement of Oct. 23, 1952, Bundesverfassungsgericht, 2 BVerfGE 1.
18. Judgement of Aug. 17, 1956, Bundesverfassungsgericht, 5 BVerfGE 85.
19. Judgement of Mar. 1, 1979, Bundesverfassungsgericht, 50 BVerfGE 290.

the statement that while fundamental rights originally and actually are individual rights of the citizen in relation to the State, recognition is at the same time given to the "objective value character" of fundamental rights. Yet these value decisions do not form — as the Court ruled unanimously — an objective order of values which would prescribe for the legislature or prohibit a certain kind of socio-economic legal order.

This does not imply the complete neutrality of the constitution towards the economic order — as has often been misunderstood since one of the Court's initial decisions — but warrants considerable judicial self-restraint on the part of the constitutional judge towards legislative acts of this kind. Another legitimate reason for abstention in this field was the uncertainty as to how the new Co-determination Act would work in practice. So if the legislative prognosis seems to be reasonable there is no legitimate ground for overruling the democratic decision of Parliament.

I myself wish to exercise "judicial self-restraint" here by avoiding a prediction as to whether future co-determination legislation requiring "full parity" would be constitutional within the reasoning of this decision. In any case, there is no doubt that the "co-determination decision" of 1979 eased the social conflict between enterprise and labor. This is an example of the integrative function of constitutional jurisdiction.

## III. The Role of Constitutional Review in a Democratic Society

As mentioned already, the fundamental aspects of constitutional review are — from the point of view of legal policy — still under discussion. Some controversial judgements of the Court, like the abortion case, were echoed by adverse criticism in the public press tending to question the justification of constitutional review against the background of a democratic society. Should eight judges really have the power to declare null and void a law which was enacted by a democratically and directly elected parliament? Different countries and peoples have, in the course of time, answered this question differently. Today we are witness to an extension of the idea of constitutional jurisdiction. The new Spanish constitution of 1978 has provided for a strong constitutional jurisdiction clearly based on the German model with the competences I mentioned earlier on.

The fundamental decision of our "founding fathers" in favor of a constitutional jurisdiction may well be explained by our historical experience. The Basic Law tried to avoid past faults and to learn not only from history — if ever possible — but from our own constitutional history. It did so first by means of Art. 79 para. 3, which declares inadmissible any amendments of the Basic Law affecting the division of the Federation into Laender, the participation, in principle, of the Laender in legislation, or the basic principles laid down in Articles 1 and 20. Article 1 deals with the protection of human dignity, declares human rights to be inviolable and inalienable and obliges the Legislature, the Executive and the Judiciary to respect the basic rights. Article 20 characterizes the Federal Republic of Germany as a democratic and social federal state, and affirms the separation of powers system. None of these principles can be altered or abolished by legal proceedings, not even by a unanimous vote of parliament. It did so secondly by creating a strong constitutional jurisdiction to defend the constitutional order. In modern parliamentary systems the majority of parliament generally supports the government and is no counter-part, not an instrument of control. The controlling function is exercised by the opposition, but this is the political minority. The constitutional jurisdiction should not play the role of the opposition, but in a very specific way its duty is to protect the minority. From this point of view, the criticism that the constitutional courts are a non-democratic power will carry no conviction as long as the majority of today must be prepared to be the minority of tomorrow; so, in the long run, the majority, too, is dependent upon the protection of the constitutional courts.

### A. *Restraints on Constitutional Jurisdiction*

Nevertheless, the FCC — though "guardian of the constitution" — must also be seen against the background of this constitution, must fit in the system of the separation of powers. James Iredell, later Justice at the Marshall Court, wrote in 1787 about the power of the courts to review laws: "That such a power in the judge may be abused is very certain; that it will be, is not very probable." Whence does this confidence come?

This is the question of restraints on constitutional jurisdiction. In this sense, on the occasion of the 25th anniversary of the FCC, I attributed to the Court "auctoritas" not "potestas". Let me give some explanation of this.

One reason is expressed in the famous words of Alexander Hamilton: "The judiciary . . . has no influence over either the sword or the purse; no direction either of the strength or of the wealth of the society; and can take no active resolution whatever." This is true as well of the FCC. Its decisions must be executed by State organs, whose acts have perhaps been held unconstitutional and void by those very decisions. The Court has no executive power of its own; it may give orders but they must be obeyed voluntarily. Here a very specific feature of a free and democratic society becomes distinct: it is the mixture of trust and distrust of the people's institutions. The whole system of separation of powers is founded on the distrust and the knowledge that power corrupts and absolute power corrupts absolutely (Lord Acton). On the other side we all know that an atmosphere of distrust alone kills liberty. A free society needs confidence as much as control.

Another reason is contained in the words of Alexander Hamilton, too. The Court cannot act on its own initiative; it only becomes active when it receives an impulse from outside and if the given procedure is observed. If nobody seizes the Court of a matter, it cannot decide.

A further restraint on the power of the FCC is that the judges are elected and appointed for a 12-year term and cannot be reelected. Even if in Germany the Court itself as an institution is placed in the foreground and not so much the individual judges, it is evident that the status of the judges is of great importance. A job as responsible and meaningful as that of a judge of the FCC is rightly limited in time.

A fourth restraint on the FCC follows from the knowledge that nobody can be sure to have found the true law. This is another essential of a free society: Nobody holds the truth. Of course, cases must be decided; this is done, however, not in certainty but only in a serious attempt to get a little closer to truth and justice. Therefore, the decisions of the Court (as any government action) are and must be open to criticism from the public as well as from the legal profession. The decisions must be convincing by their motives. The uncertainty of being right is not at all hidden. So the Court is not prevented from overruling its previous decisions. Furthermore, for a number of years now the judges have had the right to dissent from the majority decision and to adhere to a separate opinion. This also reveals that the case in question may very well be disputed and there is no simple yes or no answer.

All this leads the judge to an attitude which can be termed judicial self-restraint. Judicial self-restraint perhaps is the essential virtue of a constitutional judge. I can quote here Justice Stone: "[T]he only check upon our own exercise of power is our own sense of self-restraint."[20] Certainly, "judicial self-restraint" does not mean that the Court itself could limit its functions and powers; it has to fulfill its task. On the other hand the Court is, of course, forbidden to expand its functions and powers, but this is nothing other than the ordinary respect of one power for the other powers in a system of separation of powers. The reason for this may be that the FCC is the authentic interpreter of the Constitution; in interpreting the Basic Law the Court delineates the competences of the other powers and its own. The admonition to exercise self-restraint requires the Court to remain aware of the consequences of its work and of its responsibility of defining the Constitution which marks and determines the way of State and People.

## IV. Conclusion

The FCC takes an essential part in the task of constituting the State as a whole. The reason for the integrating effect of the Court's decisions is twofold.

It stems first of all from the role of the law and particularly of the Constitution itself in a free and democratic society. The law is, on the one side, the "instrument of government," that is, it can be used as an instrument to achieve the aims of the government majority. Law always has this functional character. But it does not exhaust itself in this function. Law also fixes the limits and draws the boundaries of all State action. It does not draw these boundaries only in a procedural sense. One cannot deny the great importance of the procedural aspect of the law. Law must even, perhaps, for the most part be understood from this point of view. But in my opinion, there is no doubt that law also contains and creates material values. To secure and to further these legally protected values is the duty of all State organs, and, especially, of the Constitutional Court.

This theoretical approach is highly disputed. It is said one would overburden the small ship — as the Basic Law is figuratively seen — by reading out of the Constitution an order of material values. Is it really possible for a constitution to anticipate the whole intellectual and political evolution of a nation?

It is true that the constitution of a free democracy must not aim to regulate all political issues down to the last detail; if it did it would itself be totalitarian. But this does not mean that material values enshrined in the Constitution must be absent altogether.

20. United States v. Butler, 297 U.S. 1, 79 (1935) (Stone, J.) (dissenting opinion).

History shows us that the absence of binding values or even value relativism tends to lead to a rule of majority which is not controlled by any material provisions but has to adapt only to some rules of procedure which may be changed if the majority is big enough. For such a majority, human rights might lose their essence and be "not more than admonitions of moderation" (Learned Hand). A regulating and just law cannot confine itself to offering but the rules of the game. Its function must be to make the integration process possible, to establish the basis for the development of political life. Not the several steps of this evolution are prescribed but the direction and the aim of the evolution is indicated. It is the main task of the FCC to elucidate this process. By its jurisprudence the Court has to formulate and reformulate the national consensus which enables majority and minority to live together or to approach each other on a common basis.

# [14]



## COMMENT

# THE MACHINERY OF LAW ADMINISTRATION IN FRANCE

GERALD L. KOCK †

For more than twenty years the classic article by Deák and Rheinstein has provided a much needed summary of the "machinery of law administration in France." [1] This period has, however, been a time of turmoil. There have been many changes, even some improvements, in the legal order. The machinery for dealing with law problems, in France as in the rest of the world, has been modified to meet the challenges of a new age.[2] But change is not new, nor has it run its full course for France. She has, in fact, only now begun a period of drastic change, a period of convalescence after a strong purgative taken to cure a sorely ill constitutional order.

President DeGaulle, during his interim premiership,[3] pursued with vigor the reform of France's law machinery which had begun with the promulgation of the first parts of the new Code of Penal Procedure.[4] In December 1958, there were issued in quick succession a series of decrees designed to make the courts more uniform throughout the country and to take account of the changes that have occurred over the years in the flow of cases that must be dealt with in the various courts. It is the purpose of this Comment to serve as a *mise à jour*, so to speak, of the Deák-Rheinstein exposition of 1936.

The judicial structure of France is perhaps most different from that to which we in the common-law system are accustomed in the existence of what amounts to two judicial systems working side by side. The picture is not that of a few specialized courts set outside the regular court structure but of a separate system of courts for trial, appeal, and review of cases which, because of the interests involved, are not within the jurisdiction of the ordinary courts. The French courts are, then, of two kinds: the ordinary, or judicial, courts and the ad-

† Teaching Associate in Law, Indiana University. J.D., 1958, University of Chicago.

1 Deák & Rheinstein, *The Machinery of Law Administration in France and Germany*, 84 U. PA. L. REV. 846 (1936).

2 Many of these changes have been treated in DAVID & DEVRIES, THE FRENCH LEGAL SYSTEM (1958).

3 June to December, 1958.

4 Promulgated in Law 57-1426 of Dec. 31, 1957, and Ordonnance 58-1296 of Dec. 23, 1958.

ministrative tribunals. Each system is complete in itself[5] and capable of deciding at all stages of litigation cases falling within its subject-matter competence. Because the courts in both systems have general jurisdiction—*i.e.*, are not limited in their functioning to only certain kinds of cases—the question of appropriate jurisdiction is often difficult to answer. Acting as arbiter of jurisdictional disputes between the two court systems there is a special court, the Conflicts Court.[6]

The following discussion will deal first with the judicial courts and then with the administrative tribunals. The Conflicts Court will be discussed with the administrative tribunals, whose jurisdiction it was created to protect. The discussion will progress in each case from the most limited or specialized courts of first instance to the court of review at the pinnacle of the pyramid.

## The Judicial Courts

### *Courts of Limited Jurisdiction*

There are a number of courts with jurisdiction limited to specific classes of cases (*tribunaux d'exception*). Much of what is brought before some of these courts would not be the subject of litigation in common-law countries, but would be left to extra-judicial negotiation or arbitration.

The industrial councils (*conseils des prud'hommes*) serve as courts for the purpose of determining disputes between employers and their employees with regard to wages, working hours, and like matters. They also serve as arbitration or conciliation agents for the settlement of disputes in trade and industry. A *conseil* is set up at the request of the municipal council of the community where one is to be established after approval by a majority of the councils of other communes[7] that are to be within its jurisdiction and by the general council of the department.[8] Its members are elected by the interest groups they repre-

[5] The judicial courts are in a way subject to the administrative system since no civil court can make a binding determination of its own competence *vis à vis* administrative jurisdiction, Laws of 1790 and 1794, whereas the Council of State (*Conseil d'état*), the highest tribunal of the administrative system, does decide what is properly within the jurisdiction of the administrative courts.

[6] See text accompanying notes 95-107 *infra*.

[7] A centralized state, France is divided for administrative purposes into ninety *départments* (not counting three in Algeria) which are again divided into 311 *arrondisements*. Within the *arrondisements* are the towns and villages (*communes*, of which there are 38,000), each with its own mayor and municipal council. When used with reference to Paris, Lyon, and Marseilles, *arrondisement* means a subdivision of the city roughly equivalent to a ward in an American city.

[8] Decree 58-1292 of Dec. 22, 1958. The initiating commune proposes the geographical bounds of authority of the *conseil*. No *maximum* limitation is fixed upon the permissible extent of jurisdiction of an industrial council, but it is provided that no city may contain more than one.

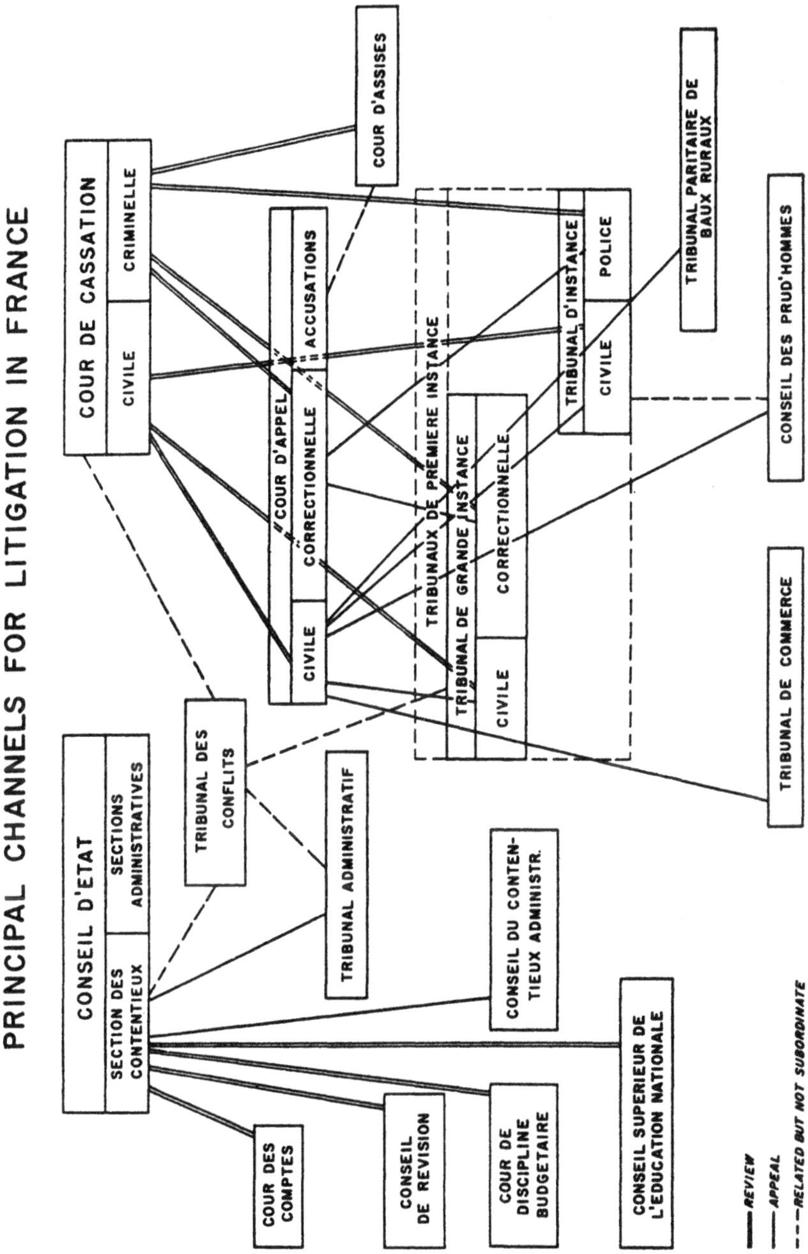
PRINCIPAL CHANNELS FOR LITIGATION IN FRANCE
COUR DE CASSATION
CIVILE
CRIMINELLE
COUR D'ASSISES
COUR D'APPEL
CIVILE
CORRECTIONNELLE
ACCUSATIONS
TRIBUNAUX DE PREMIERE INSTANCE
TRIBUNAL DE GRANDE INSTANCE
CIVILE
CORRECTIONNELLE
TRIBUNAL D'INSTANCE
CIVILE
POLICE
TRIBUNAL PARITAIRE DE BAUX RURAUX
CONSEIL DES PRUD'HOMMES
TRIBUNAL DE COMMERCE
CONSEIL D'ETAT
SECTION DES CONTENTIEUX
SECTIONS ADMINISTRATIVES
TRIBUNAL DES CONFLITS
TRIBUNAL ADMINISTRATIF
CONSEIL DU CONTENTIEUX ADMINISTR.
CONSEIL SUPERIEUR DE L'EDUCATION NATIONALE
COUR DE DISCIPLINE BUDGETAIRE
CONSEIL DE REVISION
COUR DES COMPTES
REVIEW
APPEAL
RELATED BUT NOT SUBORDINATE

sent. They need not be lawyers and they do not become members of the judiciary by virtue of their election. There are at least four members in each council—two representing employers and two representing employees. Decisions are rendered by a simple majority vote. Should a tie result, the dispute is heard again by the council, this time presided over by a judge of the civil court with jurisdiction over minor litigation,[9] who has the deciding vote. If the dispute involves more than the amount for which the *tribunal d'instance* is court of last resort,[10] appeal may be taken by either party to the local court of appeal; [11] otherwise appeal is unavailable. In any case a petition for review of the decision on the ground that the council exceeded its powers [12] may be taken before the Court of Cassation.[13] In localities where no industrial council has been established that jurisdiction may be exercised by the local court having jurisdiction over minor litigation.

There are commercial courts (*tribunaux de commerce*) with jurisdiction over litigation involving sales, manufacture, distribution and transportation of goods within limits set by decree of the government. These courts sit for the *arrondisement* [14] from which members, chosen from among the local businessmen, are elected. Decisions must be rendered by at least three judges, one of whom must be a regular judge [15] of the court. Members, except presidents are elected for two-year terms; presidents, for three-year terms.[16] Decisions of a commercial court are final if the amount involved is not more than 150,000 francs,[17] subject to a limited review by the Court of Cassation.[18] Cases involving larger sums may be appealed to the court of appeal for the jurisdiction. If no commercial court has been established in a district, that jurisdiction is exercised by the local trial court having primary jurisdiction.[19]

[9] *Tribunal d'instance*. See text accompanying notes 39-46 *infra*.

[10] See note 42 *infra* and accompanying text.

[11] See text accompanying notes 57-60 *infra*.

[12] *Pour excès de pouvoir*. This challenge is not one simply of exceeding one's jurisdiction. Any act not supportable in law can be so attacked.

[13] See text accompanying notes 61-66 *infra*.

[14] See note 7 *supra*.

[15] *Juge titulaire* as opposed to *juge suppléant* (alternate).

[16] The new provisions for the election of members of the commercial courts are in Decree 59-94 of Jan. 3, 1959. One can see developing in these provisions a sort of sub-civil service; presidents can be selected only from persons who have been judges for three years and no one can be elected as a judge who has not been an alternate for three years. See also Decree 59-348, art. 2 of Feb. 27, 1959, which provides that the number of judges each court shall have is to be fixed by decree.

[17] Approximately $300. Decree 58-1283, art. 5 of Dec. 22, 1958. The decision is final as to all cross-claims even if the total in litigation exceeds this figure. Also, the parties may agree that the decision will be final no matter how much is involved. CODE DE COMMERCE art. 639 (Fr. 51st ed. Dalloz 1955).

[18] See note 12 *supra*.

[19] Decree 58-1283, art. 1 of Dec. 22, 1958.

Equalization tribunals (*tribunaux paritaires de baux ruraux*) have been created to assure the fairness of rents in the rural districts.[20] They consist of an equal number of landlords and tenants and are presided over by the judge of the lowest civil court.[21] The recorder of the lowest civil court serves as secretary of the rents tribunal. The procedure used is that of the court from which the president and secretary are drawn. Decisions are final within the limits of the final decisions of the *tribunal d'instance*;[22] beyond that amount, or if the amount is indeterminate, appeal may be had to the court of appeal.

The courts having the jurisdiction formerly exercised by the justices of the peace are not courts of general jurisdiction, but because they are now considered as one of the new courts of first instance they will be dealt with below.[23] There are, in addition, juvenile courts[24] and military courts for each of the three armed services.[25]

### *Courts of General Jurisdiction—Trial Courts*

There are three courts of general jurisdiction within the regular judicial system—the courts of primary jurisdiction (*tribunaux de grande instance*), courts of appeal (*cours d'appel*), and a court of review (the *Cour de cassation*).

The courts of the first instance (*tribunaux de première instance*) are a new creation of the Fifth Republic.[26] They consist of two categories—the court of primary jurisdiction (*tribunal de grande instance*), having the jurisdiction and makeup of the former district courts (which courts were also called *tribunaux de première instance* or, more commonly, *tribunaux civils*), and a court having jurisdiction over minor litigation (*tribunal d'instance*), replacing the old cantonal courts and justices of the peace.[27]

The court of primary jurisdiction (*tribunal de grande instance*) has both civil and criminal jurisdiction.[28] The court consists of at

---

20 Decree 58-1293 of Dec. 22, 1958.

21 *Tribunal d'instance.*

22 See notes 40-43 *infra* and accompanying text.

23 See notes 39-46 *infra* and accompanying text.

24 *Tribunaux pour enfants et adolescents.* Ordonnance 58-1274 of Dec. 22, 1958.

25 There is, in theory, a single system of permanent armed forces tribunals, but they are composed of personnel of the service to which the accused belongs. Law of March 9, 1928, as amended by Decree of Sept. 22, 1953.

26 Ordonnance 58-1273, and Decrees 58-1281, -1284, all of Dec. 22, 1958.

27 In most of France, *juges de paix*; in the departments of Bas-Rhin, Haut-Rhin and Moselle, *tribunaux cantonaux.*

28 This represents the concept of "unity of jurisdiction" that is emphasized in the texts on French law and that leads in practice to an interesting and litigation-saving result. Since, in theory at least, it is the same court that hears all kinds of cases, it is possible in France to file in a criminal prosecution a civil claim for damage done by the accused to any claimant in the course of committing the crime.

least three judges [29] and sits in separate chambers, or divisions.[30] When a chamber is sitting to hear a civil case it is referred to as the *tribunal civil*; the criminal chamber is usually called the *tribunal correctionnelle.* The civil chambers have original jurisdiction over all civil litigation that is not limited to a special court or restricted to the administrative tribunals.[31] Their decisions (*jugements*) are final, subject to review by the Court of Cassation,[32] in cases involving personal rights of a value of not more than 150,000 francs [33] and real property producing an annual income of no more than 30,000 francs.[34] All other decisions are subject to an appeal of right to a court of appeal. The criminal chamber has trial jurisdiction over misdemeanors (*délits*).[35] Appeals from its decisions in criminal cases are taken to the local court of appeal.

Each court has attached to it a record office manned by a recorder [36] with, perhaps, one or more assistants.[37] The recorder, or an assistant, must be present at the hearings and sign the record and all judgments and orders. There is also at least one bailiff [38] whose job it is to effect service of necessary papers and to assist the president of the chamber in the performance of his duty to maintain order in the conduct of the trial.

The court established for the trial of minor cases (*tribunal d'instance*), though it does not have general jurisdiction, is also a court of first instance.[39] This is the only court in France that consists of only one judge. He has jurisdiction within his territory to hear minor civil

---

[29] There must be three before the court can decide cases. In the past, because some courts had little business, there were courts (*tribunaux rattachés*) with only one regularly assigned judge (*juge résident*); for a term of court, additional judges had to be brought in from a neighboring court (*tribunal de rattachement*). This practice will not continue. The number of courts has been reduced, and all must have three assigned judges.

[30] As regards the number and geographic distribution of the *tribunaux de grande instance*, see note 57 *infra.*

[31] See text accompanying notes 7-22 *supra* and 83-84 *infra.*

[32] See text accompanying notes 64-67 *infra.*

[33] Approximately $300.

[34] Approximately $60.

[35] Offenses are of three classes: felonies and misdemeanors, in the exclusive power of parliament (CONST. art. 34 (1958)), and *contraventions*, established by decree. For *contraventions* punishment may not exceed two months imprisonment and fine of 200,000 francs. Misdemeanors may be penalized by fine in excess of 200,000 francs and by imprisonment for up to five years; such penalty is said to be "correctional." Felonies are offenses punishable by "afflictive" or "degrading"—as opposed to "correctional"—penalties: death, deportation, more than five years imprisonment. PENAL CODE PÉNAL arts. 1, 6-9 (Fr. 52d ed. Dalloz 1955).

[36] *Greffier.* The office is a *greffe.*

[37] *Commis greffier.*

[38] *Huissier.*

[39] Decree 58-1284, arts. 1-30 of Dec. 22, 1958.

litigation involving not more than 300,000 francs[40] and to try persons charged with petty offenses against police regulations.[41] Decisions in civil cases involving no more than 100,000 or 150,000 francs,[42] depending upon the type of case, and convictions resulting in imprisonment for up to five days or fine of 6,000 francs, or both, are final, subject to review by the Court of Cassation. Appeals from decisions that are not final may be taken to the local court of appeal.[43]

The *tribunal d'instance* rides circuit, an innovation in French law.[44] It sits in several places within most jurisdictions and maintains a record office and recorder in each place where it sits.[45] In addition to his judicial duties the judge has several assigned non-judicial capacities inherited from the former justice of the peace who was conceived of as a general peacemaker and conciliator for the neighborhood within which he lived.[46]

The third regular court in the ordinary judicial system is the assizes court (*cour d'assises*).[47] This court, constituted periodically for the trial of felonies, is the only court in the French system that sits with a jury. The court itself is composed of three judges, one of whom, the president, is from the court of appeal. The other two judges are from the court of appeal or from the court of primary jurisdiction within the same district. The court usually sits for one two-week term during each quarter of the year.[48] While it is established for the trial of per-

[40] Approximately $600. A special provision for claims of several persons joined because based on a common right extends jurisdiction to 500,000 francs (approximately $1,000). Decree 58-1284, art. 15 of Dec. 22, 1958.

[41] *Contraventions de simple police* (usually called *contraventions*) are offenses punishable by no more than two months' imprisonment or fine of 200,000 francs or both. Code of Penal Procedure art. 521. See also note 35 *supra*.

[42] Approximately $200 and $300 respectively. Decree 58-1284, arts. 2, 4 of Dec. 22, 1958.

[43] Appeals from the former *juges de paix* used to be taken to the equivalent of the *tribunal de grande instance*. It is still possible for the Council of State to require by decree that cases within a very limited category be appealed to the *tribunal de grande instance* rather than to the *cour d'appel*. Decree of 58-1284, art. 35 of Dec. 22, 1958.

[44] The *tribunal d'instance* supplants the old *juge de paix*. There was one of the latter in each community as a rule, but the new courts will be less numerous. *Tribunaux d'instance* will hold court in most of the places where there were formerly *juges de paix*.

[45] Ordonnance 58-1273, art. 6 of Dec. 22, 1958. Regarding the total number and regional allocation of these courts, see note 57 *infra*.

[46] The judge, for example, within his jurisdiction presides over family councils and inventories the estates of deceased persons and of persons who are unaccountably absent for a long time.

[47] Code of Penal Procedure art. 231. The *cour d'assises* does not have general jurisdiction, but it is a regularly meeting court and is manned by the regular judiciary.

[48] For the provisions dealing with the composition of the court and the duration of its terms, see Code of Penal Procedure arts. 236-37, 240-53. For the number and geographic distribution of the assizes, see note 57 *infra*.

sons charged with felonies, its jurisdiction is at the same time more and less broad than that description would indicate. The assizes court may assume jurisdiction over only those cases that have been referred to it by the indicting chamber of the local court of appeal or that have been remanded to it by the Court of Cassation.[49] Once the court has received a case, however, whether by reference or remand, it must proceed to complete the trial and decree an appropriate penalty, or an acquittal, even if it decides that the offense charged is not a felony and should not have been sent to an assizes court for trial in the first place.

The jury that forms a part of the assizes court is quite unlike the jury known to common-law countries. The French jury sits more in the capacity of lay judges than as fact finders. There are nine jurors,[50] and if the courtroom is so constructed as to permit it they sit at the bench with the judges. The jurors deliberate and vote with the judges on both the question of guilt and the appropriate penalty.[51] A finding of guilty must be supported by at least eight of the possible twelve votes.[52] Other questions are decided by a simple majority. There is no appeal from the decree [53] of an assizes court, a rule said to be left from the day when the French jury was more like our own.[54] A petition for review of the decision may be pressed before the Court of Cassation, however.

### *Appeal and Review*

There is in France no single court at the summit of the judicial system with jurisdiction to hear appeals from and to review decisions of lower courts.[55] French law recognizes one *appeal* as a matter of right, except for small cases and decisions of the assizes courts. This appeal brings the whole record before the appellate court and amounts

---

[49] The French is *renvoi* in either event.

[50] CODE OF PENAL PROCEDURE art. 296. There were twelve from the time the English jury was copied (1791) until 1941; six from 1941 to 1945; seven from 1945 to 1958.

[51] This arrangement has been given the name *échèvinage*, though the label is not wholly accurate.

[52] CODE OF PENAL PROCEDURE art. 359. Since there are only three judges this means, of course, that a conviction must be supported by a majority of the jurors.

[53] *Arrêt*. CODE OF PENAL PROCEDURE art. 365.

[54] The French adopted both the grand and petit juries from England in 1791. In 1808 the grand jury was discontinued, but the trial jury was maintained until 1932 when the present system was adopted. For an interesting discussion of the French, English, and Scottish juries see Brethe de la Gressaye's note 13 to book VI of MONTESQUIEUX, DE L'ESPRIT DES LOIS (1950).

[55] This is true only for the regular judicial system. In the administrative court system the *Conseil d'état* does do both. See text accompanying note 86 *infra*.

to a hearing *de novo*.[56] In the event that the trial court is reversed the appellate court enters a final judgment. A case is never remanded for a new trial or for other further action by the trial court.

A *reviewing* court, on the other hand, has no authority to consider questions of fact or evidence. The record is closed, and all that remains is whether or not the questions of law discussed in the petition for review were correctly decided below. The reviewing court, if it grants a hearing and decides in favor of the petitioner, can only remand the case for a correct treatment below. A reviewing court never finally decides the case. That is done after remand.

The courts of appeal (*cours d'appel*) hear appeals from the lower courts within their jurisdiction and decide on remand cases in which the Court of Cassation has reversed the decision of another court of appeal.[57] The court consists of a president of the court, a president for each chamber and other judges as required to complete the court.[58] Judges who do not preside over a chamber are called councillors.

The court is divided into at least four chambers. There must be a chamber to hear criminal appeals from the courts of first instance (*chambre correctionnelle*) and another to serve as an indicting chamber.[59] In 1958 a social chamber was created to hear specialized civil cases.[60] And there must, of course, be one or more civil chambers to hear civil appeals from the lower courts. When the court is hearing a case that has been remanded to it by the Court of Cassation it must

[56] This appeal of right, as we might call it, is called by the French a double degree of jurisdiction (*double degré de juridiction*), indicating that they conceive of it as a right to a second trial before different judges, not, as we usually think of an appeal, simply an examination of specific alleged errors.

[57] CODE OF PENAL PROCEDURE arts. 496-520; Ordonnance 58-1273, and Decrees 58-1281, -1284, -1286 of Dec. 22, 1958.

There are twenty-seven courts of appeal each having jurisdiction over from one to seven departments. Each department has at least one *tribunal de grande instance* (in the principal city) but may have as many as seven, depending on total population, distribution of population, and difficulty of communication within the department. Thirty-nine departments have two; seventeen have three; one has four; and one has seven. There are 172 courts in all. There is at least one *tribunal d'instance* in each *arrondisement*, but there are in all 455 of these courts since fifty *arrondisements* have several. Assizes are held in each department. In departments where a court of appeal has its seat the assize court usually sits in the same city as does the court of appeal. The geographical distribution of the courts is important to litigants because of venue requirements. The privilege is waived if not timely raised, but a defendant usually may demand that he be pursued only in the courts of the area where he is domiciled, or has committed an offense, or is to perform his contract.

[58] There must be at least two.

[59] The indicting chamber (*chambre d'accusations*) hears appeals from the orders of investigating magistrates (*juges d'instruction*), decides on extradition questions, exercises disciplinary control over the judicial police, and on the basis of the record made by the investigating magistrate decides whether trial for a felony is appropriate. It is the decree (*arrêt de renvoi*) transferring his case to the assizes court that changes one subject to charges (*l'inculpé*) into an accused (*l'accusé*).

[60] The new social chamber hears appeals from cases involving social security, labor contracts, and the application of social welfare laws.

sit in solemn session (*audience solennelle, "en robes rouges"*), for which at least four judges and a president must sit. Decrees (*arrêts*) of the court of appeal are final adjudications and supplant the decision of the trial court. They are subject to review by the Court of Cassation. In addition, the courts of appeal have original jurisdiction to try civil actions brought against judges of the industrial councils, the courts of first instance, individual judges of those courts, and individual judges of the courts of appeal for recovery of damages caused by intentional unlawful acts committed in the performance of judicial duties. This unusual form of action, carried into the French from the Roman law, is the *prise à partie*.

At the head of the French judicial system is found the Court of Cassation (*Cour de cassation*).[61] This Court is a court of review, as that term is explained above. Its purpose is twofold: to keep the law pure by assuring that the courts below do not diverge in their decisions from the law as it is found in the codes and other legislative acts, and—as a part of the same task—to secure the uniformity of the law throughout the area in which it is applicable.[62]

The Court of Cassation consists of the president, five chamber presidents and sixty-three councillors. They sit in divisions as do the lower courts. There are a criminal chamber and four civil chambers.[63] The councillors assigned to civil cases rotate among the various chambers but those on the criminal side are permanently assigned.

Cases come to the Court of Cassation by way of petition for review. Petitions in criminal cases go directly to the criminal chamber where they are ruled upon. Petitions for review of civil cases go first to the first civil section,[64] which may either send the request to another, specialized chamber or itself decide it. If after a hearing the Court

---

[61] Law of July 23, 1947, as amended by Law of July 21, 1952. The *Cour de cassation* sits only in Paris.

[62] To aid the Court, sitting in sections, to maintain uniformity in its decisions a central index of decisions (*fichier central*) was created in 1947. Law of July 23, 1947, art. 10. From this beginning has developed the *Service de documentation et d'études de la Cour de cassation* manned by twenty persons of magisterial rank. See Decree 58-1281, art. 19 of Dec. 22, 1958. In addition, the first president may call into being an *assemblée plenière* composed of at least fifteen of the senior members of the Court when he feels it is necessary in order to avoid contrariety of decisions. This group meets also to hear particularly difficult cases and cases in which another section or chamber has arrived at a tied vote. See Law 47-1366, art. 41 of July 23, 1947.

[63] The civil chamber works as four specialized sections. A not unusual division of its work load would be: first section, general supervision and routing of cases; second section, divorce, tort liability, civil procedure and social security; third section, commercial problems; fourth section, labor law and land rents.

[64] Formerly (1795-1947) there was a chamber (*chambre des requêtes*) that did nothing but serve as a screening device for civil cases. It would reject the obviously unmeritorious petitions and forward the others to the civil chamber. The change was made in an attempt to speed up the work of the Court, but it seems not to have done so.

finds that the lower court correctly applied the law, it dismisses the petition (*rejet de pourvoi*) and the judgment or decree rendered below becomes final. Should the Court decide that the lower court erred, it sets aside the decision (*casse le jugement*) and remands (*renvoi*) the case to another court of the same rank as that from which it came.[65] The Court of Cassation is free to send a case to any court of the appropriate rank except that from which it came or one that has had the same case before, in the event it is the second time the case has been remanded.[66]

It has been said that the Court of Cassation judges decisions, not suits. In a very real sense this is true, for cases may be brought before it only on the ground that a law has been violated or incorrectly applied or that a court has exceeded its authority. Nothing may be considered that has not been alleged in the original petition for review, and the decision of the Court can only be to send the case back to another court to be considered.[67] No evidence may be looked to, and the findings of fact below may not be disturbed by the Court of Cassation even if there is no evidence in the record to support them.

The court to which the Court of Cassation remands a case (*cour de renvoi*) is not bound to follow the higher Court.[68] If, however, the court of remand does not follow the Court of Cassation and on review that Court, all chambers sitting together,[69] again sets the decision aside and remands the case for the same reasons, the second court to

[65] Of course, if the decision is reversed on grounds that the court below did not have jurisdiction the remand will be to a court that does have jurisdiction.

[66] The case may be remanded to the same court if the reversal does not imply any fault in those judges. This is not the usual case, however.

[67] There is provision as well for a rare kind of case in which there remains nothing to be decided on the merits. In that event the Court may reverse without remanding the case (*cassation sans renvoi*). See also note 66 *supra*.

[68] In practice, of course, they usually do so. As an excellent example to the contrary there is the recent case involving Pierre Bonnard's unsold paintings. The civil court in Paris decided that all works of art are community property. [1952] Dalloz Jurisprudence 390. The court of appeals in Paris decided that the rule held only for completed works, that sketches and unfinished canvases are not included. [1953] Dalloz Jurisprudence 405. On review the Court of Cassation decided that the trial court, not the court of appeal, had been right and remanded the case to the court of appeal in Orleans. On remand, the court in Orleans ruled that no such work of art is community property unless released for sale or exhibition before termination of the community. [1959] Dalloz Jurisprudence 440.

The source of this recognized freedom of the *cour de renvoi* may perhaps be located in the broad principle of article 5 of the Civil Code providing that in the decision of cases judges shall not hand down general, regulatory decisions. While the text will not extend so far as Dean Pound would have it, POUND, SPIRIT OF THE COMMON LAW 180 (1921), it has been taken to mean that, in the absence of statutory dictate, no judge is bound to follow another judge's opinion or even an earlier ruling he has himself made. This freedom has been curtailed by statutes govering the second remand of cases by the *Cour de cassation*. Law of July 23, 1947, art. 60; CODE OF PENAL PROCEDURE art. 619.

[69] *Toutes chambres réunies* (at least thirty-five members). Law of July 23, 1947, arts. 58-60.

which it is remanded is bound to enter a decision in conformity with the decision of the Court of Cassation.

The Court has original jurisdiction to hear *prise à partie* actions against courts of appeal, assizes courts and individual members of the Court of Cassation. No such action may be had against the Court of Cassation as a whole. For hearings on these actions, as for the second review of a case in which its first decision has not been followed on remand, all chambers of the Court must sit as a single bench. In no other cases is this necessary.

## Administrative Courts

It is in the administrative courts that the difference between the French and our own legal system is generally thought to be greatest. Disputes with the government that must, in the United States, be pursued by way of claims filed with the department of government concerned [70] are, in France, litigated before courts established for that purpose. The French system began not unlike our own. Claims were presented to the prefect (*préfet*) charged with supervising governmental interests in the department, a subdivision roughly equivalent to our states but having no powers of self-government.[71] Later, the prefect was given a council to assist in the adjudication of these claims.[72] In 1953 the prefectural councils were replaced with administrative tribunals, which have been given in addition to the prefect's claim adjusting powers a general jurisdiction that was earlier exercised in the administrative system only by the Council of State (*Conseil d'état*).[73]

### *Courts of Limited Jurisdiction*

While the administrative tribunals (*tribunaux administratifs*) are the center of the administrative system, there are a number of specialized tribunals established for particular cases.

The councils for administrative litigation (*conseils du contentieux administratifs*) serve for the overseas territories [74] the same function as that served for the national government by the administrative tri-

[70] Or, in some instances as regards the national government, actions brought in the court of claims or under special grants of jurisdiction in the federal district courts.

[71] See note 7 *supra*.

[72] The *conseils de préfecture* were created by the Law of Feb. 18, 1801. Until 1926 the jurisdiction of a *conseil* was strictly departmental. In 1926 their number was reduced and their jurisdiction became inter-departmental. Laws of Sept. 6 and 26, 1926. At the same time their subject-matter jurisdiction was somewhat expanded.

[73] Decree 53-934 of Sept. 30, 1953.

[74] Antarctic Territories, Comoro Archipelago, Dahomey, French Equitorial Africa, Ivory Coast, Madagascar, Mauritania, New Caledonia, Niger, Oceania, St. Pierre and Miquelon, Senegal, Somaliland, Sudan and Upper Volta.

bunals.[75] These local councils have general jurisdiction, but are organized differently from territory to territory. Their decisions may be appealed to the Council of State.

The Court of Accounts (*Cour des comptes*) is charged with assuring the regularity of the accounts of all officers accountable to the government.[76] Members of the court are chosen by competition and may not be removed from office. This is not a court in the usual sense, since no claim or dispute is necessary to justify an exercise of jurisdiction by it. Its function is really that of a supervisory agency. A review of its decisions may be had before the Council of State.

To ensure that public officials conduct their offices within the prescriptions of their budgets, there was created in 1948 a Court of Budgetary Discipline (*Cour de discipline budgétaire*) composed of six members appointed for three years and presided over by the first president of the Court of Accounts.[77] The court has authority to adjudge fines against public officials guilty of budgetary irregularities. Decisions of the court are subject to review by the Council of State.

The councils of revision (*conseils de révision*), presided over by the departmental prefects, have authority over disputes arising from the requirement of national defense service.[78] It is these courts which adjudicate claims to immunity from national service—on grounds, for example, that one is not of French nationality or that one is not physically capable of serving. Their decisions also are subject to review by the Council of State.

The National Education Council (*Conseil supérieur de l'éducation nationale*) is composed of fourteen high-ranking officers of the Ministry of Education, ten members named by the Minister of Education, fifty members elected by the teaching profession (public schools), and three representatives of the private schools.[79] The council has general supervision over all curricular changes in the schools and, as a court, hears appeals from decisions of and disciplinary action taken by the academic councils and university councils, both of which in addition to their administrative duties have jurisdiction over disciplinary matters and disputes concerning the operation of their schools. Decisions of the Education Council are subject to review by the Council of State.

There are more than forty other administrative jurisdictions and commissions created to settle claims and disputes, but they are limited

[75] Ordonnances of Aug. 21, 1825 and Feb. 9, 1827; Decrees of Sept. 7, 1881 and Jan. 20, 1958.

[76] Laws of Sept. 16, 1807, May 16, 1941, Feb. 2, 1943 and Dec. 31, 1949; Decree of Nov. 22, 1951.

[77] Laws of Sept. 25, 1948 and Aug. 8, 1950.

[78] Laws of March 31, 1928 and Jan. 22, 1931.

[79] Law of May 18, 1946.

in their scope, often coming into existence only when a particular case arises and then dissolving again for years.

*Courts of General Jurisdiction*

Thirty-one administrative tribunals (*tribunaux administratifs*) have been established for the adjudication of administrative disputes.[80] Each tribunal is composed of a president and three or four councillors, one of whom serves as government commissioner.[81] The administrative tribunals can sit only if there are three members present. Should a member of the tribunal be disqualified or absent, the vacancy may be filled either from the membership of a neighboring tribunal or from among local attorneys (*avocats*). It is not usually considered desirable to use local attorneys for this purpose because they are inclined to apply the rules of the private law with which they work in the ordinary courts rather than the public law rules evolved for the administrative system.

The competence of the administrative tribunals extends to any subject matter that may be brought before them,[82] since they are courts of general jurisdiction. Their jurisdiction is limited, however, with regard to the parties whose disputes they may consider. Litigation before the administrative tribunals must involve the rights or obligations of one of the administrative persons (*personnes administratives*)—the state, communes, departments, public establishments[83] or professional orders.[84]

*Appeal and Review*

Decisions of the administrative tribunals are open to appeal to the Council of State.[85] That body's place at the summit of the administrative system invites comparison with the Court of Cassation, which

[80] Law of July 22, 1889; Decree of Sept. 30, 1953. There are twenty-four in France, three in Algeria, and one each in Martinique, Guadeloupe, Réunion and Guiana.

[81] In Paris the court has one president, five section presidents, twenty-five councillors and ten government commissioners. The role of a commissioner (*commissaire*) is similar to that played by the public ministry before the regular judicial courts. See text accompanying notes 114-16 *infra*; note 118 *infra*.

[82] Except for those subject matters for which the special *juridictions d'exception* have been created. See notes 74-79 *supra* and accompanying text.

[83] *E.g.*, schools, chambers of commerce, welfare agencies, National Office of Navigation, *l'Électricité de France*.

[84] *E.g.*, The Order of Advocates, The Order of Medical Doctors, The Order of Midwives, The Order of Architects.

Not all litigation involving these various parties goes to the administrative tribunals, only that which involves them as administrative (public) organs. For example, where a prefect is acting as guardian of the property of a minor who is a ward of the state, his duties are prescribed by the civil code, and any litigation growing out of them are private law disputes and must be taken before the civil courts.

[85] Laws of May 24, 1872 and Dec. 18, 1940; Ordonnance of July 31, 1945; Decrees of Dec. 12, 1950, Nov. 19, 1955 and Dec. 27, 1956.

we find at the top of the ordinary judicial system. In fact, the Council of State has much broader powers than has the Court of Cassation, even in its judicial duties. The Council's broader jurisdiction is evident from its power to hear appeals from the administrative tribunals and their equivalents in the overseas territories. It reviews final decisions of administrative commissions and courts just as the Court of Cassation reviews decisions of the judicial tribunals.[86] And in addition to its judicial functions the Council of State has the position indicated by its name—it is an advisory council to the government.[87]

The Council of State has a size and structure as formidable as its varying duties. There are one hundred sixty-six members in all, not counting its titular president, the President of France.[88] There are fifty-eight auditors[89] who read records and prepare reports for the seniors. Next in rank above the auditors are fifty-one masters of requests,[90] then fifty-one councillors of state in regular service.[91] Filling the complement are five section presidents and one vice-president. Provision has been made for renewable one-year appointments for twelve additional councillors (*conseillers en service extraordinaire*) to help keep the Council from falling behind in its work.

86 Until the new reform provisions the *Conseil supérieur de la magistrature*, see note 110 *infra* and accompanying text, was, in effect, simply the *Conseil d'état* sitting in another capacity. This had the interesting result of having the judges of the Court of Cassation subject to review by the *Conseil d'état*.

87 Created by Napoleon in 1799 (Constitution of 22 Frimaire an VIII) as a sort of privy council, it was to work on the preparation of the civil code and also to serve as legal advisor. In the latter capacity it was called upon to recommend to the First Consul the action to be taken by him, as chief of state, on claims for redress from official action. From this beginning the present system of administrative tribunals has grown. While the fortunes of the Council of State have not been uniformly good in all periods, it has in general become increasingly important over the years. An excellent demonstration of its current prestige is the provision that some legislative pronouncements cannot be validly issued without the prior advice of the Council of State. CONST. arts. 37-39, 92 (1958).

88 Or the Minister of Justice as his deputy.

89 *Auditeurs.* The auditorship was created as an apprenticeship during which candidates for the bench were to "listen and learn," but work was soon found for them.

90 *Maîtres de requêtes.*

91 The principal source of judges for the *Conseil d'état* is the National School of Administration (*Ecole nationale de l'administration*). That school was created in 1945, Ordonnance and Decrees of Oct. 9, 1945, to train candidates for the civil service. Students are admitted by competitive examination and must be university graduates unless they already are employed in the government. The lowest ranking members of the *Conseil d'état*, the *auditeurs*, are chosen by competitive examination from among the school's graduates. Three-fourths of the appointments to the next higher grade, *maître de requêtes*, must be chosen from among the auditors. Two-thirds of the councillors, the highest ranking members, must be chosen from among the masters of requests. Most of the members of the *Conseil d'état* are therefore career members holding seats from the time of their graduation from the civil service school until retirement age. The provision permitting appointments of members from outside the ranks at each level above the first enables the government to add to the bench particularly talented men who have not chosen administration as their initial careers. These men are often chosen from the higher levels of the executive departments.

The litigation section of the Council of State is composed of a president, a deputy president, at least twenty-three councillors, seven councillors from administrative sections of the Council and enough auditors and masters of requests to fill the positions of government commissioners [92] and *rapporteurs*.[93] The section is divided into eleven sub-sections with three or four members each. These sections divide the work, some deciding cases and others conducting preliminary hearings (as *organes d'instruction*). For very important cases there is provision for a plenary assembly consisting of the vice-president of the Council of State, the president and deputy of the litigation section, the presidents of the sub-sections, four councillors elected from the administrative sections, and a *rapporteur*. The largest part of the Council's judicial business is made up of appeals from the administrative tribunals, though, as noted above, it also serves as a court of review. In addition, it has original jurisdiction in some cases: reserved to it are challenges to decisions of the President of France or of the Council of Ministers and the invalidation of decrees as unconstitutional or contrary to law.[94]

## The Conflicts Court

Given two systems of courts, both of which have general subject-matter jurisdiction but nonetheless limited competence, there are cases where very difficult jurisdictional questions can arise. If a man should file his claim in a civil court and have it dismissed for want of jurisdiction, then file in the administrative court only to be dismissed again for the same reason, what can he do next? If a man has a claim against a local agency and attempts to invoke the jurisdiction of a civil court where he believes he will be more sympathetically treated, what can the agency do to get the case to an administrative court, where *it* expects greater fairness? The difficulty is compounded inasmuch as the ques-

[92] The function of the commissioners, who appear before the *Conseil d'état* and the administrative tribunals, is similar to that of the public ministry (*le parquet*) for the ordinary courts. See notes 114-16 *infra*.

[93] See note 98 *infra*.

[94] A controversy presenting as its principal question the invalidity of a decree or act of a governmental officer on the ground that it is in *excès de pouvoir* is within the original jurisdiction of the *Conseil d'état* and must be brought there whether it is initiated by a private person or a government official. Decree of Sept. 30, 1953, art. 2. If the controversy arises from an alleged invasion of a contract right by the decree that is attacked, the case must be taken in the first instance before an administrative tribunal, which has the power to declare a decree unconstitutional or contrary to law if such a declaration is appropriate to a contract action otherwise properly before it. Soc. anon. des Grands Travaux de Marseille, Conseil d'état, [1955] Dalloz Jurisprudence 579. The *Conseil d'état* has, during most of its history, declined to consider the question of legality of any act of the Parliament. Examination of the constitutionality of proposed legislation is reserved to the *Conseil Constitutionnel* by title VII of the 1958 Constitution.

tion of conflicting competence cannot be finally decided by any civil court, even the Court of Cassation.[95] To solve these problems there is in France a most extraordinary court, actually more remarkable for what it is not than for what it is.

The Conflicts Court (*Tribunal des conflits*)[96] is one of the strongest benches in France. Yet it is almost never heard of outside professional circles; it hears fewer cases than any other court (though it has existed since 1848), it decided no case on the merits until 1933 and even now only rarely does so, and it is absolutely prohibited from arriving at an independent interpretation of the law governing the merits of a case. Its sole purpose is to keep the two judicial systems from trenching on each other's territory.

Because the Conflicts Court hears so few cases, no separate personnel has been established for it. The Court consists of three councillors from the Court of Cassation and three councillors from the Council of State, elected from their respective Courts for three-year terms. These six men in turn elect two more, usually one councillor each from the Court of Cassation and the Council of State. The president, who casts the tie-breaking vote,[97] is the Minister of Justice. Attached to the Court are public counsel (*ministère public*), two of whom are masters of requests in the Council of State and two of whom are advocates general (*avocats généraux*) before the Court of Cassation. These men serve more as additional *rapporteurs*[98] to the Court than as counsel as they are found with the other courts.[99] The practice has grown up that when the *rapporteur* is from one system, judicial or administrative, the counsel who reports on the case is from the other.

The usual way for a case to be brought to the Conflicts Court is for the prefect of the department concerned to file with the civil court that has taken the case a petition requesting that court to renounce its jurisdiction (*déclinatoire de compétence*) on grounds that jurisdiction properly belongs to the administrative system. If the court does so, there is no conflict; the plaintiff must take his case to the administrative tribunal. Should the court deny the prefect's petition,[100] the prefect must, if he chooses to pursue the matter, issue a decree setting

[95] See note 5 *supra*.

[96] Laws of May 24, 1872 and April 20, 1932.

[97] This has been necessary only six times since 1872.

[98] A *rapporteur* is the councillor assigned to give special attention to the case and report on it to his fellow judges. This is a practice of most of the collegiate courts in France.

[99] Regarding the role of public counsel before the regular judicial courts and the role of government commissioners before the administrative tribunals, see text accompanying notes 114-16 *infra*.

[100] The trial court should suspend the trial for fifteen days to give the prefect time for his next step.

out the conflict, which has the effect of suspending the civil court's jurisdiction to enter a final judgment until the Conflicts Court has ruled on the question. This decree serves to vest jurisdiction of the conflict in the Conflicts Court. That Court must decide the question within three months;[101] if the civil court has not received the decision of the Conflicts Court within four months it may proceed with the case as though a decision in favor of its jurisdiction had been rendered.

If a petitioner with the same claim against the same defendant, in the same capacity, based on the same facts and law is turned away from each system of courts on the theory that the other has jurisdiction, he too may gain help from the Conflicts Court. He then petitions that Court to reverse (invalidate) one of the decisions refusing to exercise jurisdiction. The court whose decision is invalidated must take the case.

The third type of case that can be taken before the Conflicts Court is the only one in which that Court has power to decide a case on the merits. At approximately seven in the evening of September 13, 1922, two automobiles collided at an intersection of national highways numbered 88 and 63. One was a Ford motor car driven by a M. Bornon and the other was a Panhard truck, a government vehicle, operated by military personnel. Senator Rosay (or Rozay), a passenger in the Ford, was badly injured. The Senator filed his claim for damages in the Council of State.[102] That Court acknowledged its jurisdiction but decided that since the civilian driver was at fault[103] it could not make an award. In the civil courts the Senator was told that the military driver was the culprit[104] and that, therefore, no binding judgment could be entered except to relieve M. Bornon from liability. This litigation took until December 1926, and Senator Rosay had nothing for his pains but attorneys' fees. In 1932 the legislature, "astonished that in our day there can still be claims for which no judge can be found,"[105] acted to correct this case. The Law of April 20, 1932 (retroactive to April 1922) gave one in Senator Rosay's position the right within two months

[101] The decisions open to the Court are: (1) that the conflict procedure was not regular in form and that therefore it has no jurisdiction; (2) that it is not appropriate to decide the question since the plaintiff below has abandoned his case; (3) that the civil court is competent and that therefore the *arrêté de conflit* should be invalidated; (4) that the civil court is not competent and that therefore the *arrêté de conflit* should be affirmed.

[102] Until 1953 the administrative tribunals—and the *conseils de préfecture* that preceded them—had no general jurisdiction.

[103] He turned too close to the embankment, swerved, and was on the wrong side of the road.

[104] He was going too fast, failed to signal his coming, and failed to give the right of way to the vehicle on his right.

[105] Note of René Martin, [1932] Dalloz Recueil périodique et critique, pt. 4, p. 273.

after the decisions of the courts of first impression became final (or six months after the effective date of the law) to petition the Conflicts Court for redress. That Court then had jurisdiction to decide the case on the merits. The Court would combine the two records below, gather more information if it thought it was needed, and decide the dispute as among all the parties.[106] In 1957 the regular courts were given jurisdiction over automobile accident cases involving official vehicles.[107] As this was the most fruitful source of litigation taken before the Conflicts Court under the law of 1932, that body of cases will be reduced for the future, but, since it was not limited to automobile cases, the jurisdiction has not itself been abolished.

Decisions of the Conflicts Court have an effect of res judicata and are not subject to appeal or review.

## The Magistrates

### *Judges*

Since the days of the monarchy the group of men qualified as magistrates has been divided into two groups according to their functions. The magistrates of the bench (*de siége*) fill the positions of judges in the regular courts.[108] They are promised independence from the government of the day by the Constitution,[109] and the High Council of the Judiciary (*Conseil supérieur de la magistrature*) has been created[110] to ensure that independence. The council, with its full membership,[111] meets at the call of the President of France to advise on promotions and appointments among the judiciary.[112] With the political members excluded,[113] the council sits as a court to decide upon disciplinary action against judges.

[106] In the Rosay case, the Court ordered that the damages, including the costs of all the fruitless litigation, be paid half and half by the government and M. Bornon.

[107] Law 57-1424 of Dec. 31, 1957.

[108] *Tribunaux de première instance, cour d'appel, Cour de cassation.*

[109] CONST. art. 64.

[110] CONST. arts. 64-65; Ordonnance 58-1271 of Dec. 22, 1958.

[111] The President of France, president; the Minister of Justice, vice president; three members of the Court of Cassation, one of whom must be an advocate general; three judges from the courts of appeal or lower courts; one councillor of state; two persons not belonging to the magistrature and not public officials or practicing advocates. Ordonnance 58-1271, art. 1 of Dec. 22, 1958.

[112] Magistrates, both those who sit as judges (*de siége*) and those who are members of the parquet (*debout*), are appointed from among law graduates who have successfully passed a competitive examination. Once appointed these men all become members of the magistracy, a civil service. Provision is made, in addition, for appointment of men from high executive or administrative office and law faculties who have the required training in law. Candidates appointed after examination start at the lowest courts and progress up the hierarchy by promotion. Some of the highest ranking positions are filled directly by presidential appointment. Ordonnance 58-1270, and Decree 58-1277, both of Dec. 22, 1958.

[113] When only the judicial members are sitting, they meet at the chambers of the Court of Cassation and are presided over by the president of that Court.

### *The Parquet*

The other branch of the magistracy does not enjoy so insulated a position. Subject to more political control, though they may not be appointed or dismissed by the government except through procedures hedged with safeguards,[114] they serve a function quite unknown to the common law where the outcome of litigation is left entirely to the two adverse parties. In France there has been added a third voice, that of the public interest. Attached to all but the minor courts [115] are trained counsel whose duty it is to represent the law and the people; these men constitute the public ministry (*ministère public*, often referred to as the *parquet*).

In criminal cases the public ministry serves a dual role that seems at first sight to destroy the reality of their service as a third party. The public ministry are officers of the state and, as such, are directly involved in the investigation and prosecution of all criminal cases before the court to which they are attached. Yet it appears in practice, as it is intended in theory, that the public ministry is able to retain a large measure of impartiality even though it is the agent of prosecution.[116] The *ministère public* is a hierarchy headed by the Minister of Justice and the members of that hierarchy are subject to the orders of their superiors. The most unique aspect of this position, however, and the mechanism through which the third party in fact enters criminal litigation, is the limit that has been assigned to authority from above. The public minister must brief and submit to the court in writing the position of his superiors, but when it comes time for his oral presentation he is free to present any position that he feels, in good conscience, is the correct one. The French have a phrase that very aptly describes the case: *la plume est serve, la parole est libre.*

The public ministry is represented before the courts of primary jurisdiction by a procurer of the Republic and his deputies, before the courts of appeal by a procurer general and his deputies, and before the Court of Cassation by the Procurer General to the Court of Cassation and two advocates general (*avocats généraux*) for each chamber or section.

### *The Administrative Tribunals*

Councillors of the administrative tribunals outside Paris are divided into two civil service ranks or classes. The second class is se-

[114] See note 112 *supra.*

[115] No representative of the *ministère public* is regularly assigned to the *tribunaux d'instance* or various *tribunaux d'exception.*

[116] It should be noted here that the same representative of the *parquet* who participated in making the record before the examining magistrate does not participate at the trial.

lected from among graduates of the National School of Administration (*École nationale d'administration*) who have been admitted to practice before the litigation bar of the Council of State. Three-fourths of the councillors of the first class are chosen from the councillors of the second class. The remaining one-fourth of the posts are filled by the government as it chooses.[117] Three-fourths of the posts of president of administrative tribunals and councillors of the tribunal of Paris must be chosen from councillors of the first class from outside Paris. The remaining one-fourth are chosen by the government as it wills. The president of the administrative tribunal of Paris may be chosen from section presidents of that court or from members of the Council of State.

Attached to the administrative courts there are government commissioners who serve there the function of the public ministry.[118] These men, though, are appointees of the administrative branch of government; they are not members of the magistracy and have a different course of training and different procedures for appointment and promotion.[119] They are not, of course, assured independence since they are a part of the administration. In fact, however, they are probably subject to no more interference than are their counterparts in the ordinary judicial system. The dual court system has worked as satisfactorily as it has largely because of an absence of political meddling.

117 The government is not, however, completely free. It must comply with certain requirements prescribed for the public administration under the scheme detailed in Decree 53-936 of Sept. 30, 1953 and modified in Decree 54-599 of June 11, 1954.

118 There is no separately organized *parquet* for the administrative system. The duties of the public ministry are fulfilled by regular members of the administrative tribunals and Council of State who serve temporarily as government commissioners.

119 Ordonnance and Decree of July 31, 1945; Decrees of Sept. 30, 1953 and June 11, 1954.

# Part V
# Criminal Courts, Prosecutors and the Inquisitorial Process

# [15]

# Structures of Authority and Comparative Criminal Procedure

**Mirjan Damaška**[†]

TABLE OF CONTENTS



† Professor of Law, University of Pennsylvania.

Structures of Authority and Comparative Criminal Procedure

It is apparent to the most casual observer that a great divide separates the two systems of criminal procedure devised by Western man over the past eight centuries. When the comparatist turns his view from the Continent to the English speaking world, he encounters contrasts so striking that the great diversity existing within each legal culture pales in significance. Unfortunately, however, although it is an easy matter to enumerate countless striking differences between the two systems, it is far more difficult to investigate the extent to which these differences in detail can be traced to more fundamental differences in the way the two systems conceive of the nature of justice, order, and law itself.

The conventional contrast between the two systems is one that emphasizes the adversarial (or accusatorial) aspects of the Anglo-American process, and the nonadversarial (or inquisitorial) character of the continental mode of proceeding. This dichotomy, no matter how refined, fails to account for many important variations between the two systems, especially if one's focus moves away from the trial stage, and if one discards a preoccupation with legal mythology to consider law as it is actually applied.[1]

In this article I shall argue that previously inexplicable differences between the continental and Anglo-American systems can be understood once the conventional trial-centered models are displaced by another set of organizing concepts. These concepts are intended to suggest that divergences in procedural arrangements are, to a considerable extent, related to larger divergences in the conception of the proper organization of authority characteristic of the Continent and the English-speaking world.

To this end I shall offer two models of authority,[2] the hierarchical

1. Notwithstanding the relatively narrow focus of the conventional dichotomy, the rival procedural types springing from it are variously characterized. I have attempted elsewhere to trace diverse ways in which the contrast between adversary and nonadversary procedures can be conceived, and have tried to isolate the opposition most fruitful and illuminating for comparative analysis. This, I believe, is the contrast between the procedural structure of trial as a party contest and as an official inquiry. *See* Damaška, *Evidentiary Barriers to Conviction and Two Models of Criminal Procedure*, 121 U. PA. L. REV. 506, 554-78 (1973). The trial-centeredness of the polarization creates many problems, only one of which resides in the fact that the trial is much less crucial a stage in the continental than in the common law system. One cannot deny, however, that the conventional dichotomy possesses an illuminating force, transcending the trial stage of the criminal process. *See* note 109 *infra*.

2. *See* notes 6, 74 *infra*. As *cognoscenti* will readily notice, my argument is, in a general way, inspired by a number of Weberian concepts and ideas. Indeed, the hierarchical model is in many respects an effort to adapt Weber's bureaucratic model to the particular problems of criminal procedure. The coordinate model, however, has no simple Weberian analogue. This should not be surprising, given the fact that patterns of authority characteristic of the Anglo-American system seem to elude Weberian typologies.

and the coordinate, to illuminate respectively the continental and the Anglo-American systems. For heuristic purposes, each model is premised on a very different view of the nature of justice, without any intention to imply that specific conceptions of justice historically precede or causally determine particular patterns of organizing authority.

To many tastes, the development and use of procedural models is an overly abstract scholarly genre. But consider that comparatists are, in a sense, men without a country; their efforts at comprehensiveness, and their separation from the comfortable and the familiar, necessarily invite a reliance upon the abstract. I concede that there are levels of analysis at which procedural models are generally misleading stereotypes or lifeless clichés. They are also simplifications; but this is precisely their *default de qualité,* indeed their virtue. They are used to liberate us from the tyranny of details, so that we can discern the overall distinguishing attributes of complex phenomena. They will be as useful as our purposes are precise and well-defined. Although my models of authority are mainly provisional markers toward more specific theoretical constructs, I hope to show that even in this crude form they are useful analytic tools, and possibly pedagogical devices.

In an effort to prove the explanatory power of the two models of authority, I have chosen numerous examples.[3] I do not claim, however, that they were randomly selected and just happen to be consistent with my constructs. Rather, I tried to use as illustrations those features common to actual procedures that are of some interest in themselves. Some, notably those concerning the appellate process, have not been previously elucidated from a comparative standpoint. Others, such as prosecutorial discretion, can easily be misunderstood by commentators, because similar phenomena often subtly change in the radically divergent climate of the two legal cultures. Finally, some

It is needless to dwell here on the controversy over whether there is a meaningful difference between ideal types conceived primarily as heuristic devices and models purporting to describe the most general features of empiric phenomena. On Weber's views concerning ideal types, see M. WEBER, ESSAIS SUR LA THÉORIE DE LA SCIENCE 185 (1966); R. DAHRENDORF, CLASS AND CLASS CONFLICT IN INDUSTRIAL SOCIETY 40 (1959). Even if there is an element of "as-if-ness" about some procedural models, they can still be useful as illuminating metaphors; *cf.* A. RAPOPORT, OPERATIONAL PHILOSOPHY 203 (1953).

3. I make no claims that variables in the polarization represented by my models were derived in a rigorous methodological fashion. For a perceptive discussion of dangers lurking in the selection of variables, see Abel, *A Comparative Theory of Dispute Institutions in Society,* 8 LAW & SOC'Y REV. 217, 240-42 (1974).

illustrations, such as different degrees of bureaucratization on judicial panels, are offered as striking contrasts between the systems.

Since all these areas that I discuss bristle with technical details, many of them Lilliputian and deeply bracketed within local contexts, I must occasionally use a very broad brush; misgivings about some rather robust statements will be allayed in the footnotes. Moreover, for brevity's sake, I shall, whenever possible, appeal to the reader's knowledge in an invitation to rearrange into new configurations what is already known.

## I. The Hierarchical Model

### A. *General Characteristics*

#### 1. *The Object of Hierarchy*

The system of values underlying the hierarchical model is characterized by the high premium placed on certainty of decisionmaking. This preference directly affects the tradeoffs with other recognized goals of the criminal justice system, especially the desire to achieve justice in the special circumstances of each individual case. Whenever the consideration of individualized circumstances prevents the conversion of the bases of the particular decision into a general, certain formula, such consideration must be forgone.[4] If one were to seek a deeper motivation for this great emphasis on certainty, the attitudinal keynote of the hierarchical model would probably be located

4. This, of course, is the logic of the model. In actual continental systems certainty is not inflated to an absolute dogma; there are well-recognized situations in which it must yield to competing values. The reconsideration of finally adjudicated cases in the interest of justice offers such a counterpoint. It is true, however, that the continental machinery of criminal justice attributes a significantly greater relative weight to certainty than do some other systems. On this issue, criminal justice mirrors more general characteristics of the continental legal system. *See* J. MERRYMAN, THE CIVIL LAW TRADITION 50-58 (1969). Merryman is critical of the continental emphasis on certainty, which he claims is much too abstract. "Like the queen in chess, it can move in any direction." *Id.* at 50. Note, however, how differently the problem appears in the continental fabric of beliefs. Particularized justice is regarded by a continental lawyer as so elusive and endlessly debatable that he would more readily use the chess metaphor in talking about individualized justice than certainty, which implies the consistent application of a cruder standard. From this perspective it is better to apply across the board a criterion for decision which is just in an average case, than to risk floundering in the sea of particulars; at least one has evenhandedness and uniformity. As we shall see later, the counterassertion of a lawyer in a common law system is that such a position amounts to a quintessentially Procrustean administration of justice.

in the rationalist desire to impose a relatively simple order on the rich complexities of life.

### 2. *The Hierarchical Organization*

Certainty in decisionmaking requires that uniform policies be developed. This is indubitably a centripetal striving, leading quite naturally to the centralization of authority. Thus, incumbents of authority positions have no autonomous powers: authority is only delegated to them and its exercise must be closely watched.

This leads to another derivation from the basic orientations of the hierarchical model. Any structure of authority organized along its lines, except the very small ones, is inexorably driven toward rigorous hierarchical ordering. Three attributes of such ordering are important for my purposes. The first is a precise delineation of the province of each official: he must be pinned down to an exact spot determined in relation to the dominant center. Positions of super- and sub-ordination must be sharply defined and unmistakable, almost in a reenactment of the medieval adage *"nul homme sans seigneur."* All ambiguities in hierarchical relations are viewed as a sorry state of affairs to be quickly remedied; duplicate and overlapping spheres of authority are abhorred. The second attribute of strict ordering is that authority is allocated along a gradient of importance; the higher one climbs the "scalar" of hierarchy, the more comprehensive and important the authority one acquires. Put differently, there is a pronounced inequality among officials on various hierarchical echelons, especially in terms of the kinds of questions delegated to each for decision. The third attribute concerns the interrelationship of officials at the same level, and leads to the separation of office and incumbent: Where an individual official is delegated authority to make a decision, the decision can be changed only by hierarchical superiors. Thus it is binding on all coequal officials, and becomes a decision of an administrative unit. On the other hand, where a decision is collective, it must express the will of the group as a readily identifiable object of superior review. The group is transmogrified into an institution which assumes a life of its own, distinct and apart from the individuals comprising it.

The more freedom officials retain, the more difficult it becomes to achieve certainty and uniformity of decisionmaking. Accordingly, the hierarchical model strives to guide its officials by outcome-determining normative propositions in as many situations as can be anticipated. The more precise the directives contained in these propositions, the better. Directives must be sufficiently rigid that they cannot be altered or evaded when officials applying them feel they lead to undesirable outcomes. To remedy such regrettable situations is not the business of officials in the hierarchical model. Yet the desire for precision and comprehensiveness of normative propositions creates a difficulty: Precise directives covering wide areas of experience can easily conflict. Hence there are strong demands in the hierarchical model for the ordering, systematization and simplification of the normative universe.

What emerges from this brief description is that the use of "official discretion" is viewed with disfavor.[5] Essentially, the exercise of discretion represents a necessary evil in the hierarchical model, an evil to be tolerated so long as more precise guidelines for official action cannot be formulated.

Intimately linked to the "brooding omnipresence" of hierarchical review is the great importance attached to official documentation and bureaucratic techniques. All official decisions must be recorded and traces of all other official activity preserved for possible supervision by higher officials. To facilitate the work of the latter, standardization and formalization of official documents and reports are demanded.

The foregoing features of the hierarchical model influence officials' perceptions of their roles. Consider, for instance, the ideal of official decisionmaking: This process is one in which clear directives are applied to accurately determined facts. The personal views of officials as to the desirability of the outcome of this process must be considered irrelevant. Officials are "servants," members of the service class merely administering normative standards which are supplied to them. If they were permitted to question these standards and depart from them when they deemed it appropriate, the very foundation of the hierarchical model would be shaken; the certainty and predictability of official decisions would be endangered. Since few areas are free from normative intrusion, and since the systematic organiza-

5. Because of the relatively recent debate in Anglo-American legal theory concerning the meaning of discretion, a definitional remark is in order here. As used in this essay the term is not limited to situations of full official freedom from the application of normative standards. It is intended also to cover those situations in which an official is guided by vague standards, making predictability difficult. *Compare* Dworkin, *The Model of Rules*, 35 U. CHI. L. REV. 14, 32-40 (1967), *with* A. DE LAUBADÈRE, TRAITÉ DE DROIT ADMINISTRATIF 261-62 (6th ed. 1973) (discussing the French concept of *pouvoir discrétionnaire*).
Of course, "discretion" appears differently when, rather than used as a point of contrast between systems, its uses (and the shortcomings of those uses) are examined within a single system. *See* Rosett, *Discretion, Severity and Legality in Criminal Justice*, 46 S. CAL. L. REV. 12 (1972).

The Yale Law Journal Vol. 84: 480, 1975

tion of normative criteria achieves a degree of insulation from external considerations, the problems involved in decisionmaking appear essentially as nonpolitical, technical tasks.

What are the most important qualifications for a position in the official hierarchy? An office holder must be a technical expert capable of efficiently applying normative standards, irrespective of what interests are thereby served. A good official is also one who has mastered the bureaucratic skills that permit the smooth functioning of the hierarchical authority structure. Generating bureaucratic minutiae is not regarded as an irksome chore, preventing an office holder from performing more important tasks. Rather, the deft handling of files and similar bureaucratic techniques are accepted as essential skills of proficient officials.

Role expectations are reinforced by a variety of mechanisms within the hierarchical model. Prominent among these mechanisms are the training for official positions, recruitment techniques, and the system of promotions. Entry into a strictly ordered officialdom begins at the lowest rung of the hierarchical ladder. Established people will seldom be willing to begin at the bottom, and thus an entrant will typically be a technically skilled young man who has undergone both systematic instruction in the normative system and practical training in bureaucratic techniques. His aptitude may be tested by entrance examinations. Because there is practically no lateral entry to higher positions, important officials will be those who have ascended the ladder of hierarchy through periodic promotions which depend, at least to some extent, on performance evaluations by one's superiors.

To this cursory sketch of the hierarchical model a few reflections must be added by way of transition from the description of the model to its comparison with actual continental systems.[6] Of course,

6. The proximity of the hierarchical model to a number of Weberian ideas is obvious. The aspirations of the model may be viewed as premises underlying the "logically formal rationality" of legal thought as understood by Weber. The organization of the model incorporates, both explicitly and by implication, many constituent elements of the "bureaucratic" (or "legal") type of domination (*Herrschaft*). *See Max Weber on Economy and Society* xxxi-xxxiv (M. Rheinstein ed. 1954). The most important deviation of the hierarchical model from Weber's bureaucratic authority is the absence in the former of the impersonal, detached style of exercising authority. The comparison of *modern* continental and Anglo-American system on this score is exceedingly complex and of uncertain outcome. *See* note 74 *infra*.

I have neglected to emphasize the impersonality of orders within the hierarchy, for I believe that in all bureaucracies a strong feeling of personal dependence remains. Many will claim that Weber believed that the structure of power determines legal order rather than *vice versa*. Because I sketch the hierarchical model as originating in the quest for certainty and order, I may be interpreted as implying that certain value orientations precede patterns of authority. I make no such claims. *See* note 158 *infra*. For a thoughtful and very lucid recent discussion of the relationship between political structure and legal thinking in Weber's work, see Trubek, *Max Weber on Law and the Rise of Capitalism*, 1972 Wis. L. Rev. 720, 731-35.

discrepancies will exist between the demands of the hierarchical model and the reality of systems which it approximates.

For example, with respect to official decisionmaking, one cannot seriously expect that an authority structure can be devised in which normative propositions completely determine the outcome of decisions. The latter can seldom be complete and inexorable derivations from normative standards. But even if the ideal of decisionmaking in the hierarchical model were both logically and psychologically an impossibility, this hardly implies that decisionmaking is independent of variations in the structure of authority or that the folklore developed by such structures can be relegated to the realm of myths having no operational significance. Indeed, the relative weight of the normative variable in the equation of factors determining the actual official decision seems to change significantly from one type of authority structure to another.

B. *The Hierarchical Model and Continental Reality*

At first the scene on the Continent seems too vast and complex to handle. Important variations can be observed from country to country, and many factors of diverse origin pull actual systems of criminal justice away from the hierarchical model to a degree one cannot easily determine. Nonetheless, a general continental pattern can be discerned from these features: the strong tendency to arrive at uniform policies through the centralization of authority; the rigorously hierarchical ordering of agencies participating in the administration of justice; the preference for precise and rigid normative directives over more flexible standards; and, finally, the great importance accorded official documentation. This general, bureaucratic style of exercising authority tends to be sustained everywhere by chosen methods of training, recruiting and promoting officials. It is around these foci that my presentation will revolve.

1. *Centripetal Decisionmaking*

a. *Police Forces and Public Prosecutors.* It is commonplace that centralization of both the police and the prosecutorial corps remains the dominant structural principle of all continental systems.[7] Central

7. Continental police forces are usually subordinate to the Minister of the Interior. In some countries, there are police forces with no organizational unity. Thus, for instance, some systems assign a segment of the police force to the Ministry of Justice, and it is only this segment which is entitled to participate in the criminal process. The rest of the

authorities issue binding general directives to local officials and can give specific instructions on the handling of a particular case.[8] Even where, sporadically, a degree of local independence is cultivated, local police and prosecutors are far from being important local potentates. Although the federal system of some continental countries may occasionally lead to the absence of organizational unity on the national level, strong forces are at work to coordinate law enforcement among federal units and establish uniform national policies.[9]

b. *The Judiciary*. Turning to the continental judiciary, the picture becomes much more complex because of cross-currents and offsetting tendencies. I shall first consider those characteristics of the judicial organization that accord with the hierarchical model, and that deal with features that seem to deviate from it.

There are in the continental judicial systems[10] two decisive weap-

police remain under the Ministry of the Interior. This is, essentially, the French pattern of division between the "judicial" (law enforcement) and "administrative" (peacekeeping) branches of the police force. *See* G. STEFANI & G. LEVASSEUR, PROCÉDURE PENALE 347-68 (2d ed. 1962). Even in this case, however, police forces are ultimately responsible to an important member of the central government. Attempts have been made to transplant a decentralized pattern of police organization to countries with a different tradition; most of these experiments, however, have failed. *See, e.g.*, Nakahara, *The Japanese Police*, 46 J. CRIM. L.C. & P.S. 583 (1955) (Japanese experience with American ideas).

Continental offices of public prosecution are strictly centralized. For the French *Ministère Public*, see G. STEFANI & G. LEVASSEUR, *supra*, at 460. True, there is the oft-proclaimed freedom of the French prosecutor to deviate from directives of his superiors in his *oral* arguments in court; but this folkloric proclamation has been termed "a joke" in its practical effects. *See* VILLÉRÉ, L'AFFAIRE DE LA SECTION SPECIALE 270 (1973). For the West German system, see Jescheck, *The Discretionary Powers of the Prosecuting Attorney in West Germany*, 18 AM. J. COMP. L. 508, 511 (1970). On the Russian prosecutor, see H. BERMAN, SOVIET CRIMINAL LAW AND PROCEDURE 109-17 (1966). Relatively speaking, Dutch prosecutors have a degree of local independence. *See* Rosett, *Trial and Discretion in Dutch Criminal Justice*, 19 U.C.L.A. L. REV. 353, 364-65 (1972).

8. On the limits of this subordination see Jescheck, *supra* note 7, at 511. *See generally* Vouin, *The Role of the Prosecutor in French Criminal Trials*, 18 AM. J. COMP. L. 483, 487-89 (1970).

9. This is, for example, the case in West Germany, where the police and prosecutorial offices are organized on the state, not federal, level. But a striving for uniformity is nevertheless obvious. *See Richtlinien für das Strafverfahren*, in STRAFPROZESSORDNUNG (T. Kleinknecht ed. 30th ed. 1972). In this connection it must also be noted that, for the sake of uniformity, both substantive and procedural criminal law tends to be heavily "federalized" in all continental federations. The Soviet Union is only an apparent exception, because the constituent republics are bound by federal model legislation in both procedure and substance. Swiss cantons in the field of procedure, and the Yugoslav constituent republics in substantive law, can more properly be viewed as minor deviations from the prevailing continental pattern of "treating" criminal law essentially as a federal matter.

10. In federally structured continental countries there are no parallel hierarchies of federal and state courts. The only federal court is the supreme court, placed at the apex of the national hierarchy of regular courts. In case of a conflict between state supreme courts and the federal supreme court, various mechanisms exist for bringing the issue to the latter for resolution. For an example in West Germany, see E. KERN, STRAFVERFAHRENSRECHT 32 (8th ed. 1967).

Outside the area of our interest, *i.e.*, courts of general jurisdiction which consider criminal cases, the prevailing continental pattern displays a multiplicity of independent judicial hierarchies. Rather than a unified court system for the whole country with a single supreme court, there will be special commercial and administrative courts, perhaps

ons to cope with centrifugal tendencies in administering criminal justice. One is the comprehensive and widely used system of appeals; the other, the comparatively weak forms of lay participation in adjudication.

The comprehensive system of appellate review has a long record on the Continent. Those wishing to trace its history must venture deep into the hidden origins of the modern state, when continental rulers began to build bureaucracies to establish their control over previously independent provincial and local authorities.[11] As befits a system in

even a special constitutional court. The historical reason for this deviation from the ideal of rigid centralization originate in attitudes very close to what I have described, in the administration of criminal justice, as the attitudinal keynote of the hierarchical model. Yet it would be a serious mistake to believe that this multiplicity of hierarchies, with the unavoidable conflicts arising therefrom, seriously affects the unity of the legal system in continental countries; everywhere mechanisms have been developed to settle inter-hierarchy conflicts. *See* R. SCHLESINGER, COMPARATIVE LAW 350 (3d ed. 1970).

11. The origin of the appellate system in Western civilization is usually traced back to the post-classical Roman idea that judges exercise their authority by delegation from the emperor. *See* T. MOMMSEN, RÖMISCHES STRAFRECHT 980 (1899). Appellate review was, however, alien to early medieval society; it is fair to say that appeal was "reinvented" after 1100 A.D. when institutions of the modern state began slowly to emerge.

This movement began in connection with the centralization within the Roman Catholic church, as a network of ecclessiastical courts developed with the Pope as *judex ordinarius omnium*. Soon afterward, accompanying royal centralization, the appellate process became firmly entrenched in the French legal system. Under the famous Criminal Ordinance of Louis XIV (1670), and probably even before, an appeal was automatic in many criminal cases. *See* A. ESMEIN, HISTOIRE DE LA PROCÉDURE CRIMINELLE EN FRANCE 177-283 (1882). Italian medieval lawyers who struck the foundation of continental *jus commune* maintained that an appeal must be permitted both from interlocutory decisions (*e.g.*, a decision to extract a confession by torture) and from final determination of the trial court. Many authorities claimed that custom or statutes could not abolish appeals in criminal matters. *See, e.g.*, 2 CONSILIA ET SINGULARIA OMNIA DOMINI HIPPOLYTI DE MARSILIIS, CONSILIUM 84, at 11 (1537) [hereinafter cited as DE MARSILIIS]. The judge who refused to transmit an appeal to the superior court was liable to punishment. *See* the opinion of *Angelus Aretinus de Gambilionibus*, in 2 Salvioli, *Storia della Procedura Civile e Criminale* in 3 STORIA DEL DIRITTO ITALIANO (P. del Giudice ed. 1927).

Nor was the defendant the only one permitted to appeal; various representatives of fiscal interest were entitled to appeal from acquittals. *See* Salvioli, *supra*. However, Italian practice in inquisitorial proceedings imposed serious limitations on the defendant's right to appeal, and in some city-states appeals virtually fell into desuetude. Later theory hedged the right to appeal in criminal matters with numerous exceptions, some of which had been advocated even earlier. *See* 1 DE MARSILIIS, CONSILIUM 1, at 1, for *crimina lese maiestatis*. Among the reasons advanced by scholars for these developments were the sufficient guarantees against error supplied and the nefarious maxim *propter enormitatem delicti licitum est iura transgredi* (laws may be disregarded because of the magnitude of crime). *See* 1 DE MARSILIIS, CONSILIUM 5, at 9. These Italian ideas were picked up by the 17th century German authority, Benedict Carpzov, and through his influence adopted in the continental inquisitorial proceedings of many countries. See B. CARPZOV, PRACTICA NOVA RERUM CRIMINALIUM IMPERIALIS SAXONICA, Pars 3, Questio 139, no. 14 (1739). This does not mean, however, that in German countries there was no review of judicial decisions in criminal matters. Some interlocutory decisions remained appealable (*e.g.*, the decision to torture the defendant). Also the investigator's file would be transmitted to a panel of "legal experts" for decision, and the decision of the latter—at least in capital cases—reconsidered by a competent ministry.

Carpzov's ideas did not remain unchallenged by his contemporaries. *See* R. STINTZING, GESCHICHTE DER DEUTSCHEN RECHTSWISSENSCHAFT 101 (1884). At any rate, appellate review, already quite refined in civil matters, was again widely permitted in criminal cases in the early 19th century. *See* Fiorelli, *Appello (Diritto Intermedio)*, in 2 ENCICLOPEDIA DEL DIRITTO 714 (1958).

The Yale Law Journal Vol. 84: 480, 1975

which decisions of subordinates are supervised by those closer to the center of power, appellate review was from its inception conceived as a comprehensive device that permitted, at least at the first level of review, a complete reconsideration of the case. Thus criminal appeal in all modern continental systems implies a review not only of alleged legal error, but also of factual findings and even the punishment imposed.[12] Nor is it surprising, in light of centuries of tradition, that appellate review gradually became associated with fairness in the administration of justice. Indeed, in modern continental countries, the "right of appeal" is usually elevated to the constitutional level. The appellate process is made very inexpensive, and is not risky for the parties.[13] In large classes of criminal cases even supreme courts can be reached as a matter of right through the mechanism of appeals. Of course, one consequence of this is that supreme courts lose control over their dockets and must handle a large volume of business. Relatively large numbers of judges must be appointed to the top of the judicial hierarchy and divided into panels, some of which specialize in the adjudication of criminal cases.[14] But the uncertainty produced while waiting for the Supreme Court to consent to decide a controversial question is almost totally absent from the continental scene, and the continental appellate mechanism is able to achieve considerable uniformity of decisionmaking on most of the important issues arising in the administration of criminal justice.

The ready availability of appellate review has bequeathed many legacies to all continental procedures. One of these must be pursued in some detail, because, as I shall later show, it explains so many

12. For simplicity's sake I apply the term "appeal" to all ordinary legal remedies. *See* note 15 *infra*. In some, but not all, continental systems, after the intermediate appellate court has spoken, further appeal is permitted only on matters of law. Sentencing problems may raise issues of "illegality" and "inappropriateness." *See* Mueller & LePoole, *Appellate Review of Legal but Excessive Sentences: A Comparative Study*, 21 VAND. L. REV. 411, 418 (1968).

13. The elimination of risk is connected with the generally accepted principle prohibiting *reformatio in peius*, *i.e.*, preventing the appellate court from using the defendant's appeal as an opportunity to modify the judgment of the court below to the detriment of the appellant. In most continental jurisdictions, the ban applies to proceedings on retrial as well; but the limits of the prohibition in this situation differ from country to country and are uncertain and controversial.

14. For instance the criminal law division (*La Chambre criminelle*) of the French Supreme Court (*Cour de cassation*) consists of one president, seventeen judges, and, of late, four judicial assistants (*conseillers référendaires*). Inconsistencies among supreme court panels can and do arise. But various mandatory devices have been developed in all jurisdictions to assure the unity of decisionmaking. For instance, a panel is not authorized simply to deviate from a prior decision of another panel, and must submit the issue to a larger body within the supreme court for resolution. Although the continental legal folklore maintains that judges are not formally bound by prior decisions—in the interest of uniformity of decisionmaking—this supposed rule does not apply to judges at the supreme court level. Paradoxically, they seem to have less potential freedom of action than lower judges.

puzzling technical contrasts between Anglo-American and continental procedural arrangements.

Where judicial decisions are normally subject to reconsideration, it is quite natural to postpone their finality and execution until the ordinary means of review have been exhausted.[15] In this situation, however, the appellate process becomes a continuation of trial adjudication. Consider the immediate impact of this development on notions of double jeopardy:[16] If an appeal is part and parcel of one single proceeding, jeopardy must be regarded as continuing until the termination of the entire criminal case. Thus, an appeal by the prosecution from an acquittal would not violate the prohibition against double jeopardy. Similarly, because convictions are also not final, it is unnecessary to explain the permissibility of a defendant's appeal by constructs such as waiver of jeopardy or other fictions. Moreover, the defendant need not seek a stay of execution; the execution of judgments is automatically postponed, at least until the time limit for the filing of an appeal has expired.

But here I have, perhaps, already gone too far into technical detail. Let me, therefore, quickly turn to the other centripetal weapon at the disposal of the continental judicial system.

A pure hierarchical model regards with great misgivings any participation of lay people in the administration of justice. The reasons for this attitude are not difficult to see: Laymen are usually unable and often unwilling to look at criminal cases through the prism of general rules. To laymen each case is a crisis, a unique human drama, rather than a representative of a general class. Thus, no matter what form it takes, lay participation always injects an element of unpredictability into the criminal justice system.

There are, however, important differences in the degree to which lay participation in adjudication conflicts with the hierarchical model. At one pole, and fundamentally antagonistic to the model, is the Anglo-American jury trial. Decentralized administration is inevitable where lay people are expected to apply local standards in determining guilt, and are even permitted to set aside the centrally imposed criminal law embodied in the judge's instructions. Furthermore, the largely inscrutable and often unchallengeable general verdict rep-

15. Medieval continental law had already elaborated a distinction between ordinary legal remedies which suspend the res judicata effect of decisions and extraordinary legal remedies to be used in exceptional situations after the judgment had become legally binding and executable. It is often mistakenly assumed that this distinction corresponds to that of direct and collateral attack in American law.

16. The continental counterpart to the prohibition against double jeopardy is the *ne bis in idem* maxim.

resents a crowning example of autonomous rather than delegated adjudicative powers.

At the other extreme, from the later Middle Ages to the French Revolution, the administration of justice on the Continent was dominated by professional adjudicators. Revolutionary times inaugurated a change. It was a period permeated by a somewhat naive intoxication with the exotic but never fully understood charm of English political institutions. It was also an epoch of great distrust of the politically reactionary judicial bureaucracy. The two circumstances in combination explain the curious phenomenon that, in the wake of the victorious French Revolution, the jury trial was transferred to the Continent, although the English ways of organizing society were quite alien to French revolutionary ideology.[17] It is important to note, however, that the broad jury discretion was not imported; from the very beginning, professional officials retained more control over the jury than was the case in England.[18] More importantly the transplanted jury, even in this adulterated form, never really became acculturated on the Continent. Without recounting here the exquisite misadventures of the continental jury,[19] suffice it to note that the jury soon suffered a decline in all European countries. Nevertheless, though somewhat distorted in the transforming screen of all ideological migrations, the idea of lay participation in the adjudication of criminal cases remained a potent political force. Because the judicial bureaucracy was never powerful enough to secure a complete reversion to professional adjudication in criminal matters, the natural result, a sort of compromise, was the adoption of a milder form of lay participation. The prevailing form came to be a mixed bench on

17. Consider only the extent to which the English jury as an autonomous decisionmaker actually conflicts with the revolutionary ideal of a judge who mechanically applies preexisting legislative norms. This is, of course, Montesquieu's idea of the adjudicator as *la bouche de la loi*.

18. The general verdict was rejected in favor of a form of special verdict, and the unanimity of jurors was never required. Although briefly, during Year V, the jury verdict was supposed to be unanimous, if unanimity could not be achieved within 24 hours, a simple majority would suffice. There was also a limited possibility of changing the jury verdict by adding new jurors if, in the unanimous opinion of professional judges, the existing jurors committed a mistake. Probably the best account of the original revolutionary jury is still A. ESMEIN, *supra* note 11, at 417-30. In addition, from the beginning the possibility existed of proceedings *in absentia*. Jury trials could not be "waived" by the defendant; even if he "pleaded guilty," the case would still have to go to the jury. The significance of these two deviations from the English model will be discussed later in connection with the ideological basis of the Anglo-American system.

19. For an excellent account, see Mannheim, *Trial by Jury in Modern Continental Criminal Law*, 53 LAW Q. REV. 99, 388 (1937). Even the French have since abolished the jury as an *independent* decisionmaker. The 1941 reforms of the Vichy government, never repealed on this point by postwar legislation, created a system in which the jurors deliberate and vote jointly with professional judges. Somewhat special is the history of the Tsarist Russian jury introduced in 1864 and abolished by the Soviet government. *See* S. KUCHEROV, COURTS, LAWYERS AND TRIALS UNDER THE LAST THREE TSARS 51-86 (1953).

which professional and lay judges sat and decided jointly, and this is still the representative continental adjudicative body in criminal matters.[20]

It would be an exaggeration to claim that the actual significance of lay assessors reduces everywhere to a mere nonfunctional political embellishment of the decisional body. But few would deny that the professional judge on the mixed bench is such a towering figure that the lay influence is rather negligible,[21] and nowhere does this influence seriously impede uniformity and predictability of decisionmaking. Moreover, an appeal lies from the mixed bench to higher courts which review the entire record, and these courts are typically composed solely of professional judges.

While it appears that all continental systems have evolved potent mechanisms to counteract centrifugal tendencies in the administration of criminal justice, a balanced appraisal must recognize departures from the ideal of strict judicial centralization. Some of these departures are simply the minimal requirements of judicial independence in all modern legal systems. But one centrifugal feature of a different sort is significant for comparative purposes.

In a centralized judicial system which sets great store by consistency of decisionmaking, one would expect to find a policy that requires judges to abide by normative standards expressed by their superiors. Strangely enough, no such policy is espoused by continental systems, at least as a matter of formal legal doctrine. Is this phenomenon, in its actual impact, a serious departure from the ideal of judicial centralization? Not quite. But to understand the development of this phenomenon one must first turn to the seemingly inapposite continental doctrine against judicial lawmaking.

One obvious source of this doctrine is the ideology which inspired the French Revolution; like most revolutionary thought, it was not

20. There are, of course, many varieties in the composition of the mixed tribunal. By way of exception, adjudication by professional judges existed solely in prewar Yugoslavia and still persists only in Holland.

21. This rather general impression has recently been substantiated by empirical research. *See, e.g.*, Casper & Zeisel, *Lay Judges in the German Criminal Courts*, 1 J. LEGAL STUDIES 135, 186 (1972); Zawadzky Kubicki, *L'elément populaire et le juge professionel dans la procédure pénale en Pologne*, 50 REVUE DE DROIT PÉNAL ET DE CRIMINOLOGIE 919, 929 (1970).

A recent Soviet study revealed that disagreements between the professional judge and lay-assessors in trial courts arise in only 18 percent of cases surveyed. Of these, only one percent involved disagreement over the guilt of the defendant. The overwhelming majority of disagreements concerned the magnitude of punishment. Indeed, sentencing is regarded by many lay-assessors as the main purpose of the criminal trial. *See* Raditnaya, *O metodike issledovanya effektivnosti uchastiya narodnih zasedatelei v osushcestvenii pravosudia*, in EFFEKTIVNOST PRIMENENIYA UGOLOVNOGO ZAKONA 195-97 (N. Kuznetsova & I. Mikhaylovskaya eds. 1973).

without a utopian element. It was predicated on the assumption that normative standards could be developed with such clarity and over so broad a range of issues that their application to individual cases would require no creative activity on the part of the judge. This restrictive role was regarded as a postulate of national legal unity and as a means of furthering legal certainty. These two values called for judicial centralization, which, after a brief interlude, became one of the important achievements of the Revolution.[22]

Since the proper business of the judiciary was to be solely the *application* of norms, rather than their formulation, judicial centralization was conceived exclusively as centralization of application. Not even the highest court could authoritatively decide the meaning of legal propositions.[23] Even on appeal, traditionally so important, review was to involve only the propriety of the process of norm application, imagined syllogistically. True, the higher court could disagree with the court below on the meaning of the normative standard for de-

22. Pre-revolutionary French courts (*Parlements*) were a centrifugal force, opposed to the unification of the law. *Parlements* had the authority to render decisions, not necessarily in the context of an actual litigation, enunciating legal views to be applied in future cases (*arrèts de règlement*). In the 18th century, conflicts between these courts and the monarchy were quite frequent, occasionally creating scandals.

> Le règne de Louis XV, jusqu'en 1770, fut fertils en conflits entre [Parlements] et le pouvoir royale, . . . et les deux partis allaient jusqu'a l'èxtreme usage de leurs droits traditionels.

A. ESMEIN, COURS ÉLEMÉNTAIRE D'HISTOIRE DU DROIT FRANCAIS 520 (1921); J. SHENNAN, THE PARLEMENT IN THE EIGHTEENTH CENTURY, THE PARLEMENT OF PARIS 285 (1968). In addition, conflicts among the 14 Parlements on many legal issues often occurred during the *Ancien Règime*. In contrast to common law judges, the French judiciary was not so definitely on the side of the middle class, in many respects judges were quite reactionary, and French revolutionary ideology was strongly antijudicial. This ideology reached countries with quite different judicial traditions. *See* note 26 *infra*.

23. Analytically this determination can take place in three situations. The first is one in which the supreme court determines general rules independently of actual litigation. This is pure judicial legislation. Another is by a determination for the case *sub judice*, *i.e.*, by a legal opinion expressed in remanding to the court below. Finally, legal opinions expressed by the supreme court in actual litigation may be considered binding in *another* similar case. The original revolutionary ideology prohibited supreme courts from making binding determination in all of these situations. M. CAPPELLETTI, J. MERRYMAN & J. PERILLO, THE ITALIAN LEGAL SYSTEM 150 (1967).

The very process of judicial interpretation, be it authoritative or not, was viewed with suspicion in the revolutionary eras. Thus, more than a century before the French revolution, English Levellers advocated a simple codification of law, coupled with a ban on judicial interpretation. *See* Shapiro, *Codification of the Laws in Seventeenth Century England*, 1974 WIS. L. REV. 428, 449-50, 455. Two French revolutionary decrees of 1790 forbade courts any interpretation of laws. *See* F. NEUMANN, THE DEMOCRATIC AND THE AUTHORITARIAN STATE 38, 141 (1957).

Less known is the fact that this radical ideology of the rising bourgeoisie was shared by continental "enlightened monarchs" in their efforts to codify the law. For instance, on April 14, 1780, a decade before the aforementioned French revolutionary decrees, Frederich II of Prussia prohibited judicial interpretation of laws. Similarly, in 1786, Emperor Joseph II of Austria prohibited interpretation of his Code. An instruction was passed in Bavaria in 1813 forbidding the writing of commentaries to the famous Bavarian Penal Code of the same year. *See id*. This alliance of monarchical and bourgeois interests in shaping the law on the Continent is a major theme in Max Weber's work. *See* MAX WEBER ON LAW IN ECONOMY AND SOCIETY 267, 279, 289 (M. Rheinstein ed. 1954).

Structures of Authority and Comparative Criminal Procedure

cision, but it could not require adherence to its views even in remanding a case for retrial.[24] Given the internal logic of the doctrine this is not a strange arrangement. If the creation of law is ultra vires for the judiciary, there cannot be any super- or sub-ordination on this issue. All judges are equally subordinated to the legislator. The strength of their legal pronouncement derives solely from supporting arguments. *Tantum valet quantum ratio probat.*[25]

As revolutionary ideology confronted the constraints of the possible, the pristine views on the role of the judge were qualified somewhat. Nevertheless, the basic contours of the doctrine remain intact to the present day and its continuing vitality can be seen as an ideal to be approximated.[26] Those inroads that have been made are in the narrow area of binding lower courts to legal views expressed by superiors on the remand of a case for reconsideration.[27]

So much then for continental legal folklore. More relevant to my purposes is the actual importance of normative standards expressed by superior courts for the decisionmaking of courts below.

Although technically not binding, these normative standards are of extreme importance in the actual operation of criminal justice.[28] Because the striving for uniformity and consistent decisionmaking

24. *See* note 27 *infra*.

25. "It is worth as much as can be proven by reason."

26. This attitude toward judicial legislation can no longer be attributed either to the traumatic experience with French judges during the *Ancien Régime* or to the relatively rigid continental views on separation of powers. A deeper explanation focuses on the continental belief that judicial lawmaking (unless guided by scholarly conceptual frameworks or legislative directives) results in casuistry, ultimately subverting legal certainty. This belief probably dates back to the rise of medieval universities; *praxis caecus in via* is an adage much older than Montesquieu. But this problem is a faded fresco I cannot even begin to restore here. For a modern reconstruction of this doctrine, see the decision of the West German Constitutional Court cited *infra* note 69.

27. In some continental countries the legal rule determined by the supreme court is binding on first remand. In the majority of jurisdictions, however, the old doctrine is partially maintained, and the first court of remand retains the option to refuse to apply the law as enunciated by the supreme court. Only if a larger augmented panel meets (*e.g.*, a supreme court session) following a second appeal will its legal view be binding on second remand. At the level of the intermediate appellate courts, the old doctrine frequently preserves its full force.

It is true that in some systems repeated decisions of supreme courts are legally binding (*jurisprudence constante, doctrina legal*), but this is usually explained in terms of custom. Decisions of constitutional courts are also legally binding, but these courts are sui generis.

Sophisticated continental theorists seem of late to recognize some additional instances in which court decisions possess legally (not factually) binding power. Most interesting of these is the case in which a supreme court announces an important legal principle (*e.g.*, that mistake of law constitutes a defense, or that debts should be revalued due to currency collapse), and this principle accords with widely held convictions of justice. *See* K. Larenz, Methodenlehre der Rechtswissenschaft 411 (2d ed. 1969).

28. On this subject the literature is truly vast. For a subtle and insightful presentation, see R. Schlesinger, *supra* note 10, at 434; *cf.* J. Merryman, *supra* note 5, at 23, 48. Unless conformity were expected, such formal opinions would be nonsensical.

is such an overriding tendency in all continental systems, a number of mechanisms have been designed to make lower courts accept legal propositions developed by superior courts.

Such mechanisms may operate outside actual litigation. In many countries, for example, supreme courts will formally enunciate advisory legal opinions; although usually not binding, these opinions in actual fact will be followed.[29] Less visible, never published, but perhaps more important are various internal recommendations and circulars on legal issues flowing from higher to lower courts on diverse occasions, such as following the inspection of lower courts or perusal of their files.

Closer to the enunciation of normative propositions in actual litigation, and appearing quite bizarre to outsiders, are the "audit" procedures by which supreme courts review final decisions "in the interest of the law."[30] Frequently their effect is solely to declare that in a decision "law was misinterpreted," but without changing the adjudication. The *effet platonique* of such supreme court decisions remains entirely incomprehensible unless their purpose is revealed as one of assuring uniformity of decisionmaking in lower courts. Finally, the pervasive appellate mechanism renders legal opinions of higher courts quite important. If the lower court judge fails to follow the legal views of his superiors, his decision inevitably will either be reversed or amended. All continental systems, mirroring the hierarchical model, have developed effective pressures against the display of obstinacy and independent assertion of views by the lower judiciary. Briefly, when the continental judge knows of a legal view expressed by his superiors and has reason to believe they still adhere to it, he will usually follow it even without any doctrinal obligation

29. Occasionally such opinions are even declared legally binding. An interesting example was the system adopted by the Tsarist Russian supreme court (Ruling Senate). Its rulings, if rendered by "super-panels" (an enlarged complement of judges), were binding on similar cases in the future. *See* N. ROZIN, UGOLOVNOE SUDOPROIZVODSTVO 85 (1916). Of course, Russian legal scholars of the time, steeped in the continental legal tradition, tried desperately to reconcile this judicial legislation with the prevailing legal folklore. In a modern reflection of the old system, Soviet supreme courts can presently also issue binding directives to courts below (so-called *postanovlenia*), and their example is followed in some Eastern European systems. But, in keeping with the orthodox continental theory of legal sources, this actual norm-creating activity is classified as one pertaining solely to the "application" of law, a supposedly automatic operation devoid of judicial creativity. *See* 1 M. STROGOVICH, KURS SOVETSKOGO UGOLOVNOGO PROTSESSA 73-74 (1968). Soviet legal theory is generally hostile to judicial legislation, which it associates with law in monopolist capitalism. *See* V. TUMANOV, BURZHUAZNAIA PRAVOVAIA IDEOLOGIIA 74 (1971).

30. A prototype of such a mechanism is the French "*pourvoi en cassation dans l'intérêt de la loi.*" *See* G. STEFANI & G. LEVASSEUR, *supra* note 7, at 757-59. Similar devices exist in Austria (arts. 33 and 282, Code of Penal Procedure), and in most Eastern European countries. *See* Rudzinski, *Soviet-Type Audit Proceedings and their Western Counterparts*, in L. BOIM, G. MORGAN & A. RUDZINSKI, LEGAL CONTROLS IN THE SOVIET UNION 287 (1966).

to do so. Whether this view happens to be expressed within or without the context of a particular case will be largely irrelevant to him. Instances in which trial judges actually use the freedom to develop legal standards accorded them by the system's folklore constitute quite rare deviations from the mode.

This does not mean, however, that continental systems have adopted in practice, although not in theory, the doctrine of stare decisis.[31] As already shown, prior decisions rendered in actual litigation have serious competitors as sources of information on legal views of higher courts.[32] But even if the first reaction of continental judges were always to reach for prior decisions, an important difference would still remain between their style and that expressed by the doctrine of stare decisis. To a continental judge a prior decision is not a "case," a solution to a real life problem in all the richness of its raw facts. What he is looking for in a decision is essentially a specification of a more general legal proposition that will cover the case before him. The facts of the decided case will seldom interest him; indeed, they may often constitute a regrettable distraction from his proper business of finding a precisely articulated standard.[33] Most of the time, an abstract legal proposition, totally denuded of the enveloping factual context, will suffice for his purposes. Gone is the flexibility springing from the "distinguishing" of cases on their facts, or emanating from broader and narrower formulation of holdings. Gone also is the freedom resulting from the various degrees of weight that can be attri-

31. It is sometimes said that, at the time of the French Revolution, continental countries rejected stare decisis, while importing many other English judicial institutions. In fact, they were only reacting to their own pre-revolutionary experience. The doctrine of stare decisis is a product of the 19th century, and did not even exist in England at the time when French political theorists looked to that country for inspiration. The necessary cohesion of the English common law was maintained at the time by the oral transmission of tradition within a small group of lawyers and judges. The stare decisis doctrine appeared only after the expansion of the judicial system broke down the cohesion of the common law. *See* A. Simpson, The Common Law and Legal Theory, in Oxford Essays in Jurisprudence (Second Series) 77, 98 (1973). Assume, however, that French revolutionists were familiar with an analogue of stare decisis, conceived as an instrument designed to assure consistency in a system where law gradually evolves from judicial decisionmaking; even so, they would have rejected such doctrine without hesitancy because it clashes irreconcilably with the view that legal standards must be formulated by the legislator rather than the judiciary.

A related but unexplored contemporary question concerns the effect of an accelerated pace of change on the doctrine of stare decisis, the essence of which is tradition.

32. An important additional source of information are commentaries written by scholars whose primary function is to maintain order in the normative universe.

33. Therefore, continental decisions will contain only the thinnest distillate of legally relevant facts. Building upon an idea expressed by T.S. Kuhn, one would say that continentals do not treat prior cases as examples shared by the profession, examples that are applied without mediation of rules. Rather from the examples (actual decided cases) they abstract rules which are to function instead of shared examples. The two processes are altogether different manners of knowing. T. Kuhn, The Structure of Scientific Revolution 192 (2d ed. 1970).

buted to precedents. The rule found in the decision either applies or it does not.[34] This difference is of great importance, because following prior decisions in the continental fashion leads to much more rigidity than is the case under the stare decisis doctrine. While the latter does not prevent the growth of law, the former easily can.[35]

Here I must return from my excursion into deviations by the continental judicial organization from the ideal of strict centralization. These deviations do not prevent the machinery of justice from maintaining a high degree of uniformity in decisionmaking, and strong pressure toward centralization remains one of the most distinguishing characteristics of all continental agencies operating in the administration of criminal justice.

### 2. *Rigid Ordering of Authority*

Preceding by several centuries the unification of law, stratified administrative structures appeared on the Continent as early as the 13th century.[36] In discussing the elaborate appellate system that resulted from this development, I have already touched on some hierarchical aspects. What remains for consideration are three characteristics of a rigorous hierarchical design suggested by the hierarchical model. As the highly defined stratification of continental police and public prosecution is too plain for argument, I shall focus solely on the organization of the judiciary.

The first characteristic is the precise delineation of responsibilities, both internally and in relation to other branches of government. In this regard, the continental judiciary clearly satisfies the requirements of a rigid ordering of authority. To begin with, consider that continental courts have no "inherent powers," and it is these powers that invest any structure with marginal ambiguity. Whatever authority is vested in continental courts derives from legislation. And in their desire to anticipate the future through legislation, continentals have settled jurisdictional issues relatively well. Waiting for a crisis to bring up basic problems before deciding them appears to be a style that produces too much anxiety for continentals. Furthermore, it is important to note that allocation of adjudicative authority

34. *See* H. Silving, Sources of Law 100, 113 (1968).

35. Ehrenzweig is probably right in claiming that the adoption of stare decisis in its continental variant would invest the continental legal system with great rigidity. *See* A. Ehrenzweig, Psychoanalytic Jurisprudence 132-33 (1971). The continental view of the legal decision explains why continental lawyers have great difficulty grasping that a legal system can grow and change by standing on precedents. They simply project their own perceptions of decisions into the common law world.

36. *See* J. Strayer, On the Medieval Origins of the Modern State 50-52 (1970).

on the Continent invariably implies both the power and the *duty* to act, so that continental courts lack the option to refuse consideration of a case.[37]

Descending to details, a few examples of precise delineation of authority must be offered. A provision allocating the same matter either to a single judge or a panel, or authorizing both the trial and the appellate judge to render or alter the same decision, would be viewed in the continental systems as a serious ambiguity to be quickly remedied. Similarly, it would be unacceptable for a judge to be able to change his decision after he has announced it, even if such power extended only for a limited time period; once the decision is announced the court loses all power over it, and only the hierarchical superior can alter it. Relatively little difficulty is ever encountered in determining the proper adjudicator and relationships of super- and sub-ordination.[38]

A second characteristic of rigorous hierarchies is the pronounced differentiation among judges at various levels, and in this the continental judiciary corresponds quite closely to the model. Let me begin with the courts of original jurisdiction.[39] A single judge will be authorized to decide only minor offenses.[40] More serious cases are allocated to a panel. If, however, serious felonies or sensitive matters such as political issues are involved, the criminal case will usually fall within the province of a higher trial court. More significantly for my purposes, many sensitive decisions that in other systems are made at the level of original adjudication are either taken away from the trial courts altogether and vested in appellate courts or removed from the judiciary entirely. For example, the idea that a trial judge could be entitled to determine whether a high government official is properly exercising his testimonial privilege, or what is and what is not in the interests of national security, appears almost preposterous from the continental perspective.[41] From such a perspective, if these

37. The *forum non conveniens* doctrine is largely unknown, as are mechanisms such as certiorari.

38. A further problem pertaining to certitude about adjudicative powers concerns judicial disqualification, which makes clear the contrasts between an autonomous and a bureaucratic decisionmaker. From a comparative law perspective, judicial disqualification in common law countries would have to be related to *voir dire*. *See* notes 96, 117 *infra*.

39. I am talking of ordinary courts of record. Punishable conduct of noncriminal nature (*i.e.*, "administrative offenses") is considered by officials other than judges.

40. The practice in Holland is contrary.

41. The West German Criminal Procedure Code accords the right to the head of state to refuse to give testimony in criminal cases if he believes this to be in the national interest. German Code of Criminal Procedure § 54(3), at 44 (Am. Series of Foreign Penal Codes, No. 10, 1965). No court is entitled to probe whether he justifiably invokes the national interest. But, if the head of state chooses to testify, even the manner in which his testimony is taken is regulated. *Id.* § 49, at 41.

problems are to be entrusted to the judiciary at all, it would seem natural to vest authority to resolve them in a judicial echelon corresponding to the rank of the government official whose acts are in question. Any other solution would be regarded as a serious disruption of elementary symmetry in the allocation of authority. Consider also the power to review the constitutionality of legislation. It is probably still fair to say that continentals regard the ordinary judiciary to be an inappropriate authority to strike down statutes as unconstitutional. If judicial review is allowed, it is entrusted to a special high tribunal which deviates in many ways from "normal" courts. It would be truly alien to this system to decentralize judicial review by authorizing ordinary trial judges to declare legislation unconstitutional.[42] Such an arrangement would introduce a serious hierarchical disharmony.[43]

Let us move up the hierarchy to appellate courts. Here, one quite frequently encounters significant hierarchical differentiation. Judges normally decide cases in small panels; some important matters, however, come within the province of super-panels whose legal views are binding on ordinary panels. In this manner internal or infra-court echelons of authority are created. As shown before, this is especially important at the supreme court level.[44] Nor is it unusual that a rudimentary hierarchy may appear even in a single panel, in the sense that rules evolve which accord certain powers to the president and other powers to the full panel. This should come as no surprise. To a considerable extent, this ranking accompanies the elaborate and extensive reviewability of decisions; later, when recruitment and promotion techniques are considered, it will become even more significant.

42. On judicial review in Europe see M. CAPPELLETTI, JUDICIAL REVIEW IN THE CONTEMPORARY WORLD 54-66 (1971). The abhorrence of a diffuse power to review the constitutionality of statutes can be explained otherwise than by the low esteem in which trial judges are held. But surely it would appear incongruous to continentals to let a low bureaucrat, often a young novice, review the legislative determination. Where this is permitted at all (as in West Germany or Yugoslavia), the trial judge can only find the statute constitutional. If he suspects its possible unconstitutionality, he must suspend the proceedings and refer the issue to the constitutional court.

43. For further examples of decisions removed from lower to higher courts because of the importance of the issue involved, consider provisions such as §§ 121, 122 of the West German Criminal Procedural Code, authorizing only higher courts to extend preliminary detention beyond a certain time limit. GERMAN CODE OF CRIMINAL PROCEDURE, *supra* note 41, at 71-72.

44. *See* note 27 *supra*. An extreme case of such differentiation, leading to the possibility of internal review, is the arrangement found in the supreme courts of the Soviet Union. *See* H. BERMAN, *supra* note 7, at 92. Higher courts in the Soviet Union can take cases away from lower courts and decide them themselves, CODE OF CRIMINAL PROCEDURE OF THE RSFSR art. 40 (1972), although this power is apparently seldom exercised. In most continental systems, however, such powers of higher courts would be an unacceptable, sometimes even unconstitutional, deprivation of the citizen's right to have "the judge determined by statute." Not even the intermediate appellate level can be skipped.

The last demand of a rigid ordering of authority is that courts be treated as units, distinct and separate from their judges. This precisely correlates with the hierarchical model.

Consider first the situation in which a matter falls within the province of a single judge. Even after a particular judge has been assigned to decide the matter, all motions and briefs must be directed to the court on which the judge sits, rather than to him personally. And when he has rendered his decision, he has spoken for the whole court. Thus, the same matter cannot be considered again by another member of the same bench thereby creating complexities and duplications. For example, a party denied bail cannot turn to another judge in the hope of obtaining it. Most of the time, however, criminal matters will be in the province of a panel whose behavior is rooted in the long continental tradition of collective decisionmaking.[45] Not surprisingly, the panel is elevated into an abstract, faceless legal creature, a sort of corporate personality. It is thus not unusual to find continental systems in which opinions are not even signed by the individual judges who wrote them. Judicial dissents are neither orally announced nor published. While many reasons are advanced in support of this arrangement, there is only one which in my view goes beyond the surface of the continental system:[46] Where a hierarchical organization created for the sake of assuring unity and certainty is not forced to be unisonous, especially at the top of the pyramid, the animating presuppositions of the whole structure are strained, and the criteria for decisionmaking become either completely elusive or affected with a germ of dissolution.[47]

45. The old French maxim *juge unique—juge inique* expresses the fear of entrusting the power to decide cases to a single person. I cannot consider here the extent to which this attitude is connected with the reluctance of continental monarchs to delegate substantial authority to a single individual.

46. Reasons frequently mentioned are the desire to prevent outside interference with the adjudicative process and to enhance public confidence in the administration of justice. *See, e.g.*, R. SCHLESINGER, *supra* note 10, at 157. Even in a rare continental jurisdiction such as Norway which permits the announcement of dissenting opinions, dissents are quite rare, especially on points of law. *See* Andenaes, *Reasons for differences of opinion on questions of law*, in 15 SCANDINAVIAN STUDIES IN LAW 29 (1971).

47. The fact that constitutional courts in a few continental systems have recently begun to permit publication of dissents perhaps only strengthens the point made in the text. Constitutional courts are viewed as "political" tribunals, deviating from the "pure" model of courts. Although judges may be permitted to disagree on political questions, even at inordinate length if they so desire, in legal matters there must be "true law," necessarily unisonous rather than contrapuntal. For further insight into the "institutionalization" of agencies participating in the administration of justice and the underlying desire for unity and order, consider the "monocratic" organization (*Führerprinzip*) of prosecutorial offices. *See, e.g.*, M. VELLANI, IL PUBLICO MINISTERO NEL PROCESSO (1970). Broader studies would probably also have to encompass differences between the common law and civil law concepts of corporate personality.

The Yale Law Journal Vol. 84: 480, 1975

3. *Preference for Determinative Rules*

It is common knowledge that officials must have considerable leeway in solving many of the problems involved in the administration of criminal justice. The exercise of official discretion[48] seems at once more natural and desirable in this area than in many others. It is therefore all the more remarkable that continental systems insist even here on guiding officials by precise standards, and are quite reluctant to be satisfied with vague principles and policies as guidelines for conduct. To outside observers, continental attitudes sometimes seem to reveal symptoms of a mind which has lost all touch with reality, whose aspirations have become utterly quixotic. This is, then, a question of great importance for comparative studies, and it must be traced from the police stage, where it is least pronounced, to the prosecutorial and judicial levels.

a. *The Police.* A general feature of continental police forces is a high degree of regimentation and pervasive regulation. This feature escapes those observers who identify regulation with *external* normative constraint on police forces. However, both a strict hierarchy and a professional tradition favor a great deal of *internal* regulation; uniformity, consistency, and internal review by superiors are routine. In fact, the saturation of police forces with internal regulation bears a strong resemblance to that of the military. As a result, the police tend to assess situations with reference to existing internal regulations. Substantial discretion tends to gravitate to higher echelons of the police hierarchy; lower levels are guided by rules and subjected to extensive internal control.

As far as external constraints are concerned, relatively few normative standards can be located in most continental codes of criminal procedure. It is startling, considering the importance of police work in all modern systems, to reflect on the meager regulation of police inquiries as compared to that of prosecutorial or judicial investigations.[49] Significantly, however, except in the area of minor crime, most continental countries refuse to concede to the police the authority to decide whether or not to invoke the criminal process. This is seldom explicit, but rather follows inferentially from a variety of arrangements. For example, in West Germany and Yugoslavia, official agencies, including the police, are legally bound to report all criminal

48. *See* note 6 *supra* on the use of the term discretion.

49. In some continental countries procedural theorists insist that the police stage precedes the institution of criminal proceedings, and that therefore the law of criminal procedure does not apply to the police. But these internally influential opinions must be rejected on a broader comparative plane.

activity to the prosecutor's office. Thus, at least as a matter of legal norm, the police must forward to the prosecutor all information on criminal conduct.[50] While it would be naive to assume that all such information actually reaches the prosecutor, this legal obligation creates a moderating influence on temptations to exploit police discretion. Also contributing to this result is the particular role of the victim in continental proceedings, to which I shall turn in discussing the continental public prosecutor.

b. *Public Prosecutors.* Although there are numerous kinds of decisions on which prosecutors can have more or less freedom from normative standards, most people would agree that the central issue is whether the public prosecutor should have broad discretion in instituting criminal proceedings. On this question, at least in cases of serious crime,[51] the practice of continental countries can be classified into two groups.

The first and larger group espouses the principle that, given the initial probability that a serious crime has been committed, public prosecutors must press charges as part of their official duty; this is the *principle of mandatory prosecution (Legalitätsprinzip; principe de legalité des poursuites).*[52] It can hardly be maintained that as a result of the operation of this principle the public prosecutor has no leeway in deciding not to prosecute.[53] But his freedom in doing so is seriously

50. *See* Jescheck, *supra* note 17, at 510; *Yugoslav Code of Criminal Procedure* articles 137, 139.

51. As regards minor crime, continental prosecutors have a great deal of leeway. Sometimes this is openly acknowledged as a matter of legal doctrine. For West Germany, see, *e.g.*, J. Langbein, *Controlling Prosecutorial Discretion in Germany*, 41 U. CHI. L. REV. 439 (1974). In a number of countries, however, for various ideological reasons, the prosecutor is expected as a matter of legal folklore to prosecute fully even minor crime. But it is not hard to find in all countries numerous alternative devices providing the prosecutor with the necessary flexibility. One such prosecutorial "cushion" lies in the substantive provisions spelling out the definitional elements of criminal offenses. Conduct which satisfies the definition but presents only insignificant "social danger" is denied the character of a crime. *See, e.g.*, art. 7(2) *Criminal Code of RSFSR;* art. 4(2) *Yugoslav Criminal Code*. Such provisions give prosecutors asylum from the rigidities of legal folklore. Rather than justifying their failure to prosecute minor crime by reasons of inconvenience or some other factor, they simply say that there is no crime at all. Thus, rationalizations change, but the actual effect is the same as under systems where the principle of mandatory prosecution does not apply for minor crime. For other alternatives see, *e.g.*, art 7 *Criminal Procedural Code of RSFSR*. This is not to say, however, that in refusing to prosecute minor crime, continental prosecutors are not bound by internal prosecutorial rules.

52. This principle was adopted by the French Revolution as a postulate of equality and disseminated throughout Europe. There are exceptions to this principle for some political offenses, juvenile delinquency and—of course—minor offenses. For such exceptions in West Germany, see Jescheck, *supra* note 10, at 513. France has since repudiated the idea of mandatory prosecution.

53. For a realistic recent appraisal of the situation in West Germany, see G. KAISER, STRATEGIEN UND PROZESSE STRAFRECHTLICHER SOZIALKONTROLLE 78-86 (1972). An unavoidable flexibility stems clearly from the appraisal of the initial probability that a crime has been committed.

limited, and there are effective pressures on him to abide by this normative mandate. Within the purview of this essay it is enough to point to arrangements whereby the victim of crime, in one way or another, can check the prosecutor's refusal to press charges.[54] In addition, there are less visible but extremely important internal constraints on the exercise of prosecutorial freedom; within the hierarchy of the prosecutor's office there are regulations guiding the decision of whether to invoke the criminal process. For instance, oral or written directions instruct the prosecutor as to the significance of first-offender status in regard to specific offenses, or the point at which property damage becomes minimal. Accordingly, prosecutors often press charges *contre coeur,* or against their personal wishes, led to their decisions by normative directives.

The second and smaller group of continental countries authorize the public prosecutor to decline prosecution, even with respect to serious crime, if such a decision appears to be in the public interest; this is the *principle of expediency (Opportunitätsprinzip; principe de l'opportunité des poursuites).*[55] It is tempting to associate this principle with broad prosecutorial freedom from normative constraints, but to do so would be a serious mistake. The victim, who partakes in prosecutorial activity under this system as well, may institute prosecution if the public prosecutor fails to do so, and this alternative restrains official discretion. More importantly, prosecutorial freedom is once again confined by extensive internal regulation, which reflects the emphasis placed on consistency and uniformity of decisions. Where rules can be formulated, instructions and circulars will flow profusely down hierarchically defined channels; where contours of experience prove elusive, frequent conferences will be convened, in efforts toward the formulation of ever more articulate guides.[56] Once established, these standards will be enforced throughout the hierarchical pyramid.

c. *The Judiciary.* It stands to reason that the vaguer the decisional standard adopted, the more difficult it becomes to reconsider the resultant decision. A judicial organization cannot be seriously committed at once to both regular review and broad discretionary powers without succumbing to a sort of institutional schizophrenia. Obviously,

54. One example is the method by which the victim can secure from the court a mandamus ordering the prosecutor to press charges (*Klageerzwingungsverfahren*). Another is the Austrian invention of a "subsidiary charge" preferred by the victim if the public prosecutor fails to prosecute. Of course, in victimless crime, external pressures on prosecutors to institute proceedings are weak.

55. This is, for instance, the present system in France, Belgium, Holland and a limited number of other European countries.

56. Only a few internal guidelines become visible—those formulated at the very top of the hierarchy and published.

then, because it values appellate review so highly, the continental judiciary necessarily favors standards as lucidly defined as possible. In the absence of the jury as the autonomous decisionmaker *par excellence,* this is not overly difficult.

Most comparatists would probably agree that continental criminal legislation, both substantive and procedural, purports to cover all problems that can be anticipated, including the very exceptional situation.[57] Permissive as opposed to mandatory language is quite rare. This, of course, furnishes to decisionmakers only the broad framework of normative standards. But broad legislative standards are made more concrete by the judicial hierarchy, both within and without actual litigation, and the normative output of higher courts is quite rigid. Consistency, mutual compatibility of rules, perhaps even an order of analysis within the resulting normative universe are maintained by "legal science."[58]

But norm-saturation is not the only relevant consideration; attitudes towards norms are also important. It would be a serious mistake to think that this attitude is independent of the authority structure. Comparatively speaking, the attitude of the continental judiciary toward normative standards can easily be classified as rigid and unbending. Norms are not regarded, even in procedure and practice outside the trial context, as instructions from which there are legitimate departures. The great deference of the continental judiciary toward legislation is one of the *loci communes* of comparative law, and this is only partially mirrored in the uneasiness of the ordinary judiciary concerning the constitutional review of statutes. Equally important is the meticulous observance of norms emanating from higher courts. In sum, rules regulating the behavior of the continental judiciary are not only relatively precise and prolific, they are also comparatively inflexible.

We can now begin to understand some intellectual habits of continental judges and the idiom of their debate. Both have struck outsiders as abstract, and yet capable of easily producing accurate answers.

57. On the substantive side, duress and necessity are good examples. With respect to procedural problems, see, *e.g.,* note 41 *supra.* The law of evidence, governed by the "principle of free evaluation," seems to be an exception. The absence of norms in this area does not significantly free the continental judge. Factual findings must be justified in his opinion and are subject to review. Low-visibility rules have developed in all judicial hierarchies regarding evidentiary questions. On the reasons for the legislative abdication in evidentiary matters see Damaška, *supra* note 1, at 514-15.

58. On continental legal science generally, see, *e.g.,* J. MERRYMAN, *supra* note 5, at 65-72. On the science of criminal law specifically, see Ryu & Silving, *Toward a Rational System of Criminal Law,* 32 REV. JUR. U.P.R. 119 (1963).

Where law is not interwoven with the tradition of deciding cases in all their intricacy, the knowledge of law is not necessarily a knowledge of details.

### 4. *Importance of Official Documents and Reports*

Implicit in the ubiquitous hierarchical control of the continental machinery of criminal justice is the importance of documentation. Traces of all official activity must be preserved for possible review by superiors. Thus files must be maintained on all official matters, and these files can be closed only in accordance with precise rules. All official activity must be recorded and even minor decisions and their justifications reduced to written form. The part played by paperwork, ministerial matters, and bureaucratic minutiae in the total effort of officialdom is quite considerable.

Documents and reports drafted by officials are highly formalized. Specific matter must be included in specific parts of documents.[59] Exposition must be succinct and summaries made whenever possible.[60] Even the style of writing is standardized: It frequently becomes arid, impersonal, and cliché-ridden.[61] Personal expression, even in a jeweled and coruscated style, is anathema. Usually, tendencies toward individualism are rooted out during one's novitiate in the bureaucracy. As a consequence, anything but an impersonal *stylus curiae* would constitute a display of bad taste and lack of professionalism.

The great importance of this wealth of documentation, most of which ends up in the file of the criminal case, cannot in candor be denied. This is lost to many continental theoretical writers, overimpressed by the reduced role of dossiers in criminal cases after the abolition of inquisitorial procedure.[62] Concentrating on the trial stage, they stress that evidence which has not been brought out during trial

59. Sometimes proper inclusion is of great practical significance. For instance, as a rule, only matter included in the "ordering part" of continental criminal judgments becomes res judicata. During their novitiate fledgling officials must learn exactly what must be included into the ordering part, and how it should read.

60. Thus, for instance, testimony will very seldom be taken verbatim. Instead, short summaries of what witnesses said filter information through the transforming screen of legal relevance.

61. There are of course differences of degree among various continental countries *inter sese*. For instance, the style of the French *Cour de Cassation* would be at the formal pole, while the Swedish judgments fall close to the other extreme. But even the latter are far removed from the personal, often lengthy expression of common law judges. *See generally* J. WETTER, THE STYLES OF APPELLATE JUDICIAL OPINIONS (1960).

62. In inquisitorial proceedings the decision was based solely on the written file. *Quod non est in actis non est in mundo* was the maxim of the day. Even in the French revolutionary assembly, enchanted as it was by English *viva vox* proceedings, reliance on anything but written documents was vigorously opposed as an attempt to "écrire sur de la neige." *Compare* A. ESMEIN, *supra* note 11, at 434.

may no longer be used in arriving at the decision, due to the "principle of immediacy."[63] But when all the usual arguments have been made, the fact remains that the dossier still constitutes the backbone of criminal proceedings. Note particularly that in almost all continental countries the presiding judge studies the file in advance of the trial, and that many important documents from the file can be read aloud in court as evidence.[64] Finally, the extent to which a cloistral calm, unperturbed by *viva vox,* permeates the appellate process must be obvious to anyone who comes from a less bureaucratic system.

### 5. *Behavior Expectations*

On this last point of comparison between existing continental systems and the hierarchical model I can be very brief, for much of what I would have to say has already been mentioned.[65] It will be recalled that the 18th century vision of decisionmaking as an automatic process of norm application has been recognized as a rationalist illusion and rejected as a practical proposition; it has remained, however, as a regulating ideal.[66] Often the obscured constituent of complex processes, this ideal can best be perceived in existing role expectations, and some of these can, I believe, be factored out as representative of the continental machinery of criminal law enforcement.

Officials are not supposed to be autonomous decisionmakers, but are instead expected to adopt the behavioral idiom of civil servants. Guidance for official activity must be sought in the corpus of official norms, so that all problems appear primarily as technical administrative questions. Professional craftsmanship is a highly valued asset.[67] When no standards for decisionmaking exist, and independent

63. *See* Damaška, *supra* note 1, at 517; H. Löhr, Der Grundsatz der Unmittelbarkeit im deutschen Strafprozessrecht (1972) (monograph on West German aspects, with comparative comments).

64. For details, see Damaška, *supra* note 1, at 519.

65. *See, e.g.,* pp. 506-07 *supra* (the rigid discipline enforced in writing decisions); p. 506 *supra* (the handling of documents and dossiers); p. 500 *supra* (the hierarchical ordering inside a given court); p. 490 *supra* (comprehensive review on appeal).

66. *See* p. 495 *supra.*

67. The tendency of continental systems to treat legal and political issues as technical problems has been noted in, *e.g.,* R. Dahrendorf, *supra* note 3, at 230; K. Mannheim, Ideology and Utopia 105 (1949); H. Spiro, Government by Constitution 285 (1959). The attitude that legal activity is more a craft and a technique than a political pursuit can be traced to Greek antiquity, where the craft of lawmaking was considered antecedent to political activity, just as in continental ideology lawmaking is subsequent to basic political choices. H. Arendt, The Human Condition 173 (1959). Professionalism creates pressures for specialization even at the top of the hierarchy which explains why continental supreme court judges sit in specialized panels. A general problem-solving capacity does not suffice; to allow litigants to supply technical knowledge ad hoc would be, in the continental view, a surrender of an essential aspect of judicial activity. Extreme specialization also exists in continental law schools. A continental instructor teaching in as many fields as American law professors would probably be viewed by his colleagues as a dilettante.

action becomes unavoidable, it must be exercised sparingly, with extreme moderation and preferably at the apex of the hierarchy.[68] Moreover, this norm-creation by officials is supposed to proceed as an activity guided by internal rules of the craft, that is, by autonomous principles of the normative order, and it should never be influenced by political, ethical or similar extrinsic values. The great hostility toward decisionmaking on the basis of such considerations clearly permeates the ideology of all continental countries. Indeed, apocalyptic consequences are feared for the legal system as a whole if officials in the law enforcement machinery are permitted to engage in such unrestrained decisionmaking. The most dreaded consequence is not the obliteration of the separation of powers, within which policy questions are for the legislator to decide; after all, this principle is often viewed, especially in the East, as a formal organizational device of dividing functions. The primary fear goes deeper. It is generally believed that decisionmaking divorced from the restraint of the normative order brings the curse of uncertainty. Uniformity is undermined and replaced by the wilderness of single instances. And in the resulting chaos law itself, gradually but inexorably, dissolves into politics.[69]

Notwithstanding important local variations, mechanisms to assure conformity of behavior to these expectations can easily be identified in all continental countries. It is probably not too far fetched to regard even university training as a factor in shaping attitudes desirable in the machinery of law enforcement. The view is there imparted that the normative order contains, at least in embryonic form, the solution to all problems. Broad panoramic vistas of neatly delineated legal fields are offered to students, and the unmistakable emphasis is probably still on acquiring knowledge of what has authoritatively been said, rather than on the manner of thinking which generated those authoritative pronouncements.[70] But, no matter what the influence of university training, the period of practical novitiate for

68. At the top, independent action is not limited to minor matters even in the criminal law area. *See* H. SILVING, *supra* note 34, at 88.

69. This apocalyptic scenario is reflected almost verbatim in a 1954 decision rendered by the West German Constitutional Court, itself a "marginal court," admittedly more politicized than ordinary courts. *See* 3 ENTSCHEIDUNGEN DES BUNDESVERFASSUNGSGERICHTS 225 (1954). And it is this vision which has prompted a famous French comparatist, looking at American law, to declare in desperation that, with the weakening of the force of precedents, law itself has been weakened. A. TUNC & S. TUNC, LE DROIT DES ÉTAT-UNIS D'AMÉRIQUE 163, 183 (1955). Judicial legislation is opposed also by the legal ideology of Marxian socialist countries. *See* note 29 *supra*.

70. Elsewhere I have tried to define the continental *mos jura docendi* (the mode of teaching law). *See* Damaška, *A Continental Lawyer in an American Law School: Trial and Tribulations of Adjustment*, 116 U. PA. L. REV. 1363 (1968).

Structures of Authority and Comparative Criminal Procedure

official positions is in almost all systems an initiation to bureaucratic techniques and modes of thinking.[71] The successful socialization into this world is then tested by entrance examinations, which are even organized for aspirants to judicial positions. Finally, the desire of career people to advance makes the system of promotions a very potent weapon in enforcing conformity with expected official conduct.[72]

## II. The Coordinate Model

### A. *General Characteristics*

#### 1. *The Object of Coordination*

Animating the coordinate model is the aim of reaching the decision most appropriate to the circumstances of each case. Certainty of decisionmaking is recognized as an important value, but is less weighty than in the hierarchical model; what appears to be the best solution in a particular case will not be readily sacrificed to certainty and uniformity of decisionmaking. Consequently, the distinction between saying that a particular decision is just and that it is in accordance with the law cannot as easily be made as in the hierarchical model. The cast of mind underlying these value preferences attaches great importance to the rich variety of experience and is skeptical of attempts to impress general structures on the complexities of life.

#### 2. *The Coordinate Organization*

The desire for particularized justice requires that officials be close to the concrete situations of life involved in the processing of cases, and, of course, that they be free from outside constraints in considering equities. If achieving particularized justice were indeed the sole concern in the coordinate model, the ideal system would be a single layer of authority; but the need for a degree of uniformity is recognized, and the necessary unification of policies cannot always be achieved through the voluntary cooperation of autonomous officials. Accordingly, more complex structures of authority must be composed.

71. *See, e.g.*, R. Schlesinger, *supra* note 10, at 95 (West Germany and France); M. Cappelletti, J. Merryman & J. Perillo, *supra* note 23, at 86, 104 (Italy).

72. *See* M. Beradt, Der deutsche Richter 7-21, 42-80 (1930) (masterful attempt to sketch the psychology of the German judge). A common law reader would find this portrayal quite inapplicable to the judiciary of his own system.

When hierarchical structures of authority must be established, the basic value orientations of the coordinate model mandate that the ordering of authority be as mild as possible. Three attributes of such a mild hierarchy are important for my purposes. Because of the aversion to defining the relation of each official to the center of authority, positions of sub- and super-ordination are not clearly delineated. The resulting ambiguities and occasional overlappings are willingly accepted as a necessary price for the fundamental commitment to autonomous official powers. In keeping with the importance of the first layer of authority, the inequality among officials on various rungs of the hierarchical pyramid is not very pronounced; essentially, they are all homologues with similar authority inherent in their positions. And lastly, when officials must be organized into a unit, they do not thereby totally surrender their independence. Office and incumbent are not fully separated. The unit does not become an institution divorced from the real people comprising it.

Because officials must tailor their decisions to the special, sometimes unique circumstances of individual situations, the desire to predetermine the outcome of cases by precise and unbending rules is repugnant to the coordinate model. This is not to say, of course, that there are no preexisting standards for decisionmaking at all. Standards do exist, but they tend to be less precise and more flexible than in the hierarchical model. The general theme of "official discretion"[73] runs like an obbligato through all aspects of official activity. Moreover, it is consistent with the model to entrust crucial decisions to independent bodies of laymen. In such a setting there is no need for officials to make a record of all their activities, or to write down and justify even minor rulings. And where written decisions and reports appear warranted, standardization and regimentation of style appear as unnecessary and irksome formalisms, perhaps not fully compatible with the dignity of official positions. Generally speaking, bureaucracy in the coordinate model is rudimentary.

The structure of authority emerging from the foregoing brief sketch generates quite different behavior expectations than those encountered in the hierarchical model. Obviously, the ideal official is not a technical expert applying normative directives, irrespective of what appears to him to be the best solution in the light of the circumstances of individual cases. Decisionmaking is not a technical or administrative problem with policy issues settled in advance, but rather involves

73. *See* note 6 *supra*.

the more exalted and responsible activity of finding the best solution to a social problem in light of the political and ethical values of the decisionmaker.

This different role expectation in the coordinate model is reflected in the requirements for official positions. The importance of both professional training and a period of apprenticeship is minimized or totally eliminated. A candidate for office is preferably an established person who has made his mark in society, a problem-solver attuned to community values. Since socialization to a bureaucratic world is not necessary, even the highest positions may be entered laterally, that is, by outsiders without previous experience in the machinery of criminal justice.[74]

### B. *The Coordinate Model and Anglo-American Reality*

As was the case with continental countries, important variations that exist among common law jurisdictions must be acknowledged at the very outset. Some countries, the United Kingdom being one, have of late inaugurated changes bringing them much closer to continental systems. Nevertheless, a general pattern can be discerned on many crucial points in all Anglo-American countries, and it is to this general pattern that my presentation is devoted.

#### 1. *Centrifugal Decisionmaking*

a. *Police and Public Prosecutors.* It may be said with only a modicum of exaggeration that both in England and in America a police system, in the continental sense, hardly exists. Although professional forces originated in the 19th century, they remain to the present day

74. The relationship of the briefly outlined coordinate model to Weberian typologies is uncertain; Weber himself found that the common law system eluded his taxonomy. Yet one might reasonably ask why the hierarchical and coordinate models are not polarized with respect to the impersonal (or detached) style of exercising authority as Weber similarly polarized the bureaucratic and various "traditional" types of authority. I think this opposition is impossible, given the unusual constellations of personal involvement in both models. Consider whether or not officials perform their duties as part of a permanent occupation; the extent of lay involvement; the visibility of individual destinies (frequently submerged in the neutral shelter of normative propositions); how many, and how crucial, the decisions made at the level of original jurisdiction; all these factors seem to turn one way. Yet other features confound this easy polarity: For example, the more elevated the position of the autonomous decisionmaker the more likely the social distance to be great between officials and ordinary persons, and this increases with an increase in autonomy. And note the role of the aims of the criminal process itself. If one of the tasks of the process is not only to consider people's activities but also their personalities (*e.g.*, in an attempt to change them), officials tend to get more personally involved in the processing of cases. Finally, I must point out the passive character of the ideal coordinate judge and add that passivity can easily lead to aloofness. The variations smudge any clear contrast between the two models on this point.

deeply imbedded in local institutions and are in most respects wholly decentralized. The jurisdiction of such police organizations as the FBI in the United States and Scotland Yard in the United Kingdom remains severely restricted.[75]

The situation is similar with respect to professional public prosecution. England still gets along without any real counterpart to public prosecutors' offices, with the "system of popular prosecution" *(actio popularis)* remaining the theoretical foundation.[76] In most American states, public prosecutors are locally elected officials with surprisingly great and virtually uncontrolled authority. Even where state attorneys general do possess some powers to coordinate local law enforcement, these powers are seldom exercised. While the federal prosecutorial arm is centralized, hierarchical subordination is negligible by continental standards.[77]

b. *The Jury*. The common law jury is a classic example of an autonomous decisionmaking body in the administration of justice. No doubt, it is also a centrifugal force. Consider only the issue of jury nullification. In the face of uncontroverted evidence, and in the teeth of clear judicial instructions, the jury may bring in a verdict of acquittal and thereby refuse to apply substantive law, whether centrally imposed by the legislature or developed through judicial lawmaking. The frequent justification for this power is that jurors must bring to bear local conceptions of justice upon decisionmaking and adjust the crude substantive criminal law to the circumstances of individual cases.[78] But even if the jury verdict is one of conviction and may therefore be set aside, decisions as to fact, law and substantive justice are so deeply entangled in the general verdict that continental review can hardly be imagined.[79]

75. Police decentralization sometimes continues even beyond the municipal level, as in New York City. *See* Danzig, *Toward the Creation of a Complementary Decentralized System of Criminal Justice*, 26 STAN. L. REV. 1, 20 (1973).

76. *See* R. JACKSON, THE MACHINERY OF JUSTICE IN ENGLAND 120 (4th ed. 1964).

77. U.S. PRESIDENT'S COMM'N ON LAW ENFORCEMENT AND ADMINISTRATION OF JUSTICE, TASK FORCE REPORT: THE COURTS 73-77 (1967).

78. Note, however, that the jury may most freely exercise this power of adjustment in favor of the defendant. They cannot blatantly alter the substantive criminal law in order to convict a defendant who would otherwise go free. The adjustment rationale is linked to the challengeability of verdicts, and ultimately to the structure of power in the criminal process. *See* P. DEVLIN, TRIAL BY JURY 89 (1956) (England). For a recent judicial discussion of jury nullification in America, see United States v. Dougherty, 473 F. 2d 1113, 1130-37 (D.C. Cir. 1973). *See generally* Kadish & Kadish, *On Justified Rule Departures by Officials*, 59 CALIF. L. REV. 905, 925 (1971); Note, *Toward Principles of Jury Equity*, 83 YALE L.J. 1023 (1974). The centrifugal potential of jury nullification is almost the same, even if it is viewed solely as a factual power rather than as a "legal right."

79. In addition, the inscrutable character of the general verdict has contributed to the relatively unrefined nature of substantive criminal law. *See* S. MILSOM, HISTORICAL FOUNDATIONS OF THE COMMON LAW 361 (1969). While the continental variant of the jury

It is true that in all modern common law systems, and especially in the United States, jurors decide only a miniscule fraction of the total volume of criminal cases. Nevertheless trial by jury remains an ever-present practical possibility; more importantly for my purposes, the jury is a paradigmatic concept around which ideologies and legal sensibilities crystalize.

c. *The Judiciary*. It is well known that England was the first Western country to develop uniform judicial institutions and to achieve unity of law. This fact alone might seem to indicate that the judiciary in common law countries is very far removed from the decentralizing ideals of the coordinate model. Curiously enough, however, many striking features of judicial decentralization survive in the modern adjudication of criminal cases. But before I turn to these features, let me engage in a temporary *petitio principii* and try to explain this curious phenomenon.

A good starting point is to recall the unique features of, and limitations on, the centralization of justice in medieval England. Discussions of centralization and the unification of law customarily concentrate on the operation of central royal courts. In an abridgment of a much more complex phenomenon, one may say that English kings created a single, rather undifferentiated system of courts of original jurisdiction for the whole country, rather than a hierarchical structure. Because of the relatively small scale of operation and the very small number of judges, it was possible to maintain in informal ways the necessary degree of unity and consistency of adjudication. Judges formed close-knit groups and regularly engaged in informal consultation.[80] No internal hierarchical differentiation or appellate system was needed to achieve uniform decisionmaking by individual judges.[81]

In discussing the administration of criminal justice, however, it is wrong to focus on central royal courts at all. They were, after all, created primarily for the legal needs of the dominant social classes, and crime usually involved hoi polloi. The disposition of the great bulk of criminal cases was entrusted to the local gentry—the justices of the peace—who acted in partnership with local juries. No need

trial adopted a form of special verdict, see note 21 *supra*, hostility toward such verdicts prevails in common law countries to the present day. For a recent example from American federal courts, see United States v. Spock, 416 F. 2d 165, 180-81 (1st Cir. 1969); *cf.* Heald v. Mullaney, 16 Crim. L. Rep. 1035 (1st Cir., Nov. 13, 1974).

80. On various techniques used to develop unity of law within royal courts, see M. Hale, The History of the Common Law of England 251-52 (1820).

81. Consider how different this historical experience is from the continental development, where the monarchs developed a many-layered bureaucracy and an appellate system which reached local levels of administration, but were never strong enough to displace local customs and unify the law.

was felt for institutionalized forms of central supervision over the work of local potentates. Various extraordinary legal devices, designed to bring matters before the central royal judges, were seldom used in criminal matters, and the administration of criminal justice remained to the 19th century "a notable essay in decentralization."[82]

Whether in royal courts or local ones, criminal cases involved one-level adjudication. Quite naturally, then, the entire criminal process became identified with the trial, and the conclusion of this stage signalled the end of the criminal proceeding.[83] This conception of the criminal process, springing as it does from decentralization, has not disappeared even now from Anglo-American law. Although obscured by the twisting route in which its implications have been circumvented or subordinated to modern needs, the importance of single-level adjudication can be observed without great difficulty; it is especially apparent in the interplay between the original adjudication and appellate review, which came relatively late to the common law world. Let me present a few illustrations from American law in support of this proposition.[84]

Because the notion has not been entirely discarded that the decision of the trial court terminates the criminal proceeding, appellate review seems to conflict with the guarantee against double jeopardy:[85] Review appears as a "new jeopardy" rather than the continuation of the original one.

Artificial constructs (such as the defendant's waiver) are invoked to avoid this conflict. Similarly, the reconsideration of acquittals appears as a violation of the prohibition against successive prosecutions for the same act. And, to the bewilderment of continental observers, the defendant must obtain a stay of the trial court's decision pending appeal.[86]

The lasting vitality of the notion of trial adjudication as final also ac-

82. T. PLUCKNETT, A CONCISE HISTORY OF THE COMMON LAW 169 (5th ed. 1956).

83. At common law, the pleas of *autrefois acquit* and *autrefois convict* prevented reconsideration of criminal cases on appeal and retrial for the same offense. This practice was reflected in the debate on the original draft of the Fifth Amendment. *See* 1 ANNALS OF CONG. 730, 781-82 (1789-1791).

84. It should be noted that England has in this century moved closer to the continental system of liberal review. However, this trend should not be exaggerated; for example, the English appeal from questions of facts and from the sentence is not a matter of right, but typically depends on leave of court. *See* R. ARGUILE, CRIMINAL PROCEDURE 171 (1969). *See* note 95 *infra*. For some useful remarks in a generally neglected area of the history of appellate remedies in common law countries, see L. B. ORFIELD, CRIMINAL APPEALS IN AMERICA 14, 56 (1939).

85. *See* Benton v. Maryland, 395 U.S. 784 (1969), *overruling* Palko v. Connecticut, 302 U.S. 319 (1937); North Carolina v. Pearce, 395 U.S. 711 (1969).

86. From the continental point of view all Anglo-American appellate remedies would be classified as "extraordinary" rather than "ordinary"; *cf.* note 15 *supra*. Since stays are nowadays granted as a matter of course where decisions are reviewable, any distinction

counts for the relatively limited scope of appeal. Leaving aside the fact that acquittals cannot be appealed on any ground, consider the comparatively severe limitations on the grounds for the defendant's appeal. Both the factual findings and the sentence imposed can hardly be challenged. Even when error can be appealed, *direct* reconsideration of the adjudication, as in the continental system, is not involved. Following the pattern quite understandable in the setting of the jury trial with its inscrutable general verdict, what is actually reviewed is the propriety of the material submitted to the decision-maker for decision, rather than his "correct" use of the material.[87] In light of the foregoing it is not at all surprising that the right to appeal is not nearly so important in Anglo-American as it is in continental systems, and that it is generally not accorded constitutional stature.[88]

The continued importance of original jurisdiction, with the accompanying lesser importance of the appellate process, invests the Anglo-American judicial system with strong centrifugal tendencies. Judges retain important autonomous powers typical of a decentralized judiciary: Like the jury, they can nullify substantive criminal law;[89] the unreviewability of acquittals gives them significant leeway in deciding evidentiary issues; and the scope of their sentencing power is astonishing by continental standards.[90] As a result, centralization of policies cannot be achieved nearly so easily as it is in the hierarchical systems.

## 2. *Mild Ordering of Authority*[91]

Beginning again with medieval England, we must recall that courts, much as amoebae in the primordial biological soup, were for a con-

has been made virtually irrelevant for the purpose of obtaining a stay. But the concept of original adjudication as a basis for res judicata and execution of judgment causes other problems which have not been clearly resolved in the case law (*e.g.*, the use of convictions pending appeal for the purpose of impeaching the defendant at another trial).

87. Typical questions explored on appeal are whether the evidence was properly admitted, or whether the jury received proper instructions. The question of whether, given the proper informational sources, the "correct" result was reached is not considered. By contrast, in continental systems, this question too is subject to review.

88. *See* Griffin v. Illinois, 351 U.S. 12, 18 (1956); Ross v. Moffitt, 417 U.S. 600 (1974); North Carolina v. Pearce, 395 U.S. 711 (1969).

89. *See, e.g.*, Model Penal Code § 2.12 (Proposed Official Draft, 1962) (purporting to codify prevailing practice).

90. Continental lawyers would object to "provisional sentencing" (*e.g.*, 18 U.S.C. § 4208(b) (1970)) as placing unacceptable pressures on defendants to conform to whatever the judge demands. Consider also the example given by D. NEWMAN, CONVICTION: THE DETERMINATION OF GUILT OR INNOCENCE WITHOUT TRIAL 178 (1966). *See* Mueller & LePoole, *supra* note 12, at 418 (on the continental system).

91. Because police forces and prosecutorial offices in Anglo-American countries are seldom centralized, I may, perhaps, be allowed to neglect any minor hierarchies existing in this area and concentrate solely on the ordering of the judiciary.

The Yale Law Journal Vol. 84: 480, 1975

siderable time quite undifferentiated. Some became stationed at Westminster; others travelled around the country, possessed by *l'humeur vagabonde*. Consistency of decision was maintained in informal ways; little need was perceived for clear and rigid internal organizational arrangements, and it was thought unnecessary to establish a judicial hierarchy linking the center with local adjudicators. Consequently a mildly hierarchical but quite complex court structure with somewhat ambiguous organizational arrangements persisted until the court reforms of the last century.[92]

It is striking that, notwithstanding the vast differences in the scale of operation, many of the mildly hierarchical features of the British court system exist in America. The most important of these features must be examined in some detail.

Characteristically, a penumbra of uncertainty exists in the circumscription of judicial authority in the United States. It springs mainly from the fact that American courts, including those in the federal system, are not "creatures of legislation" in the continental sense. Judges retain certain "inherent powers," independent of the legislative delegation of authority. Nor is there much anticipatory legislation concerning the division of authority, if only because even the lower courts possess some "rulemaking" power.[93] Indeed, legislation on what could be termed judicial competence is so meager that, with its blank areas, it appears to continental lawyers to resemble early maps of Africa. Overlappings frequently occur in the jurisdiction of courts at different levels. For instance, the trial judge, for a time, following the announcement of his decision, shares with higher courts the power to alter the judgment; moreover, a stay of execution may be sought from either the court of original jurisdiction or from the appellate court. As a final illustration of ambiguous relationships, anathema to the hierarchical model, consider the power of federal *district* court judges in habeas corpus proceedings to review state *supreme* court decisions, both in deciding whether to use the existing record and in invalidating convictions of state courts rather than merely disturbing the custody of prisoners based on such convictions.[94]

92. The latest reform, which went into force in 1972, brought the English court system closer to the simple continental model. Nevertheless, carryovers from the past (such as judges differentiated in title) remain within certain courts. *See* Grzybowski, *Court Reform in England*, 21 Am. J. Comp. L. 747 (1973).

93. Such rulemaking power, even if specifically delegated solely to the supreme courts, is almost beyond the comprehension of most continental lawyers. Courts with which they are familiar are mainly limited to issuing insignificant rules of order. Greater flexibility and, consequently, uncertainty also stem from the freedom of some American courts to refuse to consider a case falling within their jurisdiction. On the continent such a practice would be a clear instance of "*denegatio justiciae.*"

94. *See* Brown v. Allen, 344 U.S. 443 (1953).

Structures of Authority and Comparative Criminal Procedure

In accord with another distinguishing feature of the mild ordering of authority, trial judges are allocated many powers which a rigid hierarchy would either vest judges at a higher level, or deny to the judiciary altogether. An obvious example is the power to strike down legislation as unconstitutional.[95] But even more remarkable is the *cause célèbre* of a federal trial judge determining—albeit in the first instance only—the proper limits of the President's executive privilege.[96] Within the hierarchical model issues of such magnitude would never be entrusted to the lowest judicial echelon.

In yet another respect the Anglo-American judiciary is accurately represented by the coordinate model: Individual judges, even when on a panel, preserve their independence and identity. Thus, for instance, the common law system has never accepted the idea, so typical of hierarchical structures, that the court as a unit has spoken when a judge belonging to its bench has rendered his decision.[97] And, when a panel issues a decision, it need not speak with one voice; indeed, a requirement that individual opinions be forgone would run counter to basic ideas of the autonomy and dignity of judicial office. Consequently judges are entitled to deliver individual opinions, even if this implies, as in the Japanese fable of Rashomon, that the same story is recounted from various standpoints and there is no discernible opinion of the panel as such.

### 3. *Preference for Flexible Rules*

a. *Police and Prosecutors.* One of the most important tasks of the police and public prosecutors is, of course, to stand as Cerberus at the entrance gate of the criminal justice system. Their decisions concerning which cases to admit and which to exclude are notoriously difficult to regulate, especially through relatively rigid standards imposed from outside their respective organizations. Although a measure of discretion, exercised in concrete circumstances, seems at once necessary and unavoidable, continental systems have attempted to deny both the police and public prosecutors freedom from normative con-

95. This power does not exist in the United Kingdom.

96. *See* United States v. Nixon, 94 S. Ct. 3090 (1974); Reynolds v. United States, 345 U.S. 1 (1953). Compare the less dramatic problem decided by the House of Lords in Conway v. Rimmer, [1968] A.C. 910. A further example of powers that would be unacceptable in the hierarchical model is the discretion of American judges to decide whether they must disqualify themselves because of bias. A finding of such bias would in a hierarchical system be made either by the chief judge or—more likely—by the higher court. For contrasts with the continental systems, see notes 41, 43 *supra*.

97. For example, the denial of bail or of a stay of execution by one judge does not prevent his colleague on the court from granting it. *See* Holtzman v. Schlesinger, *stay denied*, 414 U.S. 1304 (1973).

straints. Similar efforts are not apparent in Anglo-American systems. Consider the decision of police officers whether to invoke the criminal process: In the absence of a centralized police organization, there is comparatively little concern with overall uniformity and thus only minimal internal regulation exists. Moreover, existing standards cannot be as effectively enforced here through internal supervision as in a rigid hierarchical police structure.

What about external constraints imposed by the courts or the legislature? Without broad participatory mechanisms such as the victim's right to invoke the initial stage of the criminal process, there is little effective control over police decisions not to investigate or arrest. Thus the freedom of police officials from normative constraints in deciding what matters to pursue, quite considerable in all systems, seems somewhat more pronounced in Anglo-American countries.[98]

While some will surely dispute this conclusion on the independence of the police, for admittedly only nuances are involved in the difference, few would be prepared to deny that the Anglo-American public prosecutor has considerably more freedom from regulation than his continental counterpart. A typical American district attorney comes quite close to the very ideal of an autonomous decisionmaker. His decisions not to prosecute are practically unchallengeable, a circumstance all the more significant because the victim of the crime does not have the right to institute formal criminal proceedings. Once the prosecutor has decided to pursue a matter, there are comparatively few legal constraints on his determination of how many charges to squeeze out of the criminal transaction,[99] and there is very little law on the question of whether charges pertaining to the same event must be pressed together or *seriatim*.[100] Moreover, prosecutorial freedom in plea-bargaining is virtually total. Finally, since there is no centralized prosecutorial organization, the great freedom of individual

98. This, I believe, is true even of those police forces which have abandoned the traditional "watchman" style and adopted the "legalistic" style of work. *See generally* J. Wilson, Varieties of Police Behaviour 140, 172 (1970). In the United Kingdom the police prosecute most offenses and their exercise of "discretion" is generally accepted. *See* G. Williams, *Discretion in Prosecuting* 3 Crim. L. Rev. (Eng.) 222 (1956).

My statement in the text should not be taken to imply that judicial control over police on the continent is generally more effective; rather, internal constraints, and the more pronounced role of the victim, are in part responsible for the comparatively less discretion available to continental police. With his large automous powers in the area of excluding evidence, the Anglo-American judge actually possesses stronger weapons to affect police work than does his continental colleague.

99. Continental criminal law seems to be much more elaborate and specific. *See* H. Silving, Constituent Element of Crime 62, 175-97 (1967).

100. In most continental systems re-prosecution following a nolle prosequi faces some double jeopardy obstacles. Unlike the common law system, where double jeopardy ideas revolve around the trial, continental countries attach jeopardy to *criminal proceedings* so that problems appear earlier and continue until the appellate process comes to an end.

prosecutors from normative constraints is not limited by internal regulations aimed at assuring the uniformity and consistency of decisions.

Such unfettered prosecutorial discretion is not very striking from the comparative perspective, for substantial official leeway from precisely articulated standards can be encountered in many criminal justice systems. It is when we turn to Anglo-American adjudicators, *i.e.*, the judge and jury, that much more considerable contrasts arise.

b. *The Adjudicators.* The Anglo-American adjudicator of criminal cases may be characterized by his freedom from settled and precise substantive law, and his flexible attitude toward rules, be they substantive or procedural.

In discussing the substantive criminal law, experts commonly assert that problems belonging to what continental lawyers would call the "general part" (such as principles of criminal liability, the unit of criminal conduct, and the definition and sufficiency of charges) are in a fluid and comparatively unrefined state.[101] That this should be so will not surprise anyone familiar with the spirit of what I have called the coordinate model. Problems of criminal law are not authoritively structured in advance, for it is feared that such attempts to capture reality in the mesh of rules may hamper the attainment of particularized justice. It is thought that the task of refining the law is done best in the context of individual cases, by people both familiar with the concrete details and attuned to community values. Unusual cases that contribute so much to the complexities of the law are infrequent, and prosecutors often decline to prosecute when such cases occur.[102]

101. One cannot deny, of course, that there is of late in almost all common law countries a great deal of very sophisticated writing on substantive criminal law problems. But this writing differs from the continental one in at least two characteristic respects. Firstly, its major effort is directed towards the criminalization decision and purposes of punishment, areas which, from the continental perspective, lie in a "meta-juridical" zone, and are more appropriately the concern of politicians, philosophers and sociologists. One finds relatively little analysis of the formal structure of substantive criminal law, particularly inspired by a desire to establish a sort of neutral algorithm for helping lawyers to arrive at a given result in dealing with substantive criminal law problems. Secondly, where analogues exist to the continental analysis of problems belonging to the "general part" of criminal law, there is almost no agreement on the conceptual matrix from which one can proceed to cumulative scholarship. Both in theoretical writing and in decisions, one tends to go back to fundamentals. Using Kuhn's language, the discipline seems to be in a "pre-paradigmatic" stage. *See* T. KUHN, THE STRUCTURE OF SCIENTIFIC REVOLUTIONS 11 (2d ed. 1970). Nor is this strange, if only in view of the fact that in common law jurisdictions criminal law has only of late become the business of lawyers. *See* S. MILSOM, *supra* note 79, at 353. If this is true of substantive criminal law, it certainly does not apply to criminal procedural law. The latter is replete with arabesques of technical refinement and is often exceedingly complex. *See* p. 527 *infra*. But, as we shall see, even in the field of procedure and evidence, many important issues are left to the discretion of the decisionmaker, and what I shall say about judicial attitudes toward substantive legal rules applies *equo rationae* to the law of procedure.

102. Under the coordinate model no rational prosecutor would bring the defendant to trial in the exceptional circumstances that constitute a borderline problem in the law. A different result may occur under the principle of mandatory prosecution.

Those cases that are brought within the criminal justice system are usually left to the adjudicator's general verdict, from which concrete standards simply cannot be distilled.[103] In sum, what to continental eyes appears as a sorry state of affairs, resembling the charmingly confusing Chagallian universe of freely floating objects, represents in the setting of the coordinate model a perfectly natural and desirable arrangement.

Much more important than the relatively large areas of substantive law that are not in fact governed by rules is the Anglo-American adjudicator's disposition toward those rules that do exist. In contrast to his continental counterpart, he finds little that is sacrosanct about them and regards certain departures as perfectly legitimate. Let me present a few examples. Of course, a judge in the Anglo-American system can question the constitutionality of rules, and such rules are therefore not inviolate; and it is obvious that where a judge can decide these constitutional challenges, basic policy issues will often surface. But even in those cases where constitutional objections to rules are not raised, precedential or legislative standards will be discarded or modified whenever they indicate a result contrary to the adjudicator's strong beliefs as to the best disposition of the case. Where departures from established rules lead to the acquittal of the defendant, the adjudicator's decision usually cannot be challenged. And even where his decisions are reviewable, his attitude toward rules will be far from deferential, and departures from them may be regarded as justifiable.

Generally, then, one can observe that rules in the Anglo-American system are not much more than guidelines for average cases, guidelines susceptible of improvement and reconsideration in light of current experience and the particular circumstances of each case. The premise of this attitude resides in the desire to achieve particularized justice.

But it is important for comparative purposes to note that, in this concept of adjudication, decisionmaking becomes inevitably enmeshed in concrete situations and even minor details. Legal questions cannot be debated *grosso modo*, and efforts can hardly be made to develop law as a system of interrelated legal standards. Adapting a felicitous phrase from another context "a tradition of behavior is not

103. Frequently questions of determining facts and establishing normative standards will be combined and treated as an issue for the jury to decide, as with negligence problems. The extent to which this arrangement discourages the development of substantive law is a more general phenomenon. *See* David, *Les caractères originaux de la pensée juridique anglaise et américaine*, in 15 ARCHIVES DE PHILOSOPHIE DU DROIT 6 (1970).

susceptible of the distinction between essence and accident; to know the gist is to know nothing."[104]

### 4. *The Informal Style*

The autonomous manner of exercising authority that is so characteristic of the Anglo-American machinery of criminal justice must inevitably decrease the importance of official documentation and bureaucratic techniques.[105] There is in the Anglo-American criminal process no real counterpart of the continental dossier; in fact, even writing judicial opinions is regarded by many judges as an opportunity for the expression of self, so that, by continental standards, many judicial opinions appear more like products of *littérateurs* than official documents. And this applies even to periods in which the common law followed what Llewellyn has termed the formal style.[106]

In this scheme, it would not make sense to suggest that decisionmaking should place great reliance on official documentation. Indeed, much of the law of evidence is designed to prevent such an occurrence. Summaries of testimony or of visits to the scene of crime, for example, assume the character of lifeless bureaucratic residues of reality, always defective, often spurious, and therefore such evidence is normally inadmissible at trial. The best substitute for the *viva vox* as a basis for decisionmaking at the trial is the full transcript, for this comes closest to reproducing the full complexity of reality that is so crucial to adjudication in the coordinate model.

### 5. *Behavior Expectations*

As a result of differences in the respective authority structures, the objective role expectations of Anglo-American officials present a sharp contrast to those engendered in continental systems. Because the goal of the common law process is justice within the individual case, re-

104. M. OAKESHOTT, RATIONALISM IN POLITICS AND OTHER ESSAYS 128-29 (1962). Bentham's remark that common law, conceived as a system of rules, is "a thing merely imaginary" is thus not as preposterous as it might initially appear. J. BENTHAM, A COMMENT ON THE COMMENTARIES 125 (C. Everett ed. 1928). *See* A. SIMPSON, *supra* note 31, at 88-99, for a modern and quite persuasive argument that common law cannot be understood as a system of rules.

105. In this area, some professionalized Anglo-American police forces come closer to the bureaucratic continental style than do other official bodies. Of late, efforts are observable to make American judges state the basic reasons for imposing a particular sentence. *See* ABA MODEL SENTENCING ACT § 10, in ABA STANDARDS RELATING TO SENTENCING ALTERNATIVES AND PROCEDURES, TENTATIVE DRAFT 333 (1967).

106. The *"chassé-croisé"* between more or less formal styles can be detected even within the "common law tradition", but such shifts are negligible when constrasted to the continental idiom. Compare decisions of the French *Cour de Cassation* with examples of the formal style offered by K. LLEWELLYN, JURISPRUDENCE 306 (1962).

course by its officials to substantive values, such as social policy or ethical considerations, is part of the very essence of their activity. Taking refuge in the neutrality of the legal craft and its universe of norms, while closing one's eyes to what appears desirable in the light of concrete circumstances, is not fully compatible with the dignity of the office. The ideal official in the Anglo-American system is not so much a professional expert as a wise problem-solver, attuned to the values of the community.

Mechanisms to sustain such behavior expectations can, at least in America, be readily located. The first influence is exerted by the system of legal education.[107]

For instance, panoramic vistas of fields of law, conceived as an orderly normative whole, are not offered at all in law school, for they would appear as hollow immensities of dubious value and of an uncertain relationship to reality. The open-endedness of issues is stressed from the very first day of school, so that freshmen will be socialized to a world in which there are few mooring places and little certainty. Most of the time in class is spent debating policy issues, making mental efforts to resolve them under professional guidance. After law school, there is neither a practical apprenticeship nor an entrance examination for official positions, although such events are crucial to the shaping of the sensibilities of continental officials. High office can be entered without any prior bureaucratic experience; candidates for official positions, even at the lowest level, are preferably prominent persons who have behind them careers as politicians or lawyers. Finally, because incumbents of official positions are established people who do not differ widely in importance and prestige on the various echelons of the hierarchy, the desire for advancement does not appear to be as pronounced.

The result of such behavior expectations and training is that the personnel manning the Anglo-American machinery of justice are relatively unwilling to tolerate the low profile and multiple constraints of bureaucracy. Officials are generally forceful and willing to make independent decisions; thus, even at the lowest echelons, few officials

107. Until recently some officials in the Anglo-American system of justice were not even required to be lawyers. In modern times university legal education has been required increasingly, for at least the judicial office, but there are still well known exceptions, such as justices of the peace and some county prosecutors. Moreover, within Anglo-American law schools, specialization is not nearly as narrow as in European universities, and the path to teaching positions is not as arduous as in most continental countries. *See* H. JACOB, JUSTICE IN AMERICA: COURTS, LAWYERS AND THE JUDICIAL PROCESS (1965); David, *supra* note 103, at 5.

display a typically bureaucratic mentality, while at the top it is not surprising to find "charismatic" personalities.[108]

## III. The Structure of Authority and the Conventional Typology of Criminal Proceedings

Two models of authority structure have now been presented. If they successfully capture some essential aspects of the contrast between continental and Anglo-American systems of criminal justice, the next inquiry then becomes their relationship to the conventional dichotomy between adversarial and nonadversarial types of procedure, where this latter set of terms is used to focus on comparisons of process *at the trial stage.*[109] Are authority structures and processing styles independent, or is one set of models, either of authority structure or processing style, ultimately subordinate to the other? This is an intriguing but very difficult question. Fortunately, for the purposes of my article, I need not explore all analytically possible or historically known combinations of authority structure and processing style in the administration of criminal justice. Nor need I consider the labyrinthine problem of which combination is analytically the best match. Instead, my attention centers on the actual combinations that present themselves in the limited field of my comparative inquiry. Accordingly, in the present part of the article I propose to consider only those issues that arise when the coordinate model is paired with adversary procedure, as is the case in Anglo-American countries, and the hierarchical model is matched with nonadversarial proceedings, which occurs in continental jurisdictions.

### A. *The Judge at Trial*

When the positions of the continental and Anglo-American judge are viewed from the different perspectives afforded by authority and process models, a curious puzzle emerges. The Anglo-American judge

108. In using this term, defined in the Weberian sense, I refer particularly to the judiciary. Notice in this connection how little specialization is encountered at the apex of the judicial hierarchy in Anglo-American countries. Charismatic leaders are not technical specialists; the necessary technical knowledge for their pronouncement is supplied to them ad hoc by the litigants, masters, or amici curiae.

109. I have elsewhere criticized the use of these models to explain the contrasting legal systems. *See* Damaška, *supra* note 1, at 561-65. Nonetheless, the descriptive force of the traditional dichotomy is not limited to the trial stage. It also illuminates the prosecutorial role before trial. In the adversary system, the prosecutor is driven into a relatively pronounced opposition to the defendant in anticipation of the trial. The police in Anglo-American countries similarly act in anticipation of an adversary trial with high evidentiary barriers to conviction. One factor that explains differences in police behavior between continental and common law systems is the greater divergence in the latter between what the police actually know and what can be introduced as evidence at trial.

The Yale Law Journal Vol. 84: 480, 1975

has great autonomous powers, but his ideal stance is that of a relatively passive umpire of the adversary process. His continental counterpart is less autonomous, but assumes an active role. It seems strange that the strong is expected to be passive, while the weak is supposed to be active; indeed, many would be inclined to view this combination as an analytical mismatch.

Attempts to explain this bizarre merger must await an analysis of those factors that affect the actual choices of structure and style.[110] In this section, I shall inquire into the features of this curious combination in an effort to illuminate the relationship between models of authority structure and models of trial design.

Let me begin by first taking the Anglo-American side of the comparison. The passive posture of the judge is historically novel[111] and far from being a general description of the judicial office. Instead, it applies only to a limited number of procedural contexts and to a restricted class of issues. Judicial passivity is the rule only during the guilt-determining phase of the trial, and there serves as the norm only with regard to the framing of the subject matter of the proceedings, the collection of evidence, and the presentation of proof.[112] Even in this limited segment of their activity, Anglo-American judges are not rigidly restricted: If a judge believes that abiding by his ideal role will adversely affect the proceedings or poorly serve the public interest, he will usually abandon his detached stance and vigorously intervene in the conduct of the trial.[113] And even though much of

110. *See* p. 529 *infra*.

111. *See* note 156 *infra*.

112. By passivity in framing the subject matter of proceedings I refer to the arrangement whereby the parties themselves determine which claims and defenses to press or to waive. In recent times some Anglo-American jurisdictions have permitted the judge to raise certain defensive issues. *See* note 137 *infra*. Where this has happened, a departure from the adversary model must be acknowledged.

By judicial passivity in collecting evidence I mean the absence of requests by the judge that the parties furnish an evidentiary source, *e.g.*, that a witness be called. Most theoretical writers would agree that if the judge goes beyond merely suggesting to the parties that particular evidence be produced, he is deviating from the adversary style. *But see* F. James, Civil Procedure 5-7 (1965). That judges should be passive in the presentation of proof is correctly viewed as less central to the ideal of adversary proceedings; asking questions of witnesses is compatible with the adversary style. United States v. Liddy, Crim. No. 1827-72 (D.C. Cir., Nov. 8, 1974); United States v. McCord, Crim. No. 73-2252 (D.C. Cir., Dec. 12, 1974) (*see* opinion of court at 17-22). But if the intensity of such judicial activism exceeds a certain point, the judge clearly deviates from his proper role. Finally, it is frequently forgotten that the stance of passivity applies a fortiori to the jury.

113. Some of these deviations from the passive role can be explained by a desire to correct the malfunctioning of the adversary system. Adversary proceedings require an approximate equality between the parties in order to function properly, and if the balance of advantage is seriously affected, the judge may intervene. If his redress of the balance helps the defendant and results in acquittal, his conduct is unreviewable. If he supports the prosecution and conviction follows, the propriety of such assistance is of course subject to review. *See e.g.*, United States v. Guglielmini, 384 F.2d 602, 605 (2d Cir. 1967). As we shall see, however, not all judicial activism can be explained along these lines.

this intervention is technically limited to suggestions to the parties, these "suggestions" will typically be heeded, for both parties will be reluctant to risk unfavorable and often unchallengeable judicial decisions on other matters. Judicial passivity, however, is recognized as an ideal posture only in limited situations. In many phases of the criminal process, such as pretrial hearings, *in camera* examinations, and the sentencing stage, passivity and aloofness come to an end. Indeed, at these junctures in the proceedings Anglo-American judges occasionally assume outright inquisitorial postures that are without counterparts in modern continental systems.[114]

And no one would be more surprised at such powers than the continental judge at trial. It is true that he is the source of most procedural activity: He is responsible for determining the subject matter of the proceedings,[115] and for securing all evidence needed for the ascertainment of the truth. During the proceedings, he not only presides over the taking of proof, but also originates the bulk of questions.[116] The continental trial judge, however, must expect superior review of all his rulings as a matter of course, and is rigidly restricted by a network of rules and customary practices. He has much less independence from normative constraints than his common law counterpart, and also much less power over the parties and other participants at the trial.[117]

It follows from the foregoing that the conventional characterizations of judicial activism in the two systems are of limited explanatory value. An analysis based on differences in the *type* of authority can provide a greater insight into a broader range of judicial activity

114. The prosecution for the break-in at the Watergate headquarters of the Democratic National Committee provides a controversial example. Judge Sirica decided that it was in the public interest to proceed to an inquiry beyond the prosecutorial charge. He refused to accept the guilty pleas (*see* N.Y. Times, Jan. 12, 1973, at 1, col. 1; at 24, col. 6) and imposed unusually harsh "provisional" sentences (up to 40 years). *See* United States v. Liddy, Crim. No. 73-1564 (D.C. Cir. Dec. 12, 1974) (*see* MacKinnon, J., dissenting, at 16-17). This second measure produced results: one defendant decided to talk, and the Watergate scandal was brought to the door of the White House.

Ever since the 19th century reforms, continental judges, whether trial or investigative, have had neither the authority to exceed prosecutorial charges nor such weapons as "provisional sentencing" to put pressure on defendants to cooperate. More generally, observe the broad equity powers of the Anglo-American judge in civil cases. It is the denial to the continental judge of comparable, flexible powers (especially of supervision) which explains more than anything else the absence of the device of the trust in the continental legal system.

115. He is, of course, confined to the prosecutor's charge, but within its limits the judge must raise all relevant issues; and thus there are, for example, no "affirmative" defenses in continental law.

116. For limited exceptions, see Damaška, *supra* note 1, at 525 n.38.

117. There is hardly a counterpart in continental systems to the contempt powers of the common law judge. Parties may also seek judicial disqualification more easily than in the common law system. *See, e.g.*, §§ 22-31, GERMAN CODE OF CRIMINAL PROCEDURE; N.Y. Times, Apr. 14, 1974, at 11, col. 1 (request for removal of Judge Sirica).

than can the traditional dichotomy between active and passive roles. Indeed, this is the case even in those areas to which the traditional view is applicable since it must admit numerous deviations from the type of judicial behavior one would expect on the basis of the traditional dichotomy.

B. *The Complexity of Procedural Issues*

Still another seeming anomaly appears when the two models of authority structure are related to the adversarial and nonadversarial styles of procedure. It will be recalled that officials in the coordinate system are free from precise and stringent legal standards, and do not regard themselves as legal technicians. But the adversary trial in which they operate has a complex structure; much of the law of evidence and procedure is intricate, replete with technicalities. In continental systems the situation is just the opposite: Nonadversary proceedings are comparatively simple, there is relatively little law of evidence,[118] yet the process unfolds before officials who perceive themselves as legal technicians and willingly assume normative constraints.

In attempting to explain this puzzle I must separately consider three issues. First, I shall determine which authority structure is likely to generate more complicated procedural law. Second, I shall inquire whether procedural complexity reduces the decisionmaker's freedom from normative constraints, and whether procedural simplicity leads to the opposite result. Finally, I shall make a few comments on the relationship between the degree of the technical complexity of law and the need for the advance training of officials, for it is this relationship that establishes the different self-perceptions of officials in the two systems.

Which model of authority structure is more likely to create legal complexities? The hierarchical model is possessed by the desire for certainty and uniform decisionmaking. But certainty and uniformity cannot be achieved without ordering, and the latter in turn implies a degree of abstraction. One cannot establish order without rearranging and eliminating whatever does not fit the order-determining principles.[119] Those who think otherwise may be likened to a gardener trying to create a formalized French garden, while refusing to trim and eliminate individual plants.

118. *But see* note 57 *supra*.
119. Examples of this are the preference for brief summaries of relevant facts rather than full transcripts and the neglect of factual description in judicial opinions.

Structures of Authority and Comparative Criminal Procedure

The coordinate model, with its strong attachment to individualized justice, is less willing to neglect the particular in the interest of ordering.[120] Denuding individual cases of those circumstances irrelevant to ordering principles appears as artificial as French topiary art seems to a devotee of the loose and free English gardening style.[121] But this too comes at a cost. The coordinate model must accept a relatively high degree of complexity in its law as the price for a relatively low degree of order in its normative structure.[122]

There is another circumstance bearing on the issue of procedural complexity. Where, as in the coordinate model, the adjudicators are autonomous and much of their decisionmaking is largely unchallengeable, procedural problems arise and assume great importance which are quite secondary or even irrelevant within other systems. At trials to an autonomous adjudicator one cannot afford to be lax in regard to potential sources of error in adjudication, since they often cannot be corrected through review. Quite naturally, then, assuring the adjudicator the proper informational input *before* he decides the case assumes central importance. This is the stage at which parties believe they can have control over the process. Intertwined with the question of guilt, structural questions as to the admissibility of evidence and the proper scope of counsel's behavior have to be litigated before

120. It was Burke, I believe, who saw the characteristic feature of liberty in the complexity of institutions and a danger of tyranny in their simplification; *cf.* G. DE RUGGIERO, THE HISTORY OF EUROPEAN LIBERALISM 99 (1959).

121. The horticultural metaphor is not so farfetched. The classical French garden strikes one as highly rational, just as rationalist attitudes underlie the hierarchical model. By comparison, the English garden seems less orderly, which accords with the Weberian idea that nonbureaucratic organizations are of low rationality. Note also that "the heated controversy during the eighteenth century between defenders of the formalized French garden and the partisans of the looser English style must surely be considered one aspect of the fight for liberalism against the rigid autocracies of the past." R. ARNHEIM, *Order and Complexity in Landscape Design*, in TOWARD A PSYCHOLOGY OF ART 125 (1972). The reader should remember this aesthetic parallel when, in the next part, I turn to the problem of ideologies supporting procedural models.

122. As far as the desire for logical symmetry and clear ordering of the law is concerned, England and continental European countries began to drift apart long before the age of codification on the Continent. Of course, I cannot offer concrete proof of the greater simplicity of continental criminal law in the precodification period; I can only invite the reader to compare a mid-17th century German book on criminal law with an early 18th century English work on the same subject. *Compare* B. CARPZOV, PRACTICA NOVA RERUM CRIMINALIUM IMPERIALIS SAXONICA, *supra* note 11, *with* W. HAWKINS, PLEAS OF THE CROWN (1824). Bear in mind that Carpzov was not a mere theorist, comfortably removed from decisionmaking, but a busy judge in Leipzig. On the other hand, Hawkins was not solely a product of empirical education, but a Cambridge graduate as well. The historical explanation of the greater ordering and intellectual symmetry of continental law is very complicated. Emphasis on different patterns of legal education as an explanatory factor goes back at least to Weber. *See* M. WEBER, RECHTSSOZIOLOGIE 197-201 (1960). For a recent exposition of this view in English, see Coing, *The Roman Law as Ius Commune on the Continent*, 89 LAW Q. REV. 505 (1973). In addition, the development of judicial administration was radically different in England than on the Continent. For the curious English development, see S. MILSOM, *supra* note 79, at 32, 37, 72, 79.

the trial is over. In this scheme it is not unusual to find a symbiosis of autonomous decisionmakers and a caste of highly skilled technical experts whose main purpose is to make sure that the adjudicator is exposed to the proper informational material.[123]

What is the situation in the hierarchical model? Because all decisions are in principle reviewable, a heavy emphasis on prophylactic rules would be misplaced and undesirable. It would only burden the consideration of the merits with "collateral" issues.[124] Moreover, without such a burden, the role of continental lawyers is correspondingly different, and their primary orientation is toward the substantive resolution of the case.

It is thus quite natural for the coordinate model to generate more complicated procedural law than does the hierarchical model. This, however, should not be taken to mean that the freedom of officials in the coordinate model is consequently more narrowly circumscribed. Rather, the attitude of such officials toward procedural and evidentiary norms is decisive. In the coordinate model, rules can legitimately be departed from and the review of such departures is comparatively limited; accordingly, procedural and evidentiary norms are not so compelling as they seem to be in the hierarchical model. Furthermore, even if the prevailing disposition toward legal propositions were the same in both models, there is a point beyond which increased complexity of law, especially in loosely ordered normative systems, objectively increases rather than decreases the decisionmaker's freedom. Contradictory views can plausibly be held, and support found for almost any position. These characteristics are, of course, much more prominent in the coordinate model than in its antipode.

These characteristics establish, and in turn are reinforced by, the different self-perceptions of officials operating within the two models. It is significant, and *not* paradoxical, that adjudicators in the procedurally less technical hierarchical model regard themselves primarily as technical experts, while their counterparts in the procedurally com-

123. It is tempting to suggest that judges in the traditional common law administration of justice are legal experts *assisting* the actual decisionmaker, rather than decisionmakers themselves. The jury is the autonomous adjudicator, while the essential function of the judge is to supervise the flow of information and to supply the jury ad hoc with any necessary technical knowledge.

124. Technical consequences of this different orientation are legion. For instance, the idea of "mistrial," so important in the Anglo-American system, is insignificant or unknown in continental countries; the notion of "fair hearing" is much less central. Moreover, the prejudicial error concept of procedure has developed quite differently in the two systems. Generally speaking, continental systems appear much more reluctant than common law systems to disturb a substantively "correct" adjudication for procedural reasons.

plex coordinate model view themselves more as general problem-solvers than legal technicians. If the individual contours of processed cases are decisive, as is the case in the coordinate model, advance knowledge of the criteria for decision is relatively unimportant. More helpful to the decisionmaker is the knowledge that can best be obtained ad hoc, in the context of litigation. The important residual of the official's own technical expertise is the normatively flexible area of practice and evidence, a rather unlikely subject for advance systematic study. More relevant to the operational demands of a coordinate system than a technical knowledge of norms is a general problem-solving capacity, social imagination, and similar nontechnical qualities.

The hierarchical model represents quite a different world. Its normative universe seems surveyable and its ordering principles, manageable information. As the importance of the particular circumstances of cases decreases, the gaining of advance knowledge of normative criteria for decision becomes a more realistic and fruitful effort. In sum, a more hospitable environment is provided for beliefs, be they illusory or not, that what is involved in making decisions is essentially a technical problem of applying predetermined legal standards.

Once again, however, my discussion of one issue has raised another, and this time broader, question. How did these curious mergers of processing style and authority structure come to pass? Is it possible that their actual choice in continental and Anglo-American countries can be related to a common determinant? It is to this question that I shall now turn.

## IV. The Criminal Process and Attitudes toward Political Authority

### A. *Procedural Models and Political Ideology*

It would betray a great deal of innocence to assume that the genesis of procedural systems reduced essentially to a more or less consistent derivation from the tenets of prevailing political ideology. The latter seldom, if ever, inexorably lead to concrete procedural choices. Furthermore, many problems of criminal procedure are matters of little controversy between ideologies, and even those ideological considerations that are relevant may be deemed less important than countervailing factors.

Consider the role of continuity of tradition. It was certainly of great importance in the gradual evolution of the common law procedure, exposed, as it was, to a variety of historical cross-currents.

The Yale Law Journal Vol. 84: 480, 1975

But even instances of ideologically motivated innovations in continental procedural history do not offer examples of procedural standards and practices written on a *tabula rasa*, but rather on a palimpsest from which the past was never completely erased.

Nevertheless, even if ideological tenets cannot causally explain specific combinations, it is worthwhile to look for possible connections between ideology and particular choices of processing style and organizing authority. In discovering affinities between ideology and criminal procedure we are actually canvassing ideological arguments advanced in support of existing procedural arrangements and in opposition to their change.

### 1. *Parental and Arm's Length Criminal Justice*[125]

Theoretical writers have attempted to articulate ideological orientations that provide an explanation for basic choices in structuring procedural authority and devising procedural arrangements.[126] In American scholarship, these efforts have led to two polar procedural ideologies. One, purporting to capture the fierce agon of Anglo-American procedure, is predicated upon the belief that an irreconcilable conflict between the individual and the state exists in the administration of criminal law. Because state officials cannot be trusted and consummate deviltry on their part cannot be ruled out, the best procedural design is one in which the individual and the state engage as adversaries in a highly formalized battle. The goal of criminal justice must be narrow, limited to the meting out of punishment for specific conduct; if it went beyond that, an unacceptable invasion of the individual sphere would occur.

Opposed to this ideology is the view that there is a basic congruence of interests, and perhaps even mutual love, between the individual and the state. Officials harbor parental emotions toward the defendant: He is viewed by them as an "erring member of the family" who has to be reconciled with and reintegrated into the community. Accordingly, state officials need not be mistrusted, they need not be limited to a passive role in the proceedings, and the ample powers they exercise need not be confiscated because of occasional abuse. Finally, the objectives of the system may be broad, encompassing even educational purposes.

125. The description in the text derives from K. LLEWELLYN, *supra* note 106, at 444; Griffiths, *Ideology in Criminal Procedure*, 79 YALE L.J. 359 (1970).
126. For an illustration of continental efforts in this direction, see G. FOSCHINI, 1 SISTEMA DEL DIRITTO PROCESSUALE PENALE 226-32 (2d ed. 1965).

This polarization of procedural ideologies, no matter how illuminating in other contexts, is unsuitable for the purpose of contrasting modern Anglo-American and continental criminal procedure. Although it cannot be denied that the parental ideology fits some systems known to history, these procedural systems can be found either in tribal cultures or in those modern societies that attempt to restrain antisocial conduct independently of state authority. While in the first case no state has yet developed,[127] it is claimed in the second that the state is moribund, and new reactions to unacceptable behaviour are harbingers of the stateless future.[128] But from the moment the state appears as a factor of any significance until such time as it actually withers away, the parental ideology may rightly be regarded with some circumspection, for it may provide a rationalization for the most brutal kinds of governmental oppression.

Leaving aside some recent but more controversial illustrations, consider the example of medieval inquisitorial procedure. Because medieval society was strongly collectivistic, and the role of government was as yet unlimited, two basic consequences of the parental ideology were present: pronounced togetherness, and a strongly "interventionist" approach to deviant behavior. Even so, the authority exercised by officials in medieval inquisitorial proceedings can hardly be explained as benevolent paternalism. The defendant did not look to the judge for guidance and protection, nor did the judge perceive the defendant *in statu pupillari*. The social distance between the typical defendant and the judges, or the heinous nature of the crime, usually prevented any real empathy among them. In serious cases the judges seldom even saw the defendant, invoking *"acta inquisitionis"* to cover a void of emotion. Thus, at least from our modern perspective, the relationship between the defendant and state officials cannot meaningfully be studied *sub specie amoris*.[129]

127. When the state has appeared but is still weak, the activity of its officials is generally limited to the supervision of contests between private individuals. Thus, while the state is still embryonic, criminal proceedings develop closer to a "battle" model than to a "parental" model.

128. Indeed, this is part of the ideological justification for East European "comradely courts" with jurisdiction, *inter alia*, over minor crimes. A system close to the parental ideology has recently been proposed for dealing with minor crime in American urban communities. *See* Danzig, *supra* note 75, at 15, 42. However, this proposal may be justified more as an abdication of state authority than as its death throes.

129. However, there are indications in contemporary sources that such "parental" justifications were attempted. Punishments for some minor crimes were claimed to have been in the miscreant's own interest (*poenae medicinales*). And even in proceedings against witches and heretics, investigators were sometimes instructed to seek the defendant's confession so that he or she could be reintegrated into the community. *See* *Bartolus de Sassoferrato* in J. HANSEN, QUELLEN UND UNTERSUCHUNGEN ZUR GESCHICHTE DES HEXENWAHNS 66 (1901). T. CAMPANELLA, CIVITAS SOLIS POETICA (1643), offers an ex-

Briefly, then, the polarization of parental and arm's length ideologies must be rejected for my purposes. Rather, to understand the ideological roots of the coordinate and hierarchical models, I shall contrast some unique features of classic English liberalism with several aspects of prevailing continental ideologies relevant to the administration of criminal justice.

2. *Classic English Liberalism as a Source for Procedural Choice*

a. *Limited Government and Diffusion of Authority.* Although it is hazardous to talk in general terms about the main themes of classic English liberalism, the views on political authority attributed to this tradition can be considered fairly representative of it. And it is precisely these views that appear quite singular from the standpoint of those continental ideologies which prevailed at the time when modern political institutions were being shaped.[130]

Within the conceptual horizons of classic liberalism, it seems as if society does best without the state at all. The state should be called in and its influence felt only in times of crises, when something goes wrong in the "self-governing" society; government is solely an arbiter in cases of conflicting interests or disputes. Under no circumstances may government legitimately impose specific beliefs upon citizens; the state is not entitled to guide and educate them in accordance with its own visions about the good life. This is paternalism—one of the strongest aversions of the classic liberal credo.[131]

Two main reasons are usually advanced for this liberal idea of limited government. The first and fundamental explanation reflects a general attitude of skepticism: Since no belief or idea regarding human affairs is exclusively or demonstrably true, it is unjustifiable to impose any such views on other people. The second reason for the ideal of limited government is related to this agnostic epistemological position: Since no one knows what is objectively best, each individual may be presumed capable of making and must be allowed to make his own

ample of a man who conceived a "parental model" of criminal justice while he languished in the dungeons of the Spanish Inquisition; *cf.* R. MARCIC, GESCHICHTE DER RECHTSPHILOSOPHIE 281 (1971). But it is not likely that such intentions to reclaim the criminal were seriously held. A totalitarian state may, however, succeed in transforming society to the degree where parental ideologies become widely accepted; *cf.* K. LLEWELLYN, *supra* note 106, at 447.

130. In what follows I deal only with the division of governmental power among competing power units. It stands to reason that this arrangement in the political system can coexist with great, even monopolistic power concentration in social and economic areas.

131. *Cf.* J. LOCKE, TWO TREATISES ON GOVERNMENT, SECOND TREATISE § 60, at 173 (1960).

choices in life,[132] no matter how strange or even foolish they may seem to others.

But even the most extreme brands of classic liberalism recognize that there are areas of social life in which continuous state intervention cannot be avoided. Where this is the case, and the administration of justice is an example in point, great concentrations of power must be prevented and the diffusion of authority is regarded as a political imperative. There are two ways in which authority may be fragmented. The more obvious method is to distribute it along a horizontal axis, among powerholders at the same level. It is this first, Montesquieuan form that has virtually monopolized the attention of both continental and Anglo-American political theorists, particularly with regard to the upper echelons of governmental structures. But while it became part of the dominant ideology in the English-speaking world, the doctrine of the "separation of powers" never really took hold in Europe, insofar as it implies the creation of independent power centers which balance one another.[133] A second way of fragmenting authority has received much less attention and is usually encountered in discussions of federalism. Yet this fragmentation is an important phenomenon, and I believe, quite typical of the intricate weave of the English political tradition of strong local self-government. It involves the allocation of authority along a vertical axis, in its "scalar" aspect; in this way, subordinated structures of government are vested with substantial autonomous powers and hence share a measure of supreme authority with the highest level of government. A mosaic of local power centers is thus created. But, as a result of the horizontal division of authority, the powers of local potentates are rather narrow, and abuses by one may be checked by the refusal of others to cooperate. It is this second form of diffusing authority, leading to minimal centralization, that

132. *See* C. MACPHERSON, THE POLITICAL THEORY OF POSSESSIVE INDIVIDUALISM 244 (1962).

133. Conceived as a separation of legislative, judicial and administrative *functions*, the separation of powers may be said to be more rigorous on the Continent than in Anglo-American countries; the judiciary is denied lawmaking powers, and the legislature is refused any judicial or *quasi*-judicial functions. But, if separation of powers is viewed as calling for the establishment of independent power centers which check and balance each other, the model becomes alien to continental political theories. Considered spurious by Rousseau, it is generally rejected because it both conflicts with the necessary unity of government and creates animated political standstills. The *locus classicus* on legal aspects of the continental variant of the separation of powers is still 2 C. DE MALBERG, CONTRIBUTION A LA THÉORIE GÉNÉRALE DE L'ÉTAT § 1, at 23-34 (1922). This famous French legal theorist thought the idea of checks and balances (*freins et contre-poids*) was tolerable in America solely because it was not extended, he mistakenly assumed, to the states, but was limited to the federal government. *Id.* at 22 n.13. On the enthusiastic American acceptance of the doctrine of separation of powers, see G. WOOD, THE CREATION OF THE AMERICAN REPUBLIC 151, 604 (1969); THE FEDERALIST Nos. 10, 47, 51 (J. Madison). In socialist countries of Eastern Europe, separation of powers is rejected on familiar Marxist grounds, as a cloak to hide the essential unity of the ruling class.

is in perfect harmony with classic English liberalism but quite alien to any influential continental political ideology.[134] Indeed, this second diffusion of authority constitutes one of the most striking features of the English political culture.

It would be incorrect to understand "liberalism" only in the context of its modern variants. The antipathy of classic English liberalism toward state intervention and strong central government may not be the attitude most congenial to the implementation of substantive liberal values. Indeed, a centralized state may further the development of liberal values, and it is by no means clear that central tyranny is necessarily worse than the tyranny of local potentates. Accordingly, the classic English liberal attitudes toward the state are not a necessary ingredient of the modern liberal credo; instead, they must be regarded as a matter of historical contingency, so that hostility toward the state is a product of ideological inertia, remaining from the days when power had not yet passed into liberal hands. Freedom, to classical liberals, was mainly freedom *from* the state, and there were only "a few presentiments" that the state in liberal hands could accomplish tasks for which spontaneous social organizations and private enterprise are insufficient.[135]

b. *Procedural Implications of Classic Liberalism.* It is hardly necessary to ask whether the ideology of classic English liberalism favors the coordinate over the hierarchical model of authority structures in the criminal process. The preference for the former follows easily from the general liberal distaste for concentrated power, and more particularly from its attachment to what I have called the vertical fragmentation of authority. Let me therefore turn to the relationship between the liberal ideology and the conventional adversarial and nonadversarial models of processing style.

In introducing this theme it is useful to step back from the usual focus for a moment and imagine the full concentration of procedural authority in the hands of only one official. An example of such a monopoly of power is the figure of the inquisitorial investigating judge. He decided on his own initiative what cases to process, and

134. Exceptions to this rule can only be found in some brands of socialist ideology (*e.g.*, the Yugoslav "self-management") which, in an attempt to disperse authority and decentralize, led to legal reforms. Excepting the area of federalism there is little political or legal literature on the vertical fragmentation of authority. Much more can be learned from writings in the area of business organizations, particularly those discussing the problems of vertical integration of firms as opposed to "autonomous contracting" in the market. *See* O. WILLIAMSON, MARKETS AND HIERARCHIES: ANALYSIS AND ANTITRUST IMPLICATIONS (forthcoming 1975).

135. *See* G. DE RUGGIERO, *supra* note 120, at 60, 135, 368.

possessed full authority to determine any issue which in his opinion required examination. Using our modern concepts, one may say that the prosecutorial, defense and adjudicative functions were merged in this role.[136] The 19th century continental reforms of criminal procedure resulted in the dissolution of this concentration of power and led to the separation of prosecutorial and adjudicative functions. Following these reforms, the continental judge could proceed only on the motion of a prosecutor, and the subject of his inquiries was limited to the offense described in the prosecutor's charge. Although motivated by independent reasons, this separation of functions is consistent with continental political ideas on the separation of powers. But, unlike the Anglo-American system, continental procedural systems refused to go beyond this point.

The additional narrowing of judicial functions in the Anglo-American criminal process cannot be justified by any influential continental theory of the relationship between the state and the individual. However, it may be understood with reference to classic English liberalism. Let me show this by considering a number of examples.

The proposition that the defendant be given a monopoly over most defense issues, and be permitted to discharge them as best he can without judicial interference, finds no support in prevailing continental political ideologies, and is generally alien to continental legal culture.[137] Classic English liberalism provides an easy justification for this arrangement: The defendant is presumed to know what is best for him, and since no one else can establish better knowledge, no official has the right to impose his views on the defendant. Within the adjudicative function that exists after the prosecutorial and defense functions have been severed, a further fragmentation may take

136. Where the judgment was rendered by a panel of judges, as was the case in serious matters, a similar concentration of functions took place. Deciding essentially on the basis of the investigative dossier, the panel was supposed to act simultaneously as prosecutors, defense counsel, and judges.

137. As part of his official duties the continental judge must raise all defense issues for which there is some support in the case. Any other arrangement is viewed as risking the conviction of an innocent person. The trend in modern Anglo-American law is away from the radical position under which the defense has a full monopoly over defense issues. For instance, some jurisdictions authorize the trial judge to raise the issue of insanity on his own initiative. *See, e.g.*, United States v. Robertson, Crim. No. 1631-71 (D.C. Cir., Oct. 22, 1974); Whalem v. United States, 346 F.2d 812, 819 (D.C. Cir. 1965). But it is significant that the drafters of the ALI Model Penal Code rejected this arrangement as "too great an interference with the conduct of the defense." MODEL PENAL CODE § 4.03, Comment at 194 (Tent. Draft No. 4, 1955).

Another consequence of divesting the judge of defense functions is that the collection of exculpating evidence becomes basically a private enterprise; *cf.* Brady v. Maryland, 373 U.S. 83 (1963). This *laissez-faire* atmosphere so pervades the Anglo-American system that the advent of "public defenders" for the indigent defendant may be viewed by many as a considerable innovation.

place if the defendant so desires. The crucial function of determining guilt can be taken away from state officials in all but minor criminal cases and vested in a group of citizens. And if the latter refuse to convict the defendant, no matter what result seems to be mandated on the basis of the ascertained facts and applicable law, their decision is in this respect sovereign.[138] Thus the Anglo-American judge's role begins to resemble the ideal role of the state in the liberal vision of society: Both state and judge are transformed into arbitrators, supervising societal conflicts. In sum, then, the limited functions of the Anglo-American judge, so central in the adversary type of trial, reflect both the idea of limited government and the horizontal division of authority.[139] But because authority is also vertically fragmented, the judge retains great autonomous powers, and, free from a comprehensive superior review, can depart from his theoretically narrow role whenever necessary to achieve justice.

The classic liberal ideology, however, provides support for more than the fundamental matrix of the adversary type of trial. Again consider the defendant's role. Continental lawyers often marvel at the degree to which crucial decisions in the Anglo-American system of criminal justice are withdrawn from state officials, and consequently withdrawn from legal norms and rational and objective decisional standards.

It is the operation of the defendant's choice, rather than of an inexorable procedural rule invoked by the state, which determines the mode of processing to be applied in his case. If he decides not to oppose the charge, an extremely informal "adjudication by consent" will typically follow, no matter how serious the offense involved. Where charges are contested, the decision whether to have a trial by jury or

138. I should reiterate at this point that I am concerned with possible liberal justifications of existing procedural arrangements, rather than trying to prove that such arrangements actually derive from liberal tenets. The division of functions between judge and jury antedates liberalism by centuries.

139. The horizontal division of authority is also noticeable in the denial to the Anglo-American judge of full authority to decide whether an arrangement between the prosecution and the defense accords with the public interest; under existing law, the judge shares this authority with the public prosecutor. It can be argued that under a pure adversary model the parties should be sovereign in their arrangements, the prosecutor acting as *sole* guardian of the public interest. A similar issue on the role of the judge also arises in connection with acceptance of the defendant's guilty plea. *See* United States v. Ammidown, 497 F.2d 615 (D.C. Cir. 1973). *See generally* North Carolina v. Alford, 400 U.S. 25 (1970).

Some scholars claim that this narrowing derives from notions about the best allocation of functions between parties to the dispute. *See* F. JAMES, CIVIL PROCEDURE 4 (1965). It is unclear, however, why such notions about optimal allocation are entertained—as far as criminal matters go—only in the Anglo-American system.

judge is again usually made by the defendant.[140] On the Continent, by contrast, separate types of processing are chosen in accordance with predetermined rules: the more severe the offense, the more elaborate the proceedings. There is very little that the defendant can do to change this arrangement, and nothing at all in case of serious crime.[141]

This division of roles also applied to the transplanted jury system which, once imported, soon suffered a decline. Throughout the jury's checkered history on the Continent, the legislature specified the catalogue of crimes, usually only of the most serious kind, which were triable to a jury. The defendant had no say on the matter, no waiver of jury trial was permitted, for the provision was *jus cogens*. Similarly, if the Anglo-American defendant *refuses* to be represented by counsel, the system cannot force him to do so, no matter how grave the charges, and despite the fact that optimal functioning from within the adversarial mode requires lawyers on both sides. The defendant has the moral right "to stand alone in his hour of trial."[142] This notion is rejected by continental systems, although defense counsel is there not nearly so crucial as in the Anglo-American system. Continental law mandates that, if certain serious criminal charges are involved, the defendant *must* be represented by counsel irrespective of his insistence on acting *pro se*.[143]

As a final illustration, consider the problem of illegally obtained

140. In legal theory, the decision concerning a jury trial does not reside exclusively in the defendant. *See* Singer v. United States, 380 U.S. 24, 25 (1965) ("We find no constitutional impediment to conditioning a waiver [of jury trial] on the consent of the prosecuting attorney and the trial judge when, if either refuses to consent, the result is simply that the defendant is subject to an impartial trial by jury . . ."). In fact, however, his choice is usually honored. *See* Note, *Government Consent to Waiver of Jury Trial under Rule 23(a) of the Federal Rules of Criminal Procedure*, 65 YALE L.J. 1032 (1956) ("Ordinarily government consent to waiver may be obtained as a matter of course . . .").

141. Where a minor crime is involved, the defendant can influence the mode of processing to some degree. Remote counterparts to pleading guilty have a long tradition in some continental countries. *See, e.g.*, the French *Ordonnance Criminelle*, Titre 14, Art. 19 (1670) (commentaries to this provision, applicable solely to minor crime, can be found in A. ESMEIN, *supra* note 11, at 275). This situation persists in modern systems. For a lucid presentation of such devices in West Germany, see J. Langbein, *supra* note 51.

But where serious offenses are involved, the case must go to trial even if the defendant fully confesses. All that the defendant's confession will effect is the shortening of the relevant criminal process. Nor can the gains to the system be compared with those arising from the avoidance of the Anglo-American trial. For some empirical data on this problem, see Casper & Zeisel, *supra* note 21, at 146.

142. *See* United States v. Dougherty, 473 F.2d 1113, 1128 (D.C. Cir. 1972) (statutory right under 28 U.S.C. § 1654 (1970)). On the *constitutional* right to *pro se* representation, see Faretta v. California, 43 U.S.L.W. 3301 (U.S., argued Nov. 19, 1974) (No. 73-5772). There is, however, no question about the *pro se* right in England, where failure to respect it is a ground for appeal. *See* The King v. Woodward, [1944] 1 K.B. 118.

143. Continental systems usually speak of "necessary defense" (*notwendige Verteidigung*). *See, e.g.*, COMPARATIVE CRIM. LAW PROJECT OF N.Y.U., GERMAN CODE OF CRIMINAL PROCEDURE § 140 (1965) [hereinafter cited as GERMAN CODE OF CRIMINAL PROCEDURE]; CODE OF CRIMINAL PROCEDURE OF THE RSFSR art. 49, in H. BERMAN, SOVIET CRIMINAL LAW AND PROCEDURE (2d ed. 1972).

The Yale Law Journal Vol. 84: 480, 1975

evidence. Continental systems are generally less hospitable to the idea that reliable but illegally obtained evidence should be rejected. Those exclusions that take place are accomplished as part of official duties and, where this occurs, even defendant's consent will not suffice to allow the use of illegally obtained evidence.[144]

Continental lawyers observing the Anglo-American criminal process have voiced fears that entrusting so many decisions to the defendant threatens his interests and may lead as well to objectively false determinations. They note, for instance, that if a defendant—for some reason best known to himself—fails to raise a defense that is both complete in law and supportable in fact, the verdict may go against him and an innocent man thereby be convicted. And they add that when issues of such strategic importance depend on the defendant's will, officials may be tempted to pressure defendants into waiving their rights to the costlier modes of processing.

These and similar objections carry decisive weight in the continental legal system, and find support in the prevailing views of the relationship of state and individual. In the framework of classical liberalism, as expressed, for example, in 19th century utilitarianism, these objections seem far weaker and too rigidly dogmatic.[145]

I could easily continue to enumerate procedural arrangements characteristic of the Anglo-American system of criminal justice that are justifiable in the context of classic English liberalism[146] but antithetical to all influential continental ideologies. What I have said so

144. Seldom will this be expressed in statutes or codes, for it is considered as self-evident in light of continental "legal science." Occasionally, however, it is expressed in legislative texts. *See, e.g.*, GERMAN CODE OF CRIMINAL PROCEDURE, *supra* note 143, § 136a (1965).

145. The marriage of classic liberalism and utilitarianism is usually taken for granted. *See, e.g.*, Smith, *Liberalism*, in 9 INT'L ENCYC. SOC. SCI. 276 (1968). It is, however, a marriage with many strains, especially if classic Benthamite utilitarianism is involved. *See* J. RAWLS, A THEORY OF JUSTICE 22-23, (1971) (especially at 29, 33). Using the concepts developed by Professor Packer, one is tempted to say that utilitarianism tends toward the "Crime Control Model," while classic liberalism (including some newer accretions with welfare state overtones) espouses the "Due Process Model." *See* H. PACKER, THE LIMITS OF THE CRIMINAL SANCTION 149-73 (1968). But on the issue discussed in the text, both marital partners, liberalism and utilitarianism, seem to concur, albeit on different grounds.

146. There is one important difference in continental and Anglo-American thinking about procedural arrangements at trial that is independent of classic liberalism, especially in its historically oldest "negative" strand that was inspired by reactions against monarchical oppression. In approaching the desirability of particular procedural arrangements, continental and Anglo-American lawyers often do not have in mind the same paradigmatic criminal case. The former imagine a case of relatively routine nature in which the hypothesis of guilt is more likely than that of innocence. The paradigm for the latter is a very close, almost Buridanian case. It is true that this difference, if indeed it exists, can be related to liberal fears of governmental persecution of the innocent, but there is a better explanation. All cases come to trial under the continental system, and the pretrial investigation screens out those in which the evidence is insufficient, thus increasing the proportion of cases in which guilt is a likely hypothesis. Cases coming up for trial under the common law system of pleading are not routine and may well be mostly "close cases."

far, however, is enough to show that classic liberalism would imply both the preference for the adversarial over the nonadversarial style, and the choice of the coordinate over the hierarchical model.[147]

### B. *The Genesis of Divergent Attitudes toward Authority*

Although it is evident that continental and English liberal political theories diverge with respect to governmental authority, the source of this divergence is elusive and undetermined. Putting this question in an Anglocentric form, why is it that the Continent is alone in its tolerance of concentrated authority? It has been fashionable, particularly in the last century, to seek the answer in the peculiarity of the English *Volksgeist*.[148] But few people nowadays would maintain that ideologies develop independently of their social context, even if, in their philosophies, they attribute autonomy to ideas. It is more likely that we may account for different perceptions of authority by studying the dissimiliar developments of political institutions in England and on the Continent. The roots of these developments are, of course, hidden in the recesses of history. But at least some of them are related to the different manner in which feudalism developed and was overcome on the Continent and in England. Renouncing, therefore, my mainly analytic perspective, I shall in this last part venture a brief historical excursus.

It is well known that feudalism appeared somewhat earlier on the Continent than in England. Many circumstances combined to make the early variant of this socio-economic structure very disrup-

147. The parallels between the liberal ideology and procedural arrangements should not be urged too far. First, liberalism as a political ideology is not without internal conflicts. It seems to vacillate between the desire to limit the role of the state and the desire to seek governmental intervention to enhance individual opportunities. Social ills may sometimes be the consequence of oppressive governmental control; at other times, the result of lack of control. Depending on historical circumstance, the balance between the two strands can cast a classical liberal as either a progressive or conservative.

Second, many characteristics of the Anglo-American administration of justice depart from liberal tenets. Consider only the fashionable emphasis on treatment and rehabilitation. Modeling people according to certain images connotes state concern with persons rather than their activities, and runs contrary to classic liberalism. However, liberalism affected substantive ideas as well as criminal procedure. Especially in debates on the limits of the criminal sanction, classic liberalism is still vital. *See* Note, *Limiting the State Police Power: Judicial Reaction to John Stuart Mill*, 37 U. CHI. L. REV. 605 (1970).

148. These views are, I think, effectively criticized by R. CAENEGEM, THE BIRTH OF THE ENGLISH COMMON LAW 86 (1973). Similar criticism can be levelled against attempts to explain the many parallels between Anglo-American and classical Roman criminal processes in terms of alleged similarities between the Roman and English "national spirits." A better explanation of these parallels is the similar pattern of structuring political authority in the Roman and English political traditions. Both political cultures display many characteristics of the coordinate model: an elaborate system of checks and balances among autonomous magistracies, duplication of functions, reluctance to abolish obsolete institutions, and slow, adventitious growth instead of deliberate intervention.

tive of order and unity. The Continent was dismembered into a kaleidoscope of virtually independent provinces, controlled by local feudal lords and only loosely bound into larger political units. In the days of slow communication and rudimentary administrative mechanisms, effective rule from a distant center was virtually impossible. As time passed, strongly entrenched regional and local political institutions crystallized. It was thus difficult for continental rulers to create exclusive states out of the existing loose confederations. To effect this gradual extension of control, rulers dispatched officials to occupy provincial and local positions of authority as agents of the central power. At first these officials were weak and perforce respected local customs and privileges. As they gained strength, however, a centralized, stratified bureaucracy emerged.[149] In areas where feudal fragmentation had caused disruptions and frustrated economic development, the emerging central rule became associated with order and stability. The final product of this development was the continental absolutist monarchy. Even progressive people who opposed such absolutism believed in the need for strong central rule; when the French Revolution destroyed the old order, for example, royal administration was expanded rather than dismantled.[150]

It was in these contexts that continental attitudes toward authority were shaped. People became adapted to strong central rule, regarding it as both antagonist and savior. Liberal cynics would probably prefer to say that people became insensitive to the evils of concentrated power in the way that Mithridates became immune to poison: by taking it in increasing doses.[151] Those who rebelled against power were few, and went to the extreme of viewing the state as intrinsically evil.[152] But even when their minds dreamed forward into the ideal

149. *See* J. STRAYER, *supra* note 36, at 50-56. The development in Italy was different from the French, and, some may think, deviating from the continental "hierarchical model", at least as far as the administration of the Communes is concerned. However, even within city-states, more than one layer of judicial administration existed, and judicial office was viewed as a delegated rather than as an autonomous function. *See* Calisse, *A History of Italian Law*, in 8 CONTINENTAL LEGAL HISTORY SERIES 145-46, 165 (1928). The Swiss experience is singular and cannot be discussed here.

150. *See* A. DE TOCQUEVILLE, L'ANCIEN RÈGIME (1933); L. HARTZ, THE LIBERAL TRADITION IN AMERICA 44 (1955).

151. Continentals accept as natural many governmental measures that seem reprehensible to Anglo-American liberals, *e.g.*, the role of identity cards. Moreover, many procedural possibilities in continental systems lie unused out of respect for authority (*e.g.*, some broad testimonial privileges).

152. It is well known that most continental liberals were not as implacably hostile to the state as classic English liberals. They believed in the need for state intervention and unity in order to prevent confusion and anarchy. Freedom to them lay not in independence *from* the state, but in turning it to liberal purposes, in taking an active part in it. *See* G. DE RUGGIERO, *supra* note 120. Only a few continental liberals regarded the state as such with antipathy. *See, e.g.*, W. VON HUMBOLDT, IDEEN ZU EINEM VERSUCHE DIE

stateless future, their imaginations did not envision an individualistic society. In their view man was ultimately a social being, a *Gattungswesen*. Significantly, when these continental rebels inspired mass movements, the exigencies of the revolutionary present were said to preempt visions of the stateless tomorrow. The concentration of power was declared an historical necessity, many social institutions were absorbed into the fabric of the state, and the stateless future was placed "on the other side of history."

The English experience was quite different and in some ways rather unique. Prior to the advent of feudalism, local notables were all but wiped out by successive invasions of the British Isles; the Norman kings, who imported feudalism, were sufficiently farsighted not to grant large, compact landholdings to their vassals. As a result, strong local power centers did not emerge. There was also the crucial circumstance of small scale, which allowed direct and very effective royal intervention throughout the land. There was no need for kings to establish a large central bureaucracy as a transmission mechanism between them and local government. Local notables, not strong enough to be feared, worked in the local administration without pay, thereby eliminating a major expense for the Crown.[153]

Notwithstanding great royal power, however, English feudalism managed to establish a measure of what we would now call constitutional restraint on its monarchs,[154] and this in the context of a feudalism that was not nearly as disruptive and centrifugal as its continental counterpart. The chaotic War of the Roses was, admittedly, succeeded by a brief intermezzo of Tudor absolutism, but this was neither so rigid nor so enduring as its later continental counterparts. The fight of the middle class against feudal restrictions resulted in the supremacy of the Parliament and a generally less radical break with the not-so-abhorrent past than was later the case in France.

This moderate social change preserved many ancient forms of government by nobility and arrested the development of modern bureaucracies. An essentially local administration by notables prevailed in England well into the 19th century;[155] indeed, because the age of administrative reforms in England was also the zenith of *laissez-faire*,

GRENZEN DER WIRKSAMKEIT DES STAATES ZU BESTIMMEN (1851). Some continental outcries against the state, such as the Nietzschean *so wenig Staat wie möglich* (as little state as possible), were placed in such ambivalent intellectual contexts that they were even exploited by totalitarian ideologues.

153. *See* J. STRAYER, *supra* note 36, at 36-37, 47.

154. *See* W. ULMANN, THE INDIVIDUAL AND SOCIETY IN THE MIDDLE AGES 51 (1966).

155. For additional details, see L. NAMIER, ENGLAND IN THE AGE OF THE AMERICAN REVOLUTION, 3-41 (2d ed. 1961).

strong centralization was never truly considered as an alternative to many increasingly obsolete administrative arrangements. While some reforms affected the administration of the criminal law, many archaic procedural ideas, some of them vestiges from the days of the emerging state, suddenly accorded with the prevailing philosophy of individualism and limited government. Rather than being rejected, they were refurbished and incorporated in the system of criminal justice which slowly assumed its present contours.[156] "The importance of being antiquated"[157] was thus vindicated with the second turn of the historical spiral. In the whole of the English experience, there is little that could have conditioned people to accept a strongly centralized bureaucratic machinery as a *conditio sine qua non* of societal order.

Transplanted to America, the classic liberal ethos fell upon fertile soil. Feudalism as a socio-economic order was skipped altogether, and strong centralist rule was never part of the national experience. While the distant English rule inspired colonists with resentment of authority, the overthrow of English dominion did not require the strong arm of concentrated power. In addition, such circumstances as the frontier society, the natural abundance of resources, and the religious legacies of 17th century Protestantism, facilitated the introduction of liberal dispositions toward authority into the American political culture to an extent astonishing even to English 19th century liberals. People never became mithridated by concentrated power.[158] It is only around the middle of the last century that the partnership between liberalism and diffuse authority came under great strain. The crises

156. Of course, some important differences between the criminal process on the Continent and in England antedated the 19th century reforms. The 13th century papal prohibition of clergy participation in trials by ordeal triggered the divergence of the two systems, although they had begun to drift apart even before. This prohibition created a vacuum in the administration of justice which was filled by different procedural arrangements in England and continental Europe. For modern perspectives on this development see R. CAENEGEM, *supra* note 148, at 84.

The adversarial style of processing criminal matters is largely a product of the early 19th century. Until the middle of that century, the pretrial phase of the process was essentially a type of judicial investigation along inquisitorial lines conducted by justices of the peace. Nor was the trial an adversary battle of counsel. Lawyers would seldom appear for the prosecution, and defense counsel were not admitted in ordinary felony cases until 1837. In this situation the judge called witnesses and examined them, and in the century prior, had also interrogated the defendant. For an account of such judicial trial examination, see Fielding's picaresque novel *Tom Jones*. H. FIELDING, THE HISTORY OF TOM JONES, book 8, ch. 11 (1906).

Evidentiary and procedural finesse, so characteristic of the adversary process, could not develop in the context of a trial without lawyers. Indeed, until the modern era, there were no law reports of criminal cases. For a realistic account of the criminal process prior to modern times, see S. MILSOM, *supra* note 79, at 353-74.

157. The phrase has been borrowed from another context in R. CAENEGEM, *supra* note 148, at 84.

158. *See* L. HARTZ, *supra* note 150, at 39-50; G. WOOD, *supra* note 133, at 150-51, 604. Perceived needs for order, so important for the opposition between the coordinate and hierarchical model, may be related to the experience with political authority.

of slavery and secession forced many liberal minds to turn to central authority as a guarantor of liberal values. It is true that, as our century progresses, many tenets of classic liberalism increasingly clash with new realities, but no alternative social theory has emerged as a dominant ideological force.

The administration of criminal law is one area in which the continued vitality of liberalism is very much in evidence, notwithstanding strong counterpressures generated by the modern system of mass criminal justice.[159] And the specter of imperious and oppressive governmental inteference in the life of the individual is still a powerful generator of procedural choices.

## Epilogue

In the first part of this article, the "hierarchical" model of authority was outlined and used to illuminate salient aspects of the continental procedural system. In the second part, the "coordinate" model was sketched and its explanatory power demonstrated by considering actual Anglo-American criminal processes. This description showed that the two systems differ significantly in the extent of the centralization of authority, the degree of its rigidity, the choice between determinative and flexible rules, the importance attached to formality and documentation, and the types of behavior expectations held by government officials.

Using this framework I next examined the connection between authority structures and criminal processing styles. Finally, I left the legal arena altogether and trespassed into the realm of political ideology. Although my narrative has not proceeded in an historical vacuum, I have not intended it primarily as a study, however superficial, of the genesis of legal phenomena. Rather, I have suggested some fundamental conceptual relationships that link certain political ideologies and particular forms of criminal justice systems.

Even if my unpardonable abridgment of history has persuaded the reader that the singular characteristics of the Anglo-American criminal process can be related to unique liberal dispositions toward gov-

159. Pressures of modern mass criminal justice to discard liberal ideology were brilliantly described by H. PACKER, *supra* note 145, at 149-73, in his depiction of the "Crime Control Model." Some procedural reforms instituted by the Supreme Court, during the 1960's, imposing positive duties on the government to help the indigent, may arguably be interpreted as a departure from classic *laissez-faire*. *See, e.g.*, Douglas v. California, 372 U.S. 353 (1963); Gideon v. Wainwright, 372 U.S. 335 (1963); Griffin v. Illinois, 351 U.S. 12 (1956).

The Yale Law Journal Vol. 84: 480, 1975

ernment authority, the reader who likes to take sociological theory with his history will probably want to continue the search for more basic factors. My discussion has already unveiled a larger problem by implication. Throughout this article I have treated continental systems as a group, lumping together Western democracies and Marxian socialist countries. This I have done in the belief that great differences among various continental systems of criminal justice pale in significance when contrasted with the Anglo-American. Does my position imply that, at least as far as the organization of procedural authority and the type of processing style are concerned, attitudes toward political authority are more important sources of procedural divergences than the social and economic structure of society?[160] This larger question comes tantalizingly close to my theme, but I must leave it aside because of the great complexity of problems involved in answering it. Thus, there is no *dénouement* to issues raised by this article, and I can unfortunately offer no deeply satisfying synthesis to the reader patient enough to follow me to the end.

160. This is inseparable from the fascinating and urgent problem of how the distinction between continental and common law legal systems relates to the opposition between capitalism and socialism.

[16]

The University of Chicago Law Review

VOLUME 41, NUMBER 3, SPRING 1974

# Controlling Prosecutorial Discretion in Germany*

*John H. Langbein*†

Among the major western legal systems, the West German is unique in its concern with controlling prosecutorial discretion. The Germans have isolated the elements of the problem, and they have implemented legislation to limit prosecutorial discretion and, indeed, to exclude it altogether in the most important cases. The German and American systems of criminal procedure differ in fundamental matters of principle and structure, and these differences restrict the direct transferability of insights and practices between the two. Nevertheless, there are also important similarities, especially in the pretrial powers and responsibilities of the prosecutorial office. Americans in search of solu-

* This article results from a period of research spent in 1973 at the Max Planck Institut für ausländisches und internationales Strafrecht, Freiburg- im- Breisgau. I wish to record my thanks to Professor Günther Kaiser, director of the criminology section, and to Professor H.-H. Jescheck, director of the institute, for making their facilities available to me; to the Alexander von Humboldt-Stiftung and the University of Chicago Center for Studies in Criminal Justice for financial support; and to Norval Morris, director of the Center, who went to considerable effort to help me organize this project. From the outset my work has enjoyed the expert guidance of Joachim Herrmann of the University of Augsburg and of Thomas Weigend, formerly a graduate student at the University of Chicago Law School, now a member of the Freiburg institute. The German prosecutor has been a figure of interest for a number of my colleagues at the University of Chicago Law School, including Gerhard Casper, Kenneth Culp Davis, Hein Kötz, and Max Rheinstein. I have benefited from their suggestions and from critiques of an earlier draft of this paper by Philip Kurland and Bernard Meltzer of the University of Chicago Law School, George Fletcher of the University of California, Los Angeles, Donald McIntyre of the American Bar Foundation, Erich Schanze of the University of Frankfurt, and Lloyd Weinreb of the Harvard Law School.

† Professor of Law, University of Chicago.

tions for our own complex problem of prosecutorial discretion should be aware of the German model.

## I. The Prosecutor's Monopoly

What we call prosecutorial discretion arises from the public prosecutor's power of nonprosecution. No society would tolerate a rule of compulsory prosecution so relentless that the prosecutor were required to institute criminal proceedings in every case, no matter how weak the incriminating evidence. The prosecutor, or the policeman who often stands in his shoes, must have the power to evaluate the evidence in advance of instituting trial. If he is convinced that a suspect's conduct did not violate the criminal law or that the evidence cannot persuade the court of the suspect's guilt, he serves the social interest by not wasting resources on a frivolous criminal trial and by not subjecting the defendant to its many discomforts. The prosecutor, being mortal, may err in his exercise of this power of nonprosecution. He may misinterpret the law, he may misevaluate the cogency of the evidence. That is a routine hazard of decision making. It does not call into doubt the wisdom of allowing the prosecutor to decide.

The prosecutor's power of nonprosecution becomes controversial when it extends beyond the power to discard hopeless cases. Prosecutorial discretion, as we shall be using the term, means the power to decline to prosecute in cases of provable criminal liability. It is the prosecutor's power to select among cases, indeed among like cases, those he shall press and those not. The public officer responsible for law enforcement is permitted to pick and choose which laws he will enforce and against which violators.

What makes this problem of prosecutorial discretion so acute in American practice is that our prosecutor has a monopoly over the criminal process. In cases of serious crime he alone procures the indictment or lays the information; and thereafter, his powers to dismiss, to compromise, or to insist on full trial are all but unlimited. No other officer and no private citizen, not even the victim, may come forward to prosecute when the public prosecutor will not. No one else may make good the prosecutor's neglect.

The omnipotence of the public prosecutor in American procedure is a sharp divergence from the common law model. In England private prosecution continues in theory to be the norm. Official prosecution is formally limited to the handful of cases brought by the Director of Public Prosecutions. "When 'the police' prosecute, the correct analysis is that some individual has instituted proceedings, and the fact that this individual is a police officer does not alter the nature of the prosecution."[1] Although public officials prosecute almost all cases, they do so in the guise of private citizens. It follows that private citizens not in uniform can (and do[2]) prosecute even cases of serious crime.

From a quite different starting point, the classical Continental criminal procedural system, the French, has also avoided creating a prosecutorial monopoly. Although the prosecutorial corps normally commands the formal public prosecution, *l'action publique*,[3] private prosecution under the rubric of *l'action civile* has acquired a significant sphere. The primary function of *l'action civile* is to permit the victim of a crime to constitute himself *partie civile* and to join a claim for civil damages to the public prosecutor's action for criminal sanctions.[4] If the public prosecutor does not initiate *l'action publique*, the *partie civile* may do it himself,[5] ostensibly in order to provide the necessary basis for his parasitic damages claim. What in fact results is akin to private prosecution. The use of this procedure has grown enormously in the present century on account of what Americans would call a relaxation of standing requirements. Trade unions, policemen's associations, and numerous other juristic persons have been allowed to deem them-

---

1 R. Jackson, The Machinery of Justice an England 155 (6th ed. 1972). For historical background, see Kurland & Waters, *Public Prosecutions in England, 1854–79: An Essay in English Legislative History*, 1959 Duke L.J. 493; Langbein, *The Origins of Public Prosecution at Common Law*, 17 Am. J. Legal Hist. 313 (1973).

2 For example, the highly publicized prosecution by Francis Bennion against Peter Hain, chairman of the Young Liberals, who was convicted at jury trial on August 21, 1972, of conspiracy to hinder and disrupt a Davis Cup tennis match at Bristol in 1969. The case arose out of protest demonstrations against White South African teams appearing at sporting contests in Britain. After the verdict the Guardian editorialized:

> The private prosecution can be a useful procedure in that it allows the police to step out of a case involving minor assault between neighbours, for example, but still allow the aggrieved neighbours recourse to the law if they desire it. . . . There is a safeguard, but it failed to operate in the Hain trial. The DPP has the power to take over a private prosecution, and then to decide whether a case should proceed. Unfortunately he did not act in this way in the Hain case. It would seem desirable that where the Director has decided there is no cause for prosecution in a case as serious as conspiracy, he should exercise his power to take over the prosecution.

Guardian (London), Aug. 22, 1972, at 10. These suggestions that private prosecution be limited to petty domestic affrays and that the public prosecutor's decision not to prosecute in serious cases be final would bring the English practice close to the German. *See* text and notes at notes 57–66 *infra*. [I am grateful to David Fleming and Peter Wallington of the Law Faculty of Cambridge University for supplying me with newspaper clippings of the *Hain* proceedings.]

3 C. Pro. Pén. art. 31: "The public prosecutor (*ministère public*) shall conduct public prosecutions (*l'action publique*) and procure the application of the law."

4 *Id.* art. 2: "Those who have personally suffered harm resulting directly from a [crime] are entitled to *l'action civile* to recover damages . . . ."

5 *Id.* art. 1: "*L'action publique* . . . may also be initiated by the injured party, under the conditions established in the present code." *Id.* art. 85: "Anyone claiming to be injured by a [crime] may constitute himself a *partie civile* by lodging a complaint with the competent [court]."

selves "victims" of crimes committed against their members.[6] Consequently, when the French prosecutor decides not to prosecute, he decides for himself and his office alone. Someone else may still invoke the criminal process against the culprit.

Although the Germans derived a good deal of their criminal procedure code in the nineteenth century from the French, they did not introduce a variant of *l'action civile* (known as the *Adhäsionsverfahren*) until the 1940s. The procedure is seldom used for civil damage claims proper,[7] and it cannot be used as in France to enable the victim (however defined) to institute the criminal case. If the German prosecutor has determined not to prosecute, the victim can bring his civil action only in tort. He is not entitled to launch a private prosecution. In Germany, with insignificant exceptions discussed below, the public prosecutor has a monopoly over the criminal process. The German law is a compelling object of comparative study for Americans, because the German prosecutor, like the American, is a monopolist.

The prosecutor's monopoly is explicitly created and protected by statute in Germany. The Code of Criminal Procedure[8] sets it forth in two consecutive sections:

> 151. The opening of a judicial investigation [meaning primarily the commencement of a "trial" (*Hauptverhandlung*)] is conditioned upon the preferring of a formal charge (*Klage*).
>
> 152(1). The public prosecutor is responsible for preferring the . . . formal charge.

These two code sections are regarded as expressing fundamental principles that have distinctive names in the literature. Section 151 is called the *Anklagegrundsatz*, roughly, the principle of the formal criminal charge. It was designed to constrain the inquisitorial judge of earlier centuries, who had been empowered to conduct the entire criminal process, from the gathering of first suspicions to final adjudication and sentencing. The *Anklagegrundsatz* bifurcates the criminal process and restricts the modern German court to the second stage. The court cannot take proofs and adjudicate until a preliminary investigation

---

6 *See* A. Beth, Die Geltendmachung zivilrechtlicher Schadensersatzansprüche im französischen Strafverfahren 32–51 (dis., Freiburg 1972).

7 For a convenient explanation of the stillbirth of this device, see Jescheck, *Die Entschädigung des Verletzten nach deutschem Strafrecht*, 13 JURISTENZEITUNG 591 (1958).

8 STRAFPROZESSORDNUNG [hereinafter cited as Code of Criminal Procedure]. The Code sections governing prosecutorial discretion were recently discussed in Jescheck, *The Discretionary Powers of the Prosecuting Attorney in West Germany*, 18 AM. J. COMP. L. 508 (1970). For a concise but now somewhat outdated English language account of the German procedure, see Wolff, *Criminal Justice in Germany*, 42 MICH. L. REV. 1067 (1944), 43 MICH. L. REV. 155 (1944).

procedure (*Vorverfahren*) has been completed, culminating in a formal, written criminal charge (variously: *Klage, Anklage* or *Anklageschrift*) setting forth a prima facie case against the accused.[9]

According to section 152(1), the preferring of this formal charge is the responsibility of the public prosecutor. German writers speak of his *Anklagemonopol*, his monopoly over the preferring of the charge. Criminal sanctions are imposed for public purposes. German law takes the position that only the state, through a specially constituted officer, should have the power to institute the process leading to those sanctions.

What the Germans have largely done, and the Americans largely not done, is to devise means to regulate the prosecutor's monopoly. The kernel of the German scheme is set out, in immediate juxtaposition to the prosecutor's *Anklagemonopol*, as the second half of section 152 of the Code of Criminal Procedure:

> 152(2). [The public prosecutor] is required . . . to take action against all judicially punishable . . . acts, to the extent that there is a sufficient factual basis.

This is the celebrated *Legalitätsprinzip* of German law (literally, the legality principle; better, the rule of compulsory prosecution). The Germans have undertaken to forbid their monopolist prosecutor the discretion to refuse to prosecute in cases where adequate incriminating evidence is at hand. This rule, together with its limitations and exceptions and the citizen's remedies to enforce it, is the subject of this study.

## II. The Origins of Prosecutorial Discretion

The contrast between the American and German law of prosecutorial discretion is sharp and invites the question of how it has come about. American law received and developed a great common law tradition of hostility to monopoly in the marketplace, and it has characteristically insisted upon limiting and checking governmental powers of every kind. How is it that Americans have managed to place one of the most dangerous of all governmental powers beyond review or control, in the hands of a nearly omnipotent prosecutor? And how is it that the Germans, whose record of controlling governmental powers has not always been distinguished, have been so alert to controlling the prosecutor?

The common law's concept of the prosecutorial function formed over centuries of predominantly private or citizen prosecution. Official or

[9] *See* Code of Criminal Procedure § 200.

public prosecution initially developed as an adjunct to private prosecution and was steeped in the forms of private prosecution, as it continues to be in England today. Those forms helped conceal the development of the professional public prosecutor in America. By the time the American prosecutor's monopoly could be perceived, new factors were operating that seemed to require expansive prosecutorial discretion—the changes in the law of criminal procedure and evidence that brought about the need for plea bargaining.

The office of the public prosecutor at common law developed within an inherited system of citizen prosecution. Throughout the Middle Ages prosecution had been left to the victim, kin, or others, who would get their story to the juries of accusation and of trial. In the fifteenth and sixteenth centuries, the local justices of the peace (JPs) were given some organizational responsibilities over citizen prosecution. When cases of serious crime were reported to the JPs, they were empowered to order pretrial detention of the suspect and to "bind over" the victim and other witnesses to prosecute—to require them to appear before the two juries on penalty of a fine for nonappearance. Lawyers were not then regularly employed in the conduct of the criminal trial, either for the crown or the defense. The trial judge called the witnesses, and the proceeding transpired as a relatively unstructured "altercation"[10] between the witnesses and the accused. The JP's prosecutorial role was mainly passive, binding over citizen prosecutors to trial. In a difficult case, however, it began to be expected that the JP would investigate on his own to discover and bind over witnesses. More exceptionally, he might continue on to exercise some forensic prosecutorial role at the trial itself—interrogating witnesses and arguing the case to the jurors.[11]

The public prosecutor at common law thus grew up in the shoes of the old citizen prosecutor, occasionally displacing or supplementing him, but more usually deferring to him. Absent professional police and professional lawyer-prosecutors, the decision whether to prosecute was still in the main left to the initiative of the victim. Hence, when professional police and their criminal counsel developed in the nineteenth century, they acceded to a role that the English still characterize as that of the private citizen.

Professional prosecution by lawyer-officers developed earlier in America than in England.[12] However, American colonial and state practice

10 SIR THOMAS SMITH, DE REPUBLICA ANGLORUM 80 (1583 ed.) (bk. 2, ch. 23).

11 For detailed discussion of the English history, see J. LANGBEIN, PROSECUTING CRIME IN THE RENAISSANCE: ENGLAND, GERMANY, FRANCE 34–54 (1974); Langbein, *supra* note 1.

12 *See* NATIONAL COMM'N ON LAW OBSERVANCE AND ENFORCEMENT, REPORT ON PROSECUTION 6–7 (1968) [Wickersham Comm'n Rept. No. 4]; Comment, *The District Attorney—A Historical Puzzle*, 1952 WISC. L. REV. 125.

took from the English JP system the notion that public prosecution was a local function, not hierarchically subordinated to the direction of the attorney general. American populism then transformed the prosecutor (along with some judges and various other local officers) into an elective officer. This reinforced the inherited pattern of discretionary prosecution. The prosecutor acquired the elective officeholder's authority to conduct the affairs of his office so as to win electoral approval.

Further, the survival of the grand jury in many American jurisdictions, including the federal system where the elective principle was not admitted, has ever worked to conceal the extent of prosecutorial discretion. The formal criminal charge is made to issue in the name of a panel of citizen accusers, but this grand jury is in truth the prosecutor's rubber stamp. It seldom refuses to indict when he insists, and still less does it exercise its theoretical power to present or indict on its own initiative. The grand jury only appears to interpose a discretion of its own. Yet the appearance has surely helped to isolate arbitrary prosecutorial practices from public resentment and reform.

More than any other factor, however, what has brought about and sustained prosecutorial discretion in America in its present dimension has been the steady accretion of evidentiary and procedural safeguards for the accused which has transformed jury trial and made the system of plea bargaining essential.

Jury trial in early modern times was a summary proceeding. A single assize judge could process dozens of felony trials in a single day. In the seventeenth century a criminal trial jury would be impaneled and hear evidence in six or seven unrelated cases before retiring to formulate verdicts in all.[13] The law of criminal evidence was primitive into the eighteenth century, the right to representation by counsel was not generalized to all felonies until the nineteenth century, and appellate review was very restricted into the twentieth century.[14] The practices that so protract modern American jury trial—extended voir dire, exclusionary rules and other evidentiary barriers, motions designed to preserve appellate issues, maneuvers and speeches of counsel—all are late

13 The mechanics of multiple trials to the same jury are described in THE OFFICE OF CLERK OF ASSIZE 12–16 (1676 ed.). The clerk should make a list of prisoners and their offenses; then "when the Jury is ready to go from the Bar, he delivereth it unto them for their better direction and help of their memory to know who they have in charge." *Id.* at 15.

14 *See* T. PLUCKNETT, A CONCISE HISTORY OF THE COMMON LAW 215, 434–35 (5th ed. 1956); 1 J. STEPHEN, A HISTORY OF THE CRIMINAL LAW OF ENGLAND 308–18 (1883); Wigmore, *A General Survey of the History of the Rules of Evidence*, in 2 SELECT ESSAYS IN ANGLO-AMERICAN LEGAL HISTORY 691, 692–97 (1908). The sixth amendment guaranteed the right to counsel half a century before the English statute of 6 & 7 Wil. IV, c. 114 (1837).

growths in the long history of common law criminal procedure. They have, however, made jury trial unworkable as a routine procedure for our burgeoning criminality and have led to the system of nontrial disposition that exists in well over 90 percent of felony cases. The system as now practiced depends on the prosecutor's exclusive authority to grant concessions in order to induce waivers of the right to jury trial.

Thus it came about that the American prosecutor fell heir to his unregulated monopoly. He stands in the shoes of an ancient citizen prosecutor. His power is often concealed by the archaic grand jury. Outside the federal system he is an elective local potentate, liberated from hierarchical control on account of being subject to theoretical review by ballot. And in our century the transformation of jury trial has forced him to erect a new procedural system, plea bargaining, on the basis of his power of nonprosecution.

## III. The German Prosecutor

The modern German rule of compulsory prosecution is also a creature of history, born in the middle of the nineteenth century together with the office of the public prosecutor. Prior to that time, the prosecutorial function had been merged in the all-encompassing work of the inquisitorial judge, who both investigated alleged or suspected crime and then adjudicated on the basis of his own investigation. By the early nineteenth century the view had become widespread that this combination of functions prejudiced the accused. "Only a judge equipped with superhuman capabilities could keep himself in his decisional function free from the suggestive influences of his own instigating and investigating activity."[15]

The prosecutorial office (*Staatsanwaltschaft*) was established as a reform, to improve the procedural lot of the accused. The responsibility for investigation on report or suspicion of crime was split from the judicial office and made the job of the public prosecutor.

### A. Criminal Procedure

The preliminary procedure (*Vorverfahren*) conducted by the prosecutor culminates with his decision either to drop the case for want of adequate factual basis or to prefer the formal criminal charge. This written charge summarizes the prima facie case against the accused and names the witnesses and any other evidence by which the charge may be substantiated. According to the *Anklagegrundsatz* of section

---

15 E. Schmidt, Lehrkommentar zur Strafprozessordnung und Gerichtsverfassungsgesetz (Teil I) 197 (2d ed. 1964).

151, only after the charge is filed may the court proceed to judicial investigation and adjudication.

Criminal procedure is still "inquisitorial" in the sense that the court[16] is itself responsible for establishing the true facts, once the prosecutor has seised it of the case by preferring the formal charge.[17] Although the prosecutor and defense lawyer may ask questions at the trial, the procedure is fundamentally nonadversarial. It is the presiding judge who interrogates the witnesses and the accused. The proofs offered by the prosecution and the defense do not bind the court, which may call additional witnesses. (The official file built up by the police and the prosecutor goes over to the court when the charge is preferred, giving the court a basis for arranging the sequence of witnesses at trial and ordering additional proofs.) The court is not bound by a defendant's confession; it interrogates the accusing witnesses in order to satisfy itself of the man's guilt, despite the confession. The prosecutor loses control over the case once he has preferred the formal charge. He is not free to drop the case without judicial consent. Nor is the court bound by the prosecutor's theory of the case; if the prosecutor's charge characterizes the events as burglary, the court may still convict the accused of armed robbery.[18]

German courts are composed of professional judges and laymen who sit and decide together.[19] The Germans do not have to contend with guiding and controlling our panel of lay jurors who formulate a verdict without the participation of professional jurists and who render it without stating reasons. Consequently, the German law of evidence is relaxed; standards of admissibility are broad, and most of the common law exclusionary rules, such as the prohibition of hearsay, are unknown. The Germans have also felt no urge to devise exclusionary rules of evidence[20] to deter abuse of powers by the police and the prosecutorial corps. German police and prosecutors are professionals, hierarchically organized and controlled from the state level and subject

[16] For the purposes of this article, it is not necessary to distinguish among the half dozen criminal trial courts in which the number of judges varies according to the gravity of the offense. For a description of these courts, see Casper & Zeisel, *Lay Judges in the German Criminal Courts*, 1 J. LEGAL STUDIES 135, 141–43 (1972).

[17] Code of Criminal Procedure § 244(2); *cf. id.* § 155(2).

[18] *Id.* § 155. The accused must be notified of the court's reformulation of the criminal liability, and he must be given an opportunity to respond in his defense. *Id.* § 265(1).

[19] Except the lowest court, the *Amtsgericht*, in which a single professional judge sits alone in petty matters.

[20] Except, of course, for tortured and similarly coerced confessions. Code of Criminal Procedure § 136a; *cf. id.* §§ 250–52. *See generally* Damaska, *Evidentiary Barriers to Conviction and Two Models of Criminal Procedure: A Comparative Study*, 121 U. PA. L. REV. 506 (1973).

to effective administrative and judicial review and discipline upon citizen complaint.

Because the law of evidence is uncomplicated and the proof-taking is largely conducted by the presiding judge, the prosecutor cuts a peripheral figure at trial. He interposes occasional questions and he makes a concluding statement to the court following the proof-taking in which he comments on the evidence and proposes a sentence should the court find the accused guilty. (Defense counsel usually does a little more questioning of witnesses at trial, but he too is customarily a relatively passive forensic performer.) In my own experience observing German trials I have never seen the legendary sleeping prosecutor, but I have seen a prosecutor reading a novel while the court conducted the proofs.

Although in his trial role the German prosecutor bears little resemblance to the forensic combatant of Anglo-American procedure, his pretrial functions are similar. He investigates (when the police have not given him a completed case) and he decides whether to prefer charges. It is this phase of his work which the *Legalitätsprinzip* regulates by insisting that he prefer charges whenever the pretrial investigation furnishes sufficient factual basis.

### B. The Logic of Compulsory Prosecution

The rule of compulsory prosecution has been operating as long as the prosecutor himself. The prosecutor was called into existence in a unique act of creation in the middle of the nineteenth century in order to remove the work of pretrial investigation from the hands of the formerly all-powerful inquisitorial judge. Some of the best minds of a great juristic age, including Savigny, as Prussian minister of justice, participated in constructing and defining the prosecutorial office. In contrast to the unplanned parentage of the Anglo-American prosecutor, the German prosecutor was conceived with considerable forethought about his duties and powers.

German writers investigated the English pattern of private prosecution, but feared that it might invite an even greater abuse than the prosecutorial bias of the procedure they were trying to reform.[21] The partisanship of a contest between private hunter and hunted seemed to them scant improvement. Their solution, therefore, was to retain and entrench the public monopoly over the criminal process, but to divide it between two main officials. The prosecutor would investigate and charge, the judge would conduct the proofs and adjudicate.

21 K. Elling, Die Einführung der Staatsanwaltschaft in Deutschland 30 ff. (1911).

The German prosecutor's office was being created to relieve the German courts of responsibility for the preliminary investigation, in order to enhance the impartiality of the courts' adjudicative work. Yet it was feared that this separation might actually worsen the position of the accused by subjecting him to the excessive zeal of a professional prosecutor. Savigny sought to prevent the prosecutor's office from acquiring such a cast by vesting it with a continuing judicial character. The prosecutor was, after all, receiving duties and powers detached from the former office of judge. To retain a judge-like impartiality for the prosecutor, the Code of Criminal Procedure has from the outset required him to gather "not only inculpating but also exculpating evidence. . . ."[22] Further, if the prosecutor believes that the trial court has erred to the detriment of the accused, for example, by setting too severe a sentence, he may appeal to a higher court on behalf of the accused.[23] Hence, in his role as leader of the pretrial investigation and in his role as public litigant to enforce the law, he is invested with the duty and the power to be impartial. In Savigny's famous phrase, the prosecutor is to be the "watchman of the law,"[24] as evenhanded an officer of enforcement as could be devised.

Savigny's conception of the prosecutorial office gave it a curious "double character"[25] as both an executive and a judicial office. The Germans were led to articulate the *Legalitätsprinzip*, the rule of compulsory prosecution, in the course of designing this hybrid. They wanted a hierarchically organized prosecutorial corps, with a chief prosecutor for each judicial district in charge of allocating and reviewing the work of his subordinates, and himself subject to review and direction by a prosecutor general and by the state minister of justice.[26] This system allows an orderly meritocratic career pattern for members of the prosecutorial corps. It permits a unitary interpretation of the law to be propounded for the whole state; and, in cases in which the

---

22 Code of Criminal Procedure § 160(2).

23 *Id.* § 296(2).

24 *Quoted in* E. Schmidt, Einführung in die Geschichte der deutschen Strafrechtspflege 331 (3d ed. 1965).

25 K. Peters, Strafprozess 139 (2d ed. 1966).

26 Gerichtsverfassungsgestz §§ 143–47. Although West Germany has a unitary national code of criminal procedure, law enforcement and the administration of justice are organized at the state level. Bavaria, Hessee, and so forth each has a ministry of justice directing the prosecutorial corps, and an interior ministry responsible for the police. However, those of the police who are put at the disposal of the prosecutor for investigatorial work are by statute made subject to his control. *Id.* § 152. There is a federal prosecutorial office, the *Bundesanwaltschaft*, but with very limited subject matter jurisdiction. *See* E. Kern & C. Roxin, Strafverfahrensrecht 41–42 (11th ed. 1972).

*Legalitätsprinzip* does not apply,[27] it permits rulemaking to guide prosecutorial discretion.

A bureaucratic prosecutorial corps subordinated to the minister of justice (a political officer of the state government) could be subjected to political pressure to abuse its considerable powers of prosecution and nonprosecution. The German rule of compulsory prosecution was designed to prevent that pressure. The German prosecutor who, for example, is ordered by his minister not to prosecute in a case of political corruption must disobey the order. Section 152(2) requires him to prosecute, and failure to do so is itself criminal.[28] Hence, although the rule of compulsory prosecution limits the power of the prosecutor, it is also a fundamental protection for him. It is the basis of the judicial character of his office, the source of his freedom from improper interference from above.

This two-sided nature of *Legalitätsprinzip* is easy for Americans to overlook, because we are so accustomed to a non-hierarchical prosecutorial structure. Although our federal system does have some points of resemblance to the German organization, the state prosecutorial systems are balkanized. Elected county prosecutors are not subject to effective higher authority, and the United States Attorneys enjoy considerable autonomy. The German system, on the other hand, gives the prosecutor a real interest in seeing to it that the rule of compulsory prosecution is adhered to. For although the rule can be enforced against him, it also shields him.

To summarize: The German prosecutor's monopoly over the formal criminal process was intentionally built into his office. The rule of compulsory prosecution appeared simultaneously, both to rid the monopoly of its dangers for the citizen and to protect the prosecutor from political intervention. The dual function of the rule mirrors the dual character of the German prosecutor's office: he is obliged to perform an executive function according to judicial standards of conduct. The rule of compulsory prosecution frees him from demands for partiality from within the executive, while opening him to demands for impartiality from without.

## IV. The Scope of Compulsory Prosecution

How can the Germans prosecute every jaywalker? They cannot and they do not. In fact, most punishable conduct falls outside the rule of compulsory prosecution and is selectively prosecuted. Nevertheless, for

[27] *See* text and notes at notes 48–58 *infra*.

[28] *See* K. Peters, *supra* note 25, at 142.

serious crime the rule retains its full vigor. *Legalitätsprinzip* has been steadily eroded in the twentieth century, but only for lesser crimes and infractions. Consequently, the rule itself needs to be understood in light of its exceptions.

A. Petty Infractions

Prosecutorial discretion is largely a resource question. American plea bargaining occurs because we lack sufficient prosecutorial and judicial resources to provide a full jury trial for every defendant entitled to it. The criminal process does not seem to have a high claim on resources. Critics have long pointed out that these resource limitations have been aggravated by so-called overcriminalization. The available enforcement resources have to be spread over a wide variety of proscribed conduct, which creates pressures for selective enforcement. There is hardly a serious American writer on criminal law today who does not urge decriminalization of a number of acts, typically victimless crimes whose proscription merely reflects moral indignation instead of more substantial public interests.

The decision to decriminalize prostitution or pornography, for example, means that conduct previously punishable shall no longer be. Decriminalization has, however, a second and less fashionable meaning, exemplified in German criminal justice: removal from the criminal process of conduct that nevertheless continues to be proscribed and punished. Since World War II the law has undergone a series of major revisions designed to eliminate from the criminal process almost all traffic violations and the bulk of economic and other public regulatory activity. The offenses remain, but they are conceptualized differently and subjected to different procedures.

Petty infractions were formerly called *Übertretungen*, translatable as lesser misdemeanors. They have now been rechristened *Ordnungswidrigkeiten* (literally, violations of order; better, petty infractions), and are regulated under a separate procedural code.[29] The procedure for processing petty infractions has four important characteristics: (1) administrative officers, primarily the police, handle these cases without the participation of the public prosecutor or the criminal courts; (2) the process is conducted wholly in writing, and there is no trial unless the citizen elects to contest the case in the criminal court; (3) the sanctions as well as the infractions are both narrowed and relabelled to avoid criminal stigma; and (4) the rule of compulsory prosecution does not apply.

---

[29] The code is the 1968 GESETZ ÜBER ORDNUNGSWIDRIGKEITEN [hereinafter cited as Petty Infractions Code], which replaced the 1952 code of the same name.

The traffic police, board of public health, or other relevant enforcement agency carries out the procedure without calling on the public prosecutor. The agency conducts a preliminary investigation, which usually amounts to no more than the policeman's observation of the speeding car, but which can involve formal questioning of a suspected violator and witnesses.[30] When the agency is persuaded that its investigation has established a violation, it issues a *Bussgeldbescheid*, a "penance money" decree. The decree orders the citizen to pay a certain sum, between 5 and 1,000 marks, unless a higher sum is prescribed by the substantive law being enforced.[31] (In traffic cases the state ministries have worked out by rule a tariff for the various infractions and aggravating factors.) The decree instructs the citizen that it becomes final unless he files an objection with the local criminal court within one week. If he does object, the administrative agency gives the file to the public prosecutor, a trial is set, and the case is processed according to the ordinary course, that is, under the Code of Criminal Procedure.

The decision to criminalize is, therefore, made by the citizen. If he does not contest the decree he must pay up, but he will not be put through the criminal process. It needs to be emphasized that this alternative procedure is no mere labelling trick, *Etikettenschwindel*.[32] To be sure, there is an element of simple relabelling in insisting on calling the penalty "penance money" rather than "fine" (*Geldstrafe*). However, important consequences differ depending on whether conduct is characterized as a crime or a petty infraction. First, penance money is not reckoned as a criminal sanction for purposes of criminal record-keeping. Second, in the event of nonpayment, the penance money decree may not be enforced by means of imprisonment. If the citizen refuses to pay, the authorities proceed by "administrative execution,"[33] which can be described in Anglo-American terminology as a set of summary modes of civil execution.

Finally, section 47 of the Petty Infractions Code provides: "The prosecution of petty infractions is remitted to the duty-bound discretion of the prosecuting authorities." The administrators who "prosecute" such cases are not bound by the rule of compulsory prosecution applicable to the offenses still labelled "criminal" and prosecuted by the public prosecutor.

This exclusion is thought to follow from the underlying theory of separating crimes from petty infractions. German writers have at-

---

30 *Id.* § 55.

31 *Id.* § 13. (The mark is currently worth about 40 American cents.)

32 E. Kern & C. Roxin, *supra* note 26, at 338.

33 Petty Infractions Code § 90.

tempted to find both qualitative and quantitative distinctions between the categories. In the qualitative sense, it has been argued that petty infractions are generally morally colorless, *mala prohibita.* They "have no social-ethical content or [they] may in any event be placed outside social-ethical consideration."[34] This notion reflects the view[35] that the essence of the criminal process is the moral condemnation attaching to its formal sanctions and its procedures. As government regulation has multiplied the number of petty prohibitions, it has cheapened the moral force of the criminal sanction. The *Ordnungswidrigkeit* procedure, by decriminalizing the morally neutral, enhances the distinctiveness of what is genuinely criminal. It rehabilitates the criminal sanction.

This attempt to distinguish *Ordnungswidrigkeiten* on qualitative grounds has not been universally accepted.[36] At least when the violations are intentional, offenses ranging from homicide to jaywalking in one sense can be regarded as ethically indistinguishable. All are proscribed for social purposes. Any willful violator may be said to offend substantially identical social interests. The only difference, it is argued, is quantitative.

The quantitative element is palpable: petty infractions are petty. They inflict a lesser quantum of social harm, and they are more lightly punished in all legal systems. When the penalty is minor in the absolute sense, and when it has been designed to avoid criminal stigma, the meticulous fact-finding and other safeguards of ordinary criminal procedure are excessive to the purpose. A short-form procedure will suffice.

The discretion of the enforcement authorities in such cases may then be subsumed under general administrative discretion. Although the authorities exercise a prosecutorial role, they are not judicial officers in the same sense that the public prosecutor is. The public prosecutor who avenges murders and robberies lacks discretion because every murder and robbery needs to be prosecuted. The community is entitled to retribution, the offender requires reformation, and maximum prosecution promotes maximum deterrence. Those imperatives are thought not to carry over to petty infractions, which are prosecuted merely when expedient, as a means of keeping order. The legislature is relatively indifferent to the details of how the administration keeps order, the precise mix of disciplinary and other steps. Highway safety is promoted not only by disciplining speeders, but by redesigning roadways.

---

34 K. Peters, *supra* note 25, at 31.

35 Also contended in the best common law thinking. *See* Hart, *The Aims of the Criminal Law*, 23 Law & Contemp. Prob. 401 (1958).

36 *See* J. Krümpelmann, Die Bagatelldelikte (1966).

The water supply is protected both by improving drainage canals and by punishing the owners of defective septic tanks.

The drawback in allowing the administrative authorities this discretion to enforce petty infractions according to their convenience is the danger that they will use the power capriciously or for improper ends. In Germany this prospect has troubled hardly anyone. The police and most other authorities are hierarchically organized from the state level. Not only are they well led and controlled, they are liable to serious departmental and judicial review for abuse of authority.

Nevertheless, there are aspects of the *Ordnungswidrigkeit* procedure that remind an American of plea bargaining. There is an inducement to the citizen not to contest the penance money decree, because if he does contest, he will be assessed costs if he loses at the subsequent trial. Yet this incentive inheres in any procedural system, civil or criminal, that both permits default judgments and charges the costs of nondefault proceedings to the loser. The crucial point in the German system is that the sanction itself—the amount of the penance money—is not systematically increased when the citizen demands a trial. It is true that the public prosecutor who then takes the case to trial is not bound by the precise sum proposed by the administrators in the rejected penance money decree. But this is because the Germans think it fundamental that the judge-like prosecutor ought never to propose a sentence to the court until he has heard all the evidence at trial. Like the court, the prosecutor must not prejudge the case. Systematically recommending a higher penalty in order to deter citizens from claiming their right to trial in petty infraction cases would be improper, and has not in fact occurred.

The inducement of a lesser penalty in exchange for waiver of defensive rights does exist, however, in the so-called warning procedure, which is a short-form version of this already short-form *Ordnungswidrigkeit* procedure. Section 56 of the Petty Infractions Code provides:

> (1) In cases of minor (*geringfügig*) petty infractions, the administrative authorities can issue a warning to the person involved and exact a warning payment (*Verwarnungsgeld*) from 2 to 20 Marks. They should impose such a warning [i.e., require payment] when a warning without warning payment is insufficient.
>
> (2) The warning according to the first sentence of subparagraph (1) is operative only if the person agrees to it after being instructed of his right to refuse [and then pays promptly] . . . .
>
> (4) When the warning . . . is operative, the act may no longer be prosecuted as a petty infraction.

The practical importance of this procedure is for the most minor traffic violations. Parking tickets and citations for lesser moving violations are generally styled as "warnings" coupled with a demand for a "warning payment." The state ministries have promulgated tariffs for warning payments, fixing the amounts by rule, a practice that the Code expressly authorizes them to undertake.[87] The warning payment is smaller than the penance money would be for the same infraction. The citizen is therefore invited to pay a lesser sum and have the infraction characterized by a still less opprobrious label, in exchange for conceding the liability and paying the penalty within a short time. The procedure can be oral and immediate: a traffic policeman may exact a payment on the spot (for which he must issue an official receipt). The administration is thereby spared the paperwork even of the regular petty infraction procedure.

The warning procedure does invite the citizen to waive defensive rights in exchange for a lesser penalty—it might be said that he is asked to "cop a plea." The procedure, however, applies only to the pettiest of petty infractions, cases where the penalties are insignificant and the stigma from suffering public discipline is least.

### B. *Strafbefehl*: The German Guilty Plea

For the remainder of this paper we shall be examining the ways the Germans process offenses that they do regard as "criminal." These offenses were formerly divided into three categories—*Verbrechen, Vergehen,* and *Übertretungen,*[88] translatable for present purposes as felonies, misdemeanors, and petty misdemeanors. The last category is now being abolished; most of these offenses are being turned into petty infractions or abolished outright; a few are being upgraded into misdemeanors. By 1975 German law will recognize only two categories—felonies and those misdemeanors that survive decriminalization. Section 1 of the Penal Code defines a felony as any crime for which the Code stipulates a minimum sentence of one year's imprisonment. In this paper we shall be speaking as though the 1975 law were now in force, in order to avoid discussing the disappearing *Übertretungen.*

The procedure we have discussed above that invites default or consent to pay penance money for petty infractions was created in imitation of the so-called *Strafbefehl* ("penal order") procedure of the Code of Criminal Procedure.[89] This too is an entirely written procedure, without trial or other appearance of the accused before a court or an

[87] Petty Infractions Code § 58.

[88] Corresponding generally to the French *crimes, délits,* and *contraventions.*

[89] Code of Criminal Procedure §§ 407–12. For the text of a model *Strafbefhl,* see K. Marquardt, Strafprozess 114 (2d ed. 1970).

officer. It applies solely to *Vergehen*, the surviving misdemeanors. It is conducted by the public prosecutor and is a mode of prosecution. For example, in a shoplifting case, when the police transmit the file to the prosecutor, he may elect to prosecute the case through the penal order procedure, instead of moving for formal trial. He is likely to do so when the facts appear to be uncontested or uncontestable, for example, when the shoplifter was apprehended in the act and thereafter confessed to the police.

The prosecutor moves in the local criminal court for the issuance of the penal order. The prosecutor drafts the proposed order, and in theory the judge reviews the file and the order before propounding the order as his own. In practice this review is generally cursory, and the order customarily contains what the prosecutor has proposed. The order has the form of a provisional judgment issued by the court: "Unless you object by such-and-such date, you are hereby sentenced to such-and-such criminal sanction(s) on account of such-and-such conduct which offends such-and-such criminal proscription(s)." The document instructs the accused that if he makes timely objection (within one week) he is entitled to a criminal trial. If he objects, the penal order is nugatory and an ordinary criminal trial will take place as though the penal order had never been issued.

The penal order procedure is normally used when the prosecutor seeks a sanction less severe than imprisonment, typically a fine. Under present law, however, he may propose by penal order a sentence of up to three months imprisonment. This provision has been criticized on the ground that imprisonment is so serious that it should not be imposed unless the court faces the man it sentences and hears whatever he has to say.[40] A statutory revision of the penal order procedure expected to come into effect in 1975 or 1976 will limit it principally to cases in which the prosecutor demands a fine or a suspension of driver's license, and will exclude imprisonment.[41] Unlike the penance money of the petty infraction procedure, however, these penalties are criminal sanctions and are entered on the citizen's criminal record.

The similarity between the German penal order and the Anglo-American guilty plea is manifest: the prosecution invites the accused to waive any defenses and consent to the punishment propounded by the prosecution.[42] There are, however, important differences.

---

40 K. Peters, *supra* note 25, at 491.

41 Entwurf eines Einführungsgesetzes zum Strafgesetzbuch (April 1972) [hereinafter EGStGB] Code of Criminal Procedure] § 407.

42 *See* Jescheck, *supra* note 8, at 515–16. The analogy to the distinctively American nolo contendere plea is even more apt. The prosecutor induces the waiver of jury trial by permitting the defendant to concede criminal liability under a less opprobrious label.

First, the penal order procedure applies only to misdemeanors, and even there only when relatively light sanction are proposed. The really troubling arena of the American guilty plea is the plea bargaining in felony cases, where the accused barters his right to jury trial for a lighter sanction. Because our right to jury trial does not extend to petty crimes,[43] plea bargaining in those cases is scant—the accused has no chips. The real parallel to the German penal order procedure is the short-form American citation practice for traffic offenses: "Pay this fine or appear in court" (variant: "Post bond and forfeit it for default on nonappearance").

Second, the German penal order might be said to invite a plea, but not a bargain. The prosecutor evaluates the case, persuades himself of the accused's guilt, and recommends a sentence. The judge passes upon the recommendation and issues the provisional judgment. The accused is not represented and does not participate in this process. He is offered the sentence on take-it-or-leave-it terms. The procedure lacks the horse-trading quality of American plea bargaining (which so offends German notions of how criminal sanctions ought to be determined).[44]

Third and most important, the penal order does not offer a lesser sanction in exchange for the guilty plea. The accused who objects to the order, demands trial, and loses is not likely to receive a stiffer sentence. Technically, a stiffer sentence could follow because the provisional sentence in the penal order does not estop the prosecutor from urging, or the court from imposing a higher sentence.[45] It is a fundamental rule of German criminal procedure[46] that the prosecutor may not formulate his demand for sentence until he has heard all the evidence. It is open to the prosecutor to take the position that the case appears more serious after trial than when he proposed the rejected penal order, and accordingly urge a higher sentence. He would, however, have to substantiate that view in order to persuade the court. In practice an increase in the recommended penalty does not seem to happen with any regularity. Hence, what the accused primarily risks in rejecting the penal order is not a greater sentence, but court costs and the notoriety of public trial. Such inducements to waive defenses,

---

43 Baldwin v. New York, 399 U.S. 66 (1970).

44 Plea bargaining is all but incomprehensible to the Germans, whose ordinary dispositive procedure is workable without such evasions. In the German press the judicial procedure surrounding the resignation of Vice President Agnew was viewed with the sort of wonder normally inspired by reports of the customs of primitive tribes. "The resignation occurred as part of a 'cow-trade,' as it can only in the United States be imagined." Badische Zeitung, Oct. 12, 1973, at 3, col. 2.

45 Code of Criminal Procedure § 411(3).

46 Already noted with regard to the petty infraction procedure. *See* text at p. 454 *supra*.

while not inconsiderable, are not comparable to the lesser sentence that the American prosecutor offers in his plea bargaining.

We need to emphasize that the penal order procedure is fully consistent with the rule of compulsory prosecution. The procedure is simply a mode of prosecution. It spares everyone the inconvenience of a trial for open-and-shut cases. An enormous proportion of German criminal prosecutions take place in the penal order format.[47] For the same reasons that most Americans do not care to go to court to contest speeding tickets, most Germans caught shoplifting do not want to go to court to contest that either.

### C. *Opportunitätsprinzip*: Explicit Prosecutorial Discretion

The German rule of compulsory prosecution, section 152(2) of the Code of Criminal Procedure, is sharply limited by the counterprinciple, discretionary nonprosecution, set forth in sections 153–154. The counterprinciple is known as *Opportunitätsprinzip*, the principle of expediency or advisability. Save for a few exceptions of no quantitative significance,[48] the scheme of discretionary prosecution applies only to misdemeanors. It has steadily expanded during this century. The basic provision is section 153 of the Code of Criminal Procedure, set out here in the slightly revised version expected to come into force in 1975 or 1976. In a case of misdemeanor

> the public prosecutor may refrain from prosecuting with the con-

[47] Earlier statistics suggest figures as high as 70 percent. *See, e.g.*, Jescheck, *supra* note 8, at 516. *See also* J. HERRMANN, DIE REFORM DER DEUTSCHEN HAUPTVERHANDLUNG NACH DEM VORBILD DES ANGLO-AMERIKANISCHEN STRAFVERFAHRENS 164 n.77 (1971). These figures include traffic offenses that are now being decriminalized as *Ordnungswidrigkeiten*; hence the present proportion of offenses handled by penal order is probably lower. (I owe this point to Professor Mirjan Damaska, University of Pennsylvania Law School.)

[48] A few discretionary provisions do extend to felonies:

(1) Cases of treason, espionage and the like are exempt from the rules of compulsory prosecution, mainly to allow spy-swapping and other political settlements. Code of Criminal Procedure §§ 153b, 153c, 153d, 154b; renumbered in EGSTGB as §§ 153c, 153d, 153e, 154b. *See* Schram, *The Obligation to Prosecute in West Germany*, 17 AM. J. COMP. L. 627 (1969).

(2) The prosecutor may decline (with judicial approval) to prosecute at all in certain cases in which the court could, on account of the strength of mitigating factors, impose no penalty whatever on the felony offender after convicting him. Code of Criminal Procedure § 153a; renumbered in EGSTGB as § 153b.

(3) When an offender has committed a series of offenses, the prosecutor need not prosecute the minor ones. Code of Criminal Procedure § 154. For example, property damage incident to a bank robbery need not be prosecuted, but the robbery itself must be.

(4) When an offender is blackmailed because of a past crime and reports the blackmail, the prosecutor is authorized to decline to prosecute him for his crime. Code of Criminal Procedure § 154c.

The justifications for discretion in these few situations are obvious: Case 1 arises out of international political necessity. Cases 2 and 3 conserve prosecutorial resources from manifest waste. Case 4 permits the prosecutor to excuse the small fry in order to induce him to turn in a more serious offender.

> sent of the court competent [to try the case], if the guilt of the actor would be regarded as minor (*gering*), and there is no public interest in prosecuting.[49]

The legislature thus authorizes nonprosecution, but subject to express standards. The prosecutor may decline to prosecute only when he is persuaded that the suspect's guilt is minor and the public interest would not be served by prosecuting. His determination requires judicial approval. Although theoretically the court can prevent the prosecutor from contravening conventional standards of interpretation of minor guilt and absence of public interest, in practice judicial approval is a mere formality. The court has no better information than the prosecutor (the official police and prosecutor's file).

In the literature this system of discretionary nonprosecution of misdemeanors is regarded as arising out of the same policies that led to decriminalization and discretionary nonprosecution of petty infractions. If the rule of compulsory prosecution were strictly applied, the growth of new categories of minor crime in the statutes and the increase of reported crimes of all types would submerge the prosecution of serious crime in a sea of less important cases.[50] In effect, section 153 provides criteria of selection in a situation where the resources to prosecute every crime are not at hand. The system: prosecute virtually every felony, and prosecute the more important misdemeanors according to the standards of gravity in section 153.

Through their rule-making authority, the ministries of justice of all the German states have propounded a code of Uniform Rules of Criminal Procedure.[51] Rule 83 attempts some further particularization of the standards of section 153. For example, to evaluate the degree of guilt of an offender, the prosecutor should compare the particular offense with other cases of the same crime in order to see whether the conduct ranks among the less serious of the genre. In addition, the public interest requires prosecution for frequently committed offenses, which show a stronger need for deterrence [shoplifting, for example]; nonprosecution of some such offenders, says the regulation, would appear to be arbitrary. Further, if the offender has been previously warned or punished for similar conduct, there is a public interest that he now be prosecuted.[52]

---

49 EGStGB: Code of Criminal Procedure § 153.

50 *See* E. Schmidt, *supra* note 15, at 219–21.

51 *Richtlinien für das Strafverfahren* (1970) [hereinafter, Uniform Rules of Criminal Procedure]. For text see T. Kleinknecht, Strafprozessordung 1525 ff. (31st. ed. 1974).

52 The operation in daily prosecutorial practice of section 153 and its regulatory gloss has been described for English speaking readers in Herrmann, *The Rule of Compulsory*

By far the most controversial of the ministerially approved standards for nonprosecution under section 153 has been a provision[53] authorizing prosecutors to treat the offender's conduct after the offense as relevant to the degree of his guilt, for example, when the offender restores property, compensates the victim, or volunteers to make a payment to a charitable organization in atonement for his conduct. Such conditional nonprosecution has been criticized in Germany,[54] because it does constitute a form of plea bargaining, and without any statutory basis. The offender or his lawyer haggles with the prosecutor, offering to waive judicial proceedings and accept a lesser "sanction" in exchange for lighter treatment (nonprosecution). Nevertheless, the revision statute expected to come into force in 1975 or 1976 expressly legitimates the use of such conditions, ostensibly to provide a basis for nonprosecution under the standards of section 153 (minor guilt, absence of public interest).[55] Professor Herrmann's study concludes that the scheme of conditional nonprosecution has until now been used mostly, although not exclusively, for traffic and other relatively trivial misdemeanors.[56] The revision legislation, however, does not limit the types of misdemeanor that may be handled in this way.

It is easy to see why this procedure appeals to both prosecutor and offender. As with the penal order mode of prosecution for misdemeanor, this mode of nonprosecution saves the prosecutor's and the court's time. The case does not go to trial. The offender saves the time and costs of trial. Much more important to him, he is spared the stigma of criminal conviction when he is allowed to settle the case by paying off the victim or making a charitable contribution. Similar arrangements have developed in American practice,[57] but without any articulated doctrinal standards like the minor guilt and lack-of-public-interest criteria of section 153.

The parallel between the short-form penal order prosecution and the conditional nonprosecution is worth stressing. Both are limited to misdemeanors—crimes of lesser social importance. Both reduce drastically the prosecutorial resources that must be devoted to such cases. These practices, by lightening the load of the prosecutor in cases of

*Prosecution and the Scope of Prosecutorial Discretion in Germany*, 41 U. CHI. L. REV. 468 (1974).

[53] Uniform Rule of Criminal Procedure 83.

[54] *See* 1 LÖWE-ROSENBERG, DIE STRAFPROZESSORDNUNG UND DAS GERICHTSVERFASSUNGSGESETZ: GROSSKOMMENTAR § 153 Anm. 17 (22d ed. 1971); Schmidhäuser, *Freikaufverfahren mit Strafcharakter im Strafprozess?*, 28 JURISTENZEITUNG 529 (1973).

[55] EGSTGB: Code of Criminal Procedure § 153a.

[56] Herrmann, *supra* note 52, at 489–93.

[57] *See* F. MILLER, PROSECUTION: THE DECISION TO CHARGE A SUSPECT WITH A CRIME 260–80 (1969).

lesser crime, bring it about that the rule of compulsory prosecution in cases of serious crime is not frustrated for want of resources.

Finally, it should be mentioned that the ministries of justice have been able to regulate section 153 by rule precisely because section 153 is the counterprinciple to the rule of compulsory prosecution, the rule which protects the prosecutors from ministerial interference. Where that rule does not apply, the ministries can bind the prosecutorial corps to the ministerial interpretation.[58] On the other hand, the significance of the ministries' rules ought not to be exaggerated. They are few and dense, and have added little to the two concepts of the statute itself—minor guilt and lack of public interest. Perhaps the relativity of both concepts makes either inherently difficult to particularize further by rule.

## V. Enforcing the Rule of Compulsory Prosecution

The public prosecutor is duty-bound to prosecute virtually all felonies and all misdemeanors that he cannot excuse under section 153 for minor guilt and lack of public interest. But what if he refuses to do his duty? What if, owing to corruption or to excess of compassion or to error, a member of the prosecutorial corps neglects to prosecute in a case in which the law demands it? And what if the case escapes the notice of his superiors in the normal course of intra-office review and discussion of cases, either through his deviousness or because it does not sufficiently stand out from the routine?

It is the prosecutorial monopoly that makes this such an extremely important question, because other officers or private citizens cannot come forward to take up the neglected prosecution. There are two ways to prevent the abuse of a monopoly—break it or regulate it. The prosecutor's monopoly would be broken if citizen prosecution were allowed as in England or France. But German law, we have seen, insists on the public monopoly of the criminal process for all but a handful of cases about to be discussed. The main German approach, therefore, has been to regulate the prosecutor's monopoly by giving citizens the right to departmental and judicial review of decisions not to prosecute.

### A. Citizen Prosecution

For a narrow class of misdemeanors, mostly designed to protect private dignitary and property interests, German law does allow private prosecution. Section 374 of the Code of Criminal Procedure lists eight such misdemeanors: trespass to domestic premises, insult, inflicting

58 E. Schmidt, *supra* note 15, at 225.

minor bodily injury, threatening to commit a crime upon another, unauthorized opening of a sealed letter or document, inflicting property damage, patent and copyright violation, and crimes proscribed by the unfair competition statute.

If the prosecutor exercises his discretion under section 153 to refuse to prosecute one of these misdemeanors, the victim may still prosecute. Citizen prosecution is not conditioned upon the public prosecutor's refusal to act,[59] as it is in France. The citizen may prosecute without having first demanded public prosecution. However, the public prosecutor may decide at any time to prefer the public criminal charge, should he form the view that it is "in the public interest" to do so.[60] If the public prosecutor does act, he takes over the primary responsibility for the case. The private prosecutor becomes a *Nebenkläger*, what we might call an intervenor with a watching brief.[61] He still has the major rights of a party: to have witnesses called, to appear by counsel, to put questions at trial, to propose a judgment to the court, and to appeal against an unfavorable result.[62]

Predictably, German law frowns on private prosecution even in this peripheral sphere. The court may dismiss the case on what we would call the pleadings, either for legal insufficiency or when it deems the defendant's guilt minor (*gering*).[63] There is also a strike suit provision, requiring the private prosecutor to provide surety for the accused's costs, and to make advance payment of court costs which will be forfeit if he loses.[64] If the case concerns any of the dignitary, as opposed to the proprietary, misdemeanors, the private citizen may not prefer criminal charges before attempting out-of-court reconciliation in a proceeding conducted by a state agency.[65] Only the victim[66] can prosecute; and German law, unlike French, has kept this standing requirement narrowly defined.[67]

Despite these limitations, private prosecution does diminish the significance of the power of the public prosecutor under section 153 to decline to prosecute these misdemeanors. Even if the prosecutor finds the

59 Code of Criminal Procedure § 374(1).

60 *Id.* § 376.

61 *See id.* §§ 377, 395.

62 *Id.* §§ 374, 384, 386, 390.

63 *Id.* § 383(2). One of the standards that governs the public prosecutor's decision not to prosecute misdemeanors under section 153 may thus reappear to defeat private prosecution in these special cases. The other standard of section 153, public interest, is implicitly suspended by the legislature's decision to allow private suits.

64 *Id.* §§ 379, 379a.

65 *Id.* § 380.

66 *Id.* § 374(1).

67 1 Löwe-Rosenberg, *supra* note 54, § 172 Anm. 7–8.

requisite public interest to be lacking, the victim may still prosecute out of private interest.

We have been speaking of the victim's right to prosecute in these special cases either alone or as *Nebenkläger* alongside the public prosecutor. For most of these misdemeanors, and for a few others, the victim is also empowered to veto the public prosecutor's decision to prosecute. The misdemeanors subject to this right are called *Antragsdelikte*, literally, demand offenses, crimes that the prosecutor may not pursue without a formal demand from the victim. The offenses consist mainly of intra-family trespasses (excluding the very serious ones such as incest), where criminal sanctions may do more harm than good; and minor injuries to property, person, and dignity, where the public interest is comparatively slight and prosecution is warranted only if the victim is sufficiently disturbed to desire that criminal sanctions be invoked.[68]

These procedures for private prosecution and for private veto of public prosecution apply to only limited categories of lesser offenses. They therefore have not had a major place in the German system. In general, the Germans have retained the public prosecutor's monopoly of the criminal process and have given the victim procedural rights that regulate rather than break the monopoly.

B. Mandamusing the Prosecutor

German law provides citizens with rights to administrative and judicial review of prosecutorial decisions not to prosecute. Not all citizens may claim these rights, and not all nonprosecution decisions are subject to them. Where they do apply, however, these remedies constitute significant controls over and deterrents against abuse of prosecutorial authority.

The statutory procedure bears the name *Klageerzwingungsverfahren*, literally, the proceeding to compel the (preferring of the formal criminal) charge. We can render it in Anglo-American terminology as a mandamus action for a judicial decree to require the prosecutor to prosecute—an action that common law courts will not entertain.

Anyone is entitled to make a formal demand to the prosecutor, asking him to prosecute in a particular case.[69] If the prosecutor still declines to prosecute, he must notify the complainant of this decision, and explain the reasons. When the complainant was the victim of the crime and reported it, the prosecutor's notice must also instruct him of his right to seek departmental and judicial review.[70]

[68] *See* Maiwald, *Die Beteiligung des Verletzten am Strafverfahren*, 1970 GOLTDAMMER'S ARCHIV FÜR STRAFRECHT 33, 34.

[69] Code of Criminal Procedure § 158(1).

[70] *Id.* § 171.

Only the victim may bring the mandamus action. He must first file a formal departmental complaint with the state prosecutor general. If it is rejected, he is entitled to sue. The complainant must be represented by counsel in bringing the mandamus action, but public aid may be available to defray these costs.[71] If he loses, he must pay costs, and he can be forced to post security. The state supreme court (*Oberlandesgericht*) has original jurisdiction in these cases, in which a mainly written procedure is prescribed. The victim's petition sets forth the facts that support his view and describes the putative proofs. The court may then demand to see the prosecutor's files; it may ask the accused to reply, indeed, it must do so before approving the petition; it may conduct its own proofs (for which purpose one of its members is constituted investigating magistrate). If persuaded that the prosecution is required, the court orders it to be brought.[72]

The scope of this citizen's remedy is sharply restricted by the proviso that it may not be used to contest nonprosecution when the prosecutor has invoked section 153 or the forthcoming section 153a—the statutory scheme of nonprosecution and conditional nonprosecution for misdemeanors.[73] This limitation is theoretically justified by the existence of judicial review in such cases, in that the prosecutor's decision under sections 153 and 153a requires (but routinely receives) judicial consent. The effect of the limitation, however, is to prevent development of effective judicial controls and standards for the most active area of nonprosecution. Doubtless the real justification is the same as for the statutory scheme of nonprosecution itself—conservation of prosecutorial resources, in this case sparing the prosecutor from having to litigate defensively misdemeanors that he did not think important enough to press offensively.

The mandamus remedy is thus only as broad as the rule of compulsory prosecution. It extends to virtually all felonies and to those misdemeanors that, according to settled departmental practice, the prosecutor would not include under the lack-of-public-interest rubric of section 153. The mandamus procedure permits judicial review of the prosecutor's evaluation under the rule of compulsory prosecution that he lacked "sufficient factual basis" for proceeding, that is, that there was no probable cause. "Successful *Klageerzwingungsverfahren* occur in practice with the most extreme rarity. Nevertheless, the possibility of a *Klageerzwingung* is of great importance, in that it imposes a flat

71 1 Löwe-Rosenberg, *supra* note 54, § 172 Anm. 12.

72 Code of Criminal Procedure §§ 172–77.

73 EGStGB: Code of Criminal Procedure § 172(2).

rule against improper and illegal considerations."[74] The rarity results not only from the somewhat limited range of cases subject to the mandamus action, but also from the exhaustion requirement. Departmental complaint precedes judicial review. Every complaint receives a careful review by the office of the state prosecutor general, and most erroneous decisions not to prosecute are corrected there rather than in the courts.

The Code provides that where the victim does succeed in mandamusing the prosecution, he is entitled to participate with the prosecutor as an accusing litigant (*Nebenkläger*) at the subsequent criminal trial.[75] This safeguard prevents the prosecutor from trying to sabotage at trial the case that he has been ordered against his will to conduct. The danger of sabotage, however, is not as great in the German system as it would be in ours for two reasons. First, we have seen that once the German prosecutor has preferred the formal criminal charge, he retains only a secondary responsibility for unearthing further evidence and presenting the case to the court. The charge seises the court of the official files of the case, and the active role in ordering further proofs is the court's. At trial the presiding judge leads the proceedings and interrogates the witnesses.[76] The court is not bound by the prosecutor's submissions; it may disregard his motion to dismiss or the sentence he proposes in his summation. Once the charge has been preferred, which is what the mandamus action achieves, the German prosecutor lacks the capacity for mischief that the common law prosecutor possesses on account of his forensic primacy at trial. Second, the hierarchical structure of the German prosecutorial corps must incline superiors to react to the rebuke of a mandamus against their underlings by transferring the case to other members of the office or otherwise directing and superintending diligent prosecution.

Any common law variant of judicial review of statutory standards for nonprosecution would probably have to provide for a special prosecutor on remand.

### C. Departmental Complaint

Because the mandamus remedy is limited to cases (mostly felonies) in which the rule of compulsory prosecution applies, it is not available to the citizen who wishes to challenge the prosecutor's exercise of his statutory power of nonprosecution for misdemeanor under section 153. The citizen may, however, lodge a departmental complaint against the

74 K. Peters, *supra* note 25, at 464–65.

75 Code of Criminal Procedure § 395(2).

76 Including the accused and experts, whom the Germans do not label as witnesses.

prosecutor's decision. This so-called *Dienstaufsichtbeschwerde* is not provided for in the Code of Criminal Procedure. It derives from the principle of German administrative law that the citizen is entitled to file a complaint against a public employee's neglect of duty or abuse of power. The employee, in this case in the prosecutorial corps, will have to answer to his superior regarding the complaint, and the superior will have to pass upon the appropriateness of his conduct.

In practice, this nonstatutory complaint system is administered in the same manner as departmental review of the victim's complaint in cases in which the victim may thereafter resort to the statutory mandamus remedy. The state prosecutor general receives the complaint (it is forwarded to him even if lodged locally). The prosecutor's file on the case is sent up to the prosecutor general, together with the written response of the local office whose decision not to prosecute is being challenged. The prosecutor general decides whether to sustain or overrule the decision not to prosecute. He notifies the citizen of the disposition of the complaint, but does not state reasons. The citizen may appeal an unfavorable ruling to the state minister of justice, but not to the courts.

What makes this remedy effective is the hierarchical structure of the prosecutorial corps. Prosecuting is a lifetime career, or an integrated part of a lifetime career, for German prosecutors. They wish to rise within the prosecutorial hierarchy or, as is usual in most German states, to transfer to the judiciary. Where transfer between the prosecutorial and the judicial corps is usual, it is also encouraged: no judge can aspire to the highest judicial office without a period of service as a prosecutor. Promotion of judges and prosecutors is meritocratic, based on internal review of individual performance. Prosecutors do not want citizen complaints, particularly successful complaints, on their records. Hence, German legal academics tend to believe that the risk of a *Dienstaufsichtbeschwerde* is a greater deterrent to prosecutorial malpractice than the possibility of the mandamus action.

## CONCLUSION

Major and indelible differences distinguish German and American criminal procedure. The fundamentally different trial procedure inevitably affects the pretrial process. The paternalistic notion of the bureaucratic German prosecutor as watchman of the accused's rights is still marked with overtones of the older, more authoritarian inquisitorial system that it displaced.[77] Because German trial procedure is

77 *See* Roxin, *Rechtsstellung und Zukunftsaufgaben der Staatsanwaltschaft*, 47 DEUTSCHE RICHTERZEITUNG 385 (1969).

more rapid and efficient than American procedure, and German crime rates lower, German law can insist on a full trial for virtually every felony case. The need for plea bargaining—for nontrial disposition—is not as urgent in German procedure.

Nevertheless, there are similarities between the German and American systems that make a comparison worthwhile. German procedure is not so efficient that every offense can be prosecuted. Resource insufficiency has led German law, like American, to admit the power of nonprosecution. Both systems have responded by empowering monopolist prosecutors to select which offenses they will prosecute. Unlike the Americans, however, the Germans have tried very hard to articulate and to enforce some criteria of selection that Americans ought to find at least suggestive.

[17]

LOUISIANA LAW REVIEW

Volume XXIII
December, 1962
Number 1

# ADMINISTRATION OF CRIMINAL JUSTICE IN FRANCE: AN INTRODUCTORY ANALYSIS

*George W. Pugh**

A system for administering criminal justice is a detailed tapestry woven of many varied threads. It is often difficult to understand the nature and significance of any particular fiber without at least a general appreciation of the function of other threads, and also a realization of the impact of the whole. This is certainly true of the French system.

An attempt at a comparative study of another procedural system is fraught with difficulty, for one becomes so accustomed to his own procedural patterns that he is tempted to make unwarranted translations in terms of his own institutional frame of reference. Comparative evaluation of a procedural device, on the other hand, is even more difficult, for it involves at least two aspects: whether the device functions satisfactorily in its own institutional setting, and whether utilization of the mechanism in the context of another given system would be feasible or desirable.

Since the inception of the Fifth Republic, there have been a number of changes in the French legal system,[1] including the

*Professor of Law, Louisiana State University. This article was prepared by the author for The Comparative Study of the Administration of Justice, established under the terms of a grant from the Ford Foundation to Loyola University School of Law (Chicago), and is published here with the consent of the Study.  Much of the research for the article was completed during the author's stay in France. For very valuable research aid in the preparation of this manuscript, the writer is indebted to Mr. Philippe Salvage, senior law student, University of Grenoble, France.

1. For discussion of changes made by the DeGaulle reforms, see: Anton, *L'Instruction Criminelle*, 9 AM. J. COMP. L. 441, 443 (1960); Herzog, *Proof of Facts in French Civil Procedure: The Reforms of 1958 and 1960*, 10 AM. J. COMP. L. 169 (1961); Patey, *Recent Reforms in French Criminal Law and Procedure*, 9 INT. & COMP. L.Q. 383 (1960); CODE DE PROCÉDURE CIVILE, *Table*

adoption of a new Code of Criminal Procedure.[2] The following is not intended to be a comprehensive comparative treatment or evaluation, but rather an introductory analysis of the functioning of French procedure in actual practice.[3] Before discussing the procedures themselves, a summary description of the French judicial system and the diverse roles of the various members of the legal profession will be given, for procedural rule and institutional context are interwoven and interact with each other.

## I. Judicial Organization

In France, justice is administered through two separate systems — administrative and judicial.[4] A discussion of the administrative system is beyond the purview of this summary.

---

*Chronologique*, p. 718 *et seq.* (Dalloz ed. 1962) [hereinafter cited as French C.P.C.]; Code de Procédure Pénale, *Table Chronologique*, p. 442 *et seq.* (Dalloz ed. 1962) [hereinafter cited as French C.P.P.]; Cuche et Vincent, Procédure Civile et Commerciale, no. 6 (12th ed. Dalloz Précis, 1960) [hereinafter cited as Cuche et Vincent]; Stefani et Levasseur, Procédure Pénale nos. 90-91 *bis* (2d ed. Dalloz Précis, 1962) [hereinafter cited as Stefani et Levasseur]; Giverdon et Larguier, Procédure Civile, Droit Pénal, Procédure Pénale, Ordonnances et decrets intervenus du 1 Juin 1958 au 28 Février 1959 (Montchrestien ed. 1959); Le Nouveau Code de Procédure Pénale, Études extraites de la Revue de Science Criminelle et de Droit Pénal Comparé, 1959, nos. 2, 3, 4 (1960).

In citing the Code de Procédure Civile, Code de Procédure Pénale, Cuche et Vincent, and Stefani et Levasseur, "*et seq.*" will be used where pertinent material follows the original citation, but is interspersed among related materials.

2. In 1958, the Code de Procédure Pénale was adopted, replacing the former Code d'Instruction Criminelle (enacted in its original form in 1808). The following discussion will be in the light of these reforms.

A very valuable English translation by Mr. J. Fergus Belanger of the *Code of Penal Procedure, 1st Part* was published by the United States Army in 1959.

3. To facilitate further study in particular areas, an effort has been made to provide useful references to sources in English (where available), followed by sources in French.

4. For a very good chart reflecting the organization and jurisdiction of both systems, see Kock, *The Machinery of Law Administration in France*, 108 U. Pa. L. Rev. 366, 368 (1960).

For general discussion of the judicial system, see: David & de Vries, The French Legal System (1958) [hereinafter cited as David & de Vries]; Dainow, *The Constitutional and Judicial Organization of France and Germany and Some Comparisions of the Civil Law and Common law Systems*, 37 Ind. L.J. 1, 9 (1960); Deák & Rheinstein, *The Machinery of Law Administration in France and Germany*, 84 U. Pa. L. Rev. 846 (1936); Kock, *The Machinery of Law Administration in France*, 108 U. Pa. L. Rev. 336, 368 (1960) [hereinafter cited as Kock]; Bouzat, Traité théorique et pratique de Droit Pénal, no. 957 (1951, et mise à jour 1956); Encyclopédie Juridique, Répertoire de Droit Criminel et de Procédure Pénale, Tome II, p. 939, et mise à jour, p. 436 (Dalloz 1953 et mise à jour 1962); Stefani et Levasseur, no. 411 *et seq.;* Vidal, Cours de Droit Criminel et de Science Pénitentiaire no. 772 (1949); Vitu, Procédure Pénale 29 (1957).

For a discussion of the administrative court, see David & de Vries, 64 and bibliography, 144; Deák & Rheinstein, *supra* at 858; Kock, 377; De Laubadere, Traité de Droit Administratif, no. 425 (1957); Rivero Droit Administratif nos. 131, 184 (Précis Dalloz 1962).

The highest court in the judicial system is the *Cour de Cassation,* and the *Conseil d'Etat,* the highest of the administrative. Questions of a jurisdictional nature between the two systems are decided by the *Tribunal des Conflits.*[5]

The noncriminal courts of first instance are fairly numerous and include a number of specialized courts (*tribunaux d'exceptions*),[6] one of which is the very important commerce court for commercial matters.[7] These specialized courts are generally staffed by *lay judges,* usually elected by those categories of persons affected by the specialized nature of the court's particular jurisdiction.

Minor civil cases not triable before these specialized courts are heard by the *tribunal d'instance,*[8] and more important civil cases by the *tribunal de grande instance.*[9] Petty criminal cases (*contraventions*) are tried by the *tribunal de police;*[10] criminal infractions of an intermediate nature (called *délits*), by the *tribunal correctionnel;*[11] and the gravest (called *crimes*), by the *Cour d'Assises.*[12]

The *tribunal d'instance* and the *tribunal de police* may be considered for practical purposes a single court, with civil and

5. For a discussion of the *Tribunal des Conflits,* see Deák & Rheinstein, *supra* note 4, at 863; Kock, 381; DE LAUBADERE, *op. cit. supra* note 4, at no. 477; RIVERO, *op. cit. supra* note 4, at no. 136.

6. These include industrial councils (*conseils des prud'hommes*); commercial courts (*tribunaux de commerce*) exercising very important jurisdiction relative to commercial transactions; rent courts (*tribunaux paritaires de baux ruraux*); juvenile courts (*tribunaux pour enfants et adolescents*). See Deák & Rheinstein, *supra* note 4, at 849; Kock, 367; CUCHE ET VINCENT, nos. 86 *et seq.*, 105 *et seq.*

7. CUCHE ET VINCENT, no. 108 *et seq.*

8. For further discussion of the organization and function of this court, see Kock, 370; CUCHE ET VINCENT, no. 106 *et seq.*

9. For further discussion of the organization and function of this court, see Kock, 370; CUCHE ET VINCENT, no. 90 *et seq.*

10. Roughly speaking, *contraventions* are petty offenses punishable by a maximum fine of 2000 NF (approximately $400), imprisonment not longer than two months, and confiscation of seized objects (French C.P.P. art. 464 *et seq.*) — triable before the *tribunal de police* (French C.P.P. art. 521 *et seq.*) presided over by a single judge, sitting without a jury. Patey, *supra* note 1, at 385; STEFANI ET LEVASSEUR, nos. 425 *et seq.*, 464.

11. Roughly speaking, *délits* are criminal infractions of an intermediate nature punishable by a fine in excess of 2000 NF, imprisonment from 2 months to 5 years, and other deprivations (see FRENCH PENAL CODE arts. 1, 9) — triable before the *tribunal correctionnel,* presided over by three judges sitting without a jury (French C.P.P. arts. 381 *et seq.*, 398 *et seq.*). STEFANI ET LEVASSEUR, nos. 427 *et seq.*, 464.

12. Roughly speaking, *crimes* are the most serious offenses, punishable by death, imprisonment, and other deprivations — triable before the *Cour d'Assises,* composed of 3 judges and 9 jurors (French C.P.P. arts. 214, 231 *et seq.*, 240 *et seq.*). STEFANI ET LEVASSEUR, no. 430 *et seq.*

criminal sides.[13] In this court a single, professional judge sits without a jury, while in all other proceedings in French law, multiple judges are employed.[14] Staffed by at least three judges, the *tribunal de grande instance* and *tribunal correctionnel* may likewise be considered a single court.

The only court in France employing a jury, the *Cour d'Assises*, is composed of three professional judges and nine lay jurors, who sit together to deliberate.[15] It is said that a strong presiding judge may exercise considerable influence over his fellow fact-finders, but that in Paris the lay jurors display greater independence than in the provinces. Thus, emotional appeals are perhaps more effective in Paris than elsewhere in France.[16]

The *Cour d'Assises* has jurisdiction only over persons who have been indicted for a *crime*[17] by a *Chambre d'Accusation* (the division of the Court of Appeal serving very roughly the same function as an American grand jury).[18] In order to arrive at a guilty verdict, eight of the twelve fact-finders must concur. Thus for a defendant to be found guilty, there must be a concurrence of at least a majority of the lay jurors.[19]

Except with respect to decisions of the *Cour d'Assises* and certain small cases,[20] a full reconsideration of both fact and law

---

13. STEFANI ET LEVASSEUR, no. 209 *et seq.*

14. See Kock, 371; STEFANI ET LEVASSEUR, no. 234 *et seq.*

15. The Court of Assizes generally sits for a two-week term during each quarter of the year. Kock, 372; French C.P.P. art. 231 *et seq.*; STEFANI ET LEVASSEUR, nos. 430 *et seq.*, 790 *et seq.*, 798 *et seq.* For general discussion of procedure before the *Cour d'Assises*, see BOUZAT, *op. cit. supra* note 4, at 1220; ENCYCLOPÉDIE JURIDIQUE, *op. cit. supra* note 4, at Tome I, p. 598 et mise à jour, p. 173; JURISCLASSEUR DE PROCÉDURE PÉNALE, art. 231 *et seq.* (Editions techniques); VIDAL, *op. cit. supra* note 4, at no. 853; VITU, *op. cit. supra* note 4, at 347.

In citing JURISCLASSEUR DE PROCÉDURE PÉNALE, "*et seq.*" will be used where pertinent material follows the original citation, but is interspersed among related materials.

16. So much so, that it has been facetiously stated that if a Frenchman plans to kill his wife, he should do so in Paris.

17. French C.P.P. arts. 214, *et seq.*, 268 *et seq.*; STEFANI ET LEVASSEUR, no. 760 *et seq.*

18. However, once a *Cour d'Assises* has received a case, it must complete the trial and render a judgment, even if it decides that the case is not one that should have originally been sent to it. Kock, 373; French C.P.P. arts. 231, 214, 191 *et seq.*; STEFANI ET LEVASSEUR, nos. 417 *et seq.*, 721 *et seq.*, 748 *et seq.*

19. Kock, 373; Patey, *supra* note 1, at 392.

For other questions, such as sentencing, etc., seven votes, a majority of the twelve, suffices. French C.P.P. art. 362; Kock, 373. See Patey, *supra* note 1, at 392; STEFANI ET LEVASSEUR, no. 799 *et seq.*; French C.P.P. arts. 355 *et seq.*, 359 *et seq.*

20. Kock, 373.

as a matter of right — called an appeal — before the *Cour d'Appel* is available to a litigant in French courts in both civil and criminal cases.[21] Obviously, this appeal provides for much broader review than an American appeal. Generally, the whole record (or *dossier*) goes before the appellate court, but the court is not restricted to this record; it may receive additional evidence. From numerous conversations, it seems to the writer that both practitioner and judge feel that the court of appeal may freely substitute its judgment for that of the lower court.[22] This is more understandable when it is considered that even at the original trial, much of the evidence comes to the court in written — not oral — form; demeanor evidence is of less significance than in Anglo-American courts.[23] When the court of appeal disagrees with a decision reached by the lower court, it enters the final judgment itself, and there is no remand to the lower court for entry of judgment.[24]

This "appeal" is to be distinguished from review of questions of law afforded by France's highest court, the *Cour de Cassation*.[25] This court generally has no authority to enter a judgment, but merely to upset (break or *casser*) the decision appealed.[26] When a decision by a court of appeal is upset, the case is sent to another court of appeal of coordinate rank with that from which the appeal was taken. This latter court need not render a decision in conformity with the views expressed by the *Cour de Cassation*. In such a case, the *Cour de Cassation* will *again* consider the matter — this time sitting *en banc*.[27] At this point, the *Cour de Cassation* may or may not adhere to its original determination. If it does, the case is referred to a third court of appeal, which *must* render a decision in accordance with the views expressed by the *Cour de Cassation*.[28]

21. *Ibid.* For discussion and description of the internal organization and function of the *Cour d'Appel*, see Kock, 374; French C.P.C. art. 454; French C.P.P. arts. 549, 510, 511; CUCHE ET VINCENT, nos. 98 *et seq.*, 208 *et seq.*; STEFANI ET LEVASSEUR, no. 464.

22. STEFANI ET LEVASSEUR, no. 838 *et seq.* See also French C.P.C. art. 443 *et seq.*; French C.P.P. arts. 496 *et seq.*, 512 *et seq.*, 546 *et seq.*; CUCHE ET VINCENT, no. 411 *et seq.*

23. See Comment, *Appellate Review of Facts in Louisiana Civil Cases*, 21 LA. L. REV. 402 (1961).

24. Kock, 374; French C.P.P. art. 515; CUCHE ET VINCENT, nos. 433 & 433 *bis*; STEFANI ET LEVASSEUR, no. 845 *et seq.*

25. French C.P.C. art. 213 *et seq.*; CUCHE ET VINCENT, no. 126 *et seq.*; STEFANI ET LEVASSEUR, no. 437.

26. But for very exceptional cases where a *Cour de Cassation* may consider the facts and even enter judgment, see French C.P.P. art. 622 *et seq.*

27. More technically speaking, the court sits "*toutes chambres réunies*," with at least 35 members. See Kock, 376.

28. For discussion and description of the internal organization and function

Of considerable interest to Anglo-American lawyers is the fact that in criminal cases, where appeal or review is available, it may be had at the instance of *either* the defendant or the state.[29]

Observation and conversations indicate that in general, criminal justice is administered with reasonable speed.[30] Delay in civil litigation, which is of such lamentable significance in the United States, is, unfortunately, also present in France. Except as to the *Cour de Cassation*, however, where dockets are very crowded, it would appear that the delay in civil litigation is due not so much to the crowded condition of dockets as to the lengthy civil procedures and the procrastination of attorneys, which is perhaps a world-wide affliction of our profession. In criminal cases, perhaps the reasons for celerity are that the judiciary bears so much of the onus of expediting proceedings, and that fewer means[31] to slow down the wheels of justice are available to defendants.

## II. Legal Professions

In France, law schools are designed for much more than merely training lawyers.[32] They provide a broad, philosophical education in law and related subjects pursued by a fairly large number of university students. The French law student is younger than his American counterpart; other university work is not a prerequisite for enrollment.[33] After graduation from a four-year law curriculum,[34] and frequently after pursuing advanced work in law, a very small minority of students seek entry into either the private practice of law or the *magistrature* (judges and prosecutors).

of the *Cour de Cassation*, see Kock, 375; French C.P.C. art. 213 *et seq.*; French C.P.P. art. 567 *et seq.*; CUCHE ET VINCENT, no. 464 *et seq.*; STEFANI ET LEVASSEUR, no. 853 *et seq.*

29. French C.P.P. arts. 497, 546, 567, 622 *et seq.*; STEFANI ET LEVASSEUR, nos. 840, 853, 867 *et seq.*

30. It must be noted, however, that pre-trial investigation in France is a painstaking process (see p. 13 *infra*). In serious cases, the defendant is often kept in jail awaiting trial under what is called preventive detention and there is understandably criticism of prolonged pre-trial detention. See Anton, *supra* note 1, at 453; Hamson et Vouin, *Le Procès Criminel en Angleterre et en France*, No. 2-3 REVUE INTERNATIONALE DE DROIT PÉNAL 177, 182 (1952) and references there cited; STEFANI ET LEVASSEUR, no. 277 *et seq.*

31. But see, for example, the instance of an attorney who came to an important case without his robe, and thus necessitated an adjournment. LE MONDE, July 11, 1962, p. 16.

32. DAVID & DE VRIES, 24, and authorities cited at 28.

33. The French student finishes the Lycée (or high school) at approximately age 18, but the last 2 years of his work at the Lycée correspond roughly to the first 2 years' study of an American university.

34. Dainow, *Revision of Legal Education in France: A Four-Year Law Program*, 7 J. LEG. ED. 495 (1955).

If one wishes to enter the *magistrature*,[35] he must take a very rigorous, competitive examination. If successful, as a result of recent reforms,[36] he follows an additional three-year course of intensive training at the National Center for Judicial Study (*Centre nationale d'Etudes judiciaires*),[37] divided approximately evenly between formal study and varied practical training. Members of the *magistrature* are composed of two groups — the *magistrature assise* (the seated magistrate, or judge),[38] and the *magistrature debout* (the standing magistrate, *procureur*, or public attorney, who corresponds roughly to the American district attorney and attorney general).[39] Interchange of personnel between the two branches of the *magistrature*, though quite possible, occurs much more frequently from *procureur* to judge than vice versa.[40] A cardinal principle in French law is the independence of the *magistrature*[41] from political and private pressure. Although the *procureur* is subject to the written directives of the Ministry of Justice to institute proceedings,[42] *etc.*, he retains great independence.[43] The *procureur* exercises two roles, one as attorney for the state in the sense of prosecutor of crime, and the other in behalf of society itself in the proper application of the law.[44] Even in civil cases, for example, he is authorized, and

35. French C.P.C. art. 410 *et seq.*

36. Ordinance 58-1270 of Dec. 22, 1958.

37. CUCHE ET VINCENT, no. 134 *et seq.*

38. DAVID & DE VRIES, 18, and authorities cited at 28; CUCHE ET VINCENT, no. 132 *et seq.*

39. DAVID & DE VRIES, 20, and authorities cited at 28; French C.P.P. art. 31 *et seq.*; CUCHE ET VINCENT, no. 155 *et seq.*; STEFANI ET LEVASSEUR, no. 496 *et seq.* In the *tribunal de police* for trial of minor offenses, the state is represented by the *commissaire de police*, who, however, is not a member of the *magistrature*. (French C.P.P. art. 45; STEFANI ET LEVASSEUR, no. 498.) Before the *tribunal correctionnel*, for the trial of *délits*, the state is represented by the *Procureur de la République*. (French C.P.P. art. 39; STEFANI ET LEVASSEUR, no. 498.) Before the *Cour d'Appel* and *Cour d'Assises*, the state is represented by the *Procureur Général* (French C.P.P. art. 34; STEFANI ET LEVASSEUR, no. 498); before the *Cour de Cassation*, by the *Procureur Général à la Cour de Cassation* (STEFANI ET LEVASSEUR, no. 498).

40. DAVID & DE VRIES, 21.

41. FRENCH CONST. art. 64 (1958); Kock, 384; CUCHE ET VINCENT, no. 138 *et seq.*; STEFANI ET LEVASSEUR, no. 242 *et seq.*

42. French C.P.P. arts. 33, 36, 37, 44; CUCHE ET VINCENT, no. 157; STEFANI ET LEVASSEUR, no. 500.

43. CUCHE ET VINCENT, no. 157; STEFANI ET LEVASSEUR, nos. 244, 502.

44. Dainow, *supra* note 4, at 10-11; DAVID & DE VRIES, 21; French C.P.P. art. 31 *et seq.*; CUCHE ET VINCENT, no. 158 *et seq.*; STEFANI ET LEVASSEUR, nos. 102, 505 *et seq.*

For general discussion of the role of the *ministère public*, see Kock, 385; Deák & Rheinstein, *supra* note 4, at 857; Vouin, *The Protection of the Accused in French Criminal Procedure*, 5 INT. & COMP. L.Q. 1, 7 (1956); BOUZAT, *op. cit. supra* note 4, at nos. 860, 982; ENCYCLOPÉDIE JURIDIQUE, *op. cit. supra* note 4, at Tome II, p. 425 et mise à jour, p. 328, Tome I, p. 51 et mise à jour, p. 19; JURISCLASSEUR, *op. cit. supra* note 15, at arts. 1-9, 31-48; STEFANI ET LEVASSEUR,

sometimes required, to express his views on questions of law at issue between private parties. The law specifically provides[45] that in his *oral* comments, the *procureur* is free to express whatever personal views and observations he feels are appropriate to the proper administration of justice. It seems that this freedom of oral expression is highly prized by the *procureur*, and there is a well-known and descriptive phrase "*la plume est serve mais la parole est libre.*" (The pen is subject to control, but the voice is free.)[46]

There is considerable *esprit de corps* of the *magistrature*. Although professional advancement results from the recommendations of the high council of the judiciary (*Conseil Supérieur de la Magistrature*),[47] composed in part of politically appointed personnel, it seems fair to state that the French ideal of an independent judiciary has generally been achieved.

French judges seldom achieve the individual recognition sometimes given members of the American judiciary. A court is normally composed of at least three judges, who render short per curiam opinions without dissents, and as a result of tradition, legal technique, and method of decision-writing, French courts generally play a much less important role in the development of the law than do American courts.[48] However, court decisons now seem to be accorded much more authoritative significance than formerly, and in some instances jurisprudential rules seem to bear only remote relationship to the written law.[49] This is perhaps because the French Civil Code is in essence a document approximately 150 years old.[50] Further, French judges do not undertake to review the constitutionality of legislation nor does there appear to be any school of thought, as in the United States, that the courts have inherent procedural rule-making power.[51]

no. 497 *et seq.*; VIDAL, *op. cit. supra* note 4, at no. 620; VITU, *op. cit. supra* note 4, at 45, 144.

45. French C.P.P. art. 33.

46. STEFANI ET LEVASSEUR, no. 244; French C.P.P. art. 33.

47. See Kock, 384; FRENCH CONST. arts. 64-65 (1958); Ordinance 58-1271 of Dec. 22, 1958; French C.P.C. art. 409; CUCHE ET VINCENT, no. 144.

48. DAVID & DE VRIES, 19; LePaulle, *Données fondamentales de l'administration de la justice dans les pays anglo-saxon*, 3 REVUE INTERNATIONALE DE DROIT COMPARÉ 1 (1956).

49. Compare FRENCH CIVIL CODE art. 1384 and the jurisprudential rules developed thereunder. See CARBONNIER, DROIT CIVIL, Tome I, no. 31 (collection Thémis 1957). *But see* FRENCH CIVIL CODE art. 5.

50. CARBONNIER *op. cit. supra* note 49, at Tome I, no. 13.

51. See LePaulle, *supra* note 48, at 4.

If the graduate of the French law school wishes to enter upon a legal career, but does not enter the *magistrature,* he has considerable choice in the type of law work he may wish to do.[52] Practice of law as known in the United States is fragmented into a number of different careers in France. The characteristic function of the *avocat* (corresponding roughly to that of the English barrister) is oral presentation of his client's case before the court.[53] The inheritor of a proud tradition dating back to the first half of the 14th century, the *avocat* enjoys high social standing.[54] Despite recent reforms the ambit of his professional activities remains severely restricted, and the local bar association (*Ordre des Avocats*) exercises pervasive control and supervision.[55]

In order to take the bar examination, a candidate must follow additional professional study of a practical nature. This may be accomplished after graduation, or, as frequently occurs, concurrently with a student's fourth year law school study. Even if successful on his bar examination, he is not immediately admitted to the full status of *avocat.* He must, for a period of from three to five years, depending on circumstances, serve somewhat of an apprenticeship. For the first year, except on special authorization, he has no right to argue cases, but thereafter has all the rights of an *avocat,* with certain obligations.[56] During the period of apprenticeship, he must follow a course of further training under the supervision of the local bar association.[57]

52. LePaulle, *Law Practice in France,* 50 COLUM. L. REV. 945 (1950); DAVID & DE VRIES, 21, and authorities cited at 28; CORNU ET FOYER, PROCÉDURE CIVILE 252-65, et mise à jour 1960, 45-49 (1958); CUCHE ET VINCENT, no. 132 *et seq.*; ENCYCLOPÉDIE JURIDIQUE, REPERTOIRE DE PROCÉDURE CIVILE ET COMMERCIALE et mise à jour 1962, Tome I, p. 291 et mise à jour p. 14, Tome I, pp. 292-323 et mise à jour pp. 14-19, Tome II, pp. 80-100 et mise à jour pp. 72-75 (Dalloz 1955); GARSONNET ET CÉZAR-BRU, TRAITÉ THÉORIQUE ET PRATIQUE DE PROCÉDURE CIVILE ET COMMERCIALE, Tome I, Partie I, nos. 241-73 (3d ed. 1912); 1 GLASSON, TISSIER ET MOREL, TRAITÉ THÉORIQUE ET PRATIQUE D'ORGANIZATION, DE COMPÉTENCE, ET DE PROCÉDURE CIVILE, nos. 114-53 (3d ed. 1925); MOREL, TRAITÉ ÉLÉMENTAIRE DE PROCÉDURE CIVILE, nos. 162-92 (2d ed. 1949); SOLUS ET PERROT, DROIT JUDICAIRE PRIVÉ, Tome I, nos. 892-1140 (1961).

53. CUCHE ET VINCENT, no. 170 *et seq.*; French C.P.C. art. 467 *et seq.*

54 LePaulle, *supra* note 52.

55. LePaulle, *supra* note 52, at 953. For statutory provisions, see French C.P.C. art. 467 *et seq.*

56. On his letterhead and professional card, he must style himself an "*avocat stagiaire*" rather than "*avocat.*" LePaulle, *supra* note 52, at 955.

57. This training includes attendance at court hearings; attending lectures and seminars covering, in addition to professional training, traditions of the bar and obligations owed to the court; sometimes participation in exercises of *conférence du stage,* which affords a type of moot court training; work with a senior lawyer, or in the office of an *avoué, notaire,* or *procureur*; and the handling of legal aid work assigned to him. LePaulle, *supra* note 52, at 956.

The *avoué* prepares pleadings, and acts as agent for parties in civil litigation, signing pleadings in their behalf, *etc.*[58] There is a movement of considerable force in France today to merge the *avocat* and *avoué* into a single profession, which it is felt would achieve significant economy for litigants. Tradition and other factors militate against such union.[59]

In addition to the *avocat* and *avoué*, there is the very important and highly respected *notaire*.[60] Of far greater significance than the notary public in American law, the *notaire*, in addition to being authorized to prepare the *acte authentique* (or authentic act), serves somewhat as an office lawyer and family counsellor.[61]

Many of the functions reserved in the United States to the legal profession, such as giving legal advice and drafting of legal documents for fees, may be performed in France by anyone, regardless of legal training.[62] In fact, there are numerous self-styled *agents d'affaires*[63] not subject to regulations, who perform many services that an American lawyer would consider to be an integral part of his practice. There are, of course, certain functions assigned exclusively to *avocats, avoués, notaires*, etc.

## III. Criminal Procedure and Evidence

In France, it is often said that in French criminal proceedings, as contrasted with Anglo-American, *"on juge l'homme, pas les faits"* (one judges the man, not facts). The implications of this approach are of pervasive significance.

As noted previously, the French system does grade offenses, and contemplates that in general, each of the three different classes of criminal infractions be tried by separate tribunals.[64]

58. Cuche et Vincent, no. 187 *et seq.;* French C.P.C. art. 523 *et seq.*; Hamson, *In Court in 2 Countries, Civil Procedure in England and France*, The Times (London), Nov. 15, 1959.

Somewhat similar to the *avoué* is the *agréé*, who performs an analogous function with respect to proceedings in a *tribunal de commerce*. LePaulle, *supra* note 52, at 947-48; David & de Vries, 23.

59. The position of *avoué* is purchased, and the expense to the government in reimbursing *avoués* would be high.

60. French C.P.C. art. 495 *et seq.*; David & de Vries, 24, and authorities cited at 28.

61. French C.P.C. arts. 495, 555; Cuche et Vincent, no. 191 *et seq.*

62. LePaulle, *supra* note 52, at 947; David & de Vries, 23.

63. Also sometimes called *"conseils juridiques," "jurisconsultes," "conseillers fiscaux,"* or *"contentieux."* LePaulle, *supra* note 52, at 947.

64. Roughly summarized: *Contraventions* are petty offenses punishable by a maximum fine of 2000 NF (approximately $400), imprisonment not longer than two months, and confiscation of seized objects (French Penal Code art. 464

The procedure to be followed varies somewhat accordingly.[65] For purposes of clarity of exposition, and to provide a meaningful basic understanding of the French system, procedure with respect to the intermediate type of offense (*délit*) will provide the focal point for subsequent discussion. Where deemed of significance in light of the purposes of this survey, reference to procedures for the more serious *crimes* and less serious *contraventions* will be given, either in text or footnote.

*Délits* embrace infractions punishable by imprisonment of up to five years at hard labor — corresponding roughly to the more serious misdemeanors and less serious felonies of Anglo-American law.[66] The institution of jury trial appears only in the *Cour d'Assises*, where *crimes* are tried, and is viewed with considerable skepticism by the French.[67] Frequently, by common

*et seq.*) — triable before the *tribunal de police* (French C.P.P. art. 521 *et seq.*), presided over by a single judge, sitting without a jury. *Délits* are criminal infractions of an intermediate nature, punishable by a fine in excess of 2000 NF, imprisonment from 2 months to 5 years, and other deprivations (see FRENCH PENAL CODE arts. 1, 9) — triable before the *tribunal correctionnel*, presided over by three judges sitting without a jury (French C.P.P. arts. 381 *et seq.*, 398 *et seq.*). *Crimes* are the most serious offenses, punishable by death, imprisonment, and other deprivations — triable before the *Court d'Assises*, composed of 3 judges and 9 jurors (French C.P.P. art. 214, 231 *et seq.*; 240 *et seq.*). STEFANI ET LEVASSEUR, no. 464.

65. For procedure for the *Cour d'Assises*, see French C.P.P. art. 231 *et seq.*; *tribunal correctionnel*, French C.P.P. art. 381 *et seq.*; *tribunal de police*, French C.P.P. art. 521 *et seq.*; STEFANI ET LEVASSEUR, nos. 757 *et seq.*, 777 *et seq.*, 797 *et seq.*

For discussion in English of French criminal procedure generally, see: FRANCE: COUNTRY LAW STUDY, prepared by Judge Advocate Division, United States Army Communications Zone, Europe (1961); Anton, *L'Instruction Criminelle*, 9 AM. J. COMP. L. 441 (1960); Hauser, *Comparative Law: The Criminal Law in France*, 45 A.B.A.J. 807 (1959); Freed, *Aspects of French Criminal Procedure*, 17 LA. L. REV. 730 (1957) (practice under prior law); Vouin, *The Protection of the Accused in French Criminal Procedure*, 5 INT. & COMP. L.Q. 1 (1956); Hamson, *Prosecutor and Accused: I. The Criminal Process in England and France*, THE TIMES (London), March 15, 1950, reprinted in French in Hamson et Vouin, *Le Procès Criminel en Angleterre et en France*, No. 2-3 REVUE INTERNATIONALE DE DROIT PÉNAL (1952); Hamson, *Prosecutor and Accused: II. The Examining Magistrate in France*, THE TIMES (London), March 16, 1950; Ploscowe, *Jury Trial in France*, 29 MINN. L. REV. 376 (1945) (practice under prior law); Ploscowe, *Development of Inquisitorial and Accusatorial Elements in French Procedure*, 23 J. CRIM. L. 372 (1932); Woods, *The French Court of Assizes*, 22 J. CRIM. L. 325 (1931) (practice under prior law); Wright, *French Criminal Procedure I*, 44 L.Q. Rev. 324 (1928) (practice under prior law); Wright, *French Criminal Procedure II*, 45 L.Q. REV. 92 (1929) (practice under prior law).

For references in French, see BOUZAT, *op. cit. supra* note 4, at nos. 1192-1296; ENCYCLOPÉDIE JURIDIQUUE, *op. cit. supra* note 4, at Tome II, p. 287 et mise à jour, p. 295; JURISCLASSEUR, *op. cit supra* note 15, at arts. 231 *et seq.*, 321 *et seq.*; STEFANI ET LEVASSEUR, nos. 757 *et seq.*, 777 *et seq.*, 790 *et seq.*; VIDAL, *op. cit. supra* note 4, at nos. 841-63 ter.; VITU, *op. cit. supra* note 4, at 343-71.

66. Ploscowe, *Development of Inquisitorial and Accusatorial Elements in French Procedure*, 23 J. CRIM. L. 372, 385 (1932).

67. STEFANI ET LEVASSEUR, no. 432.

consent of the parties (via a process known as *correctionnalization*) many infractions which could properly be treated as *crimes* are treated as *délits*, and are tried before the three-judge *tribunal correctionnel*, sitting without a jury.[68] Also, as a result of jury indulgence, certain *crimes* (abortions, bigamy) have been reduced legislatively from *crimes* to *délits*.[69]

Civil party intervention in criminal proceedings is one fascinating aspect of French procedure which it is necessary to keep in mind. Although difficult perhaps for a person trained in American law to understand,[70] French law provides that, in all criminal proceedings, a person who has been directly injured as a result of the criminal act may interpose a claim for civil relief.[71] Thus in one proceeding, civil and criminal liability may be, and frequently are, determined.[72] Although an injured party may always assert his claim for civil relief in a separate civil proceeding,[73] intervention in a pending criminal proceeding may be quite advantageous.[74] By this means, he can take full advantage of the investigatory facilities and prosecuting personnel of the state, the inquisitorial aspects of the proceedings, and the speed, economy, and more liberal rules of evidence characteristic of the criminal action. In addition, he reaps the psychological benefit resulting from his adversary's position as a criminally accused. Most automobile personal injury suits are handled in this manner.[75]

68. Freed, *supra* note 65, at 738; Ploscowe, *supra* note 66, at 385-86; STEFANI ET LEVASSEUR, nos. 432, 477 *et seq.*

69. STEFANI ET LEVASSEUR, nos. 432, 477 *et seq.*

70. In American law, criminal and civil proceedings are rigorously separated. For example, where civil and criminal proceedings both grow out of the same facts, the judgment in one case is generally inadmissible as evidence in the other. See MCCORMICK, LAW OF EVIDENCE § 295 (1954). *But see* UNIFORM RULE OF EVIDENCE 63(20) and comment.

71. French C.P.P. art. 2 *et seq.* For further discussion with respect to this procedure, see STEFANI ET LEVASSEUR, no. 513 *et seq.*; French C.P.P. arts. 85 *et seq.*, 418 *et seq.* For general discussion of the civil party and civil action, see: Vouin, *The Protection of the Accused in French Criminal Procedure*, 5 INT. & COMP. L.Q. 1, 7, 11 (1956); BOUZAT, TRAITÉ THÉORIQUE ET PRATIQUE DE DROIT PÉNAL, no. 852 (1951, et mise à jour 1956); ENCYCLOPÉDIE JURIDIQUE, RÉPERTOIRE DE DROIT CRIMINEL ET DE PROCÉDURE PÉNALE, Tome I, p. 39 et mise à jour p. 7, Tome II, p. 469 et mise à jour p. 337 (Dalloz 1953 et mise à jour 1962); JURISCLASSEUR DE PROCÉDURE PÉNALE, arts. 1-5, 10 (Editions techniques); STEFANI ET LEVASSEUR, no. 131 *et seq.*; VIDAL, COURS DE DROIT CRIMINEL ET DE SCIENCE PÉNITENTIAIRE, no. 619 (1949); VITU, PROCÉDURE PÉNALE 144 (1957).

72. STEFANI ET LEVASSEUR, nos. 180 *et seq.*, 513 *et seq.*, 657 *et seq.*, 820 *et seq.*

73. French C.P.P. art. 4 *et seq.*; STEFANI ET LEVASSEUR, nos. 170 *et seq.*, 184 *et seq.*

74. STEFANI ET LEVASSEUR, no. 180 *et seq.*

75. In France, there is compulsory automobile liability insurance, and thus

### *Pre-trial*

A criminal action in France may be commenced by a governmental official or a private individual directly injured by the criminal act.[76] The *procureur* has discretion,[77] subject to the order of his superiors,[78] to institute criminal proceedings. This possibility of private initiation affords protection against arbitrary governmental inaction.[79] If the governmental official does not institute the action, the injured party may do so by bringing a complaint against the perpetrator of the wrong, and at the same time constituting himself *partie civile* or civil party, claiming damages for injuries suffered by him personally.[80] As noted above, this may be quite advantageous. There are, however, certain hazards to this course of action, not present when a party simply interposes his claim for civil relief in a criminal action already instituted by the *procureur* against an individual. By taking the initiative, a civil claimant may become liable, in the event of unsuccessful prosecution, for damages caused the defendant[81] — no doubt a persuasive deterrent to unwarranted institution of criminal prosecution by private individuals.[82]

When a complaint (or *plainte*) is made to the police, or they have other reason to believe that a criminal offense has been committed,[83] a preliminary investigation (or *enquête*) by the police is usually held.[84] The power of the police varies, depend-

frequently in criminal cases, the attorneys for the insurance companies, through their defense of the civil liability of the company's policyholders, are active participants.

76. French C.P.P. art. 1 *et seq.*; STEFANI ET LEVASSEUR, nos. 104 *et seq.*, 140 *et seq.*, 170 *et seq.*, 496 *et seq.*, 513 *et seq.*, 569 *et seq.*, 575 *et seq.* See Sullivan, *A Comparative Survey of Problems in Criminal Procedure*, 6 ST. LOUIS U. L.J. 380, 384 (1961), for comparative discussion as to institution of criminal proceedings.

77. See Anton, *supra* note 65, at 445; STEFANI ET LEVASSEUR, no. 578.

78. See *supra* note 42; STEFANI ET LEVASSEUR, no. 500; French C.P.P. arts. 33, 36, 37, 44.

79. See Sullivan, *supra* note 76, at 385; STEFANI ET LEVASSEUR, no. 479 *et seq.*

80. See French C.P.P. art. 85 *et seq.*; STEFANI ET LEVASSEUR, no. 143 *et seq.*

81. See French C.P.P. art. 91; FRENCH PENAL CODE art. 373; STEFANI ET LEVASSEUR, no. 523.

82. See Sullivan, *supra* note 76, at 385.

83. STEFANI ET LEVASSEUR, nos. 537 *et seq.*, 384 *et seq.*; French C.P.P. art. 17.

84. For preliminary investigation, see French C.P.P. art. 75 *et seq.* For interesting procedure as to investigation where felonies and misdemeanors are discovered in the very act, see French C.P.P. art. 53 *et seq.* For discussion as to preliminary investigation by the police, see STEFANI ET LEVASSEUR, no. 537 *et seq.*

For general discussion of investigation by the police, see: Anton, *L'Instruction Criminelle*, 9 AM. J. COMP. L. 441, 442 (1960); Hamson, *Prosecutor and Accused: II. The Examining Magistrate in France*, THE TIMES (London), March

ing upon circumstances.[85] In a number of cases, a second stage of investigation is usually carried on by the very important *juge d'instruction*,[86] who serves as investigating magistrate. The *juge d'instruction* may never on his own motion assume the power and authority to investigate.[87] It can be acquired only on the request of the *procureur*, or as the result of a formal claim for damages filed by a civil party. Investigation by the *juge d'instruction*[88] is obligatory for all the most serious offenses (*crimes*),[89] and is usually required for *délits* where the perpetrator is unknown, a minor,[90] or a multiple offender.[91] It is generally optional for other *délits* and for *contraventions*.[92]

The new Code of Criminal Procedure retains the essentially secret and inquisitorial nature of the proceedings before the *juge d'instruction*,[93] but places the accused, the civil party,[94] and the prosecutor upon a more equal footing in these proceedings.[95]

The differences between French and Anglo-American law as

16, 1950; Patey, *Recent Reforms in French Criminal Law and Procedure*, 9 INT. & COMP. L.Q. 383, 389 (1960); Vouin, *The Protection of the Accused in French Criminal Procedure*, 5 INT. & COMP. L.Q. 1, 9, 14 (1956); BOUZAT, *op. cit. supra* note 71, at no. 959; ENCYCLOPÉDIE JURIDIQUE, *op. cit. supra* note 71, at Tome II, p. 539 et mise à jour, p. 359; JURISCLASSEUR, *op. cit. supra* note 71, at arts. 12-21; STEFANI ET LEVASSEUR, no. 537 *et seq.*; VIDAL, *op. cit. supra* note 71, at no. 801; VITU, *op. cit. supra* note 71, at 31.

85. Depending upon whether the felony or *délit* was discovered in the very act. Compare French C.P.P. art. 53 *et seq.* with art. 75 *et seq.* See STEFANI ET LEVASSEUR, no. 549 *et seq.*

86. For an excellent description of the function of the *juge d'instruction*, see Anton, *L'Instruction Criminelle*, 9 AM. J. COMP. L. 441 (1960). See also French C.P.P. arts. 49 *et seq.*, 79 *et seq.*; STEFANI ET LEVASSEUR, no. 412 *et seq.*

For further general discussion of the role of the *juge d'instruction*, *see*: Hamson, *supra* note 84; Sullivan, *supra* note 76, at 390; Vouin, *supra* note 84, at 4; BOUZAT, *op. cit. supra* note 71, at no. 1118; ENCYCLOPÉDIE JURIDIQUE, *op. cit. supra* note 71, at Tome II, pp. 247, 282 et mise à jour, p. 275; JURISCLASSEUR, *op. cit. supra* note 71, at arts. 49 *et seq.*, 79 *et seq.*, 92 *et seq.*; STEFANI ET LEVASSEUR, nos. 412 *et seq.*, 631 *et seq.*; VIDAL, *op. cit. supra* note 71, at no. 813; VITU, *op. cit. supra* note 71, at 55, 269.

87. French C.P.P. arts. 51, 80, 86; STEFANI ET LEVASSEUR, no. 634 *et seq.*

88. *Instruction préparatoire* or *information préalable* (synonymous terms).

89. Since the writing of this article, Ordinance no. 62-1041 of September 1, 1962, has temporarily modified this rule in exceptional cases.

90. However, investigation by *either* the *juge d'instruction* or the *juge des enfants* (juvenile judge) of *délits* committed by minors is obligatory. STEFANI ET LEVASSEUR, nos. 602, 439 *et seq.*

91. See Anton, *supra* note 86, at 445; French C.P.P. art. 79; STEFANI ET LEVASSEUR, no. 602 *et seq.*

92. French C.P.P. art. 79; STEFANI ET LEVASSEUR, no. 603.

93. French C.P.P. art. 11; STEFANI ET LEVASSEUR, no. 633. However, contradictory arguments are now possible before the accusatory chamber of the Court of Appeal, which exercises extensive supervisory powers with respect to actions of the *juge d'instruction*. Anton, *supra* note 86, at 444; Patey, *Recent Reforms in French Criminal Law and Procedure*, 9 INT. & COMP. L.Q. 383, 389-92 (1960).

94. For a discussion of the rights of the civil party, see Anton, *supra* note 86.

95. See Anton, *supra* note 86, at 444; STEFANI ET LEVASSEUR, no. 633.

to rules of evidence must be taken into consideration, even this early in the proceedings, for the statements made and evidence collected at these two phases (police and *juge d'instruction*) are generally included in the record (or *dossier*) of the case.[96] In France, the subsequent trial or hearing (*audience*) is usually quite short. The presiding judge, who is himself a fact-finder, uses the *dossier* in examining the defendant and questioning the witnesses. Counsel also employ the *dossier*[97] in their presentations, even those parts not previously developed through oral testimony.[98]

The *dossier* contains the reports prepared by both the police and the *juge d'instruction*, detailing the nature of the crime, date and place of the hearing, and a summary of the statements of each of the witnesses.[99] At each phase of the investigation, considerable evidence relative to the character and personality of persons involved in the incident is received and made part of the *dossier*. Each time a witness is heard, such things as his age, occupation, address, employer, date and place of birth, parents, and number of children are summarized succinctly, presumably so that his declarations may be evaluated accordingly and further information concerning the witness may be obtained without undue difficulty. Extensive annotated photographs and maps are usually made and included.

### *Rights of Suspect and Accused*

In order to facilitate investigation of crime, there is a means under French law (*la garde à vue*) by which a suspect or ordinary witness may be kept in custody for twenty-four hours, which, in certain instances, may be extended for an additional twenty-four hours.[100] In general, witnesses heard by the police

96. French C.P.P. art. 178 *et seq.*; STEFANI ET LEVASSEUR, nos. 568, 739 *et seq.*

97. French C.P.P. arts. 118, 183; STEFANI ET LEVASSEUR, no. 264. For further explanation as to the contents of the *dossier*, see Anton, *supra* note 86, at 452-55.

98. This is true even as to the *Cour d'Assises*. Although the jury is not supposed to have general access to the *dossier* in its deliberations (French C.P.P. art. 347), the presiding judge has studied it and the hearing has been conducted in light of it.

99. To avoid subsequent contradiction, the law provides that summaries of the witnesses' statements are signed by them. French C.P.P. art. 106.

100. See French C.P.P. art. 77 *et seq.*; for felonies and misdemeanors discovered in the very act, see French C.P.P. art. 63 *et seq.*; see Patey, *supra* note 93, at 390-91; STEFANI ET LEVASSEUR, nos. 546 *et seq.*, 562.

As a result of Ordinance no. 60-121 of February 13, 1960, the 24- and 48-hour periods are increased to 48 and 96 respectively, where *crimes* and *délits* against the safety of the state are involved.

Since the writing of this article, Ordinance no. 62-1041 of September 1, 1962

are not sworn, whereas those heard by the *juge d'instruction* usually testify under oath.[101] Any person against whom a charge has been specifically brought may refuse to testify as a witness before the *juge d'instruction*, who, after informing him of the contents of the complaint, shall notify him of this right.[102] If the person charged exercises his right not to be heard as a witness, he may be heard only as a defendant (or *inculpé*),[103] which status affords him a number of safeguards, discussed hereafter. Also, whenever there is strong and convincing evidence that a particular person has committed a crime, whether or not he has been named in a complaint, he shall not be heard as a witness, but shall be accorded the rights of an *inculpé*.[104] A suspect not entitled to the rights of an *inculpé* is obligated to submit to interrogation[105] and is not entitled to representation of counsel before the *juge d'instruction*. Apparently, at this stage, there is no French equivalent to the privilege against self-incrimination available to him.

Although a suspect may be heard many times before the *juge d'instruction* prior to officially becoming a defendant (or *inculpé*), generally once he is entitled to this status, he is to be informed[106] by the *juge d'instruction* of the acts he allegedly committed, and notified that he is free to remain silent.[107] The code article provides, however, that if the *inculpé* wishes to make a statement, it shall be received immediately. In an excellent and authoritative article on proceedings before the *juge d'in-*

---

has *temporarily* provided for a 15-day *garde à vue* (not subject to extension) in certain *crimes*.

101. French C.P.P. arts. 62 *et seq.*, 75 *et seq.*, 101 *et seq.*; STEFANI ET LEVASSEUR, no. 544 *et seq.*

102. French C.P.P. art. 104. A notation that he has been so informed must be made in the official report.

For discussion of the rights of a suspect and accused generally, see: Anton, *supra* note 86; Hamson, *Prosecutor and Accused: I. The Criminal Process in England and France*, THE TIMES (London), March 15, 1950; Hamson, *Prosecutor and Accused: II. The Examining Magistrate in France*, THE TIMES (London), March 16, 1950; Patey, *supra* note 93, at 390; Vouin, *The Protection of the Accused in French Criminal Procedure*, 5 INT. & COMP. L.Q. 1 (1956); ENCYCLOPÉDIE JURIDIQUE, *op. cit. supra* note 71, at Tome I, p. 670 et mise à jour, p. 184; STEFANI ET LEVASSEUR, no. 248 *et seq.*

103. French C.P.P. art. 104; STEFANI ET LEVASSEUR, nos. 250, 651.

104. French C.P.P. art. 105; STEFANI ET LEVASSEUR, no. 647.

105. Or be subjected to a fine of approximately $80-$200. French C.P.P. art. 109. See also French C.P.P. arts. 101 *et seq.*, 110 *et seq.*

106. But for an exceptional case, see French C.P.P. art. 115.

107. The fact that such notice has been given must be recorded in the official records. This stage in the proceedings is called the first appearance. (French C.P.P. art. 114 *et seq.*; STEFANI ET LEVASSEUR, no. 651.)

For discussion of rights of suspect and accused generally, see authorities cited in note 102 *supra*.

*struction*,[108] Professor Anton of the University of Glasgow states that it is highly probable that the *inculpé* will wish to make a statement at this time, for "in the vast majority of cases" French criminals "exhibit a quite spontaneous desire to confess all." In any event, confessions are certainly numerous.

The same code article[109] that provides for informing the *inculpé* of his right to remain silent and his option to make a statement *goes on* to provide that the judge shall advise him that he is entitled to counsel.[110] Professor Anton states that in practice, the *inculpé* is generally so informed only after he has made his statement. Although apparently there is no right to presence of counsel when an *inculpé* is formally charged by the *juge d'instruction*, and a statement by him is frequently voluntarily made at this point, thereafter, during actual interrogation or confrontation, the *inculpé* is entitled to presence of counsel, unless this right is expressly renounced.[111] But before this and any subsequent interrogation or confrontation, the attorney for the *inculpé* shall have the right, twenty-four hours in advance, to study the *dossier*.[112] However, neither counsel for the accused nor counsel for the state may speak at this hearing, except to ask questions, after receiving permission from the court.[113]

A very fascinating element in the investigatory stage is the reenactment of the crime, wherein the *inculpé* is asked to reenact what happened. It is apparently felt that, during the process of reenactment, facts not previously disclosed will emerge; even an accomplished liar may encounter difficulty in portraying a false account.[114] Photographs of the reenactment are often included in the *dossier*, very effective evidence indeed.

During the course of this investigation the *juge d'instruction's* actions and orders are subject to review, at the instance of the *inculpé* or the state[115] (even, at times, of the civil party)[116]

108. Anton, *supra* note 86, at 448.
109. French C.P.P. art. 114.
110. If the defendant wishes it, counsel shall be appointed for him. French C.P.P. art. 114.
Although an *inculpé* may freely communicate with his attorney after the first appearance, the *juge d'instruction* does have the right to prohibit communication with other persons for ten days, which may be extended to twenty days. French C.P.P. art. 116; STEFANI ET LEVASSEUR, no. 266.
111. French C.P.P. art. 118; STEFANI ET LEVASSEUR, no. 651 *et seq.*
112. French C.P.P. art. 118; STEFANI ET LEVASSEUR, nos 653, 262 *et seq.*
113. French C.P.P. art. 120; STEFANI ET LEVASSEUR, no. 655.
114. Anton, *supra* note 86, at 452.
115. French C.P.P. arts. 156 *et seq.*, 185 *et seq.*, 191 *et seq.*, 219 *et seq.*; STEFANI ET LEVASSEUR, no. 714 *et seq.*
116. French C.P.P. art. 186.

by the *Chambre d'Accusation* of the *Cour d'Appel.*[117] Although not public, hearings before the *Chambre d'Accusation* are to a large extent adversary in nature.[118]

### *Search and Seizure*

When a *crime*, and, frequently,[119] a *délit* has been discovered during the commission of the very act, provision is made for immediate search and seizure without the necessity of judicial authorization.[120] Generally, in other cases, prior to investigation by the *juge d'instruction*, the police may not undertake compulsory search and seizure in private homes.[121] Once a case is under investigation by the *juge d'instruction*, compulsory search and seizure by him or under his direction are permitted, subject to restrictions outlined in the law.[122]

### *Confessions*

The Code of Penal Procedure provides that a "confession, like all elements of proof, shall be left to the free appraisal of the judges."[123] It appears that as a result of the extensive in-

117. STEFANI ET LEVASSEUR, no. 420 *et seq.* If the *juge d'instruction* has decided, somewhat as an Anglo-American grand jury would, that the *inculpé* should be tried for a *crime* and that the case is thus one which should be tried by the highest criminal court, the *Cour d'Assises*, then *before* the defendant may be so tried, the decision of the *juge d'instruction must* be reviewed by the *Chambre d'Accusation* (French C.P.P. art. 181), which is free to reinvestigate the case, or to act upon the *dossier* prepared by the *juge d'instruction* (French C.P.P. art. 191 *et seq.*). In any event, before a person can be tried by the *Cour d'Assises*, the case must be doubly examined, first by the *juge d'instruction*, and secondly by the *Chambre d'Accusation* (French C.P.P. arts. 181, 214 *et seq.*).

118. See Patey, *supra* note 93, at 391-92.

119. In those instances where the *délit* is punishable by imprisonment.

120. For very interesting provisions outlining procedures and formalities, see French C.P.P. art. 56 *et seq.*; STEFANI ET LEVASSEUR, no. 556 *et seq.*

121. French C.P.P. art. 76; STEFANI ET LEVASSEUR, no. 545. For the very exceptional case, see French C.P.P. art. 23.

122. French C.P.P. arts. 94 *et seq.*, 151 *et seq.*; STEFANI ET LEVASSEUR, no. 659 *et seq.*

For materials on search and seizure generally, including French handling of the problem of evidence obtained as a result of illegal search and seizure, see BOUZAT, *op. cit. supra* note 71, at nos. 1145, 1161; ENCYCLOPÉDIE JURIDIQUE, *op. cit. supra* note 71, at Tome II, p. 505 et mise à jour, p. 347; JURISCLASSEUR, *op. cit. supra* note 71, at arts. 75 *et seq.*, 92 *et seq.*, 170 *et seq.*; STEFANI ET LEVASSEUR, nos. 545 *et seq.*, 556 *et seq.*, 659 *et seq.*; VIDAL, *op. cit. supra* note 71, at nos. 805, 819, 834; VITU, *op. cit. supra* note 71, at 217, 314, 337.

123. French C.P.P. art. 428; STEFANI ET LEVASSEUR, no. 343 *et seq.*

For materials on confessions, including French handling of the problem of illegally obtained confessions, see generally: French C.P.P. art. 170 *et seq.*; BOUZAT, *op. cit. supra* note 71, at no. 1098 *et seq.*; ENCYCLOPÉDIE JURIDIQUE, *op. cit. supra* note 71, at Tome I, p. 203; JURISCLASSEUR, *op. cit. supra* note 71, at *art.* 428; STEFANI ET LEVASSEUR, nos. 343 *et seq.*, 354, 356, 547 and the authorities cited therein; VIDAL, *op. cit. supra* note 71, at no. 743 *et seq.*; VITU, *op. cit. supra* note 71, at 210 *et seq.*

vestigation and interrogation carried on by the police and the *juge d'instruction*, confessions are frequently obtained. Thus often the major function of the trial is investigation of the defendant's character and the circumstances of the case in order to determine what, if any, punishment should be accorded him.

Many of the confessions are received by the police,[124] and understandably there are charges of ill-practice against them.[125] In order to prevent police brutality in examining a suspect or other witnesses, French law provides that persons held in custody (*garde à vue*)[126] have the right to a medical examination at the end of twenty-four hours detention, and the *Procureur de la République* may call for such an examination before that time.[127] Also, French law makes it a crime for a policeman to use unjustifiable force against a citizen,[128] and gives the *Chambre d'Accusation* of the court of appeal extensive authority to discipline police for misconduct.[129]

### *Appointment of Experts*

The *juge d'instruction* may on his own motion, or at the request of the defense, district attorney, or civil party, appoint experts to render an opinion on technical questions arising during the course of the investigation.[130] The procedures in this regard are very interesting, particularly because of the difficulties experienced in the United States as to expert testimony and the various efforts towards reform.[131]

---

124. STEFANI ET LEVASSEUR, no. 343 *et seq.*

125. See Hamson, *Prosecutor and Accused: II. The Examining Magistrate in France*, THE TIMES (London), March 16, 1950; Vouin, *Protection of the Accused in French Criminal Procedure*, 5 INT. & COMP. L.Q. 1, 14 (1956); STEFANI ET LEVASSEUR, nos. 256 *et seq.*, 341.

126. For a discussion of *garde à vue*, see *supra* p. 15.

127. French C.P.P. art. 64 *et seq.*; STEFANI ET LEVASSEUR, nos. 257, 547, which also provide that a record shall be made of the length of interrogation and statements received.

128. FRENCH PENAL CODE art. 186; STEFANI ET LEVASSEUR, nos. 256 *et seq.*, 344. With respect to hypnosis, "truth serum," etc., see STEPHANI ET LEVASSEUR, no. 257 and authorities therein cited.

129. See French C.P.P. art. 224 *et seq.*, discussed in JURISCLASSEUR DE PROCÉDURE PÉNAL, art. 224 *et seq.* (*Editions techniques*).

130. French C.P.P. art. 156 *et seq.*; STEFANI ET LEVASSEUR, no. 705 *et seq.* For discussion of the role of experts, see Anton, *supra* note 102, at 449; BOUZAT, TRAITÉ THÉORIQUE ET PRATIQUE DE DROIT PÉNAL, no. 1072 (1951, et mise à jour 1956); ENCYCLOPÉDIE JURIDIQUE, RÉPERTOIRE DE DROIT CRIMINEL ET DE PROCÉDURE PÉNALE, Tome I, p. 1011 et mise à jour p. 228 (Dalloz 1953 et mise à jour 1962); STEFANI ET LEVASSEUR, no. 705 *et seq.*; VIDAL, COURS DE DROIT CRIMINEL ET DE SCIENCE PÉNITENTIAIRE, no. 728 (1949); VITU, PROCÉDURE PÉNALE 223 (1957).

131. MCCORMICK, EVIDENCE § 17 (1954).

The *juge d'instruction* must give reasons for refusing a request for the appointment of experts,[132] a decision subject to immediate appeal.[133] Generally, only those experts whose names appear on a national list compiled by the *Cour de Cassation*, or on a list prepared by the *Cour d'Appel* (on the advice of the *Procureur Général*) may be appointed.[134] The experts may hold hearings and question witnesses, under certain circumstances have the defendant questioned by the *juge d'instruction* in their presence, and in the case of certain medical experts, examine the defendant themselves out of the presence of the *juge d'instruction* and counsel.[135] If the persons so appointed disagree or have reservations, this is to be stated. The parties are to be notified of the experts' report and afforded an opportunity to comment or to request the appointment of additional experts.[136] The experts may be heard at the trial of the case,[137] and if other evidence or information that emerges in the course of the trial casts doubt on the validity of the findings of the experts, the court may decide either to continue with the hearing or to postpone further proceedings until a later date for the purpose of clarification.[138]

### *Preventive Detention and Bail*

French law declares that incarceration of an *inculpé* is an exceptional measure.[139] It limits such detention to five days if the maximum penalty for the offense is less than two years' imprisonment and the defendant has no criminal record.[140] Preventive detention,[141] however, appears to be customary for seri-

132. French C.P.P. art. 156; STEFANI ET LEVASSEUR, no. 702.

133. French C.P.P. arts. 156, 185, 186; STEFANI ET LEVASSEUR, no. 706 *et seq.* Where the subject of the expert opinion is a disputed fundamental issue, at least two experts are to be appointed. Ordinance of April 6, 1960, art. 2, modifying French C.P.P. arts. 156-59. For the history of this provision, see Anton, *L'Instruction Criminelle*, 9 AM. J. COMP. L. 441, 450 (1960).

134. French C.P.P. arts. 156, 157.

135. French C.P.P. art. 164. For discussion of Ordinance of April 6, 1960, modifying French C.P.P. art. 164, permitting the defendant to agree expressly to direct examination by experts, see Anton, *supra* note 133, at 450; STEFANI ET LEVASSEUR, no. 711.

136. French C.P.P. art. 166 *et seq.*; STEFANI ET LEVASSEUR, no. 716.

137. French C.P.P. art. 168 *et seq.*

138. French C.P.P. art. 169; STEFANI ET LEVASSEUR, no. 784 *et seq.* The court shall state its reasons underlying this determination.

139. French C.P.P. art. 137.

140. *Id.* art. 138.

141. *Id.* art. 714 *et seq.*, regulated by *id.* art. 137 *et seq.* and discussed in STEFANI ET LEVASSEUR, nos. 667 *et seq.*, 680 *et seq.*

For discussion of preventive detention generally, see: Vouin, *The Protection of the Accused in French Criminal Procedure*, 5 INT. & COMP. L.Q. 1, 18 (1956); BOUZAT, *op. cit. supra* note 130, at no. 1136; ENCYCLOPÉDIE JURIDIQUE, *op. cit. supra* note 130, at Tome I, p. 725 et mise à jour, p. 192; JURISCLASSEUR DE PRO-

ous offenses.[142] The law provides[143] that preventive detention shall not exceed four months duration, except when extended for a similar period or periods by orders of the *juge d'instruction*, with written reasons. As a practical matter, such extensions appear to be frequent for the more serious crimes, and prolonged pre-trial detention in France has been severely criticized.[144]

It is interesting that French law provides[145] that, apart from exceptional cases, time served in preventive detention is to be subtracted from the sentence imposed at the trial. Although there are provisions for release, in the discretion of the court, on giving of security (*caution*),[146] these provisions are rarely utilized.[147] Instead, it appears that when felt that provisional liberty[148] is deemed appropriate, it is accorded without the formality of *caution*.

## *Trial*

The institutions of arraignment and pleas, as known in Anglo-American law, do not appear to be present as such in French law. There are, of course, ways of informing the defendant of the crime with which he is charged,[149] as noted above. Generally, there is no guilty plea in French criminal proceedings.[150] The writer has been informed that this is due to the French conception of the presumption of innocence: it is for the judge and jury to determine guilt, not the defendant. It is interesting to note that there is a possibility under French law of proceeding without the presence of the defendant.[151] But in the following discussion, it will be assumed that the defendant is in court.

---

CÉDURE PÉNALE arts. 137 *et seq.*, 714 *et seq.* (*Editions techniques*); STEFANI ET LEVASSEUR, nos. 667 *et seq.*, 680 *et seq.*; VIDAL, *op. cit. supra* note 130, at no. 826; VITU, *op. cit. supra* note 130, at 286.

142. See Anton, *supra* note 133, at 453-54.

143. French C.P.P. art. 139, as amended by Ordinance 60-529, June 4, 1960.

144. See Anton, *supra* note 133, at 453-54; Hamson et Vouin, *Le Procès Criminel en Angleterre et en France*, No. 2-3 REVUE INTERNATIONALE DE DROIT PÉNAL 177, 182 (1952), and authorities therein cited.

145. FRENCH PENAL CODE art. 24; STEFANI ET LEVASSEUR, no. 683.

146. French C.P.P. art. 145 *et seq.*

147. See Anton, *supra* note 133, at 454.

148. French C.P.P. art. 138 *et seq.*; STEFANI ET LEVASSEUR, no. 685 *et seq.*

149. See Anton, *supra* note 131, at 448; French C.P.P. arts. 104, 114 *et seq.*, 180, 217, 268, 550 *et seq.*; STEFANI ET LEVASSEUR, nos. 250, 651, 759 *et seq.*

150. For petty offenses (*contraventions*), however, there is a means by which one may voluntarily pay a fine and avoid the inconvenience of a regular hearing (*oblation volontaire* or *amende de composition*). Freed, *Aspects of French Criminal Procedure*, 17 LA. L. REV. 730, 736-37 (1957); French C.P.P. arts. 6, 524 *et seq.*; STEFANI ET LEVASSEUR, no. 771 *et seq.*

151. French C.P.P. arts. 410 *et seq.*, 487 *et seq.*, 544 *et seq.*, 627 *et seq.*; STEFANI ET LEVASSEUR, nos. 779, 829 *et seq.*

The French criminal trial (*audience*) is totally different from one in the United States.[152] Of prime importance is the *dossier*, prepared in advance by the police at the *enquête préliminaire* (or first step of investigation), and, in many cases, also by the *juge d'instruction*.[153] The *dossier* is at times lengthy indeed. As noted previously, the presiding judge has had access to it in advance of the trial, and in more serious cases, it is necessary for him to have studied it assiduously. Counsel for the prosecution, the defense, and the civil party (if there be one) have all also had access to it.[154]

The trial itself is short compared to American trials. Interrogation of the witnesses is handled almost exclusively by the presiding judge.[155] Counsel for the parties may request that the president ask certain questions, and this usually occurs from time to time during the trial.[156] Questions thus suggested, however, are not numerous, and there is nothing in French criminal procedure akin to Anglo-American examination and cross-examination of witnesses by counsel. The extensive and painstakingly prepared *dossier* is the French means of clarifying the facts in advance of trial and pinpointing whatever contradictions remain.[157]

What is necessary, and yet very difficult, for an American to understand is that, in the vast majority of French criminal proceedings, the defendant has already fully confessed several times, and does not contest the validity of his confessions. Of course, there are exceptions, but it seems to this writer, from observations and conversations, that generally by the time the trial arrives, it is quite apparent from defendant's confessions, thoroughly corroborated in the *dossier*, that he did in fact commit the act in question.[158] Since, at the same time guilt or inno-

152. See French C.P.P. arts. 381 *et seq.* (for trial of *délits*), 231 *et seq.* (*crimes*), 521 *et seq.* (*contraventions*).

For discussion of French criminal trials generally, see authorities cited in note 65, *supra*.

153. With respect to the more serious cases (*crimes*), the case must be investigated by the *juge d'instruction* and also further considered by the accusatory chamber of the Court of Appeal prior to trial by the *Cour d'Assises*.

154. French C.P.P. arts. 81, 89, 118, 183, 186.

155. STEFANI ET LEVASSEUR, nos. 327 *et seq.*, especially 336, 782 *et seq.*

156. French C.P.P. art. 454; STEFANI ET LEVASSEUR, no. 336. In cases brought before the *Cour d'Assises*, subject to certain restrictions, the *procureur* has the *right*, after the witness has given his narrative account, to ask questions directly. French C.P.P. arts. 309, 312.

157. See Anton, *supra* note 133, at 442.

158. For discussion of confessions in French criminal proceedings, see *supra* p. 18.

In a particular jurisdiction for which statistics for the 1961 term were gath-

cence is determined by the tribunal, sentence is also meted out, an extremely important consideration at the trial is determining what sentence should be given the defendant, if he should be found guilty. Naturally, this has great bearing as to the type of procedure employed, the evidence adduced, and the rules with respect thereto.

Because of the importance of the *dossier* and the role of the *juge d'instruction* in cases referred to him, it is noteworthy that this magistrate is charged with neutrality and obligated to develop for the *dossier* not merely facts favorable to the prosecution, but also those favorable to the defendant.[159] It seems fair to state that in general this obligation is actually fulfilled. Since it is for the *juge d'instruction*, in cases referred to him, to decide[160] whether an individual should be brought to trial, the standard employed by him in arriving at this decision is significant. Although the legislative texts are somewhat vague,[161] it seems to this observer that the standard actually employed is much more defendant-oriented than that used for grand jury indictment.[162] It appears that if the *juge d'instruction* is not reasonably convinced of guilt,[163] subject to review by the accusatory chamber of the court of appeal at the request of the *procureur*,[164] or the civil party,[165] the defendant does not go to trial.[166]

---

ered, approximately 94% of persons tried before the *tribunal correctionnel* (including cases which had been investigated by the *juge d'instruction*) were found guilty. It should be noted, however, that since there is no "guilty plea" for *délits* (see *supra* p. 21), many of those tried would in American proceedings have pleaded "guilty" and been sentenced without trial.

159. French C.P.P. art. 81; STEFANI ET LEVASSEUR, no. 642 *et seq.*

160. Before a person may be tried for a *crime*, however, the case must be doubly examined, first by the *juge d'instruction*, and secondly by the *Chambre d'Accusation*.

161. STEFANI ET LEVASSEUR, no. 351 *et seq.*

French C.P.P. arts. 176, 177 (1st par.), and 179 (1st par.) provide:

"176. The *juge d'instruction* shall seek to ascertain if there exist against the *inculpé* charges constituting a violation of the criminal law.

"177. If the *juge d'instruction* is of the opinion that the facts constitute neither a *crime*, a *délit*, nor a *contravention*, or that the perpetrator of the crime remains unknown, or that sufficient charges against the accused do not exist, he is to declare by an order, that there is no need to prosecute. . . .

"179. If the *juge* [*d'instruction*] is of the opinion that the facts constitute a *délit*, he shall refer the case to the *tribunal correctionnel*. . . ."

162. See A.L.I. CODE OF CRIMINAL PROCEDURE ch. 5, § 145 (1930).

163. See STEFANI ET LEVASSEUR, no. 351. For example, the writer has seen the report of a *juge d'instruction*, stating that there existed a "slight doubt," which "must be resolved in favor of the suspect," and therefore a "non-lieu" or "no true bill" was brought. The writer is informed that such handling of the "doubt" question by the *juge d'instruction* is general practice.

164. French C.P.P. art. 185; STEFANI ET LEVASSEUR, no. 742.

165. French C.P.P. art. 186; STEFANI ET LEVASSEUR, no. 745.

166. The *Chambre d'Accusation* is to employ the same standard in arriving at

The presumption of innocence, although not expressly stated in the Code of Penal Procedure, is well recognized as a fundamental concept,[167] and generally the burden of proof is clearly on the prosecution.[168] However, in petty offenses and certain exceptional cases, a *procès verbal*, prepared by public officials outside of court, drawn in accordance with strict regulations, constitutes prima facie proof of guilt, rebuttable by evidence to the contrary.[169]

At the trial, after the charge is read, the defendant is usually the first party examined by the presiding judge.[170] As is the custom for witnesses, he stands. In serious cases, with painstaking care, the presiding judge, who has studied the *dossier*, interrogates the defendant, asking him to affirm or deny the truth of the statements contained therein, both his own and those of others. The judge attempts to bring out the pertinent circumstances, both favorable and unfavorable. Questions by counsel for the defendant and the civil party may be posed through the president of the court.[171]

After the defendant has testified, other persons are heard. It should be noted that French procedure makes a distinction between witnesses and those who simply give information. Persons affected with an interest, such as the defendant,[172] the civil party,[173] and those closely related to them by blood or affinity,[174] are not permitted to testify under oath — although they may give statements and be questioned as though they were wit-

its decision as the *juge d'instruction*. See STEFANI ET LEVASSEUR, nos. 351, 736 *et seq.*

167. See Declaration of the Rights of Man, art. 9; GORPHE, APPRÉCIATIONS DES PREUVES EN JUSTICE 32 (1947); Hamson & Vouin, *supra* note 144, at 185; STEFANI ET LEVASSEUR, no. 287 *et seq*; VOUIN ET LÉAUTÉ, DROIT PÉNAL ET PROCÉDURE PÉNALE 220 (1960); Semaine Juridique, Cour de Cassation (*chambre criminelle*), 9 mars 1950, J.C.P. II, no. 5594.

168. For general discussion of burden of proof and presumption of innocence, see: BOUZAT, *op. cit. supra* note 130, at no. 1063; ENCYCLOPÉDIE JURIDIQUE, *op. cit. supra* note 130, at Tome II, p. 659 et mise è jour, p. 372; JURISCLASSEUR, *op. cit. supra* note 141, at art. 427 *et seq.*; STEFANI ET LEVASSEUR, no. 287 *et seq.*; VIDAL, *op. cit. supra* note 130, at no. 715; VITU, *op. cit. supra* note 130, at 184.

169. FRANCE: COUNTRY LAW STUDY, prepared by Judge Advocate Division, United States Army Communications Zone, Europe, 9-10 (1961); French C.P.P. arts. 537, 429 *et seq.*; STEFANI ET LEVASSEUR, no. 357 *et seq.*

170. French C.P.P. arts. 406, 410, 416, 442; STEFANI ET LEVASSEUR, nos. 781, 339 *et seq.*

171. French C.P.P. art. 442. For the rule regulating counsel's questioning of defendant in the *Cour d'Assises* see French C.P.P. 312. STEFANI ET LEVASSEUR, no. 779.

172. French C.P.P. arts. 442, 448.

173. *Id.* art. 442.

174. *Id.* art. 448.

nesses. As a result, these persons are not subject to prosecution for perjury.[175] What they say is viewed with scepticism, in light of their interest. Persons under the age of sixteen,[176] and certain individuals with past criminal records,[177] are also prohibited from giving testimony under oath. When permitted to take an oath as a witness, one swears to "tell all the truth and nothing but the truth."[178]

Persons other than the defendant usually give their testimony in narrative form, and are permitted to say whatever they feel is pertinent, uninterrupted by the objections of counsel that so often characterize American criminal proceedings. The judge, however, is in control.[179] Broad and intricately developed rules of exclusion, such as the Anglo-American hearsay rule, rule against opinion testimony, *etc.*, do not exist in French criminal proceedings.[180] The law does recognize a privilege as to professional secrets,[181] and goes so far as to make it a crime generally for an individual to reveal professional confidences reposed in him.[182]

If the testimony goes too far afield, the judge, of course, can limit it, but this seldom happens. Since the fact-finder also determines what sentence should be imposed, testimony relative to the character, family situation, background, economic status, etc., of the defendant, and even of the victim and other persons concerned in the criminal incident, may be pertinent, and are frequently discussed. Whether the defendant or the victim was previously convicted of crime, and the nature of such crime, may be presented in detail. The French statement, frequently heard,

---

175. Stefani et Levasseur, nos. 327 *et seq.*, 783. See Hamson & Vouin, *supra* note 144, at 189.

176. French C.P.P. art. 447; STEFANI ET LEVASSEUR, no. 783.

177. See FRENCH PENAL CODE arts. 28, 34, 42.

178. French C.P.P. arts. 437, 446. Witnesses before the *Cour d'Assises* shall swear to speak "without hatred and without fear, and to tell all the truth and nothing but the truth." French C.P.P. art. 331; STEFANI ET LEVASSEUR, no. 333. For the oath taken by experts, see French C.P.P. arts. 160, 168.

179. French C.P.P. art. 401; STEFANI ET LEVASSEUR, nos. 336, 782 *et seq.*

180. See BODINGTON, FRENCH LAW OF EVIDENCE 122 (1904); DAVID & DE VRIES, THE FRENCH LEGAL SYSTEM 74 (1958); Hamson et Vouin, *supra* note 144, at 187-88; STEFANI ET LEVASSEUR, nos. 315 *et seq.*, 351 *et seq.*

181. Which extends generally to lawyers, doctors, druggists, midwives, etc. FRENCH PENAL CODE art. 378; French C.P.P. arts. 109, 432; STEFANI ET LEVASSEUR, nos. 253, 257, 323, 331, 558, 649, 663, 798.

182. However, although not required to reveal criminal abortions, they may do so without being subject to criminal sanction. FRENCH PENAL CODE art. 378.

For further discussion of privileged communications in French law, see BODINGTON, FRENCH LAW OF EVIDENCE 99 (1904).

that "one judges the man, not facts," seems, indeed, to be the case.

From the broad range of testimony possible, a person accustomed to Anglo-American procedures might well imagine that a French criminal trial would be of inordinate length, but, as noted above, this is not at all the case. It must be remembered that the *dossier* has been painstakingly prepared, has been studied assiduously by the presiding judge, is readily available to the other judges, and is heavily relied upon by counsel in their presentations to the court.[183]

After all testimony has been received, counsel for the state, the civil party (if there be one), and the *inculpé* deliver oral presentations, which are frequently eloquent and moving. The summation( or *réquisitoire*) by the *procureur*, a member of the *magistrature*, is probably more restrained and judicious than its American counterpart. Employing a polished literary style, defense counsel presents his client in the most favorable light possible. Frequently, as a result of confessions confirmed beyond serious question by the fruits of the exhaustive pre-trial research reflected in the *dossier*, defense counsel does not contest his client's guilt, but instead elaborates on the psychological, sociological, and ecomonic factors which prompted the commission of the infraction. In serious cases, particularly those involving *crimes* (where juries are employed), the presentation (*plaidoirie*) of counsel is truly a masterful oration. In the publicized cases, lengthy quotations from the *plaidoirie* are frequently given by the news media (even television) and commented upon favorably or unfavorably.[184]

The judges are specifically prohibited from basing their decision on evidence other than that available at the trial.[185] They may consider all matters within the *dossier* properly acquired,[186] for it is felt that as trained professional magistrates,

183. In proceedings before the *Cour d'Assises*, the only instance in which juries are employed in French criminal proceedings, the law prohibits general access to the *dossier* during the course of deliberations. French C.P.P. art. 347.

184. See Patey, *Recent Reforms in French Criminal Law and Procedure*, 9 INT. & COMP. L.Q. 383, 394-95 (1960). Although frequently representatives of the press make sketches of the defendant, and pictures are taken prior to or after the hearings, French law prohibits photographing, broadcasting, or televising of criminal proceedings. French C.P.P. arts. 308, 403, 535; STEFANI ET LEVASSEUR, no. 258.

185. French C.P.P. art. 427; STEFANI ET LEVASSEUR, nos. 355, 803.

186. See French C.P.P. art. 170 *et seq.* as to nullification and removal of documents in the *dossier* resulting from illegal procedures during *l'instruction préparatoire*.

they can weigh the testimony and give it the value to which it is entitled.[187] In arriving at their decision, the test to be employed is "inner conviction" (*intime conviction*).[188] The nature of this test is spelled out for lay jurors (sitting for the trial of *crimes*), who are to be instructed by the president of the court before deliberation:

> "The law does not ask judges for an accounting as to the means by which they are convinced. It does not prescribe for them any special rules on which they shall make the fullness and sufficiency of the proof depend; it requires them to interrogate themselves in silence and reflection, and to seek to determine in the sincerity of their conscience what impression the proofs brought against the accused, and his defense, have made on their reason. The law only asks of them this single question, which encompasses the full measure of their duty: 'Have you an inner conviction?' "[189]

It has already been seen that the rules of evidence so characteristic of an Anglo-American criminal proceeding are generally quite unkown to its French counterpart. Possible explanations are that, except in the *Cour d'Assises*, French cases are tried before trained judges, sitting without juries, and that on the basis of the same evidence, French judges determine guilt or innocence and also mete out sentence.[190] Especially noteworthy is the frequently found provision in modern American procedure for a post-trial, pre-sentence investigation and report to the judge on the character and background of the defendant, relative to the most appropriate penal sanction for him — and that this investigation is generally unencumbered by technical rules of evidence.[191] The United States Supreme Court has stated:

187. Hamson et Vouin, *supra* note 144, at 187-88.

188. French C.P.P. art. 427; STEFANI ET LEVASSEUR, no. 348 *et seq.*

For general discussion of "*intime conviction*," see: BOUZAT, TRAITÉ THÉORIQUE ET PRATIQUE DE DROIT PÉNAL, no. 1067 (1951, et mise à jour 1956); STEFANI ET LEVASSEUR, no. 348 *et seq.*; VIDAL, COURS DE DROIT CRIMINEL ET DE SCIENCE PÉNITENTIAIRE no. 721 (1949); VITU, PROCÉDURE PÉNALE 188 (1957).

189. French C.P.P. art. 353.

190. This is also true for judges and jurors in the *Cour d'Assises*, where, sitting together, they perform the same functions.

For discussion of recent provisions affecting sentencing, see Patey, *supra* note 184, at 392-94.

191. Williams v. New York, 337 U.S. 241 (1949); McNaughton, *Judicial Notice — Excerpts Relating to the Morgan-Wigmore Controversy*, 14 VAND. L. REV. 779, 788 (1961), republished in ESSAYS ON PROCEDURE AND EVIDENCE 56, 65 (Roady & Covington ed. 1961); WIGMORE, EVIDENCE § 4 (3d ed. 1940).

Interestingly enough, since the decision as to the imposition of capital punish-

"[The sentencing judge's] task within fixed statutory or constitutional limits is to determine the type and extent of punishment after the issue of guilt has been determined. Highly relevant — if not essential — to his selection of an appropriate sentence is the possession of the fullest information possible concerning the defendant's life and characteristics. And modern concepts individualizing punishment have made it all the more necessary that a sentencing judge not be denied an opportunity to obtain pertinent information by a requirement of rigid adherence to restrictive rules of evidence properly applicable to the trial.

"Undoubtedly the New York statutes emphasize a prevalent modern philosophy of penology that the punishment should fit the offender and not merely the crime. The belief no longer prevails that every offense in a like legal category calls for an identical punishment without regard to the past life and habits of a particular offender." (Footnotes and citations omitted.)[192]

Thus the two systems, by very different means, have evolved procedures permitting consideration of factors pertinent to fitting the punishment, not merely to the crime, but also to the person.

---

ment or life imprisonment is frequently for the jury, rather than the judge, post-trial, pre-sentence investigation on this momentous question is often not available. Even here, however, matters which would be revealed at a pre-trial investigation can often be taken into consideration by the pardoning or commuting authority.

192. Williams v. New York, *supra* note 191, at 247.

# Part VI
# Courts, Lawyers and Litigation in Civil Law Systems

# [18]

## COMPARATIVE JUDICIAL STYLE

*F. H. Lawson**

Mr. J.L. Goutal is to be congratulated on breaking new ground in his able and informative article on comparative judicial style,[1] especially in his use of statistics in order to trace the lengthening or otherwise of judgments or opinions. I would not venture to comment on his article were it not that I think that his very perceptive and appreciative description of English judicial style needs to have something added to it by way of supplement. Even when account is taken of the material contained in Professor Karlen's book on *Appellate Courts in the United States and England*[2] and Dr. Rudden's article, "Courts and Codes in England, France and Soviet Russia,"[3] there appears to be room for another note on the subject.

Of course in a study of this kind one can only start from a survey of published material. The reports are indeed unlikely to lead one astray in American law, where virtually all appellate decisions are reported, or in France, where they are at any rate handed down in writing, but one misses a great deal if one confines oneself to the published English decisions. For although most House of Lords decisions are normally published, the decisions of the Court of Appeal are in principle published only where they are thought to contain a material contribution to the law. Since unpublished decisions are almost certainly shorter than published decisions, the cogency of Mr. Goutal's statistical examination of the length of English decisions may be called in question, or rather, it should perhaps be emphasized that it is confined to decisions which have been arrived at with greater than usual difficulty. I shall have more to say about this later.

The selective English practice of publishing decisions might have little significance for such a study were it not that unpublished appellate decisions have almost certainly not been handed down in writing, but delivered orally from the Bench immediately after the close of oral argument or after a very short interval.[4] A cursory inspection of the reports shows that some even of the reported judgments were delivered orally. In fact the judges in the Court of Appeal reserve judgment in only the most difficult cases. In the Civil Division they probably amount to between one-tenth and one-twentieth of the whole. I would guess that the proportion is much smaller in the Criminal Division and smaller still in the Divisional Court of the Queen's

---

* Professor of Law, University of Lancaster.

1. "Characteristics of Judicial Style in France, Britain and the U.S.A." 24 *Am. J. Comp. L.* 43 (1975).

2. (1963).

3. 48 *Tulane L. Rev.* 1010 (1974).

4. This was already noted by Karlen, supra n. 2 at 152.

Bench Division, which exercises control over the Magistrates' Courts and administrative tribunals. On the other hand, first instance decisions in the Chancery Division are fairly frequently reported.

Accordingly we must start from the position that the oral judgment is the rule. Moreover, it is based entirely on oral argument. Although "cases" are submitted in advance to the House of Lords, they can, in Professor Karlen's words,[5] "best perhaps be described as advance written outlines of oral arguments to be presented later," and although the Court of Appeal has access to the reasoning on which the judgment in the court below was based, there is nothing in English practice like the American brief.

Finally, there is no place in the English system for the judicial conference; indeed there is seldom any time for it. The judges may be able to exchange a few words during an adjournment or *sotto voce* on the Bench at the close of the argument. Then the presiding judge will usually start speaking and the others may add a few words or merely concur.[6]

All of this is highly personal. The arguments are not confined within specific limits of time,[7] though Counsel do not waste the Court's time and the judges have means of letting them know when they have heard enough. The judges consider it their business to deal with all the serious arguments that are put forward, though naturally they concentrate their attention on those that are most important. Speaking generally, they confine themselves to the arguments of Counsel, though they may open new lines of thought by putting questions. They do not find for themselves the material for decision. They do not go home to do extensive research and they have no one to help them like the American law clerks.

Moreover, English judges are taken from the ranks of successful advocates, not office lawyers, as is common in America, and they have not spent most of their life following a judicial career, as in France. Thus not only do they look to advocates for informative and persuasive arguments, but they carry their own advocacy with them to the Bench. After Counsel on both sides have sought to persuade the judges in opposite directions, the judges try to deal with their arguments and persuade them that their decisions are correct. They are, as it were, the third side of an argumentative triangle. Moreover, the judges in the Court of Appeal have to contemplate the possibility of an appeal to the House of Lords and they are, so to speak, using their judgments as advocating the point of view which they support.

---

5. Id. at 125.

6. For a candid and somewhat disconcerting account of the process by Sir Charles Russell, then a Lord Justice of Appeal, see his address, entitled *Behind the Appellate Curtain*, to the Holdsworth Club of the University of Birmingham in 1969. These annual addresses, delivered usually by eminent judges and published by the Holdsworth Club, often contain much interesting material not ordinarily to be found in print.

7. This is not peculiar to England. It is still true at least of Canada and Australia.

Hence I should prefer not to use the word justification, like Mr. Goutal, but to say that the judges are trying to persuade the profession and the public and, it may be, the House of Lords; and a judge does not change his persuasive habit when he becomes a Law Lord, that is to say, a judicial member of the House of Lords.

It would be idle to expect English judges to write in a less discursive manner than the way they speak. Judgment will be reserved in order to give the judges time for consideration, and no doubt the written judgment will usually be a more finished product. But it will be on the same general lines as an oral judgment. It will be designed to show, above all, the way a judge's mind has worked and how he arrived at his decision.

The contrast to French style and practice is admirably brought out by Mr. Goutal[8] and I need add nothing. I am very hesitant in commenting on his treatment of American opinions, but I think he misses some points. He very properly draws attention to what he calls the "statistical syllogism,"[9] that is to say, the practice of looking at the way in which a question has been decided in several jurisdictions and identifying majority and minority opinions. He very properly says that although its "substantial justificatory value is next to nothing . . . its persuasive value is extremely high."[10] An allusion to the notion of *communis opinio*, the search for which is not unknown in France until the Cour de Cassation has spoken, and the formation of something in the nature of a judicial custom, would be very much in point. Moreover, the practice is almost inevitable in a country where, except for federal questions, there is no one court of final appeal. The single ultimate jurisdiction of the House of Lords leaves no room for it in England and indeed the Judicial Committee of the Privy Council has been able to ensure substantial uniformity of common law and equity throughout the Commonwealth. This is an important reason for the greater part that precedent plays in British judicial practice than in that of France or the United States.

Secondly, the drastic curtailment of the time available for oral advocacy before American appellate courts has helped to make the preparation of argument not only a written but also a corporate enterprise, especially in the large metropolitan firms, and concurrently with the development of the judicial conference, the appellate opinion has become corporate also. I think this corporate, one might almost say bureaucratic, element in American practice has combined with the search of a *communis opinio* to cause the convergence between American and French judicial styles and their divergence from the English.

Although in all three countries the judges work upon materials, including arguments, presented to them by the practising lawyers in the case, in England the discussion takes place between the Bench and the Bar, whereas in America and France a large part of it, perhaps

8. Supra n. 1, at 45, 50-61.
9. Id. at 51.
10. Id. at 52.

the most important part, is among the judges and their auxiliaries, law clerks in the former and *avocats-généraux* in the latter.[11]

Mr. Goutal gives a valuable account of the steady increase in the length of English judgments. I have no doubt that his account of the facts is correct; but here again, as it seems to me, he misses one or two points. Inferences must be drawn with great caution from the reports of cases before the latter part of the eighteenth century. The older reporters, with a few illustrious exceptions, did not usually attempt to produce a full report. Many of the older reports are notoriously bad. Accordingly, I would attach very little importance to the evidence from this early period.

Secondly, Mr. Goutal is no doubt right in attributing the increase in the length of judgments after the 1830's to the extension of industrial, social and commercial activities involved in the Industrial Revolution,[12] but he fails to explain why the greatest increase occurred in the present century, and especially from the 1920's onwards. For such an explanation I think we must look to important changes in judicial practice.

Judgments continued to be relatively short during the period of strict pleading, which was at its height between 1834 and 1852. The concentration on a single issue would make for brevity, through concentration on a single line of argument; though even at that time it might be necessary to deal at length with a difficult point, especially if it had attracted to itself previous decisions that were hard to reconcile. Moreover, it was not until 1875 that appeals involving a "re-hearing," already characteristic of Chancery procedure, were extended to common law actions and substituted for the writ of error, which had a similar limiting effect. Third, it is only since the 1920's that the civil jury has almost disappeared from English practice, so that it is by no means so necessary as before to keep facts and law separate. It has indeed been noticed that where a judge decides both fact and law, his judgment tends to be longer than if he has to accept the facts as found elsewhere. Unlike a jury, he may feel he has to justify his findings of fact.

This is most obviously true in the actual trial of a case, but it applies also on appeal, since although the Court of Appeal normally refuses to interfere with a trial determination based upon the credibility of witnesses, it feels at complete liberty to draw inferences based on general information, experience and logic.[13]

Thus, although Mr. Goutal is undoubtedly right in emphasizing the need for sophisticated judgments dealing with the more sophisticated situations they have to deal with, a place must also be found for technical reasons associated with changes in judicial practice.

Why should there have been no such lengthening of the judgments in French Courts of Appeal? As far as one can see there is

11. See infra.
12. Supra n. 1 at 62.
13. Karlen, supra n. 2 at 86.

no legal limit to their power to deal with a case *de novo*. They feel as competent to find the correct facts as the correct law. As however it is not the practice of Courts of Appeal to hear witnesses afresh, an English lawyer is bound to wonder how they can deal adequately with primary raw facts. I well remember that question being put to an eminent French judge in a small gathering of Oxford law teachers. He replied that there was seldom any difference of opinion about them. One would have liked to pursue the matter further, but the discussion had to be drawn to a close. One reason can be stated with reasonable confidence. Oral testimony plays a much smaller part in French than in English civil practice, and as little attention as possible is paid to it. A Court of Appeal is of course just as competent as a trial judge to deal with what is in writing. On the other hand, presumptions play a greater part. In English eyes the most critical part of an English law suit is already over before the French law suit really begins. One can well understand why a French professor, after hearing my description of our Court of Appeal's handling of facts, said that its work was much closer to that of the Cour de Cassation than to that of a French Court of Appeal.

I know too little about American practice to examine critically Mr. Goutal's explanation why American opinions have not undergone the same lengthening as in England, but I suspect that the survival of the civil jury has much to answer for, the more so since, in Professor Karlen's words,[14] "if the case has been tried by jury . . . the judge's instructions usually consist of little more than abstract propositions of law, without any summary of or comment upon the evidence. If the case has been tried without a jury, there are ordinarily only formalised findings of fact and conclusions of law, without the citation of authorities." In such circumstances there is less scope for extended argument in an appellate opinion.

I wonder what would be the results of a more detailed analysis of the American cases. It should be possible to take runs of appellate decisions for short periods of time in typical appellate courts. One might then classify them according to the branch of law they deal with, comparing the opinions for length with corresponding English judgments, at the same time noting the reason for their length. One would exclude completely opinions which would not have been considered worth publishing in England.

Mr. Goutal makes an important point in noticing that there is no legal obligation on an American or an English judge to "*motiver*" his decision, that is to say, to express the reasons for it;[15] and Professor David points out that the explanation of the reasons are not really

14. Id. at 150.

15. Supra n. 1 at 56. The practice is of course otherwise. Quite recently Buckley L.J. said that he considered it a most unsatisfactory practice for a judge to give no reasons for his decision in granting or refusing an application, even of a procedural kind, that involved questions of law. "Litigants are entitled to know on what grounds their cases are decided." *Capital and Suburban Properties v. Swycher*, [1976] 1 All E.R. 882, 884.

part of the judgment, which contains merely "*le dispositif*," the declaration or order which is the result.[16] Thus the American usage which describes the exposition of the reasons for a decision as an "opinion" is prefereable to the English usage which extends the term judgment to include them.

In France, on the contrary, judicial decrees must express the motives that were decisive for the judge. The French judgment, therefore, is not shorter but longer than the American judgment. In its form and purpose it resembles the, now unusual, preamble to an American or English statute. As regards substance, the statement of reasons contained in it reads very like an entry in an American or English digest. And indeed the published report of a French case normally contains a headnote which is picked out of the judgment and reproduces word for word the statement of law which forms its major premise; but it is the work of the court itself and not of the non-judicial reporter or compiler of the digest.

Oddly enough, although the law of 16-24 August 1790 speaks of the motives that were decisive for the judge, a French judgment does not really explain why the court came to its conclusion but merely forms the premises of a syllogism. It does not explain why that formulation was arrived at. For that you will have to go to the *rapport* submitted to the court by one of its judges or to the *conclusions* of the *avocat-général*.[17] In a very important case the *rapport* or even the *conclusions* will be printed in the reports along with the judgment. Doubtless neither of them is as authoritative as the reasons contained in the judgment, which incidentally may be in disagreement with them; but it must always be remembered that in principle the judgment itself does not create a binding precedent. In contrast, the report of an American opinion or an English judgment does enjoy real authority, whereas the headnote or digest entry is viewed with a fair amount of suspicion. Had it not been for the provision in the law of 1790, perhaps the French courts might have adopted a style similar to that of American and English courts, and, by limiting the judgment to the "*dispositif*," have brought more into the foreground a "*rapport*" giving the true reasons for the decision.

A word about the syllogism. A syllogism must exist in every application of law to fact. It must always be possible to find in a judgment a major premise consisting of a legal principle or rule, a minor premise consisting of a statement of the relevant facts of a given situation, and a conclusion consisting of a subsumption of the facts within the principle or rule. In the vast majority of cases it is not difficult to identify the legal principle or rule and the relevant facts; and the application of the law to the facts is more or less automatic. If you want to emphasize its automatic character you express it openly in syllogistic form. You may also on historical grounds have to emphasize the absence of any judicial discretion or any attempt to make new

16. *Introduction à L'Étude du Droit Privé d'Angleterre* 140 (1948).
17. In the Cour de Cassation, *Procureur-général*.

law. If you are not unduly worried about the need to justify your decision, you do not emphasize the syllogistic structure, which remains latent.

A little comparative legal history is here in point. Mr. Goutal alludes to the long history of arbitrary and sometimes abusive use of judicial power that led to the self-restraint characteristic of French judges during the greater part of the nineteenth century. The English courts were preserved, largely by the openness of their procedure and the practice of reporting their decisions, from the excesses of the French *Parlements*; but the innovations of Lord Mansfield, mild as they may seem to us, provoked the violent attacks of Junius[18] and the reactions associated with the name of Kenyon, his successor as Chief Justice. In England the wave-motion had a flatter curve than in France, but it was there all the same. Moreover, the changes made in the law by the French courts, once they had recovered their self-confidence, have been more radical than those made by the English courts in the corresponding period.[19] I think that Mr. Goutal exaggerates the extent to which English judges are expected to make law and their willingness to do so. It is easy, for instance, to pay too much attention to the undoubted services performed by Lord Denning in the development of English law. He does not carry his brother judges with him in his occasional disregard of awkward precedents.

If it is not all plain sailing, the syllogism itself will not help you; the problem will be to establish the right premises. The difficulty may be to know which facts to discard in order to bring the situation within the legal principle or rule. In that case you may have trouble in formulating the correct minor premise. Or your difficulty may be in establishing the major premise, that is to say, the appropriate legal principle or rule.

Most commonly that may quite genuinely be a question of finding it, and everywhere judges feel happiest when that is the case. As Dr. Rudden says, "[t]he most frequent instance is of extending, refining, and applying" the existing law.[20] But in extreme cases—and those are the ones that are most interesting—the process will be one of creating new law, and the question will arise whether the process should be made evident in the judgment itself.

Moreover, the establishment of the major premise and that of the minor premise cannot always be kept apart. This is the explanation of what Mr. Goutal particularly notices, the prominence that English judges give to the statement of the facts and the interlocking of findings of fact and findings of law, and also of Mr. Justice Holmes's famous remark that "general propositions do not decide concrete

18. Letters of Junius, letter of 14 November 1770, quoted by Fifoot, *Lord Mansfield* 183 (1936).

19. See Tunc, "Methodology of the Civil Law in France," 50 *Tul. L. Rev.* 465-6 (1976).

20. Supra n. 3 at 1017.

cases."[21] French courts in order to make the syllogism stand out clearly, do their best, and for the most part successfully, to keep the major and minor premises separate, and for that purpose to give the appropriate legal rule or principle as general and abstract a character as possible, knowing incidentally that they are not so deeply committed to precedent as English or even American judges.

In any case, the essential task of the judge is to establish the correct premises. A more or less complete account of this process constitutes almost the whole of an English judgment or American opinion, though, in England at least, policy considerations may be kept in the background. Nothing of it appears in a French judgment, which gives only the results of the process, unless one may perhaps detect a slight trace of it in what is alluded to in Mr. Goutal's remark that "the principle will possibly be commented upon or reworded in order to fit into the hypothesis of the case."[22]

This exclusion from a French judgment of any reference to what one may call the *travaux préparatoires* on which it is based displays a strong resemblance to the character of the *Code Civil* itself in so far as it contains statements of general principle cut off from the grounds, historical or otherwise, that justified them; and, although the courts normally keep their enunciations of legal principle close to the relevant facts, occasionally they utter broad principles which would not be out of place in the Code. On the other hand the form of an American opinion, and still more obviously of an English judgment, corresponds to a general aversion to codifying the law.

The supposed aversion of common lawyers to principle is a myth however. The most recent tendencies in the development of contract and tort liability are, in England at least, in the direction of broader and broader generalization. What common lawyers are really afraid of is the authoritative verbal formulation of principle and its abstraction from the historical process. English counsel and writers on law are repeatedly warned by the judges not to take the lapidary pronouncements of famous judges literally as though they were sections of a statute. That is precisely what, in contrast, as it seems to me, French lawyers do with the pronouncements of the Cour de Cassation.

21. Lochner v. N.Y., 198 U.S. 45, 76 (1905).
22. Supra n. 1 at 45.

# [19]

JOURNAL OF LAW AND SOCIETY
VOLUME 13, NUMBER 1, SPRING 1986
0263-323X $3.00

# German Labour Courts and the British Industrial Tribunal System. A Socio-Legal Comparison of Degrees of Judicialisation

ERHARD BLANKENBURG* AND RALF ROGOWSKI**

A comparative analysis of substantive labour law and procedural practices of British Industrial Tribunals and West German Labour Courts reveals striking similarities in handling employment conflicts. Although institutional arrangements are significantly different, both labour court models are largely limited to solving disputes after dismissal, and both operate with a complex procedural mixture of negotiation, conciliation, mediation and adjudication.

While the first part of the paper presents historical background information, and while the second part discusses doctrinal aspects by comparing British and West German unfair dismissal laws, the paper focuses in a third part on degrees of judicialisation. Thereby, it tries to explain why litigation rates, plaintiffs' success, and rates of settlement are higher in West German Labour Courts compared to the British Industrial Tribunal system. Furthermore, the paper discusses differences in procedures and courtroom personnel; it is found that interaction patterns of judges or chairmen and legal representatives showed a higher degree of formalism in British Industrial Tribunals than in German Labour Court hearings. On the other hand, with respect to pre-judicial procedures Germany still lacks effective filter institutions while Britain has developed a complex system which resists early judicialisation through an interplay of negotiations in grievance procedures and official conciliation efforts. However with respect to judicial procedures, high degrees of formalisation and low success rates for the claimants in Industrial Tribunals seem to have deterrent effects on potential litigants.

* *Vrije Universiteit, Faculteit der Rechtsgeleerdheid, Postbus 7161, NL–1007 MC Amsterdam, The Netherlands*
** *European University Institute, Dept. of Law, Badia Fiesolana, I–50016 San Domenico di Fiesole (Firenze), Italy*

We would like to thank Linda Dickens of the Industrial Relations Research Unit at the University of Warwick for her support while we attended Industrial Tribunals hearings and for her assistance in arranging interviews with members of Industrial Tribunals and ACAS. We also would like to thank David Trubek for allowing us to print an earlier version as DPRP Working Paper 1984–10; to Thomas Abeltshauser, Wolfgang Daeubler, Leen van den Heuvel, Lester Mazor and Derek Sheridan (ACAS, London) who made useful comments; and to Anne Reilly who helped with the English.

## INTRODUCTION

Comparative labour law is traditionally known for going beyond the mere comparison of statutory provisions or case law. It examines specific institutional structures and determines the extent to which those structures develop around traditions of legality.[1]

Furthermore, the broader industrial relations context of labour law is becoming increasingly important for comparative studies in defining functions of labour institutions,[2] and sociological and historical factors play a prominent role in recent comparative accounts of labour law phenomena.[3]

In our yiew, comparative labour law studies could further gain from socio-legal analyses of dispute resolution and of the role that legal institutions play in dispute resolution processes.[4] The dispute resolution perspective, adopted from legal anthropology,[5] has already been used for purposes of socio-legal comparison in both theoretical and empirical studies.[6] By comparing West German Labour Courts with the British Industrial Tribunal system, we hope to provide a new focus for socio-legal comparison of dispute processing that, in our opinion, is theoretically and historically most fascinating: the administration of individual employment protection through collective institutional structures.

In order to analyse the mixture of individual and collective elements in procedures of labour dispute resolution, we shall look at *degrees of judicialisation*. Our socio-legal definition of law avoids normative dichotomising of right and wrong and, instead, views law as placed in a continuum from informal to more and more formal ways of settling disputes.[7] Thus, we define the role of legal institutions with respect to varying degrees of judicialisation emerging in the handling of labour conflicts. As we compare dispute resolution processes, we pinpoint differences in the location and inportance of labour judiciaries with respect to the forms of settlement employed. Moreover, our approach allows us to distinguish between the functions of different judiciaries and the effects they have on their pre-judicial contexts.

Our research on West German labour courts[8] leads to general theses on their restrictive character: (i) Labour judiciaries are suited for individual employment problems rather than for collective industrial conflict resolution; (ii) even with respect to claims for employment protection, the role of labour judiciaries tends to be restricted to regulating the consequences of dismissals; their direct impact on preventing dismissals or regulating ongoing employment relationships is rather limited; and (iii) labour judiciaries show a receptive attitude towards norms of industrial relations which also finds its expression in a high emphasis on conciliation and an institutionalised participation of collective industrial interest groups in decision-making.

The following comparative analysis tests these generalisations.[9] It is introduced with remarks on some of the historical and normative aspects of the British and German systems of employment protection. It then looks at the condition for mobilisation of Labour Courts and Industrial Tribunals while measuring degrees of judicialisation with respect to the intensity of third party interventionism in early stages of the conflict. Furthermore, degrees of judicialisation are analysed by comparing hearing structures and courtroom personnel as well as various "exit" options from judicial procedure in cases of successful settlements of employment conflicts outside and inside the courtroom.

## HISTORICAL ASPECTS OF LABOUR JUDICIARIES AND THEIR INDUSTRIAL RELATIONS CONTEXT IN WEST GERMANY AND GREAT BRITAIN

Industrial relations have been undergoing rapid changes in Great Britain in the last twenty years. In the past, British trade unions have been known to rely on collective bargaining power rather than on legal protection for pursuing their interests in industrial relations; British employers have been known to adhere to (the fictions of) free contracting rather than to a legal framework for regulating labour relations. From a continental perspective, in fact, British labour relations represented the "ideal type" of anti-legal culture. On the other hand, since the labour legislation of the Weimar Republic, Germany has been seen as a model for legalisation of labour relations and judicialisation of employment conflicts.[10]

The legal restraints on union behaviour and the statutory framework for employment protection which were established in Britain during the 1960s and 1970s reveal a quite spectacular tendency of convergence with their German counterpart. With the establishment of conciliatory procedures and judicial institutions for handling employment conflicts (e.g., Arbitration and Conciliation Service (A.C.A.S.) and Industrial Tribunals), the British politics of industrial relations seem to have joined the West European trend toward welfare state legal interventionism.

In the Weimar Republic, socialist lawyers like Hugo Sinzheimer and Otto Kahn-Freund helped establish a legal framework for industrial relations which was generally known as the "Economic Constitution". Adjudication of labour conflicts within the framework of the Economic Constitution was to be performed by Labour Courts (*Arbeitsgerichte*). The Labour Courts were established in 1926 after intensive political debates.[11] They replaced earlier trade courts such as the *Gewerbegerichte*, established in 1890, and the *Kaufmannsgerichte*, established in 1904. While trade courts had limited jurisdiction and covered only a few trades, the Labour Courts of 1926 could handle any problems which arose out of individual employment relationships: in fact, access was guaranteed to all categories of workers except for civil servants. In addition, Labour Courts had jurisdiction over collective labour law issues (e.g., participation rights of works councils at the shop floor level), and unions and works councils were allowed to present their claims to the new Labour Courts insofar as their grievances were based on statutory rights.

In the Third Reich, the newly created "German Labour Front" replaced both trade unions and employer associations. Labour Court jurisdiction over collective labour law issues was immediately abolished. Only individual labour law cases were left to the Labour Courts so long as they did not fall under the jurisdiction of the newly established "Courts of Social Honour".[12] Labour Courts were among the first institutions after the war to regain their pre-fascist jurisdictions; they steadily increased their jurisdiction during the 1950s. In particular, the Federal Labour Court increased its influence through decisions which supported the allegation that West German labour law, especially in collective matters, relied on case law instead of resting on "sound" statutory law.[13] In the 1970s Labour Courts acquired further jurisdiction over collective issues as a result of amendments of major co-determination laws (*Betriebsverfassungsgesetz* 1972; *Mitbestimmungsgesetz* 1976). However, in the individual labour law area only piecemeal reforms have been achieved since the enactment of the "Dismissal Protection Act" 1951 (*Kuendigungsschutzgesetz*), continuing the tradition of a 1926 Employment Protection Act for white collar workers. Among other statutes, the "Labour Law Consolidation Act" 1969 (*Arbeitsrechtsbereinigungsgesetz*) had a special impact in clarifying and slightly extending coverages and notice periods in employment protection law.

Britain began substantive statutory and institutional regulation of labour relations almost fifty years after this trend developed on the Continent. The first Industrial Tribunals with limited jurisdictions were established by the Industrial Training Act 1964. Further regulation of industrial relations was proposed by advocates for industrial democracy as well as labour economists who were concerned with "uneconomical" strikes over "small" issues, e.g., individual employment conflicts. Those discussions eventually fed into the establishment of the Royal Commission on Trade Unions and Employer Associations, chaired by Lord Donovan. The Donovan Report was released in 1968 and contains a careful description of the state of industrial relations in the mid-1960s. Although the Commission did not generally support legislation for the non-regulated, so-called "informal" sectors of industrial relations,[14] the report proposed the establishment of new "Labour Tribunals" which were to concentrate the various jurisdictions over individual employment matters within one legal body:

> . ... to make available to all employers and employees, for all disputes arising from their contracts of employment, a procedure which is easily accessible, informal, speedy and inexpensive.[15]

According to the report, this Labour Tribunal should be obliged to seek settlement before adjudication, cases should be deferred to already existing voluntary procedures as much as possible, and collective disputes should be kept out of the Tribunals and left as a matter for voluntary collective bargaining.

It is well known that experts like Hugh Clegg, the industrial relations specialist, and Otto Kahn-Freund had a major impact on the final draft of this rather moderate report. Otto Kahn-Freund, who had already taken an active part in the labour law development of the late Weimar Republic[16] and who had been forced to emigrate to England after 1933, was considered the leading British labour lawyer in the 1950s and 1960s.[17] Indeed, the chapter of the Donovan Report on Labour Tribunals reads like a former German labour lawyer's attempt to adjust the labour court model to fit British industrial relations.

The political reforms undertaken after Donovan, however, ran far short of the report's recommendations. Massive state interventions were first proposed by the Labour government's White Paper, *In Place of Strife* (1969), and then – with a different impetus against the unions – were carried out by the succeeding Conservative government in its Industrial Relations Act 1971 which also introduced unfair dismissal legislation. A National Industrial Relations Court with jurisdiction over collective conflict issues was established by this statute, thereby neglecting the warnings of the Donovan Report that labour courts were inappropriate in handling collective labour law issues. Repressive actions by the court against strikers clearly increased the already existing hostility of the British labour movement towards the courts and contributed to the eventual repeal of the Industrial Relations Act in 1974.[18] In this sense, the experience with statutory and judicial interventionism revealed the social limits of law as a regulatory instrument of industrial relations.[19]

Yet, it is historically a turning point that the legalisation of labour relations obviously had reached a point of no return by the mid-1970s.[20] The Trade Union and Labour Relations Act 1974, which repealed the Industrial Relations Act, left the provisions on unfair dismissal protection virtually unchanged. Both the Employment Protection Act 1975, which introduced the Advisory, Conciliation and Arbitration Service, and the Employment Protection (Consolidation) Act 1978 stabilised the institutional foundation for the expanded role played by the Industrial Tribunal system. Moreover, the Conservative Employment Acts 1980 and 1982 and the Trade Union Act 1985 do not seem to have seriously challenged this foundation. Although legislative amendments restricted, to some extent, Industrial Tribunals, the main emphasis of conservative reforms lies again with the (highly symbolic) politics in collective labour relations and less with employment protection.

From the preceding brief historical sketches we conclude that it is not just the short-term politics of either Conservative or Social Democratic/Labour governments when institutions of judicial remedy are established in the area of employment relations. Despite the recent attacks on state interventionism by Conservatives, there still seems to be a general acceptance of the social necessity of employment protection which characterises both German and British industrial policies. However, it seems also true that from a broader functional perspective we can observe links between the establishment of procedures for handling employment complaints and the domestication of industrial conflicts; in fact, those combinations of judicialisation and pacification seem to occur in many Western European welfare democracies which have experiences with social democratic policies creating neo-corporatist systems.

## SOME COMPARATIVE REMARKS ON BRITISH AND GERMAN UNFAIR DISMISSAL LAW

Sociologists of law would be foolish to underestimate the degree to which substantive labour law creates the normative basis for legal actions in the Industrial Tribunals and Labour Courts. It not only defines and restricts their jurisdictions, but also influences the normative expectations of the participants in a courtroom working group.

Because of the importance of complaints related to unfair dismissal in both systems – as will later become clear from our analysis of caseloads – we confine our brief comparison of substantive labour law to the statutory provisions concerning unfair dismissal.[21] We proceed by looking at the basic principles employed in reviewing dismissals, problems of eligibility, reasons for dismissal, and possible remedies.

### 1. *Basic Principles*

The principles of the two systems of employment protection can already be identified in the basic terms that define the normative basis of legal judgment concerning dismissals. While in Britain a dismissal is considered to be either fair or unfair, a German dismissal is reviewed in terms of whether or not it was "socially justified".[22]

Each of these approaches is linked to a different philosophy of industrial relations. The German idea that dismissals should be "socially acceptable" implicitly refers to social standards that are established by the industrial partners and protected and supervised by the state. The British "fair dismissal" concept, on the other hand, refers mainly to normative standards of management.[23] Only the employer's behaviour is supposed to be reviewed by the Industrial Tribunal. In this sense, fairness is a concept which is defined with regard to class-biased norms of "gentlemanly behaviour" in its application.[24] Restricting Industrial Tribunals to the review of an employer's decision may well have its roots in the anti-legalistic traditions of British industrial relations.

In addition, it has to do with the relation between employment law and private law. In both systems, we find an interplay of special labour law statutes and general private law. In the German system, sections on the "service contract" of the Civil Code are still considered as the basis of individual labour law; the employment statutes constitute an application of the general norms of the Civil Code. In the British system employment statutes are considered as supplements to the common law, but not as replacements for it. Hence, the jurisdictional basis of the Industrial Tribunals is different from that of their German counterparts insofar as it solely rests on these newly established statutes which modify the common law.[25] The basic interpretation of the law on employment contracts as it has developed under common law is still left to the ordinary courts in Britain, whereas in West Germany the Labour Courts are granted jurisdiction in all legal matters concerning employment contracts.[26]

2. *Eligibility*

Eligibility for judicial protection from unfair dismissal is restricted in both countries. With the Employment Act of 1980, the British Conservative government followed the arguments of employers from smaller firms and explicitly excluded access to the judicial review of dismissals from firms with less than twenty employees unless the worker had two years' service.[27] In Germany, only firms and administrations with at least six employees are covered by employment protection jurisdiction of the Labour Courts;[28] thus, in both countries employers of small firms are, to a certain degree, exempted from judicial review of dismissal decisions. In Britain, employees of these small firms might resort to ordinary courts under certain circumstances, but rarely seem to do so. In Germany, employees from very small firms sometimes might be able to base their claims with the Labour Courts on general provisions of the Civil Code; the Labour Court judge who handles such a case will usually not dismiss the case out of hand. Public employees are eligible for protection in both countries, but in contrast to Britain, West German civil servants are not; they must file their claims with Administrative Courts. All household employees are ineligible for employment protection in Germany.[29] Jurisdiction is, indeed, further restricted with regard to the qualifying period of employment necessary before a case can be brought to the court. German law demands an employee to have worked for at least twenty-six weeks;[30] in Britain, the period was raised from twenty-six weeks to fifty-two weeks by the Unfair Dismissal (Variation of Qualifying Period) Order 1979; and it was further raised to two years by a 1985 Order for workers being employed after the 1 June 1985.[31]

3. *Reasons for Dismissal*

There are few differences between the West German and British systems with respect to legally accepted reasons for dismissal. In bothe legal systems, the three major reasons are: conducts, capability and redundancy (*verhaltens-bedingte, persoenlichkeitsbedingte* and *betriebsbedingte Kuendigungsgruende*). These reasons cover all employer dismissals of which the employee is informed in a due notice period. "Constructive dismissal," i.e., the ability of an employee to terminate his contract due to his employer's unacceptable behaviour seems to be further developed in Britain.[32] In Germany, employees usually claim compensation rather than request reinstatement in these cases.[33]

4. *Remedies*

The major legal remedies in both systems are reinstatement and compensation. And in both systems, the law places strong emphasis on re-employment (whether the same job as before (reinstatement) or be it at a new job with the same employer (re-engagement)); thereby, compensation should only be granted if re-employment is not possible. A general right to be employed during the court proceedings (*Weiterbeschaeftigungsanspruch*) is guaranteed neither in Britain nor in West Germany.[34] Mass dismissals fall under separate provisions in West Germany; in cases of changes in the structure of the firm, which lead to dismissal of a considerable number of employees, remedies are negotiated in a social plan between management and works council.[35]

On this basis, we can generally conclude that the British employment protection law is only slightly more restrictive than its German counterpart. It is left up to the judicial bodies in both countries to interpret, adjust, and generally shape the legal norms. The basic principles of "fairness" and "social justification" grant sufficient discretion to the courts by allowing them to establish their own policies while creating rather case-oriented, concrete standards. It lies beyond the scope of our present analysis, however, to discuss whether convergence occurs on the level of these judicial standards concerning the fairness of dismissal. From our impressions of the hearings we attended, our reading of decisions and commentaries, and our studies of the literature, we find such a convergence plausible.

## CONDITIONS FOR MOBILISING LABOUR COURTS AND INDUSTRIAL TRIBUNALS

In the courts and tribunals we find only a small selection of cases that potentially could have gone to court. The selectivity of access to courts can be described as a pyramid with a large base of potential conflicts. Only a small percentage of those conflicts reach the top, i.e., the courts. This is partly due to the deliberate choice made by the parties to avoid courts and to stay clear of legal procedures; but it also has to do with the social and psychological incapabilities of the parties to use legal means. In interpreting court data, one always has to bear in mind that the court proceedings are a result of such selectivity in the pre-court mobilisation process.[36]

Nevertheless, research on legal institutions usually begins with the collecting of data at these institutions. Theoretical definitions of the data base of all conflicts that would potentially be relevant for litigation[37] are, however, often doubtful, due to the fact that they are based on estimates derived from non-reliable data sources. The unsatisfactory but unavoidable solution is to use court files to argue about pre-court selectivity by making assumptions about the kind of cases which *could* have gone to court but, in fact, did not. This is what we did by looking at files of the Labour Court in Berlin.[38]

Our first questions were related to assumptions about class justice: How does a court maintain its impartiality in an area that inherently deals with vital class conflicts? All labour conflicts include individual as well as collective aspects. The court file already indicates the degree to which the conflict might be embedded in collective relations (i.e., if the employee is represented by a solicitor or an advocate he is not likely to be a member of a union; however, if he is represented by a trade union representative he almost always is a union member). The possibility of collective interest representation, in fact, most clearly distinguishes the Labour Courts from ordinary civil or criminal courts.

According to their jurisdiction, Labour Courts and A.C.A.S. officers may handle all sorts of legally relevant conflicts that arise out of employment relationships. Looking at the kinds of conflicts which actually reach them, however, we find that the vast majority of these conflicts relate to problems that arose after the employment relationship had been terminated.

One explanation for this could lie in the general rule that relational distance tends to increase the likelihood of invoking courts. Research shows again and again that it is unlikely for parties in ongoing social relationship to resort to formal legal rules when a dispute arises. The likelihood, therefore, that labour conflicts at the shop floor level will be taken to an outside third party is rather low. Involvement of institutions like works councils or direct negotiations with the management are much more likely. However, after the employment relationship is terminated the situation changes: it becomes easier for the parties to submit the conflict to an outside third party for purposes of retrospective judgment and to have the conditions of termination assessed in legal terms.[39]

Dismissal conflicts, therefore, are more likely to be brought before courts than are conflicts within ongoing labour relationships. However, even though social relations may be terminated between an employer and his employee, only a small fraction of all dismissals does result in court interactions. Many a dismissal may be consensual (at least as to the conditions of how it is implemented) or employers may be careful not to leave any conditions for ex-post claims. But basically, we might assume that dismissal is a conflictual event to the extent that those who have been dismissed look for available reasons to, at least, "hit back". We therefore treat the total number of dismissals as data base of potential conflicts and compute the "rate of litigation" as a percentage of the best estimates of labour turnover due to dismissal that are available to us.[40] Since these estimates are not very reliable, we also compute the role of Tribunal and Labour Court actions filed in terms of the total number of people employed and in terms of the population as a whole. All three comparisons reveal large differences between the two countries, with the West German litigation rate after dismissal being at least six times higher than the British rate (taking as our most conservative basis of comparison the total number of people employed as well as taking into account available estimates of all dismissals).

The Labour Courts have experienced an increase of 40% in caseload in the last ten years. In contrast, the British Industrial Tribunals showed a steady decrease from 1976 to 1981 and a slight recovery in the last few years.[41] The A.C.A.S. caseload presented in Table 1 includes more than ten per cent of cases where no formal complaint was made to an Industrial Tribunal, but A.C.A.S. assistance was sought under special sections of the Employment Protection (Consolidation) Act 1978;[42] therefore, the caseload figures which are published by the Central Office of the Industrial Tribunals generally tend to be lower. However, it should be mentioned also that about ten per cent of the caseload of the West German Labour Courts consist of technical cases concerned with social insurance matters which usually need no hearing.

*Table 1: Comparison of Caseload of the Industrial Tribunal System and the West German Labour Courts in 1982 with Respect to Size of Population and Labour Force*

| | *Great Britain* | *West Germany* |
|---|---|---|
| Cases | 46,996 (ACAS, individual conciliation) | 386,789 (all Labour Court filings) |
| Population | 54,284,000 | 61,638,000 |
| Cases per 100,000 People | 87 | 627 |
| Registered Labour Force | 21,314,000 | 28,335,000 |
| Cases per 100,000 of the Labour Force | 220 | 1,365 |
| Cases per 100,000 of all dismissals (estimates for 1978)* | 1% | 6% |

Sources: *ACAS Annual Report* 1982, op.cit. (n.41), 66, table 11; *Bundesarbeitsblatt* 6/1983, 116; *Statistisches Jahrbuch fuer die Bundesrepublik Deutschland 1983*, 52 and 96; *Census of Employment, Employment Gazette Occasional Supplement* No.2, Dec. 1983.

* Rather vague indications taken from Rhode, *op.cit.* (n. 9), 181, *Uebersicht* 1.

Some of the differences in caseload between the British Industrial Tribunal system (including A.C.A.S.) and the German Labour Courts can be explained by referring to the Industrial Tribunals' more limited scope of jurisdiction. As already mentioned, some of these conflicts are handled by ordinary courts in Britain whereas all legal problems arising from employment contracts and also some conflicts over collective rights granted by statute can be dealt with in the West German Labour Courts. But this should account for only an insignificant part of the difference because the subject matter of cases before both, the Tribunals and the Labour Courts, is predominantly related to dismissal issues. The way in which the claim is presented may be a matter of proof and credibility – in our context, it is relevant only in the sense that in most of the cases, and in both systems, plaintiffs are employees who have been dismissed and who are trying to improve the terms of their respective dismissals. In the following Table 2, which presents official figures on subject matters, the German figures, to some extent, disguise the amount of claims which are related to dismissal because many claims for review of terms of employment, e.g., back payments or favourable references, deal with problems related to problems of termination of employment.[43]

*Table 2: Subject Matter of Disputes in the British Industrial Tribunals and in the West German Labour Courts in 1981*

| | British Industrial Tribunals | West German Labour Courts |
|---|---|---|
| Complaints Against Unfair Dismissal | 83% | 37% |
| Terms of Employment (including redundancy payments, wage claims after dismissal references etc.) | 15% | 49% |
| Other | 2% | 14% |
| | (n = 44,852) | (n = 399,269) |

Sources: *Fact Sheet of the COIT for England and Wales*, July 1982, para. 4 and 5; and *Fact Sheet of the COIT for Scotland*, February 1983, para. 7 and 8. *Bundesarbeitsblatt* 6/82, p. 136, Table 190. Every tenth West German claim involved two or more subject matters.

In looking at the cases brought before the Berlin Labour Court, we found that a high percentage of conflicts came out of small firms;[44] a similar over-representation of unfair dismissal applications from small firms was discovered by British research.[45] Given this phenomenon, it is plausible to hypothesise that courtroom litigation for the employees of small firms is, to a certain degree, the functional equivalent of what internal company grievance procedures are to employees of larger firms.[46] The plausibility of this hypothesis is reinforced by studies showing that works councils in West Germany are often absent from smaller firms (even if legally possible) and that in Britain collective representation on the shop floor is less effective the smaller the firm.[47] However, when we relate litigation figures back to the data base of all dismissals, we find that the relationship is more complicated and partly inverse: dismissal rates in very small firms with up to five employees are four times as high as those in large firms with more than 300 employees.[48] This high labour turnover in small firms is aggravated by a low propensity among employees to challenge dismissals. By relating the high occurrence of litigation by employees from small firms to their data-base of total dismissals, we find that the propensity for employees from small firms to go to court is lower than that of employees in larger firms.[49]

*Table 3: Relationship of Firm Size to Rate of Dismissal, Works Council Opposition, and Propensity toward Litigation in West Germany in 1978*

| | Dismissals by Employer per 100 Employed (1) per year | Among those Opposition by Works Council (2) (% of all dismissals) | Propensity to go to Court (3) (% of all dismissals) |
|---|---|---|---|
| Very Small Firms (1–5 employed) | 12 | – | 4% |
| Small Firms (6–20 employed) | 12 | 13% | 7% |
| Medium-sized Firms (21–300 employed) | 7 | 22% | 9% |
| Large Firms (301–1000 employed) | 3 | 28% | 9% |
| Very Large Firms (more than 1,000 employed) | 2–3 | 29% | 16% |

Source: 1) Falke *et al., op.cit.* (n.8), p.74 (Company survey).
2) Falke *et al., op.cit* (n.8), p.191 (Works Council survey).
Small firms: 6–100 employees; medium-sized firms: 100–300 employees.
3) Falke *et. al., op.cit.* (n.8), p.392 (Employee survey).
Medium-sized firms: 21–250 firms; large firms: 251–1000 employees.

As Table 3 shows, the relationship of decreasing dismissal rates and increasing rates of opposition to dismissal within the firms (as well as an increasing propensity to challenge dismissals in court) does not only apply to a comparison of very small with very large firms. Employees in small firms lose out not only because of an insufficient infrastructure of representation on the shop floor; by going to court they also make less effort to improve terms of their respective dismissals. There is no reason to assume that employers in small firms dismiss less unfairly. Rather, it appears that once there is an infrastructure of intra-firm representation of workers' interests, there is also a better awareness of and capacity for employing legal means of litigation. Rather than replacing each other as functional equivalents, intra-firm procedures and employment protection by courts complement and reinforce each other.[50]

## PROCEDURAL LEVELS IN BRITISH INDUSTRIAL TRIBUNALS AND IN WEST GERMAN LABOUR COURTS

The caseload of conflicts brought before courts is usually a mixed bag of trivial, routine cases with only an occasional occurrence of issues that present complicated substantive or evidentiary questions. Often, the mere threat of litigation is enough to make the other party give in. Private settlements within the shadow of the law, i.e., after registration with the Labour Court or the Industrial Tribunal, are common in both countries; they appear in the statistics under withdrawals. However, more than a quarter of British and German cases end with default judgments from a case; in these cases, courts are often successfully used to threaten an opponent. Some parties do not fully pursue all their options; plaintiffs, for instance, may be aware that they have overstated their claim, or defendants may be aware that they will have to compromise at some point. Both parties, moreover, often have a common interest in avoiding the time and costs involved in legal proceedings. Thus, they may both see some advantage in settling, sometimes even at third party's expense, if the terms of the dismissals are so defined that employment benefits or other insurance benefits become part of the deal.

In looking at other than private settlements, there is a striking institutional difference in how both systems achieve settlements by third party intervention. In West German Labour Courts conciliation is the mandatory first step of court procedure, allowing the judge every discretion to spend much time and effort on settlement (also inducing her or him to come back to settlement proposals at a later stage of the proceedings). Initial conciliation attempts in Great Britain are left to A.C.A.S. officers who are separate from the Industrial Tribunals. We were told that it is A.C.A.S. practice to allow a six-week period after the claim has been filed to settle the case. A hearing before an Industrial Tribunal will be automatically arranged and it will take place when A.C.A.S. fails.

*Table 4: Mode of Termination and Rates of Success in the Industrial Tribunal System (1982) and the German Labour Courts (1978) in Unfair Dismissal Cases*

| | British Industrial Tribunals (including ACAS) | West German Labour Courts |
|---|---|---|
| Withdrawal and Summary (default) Judgment | 30% | 26% |
| Settlement through Conciliation or Mediation | 35% | 60% |
| Decision and Hearings | 35% | 14% |
| | 100% | 100% |
| Success of the Applicant in the Decision | 30% | 50% |
| Out of all Applications: Reinstatement/Re-engagement Granted | 1.1% (ACAS)<br>0.4% (IT) | 4% |
| | (n = 33,109) | (n = 97,164) |

*Sources*: The *Employment Gazette*, Oct. 1983, 449; Falke *et al.*, Vol.II, *op.cit.* (n.8), 974, *Uebersicht* 4; Rhode, *op.cit.* (n.9), 192/3, *Uebersicht* 3.

The Industrial Tribunals are less likely to achieve settlements than are German judges at a later stage. A.C.A.S. conciliation is a pure intermediary institution such as those we often find in early societies.[51] It is followed by a predominantly adjudication-oriented adversary proceeding before the Industrial Tribunal. German procedure, on the contrary, has put both functions (that of mediation and of adjudication) into the hands of the same judge, allowing her or him to move back and forth between both functions at her or his discretion.

Compared to West German Labour Courts, not only are the litigation rates of Industrial Tribunals lower, but the chances of success for plaintiffs are lower as well. If an employee is dismissed in Germany, she or he may be aware that there is a sixty per cent chance of obtaining a lump sum settlement by going to court. The chances of obtaining a judgment that would grant reinstatement may even be irrelevant to her or him (whether attempts are made to implement this or not) given the likelihood of winning a lump sum settlement. Further, the fact that about fifty per cent of all plaintiffs tend to win their cases in final judgments of the Labour Courts as compared to only twenty-seven per cent in decisions of the Tribunals may also be of minor significance to her or him. West German civil procedure does not restrict the loser of a judgment at the Labour Court level to appeal only on grounds of law as is the case in Britain.

*Table 5: Levels of the Judicial Dispute Resolution Process of British and West German Labour Judiciaries (Estimates of Terminations at Respective Levels in Percentage in 1981)*

| *Dispute levels* | *Great Britain* | *West Germany* |
|---|---|---|
| | (all filings: 100%) | |
| Conciliation/ Withdrawal etc. | ACAS: 65% | Labour Court: 90% |
| Adjudication | Industrial Tribunal: 35% | Labour Court: decisions: 10% |
| First Appeal | Employment Appeal Tribunal: 1.54% | State Labour Court: 4% |
| Second Appeal | Court of Appeal/ Court of Session | Federal Labour Court |
| Third Appeal | House of Lords | (Federal Constitutional Court) |
| | (n = 44,852) | (n = 347,520) |

*Sources:* *Fact Sheet of the COIT for England and Wales*, July 1982, para. 6 and 8; and *Fact Sheet of the COIT for Scotland*, February 1983, para. 12; *Bundesarbeitsblatt* 6/82, 136/7, Tables 190 and 191.

The West German employment protection system invites the employer to pay the price of a lump sum settlement rather than engage in further litigation. Only a meagre ten per cent of all cases before the West German Labour Courts result in a decision by the bench. It seems quite apparent that these few cases contain the hard core of complicated issues. As Table 5 shows, forty per cent of those who received an unfavourable decision in a Labour Court later appealed before a State Labour Court. We, thereby, roughly estimate the rate of appeal by comparing the number of appeals with the number of decisions of Labour Courts which were rendered the year before. In contrast, the British Industrial Tribunal system appears to be more selective. Although we find that two-thirds of all cases are settled at the level of A.C.A.S. (withdrawals and conciliated agreements), a third of all cases go from here to the Industrial Tribunals and then to final judgment. Appeals are less frequent once the Tribunal has rendered its decision (this generally corresponds to the restrictions on a *de novo* hearing under common law procedure).

It also becomes apparent from Table 5 that appeals structures are different. The German appeal system is organisationally independent from the ordinary judiciary whereas the British system leads into the normal judiciary after the decision of the Employment Appeal Tribunal. The third "appeal" to the German Federal Constitutional Court is put in brackets because it is not considered to be a normal appeal but rather considered a right of the citizen to be protected against unconstitutional acts of state organs which include courts. However, it is left to the discretion of the Federal Constitutional Court to accept an appeal on constitutional grounds against a court decision, e.g., a decision of the Federal Labour Court; and constitutional appeal does not prevent enforcement of the Labour Court decisions. In general, the amount of cases admitted to be heard by the Constitutional Court is comparable to the amount of labour law cases in the House of Lords.

## COURTROOM OBSERVATIONS ON PROCEDURE

Talking to British lawyers, one frequently hears the opinion that Industrial Tribunals are particularly "informal" in their procedures. This is only true, however, relative to the procedural rules and practices of ordinary British courts. In fact, as Continental observers we were struck by the formality of Industrial Tribunal procedures when compared with the so-called "inquisitorial" procedures of West German Labour Courts.[52] In both systems, labour disputes are handled by procedures that are less formal than those of the civil courts; however, the basic characteristics of adversary versus so-called "inquisitorial" procedures stand out when British and West German courtroom interaction is taken into account. Both Industrial Tribunals and Labour Courts stress their settlement function over their adjudicatory function, but do so in such a culturally typical way that two very different procedural traditions have developed.

Continental procedure requires both parties to formulate their arguments – including the evidence that they are prepared to provide – in the briefs which either accompany the filing of the lawsuit or constitute the defendant's answer. The briefs of both sides are studied by the judge who will chair the proceedings, and as a rule are presented to the opposing side for purposes of response. In this way, a file builds up based on an exchange of the arguments and evidence offered by both sides. Yet, advocates of both sides may also contact each other by phone, or, occasionally, may meet in the halls of the court building to attempt to settle the matter out of court. The court does not learn about such out-of-court negotiations unless the plaintiff withdraws from the case or the respondent defaults.

Out-of-court settlements, however, are not as frequent in labour disputes as they are in certain types of civil suits (e.g., personal injury cases) since there is ample opportunity to negotiate in the company with collective representatives before the case is filed. Even the judge usually pressures the parties to settle prior to rendering a formal decision. The Labour Court Act requires that the judge attempts to get the parties to settle by mutual consent at the initial hearing. Some Labour Court judges take conciliation attempts quite seriously; others despise them. The difference in these attitudes may be represented by the time that a judge will allow for settlement. In the Berlin Labour Court which we observed, for example, initial hearings were given early morning time slots. Some of the more settlement-minded judges allowed on the average of fifteen minutes per hearing; some of the less settlement-minded judges allowed only five minutes.[53]

Hence, it is the judge in German Labour Courts who takes the initiative in structuring the formal proceeding as well as the case; it is rarely left to the parties or to their advocates to determine what arguments ought to be raised. The professional judge does this on the basis of the file, which allows him to prepare for the initial hearing and which continues to grow during the proceedings. The judges' attempts to get the parties to reconcile continue through all of the formal proceedings and are sometimes aided by lay representatives who sit on the bench. Settlements are often reached after both sides have specified what sort of evidence they plan to present; indeed, to avoid some of the costs of trial and uncertainties involving witnesses and other types of evidence, parties often settle at this later stage. Here, as well as after the evidence is presented, the judge may again offer an opinion as to how the case might be decided, thus giving both parties a clue as to what to expect.

In this sense, the judge is the most active actor in the courtroom and may repeatedly formulate possible terms for settlement. He does this based on his legal evaluation of the case as well as on the outcome most likely to occur. Settlement, therefore, is not achieved by the parties' anticipation of the costs of continuing the formal proceeding alone, but also by the judge's explicit view of what the settlement options of the parties are in light of what the likely outcome of the case will be if it is pursued.

It can be observed that the judge's prejudices and biases about the case which have been developed during preparation from written documents influence his questions and proposals. The Labour Court procedure is to a great exent a procedure in writing and not primarily designed to produce new facts in a hearing as seems to be the main function of the adversarial procedure. The inquisitorial style is hardly the best way to discover something new about the case which has not been hinted at in the documents.[54]

Adversary proceedings in Britain take on a radically different appearance in the courtroom. Even the most "informal" behaviour of the chairmen that we observed in the Industrial Tribunals would be viewed as very "passive" in comparison to the behaviour of their West German counterparts. The same may be said about the lay members on the bench. Usually not having much more information than the application form and the standard employer's response, the chairman and the lay members of the Tribunal have to obtain the relevant information on the case during the hearing. Their main duty is to be prepared to hear arguments and review evidence presented by the parties or their representatives. In the Industrial Tribunals, the rules of evidence of civil or criminal procedure are not followed in full, but the procedure for cross-examination and the techniques that solicitors and barristers use are employed in producing statements. Partly because non-lawyer representatives, e.g., trade union officials, lack reputation within the legal system and partly because they are not as skilled in adversary techniques as are practising solicitors, the latter tend to dominate the pattern of legal discourse. Chairmen of Industrial Tribunals only occasionally adopt an active role by asking a few questions, but lay members on the bench rarely ever do so.[55]

Indeed, it may well be that union and employer representatives on the bench are slightly more active in tribunals than their West German colleagues since the chairman of a Tribunal does not have much more information about the case than do the lay representatives. In West German Labour Courts, however, the judge who chairs the bench does have extensive knowledge of the file, while the lay representatives on the bench largely rely on what they have learned during the initial conversation. Thus it can be concluded from this that discussions in the chambers of the Labour Courts take place under more diverging information backgrounds between judges and lay members than those of Industrial Tribunals.

To an observer in the courtroom, the difference between interactions of an adversary and that of an "inquisitorial" procedure is remarkable. In a Continental courtroom, the judge asks most of the questions, and usually does not sharply differentiate between statements of law and statements of fact. A formal presentation of evidence is avoided unless there are outright contradictions in the briefs or unless some attorney insists on one with the idea of getting a higher fee. In chairing the proceeding, the German judge may shift from his role as mediator to that of adjudicator. He does not risk appeal as long as he proposes terms for a possible settlement, and, in this sense, thus acts as an arbitrator. The inquisitorial discretion that he enjoys allows him to shift back and forth between mediation, arbitration, and adjudication, using the letter of the law to encourage parties to settle.

## TRIBUNAL AND COURTROOM PERSONNEL

One reason why proceedings before Industrial Tribunals do not deviate from the formal adversary process as much as they could lies in the recruitment patterns of chairmen as well as in the solicitors' and chairmens' socialisation in adversary techniques. Chairmen of Industrial Tribunals are, as a rule, former barristers or solicitors at a late stage of their career.[56] They tend to stick to rather traditional views and learned behaviour patterns of the court room. West German Labour Court judges, on the other hand, pursue a career that is separate from that of their colleagues in ordinary civil courts. In West Germany, a law graduate has to make an early choice as to whether to join the bar, strive for judgeship, or join the civil service. West German lawyers may enter any of these careers if the second law degree is high enough, e.g., for a judicial position. If the law graduate opts for a Labour Court judgeship, she or he will usually stay with this post for the rest of her or his career. Nomination to the Labour Court rests with the Department of Labour (and not with the Department of Justice as is the case for careers in the ordinary courts). A nomination for a Labour Court judgeship has to clear a tripartite committee consisting of an equal number of members from the unions and the employer associations and of presidents of the Labour Courts.[57] Candidates may improve their chances if they have special qualifications in labour law and industrial relations. Labour Court judges are said to be "somewhat more leftist" than their average colleagues in the ordinary courts. In fact, their higher rate of membership of public service unions rather than of the federation of West German judges is a good indication of this. And their career expectations are oriented more toward appellate Labour Courts than toward ordinary courts.

The procedure for recruiting the two lay members of the bench in West Germany is not much different from that used in the Industrial Tribunals. Lay judges are nominated by the trade unions and the employer associations in both systems.[58] The West German tradition of participatory relations on many levels between trade unions and employer associations (including co-operation of the works councils and on the boards of companies) creates the background for meso-corporatist decision-making.[59] It is reflected in the non-partisan attitudes of lay judges in West German Labour Courts. One survey of lay judge attitudes in West Germany shows that lay judges see their roles as being neutral decision-makers rather than as advocates of a particular side in an industrial controversy.[60]

Finally, a few words about solicitors and other representatives before Labour Courts and Industrial Tribunals. In both legal systems, the parties are allowed to appear in court without representation. Considering the collective nature of disputes, we find that both systems offer both plaintiffs and respondents representation by their respective associations: trade union officials represent every fifth worker in Industrial Tribunals and every fourth worker in German Labour Courts. Representatives of employer associations are more likely to appear before the West German Labour Courts than before British Industrial Tribunals (excluding A.C.A.S.).

*Table 6: Representation of Parties*

| | British Industrial Tribunals (excluding ACAS) | | West German Labour Courts | |
|---|---|---|---|---|
| | *Plaintiffs* | *Respondents* | *Plaintiffs* | *Respondents* |
| *Self-representation* | 45% | 33% | 25% | 7% |
| *Others (In-house Lawyers, Friends or Associates)* | 9% | 21% | 5% | 21% |
| *Trade Union or Employers' Association Representatives* | 22% | 5% | 27% | 29% |
| *Represented by Attorneys* | 23% | 41% | 42% | 38% |
| | 100% | 100% | 100% | 100% |

*Sources*: Dickens *et al.*, *op.cit.* (n.56), 154, table 1. Falke *et al.*, *op.cit.* (n.8), Vol.II, p.627, Tab. IV/57 and p.647, Tab.IV/66.

West German Labour Court procedures appear more clearly as an interaction among lawyers since only twelve per cent of employers and twenty-five per cent of the plaintiff-employees are unrepresented, while in the British Industrial Tribunals more than one-third of both plaintiff-employees and employers still appear without any representation. On the other hand, in-house lawyers on the employers' side can be found in one out of five cases in both systems.

## CONCLUSION

In summarising, we return to our over-arching focus: a comparative analysis of "degrees of judicialisation" in West German and British dispute processing practices. Historically, we have seen that West German Labour Courts have a lead of half a century over British Industrial Tribunals in providing judicial remedies for dismissal conflicts. The Labour Courts in Germany developed within a tradition of social legislation and so-called liberal corporatism with trade union participation; from the beginning in the Weimar Republic, Labour Courts have been promoted by unions and they were accepted by employer associations. British industrial relations, however, have been more polarised, and both employers and unions have always been more suspicious of state intervention. Within the context of the Industrial Relations Act (1971–1974), British Industrial Tribunals were associated with legislation designed to control union activity; however, the unions refused to co-operate. And, although the workers' movement has become increasingly disillusioned with the operations and outcomes of the Industrial Tribunals, British employers still view the Tribunal mainly as a device to increase the costs of dismissals, rather than as an institution in which they have a vested interest.

A comparison of the caseloads of both systems shows that sceptical attitudes towards interventionist employment protection correspond to a restricted use of the Industrial Tribunal system. There were approximately 47,000 complaints which asked for individual conciliation provided by A.C.A.S. in 1982 compared to approximately 387,000 filings with the German Labour Courts.

This difference in caseloads cannot sufficiently be explained by differences in jurisdiction. In the first place, British dismissal law is only slightly more restrictive with regard to eligibility than West German law; e.g., British law requires a minimum period of work of two years at the time of the comparison before becoming eligible for employment protection, while in West Germany this period amounts only to twenty-six weeks. Secondly, although West German Labour Courts have jurisdiction in collective labour law, they handle only a relatively small caseload involving strictly collective issues.

The explanation for such differences in caseloads lies, instead, with the nature of dispute handling at the shop floor level. Disputes over dismissals are framed either as a matter for collective bargaining – thus to be handled by shop stewards or trade unions in Britain, and respectively by works councils in West Germany – or as a matter for the courts. In accordance with the general notion of the autonomy in industrial relations in Britain, formal grievance procedures have been set up by most of the larger British companies. In fact, industrial relations studies show that one of the major effects of the Industrial Tribunal system has been a collateral increase in the establishment of grievance procedures at the company level.

The German counterpart to grievance procedures are negotiations between the works councils and management. Works councils must be notified of every individual dismissal, and give their consent to a "mass dismissal". Yet, compared to the relatively greater involvement of British local representatives in grievance procedures, German works councils seem to be under-exploiting their potential power in employment protection cases; since works councils are integrated into company management by means of their co-determination rights, the representation of individual complaints takes place in a judicial forum more often than in British practice. When we extend our concept of "judicialisation" to compare the degrees of formalism attained in British and West German judicial proceedings, we find that both systems tend to combine conciliation or mediation with adjudication. There is still a major institutional difference, however: while conciliation in Britain is undertaken by means of a separate service (A.C.A.S.), the German Labour Court statutes give the courts themselves the responsibility of attempting to get the parties to settle at any stage of the proceedings. The German procedure, therefore, after an initial mediation hearing before a professional Labour Court judge is characterised by a constant intermingling of mediation attempts with formal litigation. This is enhanced by inquisitorial powers of the judges over the proceedings.

Consequently, German Labour Court judges attain a high rate of settlements: sixty per cent of all dismissal cases result in some form of settlement, compared to thirty-five per cent in the A.C.A.S. In these settlements, both sides satisfy some of their interests; the worker usually gets some monetary compensation, while the employer is made secure against future claims and costs.

Since West German Labour Court judges are very active as mediators, they are able to avoid the comparatively few procedural restrictions of the inquisitorial process. On the contrary, hearings before the Industrial Tribunals strike us as being relatively formal, even if some of the adversarial rituals are eased in comparison with British civil or criminal procedure. Legal representatives of the parties to the dispute also reinforce adversary techniques in courtroom interactions that occur, and chairmen usually remain passive towards these attempts.

In addition, low success rates of plaintiffs with regard to final decision cannot be left out when explaining limited attraction of Industrial Tribunals. In Industrial Tribunals, only about twenty-five per cent of workers who have been dismissed obtain satisfaction in adjudicated decisions, as compared to fifty per cent before West German Labour Courts. Combined with the formality of Industrial Tribunal hearings, such low success rates put strong pressure on plaintiffs to withdraw or settle their cases by some form of conciliation, and, at the same time, weaken their bargaining power. The meagre possibility of obtaining a final decision in Britain seems to constitute more of a deterrence to involving the Industrial Tribunals in the resolution of labour disputes, whereas in West Germany the principle of reconciling at least a portion of the disputed claims – which, in fact, underlies the admixture of mediation and adjudication in the West German Labour Courts – makes judicial involvement an attractive option, even if a formal claim for job reinstatement is hardly ever successful.

## NOTES AND REFERENCES

1 A rather traditional comparative law approach with respect to labour conflict institutions can be found in B. Aaron, "Administration of Justice in Labor Law: Arbitration and the Role of Courts, an International Survey" in *Festschrift fuer Otto Kahn-Freund.* (1980; eds. F. Gamillscheg, J. de Givry, Bob Hepple, J-M. Verlier), pp. 363–384. See generally the methodological remarks in R. Blanpain, "Comparativism in Labour Law and Industrial Relations" in *Comparative Labour Law and Industrial Relations* (1982; eds. R. Blanpain and F. Millard), pp. 17–34 and the warning of O. Kahn-Freund, "On Uses and Misuses of Comparative Law" (1974) 37 *Modern Law Rev.* 1 against too narrow purposes in comparative law studies.

2 The "functional" approach of comparing labour institutions with respect to their problem solving capacity is proposed, e.g., by J. Schregle, "Die Regelung von Arbeitsstreitigkeiten aus rechtsvergleichender Sicht" in *25 Jahre Bundesarbeitsgericht* (1979; eds. F. Gamillscheg, G. Hueck, and H. Wiedemann), pp. 541–554; and J. Schregle "Comparative Industrial Relations: Pitfalls and Potential" (1981) 118 *International Labour Rev.* 15.

3 Cf., e.g. W. Mueller-Jentsch, "Versuch ueber die Tarifautonomie. Entstehung und Funktionen kollektiver Verhandlungssysteme in Grossbritannien und Deutschland" *Leviathan* (1983) 118–150; he offers an interesting historical approach in comparing British and German Collective bargaining law.

[4] For a theoretical account, see W. Felstiner, R. Abel, and A. Sarat, "The Emergence and Transformation of Disputes: Naming, Blaming, Claiming . . . " (1981) 15 *Law and Society Rev.* 631.

[5] An overview of the dispute approach in legal anthropology can be found in S. Roberts, *Order and Dispute* (1979); interesting case studies are compiled in *The Disputing Process: Law in Ten Societies* (1978; eds. L. Nader and H. Todd) and *The Politics of Informal Justice*, Vol. II; Comparative Studies (1982; ed. R. Abel).

[6] R. Abel, "A Comparative Theory of Dispute Institutions in Society" (1974) 8 *Law and Society Rev.* 217 and V. Gessner, *Recht und Konflikt. Eine soziologische Untersuchung privatrechtlicher Konflikte in Mexiko* (1976).

[7] For a sociolegal concept of law as "gradual concept", see E. Blankenburg, "Recht als gradualisiertes Konzept" *Alternative Rechtsformen und Alternativen zum Recht. Jahrbuch fuer Rechtssoziologie und Rechtstheorie Bd.* 6 (1980; eds. E. Blankenburg, E. Klausa and H. Rottleuthner), pp. 83–98.

[8] Starting point for our analysis was our own empirical work on West German Labour Courts: E. Blankenburg, R. Rogowski and S. Schoenholz, "Phenomena of Legalization. Observations in a German Labour Court" in *European Yearbook in Law and Sociology 1978* pp. 33–66; and E. Blankenburg, S. Schoenholz with R. Rogowski, *Zur Soziologie des Arbeitsgerichtsverfahrens. Die Verrechtlichung von Arbeitskonflikten* (1979). Problems of settlement in court have been a main focus of this project; cf. R. Rogowski, "Die aktive Rolle des Richters im Prozessvergleich" in *Alternativen in der Ziviljustiz* (1982; eds. E. Blankenburg, W. Gottwald, and D. Strempel), pp. 171–187 (an English version appeared under the title "The active role of the judge in settling civil cases" as DPRP-Working Paper 1983–7. University of Wisconsin Law School, Madison); and S. Schoenholz, "Alternativen im Gerichtsverfahren. Zur Konfliktloesung vor dem Arbeitsgericht unter besonderer Beruecksichtigung des Prozessvergleichs" (1984) Diss. Vrije Universiteit Amsterdam. In addition to data from our own collection and from official statistics, we shall rely on data from recent empirical studies on the German Labour Court (especially J. Falke, A. Hoeland, B. Rhode, and G. Zimmermann, *Kuendigungspraxis und Kuendigungsschutz in der Bundesrepublik Deutschland.* Two vols. (1981); and *Rechtssoziologische Studien zur Arbeitsgerichtsbarkeit* (1984; ed. H. Rottleuthner).

[9] While studying the British system, we attended several Industrial Tribunal hearings and had interviews with Industrial Tribunal and ACAS personnel in spring and autumn 1983. A first attempt to compare recent British and German data on labour judiciaries can be found in B. Rhode, "Wie wirksam ist der rechtliche Kuendigungsschutz in England und in der Bundesrepublik Deutschland. Ein Vergleich von zwei empirischen Studien" in *Kuendigungspraxis, Kuendigungsschutz und Probleme der Arbeitsgerichtsbarkeit. Beitraege zur Regelung und Praxis in der Bundesrepublik Deutschland, in Grossbritannien und den USA* (1983; eds. R. Ellermann-Witt, H. Rottleuthner and H. Russig) pp. 173–196. The final results of the Industrial Relations Research Unit study on Industrial Tribunals are now available in L. Dickens, M. Jones, B. Weekes and M. Hart, *Dismissed: A Study of Unfair Dismissal and the Industrial Tribunal System* (1985).

[10] Cf. O. Kahn-Freund, "Labour Law and Industrial Relations in Great Britain and West Germany" (Written in 1978 as Preface for the German edition of *Labour and the Law*) in *Law and Industrial Relations: Building on Kahn-Freund* (1983; eds. Lord Wedderburn, Roy Lewis and Jon Clark), pp. 2-3; Kahn-Freund stated a traditional contrast between the "extra-legal nature" of British industrial relations and the "hypertrophy of legal thinking" in German relations of capital and labour. Cf. also for the British tradition of abstentionist industrial policies A. Flanders, "The Tradition of Voluntarism" (1974) 12 *Brit. J. of Industrial Relations* 352.

[11] For a discussion of the political debates which accompanied the establishment of Labour Courts, see B. Michel, "Der Kampf der Gewerkschaften um die einheitliche Arbeitsgerichtsbarkeit (1926)" in *Arbeitsgerichtsprotokolle* (2nd. ed. 1982; eds. K. Feser *et al.*) pp. 28–53.

12 For an early history of the Labour Courts in the Weimar Republic and the Nazi period, see F. Wunderlich, ***German Labour Courts*** (1946).

13 Cf. the critical appraisal in ***Kollektives Arbeitsrecht***. Quellentexte zur Geschichte des Arbeitsrechts in Deutschland, Vol. II (1975; eds. T. Blanke, R. Erd, U. Mueckenberger and U. Stracheit) pp. 248-9; it documents the development of West German labour law and the far-reaching influence of decision-making of the Federal Labour Court on West German collective labour law. W. Daeubler, ***Das Arbeitsrecht 1***. Ein Leitfaden fuer Arbeitnehmer (rev. ed. 1985) p. 33, calls this tendency "Richterherrschaft" (judicial domination) which is an autocratic form of legislation in an otherwise democratic society.

14 Considering the effective working of the informal system, the ***Report of the Royal Commission on Trade Unions and Employers' Associations*** (1968; Cmnd 3623. Chairman: Lord Donovan. London: HMSO), para. 1007, argued that legislative intervention would produce more disruption than order. Nevertheless, it called for changes with regard to industrial sectors which were lacking effective regulation through collective bargaining.

15 Donovan Report, ***id.*** para. 572.

16 Early German writings of Kahn-Freund have been collected in O. Kahn-Freund, ***Labour Law and Politics in the Weimar Republic*** (1981; ed. and transl. by R. Lewis and J. Clark).

17 The influence of Otto Kahn-Freund on the development of British labour law and industrial relations studies has been described by Lord Wedderburn, "Otto Kahn-Freund and British Labour Law" and H. Clegg, "Otto Kahn-Freund and British Industrial Relations", both in Wedderburn *et al., op.cit.* (n.10), pp.14–28 and 29–80.

18 Cf. C. Crouch, ***The Politics of Industrial Relations*** (2nd. ed. 1982) pp. 75–79; J. Farmer, ***Tribunals and Government*** (1974) pp. 74–82; and on the attitudes of the general courts towards industrial relations, see K.W. Lord Wedderburn, "Industrial Relations and the Courts" (1978) 9 ***Ind. Law J.*** 65 and J. Griffiths, ***The Politics of the Judiciary*** (2nd. ed. 1981) ch.3.

19 Cf. the title of B. Weekes, M. Mellish, L. Dickens and J. Lloyd, ***Industrial Relations and the Limits of Law. The Industrial Effects of the Industrial Relations Act 1971*** (1975).

20 Cf. R. Lewis, "The Historical Development of Labour Law" (1976) 14 ***Brit. J. of Industrial Relations*** 1. A "trend towards the juridification of individual disputes" was acknowledged to continue in the beginning of the 1980s: B. Hepple, "Individual Labour Law" in ***Industrial Relations in Britain*** (1983; ed. G. Bain) pp. 392–407 (392). Cf. also J. Clark and Lord Wedderburn "Modern Labour Law: Problems, Functions and Policies" in: Wedderburn *et al., op.cit.* (n.10) pp.81–106, who confirm the trend, while at the same time critciising it.

21 The respective statutes are the Employment Protection Act (EPA) 1975 and the Employment Protection (Consolidation) Act (EPCA) 1978, as amended, in the British case and the Kuendigungsschutzgesetz (KSchG) 1969, as amended, in the German case. As a guideline for our comparison we shall use the parameters of B. Napier, J.-C. Javillier and P. Verge, ***Comparative Dismissal Law*** (1982), especially chapter 7. Our comparison of German and British dismissal law can be read as additional information to their comparison of British, French and Quebec dismissal law.

22 Sec. 1 (1) KSchG.

23 Cf. P. Elias, "Fairness in Unfair Dismissal" (1981) 10 ***Ind. Law J.*** 201.

24 Cf. B. Bercusson in C. Drake and B. Bercusson, ***The Employment Acts 1974–1980*** with Commentary (1981) p. 33.

25 A list of 32 statutory jurisdictions of the Industrial Tribunals can be found in B. Hepple and P. O'Higgins, ***Employment Law*** (4th ed. 1981) pp. 362–4, par. 774; cf. K. Whiteside and G. Hawker, ***Industrial Tribunals*** (1975), on the origins of Industrial Tribunal jurisdiction. The Lord Chancellor may by order confer jurisdiction on Industrial Tribunals to hear claims for breach of employment contract presently dealt with by the ordinary courts: EPCA 1978 s. 131. To our knowledge, no such order has been made.

26 Sec. 2 (1) (2) of the West German Labour Court Act of 1953, as amended, establishes exclusive jurisdiction of Labour Courts in civil law disputes between employees and employers resulting from employment relations.

[27] EPCA 1978 s. 64A (1)(b).

[28] Sec. 23 (1) KSchG. This qualification does not apply in other than dismissal protection jurisdiction.

[29] Cf. W. Zoellner, *Arbeitsrecht*. Ein Studienbuch (3rd. ed. 1983) p.238. G. Trieschmann, "Ungleichbehandlung im gesetzlichen Arbeitsvertragsrecht" in *Festschrift fuer Herschel* (1982; eds. P. Hanau, G. Mueller, H. Wiedemann, O. Wlotzke) pp. 421–461, argued recently against any exemption of small employer dismissals from German employment protection.

[30] Sec. 1 (1) KSchG.

[31] S.I. 1979 No. 959.

[32] EPCA 1978 s.55 (2)(c). A short discussion of British "constructive dismissal" from a German point of view can be found in A. Doese-Digenopoulos, *Der arbeitsrechtliche Kuendigungsschutz in England*. Eine Darstellung aus deutscher Sicht (1982), pp. 34-5.

[33] Only to a certain degree is such constructive dismissal also known in West German law. In sec. 626 (*Kuendigung aus wichtigem Grund*) of the German Civil Code, there is a provision for dismissal without notice in cases of so-called "good cause". This paragraph – in conjunction with sec. 628 (compensation) of the Civil Code – legally applies to both parties of the employment contract, but is widely used only by employers. An overview of the few Labour Court rulings on "good cause" in cases involving employee dismissals can be found in G. Schaub, *Arbeitsrechtshandbuch* (5th. ed. 1983) pp. 622–4, para. 125 (VIII).

[34] Recently the German Federal Labour Court has decided that at least during appeal proceedings a dismissed worker is legally entitled to be actually employed, if he won in the first instance, BAG *Der Betrieb* 1985, pp. 55/6. In Britain, the Industrial Tribunal on request is able to order continuous employment as "interim relief" if an inadmissible reason for the dismissal is given, e.g., dismissal because of trade union activity.

[35] In Germany, local labour administrations have to be informed in cases of mass dismissal. See sec. 17 KSchG.

[36] Cf. E. Blankenburg, "Mobilisierung von Recht" (1980) 1 *Zeitschrift fuer Rechtssoziologie* 33, on the concept of mobilisation of courts.

[37] A discussion of "baselines" in litigation theory can be found in J. Griffiths, "The general theory of litigation – a first step" (1983) 4 *Zeitschrift fuer Rechtssoziologie* 145 (pp.168/9).

[38] Blankenburg *et al.* 1978 and 1979, *op.cit.* (n.8).

[39] J. Falke and V. Gessner "Konfliktnaehe als Massstab fuer gerichtliche und aussergerichtliche Streitbehandlung" in E. Blankenburg *et al.* 1982, *op.cit.* (n.8), pp.303-4, distinguish norm conflicts from personal and role conflicts. According to their concept, norm conflicts with low degrees of social interdependence are characterised by a high inclination for judicial interventions.

[40] Rhode, *op.cit.* (n.9).

[41] Cf. for West Germany: *Statistiken der Rechtspflege*, Table 15.4 in 1976, 1979, 1982 and 1985. For Britain: *Fact Sheet of the COIT*, July 1982, p.1.

[42] Advisory, Conciliation and Arbitration Service (ACAS) *Annual Report 1982* (1983), para. 4.7, p. 38.

[43] The official German Labour Court statistic registers only such claims as dismissal issues which directly ask for reinstatement. Claims, e.g., seeking payment for previous work, are registered separately. In including all dismissal-related claims, Rottleuthner in Ellermann-Witt *et al.*, *op.cit.* (n.9), p.86, reports from his Berlin Labour Court study that 61 per cent of the claims were related to problems of termination of employment.

[44] Blankenburg *et al.* 1979, *op.cit.* (n.8), pp.69–73.

[45] L. Dickens, "Wettelijke bescherming tegen onredelijk ontslag in Groot-Brittanie" in *Hoe goed werkt ontslagrecht?* (1985; eds. E. Blankenburg, L.van den Heuvel, and A. Houkema) pp. 81–102 (pp.87–90).

[46] For British literature on grievance procedures, cf. S. Anderman, *Voluntary Dismissal Procedure and the Industrial Relations Act* (1971); N. Singleton, *Industrial Relations Procedures* (1975); A. Thompson and V. Murray, *Grievance Procedures* (1976); and K.W. Wedderburn and P. Davies, *Employment Grievances and Disputes Procedures in Britain* (1969). The impact of employment protection legislation on the establishment of grievance procedures is documented in W. Daniel and E. Stilgoe, *The Impact of Employment Protection Laws*. Policy Studies Institute Vol. XLIV, No. 577 (1978); *The Changing Contours of British Industrial Relations. A Survey of Manufacturing Industries* (1981; ed. W. Brown) ch.3; and W. Daniel and N. Millward, *Workplace Industrial Relations*. The DE/PSI/SSRC Survey (1983), ch.VII. There is still not much research literature available on the functioning of German company procedures with the exception of studies on the participatory activity of works councils. See only H. Kotthoff, *Betriebsraete und betriebliche Herrschaft*. Eine Typologie von Partizipationsmustern im Industriebetrieb (1981); and A. Hoeland, *Das Verhalten von Betriebsraeten bei Kuendigungen*. Recht und Wirklichkeit im betrieblichen Alltag (1985). These studies present empirical findings on the (in)activity of works councils in legally prescribed dismissal procedures. A more general account of legal aspects of grievance settlement in Germany can be found in T. Ramm, "Labour Courts and Grievance Settlement in West Germany" in *Labour Courts and Grievance Settlement in Western Europe* (1971; ed. B. Aaron) pp. 81–157. An insightful comparative study of conciliation and arbitration procedures, mainly related to collective disputes, has been published by the International Labour Office: ILO,*Conciliation and arbitration procedures in labour disputes. A comparative survey* (1980).

[47] Research on intra-firm representation of workers is described for Britain by M. Terry, "Shop Steward Development and Managerial Strategies" in G. Bain, *op.cit.* (n.20), pp.67–91, and for Germany by Kotthoff, *op.cit.* (n.45). A comparison of shop stewards' and works council activities can be found in D. Marsden, "Shop Stewards in Great Britain, West Germany and France" (1980) 2 *Employee Relations* 4. The impact of unfair dismissal legislation on trade union activities is discussed in P. Joyce and A. Woods, "Does Legislation increase Industrial Conflicts?" (1981) 3 *Employee Relations* 2. Cf. also Dickens *et al.* 1985, *op.cit.* (n.9), ch.6.

[48] Falke *et al.*, Vol. I, *op.cit.* (n.8), p.74.

[49] Falke *et al.*, Vol. I, *op.cit.* (n.8), p.392.

[50] J. Diekmann, "Kuendigungsschutzklagen und Konjunktur" (1984) 5 *Zeitschrift fuer Rechtssoziologie* 79 (pp.91–95), points out that litigation rates per estimated number of dismissals differ significantly from one economic sector to another; high litigation rates in West Berlin showed banking and chemistry industry with high proportions of white collar workers. In the last ten years litigation rates rose in almost all sectors; in industries with high unemployment high increases in litigation occurred (for example, in the metal industry with large firms and in the food processing industry with medium-sized firms); traditionally small firm sectors and industries characterised by seasonal employment (such as hotel and construction industries) showed especially high litigation increases. The latter category makes up a considerable part of overall Labour Court caseload, also due to the fact that smaller firms generally show a higher rate of actual labour turnover because of dismissal.

[51] Cf. A. Hoebel, *The Law of Primitive Man: A Study in Comparative Legal Dynamics* (1954) pp. 114 ff., on the Ifugao monkalun.

[52] The debate on "legalism" in British Industrial Tribunals seems more concerned with trends in substantive labour law and less concerned with procedural matters. See R. Munday, "Tribunallore: Legalism and the Industrial Tribunals" (1981) 10 *Ind. Law J.* 146.

[53] The length of hearings differs significantly between the two systems. Judging from our non-representative observations, most German hearings will not last longer than twenty minutes. Rottleuthner in Rottleuthner, *op.cit.* (n.8), p.32, reports from his research that 95 per cent of the conciliatory meetings and 71 per cent of the judgmental meetings were terminated within thirty minutes. In contrast, Industrial Tribunal hearings usually last several hours and quite often a whole day: Dickens *et al., op.cit.* (n.9), Table 7.5, p.205. However, it has to be said with respect to the German system that there is an average of two hearings per case in West German Labour Courts compared to only one in Britain. A critical assessment of the average duration of German Labour Court proceedings can be found in Brandt in Ellermann-Witt *et al., op.cit.* (n.8), 119, Schaubild 2.

[54] In this context, advocates of increased inquisition in British Industrial Tribunals, like K. Williams, "Unfair Dismissal: Myths and Statistics" (1983) 12 *Ind. Law J.* 157, might be reminded that it is most likely in inquisitorial proceedings that a considerable number of written documents will have to be exchanged before the hearing, which might create even higher barriers for the unrepresented party.

[55] On the activity of lay members in Tribunals see L. Dickens, "Do Lay Members Influence Tribunal Decisions?" (1983) *Personnel Management*, 28; and Dickens *et al.* 1985, *op.cit.* (n.9), 59, p.65. During our observations we noticed a difference with respect to Scottish Industrial Tribunal lay members who generally seemed to be slightly more active than their English colleagues.

[56] Dickens *et al.* 1985, *op.cit.* (n.9), pp.53-54.

[57] Sec. 18(1) of the West German Labour Court Act.

[58] It is rather unusual to find former military officers serving as employer lay judges in the West German Labour Courts, but not so in British Industrial Tribunals. Data on the distribution of representatives in British Industrial Tribunals are presented by L. Dickens, M. Hart, M. Jones and B. Weekes, "Gesetzlicher Schutz gegen 'unfair dismissal' in Grossbritannien" in Ellermann-Witt *et al., op.cit.* (n.8), 145–172 (154, Tabelle 1).

[59] Cf. R. Rogowski, Meso-Corporatism and Labour Conflict Resolution. (1985) EUI Working Paper 85/150. Florence, *International Journal of Comparative Labour Law and Industrial Relations* Vol.I (1985).

[60] Cf. E. Klausa, *Ehrenamtliche Richter* (1972).

# [20]

# THE REFORM OF THE LEGAL PROFESSIONS AND OF LEGAL AID IN FRANCE

By

PETER HERZOG * and BRIGITTE ECOLIVET HERZOG †

## I. INTRODUCTION

ON September 16, 1972, two important new laws came into effect in France: (1) the law reforming certain of the legal professions [1] and (2) the law creating a new system of legal aid.[2] That these two laws came into effect on the same day is due to design rather than coincidence: a new legal aid scheme could not be created without close attention to the new organisation of the legal profession.[3] In fact, the two laws just mentioned are part of an even more complex scheme of law reform: beginning on September 9, 1971, the Government promulgated a series of decrees which will eventually be integrated into a new Code of Civil Procedure to replace the existing Code first adopted in 1806.[4] Since the revised procedure contained

* Professor of Law, Syracuse University College of Law, Member of the New York State Bar.

† *Avocat* at the Bar of the *Cour d'Appel* in Paris

1 Law No. 71-1130 of Dec. 31, 1971, *Journal Officiel de la République Française* (hereinafter abbreviated to J.O.) Jan. 5, 1972, p. 131, (1972) *Dalloz, Législation* (hereinafter abbreviated to D.L.), p. 38. The effective date of the Law was fixed by Art. 79.

2 Law No. 72-11 of Jan. 3, 1972, J.O. Jan. 5, 1972, p. 167; (1972) D.L. 69; for the effective date, see Art. 35.

3 This connection between the two laws was stressed in the report made to the French National Assembly on the Law on Legal Aid by its reporter, M. De Grailly: " It is important that the reform of legal aid should go into effect at the same time as the reform merging the professions of *avocat* and *avoué* so that the success of the new institution be insured by the open-minded and full cooperation of the new profession." French National Assembly, Committee on Constitutional Laws, Legislation and General Administration, Report No. 1991, p. 15 (1971).

4 Décret No. 71-740 of Sept. 9, 1971, J.O. Sept. 11, 1971, p. 9072; (1971) D.L. 362; Décret No. 72-684 of July 20, 1972, J.O. July 9, 1972, p. 7860, (1972) D.L. 438; Décret No. 72-788 of Aug. 28, 1972, J.O. Aug. 30, 1972, p. 9300; (1972) D.L. 475; Décret No. 72-790 of Aug. 28, 1972, J.O. Aug. 30, 1972, p. 9314; (1972) D.L. 486. As to the jurisdiction of courts, see Décret No. 72-789 of Aug. 28, 1972, J.O. Aug. 30, 1972, p. 9313; (1972) D.L. 486. Under the French Constitution of 1958, the French Government may enact measures in the field of civil procedure, and in a variety of other fields, by decree, even without a delegation of powers from the National Assembly. Such decrees have the force of law. In addition, the Law No. 72-626 of July 5, 1972, J.O. July 9, 1972, p. 7181; (1972) D.L. 362 makes a variety of miscellaneous changes in several matters relating to court organisation, the execution of judgments, arbitration, etc. The Law also provides for the eventual consolidation of all laws on judicial organisation in a Code of Judicial Organisation.

in those decrees has been adapted to the reforms in the legal professions, the provisions of the decrees also came, for the most part, into effect on September 16, 1972. While all these measures are part of a total scheme to modernise the administration of justice,[5] the reform of civil procedure, because of the complexities of the topic, will not be discussed here.

## II. HISTORICAL BACKGROUND

### *A. The Legal Professions*

France has never known a single, unified legal profession, analogous, for instance, to the profession of attorney-at-law in the United States. Rather, professional legal assistance is rendered by a wide variety of professionals subject to varying degrees of regulation or to no regulation at all, a state of affairs that can only be explained by historical accident.[6] Thus there was the profession of *avocat* whose members had the right to handle the oral phases of court procedure and who, increasingly, especially in large cities, also gave general legal advice outside litigation. Though the analogy could not be pushed too far, there was, obviously, some similarity to English barristers. The *avoués* handled the written phases of procedure, and were considered as "representing" the parties, that is, as being the parties' agents; before certain courts, their use was compulsory. They practised only before a single court, while the *avocats* could practise anywhere in France. There was a limited similarity between the *avoués* and English solicitors. Before the two highest French Courts, the *Cour de Cassation* (for general civil and criminal litigation) and the *Conseil d'Etat*, the *avocats au Conseil d'Etat et à la Cour de Cassation* combine the functions of the *avocats* and of the *avoués* before the lower courts. Their number is quite limited (about 60). Certain documents in the fields of matrimonial property, land transactions and succession, and some other documents must be prepared by the *notaires* and other documents in the three areas mentioned are customarily prepared by these individuals, who are legally trained.

[5] On the French Code of Civil Procedure of 1806 and its history see *e.g.*, P. Herzog, *Civil Procedure in France* (hereinafter cited as Herzog) (1967), pp. 48–53. On the relationship between the reform of the legal profession and the reform of civil procedure, see Giverdon, "Observations sur une réforme" (1972) *Dalloz Chronique* (hereinafter abbreviated D.Chr.), pp. 103, 104. On the innovations of the 1971 decree on civil procedure, see Motulsky, "Prolégomènes pour un futur code de procédure civile: la consécration des principes directeurs du procès civil par le décret du 9 Septembre 1971," (1972) D.Chr. 91 (with numerous comparative law references concerning the general principles of civil procedure).

[6] On the various legal professions in France see Herzog at pp. 66–112.

All the professions just mentioned are closely regulated.[7] Traditionally, however, the giving of legal advice as such had not been regulated in France. Consequently, numerous persons calling themselves usually *conseils juridiques* (legal counsellors) or *agents d'affaires* (literally, business agents) had been giving legal advice in France and preparing documents not reserved for the *notaires*. Such activities were not limited to individuals; especially in the fairly recent past, companies, sometimes with numerous branches, had entered the field, particularly in connection with legal problems affecting business enterprises. These companies are generally known as *sociétés fiduciaires* (" fiduciary " companies), but have nothing to do with English or American trusts.[8] Their development was helped by the rules circumscribing the fields of activities of the various legal professions and by a tendency, now much diminished, on the part of many *avocats* (whose activities were least narrowly defined by law) to view themselves mainly as oral advocates, rather than general advisers of their clients.

This state of affairs has been the subject of much criticism. Reform was helped along by one of the fundamental notions underlying Gaullist action, namely that France needed to modernise its institutions in order to compete effectively with its partners in the Common Market.[9] The idea of a reform in this field is, however, much older; as early as 1902, Georges Clémenceau had introduced a Bill in the French Parliament providing for the merger of the professions of *avocat* and *avoué*.[10] Furthermore, the example of the Alsace-Lorraine region of France, where the division of the legal professions into *avocats* and *avoués*, abolished after the German conquest in 1871 was not restored after France reacquired these areas

7 Often the exercise of disciplinary powers is entrusted by law, at least in the first instance, to the various professional organisations, membership in which is compulsory. See Herzog, *supra*, n. 6.

8 According to a recent speech by the French Minister of Justice, there are, at present about 5,000 *conseils juridiques* in France as compared with about 7,000 former *avocats* and about 1,500 former *avoués* before the courts of first instance. *Le Figaro*, Oct. 15, 1971. In contrast to the somewhat " commercial " organisation of the *sociétés fiduciaires* who may have numerous branches or subsidiaries, the *avocats* practise predominantly as individual practitioners and have an office with a minimal number of employees. In 1968, a French author found that of 3,628 *avocats* 1,277 had no employees, 1,194 had one employee and 10 only had more than seven. Laroche-Flavin, *La machine judiciaire*, p. 42 (1968). But this state of affairs is gradually changing and some larger " law firms " have come into being. *Cf. infra* text at nn. 67–69.

9 The list of reforms adopted since the Fifth Republic came into being is very large; among the more important could be mentioned the reform of the Constitution itself in 1958, a reform of the French system of judicial administration, a reform of matrimonial property law, a reform of company law, a reform concerning affiliation and many others. It will be remembered that one of General De Gaulle's favourite reform projects, the creation of new administrative regions, led to his abdication when it was rejected in a referendum in April 1969.

10 For a review of the Bill, see the Special Supplement to (1971) *Recueil Dalloz*, No. 18.

in 1918, showed that a unified legal profession had advantages.[11] The rules of the EEC Treaty concerning free movement of services and freedom of establishment [12] were some further incentive to bring the French legal profession into somewhat closer alignment with that of the other member States, quite apart from the need created by that Treaty for a more effective and efficient system of giving legal advice to enterprises and protecting their rights. In addition, over the years, a number of measures had been enacted making it unnecessary to use *avoués* in certain types of proceedings, though initially their use had been compulsory, except in the very lowest courts. As a result, a certain decline had taken place in the profession of *avoué*, their number having decreased from about 3,500 around the turn of the century to about 1,500 at present.

The idea of a reform of the legal professions was favoured by many who felt that the distinction between litigation and the giving of legal advice was artificial, since these two matters were often closely related; in their view, good service for the client required that all his legal needs be taken care of in a comprehensive manner by well-trained and adequately supervised professionals. Logically, this notion leads to a merger of the professions mainly concerned with litigious work with the *conseils judiciaires*, etc. This so-called " great reform " was favoured in particular by the *Association Nationale des Avocats*.[13] It also seems to have received the approval of the Ministry of Justice.[14] Others favoured merely what has since been referred to as the " small reform," a merger of the professions of *avocat* and *avoué* in order to save clients the trouble and expense of having to deal with two sets of professionals during litigation, a reform which, considering the relative numbers of *avocats* and *avoués* would practically amount to absorption of the *avoués* by the *avocats*. It should be mentioned that numerous members of the legal professions rejected both the " great " and the " small " reform, feeling that a more effective administration of justice in France required better equipment for the courts, more funds for personnel, and the like, rather than new legislation.[15]

[11] *Cf.* Herzog at pp. 50–51; Cahn, " Pour les avocats et les avoués d'Alsace la réforme est déjà faite," *Le Monde*, June 21–22, 1970, p. 15.

[12] Treaty Establishing a European Economic Community, March 25, 1957, 298 U.N.T.S. 140, Arts. 52–66.

[13] See, in particular, Association Nationale des Avocats, *Au service de la Justice, la Profession Judiciaire de Demain* (1966). The Association Nationale is a " private " organisation, separate from the " official " bar organisation.

[14] See the statement of Mr. René Pleven, Minister of Justice, of Oct. 25, 1969, as reported in *Gazette du Palais*, Dec. 20–23, 1969.

[15] Critical comments are numerous. See, *e.g.*, Bordier, " La réforme des institutions judiciaires," *Le Monde*, April 4, 1970 (M. Bordier is a young lawyer): Cayol, " L'Opinion des jeunes avocats," *Le Monde*, March 28, 1970 (M. Cayol is president of an association of young lawyers, the *Union des Jeunes Avocats*); Jegou, " L'Avis d'un Bâtonnier," *Le Monde*, March 28, 1970 (M. Jegou is

The law which was finally approved by the French Parliament on December 31, 1971 [16] prudently avoided extremes. In essence, it sanctions the " small reform," but it also marks at least the beginning of a regulation of the *conseils juridiques*. Furthermore, it holds out the possibility of more far-reaching reform in the future. In this connection, it is worth noting that the original draft of the law bore the title " Reform of the Legal Profession," while the law, as actually adopted has the more modest title " Reform of Some Legal Professions." [17]

### *B. Legal Aid*

The system of legal aid in France, as established by a law of January 22, 1851, since amended several times, in particular by a decree of December 22, 1958,[18] but never fundamentally changed, has often been criticised.[19] Legal aid could be granted to individuals and to certain associations if they could show that they possessed insufficient means to protect their rights in litigation. Legal aid could be granted for proceedings in civil (including commercial) and criminal courts, and to plaintiffs as well as defendants. The person seeking it had to address a petition to the mayor of his municipality or to the procurator of the Republic attached to the court where he wished to litigate. These officials then transmitted the petition to a " legal aid bureau " composed of *avocats*, *avoués*, retired judges and representatives of the French tax administration. The legal aid bureau could grant legal aid if it felt that the party who sought it had a reasonable chance of success in court, and insufficient means, taking into account the expected costs of litigation. Unfortunately, the law gave no adequate guidance for judging financial need, resulting in much inconsistency, and the need to show what amounted to a " good case " in effect led to a preliminary judgment of the matter by the legal aid bureau. While reasons had to be given for a denial of legal aid, only the procurator of the Republic, and not the parties, could appeal. When legal aid was granted, an *avocat* and an *avoué* were assigned to the party seeking it; no compensation was given these professionals from any government source, a fact which sometimes made their clients wonder whether they would really use their best

president (*bâtonnier*) of the Rheims bar). Many critical articles have been published in the *Gazette du Palais* for 1970; they are too numerous to be listed here.

[16] See *supra*, n. 1.

[17] It is interesting in this connection to compare the final text of the law with the original draft, as reviewed in a special supplement to (1971) *Recueil Dalloz*, No. 18. Even the change in title is significant.

[18] Law of Jan. 22, 1851, *Bulletin Officiel* No. 2680, 1851 D.4. 25; Décret No. 58–1289 of Dec. 22, 1958, J.O. Dec. 23, 1958, p. 11608, (1959) D.L.49.

[19] See *e.g.*, Cappelletti and Gordley, " Legal Aid: Modern Themes and Variations," (1972) 24 Stanford L.Rev. 347.

efforts. Furthermore, the *avocats* assigned most often were the youngest members of the bar (called *avocats stagiaires*) who, though having passed the bar examination and sworn the professional oath, had not yet received their final, permanent admission.[20] Consequently, applications for legal aid have in fact diminished in the last few years, apparently as a result of mistrust of the institution by the people.[21] In other countries, with better legal aid systems, no such trend was visible.[22] The law of January 3, 1972 [23] attempts to remedy existing defects and in essence to replace charity by social consciousness. In fact, while the former scheme of legal aid was called "*assistance judiciaire*" a term which has connotations of charity and welfare, the new scheme is entitled "*aide judiciaire,*" a term connoting rather ideas of social security.[24]

## III. THE REFORM OF THE LEGAL PROFESSIONS

### *A. The Merger of the Professions of* Avocat *and* Avoué

As has been noted above, the most important aspect of the reform of the legal professions is the merger of the *avocats* and of the *avoués*;[25] as also noted, the goal of a unified legal profession encompassing all individuals involved in a professional capacity in giving legal advice or conducting litigation was not accomplished. But even within the narrower compass of a merger of the professions of *avocats* and

[20] See generally, Herzog at pp. 545–550.

[21] In the Report by De Grailly, *supra*, n. 3 at p. 13, the following statistics are given concerning annual requests for legal aid:

| Year | Number of Requests |
|---|---|
| 1851 | 8,303 |
| 1935 | 115,099 |
| 1968 | 58,616 |

These statistics become even more startling if one considers the increase in litigation during the same period.

[22] For a comparison of legal aid systems in the U.K., the U.S.A., Italy and Germany see Oppetit, "L'aide judiciare" (1972) D.Chr. 41, 42–43. According to the author, the most complex legal aid system, which best insures to the poor free access to the courts, can be found in England. For a recent discussion in English, see Cappelletti and Gordley, *supra*, n. 19.

[23] *Supra* n. 2. The English example was apparently quite influential. M. De Grailly states in his report, *supra*, n. 3 at p. 67: "It is to be noted that the English system, which in many respects resembles the one proposed by our committee, has achieved substantial success."

[24] The same idea underlies the development of the French social security system, in particular since the end of the Second World War, as well as developments in other fields, such as education. For a somewhat dated description of social security in France, see Rodgers, "Social Security in France" (1953) 31 *Public Administration* 377.

[25] In fact, the merger encompasses one other profession, that of the so-called *agréés*. These individuals could perform the functions of *avocats* and *avoués* before the commercial court, but before no others; they had no monopoly and in fact their number was always quite small, probably not in excess of about 150. On the *agréés*, see Herzog, pp. 90–92.

*avoués*,[26] the reform is not complete. In particular, the reform concerns all *avocats*, but only the *avoués* practising before one of the courts of first instance (*tribunal de grande instance*); (as noted, *avoués* are limited in their practice to a particular court). The *avoués* practising before the intermediate appellate courts in France, the *cours d'appel*, remain unaffected by the reform and continue their practice as before.[27] This seems to be due more to a desire to avoid problems in the administration of justice than to a wish to protect any vested interests. In the first place, the area over which a *cour d'appel* may have jurisdiction is sometimes quite large; it thus seemed reasonable to leave the accomplishment of procedural formalities to practitioners already established at the seat of the court, rather than requiring others to travel there repeatedly. Furthermore, the procedure before the *cours d'appel* is complex, since these courts have the power to conduct what amounts to a *de novo* hearing in which all the procedural complications possible before the courts of first instance (intervention, etc.) may arise; but in addition, the *cours d'appel* also review the legal correctness of the decisions rendered by the lower courts. This double function of the *cours d'appel* [28] requires real specialists for effective practice before them, thus providing another reason for leaving the function of the *avoués* practising before the *cours d'appel* untouched.[29] In addition, their number is quite small; before the Paris *Cour d'Appel* which has a very large caseload, only about 50 *avoués* practise and the number is even smaller for the *cours d'appel* in the provinces. Somewhat similar reasons explain why the *Avocats au Conseil d'Etat et à la Cour de Cassation* were not included in the reform. The rules governing review by these high courts [30] are quite complex and can most easily be handled by specialists who devote their entire professional practice to this field.[31]

26 " Merger " means in effect that the members of either profession may now exercise the activities formerly reserved for the other. Law No. 71–1130, *supra*, n. 1, Art. 1 (1). However, by a statement addressed to the president of the local bar association, existing *avocats* and *avoués* may declare that they want to limit their future practice to the type of activity they exercised in the past. This statement can be revoked, but only once. Art. 1 (2).

27 *Cf.* Law No. 71–1130, *supra*, n. 1, Art. 4.

28 Herzog, pp. 376–420; *cf.* R. Schlesinger, *Comparative Law*, pp. 328–332 (3rd ed. 1970).

29 Lobin, " Réflexions sur certains aspects de la réforme des professions judiciaires," (1972) D.Chr. 35.

30 As to the *Cour de Cassation*, see Herzog, pp. 421–466. As to the *Conseil d'Etat* (Council of State) see *e.g.*, B. Schwartz, *French Administrative Law and the Common Law World*, pp. 192–249 (1954).

31 It should be remembered in this connection that the members of the new profession of *avocat* will be able to present oral argument before the *cours d'appel*, as *avocats* always have, but will not be able to act as parties' agents before them, that function being reserved to the *avoués* practising before those courts; before the *Cour de Cassation* and the *Conseil d'Etat*, however the *avocats au conseil*

The merger of the professions of *avocat* and *avoué* means that, with the exceptions indicated in the preceding paragraph, the members of each of those (former) professions may engage not only in the activities previously reserved to them, but also in the activities formerly reserved to the other profession. In other words, the members of the new profession created by the merger may present oral arguments in court as well as carry out all the necessary procedural formalities and act as their clients' agents for litigation. For these activities, the new profession has a monopoly, protected by criminal sanctions [32] except in certain limited instances.[33] But all former distinctions have not been abolished. The members of the new profession are able to present oral argument before courts anywhere in France, as was true of the *avocats* before the merger of the professions [34]; but as far as the functions formerly exercised by the *avoués* are concerned, namely to perform the procedural formalities and to act as a party's agent for litigation, territorial limitations exist. Normally, these functions may be exercised only before the *tribunal de grande instance* (court of first instance of general jurisdiction) which has jurisdiction for the area in which the member of the profession has his official residence. However, where an official regional bar association (*barreau*, of which all resident lawyers must be members) encompasses an area in which several *tribunaux de grande instance* function, its members may exercise the functions formerly reserved for the *avoués* before all these courts.[35] As noted, the *avoués* practising before the *cours d'appel* have not been merged with the *avocats*. Consequently, the members of the new profession may present oral argument before the *cours d'appel*, but not act as the parties' agents for litigation before them. And, as also noted, *all* aspects of practice before France's highest courts, the *Cour de Cassation* and the *Conseil d'Etat* remain reserved for the *avocats au Conseil d'Etat et à la Cour de Cassation.*

The merger of the professions of *avocat* and *avoué* means the abolition of a peculiarity going back to pre-revolutionary France, namely, the sale of *avoué's* offices. Under existing law and custom, the number of *avoués* before any one court was limited; while one

*d'Etat et à la Cour de Cassation* perform the functions formerly allocated to *avocats* and *avoués* in the lower courts; hence the *avocats* have no role whatever before these two courts, except in the limited instances in which the use of *avocats au Conseil d'Etat et à la Cour de Cassation* is not required.

32 Law No. 71–1130, *supra*, n. 1, Art. 72.

33 Law No. 71–1130, *supra*, n. 1, Art. 4 (2). In some cases, mainly involving small claims and matters related to labour law and social security, and a few others, a variety of persons (sometimes trade union officials, sometimes various other individuals) may appear in court for parties. See Herzog, pp. 66–67.

34 Law No. 71–1130, *supra*, n. 1, Art. 5 (1).

35 Law No. 71–1130, *supra*, n. 1, Art. 5 (2) and (3). In the Paris region, there are some other exceptions to the rule just mentioned.

had to be appointed an *avoué* by the Ministry of Justice, which meant that all legal qualifications concerning legal education, years of clerkship, etc. had to be fulfilled, the Ministry of Justice appointed only individuals who had been " presented " to it by a retiring *avoué* or by the heirs of a deceased *avoué*. Of course, the retiring *avoué* (or the heirs) was paid a substantial amount for this presentation; in substance, then, each *avoué* practising in France purchased a monopolistic position and expected to sell it upon retirement.[36] No such rule or custom had prevailed as to the *avocats*. A person could become an *avocat* upon fulfilment of the legal requirements as to education, experience, character, etc. without regard to the number of *avocats* already in practice and without any obligation to buy anybody else's practice. The new, merged profession follows that rule. Consequently, the *avoués* now exercising their profession lose the right to " present " their successor, that is, in substance, to sell their office.[37] It was felt that the loss of that right entailed a real deprivation of property for which compensation had to be paid. Consequently, a compensation scheme for the *avoués* was devised. The scheme has been criticised by some on the ground that the compensation given is far from " prompt, adequate and complete." [38] Compensation is paid through a newly organised fund with corporate personality, but under the control of the Minister of Justice and of the Minister of Economic Affairs and Finance. The Fund receives the proceeds of a new, so-called " para-fiscal " tax on lawsuits; it may also float loans guaranteed by the French State.[39] The Fund pays the indemnity to all *avoués*. The amount of compensation is between 4 and 5·5 times the average net income of the *avoué* in the last five years.[40] For *avoués* who have become members of the new profession, the indemnity will not be paid at once, however, but in instalments spread over six to eight years, depending on the amount to be paid. Unpaid instalments will be increased automatically to some extent in case of increases in the cost of living.[41] In some instances compensation is payable immediately, or at any rate within a year: this is mainly true in the case of deceased *avoués* (the payment is made to their heirs) and of *avoués* over 70 who chose not to join the merged profession; it is also true of *avoués* who have been repatriated from

36 See Herzog, pp. 83–84, 86. The present rule is based on a law enacted in 1816, but the practice has roots long antedating the French Revolution.

37 Law No. 71–1130, *supra*, n. 1, Art. 2.

38 Giverdon, *supra*, n. 5 at p. 107.

39 Law No. 71–1130, *supra*, n. 1, Art. 28. The details as to the operation of the Fund are contained in Décret No. 72–336 of April 21, 1972, J.O. May 3, 1972, p. 4563, (1972) D.L. 228. The " para-fiscal " tax has been established by Décret No. 72–337 of April 21, 1972, J.O. May 3, 1972, p. 4566, (1972) D.L. 232.

40 Law No. 71–1130, *supra*, n. 1, Art. 29.

41 Law No. 71–1130, *supra*, n. 1, Art. 32.

Algeria. Detailed rules on compensation are complex.[42] The exact amount of compensation is to be determined by regional commissions composed of representatives of the professions involved and of the Ministry of Finance, and presided over by a judge or procurator (*magistrat*) appointed by the Minister of Justice. Appeal to a Central Commission and further review by the Council of State (*Conseil d'Etat*) is possible.[43]

### B. *Rules Governing the New Profession*

The members of the new, merged profession, will be called *avocats.* They may, however, indicate their speciality (if any) following that title. Former *avoués* may also indicate that fact.[44] As noted before, they will be able to act as their clients' agents for litigation, carry out all procedural formalities and present oral argument, subject to the exceptions also noted. They may represent clients before administrative authorities.[45] Of course, they are entitled to give legal advice, and to prepare most legal documents. However, in this field, the members of the new profession have no exclusive rights; the *conseils juridiques* (and to some extent, other persons) may continue to perform these functions (subject to the restrictions to be discussed later). Some functions in this field are also performed by other "regulated" professions, such as the notaries.

Since all the members of the new profession now have the possibility of "representing" clients and thus also of handling clients' funds (this was formerly possible for the *avocats* only to a rather limited extent),[46] it was felt that the measures formerly existing in both professions for the protection of clients had to be continued and even strengthened. Each member of the new profession must now carry either individual malpractice insurance or malpractice insurance under a group policy entered into by the bar association (*barreau*) to which he belongs. He must either carry separate insurance or have some other form of guarantee (which may also be provided by the bar association) to secure the return of funds obtained on behalf of

42 Law No. 71-1130, *supra,* n. 1, Arts. 30, 31, 33. Procedural rules are contained in Décret No. 72-336, *supra,* n. 39, Arts. 14-31.

43 Law No. 71-1130, *supra,* n. 1, Art. 41. A series of decrees (Décrets No. 72-758—72-764 of Aug. 8, 1972, J.O. Aug. 19, 1972) make it easier for former *avoués* who do not wish to become members of the new merged profession, to join one of the other regulated legal professions; in some instances, these rules also apply to *avocats.*

44 Law No. 71-1130, *supra,* n. 1, Art. 1 (1).

45 Law No. 71-1130, *supra,* n. 1, Art. 6.

46 Until 1954, only the *avoués* handled clients' funds, since only they were considered as their clients' agents; the *avocats* did not. Since 1954, the *avocats* have been allowed to handle clients' funds in some limited situations, in which parties were not required to use *avoués* but special precautions were taken to protect clients' funds against dangers of misappropriation. *Cf.* J. Lemaire, *Les règles de la profession d'avocat et les usages du barreau de Paris,* pp. 264-268 (rev. ed. 1966).

clients. A third, again separate, kind of insurance is necessary if the *avocat* wishes (and is authorised, see below) to engage in some functions somewhat outside the immediate scope of his profession by being a member of a company's board of directors or by being a trustee in bankruptcy or the like. The president (*bâtonnier*) of each bar association must keep the appropriate procurator of the Republic informed about the status of the insurance just mentioned; the procurator apparently has a certain power of supervision in the matter.[47] These measures should foster public confidence in the new profession.

Since the profession is to be " liberal " and " independent,"[48] its members are barred from engaging in certain activities. In particular, they may not engage in business activities, nor be president of a company, etc. Normally, they may not enter into a contract of employment; they may, however, perform teaching functions. If they are elected to the French National Assembly, they may continue to exercise their profession, but are subject to a number of restrictions designed to avoid conflicts of interests. The same applies to *avocats* elected to municipal councils. *Avocats* may be members of a board of directors (*conseil de surveillance*) only with the consent of their bar association. Except in certain unusual situations, and for a limited time, an *avocat* may not hold a public office, except certain elective offices, such as that of deputy to the National Assembly, or member of a municipal or departmental council.[49]

What has been said shows that the members of the new profession are intended to exercise it with as much independence as possible. In this connection it is worth noting that the original Bill, in its Article 7 provided that the *avocat* was an officer of the court (*auxi-*

[47] Law No. 72–1130, *supra*, n. 1, Arts. 26, 27. The rules as to the various types of insurance and guarantee *avocats* must maintain in force are amplified in a Décret No. 72–783 of Aug. 25, 1972, J.O. Aug. 29, 1972, p. 9279, (1972) D.L. 469. That Décret also contains fairly detailed rules as to bookkeeping procedures that must be followed by *avocats*. Clients' funds, for instance, must always be deposited in a special account used only for that purpose. Even more detailed rules as to insurance and accounting procedures are contained in two regulations issued by the Ministry of Justice also on Aug. 25, 1972, and published in the French *Journal Officiel* on Aug. 29, 1972. Furthermore, the Ministry of Economics and Finance promulgated a regulation on Sept. 18, 1972, J.O. Sept. 19, 1972, containing standard clauses for the *avocats'* professional liability insurance.

The precise language of the Décret No. 72–783 caused some controversy. An early draft of the decree seems to have contained even more detailed rules as to bookkeeping procedures, including provisions for governmental checks of *avocats'* accounts, but provoked too much opposition to be adopted.

[48] Law No. 71–1130, *supra*, n. 1, Art. 14. See also the administrative regulation implementing the law, *i.e.*, Décret No. 72–468 of June 9, 1972, J.O. June 11, 1972, p. 5884, (1972) D.L. 268, Arts. 57–69.

[49] To the limited extent that *avocats* may hold a public office, they are subject to a variety of restrictions; in particular, they may not accept any business as *avocats* which involves the governmental unit where they hold the office. Sometimes, the restrictions are even more far-reaching. Décret No. 72–468, *supra*, n. 48, Arts. 63–69.

*liaire de la justice*) who had to cooperate in the administration of justice.[50] At the insistence of the bar, this was modified, so that Article 7 of the law as actually adopted, merely states that the profession is " independent " and " liberal."

For the giving of legal advice, the drafting of documents and the presentation of oral argument in court, there are no officially prescribed fees; fees are fixed by agreement between the *avocat* and his client. However, contingent fees are illegal.[51] This is to be regretted since the experience in other countries has shown that the contingent fee system can be one way for the poor to secure effective legal counsel. The functions formerly reserved for the *avoués*, namely the performance of procedural formalities, have traditionally been governed by official fee schedules in France, and this remains the case.[52]

The professional organisation of the new profession is quite similar to that of the former *avocats*. Each practitioner must be a member of his local bar association or *barreau* which is governed by an elected executive council (*conseil de l'ordre*) and a president (*bâtonnier*), also elected.[53] The *conseil de l'ordre* should see to it that all *avocats* member of the association fulfil their duties and, on the other hand, that their interests are protected. In furtherance of its duties, it may enact by-laws.[54] It exercises disciplinary powers over the *avocats* in its association.[55] It also has some powers over the admission of young attorneys following their trial period (*stage*), which will be discussed later. Decisions of the *conseil de l'ordre* are subject to review by the regional intermediate appellate court, the *cour d'appel*.[56]

As has been noted, many new trends, such as the creation of the European Communities, the increasing complexities of new rules and

[50] *Cf. supra*, n. 10. See also Giverdon *supra*, n. 5.

[51] Law No. 71–1130, *supra*, n. 1, Art. 10.

[52] *Ibid.* Décret No. 72–784 of Aug. 25, 1972, J.O. Aug. 29, 1972. For a general discussion of the fee schedule applicable to the former *avoués* see Herzog at pp. 536–537. The " fixed " fee there mentioned has subsequently been increased from F.25 to F.36. See Dalloz, *Répertoire de Procédure Civile et Commerciale*, *Frais et Dépens* at Nos. 96–102 (Supp. 1972). A revision of the fee schedule is contemplated.

[53] Law No. 71–1130, *supra*, n. 1, Art. 15.

[54] Law No. 71–1130, *supra*, n. 1, Art. 17.

[55] Law No. 71–1130, *supra*, n. 1, Arts. 22–25; Décret No. 72–468, *supra*, n. 48, Arts. 104–126 contains additional rules on discipline, in particular as to the procedure to be followed.

[56] Law No. 71–1130, *supra*, n. 1, Arts. 12–14, 18; Décret No. 72–468, *supra*, n. 48, Arts. 26–36. Local branches of these institutions may be established in cities in which law faculties (more precisely, what since the University reforms of 1968 are called U.E.R.'s (*unites d'études et de recherches*) ) are located. In addition to these functions the institutes are also to assist the law faculties in providing some supplemental instruction of a more practical nature to law students intending to become *avocats* and, hence, to take the appropriate qualifying examination.

regulations, the emergence of multinational corporations, etc. are changing the previous emphasis of the French *avocats* on litigation. In addition, the merger of the former professions gives all the members of the new profession an opportunity to perform activities to which they were not formerly accustomed. This not only implies a need for a better legal education for new members of the profession, but also for substantial efforts in the field of continuing legal education. These goals are to be achieved by a joint effort of the various regional bar associations (no official national association encompassing all regional associations has been created), and of the French Republic. The Republic contributes part of the cost of this education, which will be dispensed at Centres for Professional Legal Education created at the seat of each regional *cour d'appel*. The teaching staff will consist of members of the profession, as well as judges, procurators and law teachers from the universities.[57]

As noted, one of the functions of the new centres will be continuing legal education. However, they also assist in the education of new lawyers. To become a new member of the profession, the candidate must have obtained the degree of *licencié* in law (requiring four years of study) or a doctorate in law (requiring additional course work and a thesis) from a French University.[58] He must then pass a professional examination, give some evidence of good character and take an oath of office as *avocat*, after which he receives the title *avocat stagiaire*.[59] This could be translated as *avocat* undergoing his apprenticeship period or *stage*. The period normally lasts three years, during which time the *avocat stagiaire* must always use that title rather than simply *avocat*. He must attend the educational programmes to be organised by the new Centres for Professional Legal Education; in addition he must, during that period, work in the office of an *avocat*, or of a *conseil juridique*, or a notary (*notaire*) or an *avoué* before the *cour d'appel*, the wide range of these options indicating that an eventual merger of all these professions is contemplated. For a period of one year, he may also work in a law office abroad, or for some public body.[60] The *avocat stagiaire* may,

57 See Décret No. 72–468, *supra*, n. 48.

58 Law No. 71–1130, *supra*, n. 1, Art. 11.

59 Law No. 71–1130, *supra*, n. 1, Art. 11; Décret No. 72–468, *supra*, n. 48, Arts. 19–25. It is to be noted that the professional examination may be undertaken only by students, who, during their fourth year of law study, or subsequent to the completion of their legal studies, have attended special courses of instruction dealing with matters of particular interest to the legal profession given at special institutes or teaching units at a university. Students having completed that course and passed the examnation are issued a special certificate, called *certificat d'aptitude à la profession d'avocat*. For the detailed rules concerning the certificate, and the course of studies and examination necessary to obtain it, see Décret No. 72–715 of July 31, 1972, J.O. Aug. 3, 1972, p. 8366, (1972) D.L. 451.

60 Décret No. 72–468, *supra*, n. 48, Arts. 37–42.

however, appear in court on his own during the *stage* period.[61] If the *avocat stagiaire* has, in the opinion of the *conseil de l'ordre*, performed his duties satisfactorily during the three-year *stage* period, he is then admitted as a regular *avocat*, with all the rights attached thereto, including the right to participate in the elections for the members of the *conseil de l'ordre*, etc.[62]

In part, undoubtedly, to facilitate an eventual merger of all the legal professions, some persons already exercising a law-related profession or occupation may become *avocats* without undergoing the three-year *stage*. Former judges, certain law teachers, *conseils juridiques* and *notaires* having a *licence* or doctoral degree in law and (in some cases) more than five years' actual experience in their profession may be admitted as *avocats*.[63] Subject to the same educational requirements, this is also possible for legal advisers employed by business firms, provided they have at least eight years' experience. (An *avocat* cannot perform the functions performed in the United States, for instance, by " house counsel," since, as noted, he may not be in an employee relationship.) The " clerks " of the former *avoués* before the courts of first instance may also, under some conditions, be admitted as *avocats* without undergoing the three-year *stage*.[64]

It is perhaps worth noting here that the new law does away with a particularly discriminatory rule formerly in existence concerning the admission of new members of the legal professions: while it is still necessary to be a French national to be admitted as *avocat*, the requirement that naturalised citizens must have been naturalised for at least five years before admission has been dropped.[65]

[61] Décret No. 72–468, *supra*, n. 48, Art. 38. In fact, he may engage in all activities in which a regular *avocat* may engage, including the giving of legal advice, but all of this only to the extent that the obligations imposed upon him—attendance at instruction, work for his employer, etc.—do not suffer.

[62] Law No. 71–1130, *supra*, n. 1, Art. 17 (1); Décret No. 72–468, *supra*, n. 48, Arts. 1, 3, 43–47. This decree also provides a procedure for judicial review of decisions of the *conseil de l'ordre*.

[63] Law No. 71–1130, *supra*, n. 1, Art. 50; Décret No. 72–468, *supra*, n. 48, Art. 44.

[64] Law No. 71–1130, *supra*, n. 1, Art. 50 (3); Décret No. 72–468, *supra*, n. 48, Art. 44 (10). The list here given is not complete; for further details see the references cited in this and preceding footnotes.

[65] The present rule is contained in Art. 11 (1) of Law No. 71–1130, *supra*, n. 1. The requirement that applicants for the bar had to be French nationals for at least five years was contained in the Code of French Nationality, *Ordonnance* of Oct. 19, 1945, (1946) D.L. 10, Art. 81 (3). This provision seemed to have been impliedly abrogated by Art. 11 (1) of the Law No. 71–1130. See Dalloz, *Répertoire de Procédure Civile et Commerciale*, *Avocat*, No. 15–2 (Supp. 1972). However, when in the autumn of 1972, the French Government proposed the draft of a revised Code of French Nationality to the French Parliament, the five-year rule of Art. 81 was still part of the new draft Code. It was, however, removed at the request of the appropriate Parliamentary Committee, so that the new Code of Nationality and Law No. 71–1130 are perfectly consistent on this point. See J.O. (Débats Assemblée Nationale), Dec. 14, 1972, pp. 6110, 6111, 6115, 6116. The authors of this article express their appreciation to Prof. Paul Lagarde of the University of Paris for information on this point.

In the past, French *avocats* traditionally exercised their profession as individual practitioners, very often from an office located in their own home. The same was true of *avoués*. Until 1954, "solo" practice was, in fact, required by law.[66] At present, there is a slow, but noticeable trend toward the creation of "law firms" of some sort, especially in some of the large urban centres, where both the need and the opportunity for professional specialisation is greatest. This trend was accelerated in 1969, when a 1966 law relating to professional partnerships (*sociétés civiles professionelles*)[67] was made applicable to the *avocats*.[68] The law on the reorganised profession now provides a variety of options: *avocats* may practise as individual practitioners, or several *avocats* may associate themselves in a simple office-sharing arrangement, or they may form a regular partnership (*société civile professionelle*).[69] In addition, an *avocat* may also work as a collaborator of another *avocat* or partnership pursuant to a written contract.[70] Such a contract is subject to review by the appropriate *conseil de l'ordre*. Some care has been taken to preserve the professional integrity of the "employed" lawyer in these instances, while, at the same time, permitting adequate supervision by the "employer" lawyers, on whom the liability towards the client

66 A somewhat restrictive form of association between *avocats* was first authorised in 1954; at that time no more than five *avocats* could associate with each other. Initially, even this limited type of "law firm" was not very prevalent, and in particular not outside Paris. See Herzog at p. 81.

67 The law on professional partnerships (*sociétés civiles professionnelles*) is the Law No. 66–879 of Nov. 29, 1966, (1966) D.L. 422. It permits the formation of *sociétés* between persons engaged in practising the same profession, in spite of contrary rules requiring individual practice. The law was to be applicable only to those professions as to which a special implementing decree was promulgated. In this article, the term "partnership" "professional partnership" or sometimes "law firm" has been employed to translate *société civile professionelle*, in order to use reasonably idiomatic English, but this is not entirely correct. In the French view, a *société civile professionnelle*, which is merely a somewhat special case of the *société civile*, enjoys legal (corporate) personality even though there is no limitation of liability; its members are fully personally liable for its obligations. In actual practice, but not conceptually, a *société civile professionnelle* is thus rather similar to an English or American partnership. *Cf.* Amos and Walton, *Introduction to French Law*, pp. 51–52 (3rd ed. 1967, by Lawson, Anton and Brown).

68 Décret No. 69–1056 of Nov. 20, 1969, (1969) D.L. 411. At the same time, a Décret No. 69–1057 of Nov. 20, 1969, (1969) D.L. 416 made the law on *sociétés civiles professionnelles* applicable to *avoués*. It would seem that a revision of the law on *sociétés civiles professionnelles* is contemplated.

69 Law No. 71–1130, *supra*, n. 1, Art. 8. As to the sense in which the term "partnership" has been used, see *supra*, n. 67. In view of the reorganisation of the legal profession, it became necessary to enact a new decree to implement the law on professional partnerships, *supra*, n. 67, to make it applicable to the new profession of *avocat* which came into being on Sept. 16, 1972. This was done by Décret No. 72–669 of July 13, 1972, J.O. July 17–18, 1972, p. 7550. Somewhat more detailed rules as to what has here been called an office-sharing arrangement (*association*) are found in Décret No. 72–468, *supra*, n. 48, Arts. 70–73. *Cf.* Sialelli, "la réforme des professions judiciaires et juridiques: profession libérale, office ministériel, société commerciale," (1970) D.Chr. 13, 15.

70 Law No. 71–1130, *supra*, n. 1, Art. 8.

remains.[71] That so many different forms of professional association between *avocats* are now possible is a clear indication that the law wishes to favour the trend in that direction, not only because some form of group practice is normally essential for a specialisation that becomes increasingly necessary, but also because modern methods of office management, which can significantly increase the efficiency and productivity of lawyers, are possible only in offices of a size adequate to warrant expenditures for necessary equipment and the like. Nevertheless, some restrictions on partnerships between *avocats* have been established, primarily to facilitate the exercise of the disciplinary powers of the bar associations over their members. Thus, a partnership (*société civile professionnelle*) may consist only of *avocats* who are members of the same *barreau*, or at least of *barreaux* located within the jurisdictional area of the same intermediate appellate court (*cour d'appel*).[72]

### C. *The Regulation of the Unofficial Legal Advisers*

The law providing for the creation of the new profession of *avocat* through the merger of the former professions of *avocat* and *avoué* for the first time also regulates the giving of legal advice by others than the members of the regulated legal professions (*avocats, notaires*).[73] Apparently there have been two reasons for this: it was felt that some control should be exercised over the numerous individuals giving legal advice in order to protect the public and the way was to be prepared for an eventual " great reform " leading to the creation of a single legal profession.[74] A special commission, which is to make proposals to the Minister of Justice for that purpose within five years, is, in fact, to be set up.[75] It has been said that this casts doubts on the future of the *conseils juridiques*.[76] However, the reform that has now gone into effect is rather limited in scope. Except as provided in a " grandfather clause " protecting to some

71 Décret No. 72–468, *supra*, n. 48, Arts. 74–81. The provisions cited in this and the preceding footnote are the first legislative or quasi-legislative recognition of a practice which has been in some use in the recent past.

72 Law No. 71–1130, *supra*, n. 1, Art. 8 (5).

73 The issue whether and to what extent the giving of legal advice by others than members of the previously regulated professions should be regulated was one of the principal bones of contention during the enactment of the law on the reform of certain legal professions. See the Report by Mr. Zimmerman, reporter, on behalf of the Committee on Constitutional Laws, Legislation and General Administration on the Bill, modified by the Senate, concerning the reform of certain legal professions. French National Assembly, Report No. 2100, T. 1, pp. 2–5 (1971–72).

74 See *supra*, text at nn. 13 and 14.

75 Law No. 71–1130, *supra*, n. 1, Art. 78.

76 Giverdon, *supra*, n. 5 at p. 112.

extent persons currently calling themselves by these titles,[77] a person may not, from now on, call himself *conseil juridique* or *conseil fiscal* (tax adviser) unless he has been registered on a special list to be established for that purpose by each procurator of the Republic. To be registered on the list, the applicant must show that he possesses the degree of *licencié* in law, or a doctorate in law, or certain other diplomas considered as equivalent, and that he fulfils the same criteria as to good character which *avocats* must fulfil.[78] Furthermore, he must have at least three years' experience as clerk of a *conseil juridique*, or of a *notaire* or of an *avocat au Conseil d'Etat et à la Cour de Cassation*, or as *avocat stagiaire*.[79] Persons wishing to hold themselves out as being a tax or other expert must fulfil additional requirements.[80]

The members of certain professions and occupations who are likely to possess extensive legal knowledge may under some conditions (including, at times, the passing of an examination) be registered on the list without full compliance with all the requirements just mentioned.[81] Persons not registered on the list of *conseillers juridiques* may not, of course, use that title, nor may they use any designation which, in the mind of the public, is likely to lead to confusion with the title *conseiller juridique* (or *conseiller fiscal, i.e.* tax adviser).[82] But as long as they do not violate that rule, persons not on the list may continue to give legal advice for compensation.[83] Fear of repercussions from unions and other organisations that provide legal advice was apparently the reason for this. However, even persons not calling themselves *conseils juridiques* and therefore not subject to the detailed regulation which now applies to the *conseils juridiques* are covered by some rules intended to insure a greater protection of the public. In particular, nobody may give legal advice on a formal basis or prepare legal documents if he has been convicted of a crime or misdemeanour involving what could best be translated as " moral turpitude," if, for the same reason, he has been suspended from some profession, or received a disciplinary penalty

77 Law No. 71-1130, *supra*, n. 1, Art. 61. Required even for persons who practised on July 1, 1971, are either the standard law degree (*licence*) (or certain equivaents), or a minor law degree known as *capacité* and three years' practice, or five years' practice.

78 Law No. 71-1130, *supra*, n. 1, Art. 54. This has been implemented by Décret No. 72-670 of July 13, 1972, J.O. July 17-18, 1972, p. 7556, Arts. 1, 2.

79 Law No. 71-1130, *supra*, n. 1, Art. 54 (2); Décret No. 72-670, *supra*, n. 78, Arts. 3, 4.

80 The following specialties may be mentioned: tax law, social legislation (this would include labour law), corporation law. Décret No. 72-670, *supra*, n. 78, Arts. 8-18.

81 Décret No. 72-670, *supra*, n. 78, Art. 5.

82 Law No. 71-1130, *supra*, n. 1, Art. 74.

83 See the report by Mr. Zimmerman, *supra*, n. 73 at p. 2.

or the like and, under some conditions, if he has been declared a bankrupt. Furthermore, the court of first instance (*tribunal de grande instance*) may, at the request of the procurator of the Republic, order any persons giving legal advice on a formal basis to cease doing so if they are guilty of conduct involving "moral turpitude," even though no criminal or disciplinary sanction has been imposed upon them for that reason.[84]

Special rules are applicable to the foreign lawyers who practise in France (predominantly in Paris). Of course, they were never entitled to hold themselves out as French *avocats,* since French nationality was always a requirement for that profession.[85] However, since their activities were limited to the giving of legal advice and to the preparation of documents, they violated no law, since these activities were not subject to regulation. This has now been changed, though to a limited extent only. Foreigners may give legal advice in France and prepare documents only in matters principally related to foreign or international law; furthermore, they must be registered on the list of *conseillers juridiques* to be established by the procurators of the Republic. Both limitations are inapplicable to individuals who are nationals of member States of the European Economic Communities, to individuals of States who permit French nationals to exercise the activities they wish to exercise in France [86] and to individuals who effectively practised in France on July 1, 1971.[87] For foreign "law firms" however, separate rules prevail, which will be discussed below. Since French nationality is a requirement for the profession of *conseil juridique* only to the extent just mentioned, nationals of member States of the European Economic Community may exercise that profession in France (subject to the general French rules relating to aliens) without waiting for the enactment, by the Council of the European Communities of rules concerning the liberalisation of freedom of establishment in the legal field.[88]

It has been mentioned above that the giving of legal advice in France, especially in fields of law relating to business activities, is often performed by companies, frequently of large size, called *sociétés fiduciaires.*[89] In the future, *conseils juridiques* will be able to establish new firms only in the form of the special partnership for pro-

[84] Law No. 71–1130, *supra,* n. 1, Art. 67.

[85] See *supra,* n. 65.

[86] Law No. 71–1130, *supra,* n. 1, Art. 55.

[87] Law No. 71–1130, *supra,* n. 1, Art. 64.

[88] On the current status of the proposals of the Commission of the European Communities concerning directives relating to freedom of establishment for lawyers, tax advisers, etc., see European Communities, Commission, *Fourth General Report on the Activities of the Communities* at No. 53 (1971); *Fifth General Report on the Activities of the Communities* at Nos. 156, 157 (1972).

[89] See *supra,* n. 8; *cf.* Sialelli, *supra,* n. 69.

fessional people called *société civile professionelle*.[90] Existing *sociétés fiduciaires*, however, may ask to be registered on the list of *conseils juridiques* provided within five years from September 16, 1972, all their shares will be in the form of " nominative " shares (issued in the name of a definite person), more than half the total capital is owned by *conseils juridiques*, *conseils juridiques* hold all the positions in the top management of the company and on the board of directors, and new members are not authorised to join the company except with the permission of the shareholders, or the board of directors.[91] *Conseils juridiques* may practice only as individual practitioners, under what amounts to a contract of employment with another *conseil juridique*, under a simple office-sharing arrangement or in the two forms just mentioned.[92]

Foreign law firms are more restricted under the new legislation than individual practitioners. *New* foreign law firms will not be able to set up offices in France since, from now on, firms may act as *conseils juridiques* only if organised under the typically French form of partnership known as *société civile professionelle*; a foreign firm would, of course, not be organised in that way. It will make no difference that the firm restricts its activities to the field of foreign and international law, since even with that restricted practice foreigners must be registered on the list of *conseils juridiques*, and this is not possible for firms not organised in the form of a *société civile professionelle*.[93] An exception exists only for firms which are established in countries belonging to the European Economic Communities, or in countries granting reciprocal rights to French nationals.[94]

What has just been said is subject to one qualification, though a qualification subject to partial withdrawal. Firms (the French text uses the term *groupements*, intended to refer to any type of association between individuals regardless of its precise legal nature) established pursuant to foreign law may continue to exercise their activities

90 Law No. 71-1130, *supra*, n. 1, Art. 62. The *sociétés civiles professionelles* composed of legal advisers will, of course, be governed by the Law No. 66–879, *supra*, n. 67. In line with the requirements of that law (see also n. 68, *supra*), a special decree had to be enacted to make the law applicable to the *conseils juridiques*. Décret No. 72–698 of July 26, 1972, J.O. July 30, 1972, p. 8177, (1972) D.L. 447. Of course, these provisions do not prevent practice in the form of a simple office sharing arrangement, but do prevent the creation of new *sociétés fiduciaires*.

91 Law No. 71-1130, *supra*, n. 1, Art. 62.

92 Law No. 71-1130, *supra*, n. 1, Art. 58.

93 Law No. 71-1130, *supra*, n. 1, Art. 55. In his Circular of Oct. 16, 1972, J.O. Oct. 25, 1972, p. 11151 relating to *Conseils Juridiques*, the Minister of Justice, interpreting the applicable legislation, states specifically that henceforth it will be impossible to establish law firms organised in a form other than as a *société civile professionelle* so that partnerships in particular will be excluded. It is worthy of some note that the Circular uses the word " partnership " in English in the text.

94 See the Circular of Oct. 16, 1972, *supra*, n. 93. Chap. 3, s. 1 (2).

in France if they were established there before July 1, 1971. But this "grandfather clause" is subject to a number of conditions. All the members of the firm practising in France must be registered on the list of *conseils juridiques*; they must also be able to "represent" the firm, that is, to bind it legally. As interpreted by the French Ministry of Justice, this means that, for instance, in the case of a firm which is part of an American partnership, at least one of the partners must be located in France. Furthermore, the exception for existing firms applies only to firms which have as their general purpose the "performance of the activities mentioned in Article 54" of the law relating to the reorganisation of the legal professions. This obviously means the giving of legal advice and the preparation of legal documents not related to litigation, but does not include any type of litigation. The provision gave rise to the fear that no foreign law firm which conducted any kind of litigation would be able to benefit from the "grandfather clause" mentioned; existing American law firms in Paris, in particular, would have been affected. Fortunately, the Minister of Justice interprets this provision to mean only that the branch of the firm operating in France is limited to the giving of legal advice and the preparation of documents. The activities of the firm outside France are not material.[95]

The French Government may, by decree, limit foreign law firms and their members to the practice of foreign and international law if their home country does not, within five years, grant reciprocal rights to French firms.[96] This provision was obviously intended as a bargaining weapon. It would seem to have little purpose in connection with countries such as the United States, where the federal Government, which is in exclusive charge of foreign relations, does not (generally) regulate the legal profession, and the States, which do, may not ordinarily negotiate with foreign governments.

The new law contains fairly detailed rules on the manner in which the *conseils juridiques* must exercise their profession; these rules are somewhat similar to those applicable to *avocats*; they may have been enacted with the eventual unification of the professions in view. In a provision identical to that governing the *avocats*, the law declares the profession of *conseils juridiques* to be incompatible with any outside activity which could jeopardise the "liberal" character of the profession and the independence of the person exercising it. This

[95] Law No. 71-1130, *supra*, n. 1, Art. 62. *Cf.* the Circular of Oct. 16, 1972, *supra*, n. 93, Chap. 3, s. 2 (2).

[96] Law No. 71-1130, *supra*, n. 1, Art. 64 (3). Since many of the foreign law firms concerned by this rule have their main base in New York, the question arises whether the rule in the *Matter of Roel*, 3 N.Y.2d 224, 144 N.E.2d 24, 165 N.Y.S.2d 31 (1957) should not receive limited legislative modification in order to provide some degree of reciprocity.

means, for instance, that a *conseil juridique* may not engage in business in any form.[97] The *conseil juridique* is also, in the same way as the *avocat* obliged to carry insurance to cover his professional malpractice and a separate insurance or guarantee to insure the return of all clients' funds he may hold.[98] As a further protection of clients, *conseils juridiques* are subject to disciplinary sanctions; here, however, there is a difference with the *avocats*; while, as noted, disciplinary power over the *avocats* is exercised by their own bar associations, disciplinary power over the *conseils juridiques* is exercised by the court of first instance, the *tribunal de grande instance*, acting at the request of the procurator of the Republic.[99]

### *D. Conclusion*

The reform legislation, which has been briefly described above, and which has been quite controversial, must now be put into effect. This will undoubtedly require a change in some ingrained attitudes—though, to be sure, the legal profession in France has been in a process of change before the reform legislation, and that change would have gone on even without it. What the exact effect of the changes will be is difficult to assess. The proponents of the new law hope that, together with the procedural reforms already enacted and those contemplated, it will make law-suits less expensive and less time consuming. Some people opposing the reform have doubts about this, feeling that the close personal relationship the *avoués* had with the courts before which they were practising had a beneficial effect on the efficiency of the court system which will now be lost. There is also some feeling that the reform will lead to the creation of an increasing number of law firms composed, perhaps, of several *avocats* who might, to some extent, specialise in various areas of substantive law and of one, normally a former *avoué*, who would be concerned with the procedural aspects of the firm's practice. Others doubt such a development will occur. If such a development

[97] Law No. 71-1130, *supra*, n. 1, Art. 56. Décret No. 72-670, *supra*, n. 78, Arts. 47-52. The provisions have been modelled on those governing *avocats*.

[98] Law No. 71-1130, *supra*, n. 1, Art. 59. This has been implemented in considerable detail by Décret No. 72-671 of July 13, 1972, J.O. July 18, 1972, p. 7665. Further implementation has been provided by regulations (*arrêtés*) of the Minister of Justice of Aug. 4, 1972, published in the *Journal Officiel* of Aug. 19, 1972 and dealing with the accounts *conseils juridiques* must keep, with the certificates of insurance necessary to show that the *conseils juridiques* have the required insurance coverage, and a variety of related matters. This detailed regulation is obviously intended to protect clients, since *conseils juridiques* often handle their clients' funds in connection with investments and the like for which they give their clients legal advice.

[99] Law No. 71-1130, *supra*, n. 1, Art. 60; Décret Nr. 72-670, *supra*, n. 78, Arts. 73-86. In addition, the procurator of the Republic exercises a certain general supervision.

happens it is likely to be restricted to Paris and a few other large urban areas, where the (former) *avocats* have traditionally been more influential than the *avoués*. In rural areas, where the contrary had sometimes been the case, the creation of firms is less likely; indeed, some people fear that the former *avoués* will make substantial inroads into the practice of the former *avocats*, at least in the immediate future. The reform should, however, contribute, at least to some extent, to a more effective legal profession in France. Its total impact will undoubtedly depend also on some outside factors, such as improvements in the court system, procedural reform and the manner in which the new system of legal aid will be implemented.

## IV. THE REFORM OF LEGAL AID

### *A. Reasons for the Reform; Persons Entitled to Aid*

The law reforming the French system of legal aid [100] is, as has been noted, part of a comprehensive scheme for the reform and modernisation of French legal institutions.[101] It attempts to deal with the four objections most commonly raised against the existing French legal aid system, namely (1) the arbitrariness in the granting or denial of legal aid, resulting in substantial regional disparities; (2) the inflexible character of legal aid, which could only be granted in full or denied, without any possibility of adapting the amount of aid to the needs of the party requesting it; (3) the burden imposed by legal aid on the members of the legal profession, the French Republic providing no compensation whatever for services rendered to legal aid recipients; and (4) the review by the legal aid bureaux of the merits of the case.[102]

To deal with these defects, the new law adopts essentially objective criteria for the granting of legal aid,[103] and partial grants of legal aid are possible.[104] Full legal aid can be granted to individuals (and also to some non-profit associations) whose monthly income is less than F.900; partial legal aid can be granted to all persons with a monthly income below F.1,500.[105] While these figures do not seem

100 Law No. 72–11 of Jan. 3, 1972, J.O. Jan. 5, 1972, p. 167, (1972) D.L. 69.

101 See *supra*, nn. 1–5. Oppetit, " L'aide judiciaire " (1972) D.Chr. 42.

102 For a good review of the objections to the prior state of affairs, see the French Senate Report No. 25 of 1971–72 presented by Senator de Montigny on behalf of the Committee on Constitutional Laws, Legislation, Universal Suffrage and General Administration at pp. 4, 5. See also the Report to the French National Assembly by M. de Grailly, *supra*, n. 3 at pp. 6–9.

103 *Cf.* the Report by M. de Grailly, *supra*, n. 3 at p. 11.

104 Law No. 72–11, *supra*, n. 100, Art. 2.

105 *Ibid.* However, while the F.900 limit for the grant of complete legal aid is of general application, the F.1,500 limit for the grant of partial legal aid represents merely an upper limit. More detailed rules setting varying amounts depending on the nature of the court before which the action is pending and on its nature

excessively generous, they will give a very substantial number of individuals access to legal aid,[106] particularly because these figures are adjusted upwards for persons with dependants, and can be modified in the annual budget Bill (*Loi de finances*)[107] thus making some adjustment to the increase in the cost of living possible. A proposal by the Committee on Legislation of the French National Assembly, which would have set the maximum income for legal aid at twice the minimum wage (S.M.I.C.),[108] which, in France, is automatically increased when the cost of living index moves upwards, and is also adjusted upwards in correlation with some other economic indicators, was not adopted.[109]

In order to establish the amount of monthly income, the legal aid bureau must take not only actual revenues into consideration, but also the value of the property owned by the applicant excluding, however, the value of his residence.[110] The law does not specify in what manner the monthly income figure must be adjusted if the applicant owns property. The rule that the value of a personal residence is not to be taken into consideration for the grant of legal aid is welcome; under prior law, persons of very modest means, but who owned their own home were occasionally denied legal aid on the ground that they were "landowners." Family allowances, which are a substantial addition to family income in France, are not to be taken into consideration in arriving at monthly income; however, the income of the applicant's spouse and of other persons living in his home may be included. It should be noted, on the other hand, that a person's general standard of living may be used as a basis for refusing legal aid.[111]

In addition to the situations in which the grant of legal aid is more

have been established by a decree implementing the law, *viz.* Décret No. 72-809 of Sept. 1, 1972, J.O. Sept. 3, 1972, Art. 66. The amount of legal aid granted diminishes as the recipient's income approaches F.1,500. *Ibid.*, Art. 77. The income limits mentioned throughout this discussion on legal aid must be increased by F.100 for each dependant. *Ibid.*, Arts. 67, 68.

106 It has been estimated that about half of all the French families have a monthly income (not counting family allowances which have to be disregarded for the purposes of legal aid) of F.900 or less and a majority of all French families (perhaps about 75 per cent.) have an income, calculated as mentioned above, of less than F.1,500 per month. See the Report by M. de Grailly, *supra*, n. 3 at p. 14. If these figures are correct, legal aid is likely to be demanded in a large number of cases. M. de Grailly estimated that, in spite of the considerable number of suits brought by corporate entities, the income structure of litigants in France was not too different from the income structure of the population in general.

107 Law No. 72-11, *supra*, n. 100, Art. 2.

108 The abbreviation stands for *salaire minimum interprofessionel de croissance* which one could translate as "general, upwards variable, minimum wage."

109 Report by M. de Grailly, *supra*, n. 3 at pp. 23, 24.

110 Law No. 72-11, *supra*, n. 100, Art. 15.

111 *Ibid.*

or less mandatory, the law also permits a " discretionary " grant of legal aid to persons not coming within the income limitations mentioned, but whose application appears particularly meritorious in view of the purposes of the litigation or the anticipated expenses involved in it.[112] Though this rule is, in some respects, similar to the provisions of the earlier law which were criticised because they allowed too much discretion in evaluating the need for legal aid, it brings flexibility to the mandatory rules on maximum income, and is thus a welcome safety valve.[113] Persons entitled to supplemental social security benefits from the so-called National Solidarity Fund, that is, the aged, are entitled to legal aid without any proof as to their income.[114] This enables old people to obtain legal aid without a great deal of paperwork that may be particularly burdensome for them. Special, favourable rules for the grant of legal aid have, for some time, benefited various categories of persons, such as victims of persecution during World War II. These rules remain unchanged.[115]

Because of the large percentage of aliens living in France [116] it is significant to note that the new law authorises all aliens having their " habitual residence " in France to receive legal aid.[117] This makes the former debate whether aliens not protected by treaty could receive legal aid largely academic. Of course, any more far-reaching treaty provisions protecting nationals of any particular country remain unaffected.[118]

Legal aid may be granted to either the plaintiff or the defendant, but some distinction between the two remains. While the defendant apparently receives it automatically, the plaintiff must show that his suit is not obviously subject to dismissal on procedural grounds

[112] Law No. 72-11, *supra*, n. 100, Art. 16.

[113] See the Report by M. de Grailly, *supra*, n. 3 at p. 23.

[114] Law No. 72-11, *supra*, n. 100, Art. 15 (4).

[115] Law No. 72-11, *supra*, n. 100, Art. 32.

[116] The total number of aliens in France is about 3 million out of a total population of about 50 million. See European Communities Commission, *The Enlarged Community in Figures*, p. 3 (1972); 1 H. Batiffol & P. Lagarde, *Droit International Privé*, p. 186, n. 6 (5th ed. 1970).

[117] Law No. 72-11, *supra*, n. 100, Art. 1. Habitual residence apparently refers to residence as a matter of fact, without regard to intent. *Cf.* De Winter, " Nationality or Domicil " (1969) 128 Hague Ac.Int.L.*Recueil des Cours* 347, 419.

[118] Under the prior law, it was a debated question whether, in the absence of a pertinent treaty, legal aid could be granted only in cases of reciprocity. See F. Dawson and I. Head, *International Law, National Tribunals and the Rights of Aliens*, pp. 141–142 (1971). Numerous conventions, including the Hague Convention on Civil Procedure (Convention Relating to Civil Procedure, signed on March 1, 1954, 286 U.N.T.S. 265), Arts. 20–24, provide for legal aid for aliens. For a listing of other conventions applicable in France see Lagarde, " Assistance Judiciaire," in 1 Dalloz, *Répertoire de Droit International* at Nos. 2–8 (1968).

(*irrecevable*) or without meritorious character.[119] Though this formulation is more cautious than the corresponding formulation of the prior law, it is unfortunate.[120] While relatively objective criteria can be used to determine when an action is manifestly subject to dismissal on procedural grounds it will rarely be clear beyond doubt that an action is unfounded on the merits; it is thus to be feared that the legal aid bureaux may be tempted, in effect, to prejudge the merits.

### *B. Scope of Legal Aid: Compensation of Attorneys and Others Providing it*

Legal aid may be granted in all civil cases, even in those involving mere *ex parte* applications (*juridiction gracieuse*).[121] Unfortunately, the new law does not apply to defendants in criminal cases, who remain governed by the earlier legislation,[122] though it applies to private parties who join in a criminal action as parties plaintiff to claim damages, as is possible in France.[123] Legal aid may be granted for proceedings before the entire hierarchy of administrative courts.[124]

Legal aid covers all kinds of court costs or of costs for documents which must be submitted to the court, including court clerk's fees, fees of experts, expenses of other types of proof proceedings, etc.[125] All these expenses are now fully borne by the Government, unless only partial legal aid is granted.[126] Furthermore, counsel is assigned to all parties having been granted legal aid. The actual assignment of counsel is made by the president (*bâtonnier*) of the local bar association, after it is notified of the grant of legal aid.[127]

The most innovative, and at the same time the most controversial aspect of the new law—because of it, a strike of all French *avocats* had been threatened [128]—is the provision for government payments to *avocats* handling legal aid cases.[129] This provision, in spite of its

119 Law No. 72-11, *supra*, n. 100, Art. 3.

120 *Cf.* the Report by M. de Grailly, *supra*, n. 3 at p. 24.

121 Law No. 72-11, *supra*, n. 100, Art. 4 (1).

122 Law No. 72-11, *supra*, n. 100, Art. 4 (2). (*Cf.* text at nn. 18–20, *supra* and 142, *infra*.)

123 Law No. 72-11, *supra*, n. 100, Art. 4 (3). On the possibility of claiming damages in a criminal proceeding, see Code de Procédure Pénale, Arts. 3–10; *cf.* Herzog at p. 138.

124 Law No. 72-11, *supra*, n. 100, Art. 4 (2).

125 Law No. 72-11, *supra*, n. 100, Art. 8.

126 Law No. 72-11, *supra*, n. 100, Art. 9.

127 Law No. 72-11, *supra*, n. 100, Art. 23. However, if a particular *avocat* has agreed to represent the client, he will normally be designated, though the agreement is subject to approval by the president of the bar association.

128 This was a topic quite frequently discussed by *avocats* in 1971. *Cf. Le Figaro*, Dec. 16, 1971.

129 Law No. 72-11, *supra*, n. 100, Art. 19. Because many French *avocats* strongly objected to this on the ground that the fixing of a fee by some government

controversial character undoubtedly means real progress. Until now, *avoués* could recover their fees only if their legal aid client won and the other party thus had to pay expenses, which included the *avoué's* fee; *avocats* could recover their fee only in some exceptional circumstances.[130] Article 19 of the new law now provides that the (new type) *avocat* to whom a legal aid case has been assigned receives an "indemnity." The use of that word clearly indicates that the *avocat* is not to receive the normal fee for equivalent work, but only a limited compensation for his time and out of pocket expenses. The amount of the indemnity is established by the legal aid bureau, taking into consideration the difficulty and amount of work of the *avocat*, but it may never be more than F. 600. Details are regulated by an implementing decree promulgated by the Government. If the applicant for legal aid is granted full legal aid, the amount determined by the legal aid bureau is paid to the *avocat* by the Government. If only partial legal aid is granted, a percentage of that amount is paid to the *avocat* by the Government and the applicant must pay his *avocat* an additional amount to be determined by the legal aid bureau, taking into account the applicant's financial situation.[131]

As noted above, the provisions just mentioned have led to vigorous opposition on the part of the *avocats* who, on that issue, have been nearly unanimous, as they have not been on the issue of merger with the *avoués*. Obviously, they feel that in the future, as in the past, they, rather than the Government, will bear part of the cost of legal aid, since the indemnity to be paid by the Government is likely to be substantially smaller than a normal fee. But beyond this they fear—and this is probably the most important reason for their opposition—that the fixing of fees by the legal aid bureaux may be the first step towards the establishment of a fee schedule for *avocats* in all cases, thus leading to at least a partial loss of their prized independence.[132] It may be feared that, in view of the opposition of so

agency, and the payment of a fee to them by the government would deprive them of their independence, the committee of the French National Assembly reporting on the legislation suggested instead the creation of a Legal Aid Fund to be administered by the *avocats*, which would receive funds from parties having been granted only partial legal aid, a subsidy from the government, and various other revenues, including part of a fee levied in all civil cases. See Report by M. de Grailly, *supra*, n. 3 at pp. 37–39. The provision, obviously modelled on English precedent, was left out of the statute as enacted at the insistence of the Minister of Justice, M. Pleven. *Cf.* Oppetit, *supra*, n. 101 at p. 45.

130 Herzog at pp. 543, 549.

131 Law No. 72-11, *supra*, n. 100, Art. 19. Décret No. 72-809, *supra*, n. 105, Arts. 76 (containing detailed table indicating the amounts to be awarded in various situations), 77, 78.

132 It is to be noted in this connection that the *avocat* may not ask his client for any supplemental payment. If he received a fee from his client before legal aid had been granted, that fee must be deducted from the sum fixed by the legal aid bureau. Law No. 72-11, *supra*, n. 100, Art. 21.

many members of the bar, the previous practice of assigning most legal aid cases (except, generally, the most difficult ones) to the relatively inexperienced *avocats stagiaires* may be continued, though it was one of the purposes of the new legal aid scheme to modify that practice. Rather obviously, the new legislation is not as unfavourable to the *avocats* as some of them have claimed, and, in fact represents substantial progress; it is, nevertheless hard to understand why the law does not also require certain other persons connected with litigation, such as experts to forgo some part of their normal fee.[133]

### *C. Procedure for the Grant of Legal Aid*

Legal aid will be granted by " legal aid bureau " established at the seats of the *tribunaux de grande instance* (courts of first instance), *cours d'appel, Cour de Cassation,* and before the hierarchy of administrative courts.[134] Generally speaking, legal aid must be requested from the bureau established at the court before which the matter for which legal aid is sought is pending, or where it is to be brought. Review of a decision may be sought from the bureau established at the court which is hierarchically superior to the court where the legal aid bureau, whose decision is to be reviewed is sitting.[135] Review of decisions of the legal aid bureaux established at the *Cour de Cassation* and the *Conseil d'Etat* may be sought from a central legal aid bureau established at the Ministry of Justice.[136] Unfortunately, the rule that review may be sought only by the procurator of the Republic (or procurator-general) acting as a kind of representative of the public interest, but not by the applicant, has been continued from the old law.[137]

Generally speaking, the legal aid bureaux consist of an equal number of government representatives (civil servants) and of representatives of *avocats* and certain other individuals, such as process servers (*huissiers*) who may have to assist parties. An active or retired judge or procurator, or a retired *avocat* or *avoué* acts as chairman.[138]

Legal aid may be withdrawn from a person to whom it has been granted, if he has made false statements in order to obtain it. Legal

133 Art. 8 (d) of Law No. 72–11, *supra,* n. 100 would seem to indicate that experts (who are court-appointed in France) are entitled to their normal fee.

134 Law No. 72–11, *supra,* n. 100, Arts. 10 and 11. Detailed procedural rules are contained in Décret No. 72–809, *supra,* n. 105, Arts. 1–61.

135 Law No. 72–11, *supra,* n. 100, Art. 18.

136 Law No. 72–11, *supra,* n. 100, Art. 11 (5).

137 Law No. 72–11, *supra,* n. 100, Art. 18 (2). Requests for review by the central legal aid bureau must be made by the Minister of Justice.

138 Law No. 72–11, *supra,* n. 100, Art. 14.

aid may be also withdrawn if, while the suit for which it has been granted is pending, its recipient obtains such large additional funds that, had he had these funds at the beginning of the suit, legal aid would not have been granted.[139] If legal aid is withdrawn, all court costs, fees of *avocats* and the like, become immediately due and their payment may be required.[140] In addition, if a person who has been granted legal aid wins his case and obtains a recovery which is so large that he would not have been granted legal aid had he owned the sum recovered before the beginning of the suit, his *avocat* may ask to be paid his normal fee, but only after the decision has become final (no longer reviewable) and if the president of the local bar association (*bâtonnier*) approves.[141] The recovery has no other effect on the grant of legal aid.

### *D. Conclusion*

In spite of the hostility of many members of the bar, the law on legal aid is undoubtedly an important step forward in the efforts to provide equal justice for all. In a sense it is even more to be regretted that the law has a number of imperfections. On one hand, in many respects, the law is not very clear. More important is the incomplete character of the law. As already noted, it does not apply to defendants in criminal cases; these must still rely on the 1851 law as amended. Thus counsel assigned to them receive no compensation, a matter to be regretted in the interest of the defendants as well as of the *avocats*, and in particular the *avocats stagiaires* for whom assigned counsel cases in the criminal field represent a heavy burden.[142]

In addition, legal aid remains limited to litigation. M. de Grailly, the reporter for the law when it was in committee, strongly urged the French Parliament to complete this legal aid system by the creation of a comprehensive scheme for providing legal advice to

[139] Law No. 72–11, *supra*, n. 100, Art. 29.

[140] Law No. 72–11, *supra*, n. 100, Art. 30. The decision withdrawing legal aid must indicate to what extent payment (or repayment) may be demanded.

[141] Law No. 72–11, *supra*, n. 100, Art. 22. It would also appear that if the person having been granted legal aid wins his case, his opponent is obliged to pay, as part of the costs and disbursements for which he is liable, the fees for the performance of procedural formalities contained in the official fee schedule. See Décret No. 72–809, *supra*, n. 105, Arts. 91–94. This would be a small additional compensation for the *avocat* having taken care of such formalities As previously noted, the losing party has no obligation to pay anything towards his opponent's expenses in compensating his *avocat* for oral argument in court See nn. 51, 52 and 130 and the text accompanying them.

[142] Oppetit, *supra*, n. 101 at p. 45. The committee reports, cited *supra*, nn. 3 and 102, give no reason why defendants in criminal cases were excluded, but indicate quite clearly that this provision was found in the original Bill proposed by the Government and was not changed (except for a clarificatory amendment) in either House.

persons in need.[143] His urgings were not heeded, undoubtedly because of an attitude, not entirely untypical in France, which views law too narrowly in terms of litigation.[144] In many other countries free legal advice is widely available to those unable to pay for it. It is hardly necessary in this connection to mention the English system of legal aid, but provisions for free legal advice exist also in other countries, such as the United States (through legal aid societies and the neighbourhood legal services offices sponsored by the federal Office of Economic Opportunity), in Germany, Austria, etc.[145] It is to be regretted that these examples were not followed in France in some manner.

## V. GENERAL CONCLUSIONS

For some time France has, beyond doubt, been engaged in a strenuous effort to modernise its legal institutions, including its court system, its legal profession and a portion of its substantive law. This effort began at the very time the Fifth Republic came into being, and is still going on. It is noteworthy that these reforms have not followed general civil law tradition and taken the form of one or more new or revised codes comprehensively regulating a large field of law; instead, the approach has been much more tentative and pragmatic; changes have been made over a relatively long period of time; things that were not feasible at one time were postponed to a later period, statutes were often enacted in rather general terms, leaving much detail for more easily amended implementing decrees, etc.[146] In the preceding pages, only a small part of this movement for reform has been described. But what has just been said indicates that it is very difficult to give a final evaluation, even of that limited area. A reform of the legal profession and of legal aid can be called successful if it results in effective legal representation and sound legal advice for all those who need it, whether they are able to pay for it or not, and at the same time preserves the independence of those who provide legal services to the public, an independence without which the

143 Report by M. de Grailly, *supra*, n. 3 at p. 17. It should be mentioned in this connection that a few municipalities in the Paris region have instituted legal advice bureaus. Oppetit, *supra*, n. 101 at p. 45, n. 27. In addition, in Paris itself, the Paris bar association operates a legal consultation service where an older *avocat* assisted by some young *avocats stagiaires* giving free legal advice. The service operates in the Palace of Justice on two afternoons a week. It seems to be used by about 2,000 persons a year. J. Lemaire, *supra*, n. 46 at pp. 197–201

144 This attitude was also responsible in the past for the tendency of the *avocats* to devote little attention to the giving of legal advice, as opposed to litigation, and to the consequent growth of groups of unofficial legal advisers. *Cf. supra*, nn. 8 and 13 and accompanying text.

145 See generally, Cappelletti and Gordley, *supra*, n. 19 (with numerous comparative references).

146 *Cf.* Motulsky, *supra*, n. 5.

complete protection of the citizens' rights is hardly possible. On the other hand, the precise nature of the rules governing the legal profession or professions cannot be determined *a priori*; these rules must vary in part in response to the nature of the judicial and other institutions with which the legal profession deals. Whether the reforms which have been described above will be beneficial will therefore depend in large measure on all the additional reform measures which are planned; it will also depend in no small way on the extent to which the French Government will be willing to modernise its court system through practical rather than legal means—by supplying it with modern equipment, additional judicial and non-judicial personnel, and the like. This is perhaps an unsatisfactory conclusion; but at least it means that enough flexibility is built into the current system that problems can be solved as they arise, provided the will to do so is present.[147]

[147] The authors of this article have received information on the topics discussed from a number of individuals, including M. Pierre Bellet, formerly Presiding Judge (*Président*) of the *Tribunal de Grande Instance* in Paris, and now Presiding Judge of one of the panels (*Président de Chambre*) of the French Supreme Court (*Cour de Cassation*); M. Pignot, President of the *Union Nationale des Avocats*, M. Tinayre, President of the *Association Nationale des Avocats* and M. Ribadeau-Dumus, former *avoué* (now *avocat*). The information supplied was most helpful in providing background for the issues discussed. The authors of this article are obviously alone responsible for any errors contained in this article, and any opinions expressed in it.

It may be of some interest to persons interested in further dealing with the matters discussed here that the French law publishing firms Dalloz-Sirey and Gazette du Palais have recently jointly published a brochure entitled *Réformes-Procédure Civile, Professions Judiciaires et Juridiques, Aide Judiciaire-Recueil des Textes* (Paris 1972), collecting the statutes, decrees, regulations and circulars enacted in France on the topics mentioned since the autumn of 1971.

After this article had gone to press, a number of cases were decided dealing with the issue to what extent the new legislation had changed the rules concerning the fees of *avoués* who had now become *avocats* in instances where the statute and implementing decrees had nothing specific to say about the question. For a decision that the old rules remain in force, see *Primault* v. *Jean*, Feb. 2, 1973, (1973) D.J. 182 (Tribunal de Grande Instance, Laval) with an extensive note by Professor Givord. See also *Ministère Public* v. *Dutreix*, Nov. 28, 1972 (Tribunal de Grande Instance, Paris) and *Ministère Public* v. *Ros*, Sept. 25, 1972 (Tribunal de Grande Instance, Lyons) both in (1973) *Dalloz Sommaire* 37.

# [21]

# THE LEGAL PROFESSION: COMMENTS ON THE SITUATION IN THE FEDERAL REPUBLIC OF GERMANY *

IN 1938, some years after the world's economic crisis had dealt a heavy blow to the self-confidence of the leading technical and economic powers, the American sociologist Talcott Parsons delivered a much noted lecture on "The Professions and Social Structure." [1] Against the background of the crisis and of the controversial remedial action by the huge new bureaucracies of the New Deal, Parsons drew attention to the professions. In the classical occupational roles of physicians, of priests and of lawyers, Parsons could show a sociological modal which seemed to offer a way out. In all professional roles three characteristics are combined, first, a highly developed technical competence based on a specialised education, secondly, a universalistic unbiased and objective practice and, thirdly, an orientation towards typical dangers and societal values which is primarily non-economic and not directed towards profit. It cannot be overlooked that there was an additional fourth point, the expectation that it was possible to combine those three elements in the professional practice of an individual practitioner. Thus one could, it seemed, abandon utilitarianism but preserve individualism. Thus one could endow an old tradition of professional ethics—the medieval tradition of the partes *seu officia*—with the attributes of modern society, namely with the differing "pattern variables" of universalism and specificity. Thus one could avoid contrasting individuals and the public and show, nevertheless, to what extent individual action determines social structures. Finally, Parson's concept of the profession contained a claim for the élite and, at the same time, was open to include managers, pharmacists, nurses—or even everybody? [2]

The following comments are intended to examine this conception which is relevant for social theory and policy alike. The field of our study will be limited vocationally and regionally: let

* Wilson Memorial Lecture, University of Edinburgh, May 2, 1974.

1 *Social Forces* 17 (1939) pp. 457–467, reprinted in: *Essays in Sociological Theory Pure and Applied*, New York 1949, rev. edition New York 1954.

2 Compare Harold L. Wilensky, "The Professionalization of Everyone," *The American Journal of Sociology* 70 (1964), pp. 137–158.

me take as an example the lawyers in the Federal Republic of Germany. I hope to pursue the interests of Sheriff and Dr. Nan Wilson in testing a sociological theory in its relation to law and to lawyers.

## I

An analysis which is to meet theoretical standards and, at the same time, is intended to grasp particular historical developments in a defined cultural and regional area must indicate the point where these two aspects are linked together. The result of such a study must be the formulation of a problem which stimulates different historical developments and particular national expressions; a problem which can be resolved in different ways according to the concrete context in which it occurs.

My starting-point is a theory of social systems. Presumably the formation of a profession of lawyers greatly depends on the degree to which a particular social system for legal affairs has been differentiated in the context of the system of the whole society. According to the definition by Thomas Hobbes: " By Systemes; I understand any numbers of men joyned in one Interest, or one Businesse,"[3] this would have to be differentiated under the specific aspect or " Businesse " of law. Wherever such a development takes place, the communication inside such a legal system assumes particular forms. It submits itself to specific conditions of success and differs in this from the ordinary communication of everyday life.

Now it appears to be one of the main features of specifically juridical communication that it is always related to texts—to laws, decisions of courts, authoritative doctrine in faculties or formulated contracts or forms of contracts—by which a legally significant content is laid down or to be laid down. It might be arguable to what extent these texts are binding or open to manipulation. But, leaving this question aside, the mere fact that communication between lawyers is laid down in the form of these texts presumably has far-reaching consequences for the chances of forming a profession, but also creates specific dangers for the coherence of the profession. Some simple questions arising here are: How many texts are there and how many individuals who are concerned with the texts? What about the ratio between the number of texts and the number of individuals? Is there a minimum size where the

[3] *Leviathan*, chap. XXII.

formation of a profession takes off, and are there limits to its growth which the profession cannot exceed without collapsing?

It is obvious that in any highly developed legal system with comprehensive jurisdiction, continuous legislation and a great number of publications coming from universities, the amount of texts produced by far surpasses the capacity of the individual practitioner. This is taken into account in a two-fold way. On the one hand, ever more narrow specialisations are being developed. My solicitor who gives me counsel in matters concerning the law of building has to ask his colleague when a problem concerning transport law has to be resolved. On the other hand, the integration of the profession is reduced from common knowledge of texts and common opinion about them to the mere possibility of finding and judging the relevant texts. Something like a " law of anticipated capacities "—to vary a well-known formulation by Carl Joachim Friedrich—prevails for the processes of communication. Both ways of coping with this excess of material slacken the coherence of the profession.

A second aspect follows from a characteristic feature of communication by means of texts: it points towards a larger community of others who form their opinion too, and it receives its significance from this co-orientation. This means for lawyers that the quality of their interpretations or formulations of texts depends on the reception on the part of other lawyers. The individual lawyer, whatever place he is working in, cannot achieve any success autonomously; he is thrown back upon adequate resonance. The most elegant legal construction is of no use if nobody is able to understand or to follow it, and a refined sense for the limits of justifiable interpretation is of no avail when a floodtide of politics washes away all scruples. Therefore quality can be heightened only inside the system, and success depends on professionally qualified processes of communication and not primarily on an individual ethos.

This characterisation leads to a peculiar ambivalence which in this form does not occur in other professions. The network of communication which keeps the profession of lawyers together depends on both the quality of texts and the quality of persons. It cannot escape its dependence on formulations, and on instances alike. German lawyers have had experience with both conditions of professional communication to a point which tends to the extreme. On the one hand they have known a tradition of carefully formulated, dogmatically reasoned statutes on which they are able to have brilliant scholarly arguments. And, on the other hand, they have experienced that a change affected by political pressure—a change not so much of texts, but rather of persons and instances—radically destroys the professional system of communication within a few years: the experience of national-socialism.[4]

When forming a judgment about the situation of the profession of lawyers, and its future prospects, one is bound to have regard, above all, to the corresponding system of communication, and in more detail to problems concerning the relative number and distribution of lawyers in society, to their dependence on texts and on patterns of organisation, to historical origins and to the type of qualitative requirements, and to the chances of enforcing the latter in society.

## II

Having considered these more general aspects I now want to limit the scope to the present situation of lawyers in the Federal Republic of Germany. Let me first look into matters of size and distribution. The field of our study is so large that personal acquaintance or contacts in the framework of the upper strata of society cannot be considered as a means of integration. There are about 100,000 fully trained lawyers in the Federal Republic. About 3,000 candidates each year pass the second state examination which opens the way to legal occupations. These young people have access to different careers, among these being, without further requirements, posts of judges. The absolvents go, in roughly equal proportions, into the judiciary, into the civil service, into the private legal profession, and, in a somewhat lesser degree, into business. According to the results of a survey, to quote an example, 16 per cent. of law graduates in 1971 became judges, 7 per cent. public prosecutors, 23 per cent. public administration officials, 24 per cent. advocates and solicitors, and 10 per cent. went into business. Another 10 per cent. was made up by other occupations for lawyers.[5] This distribution already shows that there is no clear concentration on one career. With the background of legal training widely diversified occupational fields are accessible: one can go into service with public authorities, but is not bound to do so.

[4] Compare for this Bernd Rüthers, *Die unbegrenzte Auslegung: Zum Wandel der Privatrechtsordnung im Nationalsozialismus*, Tübingen 1968.

[5] Compare Heinz Recken, "Berufswahl der Juristen: Ergebnisse einer umfassenden Befragung," *Zeitschrift für Rechtspolitik* 6 (1973), pp. 124–127. It should be noted that only 46 per cent. of the persons asked reacted.

Careers in the huge bureaucracies of State or business are open, and so is the independent position of advocate or solicitor. One can rely on security or on success; one can regard the settlement of legal disputes as one's vocation for life or one can, in the process of a career in an organisation, depart from specifically legal matters. In addition, there is the choice between fields of law of very different kinds.

This openness in the choice of a profession is a relevant motive for entering a law faculty. Thus it is not surprising that the motives of lawyers for choosing law as a university subject or as a career hardly show a particular structure, either as to personality features or as to professional values. This has been demonstrated by an empirical study carried out by Renate Mayntz and myself on behalf of the Studienkommission für die Reform des öffentlichen Dienstrechts, the German counterpart to the Fulton Commission.[6] The study reveals hardly any differences between lawyers and other graduates, as far as occupational choice is concerned. Variations of personality structures and interests create divergences only in the second stage of the choice between careers, namely when lawyers are faced with the alternative of becoming judge or advocate/solicitor.

Particularly interesting is the self-selection for the posts of judges. This career is, in Germany, as has already been mentioned, immediately accessible after the second state examination. It attracts young people from the upper classes slightly more than other occupations open to lawyers, particularly children of senior servants of public authorities.[7] One should in turn expect that this group shows to a larger extent personal characteristics typical of the upper classes: flexibility, toleration of ambiguities, internal attribution of success and failure, readiness for risks. The opposite is true.

---

[6] Compare for an evaluation of the material with special reference to lawyers: Elmar Lange/Niklas Luhmann, Juristen: Berufswahl und Karrieren, Verwaltungsarchiv 65 (1974), pp. 113–162. Another study, based on a comparison between sociologists and lawyers, has shown, on the other hand, marked differences which presumably have to be ascribed to the sociologists rather than to the lawyers. Compare: Renate Mayntz (ed.), *Soziologen im Studium: Eine Untersuchung zur Entwicklung fachspezifischer Einstellungen bei Studenten*, Stuttgart 1970.

[7] Translator's note: The term "öffentlicher Dienst," public service, in Germany comprises any occupation with any department, authority, corporation of the state in the broadest sense. Among these are certain groups whose terms of employment are governed by statute and part of public law; these are called "Beamte" and embrace, *e.g.* civil servants, teachers, local administration officers, but also loco-men, and postmen. This will be translated by "public servants." Members of the armed forces and judges are under special, though very similar, regulations. Administration in government departments and local government is referred to as "public administration." For senior posts in public service (höhere Beamte), here translated as "senior public servants," as a rule, academic training is required.

The selection runs against the trend one would expect, looking to the origins of the absolvents. The candidates for judicial careers, for instance, show a lesser degree of professional ambition. They tend to attribute events rather to circumstances than to themselves, they are less prepared to take risks and less capable of tolerating ambiguities. Their professional values are concentrated on security and on independence of their salaries from success or failure; they are directed more towards order than towards enterprise. In short, they are typical "Beamte." Indeed, and this might be interesting for a comparison with the United Kingdom, these features typical of "Beamte" are far more marked among the candidates for judicial careers than among those for public administration. The private legal profession, as far as these qualities are concerned, rather attracts the opposite type of personality.

If it is possible to generalise these results of a first empirical study, then they imply that the legal profession first attracts a fairly mixed selection out of the middle and upper classes of society and only differentiates afterwards. Therefore one is bound to assume that the profession as a whole is composed of heterogeneous elements, as far as values, interests, and attitudes are concerned, and is only differentiated within itself with regard to typical roles. These conditions are not very favourable for the internal coherence of the profession, let alone its efficiency as a political factor in society.

A second point reaffirms this result. Normally, the decision to opt for one of these careers is taken for the rest of one's life. They lead lawyers into very different roles and fields of social contact. Accordingly, their "reference groups," as sociologists put it, differentiate. A judge in a lower court might look up to the judges in the courts of higher instance and might clandestinely keep a check list in his office desk on which he puts down how many of his judgments are appealed against and how many of them are affirmed or reversed. A senior civil servant in a ministry will try to be prepared for a change in the political leadership of his department by means of personal contacts and the arguments he will be able to employ. An advocate will depend to a highly varying extent on his clients, so that in an extreme case he might hardly differ from an auditor in a large company. With these remarks I do not want to contend that lawyers in the Federal Republic or elsewhere bend or even break the law in the interest of their clients or employers. What I mean is that to lawyers, according to their professional situation, different legal provisions and problems are relevant, and in developing the law they are aware of distinct needs and follow different "opinion leaders." Nor does the problem lie, in spite of many current denunciations, in our having "a class system of justice," nor in the alleged reactionary views of lawyers. More important is the previous question, namely, to what extent does professional coherence still exercise any influence at all.

As to this there is a lack of empirical studies, and it would be difficult, for methodological reasons, to carry them out. Nonetheless, the present scene in the Federal Republic offers a good field for observation. A radical, almost blind, political moralism is spreading and penetrating with the change of generations into radio stations and publishing houses, into political parties and gradually also into government departments, to say nothing about universities.[8] The blood-letting of my generation in the war and intellectual neglect in the period of reconstruction after 1948 make themselves felt; there seems nothing to offer in opposition to that trend. Switchboards in bureaucracy make some delaying resistance possible, but they do not provide for the formulation of plausible alternatives, of fresh ideas. Thus no confidence in the possibility of other circumstances can arise, not even confidence in political influence. The majority is speechless.

In this situation lawyers show a remarkable resistance against spasmodic politism. They think in normative terms anyway and are therefore immune against naïve moralising. They are accustomed to see battle-lines and antagonisms related to single cases and not as universal social battle-lines over which the fight for and against the good society takes place. Lawyers have been taught to ask first what are the valid rules before judging behaviour. And they are skilled to decide a matter quickly on the basis of a few premises and little information by exact reduction to a few relevant points. All this makes for detachment.

## III

But can this detachment be more than a mere mental attitude, more than the customary narrowness of one's own actions and abilities? Can it also be—or become—a political factor?

[8] Also congresses of sociology of law are exposed to this tendency and are blamed for only "producing knowledge for domination." See the paper by Erhard Blankenburg Wolfgang Kaupen/Rüdiger Lautmann/Frank Rotter, who are among the most alert sociologists of law in the Federal Republic, and the reply by Helmut Schelsky, in: *Jahrbuch für Rechtssoziologie und Rechtstheorie* 3 (1972) p. 600 *et seq.*

To put the question in another way: does the profession have a kind of leadership, a centre for the formation of opinions which can react quickly to rapidly changing political circumstances?

The answer to this question cannot be a clear Yes or No. First of all one has to take into account that Germany has a centre of government, but no capital and no metropolitan society comparable to Paris, Madrid, Stockholm, Warsaw—I do not know whether I should mention London to an Edinburgh audience. Berlin never quite reached this position of a social metropolis and today exists merely as a problem. Therefore we lack that level of condensed interaction at which standards of opinion are set and can be controlled. A single writer behaves as conscience of the nation—and nobody tells him that he is making a fool of himself. Professors resort to advertisements to make known their political opinions—and nobody tells them that they are making fools of themselves.[9] In this situation also a profession like that of lawyers must do without interaction in the framework of a community of leading members of society. This is replaced by organisation, and specifically by an organisation which distributes the lawyers, according to the principle of separation of powers, into two powers.

Let us first consider ministerial bureaucracy. Inside government departments lawyers perform an important, if not a dominant, role. It is inferred from the rule of law that for all legally relevant decisions only lawyers can assume responsibility and that therefore only they can give the final signature. This means in practice that leading posts have to be filled by lawyers—a principle of course often contravened, but followed to a large extent. As far as I know, nobody has ever had the idea of reserving the final responsibility for all decisions which involve expenditure to an economist. So deeply rooted is the emphasis on the rule of law in German constitutional thought, reinforced of course by the experience of National-socialism.

The practical result of this pattern of orientation is that lawyers are over-represented in government departments. In a sample which I undertook I found among the university graduates in the federal ministries 58 per cent. lawyers, in the ministries of the Land Niedersachsen (Lower Saxony) as many as 62 per cent. lawyers.[10]

[9] With the exception of Helmut Schelsky, *System überwindung, Demokrahisierung und gewaltenfislung: grundsahkouflkte der Bundesrepublik*, München 1973 p. 38 *et seq.*

[10] From the survey carried out on behalf of the Studienkommission für die Reform des öffentlichen Dienstrechts, already referred to above; figures are not published elsewhere.

In the whole senior public service in Western Germany, however, one finds only 13 per cent.[11] Moreover, lawyers are represented above the average in leading positions at all levels of administration; consequently they have much better chances of promotion and earn, on average, slightly higher salaries than other university absolvents.[12] Such a massive disproportion obviously has some effect. It determines the performance levels and performance limits of administrative bureaucracy and, in this way, indirectly also determines what is politically possible or impossible. Again, this does not mean that the bureaucracy is reactionary or hinders reforms; however, it does mean that it deals with questions concerning reforms mainly from the angle of changing legal provisions. There is, to quote one example among many others, evidence in the field of educational policies in schools and universities that only a few issues can be moulded into legal provisions regulating conflicts and limiting competences and, in this shape, can be reformed continually. On the other hand it seems that moulding the contents of education has been planned only very recently and not with great success. Ever new reforms of the legal framework, pressing on one another and already out of date when executed, are only symptoms of a cleary discernible decline.

To some extent, it is true, this disproportion of juridical perspective is corrected under the pressure of external facts. Lawyers are by no means restricted to working with legal problems and deciding them. To a large extent they are engaged outside the scope of their training, and in these cases one uses lawyers only because they are able to ascertain and also to decide, if necessary, legal questions which might arise. Administrative staff educated in law are aware, in their opinion about their jobs, that the technical legal aspect has receded; they tend to emphasise it in conversation. Presumably this is a motive in the choice of that particular career, and it is, more-

[11] Compare: Statistisches Bundesamt Wiesbaden, Fachserie L (Finanzen und Steuern), Personalstrukturerhebung am 2. Oktober 1968: Personal von Bund, Ländern und Gemeinden, Stuttgart/Mainz 1971, p. 18. These statistics, however, are based on the whole senior public service and include 13.8 per cent. which are not university absolvents.

[12] Compare Niklas Luhmann/Renate Mayntz, *Personal im öffentlichen Dienst: Eintritt und Karrieren* (*Staff in Public Service: Entry and Promotion*), Baden-Baden 1973, p. 142 *et seq.*; Gerhard Brinkmann, "Die Diskriminierung der Nichtjuristen im allgemeinen höheren Verwaltungsdienst der Bundesrepublik Deutschland: Test einer Hypothese durch einen Gehaltsvergleich zwischen der Bundesrepublik und den U.S.A.," in: *Zeitschrift für die gesamte Staatswissenschaft* 129 (1973) pp. 150–167. Compare also: Thomas Ellwein/Ralf Zoll, *Berufsbeamtentum: Anspruch und Wirklichkeit: Zur Entwicklung und Problematik des öffentlichen Dienstes*, Düsseldorf 1973, particularly p. 176 *et seq.*

over, found in the empirical analyses of these activities.[13] Even advising the legislature is asking too much. For lawyers cannot draw standards for law reform from the existing law, and in German universities they are not educated for "law policy."

The fact that lawyers in public administration have a sense of distaste towards politics, particularly towards party politics, has remained unchanged. Many of them have joined a party to overcome a hurdle in their career. Nevertheless a paramount majority objects to party-political influence on the filling of senior posts and on the conduct of public administration.[14] It seems that the opportunism which is reflected by joining a party for the sake of promotion rather reinforces this rejection. Incidentally, the distaste is more clearly marked among other university absolvents than among lawyers. Public servants object only to concrete interference by parties with the administrative machinery. This attitude appears to them to be reconcilable with a basic approval of democracy as polity, with parliamentary legislation and with the functions of political parties in the general process of legitimation. Only the younger generation is more open-minded towards the concrete interests of party politics; perhaps one also simply adapts to the well-established reality.

Against the background of this description the question arises: is the legal profession as a whole a factor in this relationship? Does the reference group, the profession of lawyers, support the lawyers in public administration in their defence against what they feel as meddling by political parties? Does it provide them with arguments at hand, or social relations, or at least ideals?

Taking a realistic view, one can hardly answer these questions in the affirmative. The only relevant factor, again, is organisational; the fully developed jurisdiction in matters of public law as well as of constitutional law. In questions which can be grasped legally, lawyers in public administration, faced with politics, are able to rely on the courts: either on well established tendencies in their decisions or on new trends they can somehow detect. The courts, devised to protect the citizen against the State, at the same time

[13] Compare Gerhard Brinkmann/Wolfgang Pippke/Wolfgang Rippe, *Die Tätigkeitsfelder des höheren Verwaltungsdienstes: Arbeitsansprüche, Ausbildungserfordernisse, Personalbedarf*, Opladen 1973, p. 346 *et seq.*

[14] See in connection with this for particular samples in public administration: Eberhard Moths/Monika Wulf-Mathies, *Des Bürgers teure Diener*, Karlsruhe 1973 (concerning junior civil servants in the Federal Economic Department); Luhmann/Mayntz *loc. cit.*, p. 255 *et seq.*, and particularly on lawyers in public administration Lange/Luhmann *loc. cit.*

serve to protect the legal opinions of public servants against politics. This very fact forces the courts themselves to pay attention to questions of political opportunity and reasonableness as well as to questions of administrative efficiency, by giving them status as technical legal questions.[15]

## IV

With these considerations we shift our view towards the members of the judiciary. Here, if anywhere, we have to look for a backbone to the profession. Here the function of lawyers is unquestionably evident, here they genuinely work with legal problems, here, under all political challenges, the need for their existence is undisputed.

There is indeed some evidence for the retreat of the profession on its core function and of a consolidating organisation in this area. In the Federal Republic there are about 13,000 full-time judges.[16] As far as policies in relation to public service are concerned, the judges have pushed through the separation of their terms of employment from the law governing the rest of public service: there is now a particular Judges Act. Furthermore, the creation of particular ministries for the administration of justice is under consideration. They would take over administrative matters concerning judges and the organisation of the courts, and they would represent them politically. This, however, amounts only to a symbolic reform. On this neither the judge nor his self-respect can live. The salary of judges who take up this career depends on the level of entry salaries for all other graduates in public service, since they are chosen among fresh absolvents. The prospects of promotion are dependent on the hierarchical structure of the judiciary. Whereas other branches of public service managed in the last few years greatly to increase the number of their senior posts by establishing urgent need with much imagination, in the judiciary the rigidity of the organisation stood in the way of doing so. The much complained of problems of filling junior posts, as to quantity and quality as well, show how the courts lag behind. And this will increase the trend towards the selection of the rather inferior type of entrants referred to above.

---

[15] Compare *e.g.* Josef Isensee, *Verwaltungsraison gegen Verwaltungsrecht: Antinomien der Massenverwaltung in der typisierenden Betrachtungsweise des Steuerrechts*, Steuer und Wirtschaft 1973, pp. 199–206.

[16] Compare *Statistisches Jahrbuch* 1973, p. 112 for a more exact classification according to the branches of judiciary.

In spite of poor equipment and strong tendencies towards bureaucratic mass-scale manufacturing of decisions, the judiciary is gaining more independence. The authority which decides in the last resort the legitimate employment of physical force has a political function which cannot be eliminated. Relations between politics and its most extreme instrument, physical force, have always been a problem in Germany: either it is used too much or too little. In view of this oscillation it proves useful to shove off political problems on to the courts. Here the conditions for the employment of force can be decided in a complex legal jargon, and in this way conflicts can be regulated before force is actually employed. Here one sometimes finds courage for politically unpopular decisions. Such a counterweight is of some importance in a democracy of the kind existing in Germany, which reflects continually upon its own political sensitivity and, in doing so, can reduce itself to incapacity for making any decision.

This counterweight, it is true, can be used only very seldom. A decision like the judgment of the Bundesverfassungsgericht, the Federal Constitutional Court, on the minimum participation of professors in the making of decisions concerning their universities, is rather an exception. First of all, an ever increasing part of social rules and social conflicts eludes the reach of judicial decisions—particularly the most important problems in the field of economics, and also most of the internal conflicts in organisations.[17] The air controllers' strike last year is a good example of the impotence of the law. And even in a case where it is possible to submit a conflict to the courts, the aspects under which this is done are often marginal or specialised to such an extent that the decision does not settle the conflict but only allocates the weapons in a different way. And a second filter comes in, namely the motivation of private individuals to raise an action and to get their rights by long-drawn-out proceedings—a factor which is not in itself in proportion with the political significance of an issue. Therefore a successful combination of politics and jurisdiction is coincidence rather than a feature of our system—and this may be the only reason why a considerable degree of political neutrality on the part of the judiciary can be sustained.

[17] See the hint by Enrico di Robilant, "Il diritto nella società industriale," *Rivista Internazionale di filosofia del diritto* 50 (1973), pp. 225–262, towards increasing "normazione surettizia" (clandestine regulating). Compare also Vilhelm Aubert, "The Changing Role of Law and Lawyers in Nineteenth- and Twentieth-Century Norwegian Society," *The Juridical Review* 17 (1972) pp. 97–112 (105). I am able to confirm this for the Federal Republic.

There is no lack of attempts, however, to render the political function of the judiciary a topic for critical discussion. The challenges range from farcical plays about court proceedings to studies in sociology of law, consciously conceived with a view to political ends and attempting to prove that judges exercise reactionary domination which stabilises the system.[18] The vast majority of full-time judges react in an allergic way to such sociological attacks. Sociologists are defeated as broadly as they challenge lawyers. And rightly so! To the accusation of stabilising the system the only answer, indeed, can be: so what?

## V

But, admittedly, this is not yet the answer to the question: what brings about professional identification and thus coherence to lawyers in the judiciary? If one follows the sociological theory for academic occupations, this coherence might consist of improved chances of agreement based on commonly recognised values and attitudes. There is, furthermore, the advantage of the possibility of taking knowledge for granted. Interaction is much easier when one can presuppose that one's partner knows the relevant statutes, sections or cases like oneself, or at least that he can be put into the picture with a few clues. But, is this enough to be a basis for social position and responsibility for a justifiable claim to respect, regard, obedience by others? To put it another way, do the vocational skill of lawyers and the integrity of their values contribute to the reputation of the institutions they work in?

It does not make much sense to answer this question with an absolute Yes or No. However, it is possible to point out some tendencies.

A claim to "scientific" consistency in juridical knowledge and practice has always been a characteristic of the German legal tradition. This is connected to a very broad and diffuse notion of science, applicable also to the classical disciplines. You do not study simply "law," but "legal science," the faculty is called "faculty of legal science," not "law faculty." With this in mind, efforts have been made to bring the legal material into a dogmatic, systematic order.

[18] Compare Wolfgang Kaupen/Theo Rasehorn, *Die Justiz zwischen Obrigkeit und Demokratie*, Neuwied—Berlin 1971; Karl-Dieter Opp/ Rüdiger Peuckert, *Ideologie und Fakten in der Rechtsprechung*; *Eine soziologische Untersuchung über das Urteil im Strafprozeß*, München 1971; Rüdiger Lautmann, *Justiz—die stille Gewalt*, Frankfurt 1972.

They have developed on the foundations of Roman law since the sixteenth century and have served to untie the strings which once attached law to religion and, at the same time, to make the law more consistent. This orientation towards " science " also expresses itself in the judgments of the highest courts of the Federal Republic, where they discuss scientific doctrines which come from universities, in a scholarly way. Courts quote and are quoted; thus they produce texts which demonstrate scientific scrutiny and solidarity of legal opinions—and not just the authority of the judge's office.

Therefore symptoms of a crisis in juridical dogmatics after decades spent on controversies over concepts and methods [19] have to be taken all the more seriously. At the same time, people become increasingly aware how little founded are the claims of lawyers to be scientists in a strict sense. These doubts and uncertainties nowadays fall back on university education. Important matters like civil law, criminal law, law of procedure, constitutional law were brought into statutes (or into the constitution respectively) just in time to enable legal science to switch over to the interpretation of statutes. By this very fact, however, as can be exemplified by many legal concepts, it lost much of its old sovereignty.[20] That sovereignty of ultimate and conclusive foundation which science has largely surrendered now appears as liberty of interpretation postulated by judges, and in this form it is liable to political attacks.

We must also consider other factors. Other disciplines have developed rapidly in the past hundred years and today set standards which legal science can never implement or even imitate. Therefore the lawyer nowadays is careful not to claim that he argues strictly in logical terms; logic demonstrates too clearly what would be required for doing so. The same distance is indispensable in relation to empirical social science, but is still under heavy discussion. So lawyers dwell in the first floor of a house, spacious and furnished in a somewhat old-fashioned way, without being certain whether the foundations and the roof are still in order. To a certain extent,

[19] Compare Josef Esser, Möglichkeiten und Grenzen des dogmatischen Denkens im modernen Zivilrecht, Archiv für die civilistische Praxis 172 (1972), pp. 97–130. Representatives of public law which is dogmatically systematised to a smaller extent are less sceptical. Compare the papers by Otto Bachof and Winfried Brohm on the subject: Die Dogmatik des Verwaltungsrechts vor den Gegenwartsaufgaben der Verwaltung, Veröffentlichungen der Vereinigung der deutschen Staatsrechtslehrer 30 (1972), pp. 193–244 and 245–312. See also Niklas Luhmann, *Rechtssystem und Rechtsdogmatik*, Stuttgart 1974.

[20] Knut Amelung, *Rechtsgüterschutz und Schutz der Gesellschaft* (Frankfurt, 1972), demonstrates this growing dependence of juridical dogmatics on statutes by the example of the term " Rechtsgut " (*i.e.* the social value a criminal law provision is aimed to protect).

perhaps, enough for the inmates, they will be able to make necessary repairs from inside. It will be possible to prosecute the claim for the refunding of the repair costs. But even then a certain uncomfortable feeling remains, which is difficult to articulate and cannot be translated into action.

The question arises, after the event, whether German lawyers had their wits about them when they moved into this house which belongs to the huge enterprise, science. Perhaps their British colleagues were wiser. But historical decisions are irreversible. For these historical reasons problems concerning methods and dogmatics and the question whether they should follow ways of abstract analysis or of empirical social science remain of considerable importance for the professional conscience of German lawyers. Our lawyers are taught to stylise their decision-making " cognising." And if they show some reluctance to accept this, then they do so with the attitude of the experienced practitioner, who has absolute mastery over the manipulation of professional requirements—and over their neglect.

Finally, part of this scene is that university doctrine and confidence in science appeared to give to lawyers in the nineteenth century an apolitical foundation which at the same time seemed " German " in an embracing sense, independent of the then existing territorial states. This feeling led them to lose sight of the political nature of any law. Legislation was estimated under " juridical " aspects in the light of its ability to handle figures of dogmatics. The concepts of a written constitution and of the rule of law were formulated from the angle of preventing abuses. The failure of these precautions after 1933, when abuse became usage, had been noticed, but after 1945 the only response was reconstruction and enforcement of the defences. Still today, the rule of law in Germany is thought to bc a matter of public law only, some kind of limitation of state authority. It is not held to imply action to shape life in an industrial society according to the principles of law, to distribute goods and opportunities as justly as possible, and it does not seem to entail the active participation of all citizens in legal matters. To correct this perspective which, with regard to politics, is peculiarly limited, becomes ever more difficult since the confidence of lawyers in their own devices is rather on the wane than waxing. Political experience in itself does not seem to be enough, all the more since it appears in rather negative conditions.

## VI

Finally, I want to refer this somewhat descriptive report back to the analysis I set out as an introduction. To me it seems to follow therefrom that the ethos of the individual practitioner is not as decisive for the future of the profession as the communication system among lawyers. This system is determined by dealing with texts and with experience laid down in texts. By means of common orientation towards texts which are produced for lawyers by lawyers, their profession has been able to bridge gaps between roles, such as divergences between the role of the judge and the role of the advocate, and also divergences between lawyers belonging to different organisations. In this way it is possible, in spite of the existing divergences of interests, to make interaction easier and to increase the chances of understanding or, at least, to develop common rules as to relevance and irrelevance. This facilitation of interaction and of understanding enables lawyers to give counsel to clients or organisations to which they belong, and, at the same time, by intensifying professional contacts, to gain self-consciousness and detachment from the interests they represent.

Such a system of communication has a limited capacity as to its complexity and to the pace of its change. If the boundaries are exceeded, it will react with defects of function and, in the end, with some kind of devaluation of its social importance. Sociology, in its present stage of development, cannot define these limits, either theoretically or empirically. Nonetheless, it is perhaps possible to indicate points of particular sensitivity in an analysis of individual legal systems.

As far as the Federal Republic of Germany is concerned, it can be stated that a claim to scientific methods and a political constitution with a sufficiently secured judiciary belong to the foundations of the system of law. Today these foundations are shaken to a degree which is difficult to estimate, and this, not least of all, by developments inside the legal system itself. The pace of changes in law has accelerated so much that the mutations of law can no longer be controlled by means of the hitherto existing dogmatic methods. At the same time political requirements, as far as input and output are concerned, have grown considerably: democracy, which refers to input functions, and the welfare state, which refers to output functions, are today, with us, political concepts without opponents, and in both ideas is inherent a tendency to dissolve formalistic legality and skill in handling definitions.

In this situation there are sign-posts indicating two ways out, on the basis of the hitherto prevailing professional ethos, leading in opposite directions. An expansive tendency starts with the educational system, and thus in the faculties. It expects great benefit from a legal training which is supplemented by social science. This point today is being discussed over the whole range of possibilities, up to the extreme position, according to which training in law should be replaced by training in criticising law. The opposite tendency could be called " fundamentalistic," and, indeed, a comparison with problems in the field of religion suggests itself. Here the retreat on to the indispensable core function of law is under discussion—regulation of conflicts by the judiciary, maintaining its autonomy by organisation, methods and ideology from the politically inspired legislature. Whereas the scientific tradition of German lawyers could possibly lead them in the first direction, traditional concepts of a constitution with a strong judiciary and neutralistic attitudes towards politics rather pull in the opposite direction. There are as yet no signs of a decision between these alternative courses any more than in the churches. The absence of such a decision must be taken as the most reliable symptom that the social position of the profession is on the wane.

NIKLAS LUHMANN
(Translated by TH. ELSTER)

[22]

*Cambridge Law Journal*, 49(2), July 1990, pp. 233–276
*Printed in Great Britain*

# LITIGATION-MANIA IN ENGLAND, GERMANY AND THE USA: ARE WE SO VERY DIFFERENT?*

BASIL S. MARKESINIS**

THIS paper was prompted by the *feeling* that the differences between the systems under comparison are not as great as they are commonly believed to be and by the *knowledge* that lawyers in each of these countries tend to have a vague if not distorted picture of each other's laws. The way I have tried to approach my subject has been through the use of statistics so, before I say anything about the differences between the systems, real or apparent, let me make some cautionary remarks.

## I. SOME PRELIMINARY OBSERVATIONS

The dangers entailed in the use of statistics have been emphasised by many well-known statements including Disraeli's famous aphorism about there being three types of lies: lies, damned lies and statistics. These dangers are greatly multiplied when statistics from different systems are compared. Here are some of the difficulties that one encounters; and they do not include the major one which is that as one moves from West to East the lack of legal statistics affects the researcher almost as much as the underlying suspicion that where they do exist they may either be unreliable or difficult to convert into statements meaningful to a different legal order.

* This is the text of the Atkin lecture delivered at the Reform Club in London on 9 November 1989. The statistical information given here has been derived from: the many publications of the Rand Corporation identified in the notes to the text; the Judicial Statistics for 1987 prepared by the Lord Chancellor's Department; the *Statistisches Jahrbuch* 1988; the *Handbuch der Justiz Jahrgang* 1988 and private communications from Professor. Dr Werner Lorenz, Director of the Institut für Internationales Recht der Universität München— Rechtsvergleichung; Professor Dr Christian von Bar, Director of the Institut für Internationales Privatrecht und Rechtsvergleichung der Universität Osnabrück; Dr Robert Dingwall, Centre for Socio-legal Studies, Oxford; Mr Helmut Nicolaus LL.M.(Cantab) Rechtsanwalt, Heidelberg and Mr Hans-Jorg Behrens of the University of Göttingen. Whenever I have used verbatim the text of a personal communication I have inserted it in inverted commas but, in order to avoid cluttering the text with too many notes, I have not always identified my correspondent. Grateful thanks are due to all of the above as well as to Professor Kevin Clermont of the Cornell Law School and Professor Richard Wright, of the Chicago-Kent Law School, for their helpful comments on earlier drafts of this paper.

** B. S. Markesinis D.Iur (Athen.), M.A., Ph.D., LL.D.(Cantab); of Gray's Inn, Barrister; Denning Professor of Comparative Law in the University of London, Queen Mary and Westfield College; Professor of Anglo-American Law in the University of Leiden.

1. *Courts/Judges.*

There is a vast number of different courts to be found in the various legal systems. When comparing these courts with those of other countries considerable difficulties may arise. For example, names are different and where they are the same they can, in fact, conceal different functions. Moreover, some courts are difficult to classify, *e.g.* the English magistrates' courts which are mainly staffed by lay, unpaid, part-time and, until recently, rather secretly selected men and women. Their inclusion in any statistics would seriously alter the number of judges in England and Wales. Yet, though they handle over 90 per cent. of all criminal cases, they are usually not included in the kind of calculations I shall be attempting. For my purposes this may be right since their jurisdiction in tort matters is non-existent and my main focus in this paper will be on tort law. Overall, however, their exclusion tends to falsify comparisons with other systems since they do legal work which, in other systems, professional judges have to do. Court Masters and Registrars also tend to be excluded from official calculations but, as we shall see, their omission is, for comparative purposes, even less defensible since they perform important judicial functions (including quantification of damages in personal injuries litigation) typically carried out by German or French judges. The county court Registrars in fact hear more cases than the "proper" judges so their exclusion from statistics is really quite unjustifiable. In 1987, for example, the number of judgments given by judges at hearings was 18,871. The corresponding number for Registrars was 142,528![1]

More difficult to count are Recorders (of whom there were 609 in 1987) and Assistant Recorders (of whom there were 417 in 1987). These are part-time judges and statistics show that whereas High Court judges sat for 14,152 days in 1987, Recorders and Assistant Recorders sat for a total of 22,458 days.[2] As *Table 1* thus shows, the total figure of judges in England comes to about 842. Subject to what was said previously, this must be one of the lowest figures in the world. But a relatively small alteration in the statistics to include magistrates, Court Masters and Registrars can place this country at the top of this league. And the figure of 28,000 or so still does not include those who hear disputes in Tribunals. (There are other differences between our systems and those of major European countries. For example, the average age of our judiciary, though coming down, is higher than that of France and Germany; and the

[1] Judicial Statistics (Cmnd. 428) 1987, pp. 35–6. The figures are for "money" plaints; if one includes plaints for the recovery of land, they become, respectively, 22,616 and 155,239. *Ibid.* at p. 41.

[2] *Ibid.*, p. 79.

TABLE 1

*Number of Judges in England, Germany and the USA in the mid 1980s*

| *England (and Wales)** | | *Germany* | | *USA‡* | |
|---|---|---|---|---|---|
| | | *I. Civil & Criminal* | | | |
| Appellate Judges | 34 | Amtsgerichte | 6,100 | State Courts | 8,000 |
| High Court Judges | 79 | Landgerichte | 4,685 | Fed. Courts | 1,500** |
| Circuit Judges | 393 | Oberlandes-gerichte | 1,640 | | |
| Recorders† | 72 | | | | |
| Assistant Recorders† | 52 | Bundes-gerichtshof | 128 | | |
| Registrars | 212 | | | | |
| Total | 842 | | 12,556 | | 9,500 |
| | | *II. Other Courts* | | | |
| Magistrates (approximately) | 28,000 | | 4,240 | | |
| | | *Grand Total* | | | |
| | 29,000 (?) (approx.) | | 16,796 | | 28,000** |

* This list does not include Deputy High Court Judges, Deputy Circuit Judges, Deputy County Court Registrars, High Court Masters or members of Tribunals, all of whom discharge duties carried out by judges in other systems.

† During 1987 the 79 High Court Judges sat a total of 14,152 days. 609 Recorders sat for 12,976 days and 417 Assistant Recorders sat for 9,482 days. Converting this part-time work to full-time work makes approximately 72 full-time Recorders and 52 Assistant Recorders.

‡ Judges of general jurisdiction only.

** See note 3 of text.

number of women judges is, in the higher echelons of our system, pitifully low compared with some of our closest neighbours, though this last point can be partly explained by the fact that the pool from which judges are drawn is very small and contains very few women. These, however, are matters that fall outside the scope of this paper.)

The American courts are also equally difficult to classify and available statistics vary from state to state.[3] Most statistics refer to courts of *general jurisdiction* (and in this article I use the term loosely to include state trial courts of general jurisdiction as well as federal courts exercising diversity jurisdiction) but a large number of courts

[3] The estimates given in Table 1 are taken from Professor Abrahams, *The Judicial Process* (1986) p. 23. The number of federal judges includes 9 Supreme Court Justices, 158 judges of the US Circuit Courts and 576 judges of the District Courts. To this total of 753 one should add other federal judges such as: the bankruptcy judges (232), the federal judges of the US Tax Court (19), the Court of Military Appeals (3), the Claims Court (16), the Court of Appeals for the Federal Circuit (12) and the US Court of International Trade (9). One should, perhaps also include all "senior" (*i.e.* retired) appeals judges and district judges voluntarily serving on a full or part time basis as well as US Magistrates.

of *limited jurisdiction*, each subject to different rules, also handle tort litigation. Indeed, estimates suggest[4] that of civil suits 54·5 per cent. may go to courts of general jurisdiction and 45·5 per cent. may end up in the (inferior) courts of limited jurisdiction. Thus, the figures given by most statistics concentrating on courts of general jurisdiction may often be well below total figures. (Note, however, that whereas tort litigation in courts of general jurisdiction represents about 10 per cent. of the total, in courts of limited jurisdiction the percentage of tort disputes is about 4·9 per cent. of the total.[5]) On the whole, one could say that we have good statistics for federal courts, statistics of variable quality for state courts of general jurisdiction and meagre statistical evidence for courts of limited jurisdiction.

The German courts included in this survey pose another difficulty. This is caused by the high degree of specialisation which is evident from *Figure 1*.[6] There are thus six Supreme Courts and 11 Senates in the Bundesgerichtshof (Supreme Federal Court) alone. A vicarious liability dispute, for example, could thus go to the Labour Court, the Federal Court and, within the latter, to its tort or contract section. Because of the system of cumulation of actions (*Anspruchs Konkurrenz*) many tort cases are *also* pleaded in contract. Moreover, certain types of claims, which in systems such as ours are tortious in nature, would be handled under the contractual doctrine of *culpa in contrahendo*.[7] Thus, it is not always obvious exactly how these cases are classified and counted for the purposes of statistics. *Table 2* provides some idea of the kind of work done by the various Senates (or Divisions) of the Federal (Supreme) Court and, incidentally, also provides some data about the number of final judgments given on merit (not merely on procedural grounds), the average time of hearing in the Bundesgerichtshof as well as the average monetary value of litigation. Since the average time taken to dispose of a case varies from Senate to Senate[8] the allocation of a case to a particular

[4] Kakalik and Pace, *Costs and Compensation Paid in Tort Litigation* (1986), p. 9. This and other statistical studies quoted in this paper were published by the Rand Corporation.

[5] Kakalik and Pace, *op. cit.*, p. 9 note 19.

[6] Reproduced from Markesinis, *The German Law of Torts*, 2nd ed. (1990).

[7] Thus, the equivalent of our tort case of *Ward* v. *Tesco* [1976] 1 W.L.R. 810 is BGHZ 66,51 and it was heard by the eighth civil division of the Federal Court which, normally, deals with sales of goods and leases. Since the plaintiff also won on tort grounds, the sixth civil division could also have heard the case. Finally, since *culpa in contrahendo* is a contractual doctrine the case could, in theory, also have been claimed by the seventh division which handles contractual disputes. Other divisions could handle and have handled such claims which we classify as tortious. For examples see Markesinis, *The German Law of Torts*, 2nd edn. (1990), chapter 3, section B.2. This problem of proper or, rather, consistent classification also exists at the state level in the USA where, apparently, "not all state courts distinguish tort litigation from other civil cases such as commercial and contract writs". Hensler, Vaiana, Kakalik, Peterson, *Trends in Tort Litigation. The Story Behind the Statistics* (1987), p. 6.

[8] The average time of a disposal of a case by means of a judgment on merits in the BGH is 15·8 months. For more precise details depending on the nature of the dispute see *Table 2*. The *average* time from issue of writ to judgment by the BGH seems to be 34·2 months.

FIGURE 1

*The Structure of the German Courts**

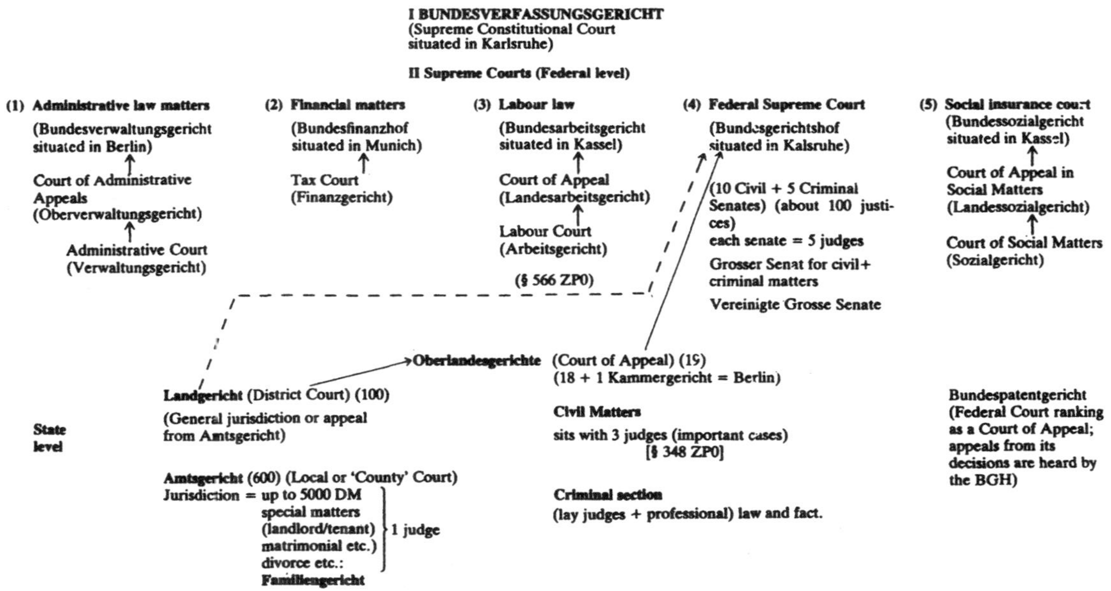


* From B. S. Markesinis, *The German Law of Torts*, 2nd edn (1990).

TABLE 2
*Bundesgerichtshof Senates, Specialisation/number of* final *judgments/average awards 1986*

| *Senate* | *Type of case considered* | *Nos of judgments* | *Average time in BGH (months)* | *Average value of claims* (ex. costs) DM |
|---|---|---|---|---|
| I | Competition, trademark | 101 | 25·4 | 188,200 |
| II | Companies, Stock Exchange Disputes | 95 | 10·4 | 473,400 |
| III | Building and planning, Bankruptcy, § 839 BGB | 82 | 16·3 | 279,500 |
| IVa | Insurance contracts | 94 | 20·3 | 165,500 |
| IVb | Family Law | 63 | 13·7 | 63,600 |
| V | Land Law | 56 | 17·3 | 328,000 |
| VI | Tort | 80 | 13·2 | 122,600 |
| VII | Contracts | 51 | 13·3 | 179,500 |
| VIII | Commercial law, landlord/tenant | 70 | 12·0 | 232,700 |
| IX | Execution of judgments | 49 | 9·3 | 211,000 |
| X | Patents, copyrights | 12 | 14·1 | 229,500 |
| | Kartellsenat | 12 | 16·4 | 426,800 |
| | Dienstgericht (staff disputes) | 5 | 7·2 | 14,000 |

Senate may also be a matter of importance. Similar considerations may also influence American litigants who have a choice between going to a federal or a state court.

2. *Writs/Claims/Filings.*

These terms are often used interchangeably but they mean different things. In this country, for example, the medical defence societies constantly talk of an "increase in claims" but we are not told how many of these claims actually turn into writs. Some knowledgeable colleagues have suggested to me that some of these claims may consist of nothing more than a letter from a solicitor which is then not followed up by any further action. Yet they are still recorded as claims, thus possibly distorting the overall impact that this information can have. The secrecy with which the medical defence societies shroud this part of their operations makes any comment on such views impossible. Difficulties are also compounded by the fact that court filings are defined in different ways in the USA. In some states, for example New York and New Jersey, civil filings are included in judicial statistics only when the case has been "placed on the calendar" or has reached "issue" or "readiness". Thus, in those two large states, a case that settles early in the process is never recorded for statistical purposes.[9]

3. *Damage awards.*

There are three major dangers here. First, the terms *average* (sometimes more accurately referred to as *mean*) and *median* are not always used precisely or consistently while the equally interesting statistical indicator of the typical award—the *mode* (*i.e.* the value that occurs most frequently)—seems to be rarely used. Secondly, there are enormous variations on the basis of (a) regions within federal states such as the USA (*e.g.* California and Chicago compared to Louisiana[10]) or even within some unitary states (*e.g.* France[11]) and (b) type of tort litigation, *e.g.* products liability and medical malpractice, compared to other tort cases (about which further on). Thirdly, the average figures given are, more often than not, stated without reference to out-of-court settlements—which account for approximately 90 per cent. of all payments; and they do not include defendants' verdicts or subsequent adjustments by means of settlements, remittiturs or appeals. In practice this can make an enormous difference. For example, in the notorious *Ford Pinto* case a jury award of US$ 125 million was subsequently reduced to US$ 3·5 million.[12] Finally, figures given are often not properly adjusted to take into account factors such as inflation. Thus, though it is generally accepted that recorded claims have exceeded the rate of inflation since the 1970s, the exact amount is not beyond dispute.[13]

[9] Kakalik and Pace, *op. cit.*, p. 7.

[10] California and Illinois (Cook County in particular) seem to have received enormous attention whereas other states are hardly ever mentioned. Even between these two states the differences can be impressive. For example, punitive damages were awarded in business/contract cases three times more often in major urban Californian jurisdictions than they were in Cook County. *Punitive Damages. Empirical Findings* (Rand publication 1987), p. 34. Punitive damages are not as easily available in Louisiana—a state with a civil law background.

[11] On this see: Viney and Markesinis, *La Reparation du Dommage Corporel—Essai de Comparaison des Droits Anglais et Français* (1985), para. 30.

[12] *Grimshaw* v. *Ford Motor Co.* 119 Cal.App. 3rd 757. Punitive damages in product liability cases have caused much discussion yet the Rand Corporation study quoted above (p. v) states that "our analyses indicate that punitive damages were awarded in only four product liability cases in San Francisco and two in Cook County from 1960 through 1984". Apparently, before 1980 60 per cent. of all punitive awards occurred in intentional torts. After 1980 the percentage dropped to 22 and business/contract cases generated 67 per cent. of all punitive awards. *Ibid.*, p. 19. About 2 per cent. of trials involving personal injury resulted in punitive awards (*Ibid.*, p. 11). In another study by a Rand Corporation team—Hensler, Vaiana, Kakalik and Peterson, *op. cit.* note 7, above, at pp. 22–3 it is said "that awards most likely to be viewed as 'excessive' . . . are most likely to be cut substantially".

[13] On this, see Galanter, "Reading the Landscape of Disputes: What we know and don't know (and think we know) about our allegedly contentious and litigious society", 31 *UCLA Law Rev.* 4 (1983) and, especially, Galanter, "The Day after the Litigation Explosion", 46 *Maryland L. Rev.* 3 (1986). For a more *nuancé* description see Hensler, Vaiana, Kakalik and Peterson, *op. cit.* note 7, above, at pp. 14–24.

In my experience the only entities which have figures are the insurance companies and, once again, they tend to guard them jealously.

## II. Why the Differences?

Despite the caveats expressed concerning the dangers inherent in statistics, comparisons can be and have been made between various legal systems. Making use of such figures, England and the USA have, in particular, often been compared and such exercises have prompted various conclusions among which the central one is that American society is much more lawyer-oriented and litigious than the English. For example, Professor Atiyah, paraphrasing Bernard Shaw, has referred to England and America as two countries

Figure 2
*Total Number* of Civil Actions*

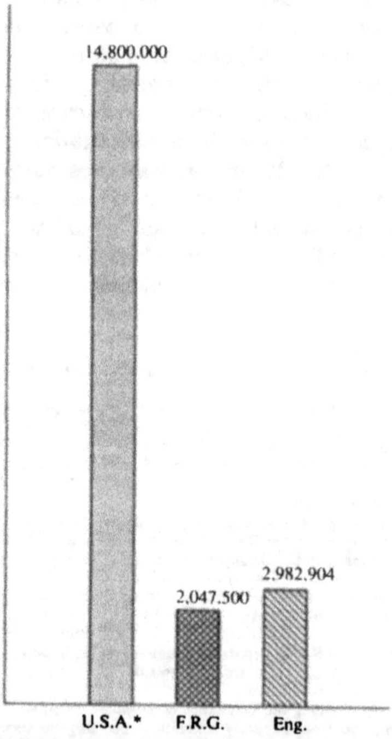


* Figures refer to filings in courts of general *and* limited jurisdictions. 54·2 per cent of this total—*i.e.* 8·02 million—are *estimated* to be general jurisdiction filings.

separated by a common legal culture.[14] *Figures 2* and *3* tend, at first sight at least, to support the view that, even allowing for the population differences, there exist important differences between the systems. However, as we shall see further on, the real differences are not to be found in overall figures but in particular types of

FIGURE 3
*Number of Tort Suits*

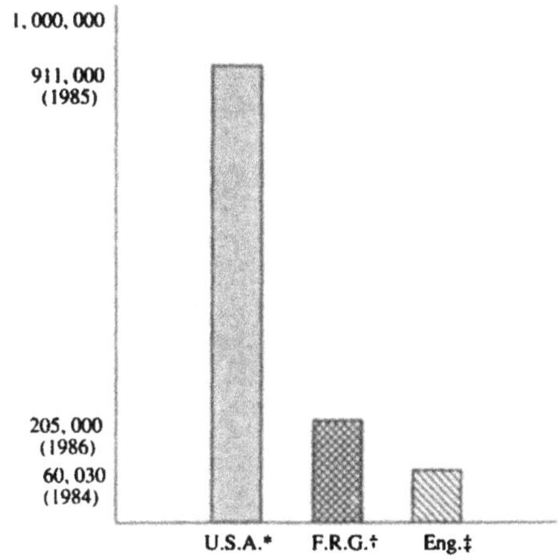


* American figures refer to filings in courts of *general* jurisdiction (see Table 1). Of the 911,000, 869,000 were filings in state courts and 42,000 in federal courts.

† This is an estimate based on (a) the percentage of tort actions fought to the end in the Bundesgerichtshof (BGH) which, over the years, has been somewhere in the order of 8 per cent. of that court's total number of decisions and (b) the opinions expressed to me that for various reasons the BGH figure is likely to be higher than the overall percentage.

‡ Judicial Statistics Annual Report 1987 (Cmnd. 428) 1988
31,470 writs issued in High Court for pers. injuries;
24,060 writs issued in County Courts for pers. injuries
In addition:
550 non-personal injury tort suits in High Court
4,920 non-personal injury tort suits in County Court

litigation. The reasons for these differences are many and some of them may have been overstressed or, conversely, understressed in importance. The use of German figures tends to support this scepticism and can introduce an altogether different dimension to the enquiry since it is obvious that the Federal Republic in some respects

[14] "Tort Law and the Alternatives: Some Anglo-American Comparisons", 1987 *Duke L. Journ.* 1002, p. 1005.

shows greater affinity with the American scene than it does with England. How, then, can we explain some of these differences between the various systems? Here, first, are some possible explanations covering the Anglo-American differences.

A number of reasons have been advanced to explain the differences between England and the USA suggested by the figures. One can go through them quickly since a number of authors have already examined them in a number of works.[15]

1. *Political judges with definite ideas for social reform.*

The paralysis of legislatures, provoked by competing lobby pressures, is a notorious phenomenon in the USA and is one reason for the fact that much of American tort reform was achieved after the Second World War by means of judicial initiatives at state level and *not*, as in England through legislative action. Another and related reason is the optimistic belief that change always entails progress. This, in turn, induces a sense of mission to improve the existing legal order that many of my American colleagues, students and legal friends display at times with endearing if somewhat naïve fervour. Judicial innovation thus fits in with the mood of a society which is physically and intellectually constantly "on the move". By contrast static or traditionalist societies like ours seek refuge in notions like *stare decisis* and opt for incremental changes and—what is worse—phased corrections of admitted errors. What, however, is most striking to a foreign observer is the American judge's *open* commitment to social reform which is often connected with the fact that many judges (a) are elected by popular vote and (b) may have run for judicial office only after they failed in their bid to capture high political office. Robert Neely, an elected member of the Supreme Court of West Virginia, unusually outspoken even by American standards, is a good example since in his many writings he has clearly expressed the attitude that I have just mentioned.[16]

2. *The pro-plaintiff bar.*

The pro-plaintiff bar effectively represented by its own organisation—the Association of Trial Lawyers of America (ATLA)—is also a well-documented phenomenon as is its influence as a pressure group both in local politics and judicial appointments. ATLA has, with evangelical fervour, been particularly active in fending off moves to undo by legislative action (promoted with equal

[15] John Fleming's *The American Tort Process* (1988) is one of the most recent and it provides rich references to further related literature.

[16] See, for example: *How Courts Govern America* (1981) and *The Product Liability Mess* (1988). For a more restrained account see Atiyah and Summers, *Form and Substance in Anglo-American Law* (1987), chapters 10 and 12.

fervour by the insurance industry) judicial decisions that were favourable to plaintiffs. The introduction of no-fault automobile plans—avoiding jury involvement—and the attempts to limit the extent of medical liability were thus strenuously opposed. Even more questionable—at any rate to non-American lawyers—is the extensive political mobilisation, often furthered by substantial financial donations, to secure the appointment of demonstrably pro-plaintiff lawyers to the highest judicial offices; or, as happened with California's Chief Justice Rose Bird, to secure her re-election as Chief Justice in the face of growing opposition towards her judicial activism, especially but not solely in criminal matters. (In my opinion the recent defeats of pro-plaintiff justices in the Supreme Courts of some states—such as Texas and California—indicate in part that the electorate may be slowly becoming aware of some of the excesses of the pro-plaintiff lobby but non-American lawyers should be slow in formulating definite opinions on such complicated issues.) The pro-plaintiff bar, however, has also had influential academic defenders who saw 19th century American tort law as deliberately subsidising nascent industrialisation at the expense of the working classes[17] and thus welcomed the pro-plaintiff decisions as an inevitable attempt by the courts to fill the gap left by a non-existent welfare state. These pro-plaintiff views may, in many respects, be closely linked to the next factor.

3. *The absence of a strong welfare state system.*

This results in many victims of accidents being left with little or no coverage for their medical treatment and, therefore, being forced to seek redress through generous tort awards. The importance of this factor is mentioned here partly because it explains the generosity (real or apparent[18]) of American tort awards—something which has often been forgotten by potential imitators on the other side of the Atlantic (for example when, in the 1970s, they became excited about American products liability law)—and partly because in some (European) systems the existence of a generous welfare system has resulted in the reduction or even total absence of a certain type of litigation which, by contrast, has been very popular in another. Thus Professor Lorenz wrote to me that "The German social security system has the effect that many cases are not litigated. A typical example seems to be *Asbestos*. Certainly, the number of illnesses and

[17] *E.g.* Horwitz, *The Transformation of American Law 1780–1860* (1977), severely criticized by, among others, Schwartz, "Tort Law and the Economy in Nineteenth Century America: A Reinterpretation" 90 *Yale L.J.* 1717 (1981); *idem.*, "The Character of early American Tort Law" 36 *UCLA L. Rev.* 641 (1989).

[18] I shall return to this point below.

even deaths due to asbestos is alarming.[19] However, thus far no asbestos case has been reported from the BGH. I have discussed the matter with my colleague Dieter Medicus [an eminent Professor of Civil Law at the University of Munich] . . . and he, too, knows of no relevant litigation." As we shall see, in this matter the UK is somewhere in between these two extremes with a tiny number of cases—apparently only twenty-nine—*tried* by courts in England, Scotland and Northern Ireland between 1970 and 1987 and rather more writs issued but settled without a final judgment. Why exactly the German social security system has discouraged this type of litigation, whereas the English has not done so, is not entirely clear. The comparative generosity of German and English social security awards is thus another topic that warrants further investigation.

4. *The presence of a large number of lawyers and the availability—in different forms—of the contingency fee system.*

These are also crucial factors as far as "easy access to justice" is concerned. The American figures in *Table 3* would, again, *appear* to

TABLE 3

*Number of Practising Lawyers*

| *England (and Wales)* | | *Germany* | | *USA* |
|---|---|---|---|---|
| Barristers | 5,369 | Attorneys | 41,724 | 674,000 |
| Solicitors | 50,337 | Attorneys/ Notaries | 7,520 | |
| | | Notaries | 1,003 | |
| Total | 55,706 | Total | 50,347 | |
| | *Judges and Lawyers per 1 million of population*† | | | |
| Judges | 16·8* | | 278 | 116 |
| Lawyers | 1,120 | | 810 | 2,808 |

* Counting only the 842 (see Table 1). The figure is thus suspect.

† Population of:

| | |
|---|---|
| *United Kingdom* | 56,972,700 |
| England | 47,254,000 |
| Wales | 2,821,000 |
| Scotland | 5,121,000 |
| N. Ireland | 1,575,200 |
| *Federal Republic of Germany* | 61,149,000 |
| *USA* | 239,283,000 |

Source: Whitaker's Almanac 1989.

[19] Thus, for example, the *Süddeutsche Zeitung* reported in its issue of 26 June 1989 that the *Deutscher Gewerkschaftsbund* (German Trade Union Association) had recorded 292 instances of asbestos-related complaints—46 of them being fatal. It would be interesting to see a comparative study of social security payments in comparable situations in England and Germany in order to explain the apparently total lack of litigation in Germany.

support this conclusion. Critics of the contingency fee system also blame this method of payment of the legal fees for much of the litigation. Defenders of the system have not only drawn attention to the shortcomings of our own legal aid scheme but have also stressed, with some measure of accuracy, that attorneys can be quite sophisticated in calculating their chances of success and will refuse to take on a case if it looks hopeless or even weak. In this context, an interesting feature of the American system is the use of in-house doctors to advise a firm whether to take on a medical malpractice case—a course of action which, apparently, leads to something in the order of 85 per cent. of potential plaintiffs being turned down by legal firms. Still, one also hears of a number of quite frivolous tort claims brought before American courts, a fact which suggests that not all lawyers are as selective; these claims also reveal something of the litigious nature of the Americans to which I shall return later in this lecture.[20]

5. *Juries.*

Here, I think, lies one of the crucial differences. According to Professor John Fleming of the University of California at Berkeley it would not be an exaggeration to say that the transformation of American tort law owes much to the surrender of most legal concepts to civil juries.[21] As a result, the ambit of many tort rules has been widened beyond the limits accepted by English law. Thus, the combined effect of lax attitudes by judges (especially trial judges) and juries has led to tort liability moving even further away from fault than it has in English law (*e.g.* product liability law); and many non-liability enclaves of English law have vanished in the USA (*e.g.* liability for certain types of omission).

The effect that juries have had on the development of American substantive tort law was recently examined by Professor John Fleming and little need be added here. For present purposes, however, three things are worth stressing—and they emerge clearly, from various statistical surveys. The *first*, clearly supported by the various Rand Corporation studies, is the juries' propensity to vary and adjust the

[20] A number of amusing/outrageous examples are given in *U.S. News and World Report*, 4 December 1978. For those who collect these stories the *Californian Lawyer*, July 1989 vol. 9, no. 7, p. 34 contains the latest outrageous example: A fifteen year old girl and her mother filed a claim against the girl's boy friend claiming $49·53 for "the cost of the shoes, flowers and hairdo (that the girl) never got to wear" because the boy "stood her up for the date. Filing the claim cost $31·75." This type of situation has, apparently, led to court filings in the past. See *U.S. News and World Report* 1978, p. 50. Stories like these, and the one with which Mr Bernard Levin entertained his readers (*The Times*, 29 June 1989) are amusing, but they are dangerously misleading if they provide, as they often do, the only conception that ordinary people have about the American system and how it works in practice.

[21] Fleming, *op. cit.*, p. 131.

amounts awarded depending on the circumstances of the accident. Thus, if the loss of two legs in a car accident will result in an average $250,000 in compensation, *the same loss to the same kind of plaintiff*, resulting from an accident in the workplace (probably as the result of a defective product) can produce, on average, three times as much compensation. The *second* thing that juries do is to relate damages to the defendant's degree of fault and his financial resources. That juries, once again, treat identical injuries differently depending on *who* is being sued does not seem to be in doubt. What does remain unsettled is the extent that jury damage awards deny equal justice. Thus, one Rand Corporation study[22] has claimed that government defendants pay three times more than private defendants and corporate defendants pay four and a half times more. The result, according to the same study, is that "where a government defendant might pay $75,000 and an individual defendant $50,000 to a severely injured plaintiff, a corporate defendant would pay $220,000. Other studies, however, suggest that the differences may be much less pronounced,[23] while yet a third study, which has focused on median awards made by Cook County juries in cases involving damage to property, distinguished between "moderate" and "serious" cases. In the first category median awards against individuals were $27,000, against corporations were $35,000 and against government entities were $41,000. In the second category the figures were $37,000 against individuals, $98,000 against government entities and $161,000 against corporations. As the study concludes "this 165 to 335 per cent. difference is staggering".[24] There is no detailed study showing to what extent, if any, judges—consciously or unconsciously—do the same thing in those systems where juries are ignored. In Germany, however, judges tend to increase the size of awards in privacy and

[22] Chin and Peterson, *Deep Pockets, Empty Pockets. Who Wins in Cook County Jury Trials* (1985), p. vii. Interestingly enough post-verdict reduction of awards is also smaller where deep-pocket defendants are involved. See: Hensler, Vaiana, Kakalik and Peterson, *op. cit.* note 7, above, p. 22. The tendency to punish corporate defendants is even greater in cases involving punitive awards. These results have been replicated by two other researchers using a mock juror experiment. As MacCoun, who reports the work in *Getting Inside the Black Box: Toward a Better Understanding of Civil Jury Behaviour* (1987), p. 34, puts it: "Hans and Ermann created a brief trial summary in which several workers received permanent lung damage following exposure to a toxic substance during a landscaping job. Students read one of two versions of the case in which the defendant was described as either 'Mr. Jones' or 'the Jones Corporation'. This simple manipulation influenced *both* liability and damage judgments. The corporation was held liable for *significantly* more claims than the individual, and awards against the corporation were *significantly* larger than awards against the individual in each category of damages: *hospital bills*, and especially '*pain and suffering*'." (Italics supplied.)

[23] See, for example, *Claim File Data Analysis: Technical Analysis of Study Results*, Insurance Services Office (ISO) Data, Inc. (1988) pp. 39, 45. Where average loss for single defendant claims (involving $25,000 or more) are stated to be $91,466 for government defendants, $90,320 for business defendants and $78,821 for individual defendants.

[24] Kelly and Beyler, "Large Damage Awards and the Insurance Crisis: Causes, Effects and Cures", 130 *Illinois Bar Journal* 140, 153 (1986).

defamation cases where media defendants are involved. And there is also anecdotal evidence to suggest that the same happens in French contract and tort law. Since, however, the open linking of damages to the degree of the defendant's fault and his status would, automatically, justify a *pourvoi* to the court of cassation, there is little evidence of such practice in the reports. *Finally*, the lack of even a relative degree of consistency in some cases of jury awards must make it more difficult for extra-judicial settlements to be reached. Thus in the mid 1980s an ABA conference was told that "the same injury might lead to a tort award ranging from $10,000 to $2 million".[25] At about the same time Judge Klein (a Philadelphia Common Pleas judge) said in *Blue* v. *Johns-Manville Corp.*,[26] "In two cases before this judge, two men had similar physical problems. They each had pleural thickening and some shortness of breath. In the case involving the man who most counsel believed to be the sicker of the two, the jury awarded $15,000. For the other plaintiff, the jury awarded $1,200,000. These results make this litigation more like a roulette than jurisprudence."

## III. What Does the Comparison with Germany Suggest?

If we look again at *Figures 2*, and *3* and *Table 1* (and allow for population differences given in *Table 3*) we see that the Germans bring approximately 55 per cent. of the total number of suits brought by the Americans but have (again allowing for population differences) almost 100 per cent. more judges (though fewer attorneys)[27] to handle their judicial load. The English, on the other hand, seem to have the *same* overall number of actions as the Americans, though when it comes to judges they tend to underplay their numbers.

If we shift to the tort scene the picture changes. If the German estimate of tort suits is correct—a big assumption as one sees from the second note to *Figure 3*—the rate of tort litigation in that country is about the same as it is in the USA. In terms of tort suits per 1 million of population that means some 3,750 suits in America as against 3,278 suits in Germany—a roughly comparable figure. England, on the other hand, reveals a different picture. Tort suits are, apparently, about three times less numerous than they are in the

25 *Towards a Jurisprudence of Injury: A Summary of the Report of the A.B.A.'s Special Committee on the Tort Liability System* (1986), pp. 2–26.

26 10 Phila. 23 (1983). This statement was quoted as one illustration of the kind of difficulties encountered in asbestos litigation by Judge Weis in the important *In Re School Asbestos Litigation* 789 F 2d. (1986). A Rand Corporation Study by Hensler, Felstiner, Selvin and Ebener entitled *Asbestos in the Courts* (1985) states at p. 42 that those problems may in part be due to the difficulties experienced by juries when "dealing with probabilistic [sic] evidence".

27 The word is used in a neutral way to avoid distinctions between barristers, solicitors, Rechtsanwalt, notaries, etc.

USA and Germany or about 1,200 tort actions per 1 million of population. In view of the above, are we right to compare ourselves with the Americans and claim that they are afflicted by a tort crisis and we are not? If so, what are the reasons that have provoked the American crisis and can they affect us as well? Should we bracket Germany with the USA and claim—as they, themselves, do not—that there is a tort crisis in Germany? Could it be that we in England have been spoilt by low rates of litigation[28] and, if so, why do we sue less in tort than other nations but, in other contexts, we are apparently willing to chance litigation as much as they do? The introduction of the German figures—despite the uncertainty that surrounds them—thus forces one to re-examine the validity of the reasons given to explain the differences between England and the USA.

The German scene makes a number of things clear. You do not need a politically-minded judiciary in order to encourage frequent recourse to the courts. Nor does the absence of the contingency fee system necessarily avoid it. (The Scottish version of the contingency fee system seems to be different.) The absence of a pro-plaintiff bar in the American style has also not discouraged Germans from going to court. Finally, a stronger social security system may make tort awards *appear* to be smaller than they actually are in terms of total compensation; and it does not always stop aggrieved citizens from having recourse to tort law. What about the legal rules: are they more or less generous to plaintiffs than the American ones?

Conventional wisdom has it that American tort rules are more generous towards plaintiffs than the English ones. But when you compare American and German tort rules the verdict does not appear to me to be uniformly in favour of one or the other system. Thus, German law blazed the trail in actions for pre-natal injuries; it is still more generous than Anglo-American law to victims of nervous shock; and it has never taken a completely hostile view towards liability for harmful omissions in the way that English (and less so American) law have done. On the other hand, it took longer to reach the levels of strict liability attained by American product liability law; and in the context of fatal accident actions, it has drawn the list of dependants who can claim damages in a more restricted way, preferring, perhaps, certainty to flexible justice (as the French do in this matter). In matters of causation it has also treated the adequate cause test in an expansive manner, not dissimilar to our foreseeability test—so much so that for some time now the trend has been to rely more on

[28] It is clear, for example, that there have been fewer asbestos-related suits in this country than there have been in the USA even though, as we shall note below, where legal action was taken it produced remarkably similar awards in both systems. Felstiner and Dingwall, *Asbestos Litigation in the United Kingdom* (1988), especially pp. 17 *et seq.* and *Table 12*.

normative tests of causation, such as the scope of the rule theory.[29]

Yet, paradoxically perhaps, one cannot find in its generous legal rules the reason for greater litigiousness since nervous shock cases, omission cases and the like never seem to have produced a formidable body of case law. On the contrary, the great generators of litigation have been such well-known causes as traffic accidents (despite the strict liability Road Traffic Act which by avoiding fault liability was meant to facilitate the compensation of victims of traffic accidents) and the related difficulties of evaluating damages for personal injury. According to the *Statistisches Jahrbuch* for 1988, a total of 160,975 such actions were instigated in 1986 of which the vast majority—123,237—were commenced in the *Amtsgerichte* (which suggests that they involved claims below 5,000 DM). The other highly litigated subjects are sales of goods (often raising tort problems as well, a total of 277,440 actions), the law concerning builders and architects (27,188), and the law of landlord and tenant (275,510 actions),[30] all well known both in England and the USA. Matrimonial disputes also account for a substantial proportion of litigation. One cannot, therefore, find here, either, a special explanation for the greater volume of litigation. Indeed, as already stated, in terms of law suits *commenced*—proportionate to their populations—the difference between the three countries compared in this paper is not as great as commonly believed. *Figure 2* suggests as much. Certain types of product liability and medical malpractice disputes may, as we shall see, provide the greatest differences with the USA in terms of number of suits brought and, above all, in the potential to lead to "mega-awards".

But if the reasons for the greater volume of litigation have not yet been identified, and all that we seem to have managed to do so

[29] For more details on all these topics see my *German Law of Tort: A Comparative Introduction* 2nd ed. (1990). In his study "Das Problem des Kausalzusammenhangs im Privatrecht" reprinted in his *Gesammelte Schriften*, I, p. 395 *et seq.*, Professor Ernst von Caemmerer reached the conclusion that the plaintiff's claim will rarely if ever fail if adequate causation is the only "corrective" device in the hands of the judge. Our foreseeability test can reach similarly outrageous results. See *Meah* v. *McCreamer (No. 1)* [1985] 1 All E.R. 367 and *(No. 2)* [1986] 1 All E.R. 943.

[30] *Statistisches Jahrbuch* 1988, p. 331. The statistics give no details about particular types of negligence litigation under para. 823 I BGB such as for example the number of medical malpractice claims that reach the courts. Thus I have only been able to find *estimates* that put the figure of claims satisfied (by Arbitration Boards *and* courts) at about 3,000. Deutsch, Schreiber and Lilie, *Medizinische Verantwortlichkeit und Verfahren* in *Medical Responsibility in Western Europe* (1985), pp. 226 *et seq.* esp. 230. Most commentators, including the aforementioned authors, draw statistical information from Professor Hans-Leo Weyers's empirical work published in *Gutachten A für den 52. Deutschen Juristentag. Empfiehet es sich, im Interesse der Patienten and Artzen ergänzende Regelungen für das ärztliche Vertrags-(Standes-) und Haftungrecht einzuführen?* Verhandlungen des 52. Deutschen Juristentages München 1978 Bd. 1, pp. 37 *et seq.* This survey, however, though replete with interesting information, invariably refers to claims met by Arbitration Boards and courts. Moreover, it seems to me to suffer from the fact that its information is: (a) about fifteen years old and (b) its estimates derived from inadequate sources.

far is to weaken the value of the explanations of the American phenomenon, the reasons for the greater number of judges are less difficult to discern. Obviously, a greater volume of litigation needs more professionals to handle it properly. Overall at the writ stage there are, as *Figure 2* demonstrates, some differences in the volume of litigation. What is important, however, is not the number of law actions *commenced*—England, for example, as *Figure 2* shows, has a higher number than Germany despite the fact that it has a smaller population—but how many of them actually run *their full course* and end by means of a judgment of the court pronouncing on the merits

**TABLE 4**

***I Civil Proceedings before the German Courts***

| | |
|---|---|
| *I Number of writs issued* | |
| (i) *Amtsgerichte* | |
| (general civil jurisdiction) | 1,306,628 |
| (ii) *Amtsgerichte* | |
| (family division) | 368,406 |
| (iii) *Landgerichte* | |
| (as court of first instance) | 353,292 |
| Total Number: | 2,028,326 |
| *II Number of actions decided in 1986* | |
| 1. *Amtsgerichte* | |
| settled out of court | 576,122 |
| undefended (resolved by court) | 353,907 |
| fought to the end | 376,599 |
| Total | 1,306,628 |
| 2. *Landgerichte* | |
| settled out of court | 175,963 |
| undefended (resolved by court) | 72,987 |
| fought to end | 104,542 |
| Total | 353,292 |
| 3. Family Division (only matrimonial) (divorce cases reported only) | |
| undefended | 29,597 |
| fought to end | 124,630 |
| 4. *Landgerichte* (sitting as court of first instance) | |
| Total | 87,981 |
| number fought to end | 48,007 |
| 5. Courts of Appeal | |
| total | 53,633 |
| fought to end | 25,668 |

of the case. Here, if we compare the figures in *Tables 4, 5* and *6*, we see that in England a remarkably low number actually reaches the very end. Moreover, if one takes the county court figure (*Table 6*), one notices that over half of these cases are resolved through

TABLE 5
*Summary analysis of Queen's Bench Division in 1986*

| | |
|---|---|
| Total proceedings commenced | 234,782 |
| Matters involved — debt | 183,199 |
| — breach of contract | 9,150 |
| — personal injury & death | 24,183 |
| — recovery of land | 5,190 |
| — other | 13,060 |
| Judgments given without trial (by default; Order 14 etc.) | 100,967 |
| Contested cases ending with judgment | |
| — personal injury and death | 2,670 |
| — other | 1,010 |
| Total | 3,680 |

TABLE 6
*The Work-load of the County Courts in 1987*

| | |
|---|---|
| All nature of plaints | 2,375,431 |
| Judgments enforced by default or with consent | 1,184,264 |
| Cases decided by formal trial | *23,248 |
| Cases decided by arbitration of Registrar | †47,841 |

* 14,675 decided by a judge
8,573 decided by a Registrar
† 45,612 after arbitration by Registrar
229 after arbitration by a judge

Source: *Judicial Statistics* 1987, p. 35.

arbitration with the intervention of one official—the Registrar—whom as I said we do not (yet) dignify with the title of "judge". Here then, we have a very significant difference between the English and German scenes.

A second reason for the need for more judges in Germany is, of course, the fact that in that system (as in all civil law systems) the judge has to do so much more in a case than his common law counterpart. So, while in the procedure of civil law courts the advocate plays, on the whole, a more passive role, the judge, in the context of the prevailing inquisitorial system, has the direction of the entire proceedings, including the examination of the witnesses and the finding of the appropriate law, assigned almost entirely to his charge. *Iura novit curia* is an expensive compliment to pay to a judge! Thus, overall, the civilian judge tends to be overworked whereas the civilian advocate tends to be underworked—at any rate in the context of litigation.[31]

Here is no place to consider the merits of the inquisitorial versus the accusatorial system; but the large number of cases that in Germany may be allowed to drag on to the end must be noted. In this context I think our system is preferable; and, I believe, a factor that contributes to this German phenomenon is the way lawyers are paid the more or less low, predetermined sums (almost invariably determined by the sums in dispute) they are entitled to claim for each case they handle. For payment is, on the whole, "front loaded" and with costs being low, compared to English and American law, the litigant seems to have little or no incentive to withdraw or compromise his action. (Note, however, that a court-approved compromise (*Vergleich*) entitles the attorney to a (usually small) additional sum (*Vergleichsgebühr*).)

## IV. What Really Makes People go to Court?

A number of reasons have, at times, been advanced to explain the differences between the scenes in the USA and England. The fact, however, that one finds analogous trends in the Continent of Europe would suggest that the reasons that we have examined briefly are, at most, local factors that strengthen other forces at work. I focus on three in particular.

The *first* is the relative cheapness of having access to the courts. Comparatively speaking, from the litigant's point of view, this is true if one compares, on the one hand, the USA and Germany and, on the other hand, England. The contingency fee system in the USA, coupled with the class action mechanism (in practice rarely used because of its complexities), punitive damages and the psychological effect that "mega-awards" can have on potential litigants, all combine to encourage more persons to chance their luck in court. The German pattern is, on the other hand, different, though it leads to the same results. Tables set the fees that can be charged and these, as already stated, are modest and are mainly related to the disputed amount. The way the remuneration is computed is difficult, but it is interesting to note that the figures given in these official tables represent

[31] "To the common law lawyer . . . the German judge will seem to be highly vocal and dominant whereas counsel will appear to act with somewhat subdued zeal:" Kotz, "The role of the judge in the court-room: the common law and civil law compared" (1987) *Tydskrif vir die Suid-Afrikaanse Reg* 35. The idea of increased judicial control over the conduct of the action is increasingly appealing to some American and British proceduralists. See: Langbein, "The German Advantage in Civil Procedure", *U. Chicago L. Rev.* 823, 858–862 (1985); Jolowicz, "Some Twentieth Century Developments in Anglo-American Civil Procedure", *Studi in onore de Enrico Tullio Lieberman* (1979), p. 217.

minimum amounts. I am told, however, that these are observed in practice—at least at the two low levels. Thus, half a million pounds in legal expenses for a defamation case (Jeffrey Archer) or a tax-evasion prosecution (Ken Dodd) are, I am told, unimaginable figures in civil law countries such as Germany or France. In any event, the fee levels seem low and, coupled with the wide availability of litigation insurance, make it relatively easy for a German citizen to sue and then think, if at all, of a possible compromise. So the Americans, by shifting the risk of litigation costs to the attorney, and the Germans, by keeping them low, tend to achieve the same objective which is easy access to the courts.

The cheapness of litigation in Germany is also reflected in their court-appointed system of experts—usually just one. These experts are paid an hourly rate of 70 DM (just over £20) a figure that may "in extreme cases" rise to 105 DM. Because the proceedings are different, and the time that an expert has to spend "in court" is also considerably less than that of his English or American counterpart, the final bill is invariably much lower. By contrast, in our system each party engages its own experts—often two or more on each side—and in many instances—including medical cases—these experts can spend many hours in court, adding significantly to the total cost of the trial. Whether they improve the chances of discovering what went wrong is, I think, a matter of some doubt. What appears to be less in doubt is the falsity of the old myth that one cannot find doctors to testify against doctors.

This cheapness must be, at the very least, an important contributory factor in the important difference that exists between England and Germany when it comes to the number of cases that are actually fought to the end. For even the system of court-approved amicable settlement of proceedings (*Prozessvergleich*), encouraged by para 279 *Zivilprozessordnung* and achieved in about 15 per cent. of cases,[32] still leaves a large number of actions to be fought to the very end, and the pre-trial phase in civil (but not criminal) cases does not cut down significantly the number of cases that reach what we would call "open court". The possibility of pre-trial discovery and the narrowing of the issue in dispute is, also, on the whole weaker than it is in English law. In one word, the legal background is in tune with the continental mentality which regards access to the courts to be free to all and not restricted to the few who can afford to litigate, let alone fight to the end. This attitude is also reflected in the appeals system, my civilian colleagues always being shocked (and, if they are judges,

[32] On which see: Stein-Jonas, *Kommentar zur Zivilprozessordnung* 20th edn. by Grunsky, Leipold, Münzberg, Schlosser and Schumann (1985) § 229. The percentage is, apparently, higher in medical malpractice cases.

not a little envious) of the minuscule number of cases heard annually by the House of Lords.

The second reason is, I think, the greater awareness that victims have in the USA and Europe of their *rights* to go to court. Freer advertising by lawyers—compared to England—insurance to cover litigation costs (in Germany) and a growing number of semi-official bodies and consumer organisations informing citizens of their rights as victims also help reinforce the feeling that recourse to the courts is, as it were, a natural right and not a privilege to be availed of rarely. An interesting illustration of this can be found in the comparison of what, for brevity's sake, I shall call the Unfair Contract Terms Acts of England and Germany, for in the latter we find that consumer organisations, as well as the contracting parties, have the right to challenge the validity of potentially unfair clauses in standard form contracts.[33]

The role of consumer-orientated bodies that inform plaintiffs of their potential rights is one that deserves much closer empirical study, so that it can be both encouraged and controlled. Here suffice it to say that in English medical cases bodies like the AVMA (Association of Victims of Medical Accidents) have contributed to making patients more alert to possible legal redress of their grievances; and there is some evidence to support the view that in the UK asbestos-related claims have been pursued more vigorously by victims who have belonged to those trade unions which have taken a more active interest in this matter than other unions.[34] To put it differently: here, as elsewhere in tort litigation, easy access to qualified para-legal counselling services may be a major determinant of the victim's decision to have recourse to the courts.

The third factor, not unrelated to the previous two but even more difficult to measure, is national temperament. How different, for example, is the American mentality on this matter? As already stated. in the USA recourse to courts—especially in personal injury cases—can be seen as a way of coping with the financial adversities of accidents in the absence of a caring state. In many cases this is a perfectly legitimate reaction. (German litigation could, in part, be explained by the plaintiff's wish to top up social security payments or, in the case of strict liability statutes, the wish to claim additional damages for pain and suffering which are not recoverable under the statutes. Furthermore, insurers' ability to invoke the defence of contributory negligence often pushes into court claims which could or should have been settled without litigation.) In other instances,

[33] The *Gesetz zur Regelung des Rechts der Allgemeinen Geschäftsbedingungen* of April 1st 1977, para. 13.

[34] Felstiner and Dingwall, *Asbestos Litigation in U.K. An Interim Report* (1988), p. 17.

however, recourse to the courts by American plaintiffs also demonstrates a low threshold of coping with the vicissitudes of life. I have more sympathy with the former explanation than with the latter. But there are other reasons. A mobile population, accustomed on the whole to a comfortable standard of living, declining family ties, looser doctor/patient relationships and the kind of loneliness that leads so many to seek psychiatric help (for companionship rather than treatment which they often do not need), also encourages, I suspect, many to go to court when faced with the slightest adversity. This may sound a harsh assessment by a foreign observer, but the former Chief Justice of the US Supreme Court Warren E. Berger expressed similar thoughts when in 1982 he addressed the American Bar Association and said: "One reason our courts have become overburdened is that Americans are increasingly turning to the courts for relief from a range of personal distresses and anxieties. Remedies for personal wrongs that once were considered the responsibility of institutions other than the courts are now boldly asserted as "entitlements". The courts have been expected to fill the void created by the decline of church, family, and neighborhood unity."[35] Well-publicised high awards may aid and abet this attitude and often result—for example in cases of foetal injuries, loss of companionship and other such claims—in what one suspects are often gold-digging actions. Pro-plaintiff judges and juries appear to be more sympathetic towards them; and, in this instance, the contingency fee system provides a further inducement to "have a go" at litigation, since many claims, because of their nuisance value, result in some payment being made to the plaintiffs. Certainly, the number of frivolous if not outrageous actions reported from time to time is not easily explained by reference to rational considerations.

Are all these factors totally absent from England? British writers have often been quick to stress that recourse to courts is seen here as an exceptional and costly move not to be undertaken lightly. Tony Weir, for example, recently suggested that in England "resort to the law is reluctant, infrequent and deplored"; and, as is often the case with the writings of this brilliant colleague, he has backed his assertion with a humorous quotation from Henry James's *An International Episode.*[36] Yet the duller world of statistics that I have described does not fully support this assertion. For even if recourse to the courts is "reluctant", it is not, overall, infrequent, as *Figure 2* demonstrates. Indeed, it is extraordinarily high given the absence of the contingency fee system and the unavailability of legal aid for victims with middle-range earnings and above.

[35] "Is'nt there a Better Way", (1982) 68 *American Bar Association Journal*, 274, p. 275.
[36] Weir, "A Strike Against the Law", 46 *Maryland Law Rev.* 133 (1986).

But the systems do show a more marked difference when we look at tort litigation. Could "temperament" (not in the sense of deploring litigation but in the sense of treating litigation as a step of last resort) explain this difference? The reputed tendency of Americans to file a suit (in order to demonstrate to their opponent that they "mean business") and then to compromise may contrast with the Englishman's attitude somehow to seek a resolution to the dispute without resorting to the courts if at all possible. Yet even this point cannot provide a complete explanation of the differences between the systems for there is in the US medico-legal field intriguing statistical evidence to suggest that only a tiny percentage of injury-producing errors leads to claims being made against insurance companies and of these an even smaller percentage develops into suits that end with a jury verdict.[37] In one sense, therefore, what we should be investigating is not only the number of filings in the systems under comparison but also the reasons which prevent disputes from developing into full-blown legal suits, the "barriers", as one of my American colleagues put it, that stop the potential disputes entering the legal stream. My own inclination is to attribute the differences in filing primarily to ignorance of one's rights and financial fears associated with litigation rather than to temperament although I suspect that in this increasingly urbanised, industrialised and cosmopolitan world, differences in national mentality are being steadily eroded. But even temperament or mentality, these most unquantifiable of factors invoked by so eminent a jurist as Professor Atiyah[38] as the *differentia specifica* between English and American law, may be changing. The medico-legal scene may, through careful analysis of the available statistics, provide a positive indication that this type of change is slowly taking place aided by greater information and specialised services being made available to victims of iatrogenic injuries and this may even not be a bad thing.

Though there is much talk these days of a medico-legal crisis, the reality is that in England medical malpractice cases form, as *Table 7* shows, a tiny minority of tort claims. The 700 or so claims made (and, be it noted, these are not necessarily writs) in 1973 had, apparently, increased to 2,000 by 1983/4 and to above 4,000 by 1987. The figure of 2,000 must be compared to the figure of about 40,000 claims made in the late 1970s, early 1980s in the USA[39] and about

[37] Daniels, "Jury Verdicts in Medical Malpractice Cases". Paper delivered to the Annual Meeting of the Law and Society Association on 11 August 1989; *idem.* "The Shadow of the Law: Jury Decisions in Obstetrics and Gynaecology Cases", ABF Working Paper No. 8806 (1988) both kindly sent to me by their author.

[38] In his article in the *Duke Law Journal* 1002, 1043 (1987).

[39] 1 American Medical Association, Special Task Force on Professional Liability, Professional Liability in the '80s, 10 (1984).

TABLE 7

*Annual Numbers of Tort Claims for Personal Injury or Death by Type of Claim, UK**

| | *Claims* 000s | % | *Payments* 000s | % |
|---|---|---|---|---|
| Employers' Liability | 114·7 | 46·0 | 90·5 | 42·0 |
| Motor Vehicle | 102·2 | 40·9 | 98·3 | 45·7 |
| Products & Services (excluding medical) | 2·2 | 0·9 | 1·7 | 0·8 |
| Occupiers' Liability | 12·2 | 4·9 | 10·8 | 5·0 |
| Medical Services (doctors, dentists, pharmacists) | 0·7 | 0·2 | 0·3 | 0·1 |

* Estimates in round numbers for 1973.
Source: Pearson Commission, Cmnd. 7054–II, 19 (1978).

*Complaints lodged with the Medical Arbitration Boards of the Federal Republic of Germany 1982–83**

| | | |
|---|---|---|
| Total number of complaints received | 16,434 | |
| Closed on procedural grounds | ·8,392 | (51% of total) |
| Cases decided on merit | 7,969 | (100%) |
| Decided in favour of plaintiff | 2,152 | (27%) |
| Decided in favour of defendant | 5,817 | (63%) [or 13% of total] |

* Source: Giesen, *International Medical Law* (1988), p. 510.

8,000 claims considered in the 1980s by the voluntary arbitration boards to which German victims of iatrogenic injuries are encouraged (but not obliged) to have resort, if possible in lieu of litigation.[40] The German figure and the apparent success rate of about 27 per cent. call for three comments. First, the overall number of German *claims* considered by the Arbitration Boards *and* the courts is, allowing for population differences, close to that of the USA but double or even treble the English figure. Secondly, how many of these claims actually turn into court actions we do not know, or at least I have not been

[40] The Boards are comprised of four members—two coming from the doctors' professional body (*Arztekammer*) and one representative (usually a lawyer) for the potential plaintiff and defendant. Their majority opinion, on liability but not, apparently, on *quantum* of damages, if accepted by the parties, will be honoured by the insurance company. Though recourse to court is always possible, the Winterthur A.G. Versicherung of Munich (one of Germany's leading doctors' insurance companies) informed me (through Professor Lorenz) that "the number of cases resolved by this sort of arbitration is considerable". These boards seem to take anything between 4–9 months to reach a decision. See Eberhardt, "*Zur Praxis der Schlictung in Arzthaftpflichtfällen*", 1986 *Neue Juristiche Wochenschrift* 747–8. Judicial resolution of medical disputes takes significantly longer—mainly because of the difficulties associated with scientific evidence.

able to discover (see however note 30 above and note 42 below). Nor do we know how many cases go *directly* to the courts, totally by-passing the voluntary arbitration boards. We do know, however, that the German Federal Court[41] has drawn attention to the increasing number of malpractice suits. Such an increase, however, can be seen across the board of tort litigation; medical malpractice cases still form a small percentage of the overall volume of tort litigation; and none of my German correspondents felt that the existing levels could be described as "alarming". Finally, it is worth noting that the success rate of 27 per cent. of *all claims* which result in some payment to the plaintiff, whether by agreement or as a result of a court award, is close to the figure given for England though, as stated, in this last case one is talking of a much lower number of total claims.[42] Since it is fair to assume that the level of medicine practised in England and West Germany must be similar, it would not appear to be unreasonable to hypothesise that for various reasons, in England, a number of injury-producing medical errors do not reach the legal system and do not result in legal redress.

*Table 8* also suggests that in England, despite alarmist cries, the proportion of claims that are successful through *litigation* does not appear to have increased significantly since Pearson: indeed it may be decreasing. The rate of abandonment of claims has also gone up: from 60 to about 75 per cent. of all claims made. What have also gone up, however are (a) the number of total claims initiated; (b) arguably the number of claims that reach court; and (c) the size of awards. *Figures 4* and *5* show the increase in the maximum individual payments made in the last 15 years (though, again, the figures—provided by the medical defence societies—are ambiguous in many respects and must be treated with considerable caution). Insurance rates have also gone up (*Table 9*), but this, I think, is mainly due to (a) defending more—often useless—cases; (b) the higher size of some exceptional awards; and (c) the profitability of insurers' investment policies which, admittedly, is a hazardous operation because of the time lag between injury, claim and payment. In England this last factor has been conspicuously ignored by all who talk of an insurance crisis and explicitly or implicitly blame the lawyers for it. As for the

[41] Press Release to the *Frankfurter Allegemeine Zeitung*, 4 Feb. 1986, p. 14. Significantly, this prestigious newspaper attributes the increased volume of claims to, inter alia, a change in mentality.

[42] Bowles and Jones, "A Health Authority's Experience", *New Law Journal* 27th January 1989, p. 119. For Germany see Deutsch, Schreiber and Lilie *op. cit.* note 30, above. According to the same authors, only 10 per cent. of claims resolved by judicial decision go in favour of plaintiffs. *Ibid.* at p. 230. Reichenbach, in "Arzthaflpflicht aus der Sicht des Versicherungsmediziners", *VersR* 1981, 807, p. 809 gives a similar figure for cases resolved by the courts. The success rate is higher—about 34 per cent.—for claims resolved through the intervention of the conciliation boards.

TABLE 8
*Claims Made on Medical Defence Societies*

*1973* (Source: Pearson Commission Report)

| | |
|---|---|
| Total | 500 |
| Abandoned | 305 (60%) |
| Settled out of court | 170 (34%) |
| Ended in Court | 25 (5%) |
| Won by defendant | 20 (4%) |
| Won by plaintiff | 1 (1%) |
| *Success rate* (claims partially satisfied through settlement or more generously compensated through court payment) | 35·4% |

*1984* (Source: Hawkins and Patterson: study based on 100 files randomly selected out of a total of 324 of the West Midland region which is the largest in the NHS)

| | |
|---|---|
| Total | 100 |
| Abandoned | 73 |
| Settled out of court | 12 |
| Pending (3 years later) | 14* |
| Lost by plaintiff in court | 1 |

* of which 9 likely to go to court

| | |
|---|---|
| *Success rate* | 12–28% |

*1987* Total number of claims reported (unofficially) by the medical defence societies. How do they fare? The last three sets of figures are *estimates* based on the Hawkins and Paterson data.

| | |
|---|---|
| Total | 4,000 |
| Abandoned | 2,920 (74%) |
| Settled out of Court | 480 (12%) |
| Pending† | 760 (14%) |

*Summary Conclusion 1973–1987 (approximate figures)*

| | |
|---|---|
| — Frequency of claims | — *up* by 700% |
| — Total cost of settlements | — *up* (no exact figure available) |
| — Abandonment rate | — *up* from 60% of claims to about 75% of claims made |
| | — Proportion of claims which succeed |
| | — *down* from 30–40% to around 25% |

† On the Hawkins/Paterson figures about 360 might end up in court. This would be 9% of the total—instead of 5% in the Pearson era. *Estimates* based on figures from studies of individual regions suggest a success rate for plaintiffs of 2–4% of total claims, *i.e.* 80–160 actions most of which probably being settled by the parties.

FIGURE 4

*Maximum Awards paid by the Medical Protection Society for Failed Sterilisation**

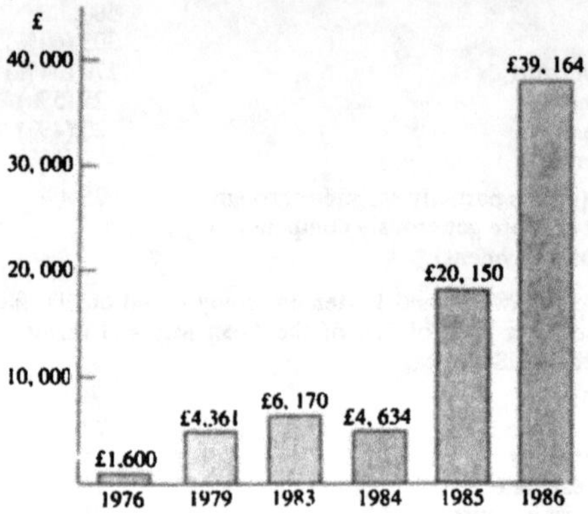


* Source: Hamm, Dingwall, Fenn and Harris, *Compensation and Accountability* (1988), 11.

USA, there is growing awareness that profit-oriented insurance companies may have been too eager to underwrite doubtful risks when interest rates were high. Bad insurance practices were thus concealed while returns from investments of premium money remained high.[43]

Comparison with Germany is interesting but again patchy, mainly because of the lack of meaningful statistics. Professor Weyers' figures are the most detailed that I have seen but I must remind the reader of the caveats expressed in footnote 30, above. Professor Weyers gives the average as 35,000 DM. At about £12,000 this is about two-thirds the average English medical *settlement* though, of course, one must stress that Weyers's figures come mainly from the early seventies. Weyers's study found that 25–30 per cent. of the claims were for 3,000 DM or less; 65–70 per cent. related to 3–50,000 DM; 2 per cent. were for 50,000 DM; and about 3 per cent. concerned 100,000 DM or more. Deutsch, Schreiber and Lilie, writing in

[43] Remarkably, this was openly admitted by R. J. Haayen, Chairman and Chief Executive Officer of the Allstate Insurance Company in a public speech given in Pennsylvania entitled "Balancing Risk and Reward" published by the Insurance Information Institute in 1987 at p. 6.

FIGURE 5

*Highest Sum Awarded in Medical Negligence Cases 1977–1987*

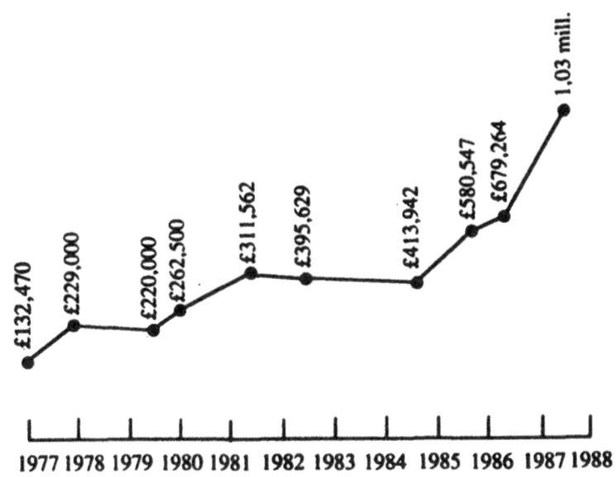


Source: M.D.U./Hamm, Dingwall, Fenn and Harris, *op. cit.*, p. 11

TABLE 9

*Defence Society Subscription Rates*

| *Year* | *Rate* £ | *Annual Increase* % |
|---|---|---|
| 1978 | 40 | — |
| 1979 | 70 | 75 |
| 1980 | 95 | 36 |
| 1981 | 120 | 26 |
| 1982 | 135 | 13 |
| 1983 | 195 | 44 |
| 1984 | 264 | 35 |
| 1985 | 288 | 17 |
| 1986 | 336 | 17 |
| 1987 | 576 | 71 |
| 1988 | 1,080 | 87 |

1985, suggest that 100,000 DM awards are "nowadays" much more common, while Reichenbach, writing in 1981, has noted that even at that time there were cases where the 500,000 DM compulsory insurance maximum coverage proved inadequate. Precise figures, however, are not given. Weyers also found that the greater complexity of medical cases tended to make them more costly to litigate than the usual tort case (the cost of litigation incurred by the loser tended to be in the order of 20 per cent. of the total amount claimed). One must remember, however, that the bulk of medical–legal disputes are nowadays resolved by the voluntary arbitration boards, referred to earlier in this paper, and the cost of presenting a claim before such boards tends to be very low. The unavailability (to me at least) of more precise figures makes further comparisons difficult. What one can say, however, is that the near-panic reaction of the British medico-insurance profession has not been reflected in Germany even though the total number of claims is greater than it is in England and the average awards similar if not higher. But then German industry in general and the insurance industry in particular here satisfactorily weathered changes in the other areas of the law which, when mooted in this country, send shivers down the spines of British industrialists. The abolition in Germany in 1972 of the state of art defence for pharmaceutical products is an example akin to our subject.

Do these figures, then, suggest that a crisis has reached our shores? An increase in willingness to litigate, yes, but a crisis, no—not yet, at any rate. But just as doctors (or rather insurers, since nowadays most doctors no longer fully pay their insurance premiums) are concerned by the increase I am interested in its causes. *Figure 6* shows that there are considerable variations among regions. Local factors seem to be at work but urbanisation is not, apparently, one of them. American studies, on the other hand, suggest that urbanisation is a factor, though it is also said that the greater litigiousness in urban areas cannot be linked to a greater concentration of lawyers, but it can be linked to a greater awareness of one's rights.

Remarkably, these figures also suggest that the average number of claims in the USA is about three to four times higher than in England and only about one-third higher than the number of claims made in some (relatively few) regions. Once again, however, note the apparent similarity of German and American figures on the total number of claims made and the calmer level of debate that prevails in the former of these two countries, which is almost certainly due to the absence of the American-style "mega-awards".

But let us return to the British scene. In my opinion, the major reason for the change we are witnessing must be greater publicity of awards and, above all, a greater effectiveness of pressure groups like

FIGURE 6
*Annual Claims per 100,000 Population*

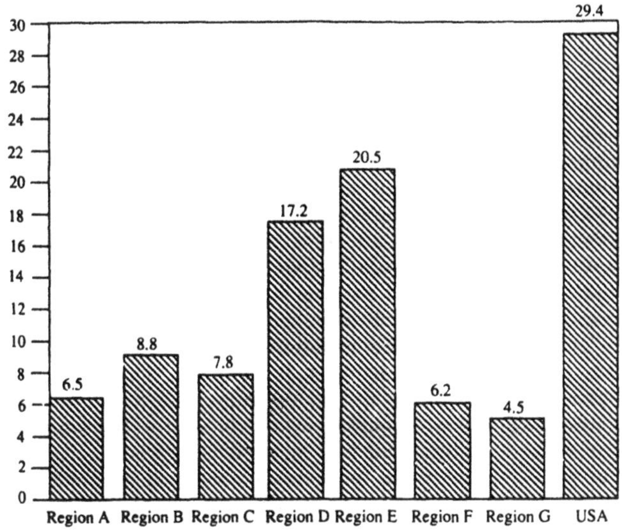


Source: R. Dingwall, forthcoming in "Health Care UK" 1989.

the AVMA which was founded in 1982 and the resulting willingness to chance marginal claims. On the whole, I would regard this as a healthy development. But there is another reason that may contribute to more claims and this is less easy to justify. The lack of any medical screening of the merits of the case at the legal aid stage of the process enables many unmeritorious claims to generate considerable defence costs by potential defendants. Clearly, more information is needed to draw firm conclusions, information which is available to the medical defence societies but which they are unwilling to release. But there is already some evidence to suggest that the national reluctance to sue, to the extent that it really exists, may be weakening where there is greater activity by pro-consumer groups and easy access to legal aid. Or, to put it more bluntly, an aggrieved Englishman will sue if given half the chance by the legal system! My overall conclusion, therefore, is that medical malpractice presents our tort system with a challenge: the challenge is not how to suppress deserving cases for the sake of a streamlined legal system, but how to separate the unmeritorious from the meritorious claim in a fair and efficient way. And once again, the study of the German system can help us decide whether the American system is "dangerous" by being outrageously pro-plaintiff or whether ours is aberrant by being excessively pro-defendant.

## V. Putting Matters into Perspective

The danger inherent in the use of figures and the difficulties of comparing (inadequate) judicial statistics from different countries were mentioned at the outset and, perhaps, should be stressed again. Yet these dangers do not, I believe, outweigh the advantages that may follow such empirical studies. Lawyers, and I am now thinking not only of British lawyers but also of continental European lawyers, should not frown upon such additional tools, especially since, if properly used, they could have an impact on the kind of policy arguments that lie concealed behind the more formal judicial reasoning. Let me give one or two examples of what I have in mind, drawing again, for convenience's sake, from the medico-legal scene.

Some lawyers and most doctors nowadays tend to talk of a real or impending medico-legal crisis; some may refer to the American scene as the apocalypse that may be about to descend on us. The latter point can, for present purposes, be disposed of briefly. The situation in America is, as I indicated, a complex phenomenon produced by many factors, institutional, political and demographic, that cannot be duplicated in this country. Imitation tendencies may, to some extent, change the medico-legal scene, but let us face it, this was a non-subject until a few years ago and any change will be seen by many—wrongly—as one for the worse. Any increase in legal activity can be interpreted as opening uncontrollable floodgates. After all, ten cases being resolved by judicial means instead of five represents a one hundred per cent. increase! Few, however, will stress (or have stressed) that greater accountability may make doctors more careful in (a) the way they conduct their profession (b) in the way they handle their patients, and (c) in the way they keep their records. If the Germans can cope, why can't we?

This is not to deny that changes are taking place and that if they are *abrupt* in manner and *substantial* in proportion, they could put the NHS under stress. But the use of statistics can help put the problems into proper perspective. For example, a different doctrine of informed consent has not, apparently, caused unbearable stresses to either the American or German systems. And the so-called phenomenon of defensive medicine may not, as some have claimed, be attributable (or substantially attributable) to changing patterns of litigation. It may, for example, be linked to the fee-for-services system which gives doctors a financial incentive to order as many tests and procedures as are technically justifiable. Is this too harsh a comment to make? I do not think it is for American doctors; nor, apparently, is it for German doctors. And in Germany, too, we have witnessed recently an increase in tests carried out *even though* there has been no outrageous rise in medical malpractice litigation. The increase must be partly linked to the overall method of remuneration.

The position in England, as far as defensive medicine is concerned, may be even less clear. Though a recent study has claimed that "defensive procedures are fairly widespread",[44] its conclusions admit that the questions did not address the problem of the respondents' perception of what is meant by defensive medicine. A knowledgeable commentator has also warned me that "the reasons people give for their actions in a survey may be very different from those that motivated the actions in the first place. We think, for instance, that it may be used as a justification for clinical interventions which are controversial between doctors and midwives: legal responsibility is a trump card for the doctor in an argument." Thus, not only is it arguable that in some—perhaps many—cases one doctor's defensive medicine may be another's good practice; it is also possible that unnecessary procedures may often be authorised because the doctor is unsure of what responsible medical practice, as judged by his peers, requires him to do.[45] In any event, one thing is reasonably clear: a doctor is mistaken if he adopts unnecessary defensive procedures because he thinks the law requires him to do so in order to protect himself. The law makes no such demands of any doctor.

Statistical work on the English medico-legal scene reveals other things. The Hawkins/Paterson study,[46] for example, vividly illustrates how time-consuming and costly is the process from complaint to writ to judgment by the court. Worse still, the "avalanche of correspondence" that this process entails often turns out to be totally wasteful since, as I have indicated, in 39 per cent. of the total number of cases investigated, the condition complained of is due to natural causes and unavoidable risks and not to doctors' errors. Could not the use of doctors on the legal aid panel prevent these cases from even getting off the ground? Moreover, what can we learn from the German arbitration boards and the way they manage to suppress the gladiatorial nature of our procedure?

Many cases also show that voluminous correspondence is produced for immensely trivial injuries (12 per cent.) that in the end are not

[44] Jones and Morris, "Defensive Medicine: myths and facts", (1989) *Journal of the Medical Defence Union* (Summer part) 40, p. 42.

[45] *Ibid.*, pp. 41, 42.

[46] "Medicolegal audit in the West Midlands region: analysis of 100 cases", (1987) 295 *British Medical Journal* 1533.

worth pursuing, while in another 6 per cent. of claims the dispute has been caused by various forms of breakdown in the doctor/patient relationship or, even, created by irresponsible speculation by other doctors or nurses not immediately involved in the case in point. It does not take radical law reform to cut down some of these instances and concentrate efforts either on compensating cases where negligence is undeniable (12 per cent. settled out of court on these grounds) or expediting the resolution of the truly disputed cases which, according to this study are about 9 per cent. Of course, one could, and one day must, envisage more radical methods of solving these disputes, which could include a no-fault non-adversarial process of compensation rather than litigation, but that is another matter.

Another point that can emerge from studying these statistical variations is the complexity of factors that lie behind them. This is a crucial point for we are apt, whenever we see an increase in litigation figures or premiums, to talk of the American crisis reaching our shores. This would, as I have indicated, tend to underestimate the many local and institutional differences that exist in the USA which are not duplicated in the UK. On the other hand, if the crucial factor is one of mentality, capacity to endure the adversities of life, access to justice and the like, then there may be some subtle changes taking place in this country which will move it closer to the pattern we find elsewhere. One thing, however, must be made clear. While increased litigation-consciousness may place great strains on the NHS and the courts, it cannot be totally condemned in all its aspects.

Moving away from the specific instances of medico-legal disputes to more general issues, does my brief and tentative survey reveal any great differences between the three different systems we have looked at? The glass of water provided for me for tonight's lecture is, at this moment, 50 per cent. full of water. I could, with equal accuracy, describe it as half full or half empty. The material that I have given you could, with a minimum of ingenuity, support a conclusion that there exist great differences or great similarities. After all, one only has to select a few "mega-awards" from the United States and the current picture of outrageous differences between the systems remains intact. Despite this, I prefer to look at things from the second angle, not least because so many of us, instinctively it would seem, opt for the first. With this as my starting point, I think one must be cautious when talking of a litigation explosion. Though there is a steady increase in litigation, the words "explosion" or "crisis" have not been used by my German colleagues. I think they are inappropriate in our case, as well; and to the extent that they can be used to describe the legal scene in the USA, I think they should be limited to certain areas, some courts and, possibly, some types of case—for example products cases (particularly latent toxic torts) and medical malpractice. Indeed, one research officer of the Institute for Civil Justice of the Rand Corporation, when giving evidence before a special subcommittee of the US House of Representatives in 1986, stated: "Increasingly, the civil justice system seems to be two different systems. One is a stable system that provides modest compensation for plaintiffs who claimed slight or moderate injuries in automobile and other accidents that have been the major source of litigation for 50 years. The second is an unstable system that provides continually increasing awards for claims for serious injuries in any type of lawsuit, and for all injuries, serious or not, in product liability, malpractice, street hazards and workplace accidents."[47]

TABLE 10
*Federal District Courts**
Filings in Selected Categories 1975 and 1984

| *Category* | *1975* | *1984* | *Per cent. change* | *Increase* | *Fraction of absolute increase 1975/1984* |
|---|---|---|---|---|---|
| Total filings | 117,320 | 261,485 | 122·9 | 144,165 | 100% |
| 1. Prisoner Petitions | 19,307 | 31,107 | 61 | 11,800 | 8·2% |
| 2. Recovery of Overpayment and Enforcement of judgments | 681 | 46,190 | 6,682·7 | 45,509 | 31·6% |
| 3. Civil Rights | 10,392 | 21,219 | 104·2 | 10,827 | 7·5% |
| 4. Social Security | 5,846 | 29,985 | 412·9 | 24,139 | 16·7% |
| 5. *Torts* (General) | 25,691 | 37,522 | 46 | 11,831 | 8·2% |
| Products Liability | 2,886 | 10,745 | 272·3 | 7,859 | 5·4% |

* Adapted from Prof. Galanter's "The Day After the Litigation Explosion", 46 *Maryland L. Rev.* 3, 16 which, in turn, is based on Director of the Administration Office of the United States Courts, Annual Reports 1975 and 1984.

The figures given in *Table 10* tend to support this assertion. They show in a summary way the increase in the volume of litigation in the federal courts between 1975 and 1984. One can, of course,

[47] M. A. Peterson, *A Summary of Research Results: Trends and Patterns in Civil Jury Verdicts*, testimony presented to the Sub-Committee on Oversight, Committee on Ways and Means, US House of Representatives on 13 March 1986 (Rand Corporation, 1986), p. 4.

immediately object that they must be treated with great caution since some 97 per cent. of claims are litigated in state not federal courts. Notwithstanding this legitimate caveat, focussing on the activity in the federal courts is advisable since: (a) the most reliable information available, on the whole, refers to the federal courts; (b) the increase in federal litigation is the one most commonly used as an example of runaway litigiousness and (c) the recent growth of filings has, apparently, been far greater in federal courts than it has been in state courts.[48] Now, if you look at these figures carefully you will see that the two major increases have taken place in categories 2 and 4 and they represent a deliberate official policy "to recover over-payments of veteran's benefits by litigation and to curtail disability benefits by summarily removing beneficiaries from the rolls". As Professor Galanter continues: "Is the 413 per cent. increase in social security cases to be understood as an outbreak of litigiousness among Social Security claimants? Does it make sense to take the 6,683 per cent. increase in recovery cases as evidence of an outbreak of litigiousness among federal officials?"

The tort increase by contrast is interesting in that it reveals two things: (a) an overall increase more or less in tune with the increase in population during the same period and (b) the bulk of the overall increase is taken up by one type of tort litigation—products liability—which, indeed, was itself dominated by two major incidents: the asbestos litigation and the Dalcon Shield disputes.[49] The recent Special Report of the Institute for Civil Justice, *Trends in Tort Litigation. The Story behind the Statistics*,[50] thus appears to be right when it claims that in the USA the "answer to the question of how much tort litigation there really is depends on which world of litigation the data describe. (i) Auto accident [and other routine personal injuries] are a steady or declining percentage of court action. (ii) Non-auto personal injury cases such as malpractice and product liability are growing moderately in state courts and more dramatically in federal courts. (iii) Mass latent injury cases have the potential for

[48] Galanter, "The Day After the Litigation Explosion", 46 *Maryland L. Rev.* 3 (1986) 15, note 44 on which this section and Table 16 are based. The National Centre for State Courts, in a *Preliminary Examination of Available Civil and Criminal Trend Data in State Courts for 1978, 1981 and 1984* (1986), based on statistics supplied by twenty states, has concluded that "During 1981–4, tort filings increased 7% while population increased 4%. For the entire period 1978–84, total tort filings increased 9%, but the population also increased by 8%".

[49] In 1981 there were some 16,000 asbestos claims which, by 1986, had grown to more than 30,000 in state and federal courts. 7,500 Dalcon Shield-related suits in 1981 had grown to more than 325,000 in the Bankruptcy court after A. H. Robins had sought the protection of Chapter 11.

[50] By Hensler, Vaiana, Kakalik and Peterson, *op. cit.* note 7, above, at p. 11. The figures in California are similar. Thus, for the period 1980–4 there were 46 punitive damages awards in personal injuries cases—6 in San Francisco, 15 in Los Angeles, and a further 15 in other metropolitan jurisdictions. Hensler, *Trends in California Tort Liability Litigation* (Rand Publication, 1987), p. 11.

explosive growth as new evidence of harms is developed." So, despite the difficulty of keeping these three categories rigidly separated, I believe that here, perhaps, lies the main difference from the European scene. Otherwise it seems that the Europeans go to court as often as the Americans or, at any rate, if they can help it, do not avoid it as the prevailing opinion would like us to believe.

This brings me to the second and, I think, really major difference. Going to court is one thing, staying there to the end is another. A system that encourages settlements must be good: a system that forces settlements through complexity and high costs may be less defensible. I have neither the time nor the expertise to attempt comparisons in procedural law; but the impression I have is that English law belongs to this second category; and this, coupled with the cost of tort litigation, may explain the lower level of tort suits in England. This is a fertile area for comparisons as the growing number of articles suggests, though one must also add that in the area of procedural law, national lawyers seem to be even more protective of their own "turf" than they are in substantive law (and we all know how unwilling they are even here to be influenced by foreign ideas).

What about the size of awards? In this paper I have only skimmed the surface of this subject, yet I should like to make five tentative observations. First, do not focus on the mega-awards but look at the median or, better still, at the mode awards in order to avoid distortions by a few mega-awards that can grossly affect average awards. Take, for example, the figure of $1·1 million which was in 1984 the average product liability award made by juries in San Francisco. The median award for the same period was $200,000 which was (and is still) a lot of money, but only a fifth of the average figure inflated by a tiny percentage of mega-awards. The Cook County, Illinois, median figure was lower—$187,000: and there is every reason to believe that the nationwide median figure would be even lower.[51] Similarly, the medical average of $1 million in San Francisco for the same period becomes a median of $156,000.[52] Or look at the punitive awards made in Cook County during 1980–84 for personal injury cases. The *average* award was $1,934 million. This makes the headlines. But this average was produced by *less than a handful* of very substantial

[51] The Administrative Office of the US Courts, Guide to Judiciary, Policies and Procedures Transmital 64, vol. XI, 1 March 1985 showed median awards in non-asbestos product cases of $70,000 (1980), $100,000 (1981) and $135,000 (1982).

[52] Hensler, *Trends in California Tort Liability Litigation* (1987), p. 5; Hensler, *Summary of Research Results on Product Liability* (1986), p. 4. Professor Stephen Daniels, in his "Verdicts in Medical Malpractice Cases", *Trial*, May 1989 reviews the collected data on all cases that went to a jury in 46 counties in 11 states between 1981–5. Daniels observes that: "Generally speaking, median awards in successful money damages cases [other than medical malpractice] in most places were below $40,000. Only four sites [out of the 46] had medians for the total verdicts over $100,000, one in California and the other three in New York city."

punitive awards (including a 1980 medical malpractice award which, in 1984 dollars, was worth $9·3 million.[53] The median award, on the other hand, was worth $82,000. If to that you add the fact that there were in Cook County between 1980 and 1984 only 14 punitive awards in personal injury cases, the whole picture changes and, with the change, much of the newsworthiness value disappears.[54] These median figures are still high—I strongly suspect quite higher than the European equivalents—but remember that they are found in some types of tort litigation only and if one looks at tort litigation across the board the levels drop even further. (The *average* tort award *nationwide* in the USA in 1985 was a mere US$29,000.)

Secondly, never forget the significant, at times outstanding, regional variations in *median* (and, of course, *mean*) awards. *Table 11* provides some idea of this phenomenon and is based on a study of 24,625 civil verdicts from state trial courts of general jurisdiction in 46 counties in 11 states covering the years 1981–85. Some medians are affected by the low number of successful malpractice suits; others, however, present variations that call for explanation. What accounts for such variations (*e.g.* between New York and Dallas)? Are they the product of different political environments (liberal/democratic versus republican/conservative)? Could they be the result of conscious jury tendencies to award more to poor victims (assuming this is so)? Could the level of services be of inferior quality in the poorer areas, inevitably leading to more malpractice? Could all these factors be combined? American researchers have offered some explanations.[55]

[53] In *Djon Pjetri and Zoja Petri* v. *N.Y. City Health and Hospitals Corporation* (20 *Trial Lawyers Quarterly* (1989) 37 ff.) the Supreme Court of the State of New York followed suit by awarding to the plaintiff who was brain-damaged as a result of an anesthesia error a total of $35,517,578 which was reduced by the Appellate Division on 1 June 1989 to $9·2 million. More piecisely the injured plaintiff received $20 million for pain and suffering; $142,000 for past medical expenses; $3 million for future medical care; $1·3 million for future loss of earnings (even though he was 32 years of age and, at the time of the accident was earning as handyman–porter $320 per week). His wife—who, incidentally, left him three years after the accident—was also awarded $3 million (reduced on appeal to $1·5 million) for "loss of services". Additionally, the jury awarded $6 million (completely set aside on appeal) to Pjetri's mother and sons who were not plaintiffs in the action! The reader can decide how much of the blame (or praise?) for this result can be attributed to the jury and how much to the trial judge.

[54] *Punitive Damages. Empirical Findings* (Rand Corporation, 1987), pp. 21–2. Peterson, in the study quoted in note 47, above, states (p. 2) that throughout the 1960s and 1970s jury awards did not change in the "bulk of lawsuits". (After adjusting for inflation, the median jury award remained almost constant in both Cook County and San Francisco—less than $20,000 during the decades. The "mega-awards", on the other hand, seriously distorted averages. Thus, "In San Francisco during the 1960's, only five cases had a value of $1 million (in 1979 dollars)—0·3% of all cases in which plaintiffs received an award. The total amount of money awarded in these million dollar verdicts represented eight per cent. of all money awarded to plaintiffs. During the 1975's, 26 cases (2·3 per cent. of all cases in which plaintiffs received an award) produced awards exceeding $1 million. These cases accounted for 30 per cent. of all money awarded in the first half of the decade and nearly half of all money awarded in the second half of 1970's. [Preliminary results for 1980–1985 indicate that] although million dollar awards occurred in less than four per cent. of all cases won by plaintiffs during this period, they now account for roughly two-thirds of all money awarded to plaintiffs." (*Ibid.* at p. 3.)

[55] Daniels, *op. cit.*, note 33, above.

TABLE 11
*Median Medical Malpractice Awards 1981–85*
(in 1985 dollars)

| *Location* | *Number of cases* | *Success rate* | *Median award* | *Expected award* |
|---|---|---|---|---|
| Maricopa, AZ | 50 | 28·0 | 124,180 | 34,770 |
| Alameda, CA | 32 | 31·1 | 141,802 | 44,384 |
| Los Angeles, CA | 305 | 30·8 | 156,520 | 48,208 |
| Sacramento, CA | 27 | 22·2 | 260,818 | 57,902 |
| San Diego, CA | 39 | 41·0 | 136,210 | 55,809 |
| San Francisco, CA | 38 | 39·5 | 187,200 | 73,944 |
| Denver, CO | 29 | 20·7 | 70,000 | 14,490 |
| Fulton, GA | 37 | 48·6 | 40,815 | 19,836 |
| Cook, IL | 134 | 33·6 | 194,326 | 65,294 |
| DuPage, IL | 28 | 17·9 | 17,280 | 3,093 |
| Lake, IL | 22 | 40·9 | 66,600 | 27,239 |
| Johnson, KS | 17 | 41·2 | 280,000 | 115,360 |
| Wyandotte, KS | 10 | 50·0 | 810,000 | 405,000 |
| Jackson, MO | 38 | 28·9 | 69,500 | 20,086 |
| Bronx, NY | 43 | 55·8 | 602,195 | 336,025 |
| Kings, NY | 150 | 46·7 | 370,100 | 172,837 |
| Nassan, NY | 121 | 29·7 | 220,316 | 65,434 |
| New York, NY | 224 | 43·3 | 255,300 | 110,545 |
| Queens, NY | 85 | 48·2 | 166,500 | 80,253 |
| Suffolk, NY | 36 | 41·7 | 351,666 | 146,645 |
| Westchester, NY | 46 | 21·7 | 276,750 | 60,055 |
| Dallas, TX | 42 | 21·4 | 58,240 | 12,463 |
| Harris, TX | 117 | 10·3 | 597,000 | 61,491 |
| King, WA | 33 | 27·3 | 130,000 | 35,490 |

Source: S. Daniels, "Verdicts in Medical Malpractice Cases", *Trial*, May 1989 (adapted from tables 1 and 2).

From the point of view of a foreign observer what matters is that these variations are probably to be found in other areas of civil litigation such as product cases and business/tort situations. The local variations may, therefore, if taken with appropriate jurisdiction and *forum non conveniens* rules, greatly influence the decision to chance litigation in the USA.

This last point deserves a small excursus; and it is well-illustrated by the Piper-Alpha disaster and the ensuing mid-Atlantic settlement. For briefly in that case the Scottish victims, desirous of obtaining higher compensation than that likely to be available locally, had a choice between three *fora*: California, de facto excluded by its *forum non conveniens* doctrine; Louisiana, riddled by technical obstacles (short limitation period; rules excluding certain dependants if others were alive) and, in any event, because of the absence of punitive damages likely to produce lower compensation than other US states; and Texas, apparently open to foreign litigants after the Court of

Appeals of Texas, overruling a trial court judgment, had in *Alfaro* v. *Dow Chemical*[56] held that there was an absolute right to bring a fatal accident action in Texas without being subject to *forum non conveniens* dismissal. Largely on the basis of this judgment the plaintiffs pressed their case threatening Texas actions and the defendants offered a settlement in October 1988. The plaintiffs were lucky. Barely a month later the Texas Supreme Court, distinctly more conservative as a result of recent elections, granted a writ of error indicating its willingness to adopt or fashion a *forum non conveniens* doctrine. Had this event taken place a month earlier the defendants would have almost certainly pitched their offers at a significantly lower level reflecting the fact that Louisiana (with all its drawbacks) would be the only realistic US *forum* left to the plaintiffs. This sequence of events, little noticed by the otherwise watchful Press,[57] thus illustrates (a) the importance of regional variations in the USA; (b) the vacillation of legal doctrine as changing political fashions shape and reshape the composition of state courts; and (c) the dangers of asserting unequivocally that litigation in the USA is always and indisputably in the interests of British (or European) victims. Here, as elsewhere, a more nuancé approach must be adopted; and contact with the USA made, if at all, through the intervention or with the assistance of British legal help. Otherwise the American judicial process could adopt the words that Thoman Mann put into the mouth of Goethe as he bid his final farewell to Charlotte Kestner: "I am the flame, and into me the poor moth flings itself . . . once I burned you . . .".[58]

Thirdly, try to compare totals, including where possible medical bills, which in the European scene tend to be concealed because they are borne by the State. These can represent a substantial part of a tort award and thus make an American award seem much larger than it really is.

Fourthly, remember that American awards—especially mega-compensatory and mega-punitive awards—are frequently and substantially reduced as a result of settlements, remittiturs and appellate court decisions.

Fifthly, bear in mind that awards are bound to be higher where salaries, stipends and the standard of living are higher and when, as

[56] 751 SW 2d 208. Writ of error granted in November 1988.

[57] I have derived much information and assistance in this matter from Mr. Graeme F. Garrett of the Edinburgh firm of solicitors of Allan McDougall and who also successfully represented a number of victims in this case.

[58] *Lotte in Weimar* (Penguin edition) p. 330. This metaphor was also used by Lord Denning in *Smith Kline, Ltd.* v. *Bloch* (No. 1) [1983] 1 W.L.R. 730, 733. Jurisdictional aspects of the points discussed in the text, above, are considered by Baade, "Foreign Oil Disaster Litigation Prospects in the U.S. and the Mid-Atlantic Settlement Formula", (1989) 7 *Journal of Energy and Natural Resources Law* 125.

in the USA, they include a substantial percentage that will go not to the victorious victim but his legal advisor. Remarkably, perhaps, one can even find court decisions openly admitting that a particular tort rule, generous to the plaintiff, is adopted precisely because it can lead to a larger award and thereby, indirectly, finance litigation. The American version of the collateral source rule has been justified on such grounds;[59] and another court came up with the same reason in order to deny subrogation rights to an insurer of medical costs.[60]

Finally, do not only be struck by the differences but also be impressed by some uncanny similarities. Note, for example, how German and English law have arrived at about £100,000 as the right figure for compensation for loss of amenities of a severely injured but conscious plaintiff.[61] Note, also, that the proportion of all claims which result in some payment in medical malpractice cases is approximately the same in both England and Germany. Finally, note the similarity in the size of average awards in asbestos claims in England and the USA—at any rate during the first phase (up to 1982) of this massive tort litigation. Let me pursue this last point further.

Recent studies on awards made in the asbestos litigation seem to support the view that there exist greater similarities between the English and American systems than has hitherto been believed. Indeed, *Table 12* reveals an uncanny similarity of awards which makes one wish that there existed more comparative data on other types of tort litigation to test the validity of my supposition about relative equivalence of awards. More remarkable still, however, are the preliminary conclusions of a study conducted by the American Bar Association and the Oxford Centre for Socio-Legal Studies which has suggested that in extra-judicial *settlements*, British asbestos victims may have done significantly better than their American counterparts.[62] Overall, therefore, if you adopt a critical approach, I suspect you will find that, though some differences persist between our systems, they seem to cease to be spectacular. My hunch is that if one attempted the same kind of study in other areas of tort litigation one would also find that the differences that exist between the systems are much less spectacular than they are commonly believed to be

[59] See *Helfend* v. *Southern California Rapid Transit District* 465 P. 2d. 61 (1970).

[60] *Frost* v. *Porter Leasing Corp.*, 436 NE 2d. 387, 391.

[61] *E.g.* 300–400,000 DM (approximately £100,000) awarded to a severely disabled, conscious, twenty-six year old plaintiff for loss of amenity and pain and suffering: OLG Nurnberg 13·7 1984, VersR 86, 173 quoted by Hacks, Ring, Bohm, *Schmerzensgeldbeträge* 13th ed. 1987. Cf: *Brightman* v. *Johnson*, *The Times*, 16 December 1985 (also reported in Kemp and Kemp, *The Quantum of Damages*, 4th ed., 1975, Vol. 2, 1–010): £95,000 for loss of amenity to a conscious plaintiff and *Lim Poh Choo* v. *Camden and Islington Area Health Authority* [1980] A.C. 174 (£20,000 for loss of amenity to an unconscious plaintiff. In 1988 values this should be about £40,000).

[62] *Asbestos Litigation in the U.K.*—an Interim Report (1988), p. 16.

TABLE 12
*Asbestos cases: Tried claims*

| *British Average Award*[1] | *US Average Award* |
|---|---|
| £-55,130 | $-220,000[2] |
| | $-116,600[3] |
| $-88,208[5] | $-100,700[4] |

[1] British awards between 1970–1987.
[2] $220,000 *includes* 47 per cent. plaintiffs' litigation expenses, *i.e.* $103,400, so amount received by plaintiff must be reduced to approximately $116,600. British costs assessed separately and added to the above figure, *i.e. not* included in figure of £55,130.
[3] This amount *includes* 53 per cent. of $30,000 punitive damages, *i.e.* $15,900. Most asbestos trials, however, did *not* result in punitive damages. The $30,000 figure is the sum of all punitive damages averaged over all trials. Rand Corporation, *Costs of Asbestos Litigation* (1983), 20 note 10. Note, however, that the first punitive awards were not made until early in 1981. In the fifteen months or so that elapsed between that date and August 1982 (when the Manville Corporation filed a petition for reorganisation and protection under Chapter 11 of the Federal Bankruptcy Code) punitive damages against Manville alone averaged at $616,000. See: P. Brodeur, *Outrageous Misconduct, The Asbestos Industry on Trial* (1985), p. 283. The cut-off rate of the Rand research may have thus affected its figures downwards.
[4] Sum excluding punitive element of $15,900. See previous note.
[5] Converted at $1·60 to £1·00.

*N.B.* Comparing the $88,208 to the $100,700 one must further bear in mind two things: (a) the American award includes elements of medical expenses covered by the NHS; (b) the difference of real wage levels between Britain and the USA.

once allowance has been made for differences in cost of medical care, standard of living and the cost and method of funding litigation. Indeed, I should not be surprised to be told that variations in the size of awards are often greater within one and the same country than they are between the median, perhaps even, average awards of some of the leading countries of the western world. Certainly France has produced some quite astounding awards which have, however, passed unnoticed by the English who choose rather to be mesmerised by American headlines. More studies of this type might well surprise us all by making the differences between the systems less pronounced.

## VI. CONCLUSIONS

The inadequacy of the available statistical information inevitably means that this can only be described as a preliminary study. Nevertheless, some broad patterns have emerged from this study which make the following tentative conclusions fairly plausible.

First, American tort law is not, as I have tried to explain in this paper, one system but many with different figures, patterns and even rules applying to each sub-category. Secondly, *overall* volumes of litigation do not appear to be significantly different in the three systems that have been compared. What is significantly different, however, is the volume of tort litigation in Germany and the USA on the one hand and England on the other. When we look at the number of cases that are fought to the end, England and the USA fall (in percentage terms) into one group and Germany into another. This may be linked to costs, procedural rules, national mentality or all three. Thirdly, the common law systems considered in this paper manage with significantly fewer judges than exist in Germany. This may be largely because they are not accustomed (or not yet accustomed) to the advantages of "managerial judging", especially in smaller cases. Fourthly, juries account for some intriguing differences between the USA on the one hand and England and Germany on the other. A closer examination of the juries' contribution to the state—crisis some would say—of modern tort law will, I think, be found to be not in their typical awards but, primarily, (a) in their capricious inconsistencies and, (b) in a small number of cases, in their outrageous generosity (especially under the non-pecuniary headings of damage currently "capped" by widely differing US statutes). For these inconsistencies trial judges may also share in the blame. These variations and geographical inconsistencies must, overall, impede the smooth conclusion of settlement. Fifthly, notwithstanding the above, I strongly suspect that the difference in median and mode awards between these three nations though significant are less spectacular than is often believed. American awards must, in particular, be discounted for legal fees, medical expenses and higher average earnings. Though there is inadequate comparative statistical evidence to support detailed comparisons, I think there is enough evidence to suggest that potential plaintiffs should not be too quick to allow themselves to be enticed to sue in American courts. The nature of their action, the location of the potential US court and the character of the defendant may be very important factors in reaching the final decision. Sixthly, while doctrinal analysis of our systems is highly developed, our knowledge of how exactly they work in practice may be less complete and thorough. The absence or neglect of empirical data may be one cause; another may be the misuse of existing data by partisan groups. The first explanation is appropriate for the European scene, the second may be relevant in the USA.

All of the above must, of course, be read with the caveat that I am neither a statistician nor a knowledgeable practitioner but a law teacher trained first as a civil lawyer and then as a common lawyer. It is, therefore, primarily as a teacher that I have spoken tonight. Like Saint Paul I have come to believe that one should be prepared to look at everything and retain what is good wherever this may come from. As a civil lawyer I have to combat the ingrained instinct to become too abstract and too conceptual; as a common law lawyer I must guard against the danger of reducing everything to the level of analytical distinctions. Both approaches have their merits. In their different ways they can produce good doctrinal analysis and provide a good picture of a particular legal system. Nevertheless, though the picture it gives is good, it is not complete so long as it underplays or ignores the impact that the institutional, political and social background can have on the operation of the legal rules. These backgrounds have, on the whole, been ignored by traditional lawyers who have been slow to avail themselves of the kind of quantitative data and institutional facts that are necessary for the wider analysis. This data, which social scientists are good at selecting, has been excluded from the traditional law schools which seem to regard it as a threatening instead of an enriching source of ideas. This point has, I believe, been well made by, among others, Judge Richard Posner,[63] and it need not be further laboured here except in order to stress that in my opinion this wider approach is particularly valid in the context of comparative studies and comparative law. That is why I have tried to adopt it tonight in an attempt to repeat the *leitmotif* of much of my work, namely that common lawyers and civil lawyers though different are *not as different* as common mythology considers them to be. My belief thus is that many if not most English and American lawyers have a very foggy image of how each other's system works in practice—an image often shaped by anecdotal evidence, media accounts or partisan literature. Despite my many caveats, I think my statistical analysis reveals a more balanced as well as a more complex situation. But I remain to the very end conscious of the dangers involved in the use of statistics; so let me end with a warning for those of you who may be showing signs of being convinced by my figures! The warning, in Lord Beveridge's words, reads as follows: "No one believes a theory except the one who formulates it; everyone believes a figure except the one who calculates it!"

[63] *The Federal Courts. Crisis and Reform* (1985) Ch. 11.

# Name Index

www.ingramcontent.com/pod-product-compliance
Lightning Source LLC
LaVergne TN
LVHW081943200926
848484LV00009B/2502

* 9 7 8 0 8 1 4 7 7 4 6 5 6 *